Encyclopedia of
Southern Literature

ABC-CLIO LITERARY COMPANION

Encyclopedia of
Southern
Literature

Mary Ellen Snodgrass

ABC-CLIO
Santa Barbara, California
Denver, Colorado
Oxford, England

Library of Congress Cataloging-in-Publication Data

Snodgrass, Mary Ellen
    Encyclopedia of southern literature   /   Mary Ellen Snodgrass.
      p.   cm.—(ABC-CLIO literary companion)
    Includes bibliographical references (p.) and index.
    1. American literature—Southern States—Encyclopedias.   2. Southern States—Intellectual life—Encyclopedias.   3. Southern States—In literature—Encyclopedias.
   I. Title   II. Series
   PS261.S515   1997   810.9/975/03 21   97041977

ISBN 0-87436-952-5 (alk. paper)

03 02 01 00 99 98 97   10 9 8 7 6 5 4 3 2 1 (cloth)

ABC-CLIO, Inc.
130 Cremona Drive, P.O. Box 1911
Santa Barbara, California 93116-1911

This book is printed on acid-free paper ∞ .
Manufacturered in the United States of America.

These were merciful men, whose righteousness hath not been forgotten.

With their seed shall continually remain a good inheritance, and their children are within the covenant.

Their seed standeth fast, and their children for their sakes. Their seed shall remain for ever, and their glory shall not be blotted out.

Their bodies are buried in peace; but their name liveth for evermore.

Let Us Now Praise Famous Men
James Agee, 1941

CONTENTS

PREFACE

The plan of the *Encyclopedia of Southern Literature* is to present literature, motifs, historical eras, writers, titles, and genres as a method of defining and exemplifying the region's contributions to American and world literature. For ease of use, I have put extensive textual commentary under genre and historical eras, as with the numerous minor poets, belletrists, and essayists who wrote during the colonial and antebellum periods, and the varied body of plays that introduced original drama and comedy to stages in the frontier South. A list of home states indicates the authors from each Southern state as well as the many writers born outside the region who are claimed among Dixie's authors, notably Lafcadio Hearn, Fanny Kemble, Alex Haley, Dorothy Heyward, Ralph Ellison, Mary Ann Shadd Cary, Charles Waddell Chesnutt, Jackie Torrence, Harry Golden, John James Audubon, and Edgar Allan Poe. The strong contribution from Virginia, Georgia, and the Carolinas reflects the population centers in Williamsburg, Richmond, Atlanta, and Charleston during the colonial period rather than any favoritism toward those four states. Separate subject commentaries peruse the influence of the frontier tradition, Fugitive Agrarian movement, late-twentieth-century writers, the life of Robert E. Lee, the Mississippi River, religious fundamentalism, Southern women, and young-adult themes in such literary works as Larry McMurtry's *Lonesome Dove*, Donald Davidson's *Lee in the Mountains*, Eudora Welty's *The Robber Bridegroom*, Harry Golden's *Only in America*, the women in Tennessee Williams's *The Glass Menagerie*, and Bette Greene's *Summer of My German Soldier*.

Entries appear alphabetically and provide textual commentary, historical background, literary analysis, and generous citations. Significant to the canon of Southern literature are extensive biographies of important contributors:

- William Faulkner, who immersed himself in Mississippi social history, as reflected in his short stories and novels, particularly *The Sound and the Fury* and "The Bear"

- Lillian Hellman, who made major contributions to American theater, feminism, and autobiography with *The Little Foxes*, "Julia," and *An Unfinished Woman*

- Richard Wright, whose painful coming-of-age in Mississippi and his self-exile in the North provided the focus of *Black Boy* and the impetus of *Native Son*

- Edgar Allan Poe, whose troubled career produced romance, detective stories, science fiction and horror, literary criticism, and the shimmering verse imagery of "Ligeia," "To Helen," and "The Raven"

- Zora Neale Hurston, who began as a social researcher and then blended regional fiction, folklore, and feminist themes in *Their Eyes Were Watching God*

- James Agee, creator of the lyric profusions in *Let Us Now Praise Famous Men*, a journalistic work that reads like a poetic salute to the South's toiling underclass

- Joel Chandler Harris, who rose from printer's devil to journalist to a voice for the West African griot by way of the fictional persona of Uncle Remus, a character who speaks the pervasive dialect of the antebellum heartland

- Margaret Mitchell, a one-title novelist whose plantation romance *Gone with the Wind* captivated readers and sent actresses stampeding to audition for the screen role of Scarlett O'Hara, a character so real that tourists still search for her home in northwestern Georgia

Beneath each entry are cross-references, primary sources, and bibliography offering additional commentary. Examples include articles on the recurrent themes of civil rights and religious fundamentalism; Internet overviews of the lives of Pocahontas and Sequoyah; travelogues of Faulkner's Rowan Oak and Thomas Wolfe's boardinghouse in Asheville, North Carolina; on-line sources describing such historic figures as Davy Crockett, Jefferson and Varina Davis, and Dr. Martin Luther King, Jr.; hypertexts of the speeches of Frederick Douglass, the Uncle Remus stories, and Dubose Heyward's *Porgy*. Audiovisual materials include television documentaries on Thomas Jefferson, William Faulkner, and Frederick Douglass; Horton Foote's teleplay "Old Man"; and "Zora Is My Name!," a dramatic video that outlines the life and art of Zora Neale Hurston.

As an adjunct to reading, lesson planning, research, or self-directed study of Southern literary themes or individual genres, titles, and authors, this volume appends self-explanatory study aids:

- a chronology of focal works from Southern literature dating from the sixteenth century to the present

- a dated list of major works from the Southern literary canon

- a list of authors and their works

- a chronology of cinema versions of major titles from the frontier canon, for example, screen adaptations of plays by Tennessee Williams and Lillian Hellman and short stories and novels by Ernest Gaines, Harper Lee, William Faulkner, Olive Ann Burns, Calder Willingham, Beth Henley, O. Henry, Alice Walker, Marsha Norman, Alfred Uhry, and Edgar Allan Poe

- a listing of primary sources either in single issue or compendia, some of which feature sketches by John James Audubon; maps of the Lewis and Clark expedition that preceded the Louisiana Purchase; speeches by Thomas Jefferson, Barbara Jordan, and Robert E. Lee; literary criticism by Hugh Holman, Margaret Walker, Ralph Ellison, John Crowe Ransom, Allen Tate, Caroline Gordon, Cleanth Brooks, and Richmond Beatty; songs collected by Alan and John Lomax; plays by Lula Vollmer, John Augustin Daly, Paul Green, Kermit Hunter, William Norment Cox, and Bernice Kelly Harris; textbooks by Robert Penn Warren, Caroline Gordon, and Cleanth Brooks; and the frontier lore compiled by James Frank Dobie and Elinore Pruitt Stewart

- a bibliography of overviews, collections, compendia, commentary, and pivotal reference works, particularly Louis D. Rubin, Jr.'s *The History of Southern Literature*, Oscar G. Brockett's *History of the Theatre*, Abraham Chapman's *Black Voices*, Oral Sumner Coad and Edwin Mims, Jr.'s *The American Stage*, Cathy N. Davidson and Linda Wagner-Martin's *The Oxford Companion to Women's Writing*, Richard Beale Davis's *Southern Writing: 1585–1920*, Eugene Ehrlich and Gorton Carruth's *The Oxford Illustrated Literary Guide to the United States*, Kenneth Estell's *The African-American Almanac*, Alexander Karanikas's *Tillers of a Myth*, Stanley J. Kunitz and Howard Haycraft's *American Authors: 1600–1900*, W. Augustus Low and Virgil A. Clift's *Encyclopedia of Black America*, Jessie Carney Smith's *Notable Black American Women*, and Dr. Robert O. Stephens's *The Family Saga in the South: Generations and Destinies*. Without doubt, the body of research in Charles Reagan Wilson and William Ferris's *Encyclopedia of Southern Culture* surpasses all other works in completeness and comprises the starting point for any study of Southern culture.

- a comprehensive index of genres, titles, authors, historical and literary events, motifs, themes, characters, and settings: for example, humor, *The Great Meadow,* Sarah Delany, Jim Crow era, Harlem Renaissance, captivity lore, film based on Southern literature, Atticus Finch, and the Mississippi Valley

Contrasting studies of the South relieve the reader of faded stereotypes of moonlight-and-magnolias or crass slave dealers. Among the living images in Southern lore are a lasting friendship in Fannie Flagg's *Fried Green Tomatoes at the Whistle Stop Cafe;* mountain men in David H. Coyner's frontier overview; immigrant neighbors in Flannery O'Connor's stories; natural backdrops in the poems of Caroline Howard Gilman; religious satire in Larry Larson, Levi Lee, and Rebecca Wackler's *Tent Meeting;* and the collaboration of George and Ira Gershwin with Dubose Heyward to produce *Porgy and Bess,* the first American folk opera. A perusal of the *Encyclopedia of Southern Literature* compels the researcher, reader, writer, teacher, and casual reader to return to Dixie's fiction and nonfiction for a lively, enthralling view of American history and culture as they exist in the South.

ACKNOWLEDGMENTS

Gary Carey
writer and editor
Lincoln, Nebraska

Reference Department
Chicago Public Library
Chicago, Illinois

Avis Gachet
Wonderland Books
Granite Falls, North Carolina

Frances Hilton
Chapter One Books
Hickory, North Carolina

Reference Department
Jackson Clinton Library
University of North Carolina–
Greensboro
Greensboro, North Carolina

Kathy Lambert-Scronce
University of North Carolina–
Greensboro
Greensboro, North Carolina

Mary A. McCay, Chair
English Department
Loyola University
New Orleans, Louisiana

Burl McCuisten
Reference Librarian
Lenoir-Rhyne College
Hickory, North Carolina

Louis Nunnery
Hickory, North Carolina

Michael Parker
English Department
University of North Carolina–
Greensboro
Greensboro, North Carolina

Lynne Bolick Reid
Catawba County Library
Newton, North Carolina

Wanda Rozzelle
Catawba County Library
Newton, North Carolina

Cindy Sears
Elbert Ivey Library
Hickory, North Carolina

Daniel E. Williams, Chair
Department of English
University of Mississippi
University, Mississippi

Many thanks to Dr. Robert O. Stephens, Greensboro, North Carolina, in whose graduate school class I first learned to love the literature of the South. And praise and thanks for the business machine management, mailing, shelving, typing, and research performed by my secretary, Andrea Pittman.

INTRODUCTION

For more than three centuries following Europe's colonization of the New World, the American South has intrigued artists with its gentle climate, varied plant and animal life, vigorous people, and ample resources. A virtual Eden, the comely land offers the traveler, explorer, settler, entrepreneur, and artist a panoply of enticements—luxuriant bays and harbors, rugged peaks and granite outcrops of the Great Smoky Mountains, genial hill country dotted with live oaks and longleaf pines, Texas grasslands, forest beauties of the Mississippi Valley, and the great Mississippi itself, the life's blood of the central plains. Over the virgin land, shapers and dreamers who established homes, plantations, and communities have left records of their contentment in letters, journals, speech, song, legend, verse, and history. Yet, as with every human idyll, the reality leans heavily toward imperfection. Displacement of native peoples and the blot of slavery forever altered the concept of a new land founded in liberty. The upheaval of the Civil War vented extremes of emotion, destroyed Southern society, and reduced the plantation origins to a shambles destined once more to feed new dreams of place and productivity. From the ruins arose a New South in a healing process drawing on the same strengths that had nourished Southern colonies. An ambitious literary movement, the Fugitive Agrarians, challenged art to examine form, substance, and imagination, and to supplant plantation-era weakness with a renewed dedication to realism. Modern and postmodern artisans who succeeded these regional beginnings have introduced Southern qualities to the national canon and to world literature, which is ennobled and enlightened by a distinct subject matter and point of view.

The creative response that has grown out of the South's experience fills a repository of life and letters with the uniqueness and energy of an area still emerging, still building on its faulty past with a determination founded on love of place and greater respect for indigenous people:

- Mary Boykin Chesnut's journals capture the clashing events and emotions that humbled the South and forced its people to rethink the basis of their prosperity.

- Sidney Lanier's "The Marshes of Glynn" expresses a transcendent immersion in nature that replenishes a poet who survived a Civil War prison.

- Mark Twain's *Pudd'nhead Wilson* attests to the hard lessons of racism; his *Life on the Mississippi* records a lifetime romance with river travel and commerce.

- James Agee's *A Death in the Family* is a gentle litany of human strengths that feed succeeding generations with his vision of loving kin, security, and acceptance.

- Harper Lee's *To Kill a Mockingbird* questions an insidious racism that crippled generations of Southerners and victimized blacks for imagined infractions of a chivalric code of white womanhood.

The spirit of the South is an amorphous blend derived from the teachers, writers, journalists, speakers, singers, fablists, and storytellers whose contributions to the American literary canon defy generalizations. The perplexing issue of what constitutes Southernness returns the questioner to the works themselves:

- the patriotic lyrics of "My Maryland," "The Bonny Blue Flag," "The Negro National Anthem," and "The Star-Spangled Banner"

- dialect in George Washington Cable's "Jean-ah Pouquelin," Julia Mood Peterkin's *Black April*, Edgar Allan Poe's "The Gold Bug," Dorothy Allison's *Bastard Out of Carolina*, and Joseph Glover Baldwin's humorous commentary on the California gold rush

- Melissa Fay Greene's sociological inquiry and Nikki Giovanni's hard-edged verse, both of which challenge stereotypes of self, race, religion, and region

- Truman Capote's prototypical journalistic novel, *In Cold Blood*, researched in part by Harper Lee

- John and Alan Lomax's collected ballads, gospels, and work songs from Southwestern and Deep South traditions

- Cynthia Rylant, Marjorie Kinnan Rawlings, Theodore Taylor, Bette Greene, and Fred Gipson's sensitive, intuitive expressions of childhood experiences that precipitate maturity

- Flannery O'Connor, William Faulkner, Carson McCullers, and Edgar Allan Poe's vivid crafting of the grotesque

- the slave narratives of William Wells Brown and Harriet Ann Jacobs and the collected anonymous slave writings in Julius Lester's *To Be a Slave*

- regional autobiographies—*Narrative of the Life of Frederick Douglass*, Jesse Stuart's *The Thread That Runs So True*, Lillian Hellman's *An Unfinished Woman*, Ellen Glasgow's *A Woman Within*, William Styron's *Darkness Visible*, Maya Angelou's *I Know Why the Caged Bird Sings*, Jackie Torrence's *The Importance of Pot Liquor*, Dick Gregory's *Nigger*, Eudora Welty's *One Writer's Beginnings*, and Marjorie Kinnan Rawlings's *Cross Creek*

- strong feminism in the writings of Angelina and Sarah Grimké, Kate Chopin's *The Awakening*, Ellen Glasgow's *Vein of Iron*, Harriette Arnow's *The Dollmaker*, Zora Neale Hurston's *Their Eyes Were Watching God*, Sara Teasdale's verse, the popular novels of E. D. E. N. Southworth, Olive Ann Burns's *Cold Sassy Tree*, and Sarah and Elizabeth Delany's *Having Our Say*

- journals and periodicals begun by area writers—*Crockett Almanac, American Mercury, Uncle Remus's Magazine, Carolina Israelite, Smart Set, Cherokee Advocate*, and *Cherokee Phoenix*

Much ink has been expended on lists of qualities that define Southern literature. The recurring elements are the love of land, sense of belonging, commitment to family and God, hearty patriotism, and resurgent traditions in folklore, language, and humor. The sterility of enumerated qualities fails to account for the astonishing intellectualism, curiosity, and grace of a literature that incorporates Allen Tate's "Ode to the Confederate Dead" and James Weldon Johnson's "The Creation," Uncle Remus's Tarbaby story alongside the Declaration of Independence, and inclusion of Mark Twain's *The Adventures of Huckleberry Finn* with Ralph Ellison's *Invisible Man*. The historical drama that fuels Alex Haley's *Roots* and *Queen* has little in common with William Styron's *Sophie's Choice*, Walter Dean Meyers's *Fallen Angels*, Sonia Sanchez's *Does Your House Have Lions?*, or Robert Penn Warren's *All the King's Men*, yet each chronicles a segment of the region's experience, whether limited to the environs or shared with the nation and world. The fervor and originality of classic Southern literature stand out from other regions by virtue of their concerns: William Gilmore Simms's addition of Native American characters to serious literature, George Washington Cable's study of the doppelgänger produced by slave masters who sired Métis children to grow up alongside heirs to plantations, Ellen Gilchrist's re-creation of amoral generations who spring from the South's flawed past, and Alfred Uhry's forgiving drama that pairs a member of the black servant class with a Jewish scion of the industrial class. Eyewitness accounts by Frederick Douglass, Ida Bell Wells-Barnett, John Ehle, Fanny Kemble, and Molly Ivins share regional inclusion among fictional scenarios by Harriette Arnow, Walter Dean Meyers, William Gilmore Simms, and Beth Henley. Lesser contributors such as Booker T. Washington, Harry Golden, Gail Godwin, Robert Harling, Ellen Glasgow, and Dubose Heyward share honors with the moguls of Southern literature—Alex Haley, Carson McCullers, James Agee, Katherine Anne Porter, Tennessee Williams, Maya Angelou, William Faulkner, Eudora Welty, and Ernest Gaines. Suited to the issues and impetus of the times, each contributes a strand to the complex ferment that generates Southern lore.

As a unit, Southern literature bears the rich, intensely satisfying qualities of any canon—the curiosity and drive of frontier literature; the passion of personal letters, journals, and poetry; the wisdom of aphorism; and the grandeur of family saga, war literature, and social doctrine. Some facets stand out as literary touchstones:

- reflections on Native Americans in the writings of Caroline Gordon, Dee Brown, Diane Glancy, and George Washington Parke Custis

- a frontier tradition evolved by Elias Boudinot, Margaret Hanley Haulee, Daniel Boone, Janice Holt Giles, Elinore Pruitt Stewart, Marjorie Kinnan Rawlings, John Beauchamp Jones, Larry McMurtry, William F. Drannan, David H. Coyner, and Sequoyah

- a body of plantation lore and the remnants of the cavalier spirit that enliven works by Harriet Ann Jacobs, John Pendleton Kennedy, Julia Mood Peterkin, and Joel Chandler Harris

- a parallel series of sketches from the mountain tradition as described by Davy Crockett, Earl Hamner, Jr., Mary Noailles Murfree, Eliot Wigginton, Jesse Stuart, James Clyman, John Fox, Jr., Charles Frazier, and Donald Davidson

- a conflicting series of historic pictures of the Civil War era as compiled and created by James Weldon Johnson, Mary Boykin Chesnut, Stephen Vincent Benét, Margaret Walker, Charles Frazier, and Charles Waddell Chesnutt

- a tradition of strong and at times eccentric and uncompromising female personae whose hardheadedness undergirds the writings of Allan Gurganus, Marsha Norman, Richard Wright, William Faulkner, Bette Greene, Tennessee Williams, Lillian Hellman, Charles Portis, Clyde Edgerton, and Truman Capote

- outdoor dramas by Paul Green and Kermit Hunter, who initiated a national demand for historic spectacle in reenactments of the Lost Colony, the life of Daniel Boone, and the Trail of Tears

- civil rights annals and protest literature by Dr. Martin Luther King, Jr., Jesse Jackson, Barbara Jordan, Eldridge Cleaver, Anne E. Moody, Dick Gregory, Ida Bell Wells-Barnett, and John Howard Griffin

- fictional works that have profited from stage and screen adaptation, as seen in *Band of Angels, To Kill a Mockingbird, Fried Green Tomatoes, Driving Miss Daisy, The Heart Is a Lonely Hunter, The Member of the Wedding, Cat on a Hot Tin Roof, The Little Foxes, The Trip to Bountiful, The Color Purple, A Streetcar Named Desire, Steel Magnolias, Bastard Out of Carolina,* and *Gone with the Wind*

Of particular note are the critical writings of H. L. Mencken, Louis D. Rubin, Jr., W. J. Cash, Edgar Allan Poe, Sidney Lanier, and a consortium of teachers and writers from Vanderbilt University, whose impetus enabled Southerners and outsiders to examine the direction the region has taken from early settlement into the twentieth century. Overall, Southern literature presents a detailed reflection on the first English colonies, early frontier spirit, scientific study of swampland and bird life, displacement of Native Americans, the expedition that preceded the Louisiana Purchase, the slave trade and resultant abolitionism, conclusion and aftermath of the nation's only civil war, and the growth of the civil rights movement. The immediacy of Southern themes sets them apart from all other bodies of literature, whether contained in the young-adult novels of Mildred Taylor; social criticism of Walter Hines Page, George Washington Cable, Henry Grady, Mary Ann Shadd Cary, and Booker T. Washington; gothic romances of Edgar Allan Poe; speeches of Patrick Henry, Jefferson Davis, Barbara Jordon, and Dr. Martin Luther King, Jr.; documents and apologias by Varina Davis and the framers of the Edenton Tea Party; or local humor found in Augustus Baldwin Longstreet, Florence King, Clyde Edgerton, Joseph Glover Baldwin, Molly Ivins, Johnson Jones Hooper, and Fannie Flagg. The perceptions of Kate Chopin, Francis Scott Key, O. Henry, and Colonel William Byrd maintain an integral place in the unfolding American literary tradition, as do the contemporary additions of Melissa Fay Greene, James Dickey, Alice Walker, William Styron, Alice Childress, and Pat Conroy. Taken as a whole, the Southern canon is a cherished record of the region's vital contribution to American culture.

ABC-CLIO LITERARY COMPANION

Encyclopedia of
Southern
Literature

AGEE, JAMES

Appreciation for the artistic, sometimes flamboyant writings of James Rufus Agee, a lyric genius and skilled modern imagist, is an acquired taste. Critics and readers who claim him as the mid–twentieth century's willful prodigy retrieve from neglect one of the extraordinarily gifted upstarts from the South. Born in Knoxville, Tennessee, he derived substance and point of view from his Cumberland Mountain heritage and broadened his knowledge of rural life by spending summer vacations bucking wheat bales in Kansas and Nebraska. Experience with humble, working-class harvesters contrasts his educational milieu—the classes at St. Andrews' School, Exeter, and Harvard that prepared him for literary stardom. Before graduating from college in 1932, he won a poetry prize from the Harvard *Advocate* and briefly pursued the stirrings of a poetic muse in his only poetry collection, *Permit Me Voyage* (1934).

Thriving in Frenchtown, Massachusetts, Agee worked in an improbable spot for a lyricist—the editorial staff of *Fortune*, which dispatched him to Alabama near the end of the Depression to observe and write about sharecropping. From a live-in experience among farmworkers evolved *Let Us Now Praise Famous Men* (1941), a moving, humanistic tribute to common labor illustrated with black-and-white candid photographs by his colleague Walker Evans. Both passionate and probingly candid, the sheaf of interconnected essays shimmers with his idiosyncratic blend of image and reportage. Similar to journalist Jack Reed's immersion in the Mexican Revolution in *Insurgent Mexico*, Agee's loss of objectivity uplifts pedestrian journalism to poetry, a violation of the expected order that unnerved some critics, who lambasted him as an out-of-control romantic posing as reporter.

After residing among the Ricketts, Gudgers, and Woods in the environs of Birmingham, Agee sets to work on a literary portrait, identifying himself and Evans as spy and counterspy. Unashamed to report that he has a lot to learn about poverty, Agee covers the commonalities of agrarian life—boots and overalls, tools, crops, one-pot meals eaten without savor or recognition, and a bare mattress on which to stretch out at night. Agee's unprecedented use of spacing, lowercase letters, colons, and semicolons metes out the elements of after-dinner activity, the cool of the evening when workers breathe free before readying themselves for sleep and another day of toil:

and when the women are through, they may or may not come out too, with their dresses wet in front with the dishwashing and their hard hands softened and seamed as if withered with water, and sit a little while with the man or the men: and if they do, it is not for long, for everyone is much too tired, and has been awake and at work since daylight whitened a little behind the trees on the hill, and it is now very close to dark, with daylight scarcely more than a sort of tincture on the air. . . . (Agee 1960, 66)

At the outer edge of sleep sound the katydid, whippoorwill, and owl and the other night noises indigenous to the South. The rooster's crow calls the sleepers back to the endless round of farm and orchard work. Like dumb beasts, they center their being in the unrelenting cycles of nature.

In the greater realm of rural life, Agee tells of limited schooling and church meetings, rare purchases, and rarer expenditure for entertainment. At a time when cash is scarce, he expresses the values of lamplight and a family Bible, and the urgent need for improved hygiene, transportation, and medical care. Beyond physical needs range the affective demands of the spirit—the inarticulate cry for respect and acknowledgment. Agee's words batter the brutality of a life that works a body like a machine. He declares that

the ends of this work are absorbed all but entirely into the work itself, and in what little remains, nearly all is obliterated; nearly nothing is obtainable; nearly all is cruelly stained, in the tensions of physical need, and in the desperate tensions of the need of work which is not available. (Agee 1960, 290)

At the heart of the sharecropper's desperation, Agee elucidates with scriptural eloquence the plainness and repetitiveness of the farm laborer's existence.

At the close of his emotional sojourn with Southern society's bottom layer, Agee demands that poverty be assessed, challenged, and eradicated. In an ardent address to the reader he pleads, "let us then hope better of our children, and of our children's children; let us know, let us *know* there is a cure, there is to be an end to it, whose beginnings are long begun, and in slow agonise and all deceptions clearing." (Agee 1960, 398–399) His final paragraph is the Lord's Prayer. A postlude casts its glance back at the swollen belly of the sharecropper's wife, Ellen. Awed by a vision of sharecrop labor's self-perpetuation, the author witnesses "a thing so strong, so valiant, so unvanquishable, it is without effort, without emotion, I know it shall at length outshine the sun." (Agee 1960, 402) The poem serving as epilogue declares that the humble shall not die unremembered.

From 1939 to 1948, Agee wrote for *Time* and reviewed films for *Nation*. One of the first serious cinema critics, he loved movies and wrote about cinema art for *Life, Partisan Review,* and *Sight and Sound.* Eager to be a part of the visual dimension, he departed print journalism to write for Madison Avenue and Hollywood. His credits cover a respectable body of screenplays—*The Quiet One* (1949), *The Night of the Hunter* (1955), *Face to Face* (a two-part adaptation of Joseph Conrad's *The Secret Sharer* and Stephen Crane's *The Bride Comes to Yellow Sky*) (1952), and Agee's most famous movie play, *The African Queen* (1951), co-authored with John Huston as a comic vehicle for Humphrey Bogart and

Katharine Hepburn. Agee returned to the novel with an autobiographical bildungsroman, *The Morning Watch* (1951), a flawed, immature novella that describes a teenager (obviously Agee in boyhood) attending a parochial school in Tennessee. The work anticipates his classic novel, *A Death in the Family* (1956), a Pulitzer Prize–winner published posthumously after Agee's death from a heart attack on May 16, 1955.

A contender for Southern literature's most invitingly lush childhood scene, *A Death in the Family* was meant as a monument to Agee's father. The opening sequence, "Knoxville: Summer 1915" (published separately in *Partisan Review* in 1935), grows from organic material that Agee may have developed subconsciously since childhood. Richly overlaid with sense impressions on a summer evening, the setting is a quilt on a Knoxville lawn, where the speaker observes the sounds of children playing and home owners hosing the grass. Departing from prose, Agee inserts eight lines of verse that describe traditional rhythms and sights, recalling "Parents on porches: rock and rock: From damp strings morning glories: hang their ancient faces." (Agee 1969, 15) Lying inert with parents, aunt, and uncle, the speaker, six-year-old Rufus, gazes at stars as the talk recedes into a background accompaniment. Limp in the early stages of sleep, he relaxes his hold on consciousness and acquiesces as his body is lifted, cradled in strong arms, and delivered safely to bed. In token of the beneficence of his childhood, he wishes God's grace on the protective adults of his family: "May God bless my people, my uncle, my aunt, my mother, my good father, oh, remember them kindly in their time of trouble; and in the hour of their taking away." (Agee 1969, 15)

The benediction ends with the query of the initiate, who questions his beginning and his place in the human scheme: "Sleep, soft smiling, draws me unto her: and those receive me, who quietly treat me, as one familiar and well-beloved in that home: but will not, oh, will not, not now, not ever; but will not ever tell me who I am." (Agee 1969, 15) Like the organ diapason drawing a worshipper into meditation, the prologue pulls the unsuspecting reader into the central conflict, which reprises Agee's dismay at his father's death in a car accident when he was six. Expecting the decline and possible death of his grandfather, Rufus recalls the late-night departure of his father alone by car to a nearby town. Rufus and his mother are jolted by a freak accident that forces the car off the road and kills his father, Jay Follett, with one quick blow of the chin against the steering column.

The misgivings and regrets that accumulate around an unforeseen death disrupt Rufus's security, recasting him as half orphan. The adults ponder their interpretations of what is important. The priest, Father Jackson, counsels Mary Follett on the altered service for people like Jay, who was never baptized. The abrasive behavior of the clergyman annoys the family, but Mary endures. Beyond her concerns, Rufus whiles away a day out of school, basks in attention, dutifully buttons his baby sister Catherine's romper, then withdraws to his father's chair to breathe in aftershave and tobacco smells that resurrect the good man who had sired and raised him. At the grave, as Rufus's uncle Andrew rails at the unfeeling priest, Rufus concentrates on a butterfly, the frail symbol of spirit that graces a scene otherwise concluded in bitterness and silence. After the author's death, playwright Tad Mosel adapted the novel to play form for *All the Way Home* (1960), also a Pulitzer Prize recipient. Agee's reviews were collected in a two-volume compendium entitled *Agee on Film* (1958); his correspondence with a high school mentor appears as *Letters to Father Flye* (1962). (Agee 1960, 1966, 1969; Bradbury 1963; Bradbury 1996; Ehrlich and Carruth 1982; King 1980; Kunitz 1942; Lowe 1994; Monaco 1991; Rubin et al. 1985; Stein 1979; Zeno 1995)

ANGELOU, MAYA

A true eclectic and a vital force among African-American women, Maya Angelou is the product of the mothering and Bible guidance of her paternal grandmother, Annie "Momma" Henderson, and the riotous urbanity and insouciance of divorced parents. Born Marguerite Johnson on April 4, 1928 in St. Louis, Missouri, Angelou is one of the South's literary matriarchs. A self-directed learner, she read English classics, the beginning of her love affair with literature. She idolized as best friend and comrade-in-mischief her older brother, Bailey Junior, who reduced her first name to Maya when she was a toddler. The two are the only children of Vivian "Bibbie" Baxter, a nurse and bon vivant faro dealer, and Bailey Henderson, Sr., a self-important doorman and Navy chef. After her parents' separation in 1931, three-year-old Maya was delivered to her grandmother and uncle, who welcomed her to Stamps, Arkansas, a wide spot in the road on the Texarkana border.

In the cultural sterility of the Southern outback, Angelou's most colorful Depression-era memories derive from the milieu of the Wm. Johnson General Merchandise Store, her grandmother's variety store and food service. In a reminiscence of childhood in the South, she speaks of the meanness of Stamps, where the only white entrepreneur was the owner of a cotton gin:

> On our side of town, called quarters (a lingering term used wistfully by whites), all the men were dirt farmers, and those women who did not work with their husbands in the bottom land and many who did, took in washing, ironing, and actually left their homes to go to care for the houses of women only a little better off than they, economically, but who believed that their white skin gave them the right to have Negro servants. (Angelou 1982, 132)

The dreary whites-over-blacks social structure inspired Angelou to vow never to return to the demeaning South, a promise she kept until she was 40 years old. The sole mentor she considered worthy of emulation was Momma Henderson, whom Angelou fantasizes as the magician who waves her handkerchief at a snooty dental assistant to "[turn] her into a crocus sack of chicken feed." (Angelou 1970, 162)

In 1936, Angelou escaped the Bible Belt to return to St. Louis, where she was swayed by citified ease, entertainments, and promise. Coddled by her elegant mother, Bailey's ideal woman, Maya grew self-conscious of her rangy, six-foot-tall body and overlarge hands and feet, which contrasted with the stylish, liberated, five-foot, four-inch Bibbie Baxter, who could shimmy, mix drinks, sweet-talk admirers, and shoot a pistol when a flirtatious male got too close or too demanding. Life with the Baxter clan, including a part-German grandmother, invalid grandfather, and three Mafiaesque uncles, replaced Angelou's fear of Ku Klux Klan retaliations with the St. Louis–style political power wielded by Grandmother Baxter, a ward boss not to be trifled with. Her rule extended to Mr. Freeman, Vivian's seedy, live-in boyfriend, whom Angelou depicts in *I Know Why the Caged Bird Sings* (1970) as a coaxing pedophile. Freeman rapes Maya and threatens to kill her brother if she divulges his dirty secret. The episode climaxes in a fitting demise—the Baxter brothers kick Freeman to death behind a slaughterhouse.

To counter guilt that she caused Freeman's violent death, Angelou willed herself mute. Unable to cope with a high-strung daughter, Vivian returned her to the safer microcosm of Stamps. With Momma's gentle-hard touch and "lessons in living" from a polite matriarch named Bertha Flowers, Maya regained her voice by reciting classical verse. (Angelou 1970, 83) In 1940, she graduated from Lafayette County Training School at the top of her eighth-grade class. Reestablished in Los Angeles with Bibbie, she later moved with the family to Oakland and then to the Fillmore district of San Francisco, where her mother gave up nursing for gambling. Angelou learned to love her stepfather, Daddy Clidell Jackson, a real estate investor who offered her security and acceptance.

Angelou continued her studies at George Washington High School, studied dance at the California Labor School, worked as the city's first female streetcar conductor, and graduated from Mission High a few weeks before the birth of Clyde Bailey "Guy" Johnson, her only child. In humorous reflection on her concealed pregnancy, she writes:

> That evening, in the bosom of the now-dear family home I uncoiled my fearful secret and in a brave gesture left a note on Daddy Clidell's bed. It read: Dear Parents, I am sorry to bring this disgrace on the family, but I am pregnant. Marguerite. (Angelou 1970, 244)

According to her autobiography, Angelou requires Bibbie's forceful nudge to welcome a fragile infant into her bed. The tender scene works out as her mother predicts. She whispers, "See, you don't have to think about doing the right thing. If you're for the right thing, then you do it without thinking." (Angelou 1970, 246)

Gather Together in My Name (1974), the second and least admirable installment of Angelou's multivolume autobiography, tells of her postadolescent rush to adult independence. Liberated from the suffocating prissiness Momma had demanded in Stamps and from Bibbie's watchful eye, she waits tables in nightclubs, clerks in a record shop, works in a bordello, cooks in a bistro, and dances exotic numbers onstage to support herself and her infant son. In typical Angelou style, she narrates a candid learning experience with prostitution:

> I had expected the loud screams of total orgasmic release and felt terribly inadequate when the men had finished with grunts and yanked up their pants

without thanks. I decided that being black, I had a different rhythm from the Latinos and all I had to do was let myself learn their tempos. (Angelou 1974, 167)

At luck's basement level, she opted out of turning tricks and sampling heroin, packed up her child, and returned to Bibbie. At age 22, Angelou married Greek-American Tosh Angelos, but ended the two-year relationship, which she describes in *Singin' and Swingin' and Gettin' Merry Like Christmas* (1976), part three of her life story. She left Guy with her mother and began studying dance with Pearl Primus and Martha Graham. Angelou's professional career in dance began with a road show of *Porgy and Bess*, which was making a government-sponsored tour of Africa and Europe. On her return to California, she settled in Sausalito and altered her aims from dancing to writing.

After migrating to New York, Angelou joined the Harlem Writers Guild while continuing her music career with singing at the Apollo Theatre and minor roles in off-Broadway productions. Her residence ended in 1961 when she moved to Cairo; after marrying South African politician Vusumzi Make, she moved to Johannesburg. Angelou was disappointed in their relationship, which Make tyrannized according to his Old World patriarchal principles and predilection for adultery. Liberated and again choosing her own way, she flourished as a reporter and associate editor for the *Arab Observer*, an English news journal. After a near-fatal car accident crippled Guy, Angelou moved to Accra, Ghana, to supervise his rehabilitation. She found work administering the School of Music and Drama, for which she wrote original musicals, and edited the *African Review*, a political monthly. In *All God's Children Need Travelin' Shoes* (1986), her reflection over residency in Africa, an epiphany emerges as she prepares to fly home from Accra:

Many years earlier I, or rather someone very like me and certainly related to me, had been taken from Africa by force. This second leave-taking would not be so onerous, for now I knew my people had never completely left Africa. (Angelou 1986, 305)

Receptive to the essential spot in her life held by the arts, she honors the bit of Africa that survives in blues, gospel, dance physique, and laughter.

Pining for California and restless for change, Angelou returned to the United States to describe transitions in her style and outlook in *The Heart of a Woman* (1981). Maturing from the picaresque era of her escapades, she became a disciple of civil rights champions Bayard Rustin, Ralph Abernathy, and Dr. Martin Luther King, Jr., collaborating with actor and comedian Godfrey Cambridge on *Cabaret for Freedom*, a fund-raiser for the Southern Christian Leadership Conference. At the urging of James Baldwin and Jules and Judy Feiffer, she wrote *I Know Why the Caged Bird Sings*, a Book-of-the-Month Club selection and National Book Award nominee. An immediate hit, it earned classic status on feminist and multicultural book lists.

Among other poignant, introspective black autobiographies, her reflections stand out as a readable and valid representation of African-American womanhood. The two-hour film version, which was showcased on the *Saturday Night*

Poet Maya Angelou reads "On the Pulse of the Morning" during William Clinton's first presidential inauguration, January 20, 1993.

Movie on April 28, 1979, starred Constance Good as the young Maya and Esther Rolle as Grandmother Henderson.

After marrying building contractor Paul de Feu in 1973, Angelou made a new home in Sonoma, California. A powerhouse of creative ideas, she wrote the screenplay *Georgia, Georgia* (1971) as well as music, novels, more segments of her autobiography, and verse collections, including *Just Give Me a Cool Drink of Water 'fore I Diiie* (1971; nominated for a Pulitzer Prize), *Oh Pray My Wings Are Gonna Fit Me Well* (1975), *And Still I Rise* (1978), and *Now Sheba Sings the Song* (1987), a verse tribute to strong black women. Angelou centers much of her writing on the tribulations of woman, as exemplified by "Momma Welfare Roll" (1978), a verse portrait of an overweight, hard-working parent who challenges the public's stereotype of lazy people living on welfare. Calling herself "too fat to whore, too mad to work," the speaker challenges a "den of bureaucrats" by demanding her share of funds and snorts, "They don't give me welfare. I take it." (Angelou 1993, 139)

Angelou has played in off-Broadway productions of Jean Genet's *The Blacks* and in an adaptation of Sophocles's *Ajax;* she gave a Tony-nominated performance as Kunta Kinte's grandmother in the television miniseries version of Alex Haley's *Roots* (1977). In addition to guest appearances on television talk shows, a ten-part PBS special on African tradition in American life, and participation as guest interviewer for *Maya Angelou's America: A Journey of the Heart* (filmed in her hometown), she scripted *Sister, Sister* (1979), which aired on NBC-TV in 1982 and starred Diahann Carroll, Robert Hooks, and Paul Winfield. In the mid-1980s, she returned to autobiography with *All God's Children Need Travelin' Shoes* (1986), a memoir of her sojourn in Ghana.

Angelou has earned an array of honors commensurate with her talents. In January 1993, President Bill Clinton invited her to follow in the footsteps of Robert Frost by composing a poem to celebrate Clinton's first inauguration. Completing the work in six weeks, she produced "On the Pulse of the Morning," a richly evocative symbolic montage of rocks, dinosaurs, trees, rivers, and other elements from the natural world. At the core of her message is a hint of Negro spiritual: "Yet, today I call you to my riverside,/If you will study war no more. Come,/Clad in peace. . . ." (Angelou 1993, 4)

She continues speaking, performing, and teaching as a major part of her lifetime appointment as the first Reynolds Professor of American Studies at Wake Forest University in Winston-Salem, North Carolina. She holds honorary doctorates from Oberlin College, Smith College, Mills College, Mt. Holyoke, Boston College, Spelman College, Rollins University, University of Arkansas, North Carolina School of the Arts, and Lawrence University. Other awards include the *Ladies' Home Journal* 1976 Woman of the Year in Communications, Candace and Horatio Alger awards, *Essence* magazine award, induction into the Women in Film Hall of Fame, the Golden Eagle award from PBS for a 1977 documentary entitled *Afro-American in the Arts*, a Rockefeller grant and Yale University fellowship, 1983 Matrix Award from Women in Communications, appointment to the North Carolina Arts Council and the American Revolution Bicentennial Council, and nominations for a Pulitzer Prize and a Tony. (*Afro-American* 1985; Angelou 1970, 1974, 1982, 1986, 1993; Angelou and Neubauer 1987; Bailey 1984; Banerjee 1990; Bloom, Lynn 1985; Bogle 1988; Bradbury 1996; Elliott 1989; Hine et al. 1993; Houtchens 1993; Lewis 1981; McPherson 1990; Oliver 1983; Shapiro 1993; Shuker 1990; Smith, Sidonie 1973; Stepto 1979)

See also Haley, Alex; *I Know Why the Caged Bird Sings;* poetry of the South.

THE AUTOBIOGRAPHY OF MISS JANE PITTMAN

In his intriguing framework novel *The Autobiography of Miss Jane Pittman* (1971), Ernest James Gaines creates an eerie realism in the idiom and character of Miss Jane Pittman, the intransigent plantation matriarch who bulldozes her way through experience, prestige, and sheer chutzpah. Similar to the female protagonists in Margaret Walker's *Jubilee* and Alice Walker's *The Color Purple*, this quasi-genuine survivor of the Civil War, Reconstruction, and civil rights movement effectively silences an unnamed teacher, the quavering interviewer seeking realistic slave narratives for classroom use. In the summer of 1962, Mary Hodges, Jane's caregiver, halts the intruder, but Jane agrees to cooperate with a hundred-year memoir, which friends amend and explain when memory fails. The novel concludes at a momentous confrontation with racism—Miss Jane's matter-of-fact sip at a courthouse water fountain in defiance of a whites-only ordinance. The deed is one of many high points in her life, which ends eight months after the interview. At the funeral, well-wishers and friends who lived similar episodes reiterate moments from Miss Jane's fight for equality.

Gaines links his protagonist to the past by picturing her at significant moments in Southern history. He introduces her at Bryant Plantation as Ticey. A child herself at age ten, she takes charge of the master's children. Two years later, while the master and adult slaves cower in the swamp during the height of Union insurgency, Ticey ventures into the open to draw water for "Secesh" stragglers. Shortly before the formal end of slavery, she encounters Corporal Brown heading a Yankee cavalry troop. Moved by her youth and spunk, he spares her the task of hauling water for men and horses, and dispatches a trooper in her place. He rescinds the ignoble slave name and calls her Jane, after his own daughter. Pertinacious and buoyed by hope, Jane throws off subservience, even after her owner calls for whipping and reassignment to fieldwork when Jane refuses to answer to the name Ticey.

The author dramatizes the arrival of freedom with a formal reading of Lincoln's Emancipation Proclamation. Having no kin to bind her to Bryant Plantation, Jane joins a clutch of newly liberated slaves who wrap apples and potatoes in spare garments to feed themselves on the trek north. She fantasizes that she will reach Ohio and locate her hero, Corporal Brown. Led by Big Laura, a sturdy, mythic figure similar to Harriet "Moses" Tubman and symbolized by the flint and steel she carries to light cook fires, the party moves out with no knowledge of maps or directions. Gaines stresses the group's naïveté and lack of forethought when they cross paths with a vindictive gang of "paterollers." The violent murder of Laura and the abandonment of her infant son Ned to Jane's care sets the parameters of the remaining narrative, in which Jane considers herself Ned's mother and protector.

Gaines depicts the minuscule progress of ex-slaves during Reconstruction as Jane, still determined to reach Ohio, struggles on with Ned in tow. Sketchy reports of the Freedman's Bureau incline them toward the corrupt resettlement houses that force ex-slaves into a new form of servitude. Pragmatic about the

absence of education and experience, Jane negotiates for work on the plantation of a typical scalawag, ominously named Mr. Bone. Blacks learn the hard
lesson of emancipation: Whereas former masters protected slaves like valuable
livestock, on their own and stripped of value as breeders and laborers tied to
the plantation, slaves must rely on themselves. A wise man called Unc Isom
explains, "Before now they didn't kill you because you was somebody chattel.
Now you ain't owned by nobody but fate." (Gaines 1971, 13) At this point, the
novel swells the theme of secondhand motherhood in Jane's faithful care of
Laura's Ned. A contemplative youngster marked for activism, he alters his name
to Edward Stephen Douglass, one of many blacks who model their ambitions
on the life of Baltimore-born ex-slave Frederick Douglass, a national model of
courage and dignity. Sure and vicious comes retaliation from groups like the
"Ku Klux Klans, the White Brotherhood, the Camellias o' Luzana." (Gaines
1971, 68) In adulthood, Ned trades roles with his foster mother and rebukes
himself for leaving Jane vulnerable. He gives up on the South, migrates north
to Kansas, and serves in Cuba during the Spanish-American War.

The regional qualities of Gaines's fiction surface in the intervening years.
Dialect pronunciations—hyphen/hydrant, Beero/Bureau, Singalee/Senegalese,
jeck/jerk, retrick/rhetoric, gorilla tragedy/guerrilla strategy, fedjal/federal,
S'mellin'/Schmeling, lectwicity/electricity, and Luzana/Louisiana—connects
Jane to time and place. Freed of responsibility for the first time since age ten,
she marries bronc-buster Joe Pittman, a widower, who adds his two girls, Clara
and Ella, to their family circle. The Pittmans find work on the Texas-Louisiana
border. In a touchingly feminine grasp at happiness, Jane seeks out Madame
Eloise Gautier, a voodoo sorceress, who bungles an attempt to save Joe from a
satanic stallion and heaps guilt on Jane for bringing a barren womb to their
marriage. Jane mourns,

> When Joe Pittman was killed a part of me went with him to his grave. No man
> will ever take his place, and that's why I carry his name to this day. I have
> knowed two or three other men, but none took the place of Joe Pittman, I let
> them know that from the start. (Gaines 1971, 98)

Once more, Jane survives tragedy, but the growing burden of loss sets the pattern for more cultural struggles that try even Jane's hardihood.

Gaines returns to the voodoo arts to counter a more virulent form of evil.
While living amicably among Cajuns at the time of Ned's return south, Jane
confronts Albert Cluveau, a friend/monster who is both her fishing companion and the obsessed bayou hit man hired to assassinate Ned. The novel's ominous rising action parallels the Sermon on the Mount and the writings of Booker
T. Washington in Ned's uplifting sermon calling for loyalty to black heritage,
pride, and newly won American citizenship. Jane's prophetic dream precedes
the return of Ned's corpse:

> When the others came in from the field and heard what had happened they
> knelt down right there and cried. They didn't want go [sic] near him when he
> was living, but when they heard he was dead they cried like children. They ran
> up to the wagon when it stopped at the gate. They wanted to touch his body,

Miss Jane Pittman (Cicely Tyson) relates her century-long story to a reporter (Michael Murphy) in a scene from *The Autobiography of Miss Jane Pittman*, a 1974 made-for-television movie based on the 1971 novel by Ernest James Gaines.

they wanted to help take it inside. The road was full, people coming from everywhere. They wanted to touch his body. When they couldn't touch his body they took lumber from the wagon. They wanted a piece of lumber with his blood on it. (Gaines 1971, 116)

The immediacy of grief and outrage recasts the humble country cortege for a local martyr as a miniature of the slow train that bore Abraham Lincoln's coffin past mourning throngs.

To normalize Jane's 110 years, Gaines counterbalances woe by setting her in the pro-black governorship of Louisiana's legendary Huey "Kingfish" Long, the era of athletic strides of Joe Louis and Jackie Robinson, and the rise of Dr. Martin Luther King, Jr. In many ways, Jane is everywoman, particularly in her yearning for a stable home and children. A victim of sexual abuse, whipping, and humiliation, she looks to males like Corporal Brown, the Dodgers, and Jimmy "The One" Aaron for strength, but finds a powerhouse in her own spirit. Canny in negotiating with greedy, crazed, and predatory people, she maintains the strong standards that buoyed her in the past. A character modeled on protester Rosa Parks, she is swept into the spirit of civil disobedience the morning that Jimmy, the chosen savior, is felled. As Gaines reflects on her odyssey from Bryant Plantation to the Bayonne courthouse, he indicates that no trial seems trivial, overstated, or happenstance. Tottery but adamant, Jane performs a courageous gesture against bigotry that proceeds as predictably from the stubborn, proud Ticey of the 1860s as the blossoming of the century plant.

A triumph of fiction, Gaines's protagonist dominates Southern literature's departure from breast-beating and muckraking to a subtler, more incisive study of racial disharmony. Miss Jane's life span during a lengthy era marked by war, unrest, social revolution, and racial confrontation mingles the destinies of slaves, Southern plantation hierarchy, free blacks, and bayou Creoles. The novel was re-created on January 3, 1974, by Prism/Tomorrow Entertainment in a CBS made-for-television movie, *The Autobiography of Miss Jane Pittman*. Scripted by Tracy Keenan Wynn, the film earned nine Emmys, including recognition for the star, Cicely Tyson. Her skillful makeup produced the corrugated face of the 110-year-old ex-slave who quietly states her intention: "I will go." (Gaines 1971, 245) The editor comments in his introduction on Jane's oneness with her people: "Miss Jane's story is all of their stories, and their stories are Miss Jane's." (Gaines 1971, viii) (Babb 1991; "Black and White" 1997; Bradbury 1996; Briggs 1997; Bruck 1977; Bryant 1972, 1974; *Contemporary Authors* 1994; *Dictionary of Literary Biography* 1978, 1984; Gaines 1971, 1978, video 1993; Gaudet and Wooten 1990; Gayle 1975; Gerber 1971; Hicks 1981; Hudson, Theodore 1985; Laney 1994; Maddocks 1971; Magnier 1995; Martin 1973; Martin and Porter 1995; O'Brien 1973; "Our Culture" 1997; Peterson 1993; Ploski and Williams 1989; Sheppard 1993; Snodgrass (*Literary Maps*) 1995; "Southern Cross" 1973; Stephens 1995; Stoelting 1971; Summer 1993; *Video Hound's* 1994; Wilson and Ferris 1989; Wolff 1969)

See also Gaines, Ernest J.

THE AWAKENING

Rejected as unwholesome and blatantly vulgar by American traditionalists, *The Awakening* (1899), Kate Chopin's masterpiece, has survived late Victorian prudery and blossomed into a radical feminist classic. A *fin de siècle* realist dubbed "St. Louis's Littlest Rebel," Chopin displayed a command of themes of liberation and self-fulfillment early in her career. (Papke 1990, 21) In an early sketch, "Emancipation: A Life Fable" (1869), she pictures a timid, introverted animal of an unnamed species. Born in a cage, it awakens from daily ennui to an open door. After hesitant attempts, the timorous beast forces itself into the "spell of the Unknown," drinks from a fetid pool, and never returns to confinement. (Chopin 1983, 177) From the time of this modest fictional allegory, Chopin warns of the pitfalls of a daring emotional jailbreak and advises the neophyte that spiritual freedom can result in "seeking, finding, joying and suffering." (Chopin 1983, 178) Prefiguring the biological determinism of Jack London, she acknowledges the savagery that awaits the unleashing of the human animal; anticipating Theodore Dreiser and D. H. Lawrence, she understands that adherents of the social order can beset the unwary who venture too far beyond their preassigned places.

Opening *The Awakening* in Louisiana's Grand Isle on the Gulf of Mexico at a summer enclave run by Madame Aline Lebrun, Chopin posts a green-and-yellow caution sign in the form of a caged parrot screaming inchoate warnings: "*Allez vous-en! Allez vous-en! Sapristi!* That's all right." (Chopin 1983, 43) Chopin reveals Edna Pontellier as a typical wife locked in the stiflingly sheltered existence that suits the social dictates of the 1890s. She and her husband Léonce, who regards her as "a valuable piece of personal property," relax in middle-class comfort with the Ratignolles and other refined New Orleans vacationers. (Chopin 1983, 44) Léonce's weekly trips into town to work at the brokerage, gamble, and visit his club leave Edna in charge of four- and five-year-old sons Etienne and Raoul. Without a male chaperone, she is open to the flirtation of Robert Lebrun, a winsome young bachelor. Chopin introduces Edna's self-analysis and latent eroticism with an inexplicable fit of weeping. After hearing Adèle Ratignolle tell a male guest of her accouchement, Edna is dismayed that she lacks such wifely passion for pregnancy and childbirth. When measured against Adèle's devotion to motherhood, Edna concludes that she is not a "mother-woman" because she could never sacrifice self for her children. (Chopin 1983, 51)

Chopin moves Edna farther from shelter after severing her ties from staid, predictable New Orleans. Released from urban strictures on married women, she enters a reckless emotional turbulence caused by disaffection for the bourgeois life and an urge for more interesting arrangements and experiences. The lure is "the voice of the sea," which addresses the needs of the soul at the same time it embraces her body in a sensuous, enveloping warmth. The summons chimes the beginning of an inner awakening that is "seductive, never ceasing, whispering, clamoring, murmuring, inviting the soul to wander for a spell in abysses of solitude; to lose itself in mazes of inward contemplation." Anticipating the resolution, Chopin warns,

> But the beginning of things, of a world especially, is necessarily vague, tangled, chaotic, and exceedingly disturbing. How few of us ever emerge from such beginning! How many souls perish in its tumult! (Chopin 1983, 57)

The author's skillful re-creation of an inner scenario alludes to the costs that Edna will face by subverting proprieties. By approving her buoyant courage, however, Chopin validates the daring overthrow of accepted sex roles for women, even if divergence precipitates destruction.

In the emotion-charged company of Creoles, Chopin deepens Edna's stressful introspection, which she alleviates with sea bathing. Tentatively freeing herself from a conventional marriage, she lets Robert, her hovering beau, teach her to swim in the gulf; after a vision of drowning overtakes her, she returns to shore. From this point to the end of the novel, the deep water prefigures her liberation and self-expression, both significant discoveries during a crisis that finds her "[idle, aimless], unthinking and unguided" and tipsy with a newfound freedom initiated by complete candor. (Chopin 1983, 61) She recalls having crushes on three men during her girlhood in Kentucky and reminisces that she married Léonce, a Creole and Catholic, as a youthful rebellion against her Presbyterian upbringing. A prelude to her revolt against their marriage occurs on

August 28, when Mademoiselle Reisz's fervid piano recital chokes Edna with tears. The pianist notes that Edna is the only member of the audience worth playing for. At Lebrun's urging, she swims far into the gulf "where no woman had swum before," and exults in the space and solitude of the deep. (Chopin 1983, 71) Ignoring Léonce's command to come to bed, she rocks in a hammock, a suspended state that suggests her suspension of old, outworn mores and a free-floating release from stress, marital tedium, and Léonce's dominance. Chopin laces the scene with irony: Both Robert and Léonce treat Edna like a child by being overly solicitous about her health and comfort.

Placing the protagonist in a daylong dalliance with Robert, Chopin extends Edna's cultivation of carnal fantasies. The next day, Edna ventures farther from conventionality while attending worship services across the Barataria Bay at Grande Terre. Grown drowsy during the service, she allows Lebrun to escort her from church to Madame Antoine's, where she sleeps away the day, dines with her beau, and returns late in the evening in a sailboat. When the summer flirtation ends, Edna despairs and returns home to Esplanade Street, an appropriate manse for her class, where she enjoys the best of china, silver, draperies, furnishing, and *objets d'art*. The primary reason for Léonce's exquisite home is not personal pleasure but the currying of business and social connections. Sunk in self and wearied by the accoutrements of her class, Edna thwarts him by neglecting wifely duties, which require her to direct the cook and nanny and run the household in a manner consistent with contemporary standards and tastes. After quarreling with her husband, she removes her wedding band and strives to trample the hard metal with her heel. The act suggests the difficulties she will face when she attempts to stamp out the conventionality that burdens her spirit.

As her protagonist becomes "the brave soul," Chopin glimpses from the perspective of three conventional males the change that seizes and reshapes Edna. She absorbs herself in her atelier. She angers her father by refusing to attend a family wedding and befuddles her husband, who cajoles in paternal fashion, "Why, my dear, I should think you'd understand by this time that people don't do such things; we've got to observe *les convenances* if we ever expect to get on and keep up with the procession." (Chopin 1983, 101) Like a parent questioning a pediatrician about a peevish child, Léonce asks Dr. Mandelet how to manage Edna's moodiness. The doctor encourages Léonce to be patient while she acts out the "fierce unrest" that impels her shifting personality. (Chopin 1983, 123)

Outside the Pontelliers' domestic contretemps, external forces push Edna again onto a sea of unstable emotions as she attempts to align incompatible selves. Mademoiselle Reisz, her confidante and guide in the world of art, encourages Edna's soulfulness and defiance of custom but warns, "Be careful; the stairs and landings are dark; don't stumble." (Chopin 1983, 116) Reisz passes on a letter from Robert in which he states his hesitance to pursue a married woman. When Edna's husband takes an extended business trip to New York, she exults in controlling her own life, takes stock of her personal contribution to their lavish household, and departs from his control by moving into a four-room cottage around the corner. For the sake of the children, she dispatches them to their grandmother's care. Unencumbered by domestic duties, Edna tolerates the blandishments of Alcée Arobin, a shallow roué, and hosts a lavish dinner party that ignites rumors about her liberated lifestyle. Her profligacy prompts Léonce to pen a note of disapproval, but she ignores him, takes to the pigeon house, and enjoys observing the world with her own eyes from a new perspective.

The conclusion to Chopin's novel draws on the tenuous nature of circumstance, the subject of "At the 'Cadian Ball," an earlier story of flirtation halted at the brink of consummation. In February, after Edna reunites with Robert, he begs her to stay with him and ignore a summons to attend Madame Ratignolle, whom Dr. Mandelet and Monsieur Ratignolle have abandoned in tortuous labor of another childbirth. The vignette of Edna's return to an empty house replicates the bleakness of her heart. She seeks the seaside where she first learned to swim, strips off her clothing, and pushes out to sea to the extent of her strength. Chopin links birth and water images with the discovery of self, which acquaints Edna with unknown territory: "She felt like some new-born creature, opening its eyes in a familiar world that it had never known." (Chopin 1983, 175) A merged image of Eve in Eden and Sandro Botticelli's painting of Venus arising from the sea, Edna steps into surf that twines about her ankles like serpents.

Chopin equips Edna with a tenacity that accepts bodily death in exchange for birth of a free and unencumbered self. Determined to reach a full sense of being and discover innate talents and sensibilities stifled by marriage and household routines, she refuses to look back, stroking on and on, thinking about a green meadow and daring herself to have courage. Her last sensations resurrect the calls of her father and sister and the barks of a dog chained to a tree. Although her fantasies about liberation have proved false and she has lost life, lover, husband, and sons, she has learned to navigate on her own terms. If a quiet meal at Catiche's, a sumptuous dinner party, an afternoon of painting in reflected light, and the whispered declaration of Robert's love have satisfied an inner cry for sustenance, she does not die wanting. (Blain et al. 1990; Bloom 1987; Bonner 1988; Boren and Davis 1992; Chopin 1983; Christ 1980; *Contemporary Authors* 1994; Davidson and Wagner-Martin 1995; Davis et al. 1970; Guilds 1970; Jones 1981; "Kate Chopin" 1996; "Kate Chopin Project" 1996; "Kate Chopin's *The Awakening*" 1995; Koloski 1988; Martin 1988; Massey 1996; Papke 1990; Quinn 1936; Rubin et al. 1985; Skaggs 1985; Stein 1979; Toth 1993)

See also Chopin, Kate.

BLACK BOY

The most riveting black autobiography written before World War II, *Black Boy: A Record of Childhood and Youth* (1945) went through numerous revisions until it produced the comprehensive statement intended by author Richard Wright. In its final version, the book dramatizes damning evidence of racism in the American South during the height of the Jim Crow era. Wright's taunting title epitomizes the self-denigration of his youth. An introspective loner from an early age, he rejects the stereotype of the pickaninny—the shuffling, mindless, sunny-faced black who endures indignities to avoid the stress and menace caused by acting normally among disapproving whites. In a bitter farewell to his homeland, he comments:

> The white South said that it knew "niggers," and I was what the white South called a "nigger." Well, the white South had never known me—never known what I thought, what I felt. The white South said that I had a "place" in life. Well, I had never felt my "place"; or, rather, my deepest instincts had always made me reject the "place" to which the white South had assigned me. (Wright 1966, 283)

Bristling with old scores to settle, Wright narrates the dismal family situation that offers him no haven from Southern violence. Wracked by violence, degradation, and devaluation on all sides, he takes refuge in dreams of flight to the North, where he can live unhampered by diminished expectations and develop his talent for writing.

In the opening scenes, four-year-old Richard Wright commits a symbolic act of defiance by setting fire to broom straws and white curtains in his family's cabin outside Natchez, Mississippi. He introduces the motif of free-floating guilt and dissatisfaction with self after he abandons his ailing grandmother near the flames and burrows under the cabin floorboards next to the brick chimney to escape punishment. The family's dismay at his misdeed results in a whipping so severe that the child lapses into unconsciousness. The dire situations that mark Wright's childhood grow from this initial episode into increasingly harsh confrontations, climaxing in his determination to quit the South and join the exodus of blacks to the ghettos of Chicago.

The major motif in Wright's youth is chaos—a perpetual disruption of school, work, friendships, and family contentment. Tossed among relatives, he recalls journeying up the Mississippi River to Memphis on the *Kate Adams;* living with his aunt in Elaine, Arkansas; and settling in the two-story frame house in Jackson, Mississippi, tyrannized by his light-skinned granny, Margaret Bolden Wilson, a sour-faced ex-slave. He typifies her fervid Southern fundamentalism in vivid glimpses of piety:

> Granny was an ardent member of the Seventh-Day Adventist Church and I was compelled to make a pretense of worshipping her God, which was her exaction for my keep. The elders of her church expounded a gospel clogged with images of vast lakes of eternal fire [and] ...the Second Coming of Christ; chronicles that concluded with the Armageddon; dramas thronged with all the billions of human beings who had ever lived or died as God judged the quick and the dead. (Wright 1966, 113)

Much of his perpetual war with Granny derives from her relentless rule of all aspects of family behavior. His memories of literature begin with *Bluebeard and His Seven Wives*, which Granny condemns as "Devil stuff." (Wright 1966, 47)

In a glimpse of ruined innocence, Wright juxtaposes fictional violence alongside the real thing. As the protagonist journeys to the tidy, fenced-in bungalow of his Aunt Maggie and Uncle Hoskins, his imagination moves from Bluebeard to typical male reading material of his era—Zane Grey's *Riders of the Purple Sage, Argosy*, and western and detective magazines. Melodramatic bloodshed on the pages contrasts the boy's real experiences, beginning with the unforeseen shooting of Uncle Hoskins, a local tavern keeper murdered by whites to end competition with a black entrepreneur. Again on the road, Wright's family moves to Jackson and then to West Helena, Arkansas, where they share a duplex apartment with prostitutes.

The author envisions his childhood self in a perpetual state of enslavement. Ella Wright's invalidism, brought on by a paralytic stroke, resituates Wright and his brother in the power of Granny, who separates them by placing each with a relative. Richard's dilemma surfaces in arguments, misunderstandings, scoldings, and sleepwalking episodes. While living with his Aunt Jody and Uncle Clark in Greenwood, Mississippi, he is terrified by stories that his room may be haunted by a ghost.

His misery is compounded when he returns to Jackson, where his mother undergoes an unsuccessful surgery to relieve a blood clot. As Ella Wright loses control over her son, Granny Wilson tyrannizes multiple aspects of his life, robbing him of amenities, limiting amusements, and rearing him on Bible readings and platitudes, all-night prayer meetings, and an insubstantial daily family menu consisting of a meatless roast made of peanuts accompanied by greens, flour gravy, and mush. He remembers that

> Granny intimated boldly, basing her logic on God's justice, that one sinful person in a household could bring down the wrath of God upon the entire establishment, damning both the innocent and the guilty, and on more than one occasion she interpreted my mother's long illness as the result of my faithlessness. (Wright 1966, 114–115)

He develops skill in ignoring Granny's twisted zeal and grows callous toward "all metaphysical preachments." To mask the growling of his stomach, he fills up on water from the schoolyard hydrant before going to class. Paramount to Wright's escape from poverty, fundamentalist piety, and ignorance is a mounting defiance. He wars against the didacticism of home, church, and school, where organized sports such as baseball are labeled a sin. Classes taught by his Aunt Addie result in public humiliation after he is injured in a brutal game of pop-the-whip, an activity she oversees, with delight in his eventual injury. The author depicts him in the role of self-rescuer. As a symbol of autonomy more than threat, he begins sleeping with a knife under his pillow. He quits his grandmother's church and insists on working Saturdays to acquire money for school clothes. Because Ella Wright maneuvers him into joining a mainline Protestant church, he agrees to be baptized. The episode concludes with a standoff against his uncle, whom he holds at bay with a razor.

Wright lauds his protagonist's courage and expresses the fulfillment of his initial composition after young Richard distinguishes himself at age 15 with "The Voodoo of Hell's Half-Acre," a story published in the *Southern Register*. A number of insufficient part-time jobs precede the last stage of his migration north. In November 1925, he settles temporarily in a rooming house in Memphis, eats well for the first time in his life, and acquires some street smarts while working at an optical company.

Self-support is sweet after years of living on family charity. With a library card borrowed from Mr. Falk, Wright forges notes that net him important literary works of his era—Baltimore critic H. L. Mencken's *A Book of Prefaces*, novelist Sinclair Lewis's *Main Street*, and Theodore Dreiser's *Sister Carrie* and *Jennie Gerhardt*, both monumental naturalistic fiction of the 1920s. Immersed in literature, Richard devours the works of Guy de Maupassant, Stendhal, Arnold Bennet, André Gide, Maxim Gorky, Joseph Conrad, Charles-Pierre Baudelaire, Anatole France, T. S. Eliot, Henrik Ibsen, H. G. Wells, Emile Zola, Honoré de Balzac, Thomas Hardy, and Friedrich Nietzsche. He is free from Granny's rule, and the nuclear family bolsters his dream of leaving the South by helping him move to Chicago with his aunt until he can save enough to send for his mother and brother.

In 1925, Richard makes his final move by joining black flight to Chicago, where he anticipates leaving behind the Ku Klux Klan, Jim Crow, job discrimination, religious fanatics, and subservience to hostile whites. He recalls:

> When I was already in full flight—aboard a northward bound train—I could not have accounted, if it had been demanded of me, for all the varied forces that were making me reject the culture that had molded and shaped me. (Wright 1966, 281)

Filled with the youthful intellectual's idealism, he longs for a life beyond the South where he can secure dignity and fulfillment. (Bain 1979; Baker 1972; Barksdale and Kinnamon 1972; Bloom 1987, 1988; Bradbury 1996; Butler 1991; Chapman 1968; Fabre 1990; Gayle 1980; Low and Clift 1981; Ploski and Williams 1989; Popkin 1978; Salzman et al. 1996; Trotman 1989; Walker 1988; Webb 1968; Williams 1970; Wilson and Ferris 1989; Wright 1966)

See also Mencken, H. L.; *Native Son*; Wright, Richard.

BOONE, DANIEL

A historical hero-turned-myth, Daniel Boone represents the westward-seeking wave of Southern pioneers. Of British extraction, the Boone family has established itself in the American psyche as the prototypical land-hungry clan of settlers. Boone's rise from backwoodsman to legend prefaces the American dream, an amalgam of ample land for settlement, hard work, and determination. Exploits of the famed Kentucky settler were the model for the Boy Scouts, originally called the "Sons of Daniel Boone." So much has been written about his life, leadership, and adventures that historians have long realized he could not have been in all the places and performed all the deeds that cling to him. Folklorists surmise that the Boone canon grew at the storyteller's whim, because colorful stories about unknown woodsmen and Indian fighters sounded better when linked to a real hero with the stature and renown of Daniel Boone.

An emigrant Southerner, Boone came from a Quaker family of skilled crafters and traders prominent in North Carolina, Kentucky, Pennsylvania, and Missouri. Fiction tends to characterize him as a semiliterate, patriotic hunter, trailblazer, and two-fisted Indian fighter. However, the stereotype is too limited by the image of an outdoorsy he-man to accommodate his service as a statesman, land speculator, and empire builder. Born the sixth of the 11 children of Squire and Sarah Morgan Boone on November 2, 1734, in Exeter, Pennsylvania, he spent his childhood in a log farmhouse. Although Boone received little formal education, he applied himself to learning wilderness skills. Unsuited to the limited cycles of agrarian life, he kept active in sharpshooting, hunting, tracking, and driving wagons for General Edward Braddock's forces at Fort Duquesne in Pittsburgh. The peripatetic Boone family moved south to the Shenandoah Valley when Daniel was 16. Within two years they pulled up stakes for another move, this time farther south along the Blue Ridge Mountains to the acreage of Squire, Daniel's brother, in the Yadkin Valley, North Carolina's western frontier.

A tall, rangy, ruggedly handsome pathfinder at age 22, Boone settled down long enough to wed Rebecca Bryan, who became the mother of their ten children, and established his family in Rowan County. Ostensibly for Rebecca and the children, but more likely to suit his rambling notions, he set out to explore open land as far south as Pensacola, Florida. From friend John Finley he learned of the beauties of "Kentucke." Before sampling the land west of the Shenandoah Valley, he built four more cabins along the Yadkin River, the last at Halman's Ford, southeast of Boone in Watauga County, North Carolina. Over a nine-year period, lengthening hunting expeditions along the Blue Ridge brought him north to Abingdon, Virginia, and closer to Kentucky.

In 1774, when a Cherokee tribe in the Appalachians sold 20 million acres to the Transylvania Company in exchange for $50,000 worth of goods, Boone assisted the traders by heading the wagon train that ferried their merchandise west to Watauga. Another task moved Boone east after he took charge of defending Fort Dobbs in Statesville, North Carolina. At last free of moneymaking responsibilities, he followed his dream to the fabled land of "Kentucke."

While exploring Warrior's Trace, a Cherokee war trail to northern tribes now immortalized as the "wilderness road," he set foot on virgin country teeming with wildlife. Around 1820, he reminisced about the splendid country that won his heart:

> I have traveled over many new countries in the great Mississippi Valley; I have critically examined their soils; their mineral wealth; their healthful climates; their manufacturing situation; and the commercial advantages given them by nature. I have discovered where these endowments were given most bountifully in many localities, singly and in groups, but I have never found but one Kentucky—a spot of earth where nature seems to have concentrated all her bounties. (Botkin 1944, 279)

The land resolved his quandary: how to roam free and hunt game while performing the duties of a family man. The answer lay in the Cumberland Gap. Returning to his family after a three-year absence, he vowed to introduce them to the teeming game and peaceful dells of Kentucky.

Boone sold his North Carolina acreage and led a wagon train of five families northwest across the Great Smoky Mountains. En route, he lost six adults to Indian attack, including his son. The inauspicious beginning temporarily sidelined his planned community. In 1775, an entrepreneurial group engaged him to mark a trail to Kentucky and build a fort. Boone fulfilled his contract and established Fort Boonesboro near Harrodsburg. Determined that the fledgling community would survive, he fought Shawnee along Licking River and recovered from them his daughter Jemima and two other females, a dramatic rescue that James Fenimore Cooper recast in his historical novel *The Last of the Mohicans* (1826), the most popular of the five Leatherstocking Tales. In 1778, the same tribe captured Boone at a salt lick and held him from February until September. During his residence among the Shawnee, Chief Blackfish adopted him as a replacement for his dead son. To prevent Blackfish from raiding Boonesboro, Boone escaped to rally the community, which survived a two-week siege. Following a year's retreat to North Carolina, he set out late in 1779 to build a new settlement, Boone's Station, near Athens on the Kentucky River.

In penetrating the frontier, Boone and his followers paid the price of constant vigilance against Cherokee attacks, which killed his brother Edward in 1780 and his son Israel in 1782. He served as lieutenant colonel in the Virginia militia during the Revolutionary War and was elected to the state legislature in 1781, 1787, and 1791. When peace was assured, the Boones moved once more to Maysville, Kentucky, where Daniel opened a tavern and freelanced as county surveyor and land agent. Already renowned for pluck and optimism, he learned of an unauthorized biography, *The Adventures of Col. Daniel Boon* [sic], *Containing a Narrative of the Wars of Kentucke*, a romanticized chapter in *Discovery, Settlement and Present State of Kentucky* (1784) by Pennsylvania schoolteacher and land speculator John Filson. Boone was flattered by the melodrama, composed in absurdly elevated diction:

> Thus situated, many hundred miles from our families in the howling wilderness, I believe few would have equally enjoyed the happiness we experienced.

I often observed to my brother, You see now how little nature requires to be satisfied. Felicity, the companion of content, is rather found in our own breasts than in the enjoyment of external things: And I firmly believe it requires but a little philosophy to make a man happy in whatsoever state he is. (Rose 1995, 1)

By 1789, discontent once more spurred Boone to push on to Point Pleasant on the Ohio River, where he earned his living as a grain and meat supplier for the U.S. military. A poor businessman, he shortly abandoned contracting and returned to hunting from his cabin in Charleston, West Virginia.

Advancing age did not rob Boone of wanderlust. In his late sixties he was arrested for debt and suffered a serious hunting accident. A late-in-life soldier of fortune, he moved his extended family farther west to Femme Osage, Missouri, where the Spanish governer conferred on him a land grant, Spanish citizenship, and the office of syndic, a municipal magistrate. After the U.S. government acquired the land through the Louisiana Purchase during Thomas Jefferson's presidency, Boone lost most of his claims, but in 1814 he successfully petitioned Congress for 850 acres near St. Louis, Missouri. Late in his many-faceted career, he held a judgeship in St. Charles County, Missouri, where he was living with his son Nathan at his death on September 26, 1820. The bodies of Rebecca and Daniel Boone were moved to Frankfort, Kentucky, in 1845.

Much Boone lore was published during his lifetime. In 1813, Virginian Daniel Bryan, a distant relative and champion of Daniel Boone, ignored the fact that

Daniel Boone (1734–1820) rescues Betsey and Frances Collanay, who had been kidnapped by Indians. This exaggeratedly heroic painting shows the regard in which Boone's countrymen held him.

Boone and his followers fled the fussy refinements of civilization and its onerous taxes. The poet chose to extol him with *The Mountain Muse: Comprising the
Adventures of Daniel Boone; and the Power of Virtuous and Refined Beauty*, an ambitious epic poem composed in high Miltonic style. Crediting the unlettered
woodsman with bestowing enlightenment on Kentucky, Bryan proclaims the
reign of freedom, science, and religious truth, which counterbalance the dangers of cruelty, death, and superstition. He lauds "the Glowing Guardians, fill'd
with views sublime/Their lofty minds, their enterprising power awak'd" and
honors Boone's enterprise in bringing "Politic Wisdom [to] Columbia." (Rose
1995, 2)

A flood of Boone material—both erudite and down-to-earth—continued
through the nineteenth century. The works typify the era's tendency toward
long, involved titles. The year of Boone's death, Samuel L. Metcalfe published
*A Collection of Some of the Most Interesting Narratives of Indian Warfare in the West,
Containing an Account of the Adventures of Daniel Boone, One of the First Settlers of
Kentucky* (1820), in which the author casts the woodsman as a skilled negotiator
and defender of settlers from wilderness perils. Two decades later, John
Beauchamp Jones, an editor and novelist from Baltimore, wrote *Wild Western
Scenes; A Narrative of Adventures in the Western Wilderness, Forty Years Ago; Wherein
the Conduct of Daniel Boone, the Great American Pioneer, Is Particularly Described*
(1841), a frontier thriller replete with ultraheroic deeds. A quarter century after
Boone's death, Kentuckian Theodore O'Hara composed an elegy to Boone, "The
Old Pioneer" (1845), a work more in keeping with reality. In 1851, George Caleb
Bingham accentuated the prevailing reverence for Boone's heroism with a dramatic painting depicting the arrival of settlers to Kentucky via the Cumberland
Road. Vivid chiaroscuro shows Boone in the lead and Rebecca sidesaddle on
his horse in a Madonnaesque pose. The dark, forbidding landscape implies
that the settlers moved resolutely through danger and dispelled the gloom of
the wild by importing the light of civilization. In 1854, romantic novelist and
historian Timothy Flint published *The First White Man of the West, or The Life and
Exploits of Col. Dan'l. Boone, the First Settler of Kentucky; Interspersed with Incidents in the Early Annals of the Country*. In prose and verse, Flint lauded the
settlement of Boonesboro, which he proclaimed "the garden of the West" in
token of its Edenic qualities. (Rose 1995, 2)

In addition to biographies, the majority of overviews of the early frontier
feature the prototypical figure of the Kentucky woodsman. W. H. Bogart comes
close to conveying a believable image of Boone in *Daniel Boone and the Hunters
of Kentucky* (1857). Bogart is hesitant to claim that Boone intentionally blazed a
trail or built a segment of Western civilization. To prove his point, he stresses
the nation's need for a hero, who was invented out of frontier episodes that
suited the purpose of the mythmaker. A regressive step in Boone biography
appeared in 1884 in historian and juvenile author Edward Sylvester Ellis's *The
Life and Time of Col. Daniel Boone, Hunter, Soldier, and Pioneer*, which returns to
the flaunted image of the wise, honest woodsman, led by God to establish
America's right to the frontier. A sympathetic biographical note in Theodore
Roosevelt's *The Winning of the West* (1889) credits Boone with the love of solitude

in the wild and with furthering the expansion of white settlement far from the seaboard, thus weaning the nation from ties with Europe. Perhaps the most lasting image of Boone occurs in the fictional Natty Bumppo, the virtuous, doughty loner of Cooper's Leatherstocking Tales.

In the twentieth century, Boone's myth holds steady, particularly among the young. Travel writer Stewart Edward White's inspirational biography *Daniel Boone: Wilderness Scout* (1922) tempted young boys to set their sights high by following the revered trailblazer's example. Kentuckian Elizabeth Madox Roberts wrote *The Great Meadow* (1930), a historical novel about Daniel Boone, female pioneers, and their role in the establishment of Old Fort Harrod, Kentucky's first settlement, in Harrodsburg. In contrast to the view of Boone-the-monument, poets Rosemary Benét and Stephen Vincent Benét depicted Boone as a destroyer in *A Book of Americans* (1933) with an enigmatic four-line stanza:

> When Daniel Boone goes by, at night,
> The phantom deer arise
> And all lost, wild America
> Is burning in their eyes.
> (Benét and Benét 1933, 45)

More often positive than denigrating, the Daniel Boone legend has served notable outdoor dramas, particularly Jan Hartman's *The Legend of Daniel Boone* in Harrodsburg, Kentucky, and Kermit Hunter's *Horn in the West* (1952) in Boone, North Carolina, which describes Boone's role in aiding settlers during the social and political turmoil that accompanied the Revolutionary War. (Benét and Benét 1933; Botkin 1944; Correll 1961; "Daniel Boone" 1996; "Daniel Boone: American Pioneer" 1996; Ehrlich and Carruth 1982; Faragher 1995; Gillett 1952; Gislason 1996; "Horn in the West" 1990; Lamar 1977; "Legend" 1972; Rose 1995; Rubin et al. 1985; Stein 1979; Waldman 1990; Wilson and Ferris 1989)

See also theater in the South.

 CABLE, GEORGE WASHINGTON

An early realist and eloquent spokesperson for Creole-American culture, George Washington Cable validated the importance of the regionalist to national literature with a diverse body of romance, historical fiction, and inclusive multiracial essays and stories. He was a noted social reformer, like Joel Chandler Harris, and built his reputation by re-creating the dialect stories of a minority people and blending chivalric nostalgia with voodoo, miscegenation, slave revolts, mistreatment of slaves and prisoners, family feuds, and other breaches of liberty, religion, and Southern tradition. His major contribution to the American canon is an authentic Creole patois and a clear perception of the complex stratified society that emerged in Louisiana as waves of immigrants and slaves settled the bayous and waterways. Threaded among his plots like the winding alleyways of the Vieux Carré are such local names as Tarbox, Jules St. Ange, Count de Charleu-Marot, Kookoo, Injin Charlie, 'Tite Poulette, Madame Délicieuse, and 'Thanase. Romantic settings range from Café des Exiles to Belles Demoiselles Plantation, names redolent with elegiac beauty.

Lauded as the first modern Southern author and critic, Cable published his first eight short stories in *Old Creole Days* (1879). At its heart is "Jean-ah Pouquelin," a lyric, tightly configured short story, published in *Scribner's* magazine in May 1875. Richly evocative passages introduce an explosive era of land development and the title character's isolated house on the marsh, a looming monstrosity that resembles "a gigantic ammunition-wagon stuck in the mud and abandoned by some retreating army." (Cable 1890, 198) A morality tale of brotherly loyalty, the suspenseful action builds on the rumors of a will-o'-the-wisp lighting Pouquelin's windows and suspicions of piracy and murder that cling to the fiery old recluse, a former indigo planter who defies a flustered bureaucrat plotting a road through private property. A darkly comic exchange in patois and broken English concludes at an impasse, with Pouquelin curtly reminding the official, "I mine me hown bizniss. Dat all right? Adieu." (Cable 1890, 206)

Cable's story rises to a touching, dramatic conclusion as Little White, a spineless office underling, creeps on all fours to Pouquelin's house to look for clues to determine whether the old man killed his own half brother and to locate the source of a foul smell, an olfactory image of Pouquelin's reputation among the city's bourgeois elite. Before White can convey an explanation of the mystery, a raucous group plans a *charivari* (the French term for "tease"), which developed into an American social mechanism meant to ridicule, harass, and intimidate. At 3:00 A.M., White halts the merrymakers as the missing brother, depigmented from leprosy, appears at the gate alongside a mute servant who lifts Jean Pouquelin's corpse from an oxcart. Cable concludes the story with hushed, respectful tones:

> For a moment more the mute and the leper stood in sight, while the former adjusted his heavy burden; then, without one backward glance upon the unkind human world, turning their faces toward the ridge in the depths of the swamp known as the Leper's Land, they stepped into the jungle, disappeared, and were never seen again. (Cable 1890, 229)

The story, frequently studied in Southern fiction classes, bears the gravity of a fable and the exotic trappings of a romance. Cable followed his initial success in short fiction with more complex works: a protest novel, *The Grandissimes* (1880); the novella *Madame Delphine* (1881); and a historic overview, *The Creoles of Louisiana* (1884), the outgrowth of a factual report to the U.S. Census Bureau four years before.

Although not himself a Creole, the author had just cause to write of Louisiana's Métis heritage. Cable was of Virginian and Puritan New England ancestry, the fifth of six children of Rebecca Boardman and merchant George Washington Cable, Sr., born October 12, 1844, in New Orleans, the South's Creole capital. In 1858, following a season of flood and fever, his father suffered a series of business reversals and died suddenly, leaving Cable and his sister Mary Louise to support the family. Cable was clerking in a wholesale grocer in 1863 when his mother and sisters were ousted from the city for refusing to pledge allegiance to the Union. Although physically undersized, he asserted his Confederate loyalty and joined the Fourth Mississippi Cavalry. Cable spent his time off studying Latin, mathematics, and the Bible. In Alabama, he served as scribe to General Nathan Bedford Forrest during the manumission of Forrest's slaves.

After General Robert E. Lee's surrender to General Ulysses S. Grant at Appomattox, Cable, like most members of the fallen Confederacy, returned to his homeland to recuperate. He healed slowly from an arm wound and recurrent fever, and entered a quiet period during which he first began to write. His evocative passages of New Orleans atmosphere prove the importance of place to his life and work. In *Madame Delphine*, a novella first published in *Scribner's* magazine in 1881, the text exudes the honeyed ambience of the city's architecture and decor:

> Yet beauty lingers here. To say nothing of the picturesque, sometimes you get sight of comfort, sometimes of opulence, through the unlatched wicket in some *port-cochère*—red-painted brick pavement, foliage of dark palm or pale banana, marble or granite masonry and blooming parterres; or through a chink between some pair of heavy batten window-shutters, opened with an almost reptile wariness, your eyes get a glimpse of lace and brocade upholstery, silver and bronze, and much similar rich antiquity. (Cable 1890, 2)

George Washington Cable (1844–1925)

While learning the elements of the writer's trade, Cable was forced to take any paying work he could find in the Reconstruction era's irregular economy. From messenger and surveyor he advanced to reporter for the *New Orleans Picayune*, but relinquished his job because it violated his strict religious tenets, which forbade attending theatrical performances.

Largely self-educated through rigorous study of French and history, Cable fortunately landed an office job at the A. C. Clark & Company cotton warehouse, where he squared accounts and typed business letters. After marrying Louise Burling Stewart Bartlett in 1869, he began turning his avocation into a career and relied on the friendly critiques of an informal writing club for encouragement. Initial submissions of poetry and sketches found no takers. His first success came in October 1873 with the publication of "'Sieur George" in *Scribner's* magazine, the first of a lifetime of writing on New Orleans stories and themes. In 1879, he left commerce at the collapse of the cotton company and launched a full-time career in writing. Over four decades, he completed short and long works of fiction, social reform, history, and a diary.

An observer of the decline of the aristocratic South, Cable wrote articles for the *New Orleans Picayune* under the pen name "Drop Shot." His motifs reflect a sensitivity toward race relations, a dislike for aristocratic arrogance, and a genteel insistence on courtesy and respect. While researching documents about Creole settlers in Teche and Attakapas in western Louisiana, he gathered material for *Old Creole Days*, which he first published in *Scribner's* magazine. He is best remembered for the story of Bras-Coupé, a victimized African slave whose destruction is the core event in *The Grandissimes*. Unable to accommodate the changes in his beloved Louisiana, Cable spent his last years penning nostalgic romances, beginning with *The Cavalier* (1901). Critics comment that the twentieth century found him detached from his source and rapidly losing touch with the Creole South that gave him a start.

Midstream in his career, Cable settled in Hartford, Connecticut, and established an amiable relationship with Mark Twain, who describes Cable in chapters 44 and 47 of *Life on the Mississippi*. On a walking tour of New Orleans in which Cable led Twain and Joel Chandler Harris about the city's landmarks, Twain came to admire Cable for his mastery of the French dialect and his insider's knowledge of city history and ambience. A fan of "Jean-ah Pouquelin," Twain was pleased to hear Cable read the story aloud, and remarked that the author had gotten into difficulties with living citizens who bore "next-to-impossible French names" that he had either contrived or borrowed from history for his stories, as with Pouquelin, the real name of French playwright Molière. Twain declares the living victims were "a good deal hurt at having attention directed to themselves and their affairs in so excessively public a manner." (Twain 1990, 307)

Teaming for a four-month cross-country lecture tour in 1884 and calling themselves the Twins of Genius, Cable and Twain traveled by rail over the East and Midwest and gave readings from their works. Beginning in Hartford, they made over a hundred stops before ending their collaboration in Washington, D.C., on February 28, 1885. Cable sometimes sang from a ready repertoire of Creole ballads and earned audience approval for his performance, but he bored the rambunctious Twain with piety. In a letter to William Dean Howells, Twain groused:

> Mind you, I like him; he is pleasant company; I rage and swear at him sometimes, but we do not quarrel; we get along mightily happily together; but in him and his person I have learned to hate all religions. He has taught me to abhor and detest the Sabbath-day and hunt up new and troublesome ways to dishonor it. (Rubin 1969, 168)

The tour wound down as the two egos bumped together—Twain chafing Cable with his florid ego and uncouth oaths; Cable annoying Twain by scrimping on meals, snitching stationery from hotel rooms, and extending his reading from *Dr. Sevier* with a melodramatic tag. Unflattering reports to the media assured Cable that Twain had besmirched Cable's character and behavior. Their spat halted the tour and soured their friendship.

Cable's reputation as a supporter of civil equality for blacks ended his chance of retiring amicably in New Orleans or any other part of Dixie, where he was reviled as a "Southern Yankee." (Guilds 1970, 228) After the publication of "The Freeman's Case in Equity" (1885) in *Century* magazine, in 1886 he moved with his frail wife and seven surviving children to Northampton, 15 miles north of Springfield, Massachusetts, where his mother, sisters, nieces, and nephews joined them. After his wife's death in 1904, he married Eva Colegate Stevenson, a blue-stocking from Kentucky whose intellectual and musical pursuits paralleled his own. Upon her death in 1923, he married an old friend, Hannah Cowing, who survived him. During his years in New England, he taught at Smith College, where his six children were educated free of charge. With a grant from Andrew Carnegie, Cable founded the Home Culture Clubs, a populist educational institute that elevated working-class members through cultural seminars, concerts, and lectures. The concept spread to 13 states and Canada.

Still entranced by the beauties of Louisiana and the evils of racism even though he had long since given up residence and employment in the South, Cable wrote two volumes of polemical essays: *The Silent South* (1885) and *The Negro Question* (1890). In the latter, he expanded on his experience in the South, both before and after the Civil War:

> Majority rule is an unfortunate term.... In fact a minority always rules. At least it always can. All the great majority ever strives for is the power to choose by what, and what kind of, a minority it shall be ruled. (Cable 1898, 41)

By mulling over late-nineteenth-century racial issues, he was able to blend Northern mercantile acumen with Southern humanity. He wished for his home region a profound prosperity tempered by magnanimity:

> May the South grow rich! But every wise friend of the South will wish, besides, to see wealth built upon public provisions for securing through it that general beneficence, without which it is not really wealth. (Cable 1898, 52)

In addition to learned and humane contemplations of social betterment, Cable's later publications include social protest in "Posson Jone' and Père Raphael" (1909), regional vignettes in *Strange True Stories of Louisiana* (1889) and *Strong Hearts* (1899), and picturesque re-creations of the Old South in the novel *Dr. Sevier* (1884). He returned to the Civil War for the plots of *John Marsh, Southerner* (1894); *Kincaid's Battery* (1908), an autobiographical spy novel; *The Cavalier* (1901), a psychological thriller; *Bylow Hill* (1902); and *Gideon's Band* (1914). *Bonaventure* (1888), an episodic romance published in *Century* in 1887 and 1888, is one of his most historic fictional works. The action turns on the Louisiana settlement of Acadian exiles from Nova Scotia, a fervid community whose story had been told by Henry Wadsworth Longfellow in his heroic poem *Evangeline* (1847).

Cable remained in New England except for winter vacations in St. Petersburg, Florida. On one of these excursions, January 31, 1925, he died. Much admired and mourned by his Northern contemporaries, he was buried in the Bridge Street Cemetery in Northampton rather than returned to the family plot in New Orleans. (Bradbury 1963; Bradbury 1996; Cable 1890, 1898, 1957, 1969; Cunliffe 1987; Ehrlich and Carruth 1982; "George W. Cable" 1994; Gross 1971; Guilds 1970; Kunitz and Haycraft 1938; Petry 1988; Quinn 1936; Rasmussen 1995; Rubin 1969; Rubin et al. 1985; Stein 1979; Stephens 1995; Trent et al. 1946; Twain 1990; Wilson and Ferris 1989)

See also The Grandissimes; the Mississippi River.

CAPOTE, TRUMAN

More self-touted sophisticate than literary prodigy, Truman Capote became one of the most recognizable and talked about of late-twentieth-century expatriate Southerners. An ostentatious dresser, gossip, and social climber, he acted the part of a fey, secretly wicked boulevardier, offending conservative elements with the rococo settings and campy, exaggerated mannerisms associated with homosexuality. Café society near his residence in the United Nations Plaza and summer residents in the Hamptons on Long Island and in Verbier, Switzerland, alternately admired and loathed his snippy, camera-loving public mask. Partially because of Capote's whimsical dress and mannerisms, his works received catty reviews, particularly after he promoted new books in the media. Over a 40-year career, his chief contribution to literature was *In Cold Blood* (1965), the journalistic novel he initiated after reading in the *New York Times* a short article about the murder of the Clutter family. Capote carefully collected details and molded them into innovative, nonfiction, current events fiction, a new wrinkle in the literary market. The book was selected by the Book-of-the-Month Club and won a National Book award and an Edgar from the Mystery Writers of America.

A New Orleans native, Truman Streckfus Persons Capote, born September 30, 1924, bore the surname of his mother and Cuban stepfather—Lillie Mae Faulk Persons, a former Miss Alabama, and Joseph G. Capote, an attorney and businessman. He was shy and sensitive from age four after his parents divorced. At age six, he felt like a turtle on its back and longed to be a tap dancer or guitarist—anything but an abandoned child. In winter, he lived with his mother and stepfather on Park Avenue in New York City. Summers spent in Louisiana introduced him to the Mississippi River, where his natural father, J. Archulus Persons, operated the Streck Steam Boat Line. After his mother sent him to live with an aunt in Plaquemine, Louisiana, and then with her reclusive elderly sister, Aunt Nanny "Sook" Faulk, Capote shared a friendship with novelist Nelle Harper Lee, his cousin, who lived next door to Sook in Monroeville, Alabama.

Capote immortalized Aunt Sook as the old lady in "A Christmas Memory" (1956), a holiday favorite. Speaking in first person as the child growing up with a perpetually youthful older woman, he says:

> I am seven; she is sixty-something. We are cousins, very distant ones, and we have lived together—well, as long as I can remember. Other people inhabit the house, relatives; and though they have power over us, and frequently make us cry, we are not, on the whole, too much aware of them. (Capote 1978, 170)

His genial memoir depicts holidays enriched by the making of fruitcakes and homemade Yule decorations and gifts—each makes a kite for the other. As though loathe to loosen his hold on the elderly woman, the speaker states bluntly, "Life separates us. Those who Know Best decide that I belong in a military school." (Capote 1978, 179) The story concludes with the death of Queenie (the real name of Aunt Sook's brown-and-white feist) and the passing of the fictional old lady, who slips away like a kite loosed from its string.

In his youth, Capote refused to apply his brilliant mind to classroom study, but pursued literary interests and studied the masters. His favorites were Henry James, Virginia Woolf, Edgar Allan Poe, Willa Cather, Ernest Hemingway, and Sarah Orne Jewett. At age ten he won a short-story contest sponsored by the *Mobile Press Register*. Of his childish exposé "Old Mr. Busybody," he told an interviewer:

> I had been noticing the activities of some neighbors who were up to no good, so I wrote a kind of *roman à clef* called "Old Mr. Busybody" and entered it in a contest. The first installment appeared one Sunday.... Only somebody suddenly realized that I was serving up a local scandal as fiction, and the second installment never appeared. Naturally I didn't win a thing. (Hill 1958, 132)

The title and genre proved prophetic of the egregious kiss-and-tell role he created for himself after becoming a much-photographed, often-mimicked public figure.

Capote passed through a succession of private schools, including Trinity School and St. John's Academy in New York, and attended Greenwich High School in Greenwich, Connecticut. At one point, an exasperated principal urged his parents to place him in an institute for the subnormal. Obviously misunderstood, Capote soured on education at the age of 17, took up drinking anything from blackberry wine to liquor to ease his angst, and moved to New York to become a writer. His first foray into publishing was a lackluster day job as researcher, news clipper, and cartoon cataloger for *New Yorker* magazine. At night, he read film scripts and wrote anecdotes for a digest. Other part-time jobs busied him at writing political speeches, dancing on a riverboat, telling fortunes, and painting on glass.

In 1941, Capote published an unassuming piece, "My Side of the Matter," for *Story* magazine, and his early promise quickly developed into mastery. In retrospect, he explained the method that won readers:

> Finding the right form for your story is simply to realize the most *natural* way of telling the story. The test of whether or not a writer has divined the natural

> shape of his story is just this: after reading it, can you imagine it differently, or does it silence your imagination and seem to you absolute and final? As an orange is final. (Hill 1958, 133)

The technique worked for Capote. In 1948, critical response to his first major work, an autobiographical novel called *Other Voices, Other Rooms*, boosted him from Southern regionalist to literary mascot of the literati.

Other Voices, Other Rooms was a prelude to novels, plays, a memoir, short fiction, columns, television plays, journalistic essays and travelogues, and screenplays, which he completed in a lifetime of sporadic writing binges. His style lay in the realm of imagination, the spiritual plain between fantasy and naturalism. An idiosyncratic example is "New Orleans," a vibrant essay in *Local Color* (1946), in which he develops texture through intense study of details as demonstrated by this comment on beverages:

> The torn lips of golden-haired girls leer luridly on faded leaning house fronts: Drink Dr. Nutt, Dr. Pepper, Nehi, Grapeade, 7 Up, Koke, Coca-Cola. N. O., like every southern town, is a city of soft-drink signs: the streets of forlorn neighborhoods are paved with Coca-Cola caps and after rain, they glint in the dust like lost dimes. (Capote 1946, 5)

A seemingly unplanned montage of images, assonance, consonance, and simile produces Capote's signature commentary—loose to the point of insouciance, but subtly shaped and placed by a master of mosaic. Keen to the rhythms of the city he once called home, he concludes with a saucy, Big Easy fillip, *"I want a big fat mama with the meat shakin' on her, yes!"* (Capote 1946, 12)

Capote's offhand work schedule required notepad and pen, coffee, cigarettes, and a bed or couch. He once commented, "I've got to be puffing and sipping. As the afternoon wears on, I shift from coffee to mint tea to sherry to martinis." (Hill 1958, 138) Prolific for all his insouciance, Capote succeeded in the genres he took up. Two of his stage plays—*The Grass Harp* (1952), which he adapted from his 1951 autobiographical novel by the same name, and *House of Flowers* (1954)—and a 1971 musical version of *The Grass Harp* appeared on Broadway. When unhappy memories of his tenuous childhood threatened to swamp him after his mother's suicide in 1953, monetary success enabled him to roam Europe, bask in applause from the French, and live in a villa in Taormina, Sicily, with his longtime mate, novelist Jack Dunphy. The two-year respite was the most tranquil of his life.

An eclectic reader and collector of the era's literature, Capote studied the best of print mentors, from Colette to James Thurber, Somerset Maugham to Jean-Paul Sartre. Of the Southern canon, he admired the prose fiction of Flannery O'Connor, William Styron, Carson McCullers, James Agee, Eudora Welty, Thomas Wolfe, and Katherine Anne Porter. His reputation grew as his style took on individual traits—a Faulknerian gothic decadence, gently whimsical memoir, and lavish Wildean symbols. His most enduring titles include the novel version of *The Grass Harp* (1951), *The Muses Are Heard* (1956), *Breakfast at Tiffany's* (1958), and *The Thanksgiving Visitor* (1968), which was serialized in *McCall's* magazine and is frequently anthologized in grade-school textbooks.

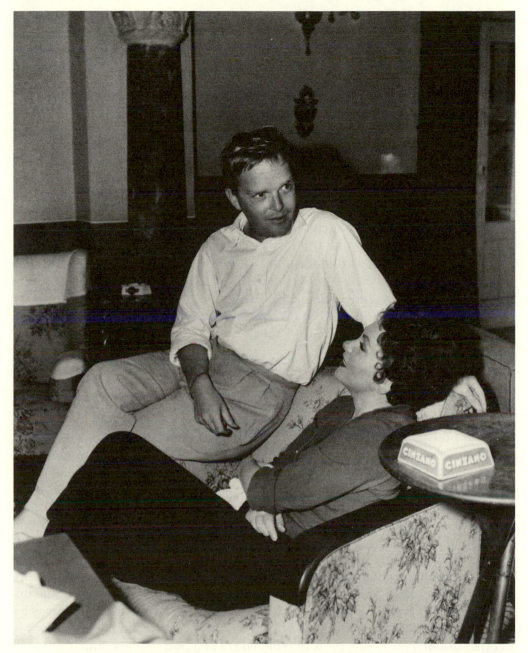

Truman Capote (1924–1984) talks with Italian actress Gina Lollobrigida in Ravello, Italy, during the 1953 filming of *Beat the Devil*, a movie based on his screenplay.

Dissatisfied with fictional genres, Capote decided to study a real crime and adapt details into a new form of fictional reportage. Accompanied by Harper Lee on his initial fact-finding study to Holcomb, Kansas, Capote took 6,000 pages of notes, then retreated to his Swiss hideaway to shape a gruesome murder into chilling, brisk-paced prose. Beginning with events in mid-November 1959, and culminating with two hangings on Wednesday, April 14, 1965, *In Cold*

Blood juxtaposes the bad with the good—killers, victims, investigators, neighbors, family, and friends connected with the execution of the prosperous Herbert William Clutter family of Holcomb, Kansas. Clutter, a successful 48-year-old wheat farmer, lives with his semi-invalid wife Bonnie, their 16-year-old daughter, Nancy, and 15-year-old son, Kenyon. On Saturday, November 14, 1959, predatory ex-cons Perry Smith and Richard Hickock enter the house, awaken Herb, slice telephone wires, and demand the family safe.

Capote's meticulous details verge on Southern gothic. Clutter's throat is cut, then Hickock blows Clutter's head off with a shotgun. The criminal duo tie Kenyon to a steam pipe and shoot him as well as Nancy and Bonnie. The killers net pocket change, Kenyon's radio, and a pair of binoculars, a melodramatic set of symbols that reflect the voyeuristic public's eyes and ears. The pair go on a check-passing spree that concludes in Mexico, where they board the *Estrellita* and enjoy the high life. Broke and restless, Hickock and Smith roam the Southwest until Floyd Wells, an inmate at the Kansas State Penitentiary, confesses to Warden Hand that he inspired Hickock's crime. Tried in a Kansas courtroom in March 1960 and sentenced to hang, they face execution, delayed by several appeals. The author, who had become obsessed with the psychopathic killers, attended the hanging and received a sealed envelope of cash left him by Smith.

In collecting material for his nonfiction novel, Capote offended locals by asking insulting personal questions that might reflect on the motivation and execution of the murders. However, after the killers were apprehended, residents became interested in the author's fictionalized evaluation, which was six years in production. Retracing the killers' movements from Mexico to Florida and interviewing other condemned criminals on death row, Capote produced an appealingly picaresque set of details that resulted in commercial success. The serialized book appeared in the *New Yorker* in four installments. Columbia Pictures filmed it in 1967.

Capote continued composing the seemingly effortless observations and reflections that fleshed out *Miriam* (1982), and in 1983 undertook a man-about-town column for *Esquire* entitled "Observations." During this fertile period, he entertained himself by posturing on television talk shows as the witty, naughty insider and acted in *Murder by Death* (1976), a Neil Simon burlesque of the detective genre. Over a 15-year period, Capote terrorized his acquaintances by threatening to publish a parallel of Marcel Proust's *Remembrance of Things Past*— a confessional *roman à clef*, parts of which he read aloud to television interviewers. Capote's public torment so infuriated his victims that he sank from in-crowd darling to social pariah and withdrew into Nembutal, Valium, booze, and psychoanalysis. Two attempts to dry out landed him first in a Connecticut hospital, then the Smithers Alcoholic Rehabilitation Center in New York. At his death in California on August 25, 1984, from phlebitis, liver failure, and multiple addictions, a posthumous edition of his memoir was issued as *Answered Prayers: The Partial Manuscript* (1986). The work, which was serialized in *Esquire,* is much slimmer than the full-blown exposé Capote had promised, leading friends and colleagues to two assumptions: Either he changed his plans and destroyed the more scathing segments, or else he hid his manuscript so well that it eluded his executors.

In addition to awards for *In Cold Blood*, Capote won numerous honors for other works, including three O. Henry awards, a National Institute of Arts and Letters award, and an Emmy for the film version of "A Christmas Memory," which aired on ABC-TV on December 21, 1966. Other works have been produced on film and videotape, including *Breakfast at Tiffany's* (1961), a star-laden vehicle for Audrey Hepburn's pixieish mannerisms; John Huston's *Beat the Devil* (1954), a talky spoof of *The Maltese Falcon* starring Humphrey Bogart, Jennifer Jones, Gina Lollobrigida, Robert Morley, and Peter Lorre; *The Innocents* (1961), a restaging of Henry James's *The Turn of the Screw*, featuring Deborah Kerr and Michael Redgrave; *Among the Paths to Eden* (1967); and *The Thanksgiving Visitor*, an ABC-TV movie aired in November 1968. *The Grass Harp*, filmed in 1997, showcases Capote's skillful juxtaposition of greedy commercialism with innocence in the story of the attempted fleecing of a gentle old woman who bottles a cure for dropsy. She flees from pursuers by taking refuge with a collection of misfits in a woodland treehouse. The movie won accolades for casting: Piper Laurie as the ethereal Dolly Talbo, Walter Matthau as the winsome Judge Cool, Sissy Spacek as Dolly's greedy sister Varina Talbo, Jack Lemmon as the villainous Dr. Ritz, and Joe Don Baker as the rooster-hugging sheriff. Capote recorded *Children on Their Birthdays* (1950) for Columbia records and Harper Caedmon audiocassettes; other readings are available from American Audio Prose. (Bradbury 1963; Bradbury 1996; Capote 1946, 1965, 1978, 1987; Cunliffe 1987; Ehrlich and Carruth 1982; Fleming 1978; Hallowell 1977; Hendrix 1964; Herzberg 1962; Hill 1958; King 1980; Kunitz 1942; Malin 1968; Moates 1989; Ruas 1985; Wilson and Ferris 1989)

See also Lee, Harper; *To Kill a Mockingbird*.

CHOPIN, KATE

An original in the regionalist canon and a pivotal figure among American feminists, Kate Chopin found success with her classic iconoclastic novel *The Awakening* (1899), a literary monument to women's emancipation. Unfortunately, the work carried the seeds of destruction. According to critical comment at the end of the nineteenth century, the author offended sensibilities by being too free with sordid, shocking details of sexuality and wifely rebellion. Mossbacked patriarchs, who considered her a pornographer and scurrilous exhibitionist, lambasted her works on a rising scale that ranked them from offensive to scandalous, even perverse. Reclaimed in the 1970s with the advance of woman-centered writing, she holds a place alongside classic feminist authors including Willa Cather, Sarah Orne Jewett, Edith Wharton, and Mary Hunter Austin.

Like the works of George Washington Cable, Lafcadio Hearn, Grace Elizabeth King, and Shirley Ann Grau, Chopin's literary milieu owes much to the Creole South, where she set her vivid social writings. Born February 8, 1851,

Kate Chopin (1851–1904), photographed in October 1876

Katherine "Kate" O'Flaherty Chopin was a native of St. Louis, Missouri, far north of the Louisiana she eventually called home. She was the pampered daughter of Eliza Faris, a belle of the French Creole bourgeoisie, and immigrant Thomas O'Flaherty, a canny Irish merchant. She experienced a major loss in 1855: Her father invested in the Pacific Railroad and was killed on the train's first run when a trestle collapsed into the Gasconade River. A second tragedy took the life of her half brother George, a Confederate soldier who died of typhoid fever in a Union military prison in Arkansas in 1863.

As a scion of the privileged, Chopin enjoyed the best of St. Louis society. Her aristocratic great-grandmother, Madame Victoire Verdon Charleville, spoke only French to Kate, told her stories about Acadian and Huguenot pioneers, taught her piano, and set an example of the resolute Old South matriarch. Further influence on Chopin's moral upbringing came from her mother, a religious fanatic who insisted on strict Catholicism. To escape religious absolutism, Chopin withdrew into music and fiction. She practiced piano daily and read widely among folktales, verse, the novels of Sir Walter Scott and Charles Dickens, and contemporary romances. She boarded at the Academy of the Sacred Heart, where a nun, Mother O'Meara, encouraged her to write.

Beyond the constraints of home, Chopin reveled in the deliciously picaresque tales of Creole and Cajun St. Louis. She attuned her reading tastes to Molière, Guy de Maupassant, Walt Whitman, and Sarah Orne Jewett, all of whom influenced her development as a consummate fiction writer. Properly presented to society at age 20, she made a drastic change in role models when she served as companion to a married opera star, a woman who lived on her own in New Orleans who demanded a degree of privacy and tolerance unheard of in Chopin's limited experience.

A year after Chopin's liberation from childhood mores, she wed Oscar Chopin, son of a wealthy Creole physician. As a financier and cotton factor, Oscar could afford to spend lavishly on his beautiful bride. He treated her to a three-month European honeymoon, regular attendance at artistic functions, and a fully staffed home in New Orleans's American district. Rid of the domestic drudgery that ordinary women assumed as a way of life, Chopin patronized the opera and theater, vacationed on chichi Grand Isle, dressed in brightly colored fashions, and strolled the city while smoking cigarettes, a daring public display for women of the late 1800s. According to her journal, she relished studying New Orleans architecture, chatting with passersby, and gathering details of community life.

After Oscar Chopin's business failed, he left the comforts of city life and moved his wife and children—sons Jean, Oscar, George, Frederick, and Felix—to his family's extensive holdings on the Cane River in Natchitoches, where Chopin gave birth to Lelia, her only daughter. Oscar's tyrannic father, Dr. Victor Chopin, ruled his son's household with a fierce autocracy, and oppressed and abused local blacks. While Oscar's brother Lamy managed the family plantation, Oscar settled in an antebellum home constructed of cypress heart and slave-made brick. He opened a general store and oversaw several small plantations. This period introduced Chopin to the working-class and agrarian elements of Louisiana river culture. Involvement with local people supplied the dialect, superstitions, and Cajun lore that permeate her short stories.

Widowed after Oscar died of malaria in January 1883, Chopin assumed his considerable debt and the role of manager of their estate. She had a brief fling with planter Albert Sampité and continued managing the cotton plantation near Cloutierville until family business called her to St. Louis during the illness of her grandmother O'Flaherty, who died in 1884. Wearied by the demands of farming and eager to return her children to a more salubrious climate, Chopin resettled in Missouri with little regret. The next year, the death of her mother overwhelmed her with yet another family loss. At the prompting of Frank Kolbenheyer, her family physician, she overcame depression by reading Charles Darwin, Thomas Henry Huxley, Herbert Spencer, and other philosophers of the period, as well as Johann Goethe and strong female writers Germaine de Staël, Jane Austen, Charlotte Brontë, and George Sand. Although her life was overrun by parental responsibilities, she began composing local cameos, poetry, children's stories, a play, translations, critical essays, and short fiction and opened a Thursday salon for writers, artists, and editors. She immediately sold her elegy "If It Might Be" (1889) to *America* magazine and her first published story, "Wiser than a God," in the December 1889 issue of the *Musical Journal of Philadelphia*. She found a publisher for a first novel, *At Fault* (1890), which introduced the settings of central Louisiana to American literature.

Chopin followed a string of successes with *Bayou Folk* (1894), a collection of 20 stories containing "Désirée's Baby," an unusually candid plot on the theme of miscegenation, which she had published in *Vogue* in December 1893. The story of Désirée's marriage to Armand Aubigny, a Louisiana planter, turns on the ironies surrounding the birth of a child with negroid features. Armand drives his innocent wife into the bayou, from which she never reemerges. As he stokes a fire with the child's willow cradle, silk and velvet gowns, laces, embroidery, bonnets, gloves, and love letters from Désirée, he discovers a page written by his mother promising his father that "Armand will never know that his mother, who adores him, belongs to the race that is cursed with the brand of slavery." (Chopin 1983, 194) The beginner's luck of Chopin's first effort ceased with a second novel, *Young Dr. Gosse*, which found no takers. Its failure turned her attention to shorter works, at which she excelled. Published in *America, Atlantic Monthly, Century, American Jewess, Vogue, Youth's Companion, Criterion, St. Louis Dispatch, Harper's Young People,* and other periodicals, she throve on the achievement of four dozen sketches, which critics praised for their command of dialect, characterization, evocative settings, and restrained irony.

Chopin selected her best work for a second collection, *A Night in Acadie* (1897). Among them is "Athénaïse," an intense sketch on wifely rebellion that introduces themes and attitudes she later develops in *The Awakening*. First published in *Atlantic Monthly* in August 1896, the story tells of the spirited French-Creole wife of Cazeau, a coarse farmworker who sees in her averted eyes after only eight weeks of marriage that their union is a mistake. In a funk at the dinner table, he complains "Dat beat me! on'y marry two mont', an' got de head turn' a'ready to go 'abroad. Ce n'est pas Chrétien, ténez! [Indeed, it isn't

Christian!]" (Chopin 1983, 230) Set on retrieving Athénaïse on the third day, he stares down her brother Montéclin Miché, who condones her separation: "If you don' wan' to go, you know w'at you got to do, 'Th'naïse," fumed Montéclin. "You don't set yo' feet back on Cane River, by God, unless you want to,—not w'ile I'm alive." (Chopin 1983, 236) Against the pull of two strong males, Chopin depicts her protagonist's willful behavior in a mad pony ride, "with the wind inflating her skirt balloon-like about her knees, and her sunbonnet falling back between her shoulders." (Chopin 1983, 236) Athénaïse grudgingly returns to her husband, but often sleeps on the lounge. The spiritual and physical chasm widens with a second flight, this time to New Orleans. She returns in her imagination to her departure, "that dark and truly dangerous midnight ride along the 'coast' to the mouth of the Cane River!" (Chopin 1983, 246)

Chopin depicts the discontent of the protagonist in choices that bring Athénaïse no peace. In giving herself to Monsieur Gouvernail, a punctiliously courteous newspaper editor, she maintains distance, allowing their intimacy to emerge slowly with guarded glimpses of her true self. As he strokes her hair and embraces her, she settles into his arms: "Before releasing herself she kissed him against the neck; she had to love somebody in her own way!" (Chopin 1983, 256) At first moody and homesick, she has an awakening of passion that sends her on an optimistic walk about the neighborhood. Her stop to greet the oyster seller and hold the woman's unwashed baby prefigures her own blossoming. As the clitoral shape of the oyster foretells, Athénaïse is pregnant and joyously returns to her brother, who hands her over to Cazeau. Their embrace unites them for the first time in an emotional oneness. A dissenting note of regret in the brief sketch issues from the gentlemanly Gouvernail, who complains, "By heaven, it hurts, it hurts!" (Chopin 1983, 260)

At age 48, Chopin faced an impasse in her career with the publication of *The Awakening*, a frank study of the financial and sexual liberation of a pampered New Orleans wife from bourgeois matrimony. Public consternation at her bold breach of contemporary morality condemned the novel for being too sensual and anti-Victorian. A negative critique printed in the *New Orleans Times-Democrat* on June 18, 1899, sniffs self-righteously at a novel that centers on the mere "gratification of a passion." The critic thunders:

> In a civilized society the right of the individual to indulge all his caprices is, and must be, subject to many restrictive clauses, and it cannot for a moment be admitted that a woman who has willingly accepted the love and devotion of a man, even without an equal love on her part—who has become his wife and the mother of his children—has not incurred a moral obligation which peremptorily forbids her from wantonly severing her relations with him, and entering openly upon the independent existence of an unmarried woman. ("Kate Chopin's *The Awakening*" 1995, 1)

The unidentified spokesperson for the *Times-Democrat* castigates the author's "undercurrent of sympathy" for the protagonist, Edna Pontellier, and her violation of male-centered tenets of marriage by failing to censure Edna for abandoning her husband's children.

The scorned novel earned only $145 over a three-year period, but it brought Chopin to the attention of critic Edmund Wilson, who admired the work's unflinching re-creation of male-female relationships and its defiance of sentiment, the overriding mode of feminist novels of the late Victorian period. Initially undeterred, Chopin produced another novel, *An Avocation and a Voice*, which remained unpublished in her lifetime. By the turn of the century, she gave up writing completely. Ironically, the silencing of Kate Chopin occurred only a year before the death of Queen Victoria, the historic end to a period of enforced female domestication modeled on the queen's example of wifeliness and motherhood. On a two-day trip to the St. Louis World's Fair during August 20–21, 1904, Chopin suffered a cerebral hemorrhage and died August 22. She was buried in St. Louis's Calvary Cemetery.

Within three decades, supporters lifted Chopin above the notoriety of her final years. No longer classed as a Creole local colorist on a par with George Washington Cable, she was recognized as a keen observer of psychological forces within marriage and of such forbidden subjects as homosexuality, marital abuse, single motherhood, insanity, repressed sexuality, miscegenation, prostitution, and venereal disease. European and Japanese readers lauded her social and domestic commentary and unfettered passion. Feminists listed her among the major antipatriarchal writers of Europe, including Gustave Flaubert, Henrik Ibsen, Isak Dinesen, and D. H. Lawrence. Her papers are housed in the offices of the Missouri Historical Society; her handsome balconied home in Cloutierville, which has been turned into a bayou folk museum, is marked with a plaque honoring her achievements. In 1982, Bob Graham directed *The End of August*, a nostalgic film adaptation of *The Awakening*. (Blain et al. 1990; Bloom 1987; Bonner 1988; Boren and Davis 1992; Bradbury 1996; Chopin 1983; Christ 1980; *Contemporary Authors* 1994; Davidson and Wagner-Martin 1995; Davis et al. 1970; Guilds 1970; Jones 1981; "Kate Chopin" 1996; "Kate Chopin Project" 1996; "Kate Chopin's *The Awakening*" 1995; Koloski 1988; Martin 1988; Massey 1996; Papke 1990; Quinn 1936; Rubin et al. 1985; Skaggs 1985; Stein 1979; Toth 1993)

See also The Awakening; Cable, George Washington.

THE CIVIL WAR ERA

The Civil War scratched out an irrevocable line of demarcation for American history and culture. The fight between North and South cost the nation its innocence, but proved that the framers of the Constitution had established a firm foundation in law for the American experiment in democracy. Just as the shakeup in Rome after the death of Julius Caesar hurtled writers into a protracted wrangle over Republican values and political aims, the American war years and beyond forced Southern writers into two camps—those who looked to the future with hope and enthusiasm, and the nostalgic minority who could not pull free of the past. Continuing into the twentieth century, the challenged beliefs of the Civil War era remain at issue, like Marley's ghost, still surfacing in their dreary trappings to dog the novelist, dramatist, poet, and essayist.

The literary perpetuation of the Old South was sometimes no more difficult than ignoring the "late unpleasantness," as euphemists called the War between the States. A popular essayist, William John Grayson of Beaufort, South Carolina, stated his conservative views in *The Hireling and the Slave* (1854), which defended slavery from a gentlemanly, elitist point of view. After Lee's surrender at Appomattox, Grayson published *James Louis Petigru: A Biographical Sketch* (1866), in which he salutes a friend who stood on the opposite side of the slavery issue. For different reasons, black storyteller Caesar Grant of Johns Island, South Carolina, reset black protest into myth in "All God's Chillen Had Wings," a popular fantasy that depicts belabored blacks sprouting wings to fly away from bondage. Alabama attorney Richard Capel Beckett, who supervised corn and flour mills in Monroe County, Mississippi, during the 1860s, poked fun at a scalawag named Woodmansee, whom he labeled "prince of smooth carpetbaggers." In a witty essay, Beckett relates how a doctor, who was treating Woodmansee for a head wound, shaved the sound side of the man's skull and plastered it with bandages, leaving the bloody side gashed and matted with blood, an image emblematic of the literary dichotomy formed of the opposing realistic and antirealistic views of the South.

Deliberately removed from the heated social and political turmoil that threatened to dismember the Union are genteel antebellum verses that look beyond the mounting dissension between North and South. Poet Alexander Beaufort Meek produced a splendid nature poem, "The Mocking Bird" (1857), a Keatsian ode that calls for gladness, jest, and pleasure in nature. Similar in tone and style are the delicate verses of John Banister Tabb, a former prisoner of war at Point Lookout, Maryland, who returned to Richmond to teach English at St. Peter's Boys School. His poetry, published in 1882, contains postwar trauma without a description of battles or heroics. Poems such as "Kildee," "The Snow-Bird," and "Compensation" remind the reader that some sufferers concealed their hurts and quietly returned to civilian duties. A four-line ode to private hells, "My Secret" speaks plainly Tabb's internal torment:

'Tis not what I am fain to hide
That doth in deepest darkness dwell,
But what my tongue hath often tried,
Alas, in vain to tell.
(Parks 1970, 204)

In a gesture toward the multicultural South, Georgian Charles Colcock Jones reflected on traditional Southern lore with *Negro Myths from the Georgia Coast Told in the Vernacular* (1888). William Elliott, a gentleman farmer and after-hours writer, produced detailed sporting vignettes for coastal South Carolina newspapers, such as the divvying up of meat in "A Deer Hunt" (1846): "And see that brave array of haunches! that is a buck of two years,—juicy, tender, but not fat,—capital for steaks!" He declares that a better use of venison is for gifts and says, "the worst use you can make of your game is to eat it yourselves." (Fulton

Jefferson Davis, president of the Confederate states between 1861 and 1865, poses with his second wife and First Lady of the Confederacy, Varina, who became a memoirist of the era.

1917, 26) Late in the postwar era, another jovial writer, Richard Malcolm Johnston, reflected on the antebellum South with dialect humor known as the *Dukesborough Tales*. His most successful include "Old Mark Langston" (1884), "Mr. Absalom Billingslea and Other Georgia Folk" (1888), and "Widow Guthrie" (1890).

On the realistic side of Dixie's literature, writers and orators who removed themselves from the jollity and romance of the antebellum South refused to see the regional immorality in rosy hues. An unusual figure in this era, William Wells Brown, an escaped mulatto slave, forced the issue of slavery. Born in Lexington, Kentucky, he lived in Louisiana when his mother was placed on the auction block at a New Orleans slave warehouse. After working for the *St. Louis Times* in 1834, he took a job on a riverboat; with the assistance of Quakers on the Ohio Underground Railroad, he then fled to Canada. Like Frederick Douglass and Harriet Jacobs, Brown educated himself and put his knowledge to use to release others from servitude. As a lecturer, agent, and writer for the Massachusetts Anti-Slavery Society, he traveled the country, speaking on equality for blacks and women, temperance, and nonviolence. He attended the Paris Peace Conference in 1849, and toured England during the period when the Fugitive Slave Law increased the danger of arrest. He published two works: a personal history, *The Narrative of William Wells Brown; a Fugitive Slave* (1851), and *The Anti-Slavery Harp* (1852), a verse collection. His travelogue, *Three Years in Europe; or, Places I Have Seen and People I Have Met* (1852), was another first for black literature.

A year before Brown purchased his freedom from his former owner, Enoch Price, he published an intriguing psychological novel, *Clotelle: A Tale of Southern States* (1853). Originally subtitled "The President's Daughter: A Narrative of Slave Life in the United States," the work is called the first black novel, although Harriet E. Wilson's *Our Nig: Or Sketches from the Life of a Free Black in a Two-Story White House, North, Showing That Slavery's Shadows Fall Even There* (1859) technically preceded the American printing of Brown's novel by five years. *Clotelle* is a shrewd piece of propaganda, but is marred by extensive coincidence and mawkish recriminations and forgiveness. Brown uses drama, suspense, and irony to exploit prevailing rumors that Thomas Jefferson sired a daughter by his mulatto concubine, Sally Hemings, and sold the girl in New Orleans for $1,000. In chapter 2, Brown heightens the melodrama of the sale after the bidding stops at $2,000 and the auctioneer guarantees the girl's virginity:

> This was a Virginia slave-auction, at which the bones, sinews, blood, and nerves of a young girl of eighteen was sold for $500; her moral character for $200; her superior intellect for $100; the benefits supposed to accrue from her having been sprinkled and immersed, together with a warranty of her devoted Christianity, for $300; her ability to make a good prayer for $200; and her chastity for $700 more. This, too, in a city thronged with churches, whose tall spires look like so many signals pointing to heaven, but whose ministers preach that slavery is a God-ordained institution! (Davis et al. 1970, 416)

Brown concludes the auction scene with a reminder that the farewells of slaves are permanent. In protest against the sufferings of three generations of black females, the book exploits its setting during Jefferson's term of office and exaggerates with dramatic irony the pursuit of Isabella, Clotelle's mother, to the Potomac River, where she drowns in sight of the White House. The falling action lauds the Union Army, for which Clotelle's father, Henry Linwood, dies fighting the Confederacy. Clotelle becomes a relief worker among Confederate prisoners and turns her father's land into a freemen's academy. Eagerly read by Union soldiers, the novel was touted as the first written by an American black author.

Brown's writing career proceeded from the prewar years through Reconstruction. The first black dramas—*Experience; or, How To Give a Northern Man a Backbone* (1856) and *The Escape, or A Leap for Freedom* (1858), a satire on slavery—he delivered along with other original plays in public readings, but he never produced his works on stage. Brown's last titles include three histories—*The Black Man: His Antecedents, His Genius, and His Achievements* (1863), *The Negro in the American Rebellion: His Heroism and His Fidelity* (1867), and *The Rising Son; or, The Antecedents and Advancement of the Colored Race* (1874)—and a memoir, *My Southern Home; or, The South and Its People* (1880).

For white writers dismayed by the war to end slavery, a different set of priorities fueled literary themes. Prefiguring the grief he endured as a military colonel of an Alabama regiment, Theodore O'Hara wrote a mournful war poem, "The Bivouac of the Dead" (1847), which takes its details from the Mexican War. From the same war, Henry Rootes Jackson, a Kentucky poet, expressed yearnings for home in "Red Old Hills of Georgia" and "My Wife and Child," both nostalgic poems in *Tallulah, and Other Poems* (1850). Torn between issues and loyalties, orator Alexander Hamilton Stephens clung to the South, but his impassioned speech, "A Plea for Union" (1860), urged calm forbearance rather than secession. A year later, Senator Jefferson Davis made his farewell address to Congress by interpreting the Declaration of Independence from an individualist stance. Under its provisions, he declared it imperative that principled citizens withdraw from a perversion of the original union and, abjuring hostility and vengefulness, discharge all civic duties without giving injury. His inaugural address, delivered in Montgomery, Alabama, on February 18, 1861, makes a case for a separate Southern nation based on indigenous agrarian principles:

> An agricultural people, whose chief interest is the export of a commodity required in every manufacturing country, our true policy is peace, and the freest trade which our necessities will permit.... There can be but little rivalry between ours and any manufacturing or navigating community, such as the North-eastern States of the American Union. (Davis 1997, n.p.)

Davis concludes that an independent set of states is the best method of restoring tranquillity, which he is willing to fight for. As though searching for a positive omen he remarks, "It is joyous, in the midst of perilous times, to look around upon a people united in heart, . . . where the sacrifices to be made are not weighed in the balance against honor and right and liberty and equality."

In an address to assembled representatives in Montgomery on April 29, 1861, Davis announced the framing of a Confederate constitution ratified by all seceding states. At this session, he referred directly to the institution and purpose of slavery:

> The climate and soil of the Northern States soon proved unpropitious to the continuance of slave labor, whilst the converse was the case at the South. Under the unrestricted free intercourse between the two sections, the Northern States consulted their own interests by selling their slaves to the South and prohibiting slavery within their limits. (Davis 1997, n.p.)

Declaring the sale a bogus exchange, Davis accused Northern congressmen of plotting hostile measures to deny the South ownership of slaves. He blamed fanatics for luring slaves into discontent, revolt, and flight, and lambasted Congress as "the theater of agitation and aggression," where bitter hatred stirred both sides to war. He estimated that the population of slaves had risen from 600,000 in 1789 to more than 4 million at the formation of the Confederacy, and asserted that they were necessary to supply the entire nation with cotton, rice, sugar, and tobacco.

Apart from the political crucible, John Esten Cooke, author of seven reflections of battlefield experiences, composed a memoir and biography of the Civil War. During the worst of the fray, he continued to think high thoughts and wrote *The Life of Stonewall Jackson: A Military Biography* (1866), followed by *Surry of Eagle's Nest* (1866), which he filled with distressing scenes of the wounded and dying. The most significant of his reflections is the loss of General Stonewall Jackson, who was accidentally shot by his own forces. Cooke recalls the groan that escaped Jackson as his mangled arm was sheared from his shoulder in what seemed an undeserved blow to the hero of Manassas and Port Republic. Cooke regrets the romantic setting "in the tangled and lugubrious depths of this weird Wilderness, with the wan moon gliding like a ghost through the clouds—the sad notes of the whippoorwill echoing from the thickets." (Beatty et al. 1952, 451–452) His imagist bent perceives a bursting shell as a shower of stars, a cosmic omen of the fallen hero of a hundred engagements, the South's idol. Like many whose idealism was shattered by loss, Cooke composed *A Life of Robert E. Lee* (1871), one of the many rehashings of strategy and circumstance. With a nod to the exigencies of feeding a defeated land, he proposed intensive agricultural techniques in *The Heir of Gaymount* (1870).

His life altered by historical events, Mississippian Irwin Russell, a precocious eight-year-old when the Civil War began, received a sketchy education because of his state's involvement in the hostilities. He completed a law degree in St. Louis and wrote verse while working for newspapers. Multiple losses during a yellow fever epidemic cost him his father and fiancée. Ten days before his own death in 1879, Russell composed a reflective holiday piece, *Christmas-Night in the Quarters* (1878), recalling the South in less formidable times. The memory of a late December frolic opens with "darkies [holding] high carnival." In the segment called "The First Banjo," Russell creates a folk legend about Noah and the flood. In the midst of a 40-day rain, Noah takes a ladder; makes a bridge, neck, and apron for his banjo; and strums with a thimble over his finger:

De' possum had as fine a tail as dis dat I's a-singin';
De ha'rs so long, an' thick, an' strong,—des fit for bango-stringin';
Dat nigger shaved 'em off as short as wash-day-dinner graces;
An' sorted ob 'em by de size, from little E's to basses.
(Parks 1970, 213)

The ringing banjo solo concludes Yule night revelries. At the first streaks of dawn, celebrants return home. Santa Claus, who is loathe to go, departs over a fence, leaving a lad to ponder: "Ef Santa had been born a twin! We'd hab two Chrismuses a yeah—Or p'r'aps *one* brudder'd *settle* heah'!" (Parks 1970, 214)

A number of women found the war era surprisingly open to their writings. Emma Dorothy Eliza Nevitte Southworth, composing under the pen name E. D. E. N. Southworth, turned out 60 novels and plays, including *India* (1853), an abolitionist novel of social protest. Alabaman Celeste Le Vert published a travelogue, *Souvenirs of Travel* (1857); Mary Ann Harris Gay observed the Union siege of Decatur and the fall of Atlanta, which she described in *Life in Dixie during the War* (ca. 1856). While residing at her husband's Georgia plantation, English actress Frances Anne "Fanny" Kemble despised the cruel methods by which overseers worked the family's several hundred slaves. She produced *Journal of an American Residence* (1835), an antislave memoir. Ironically, she wrote under her married name, Frances Anne Butler, but negative reponse to an outsider's criticism ended her marriage. She reprised the work at the beginning of the Civil War with a popular sequel, *Residence on a Georgia Plantation, 1838–1839* (1863), a fierce memoir focusing on the misery of black breeders and concubines. Also an immigrant to the South, New Englander Caroline Lee Whiting Hentz was hailed a prodigy in her early teens with the completion of poetry, a novel, and a five-act tragedy. After her marriage to Frenchman Nicholas Marcellas Hentz, she lived in the South and wrote "Fatal Cosmetics" for *Godey's Lady's Book* as well as numerous other fictional works. Set below the Mason-Dixon Line were *Linda: or, The Young Pilot of the Belle Creole* (1850); a popular romance, *The Planter's Northern Bride* (1851); followed by *Marcus Warland* (1852) and a story collection, *The Banished Son and Other Stories of the Heart* (1856), published the year of her death. A West Virginian who turned a profit from dime novels, Mittie Frances Clark Point earned $6,000 annually with romance thrillers such as *The Bride of the Tomb*, which she wrote under her husband's name, Alex McVeigh Miller. Mississippian Susan Dabney Smedes composed a salute to the past with *Memorials of a Southern Planter* (1887), in which she recounts the loss of the Burleigh plantation, auctioned and sold in 1866. Lizette Woodworth Reese, a native of Waverly, Maryland, taught high school English and wrote nature poetry, published in *A Branch of May* (1887), and a restrained autobiography, *A Victorian Village* (1929), which details the quiet splendors that tinge her most insightful poems, "April Weather," "Spicewood," and "Today."

Other writers blended their visions with the realities of carnage. John Williamson Palmer, a physician from Baltimore, published *For Charlie's Sake, and Other Ballads and Lyrics* (1901), which contains "Stonewall Jackson's Way." The speaker exults with admiration and trust for a fighting leader:

He's in the saddle now. Fall in!
    Steady! the whole brigade.
Hill's at the ford, cut off; we'll win
    His way out, ball and blade.
What matter if our shoes are worn?
What matter if our feet are torn?
Quick step! we're with him before morn
    That's Stonewall Jackson's Way.
(Parks 1970, 151)

Henry Lynden Flash echoes the adulation for Jackson with "Stonewall Jackson" (1865), a regret for the wound that brought down the stalwart general, whom he calls "the Moses of the South." (Fulton 1917, 262) A poet who did not survive the war, Georgian Thaddeus Oliver composed "All Quiet along the Potomac To-night" (1864), a flowing piece in graceful dactylic meter reprising the moment of peace that follows a picket's death in the line of duty.

Women produced a significant share of Civil War commentary. Mary Ravenel de La Coste, a Savannah poet, taught French and wrote verse when the war moved her to speak. Her emotional farewell to an unnamed soldier, "Somebody's Darling" (ca. 1864), is set in a hospital ward, where a boyish young casualty dies in anonymity. To preserve his valor, de La Coste implores,

Kiss him once for somebody's sake;
    Murmur a prayer both soft and low;
One bright curl from its fair mates take—
    They were somebody's pride, you know.
(Fulton 1917, 265)

Caroline Augusta Ball's "The Jacket of Gray" (1866) follows a similar regretful mood and delivery as she repines the loss of a loved one. She hears victory shouts override prayers and envisions a cold battlefield where the victim's blood stains a once-spruce gray tunic. Less lugubrious is the medieval touch of Margaret Junkin Preston's "The Soldier Boy" (ca. 1865), building on an image of the tempered blade, which outlives the hand that wielded it.

In an opposite mood, William Gordon McCabe, textbook author and critic, wrote a pensive poem about dreams of sweethearts at home in "Dreaming in the Trenches" (ca. 1864). His "Christmas Night of '62" (ca. 1865) returns to the theme of longing as phrased by a man who believes "My home is in the bivouac." (Fulton 1917, 257) Albert Pike, a Massachusetts native who settled in Arkansas, wrote an inspirational battle cry, "Dixie" (ca. 1865), that urges the hardy soldier:

Swear upon your country's altar
Never to submit or falter,
Till the spoilers are defeated,
Till the Lord's work is completed.
(Fulton 1917, 245)

More successful as a military song was Irish immigrant Harry McCarthy's (or McCarty's) "The Bonny Blue Flag" (ca. 1861), a resounding rally with an uplifting chorus: "Hurrah! Hurrah! for Southern rights, Hurrah! Hurrah for the Bonny Blue Flag that bears a Single Star!" (Fulton 1917, 246) The verses were so inflammatory that General Butler ordered anyone singing, playing, or whistling the tune in the confines of New Orleans to be fined $25. The oft-sung war anthem inspired a scene in Margaret Mitchell's *Gone with the Wind*, in which Melanie Wilkes offers a comparison between Rhett and Scarlet O'Hara's child's eyes and the Confederate flag. The analogy sticks; Eugenia Victoria Butler is dubbed "Bonnie Blue."

After reading about gallant home folks in the *New Orleans Sunday Delta*, James Ryder Randall was stirred to honor his homeland in "My Maryland" (1861), a hymn he hoped would encourage the state to join the Confederacy. According to legend, Southern spy Belle Boyd sat in a GAR prison and sang Randall's Maryland theme song so pertly that she reduced fellow Confederates to tears. Joseph Blyth Allston, son of General Joseph Allston, was imprisoned at Fort Delaware and awaiting release when he wrote "Stack Arms" (1865), a mixture of emotions that recalls the end of war as well as the finality of a lost dream of Southern autonomy. Imagist John Reuben Thompson wrote less grandly of war's waste in "Music in Camp" (1867), a pensive study of the Blue and the Gray camped on opposite sides of the Rappahannock River. The thin strand that holds the image together is the playing of "Home, Sweet Home," a binding memory that loosens emotions as though they are summoned by a sprite. Men on both sides grow teary-eyed and think of home and family as the simple melody withdraws from their hearts the urge to kill.

Another journalist, Georgia Eliza Frances "Fanny" Andrews, a botany teacher and author of scientific articles, speaks more realistically of terror and destruction. Reflecting on Civil War experiences at her family's plantation and her sister's home outside Albany, Andrews composed *The Wartime Journal of a Georgia Girl* (1908), in which she recalled socials, hardships, and the plight of Varina Davis, the Confederacy's First Lady, during her family's flight from Union captivity. Describing the scorched earth in her home state, she says,

> I used to feel very brave about Yankees, but since I have passed over Sherman's track and seen what devastation they make, I am so afraid of them that I believe I should drop down dead if one of the wretches should come into my presence. (Kerber 1986, 129)

She quotes Sherman's aim to destroy every blade of grass in southwest Georgia. Of her own privations she declares, "I can stand patched-up dresses, and even take a pride in wearing Confederate homespun, where it is done open and above board, but I can't help feeling vulgar and common in coarse underclothes." (Kerber 1986, 130) The shaky political situation of April 1865 causes her to write that everyone challenged outsiders and shot anybody who menaced or acted like a spy. Trains departing from the worst of Georgia's mayhem carried people hunched on the steps and clinging to doors and aisles. Andrews and the rest traded on rumor and sensational reports in lieu of real news.

The pain of realism permeates Andrews's comments later in the spring of 1865. Realizing that the South was sinking, she described with journalistic accuracy, "No more gay uniforms, no more prancing horses, but only a few ragged foot soldiers with wallets and knapsacks on, ready to march—Heaven knows where." (Kerber 1986, 136) Her own household was at odds, with her father and mother staunch Unionists and she and her brothers "red-hot Rebs." Her father became so angry at her disdain for the flag that he threatened to send her to her room for a week, even though she was 25 years old. Evenhandedly, she admitted that her father was right about secession being a mistake and wished that her family had freed their slaves in exchange for some government compensation. She concluded, "but now the thing is done, and there is no use talking about the right or the wrong of it." Still smarting with the fall of "Lee and his glorious army," like so many loyal Southerners, she preferred to be wrong with the Confederacy than "right with a gang of fanatics that have come down here to plunder and oppress us in the name of liberty." (Kerber 1986, 138) Late summer entries to her journal report that carpetbaggers, stragglers, and free Negroes conspire in a murderous cabal against Southerners.

With an insider's vision of defeat, Varina Howell Davis, Jefferson Davis's second wife and the Confederacy's First Lady, wrote memoirs and apologias for her husband, whom she felt was compromised by his role as president of a failed government. After his death, she honored his memory with a two-volume biography, *Jefferson Davis, Ex-President of the Confederate States of America; a Memoir* (1890). The burden of supporting her children taxed her strength and compromised meager resources, which had been confiscated while she and her husband were imprisoned after the war. Varina moved to New York with her daughter, Varina Anne Jefferson "Winnie" Davis, and took up a genteel literary career, penning sketches and magazine articles primarily for the curious. On December 13, 1896, she published "Christmas in the Confederate White House" in the *New York World*. The concise vignette depicts a subdued exchange of gifts with family and slaves, who were gracious and supportive of the Davis family. Among her concerns were a suitable recipe for mince pie, a tree for orphans, and the enjoyment of gifts from supporters, including bars of soap made from rendered ham fat. She concludes with a youthful cotillion, called a "starvation party" because there was music but no refreshments.

Returning veterans and civilian victims of the war and its economic hardships were unable to rid themselves of the ghosts of the 1860s. In the months following the war's end, Confederate spy Belle Boyd wrote her memoirs and launched a lecture tour. A South Carolina surgeon, John Dickson Bruns, returned from war with haunting memories of insurgents threatening Charleston. In 1865, he wrote "The Foe at the Gates," beginning each stanza with "Ring round her!," a cry meant to arouse to action both military and noncombatant to rescue the city from scarlet rain, the blood-rich torrent that accompanies "The last grand holocaust of Liberty." (Parks 1970, 156) Immediately after the Confederacy's demise, Cornelia Phillips Spencer shaped an eyewitness history, *The Last Ninety Days of the War in North Carolina* (1866). In Mississippi, Katherine Sherwood McDowell, a short-story writer and protégé of Henry Wadsworth Longfellow, kept a journal of the Reconstruction era, which she wrote under the masculine pseudonym Sherwood Bonner. Mary Ann Loughborough wrote of the Mississippians' travail in *My Cave Life in Vicksburg, with Letters of Trial and Travel* (1864). Sarah Morgan, a Louisiana diarist, composed an untitled eyewitness account of the naval siege of Baton Rouge. She angrily opposed the flying of the Union flag and mourned the ruin of her family home, where corpses lay unburied. In dismay at the destruction and looting of her room, she wrote, "Precious letters I found under heaps of broken china and rags; all my notes were gone, with many letters.... Bah! What is the use of describing such a scene!" (Sherr and Kazickas 1994, 167)

Fellow diarist Mary Boykin Chesnut, daughter of the governor of South Carolina, was steady of nerve, well read, and quick-witted, all requisites for the task of commenting on the events of the Civil War. She kept a dozen detailed journals from 1861 to 1865 filled with day-by-day accounts of her popular salon and war news, highlighted by her view of the firing on Fort Sumter, hatred of slavery, compassion for slaves beset by vicious overseers, and contempt and loathing for the institution of marriage, which restrained her in another form of servitude. Her terror on the night of April 12, 1861, at the Planters Hotel in Charleston seems genuine:

> I do not pretend to go to sleep. How can I? If Anderson does not accept terms— at four—the orders are he shall be fired upon. I count four—St. Michael chimes. I begin to hope. At half-past four, the heavy booming of a cannon. I sprang out of bed. And on my knees—prostrate—I prayed as I never prayed before. (Chesnut 1981, 46)

The entry moves along at a jog-trot pace. Hurriedly dressed in two gowns and a shawl, Chesnut is filled with the anxieties that accompany uncertainty but does not give in to panic. As shells burst over the fort, she ponders the fate of her husband, James Chesnut, who is rowing in "that dark bay." She reports that women pray on the housetops while men curse. As the bombardment continues, the fragmented night sky flashes with sudden explosions.

In 1864, as the war drags on and the South suffers more hunger, deaths, casualties, and discouragement, Chesnut maintains a front-row observation in minute detail that is often caustic but typically candid, and alive with gossip and personal commentary on the people around her. In fervent dramatic monologue, she ponders the state of fellow citizens—aristocrats, the governor's staff, President Jefferson Davis and his family, the South Carolina sandhill working class, yeomen, soldiers, and the slaves for whom the war is being fought:

> God help my country! I think we are like sailors who break into the spirits closet when they find out the ship must be sunk. There seems to be a resolute determination to enjoy the brief hours and never look beyond the day. I now have no hope. (Sherr and Kazickas 1994, 404–405)

Like others of her privileged social stratum, she realizes that the aristocratic social world is disintegrating and that the demise of slavery will end the niceties of upperclass life. Not given to whimpering, she allows herself a heartfelt bay at the dark night. Her anguish blends with the calls of whippoorwills and the shriek of screech owls.

The unforeseen outcome of civil war precipitates a pell-mell flight among Chesnut's contemporaries to Charlotte and Lincolnton, North Carolina, to escape Yankee aggressors. She is grateful to people who assist her on the road from Charleston, but maintains her distance from unkempt refugees. She encounters a "poor soldier, shaggy, scrubby, ill looking," who offers her hardtack in exchange for softer fare. Chesnut willingly hands him the "best in my lunch basket," but refuses to touch his humble food. She congratulates herself on having the spunk to boil her own eggs and wash her tea dishes, tasks usually relegated to Ellen, her black maid. (Chesnut 1981, 231)

Like most of the South's moneyed class, Chesnut suffered a steady attrition of goods and property after the war and learned to make do on a homely butter-and-egg business. To suit the tastes of postwar readers, she gave up a plan to turn memoir into fiction, which she had planned to entitle "The Bright Side of Richmond: Winter of 1864—Scraps from a Diary." Instead, she refined seven volumes of her 400,000-word memories, removing personal prejudices, mentions of slavery, gossip and trivia, and unflattering details. The revised memoir was published posthumously in 1886, the year of her death, and again in 1905 as *Diary from Dixie*, containing a third of her original commentary. It was reprised in 1981 as *Mary Chesnut's Civil War*, winner of a Pulitzer Prize for history. In the twentieth century, Maryland poet Adrienne Rich set Chesnut's images in elegiac verse, "Charleston in the 1860s: Derived from the Diaries of Mary Boykin Chesnut," a poetic narrative mourning the years of fear, bondage, loss, and death that reduced Charleston to a charnel house. In May 1997, the Actor's Theatre of South Carolina presented at the annual Spoleto Festival in Charleston *A World Kicked to Pieces: Mary Boykin Chesnut on Love and War*, a play that premiered in October 1996 in the Fine Arts Center of Kershaw County in Camden, South Carolina, Chesnut's hometown.

Chesnut's contemporary, Caroline Howard Gilman, was born in Massachusetts but spent much of her adult life in South Carolina. In her youth she kept a journal, *Rose Bud* (1832), and published a pro-slavery memoir, *Recollections of a Southern Matron* (1837); a gothic novel, *Love's Progress* (1840); and two poetry collections, *The Poetry of Traveling in the United States* (1838) and *Verses of a Lifetime* (1849). Daybooks and poems evidence her delight in the landscape around Charleston. On a journey up the Cooper River, she composed "Let Us Go to the Woods" (1838), a verse tribute to pinks, azaleas, touch-me-nots, phlox, starflowers, and butterfly weed. However, like Mary Chesnut, Gilman penned letters that relate a gravely altered outlook—from the optimism of nature lore to the misgivings at prewar hostilities. In a letter to her daughter, Gilman remained stoic: "We do see all the worst threats of the North in our paper and so are prepared, but you cannot see the calm, indomitable spirit that prevails all over the South." (Sherr and Razickas 1994, 405–406)

Journalism profited from the aggressive women who edited, wrote, and published newspapers and literary reviews. Actively composing editorials and articles for a half century, West Virginian Anne Newport Royall issued *Sketches of History, Life and Manners in the United States* (1826). A crusading newspaperwoman and the first to publish a newspaper, she established two papers in

Washington, D.C.—*Paul Pry* and the *Huntress,* for which she interviewed 13 presidents. Still active in the mid-1800s, she openly supported the Union and pressed for its sovereignty. Maryland tractarian Anna Ella Carroll wrote propaganda for the Lincoln administration and devised the Civil War battle strategy used in the Tennessee campaign. In Louisiana, poet and pioneer newspaperwoman Eliza Jane Poitevent Holbrook Nicholson edited, then published the *New Orleans Picayune* and pursued lyric verse privately in 1873 under the pseudonym Pearl Rivers. Mississippi author Sarah Anne Ellis Dorsey assisted Jefferson Davis in the research for *The Rise and Fall of the Confederate Government* (1881). A reflective relief worker from New Brunswick, Sarah Emma Evelyn Edmonds was a cross-dresser who served in a Michigan regiment under the name Frank Thompson and fought at the battles of Bull Run and Fredericksburg. She married and settled in Texas, where she wrote a fictionalized memoir, *Nurse and Spy in the Union Army* (1865). From the opposing point of view, Alabaman Kate Cumming wrote *The Journal of Hospital Life in the Confederate Army in Tennessee* (1866), which contains the carnage of the Battle of Shiloh.

Mary Ann Shadd Cary, a contemporary of these female journalists and researchers, was the daughter of free blacks who were active agents of the Underground Railroad. A graduate of Howard University law school and the first black female to practice law, she became a successful abolitionist tractarian, editor, interviewer, and investigative reporter. After moving to Windsor, Ontario, with her brother Isaac she published the *Provincial Freeman,* a newspaper aimed at providing crucial data and advice to fugitive slaves far from their families in the South. In her pamphlets *Hints to the Colored People of North America* (1849) and *A Plea for Emigration, or Notes on Canada West, in Its Moral, Social and Political Aspect* (1852), she furthered arguments that newly freed blacks should rely on themselves and turn from government agents, philanthropists, missionaries, and shysters, who robbed them of pride and bilked them of their money. Through polemical articles and lectures, her curt, abrasive manner and blunt dismissal of do-gooders put her at odds with prominent abolitionists, but her call for self-reliance and financial independence inspired readers to be wary and think for themselves.

A journalist of the Jim Crow era, Ida Bell Wells-Barnett wrote investigative reportage on lynching, published in the *Memphis Free Speech and Headlight, A.M.E. Church Review, Living Way, Memphis Watchman, New York Age, Indianapolis World,* and *Chicago Conservator.* Her collected articles appeared as *Southern Horrors: Lynch Law in All Its Phases* (1892). The next year, she protested the exclusion of black achievements from the Chicago World's Fair with *The Reason Why the Colored American Is Not in the Columbian Exposition* (1893). She stirred more controversy among racists with *A Red Record: Tabulated Statistics and Alleged Causes of Lynching in the United States, 1892–1893–1894* (1895). After conducting a lecture series in Great Britain, she returned to the fray with *Mob Rule in New Orleans* (1900).

As the antebellum South moved into decline, spirited authors—Dilue Rose Harris, James Matthew Legaré, Philip Pendleton Cooke, Hugh Swinton Legaré, Sam Houston, Charles Étienne Arthur Gayarré, John Esten Cooke, and John

Pendleton Kennedy—looked away from violence. Philip Pendleton Cooke, an aristocratic attorney, published such genteel nature poems as "The Mountaineer" and "Florence Vane" in *Froissart Ballads, and Other Poems* (1847). Hugh Swinton Legaré, the attorney general under President Tyler, wrote notebooks of learned essays, travelogues, and amiable sketches, which his daughter published in 1846 as *Writings of Hugh Swinton Legaré.* His journal, *Southern Review,* rivaled the best literary periodicals in the country. His kinsman James Matthews Legaré produced some of the enduring nature poetry of the era. The best, "To a Lily" and "Haw-Blossoms," were collected in *Orta-Undis, and Other Poems* (1848).

Mobile novelist Augusta Jane Evans Wilson, the first female author to earn over $100,000, had considerable experience in writing before the Civil War. The foremost Southern novelist of her day, she published 60 titles, beginning with *Inez: A Tale of the Alamo* (1855), an abolitionist social protest written during her teens. *Beulah* (1859), a popular novel derived from her wartime nursing experiences, preceded *St. Elmo* (1866), a Dixie blockbuster that has been called the most loved and hated work of its time. This sweeping romance novel, which preceded Ellen Glasgow's popular romances and Margaret Mitchell's *Gone with the Wind,* exploits the erotic attraction between the pious Edna Earl and St. Elmo Murray, a "mad, bad and dangerous to know" hero. (Evans 1992, v) Edna states her belief in high-mindedness in chapter 30 by reciting from a lecture she had read on architecture:

> You must love the creatures to whom you minister, your fellow-men; for if you do not love them, not only will you be little interested in the passing events of life, but in all your gazing at humanity, you will be apt to be struck only by outside form, and not by expression. It is only kindness and tenderness which will ever enable you to see and in the paleness of those fixed faces which the earth's adversity has compassed about, till they shine in their patience like dying watch-fires through twilight. (Evans 1992, 295)

In high Victorian style, the lofty ideals guide St. Elmo and Edna through a troubled courtship, which concludes with a villainess groveling in the grass as the couple clasp in true devotion. Their elevated romance inspired C. H. Webb to pen a parody, *St. Twel'mo, or, The Cuneiform Cyclopedist of Chattanooga* (1867).

Much of Wilson's writing was too philosophical to be memorable, but in an era that offered few lucrative or fulfilling professions for women, she found her work remunerative and satisfying. She captured some of the war and Reconstruction angst in her letters, in anonymous articles in the Mobile press, and in *Macaria; or Altars of Sacrifice* (1864), a pro-Confederate novel that had to be smuggled across the Mason-Dixon line after Union authorities declared it contraband. A contemporary, Virginian Mary Virginia Hawes Terhune, also a successful novelist and writer of household advice over six decades, wrote reflections of Wilson's life, including the war years. ("Augusta Evans Wilson" 1996; Blain et al. 1990; Bradbury 1996; Buck 1992; Chesnut 1981, 1984; Clinton 1994; Davidson and Wagner-Martin 1995; Davis 1996; Davis 1997; Davis et al. 1970; Ehrlich and Carruth 1982; Evans 1992; Faust 1988; Gilman 1838; Hibbard 1931; Johnson and Malone 1930; Kerber 1986; Kunitz and Haycraft 1938; "Mary

Boykin Chesnut" 1996; Mullane 1993; Parks 1970; Ravitch 1990; Rutherford 1907; Sherr and Kazickas 1994; "Slave Narratives" 1997; Spiller and Blodgett 1939; Sullivan 1995; Thorp 1955; Trent 1905)

See also the colonial and federalist eras; Douglass, Frederick; *Gone with the Wind;* Harris, Joel Chandler; Lee, Robert E.; the Mississippi River.

THE COLONIAL AND FEDERALIST ERAS

From the discovery of the New World until the establishment of peace with Native Americans and a stable government, literature deriving from the South tends toward a serious and political purpose. The hallmark of this era is the work of Captain John Smith, Jamestown's savior, who produced *A Map of Virginia with a Description of the Country, the Commodities, People, Government, and Religion* (1612). A propagandist for New World settlement, Smith meticulously counters naysayers who consider the colonies a boondoggle. To prove his project worthy of the Crown's support, he paints an appealing word picture of the area's flora and fauna:

> Virginia doth afford many excellent vegitables and living Creatures, yet grasse there is little or none, but what groweth in lowe Marishes: for all the Countrey is overgrowne with trees, whose droppings continually turneth their grasse to weedes, by reason of the ranckness of the ground which would soone be amended by good husbandry. (Gallay 1994, 22)

Careful to speak practically, Smith avoids rash promises of utopia in the new hemisphere, a fault of early Spanish writings, which predicted that Eldorado lay fallow and ripe for the taking. Nearly a century later, John Lawson composed a similar overview of resources in *New Voyage to Carolina* (1709), in which he acknowledges that Europeans in the New World labeled Indians a nuisance and menace, but admits that he and other intruders are usurpers of land that really belongs to native peoples. In 1775, an Irish trader, James Adair, compiled his observations from extensive commerce with South Carolina tribes in *The History of the American Indian*, an objective study of government and public affairs among coastal bands of Cherokee, Catawba, Choctaw, and Chickasaw.

Europe's interest in the semitropical land of Florida encouraged a definitive study and publication of precise descriptions covering heat, rainfall, native plants and animals, and aborigines. In 1775, Bernard Romans published *A Concise Natural History of East and West Florida*, a travel guide for colonists thinking of settling in Florida. Romans advises emigrants to carry a year's provisions and to buy black slaves on the East Coast before traveling south, where dense growth requires constant taming. The most valuable study of colonial Florida, *Travels through North and South Carolina, Georgia, East and West Florida* (1792), derives from the experiences of William Bartram, a botanist who collected specimens and kept a journal of his study of plants, animals, and members of the Cherokee, Muskogee, Seminole, Chickasaw, Choctaw, and Creek Nations. Of these native peoples, he describes handsome physical build, dignified countenance, and skin tones that vary from reddish brown to copper. Bartram regrets that the vices of the Old World have tempted Indians, but he is astonished to find a firm resistance in natives who live side by side with offensive Europeans.

After settlement stabilized and colonies became productive and safe for families, Southern writings remained businesslike and tended toward the more cerebral, pragmatic genres of debate, oratory, state documents, farm journals, religious treaties, and personal and business letters. Native American lore comprised oral, symbolic, and pictographic transmission, such as that found in the Mississippi Valley mound culture and rock inscriptions throughout the Caribbean. For plantation women, an entrenched androcentrism brought from Europe and bolstered by an oppressive, antifemale religious hierarchy forced females, young and old, into the limited mold of daughters, wives and mothers, cooks, midwives, indentured servants, and the pariah class composed of concubines, barkeeps, and slaves. Denied the education and cultivation that precedes writing, women found modes of expression in their daily affairs. Extant household daybooks, journals, and letters contain the treasured cameos that have entered the canon of colonial and federalist literature since the rise of feminism in the 1960s.

The body of literature composed by Southern women attests to bright, active minds, among them the prolific letter writer and diarist Eliza Lucas Pinckney, whose comments supply valuable data about the South Carolina gentry, their slaves, and the establishment and operation of plantations. Letter writer Rachel O'Connor, born in Louisiana in 1774 and twice widowed, managed a plantation and wrote frequently about her difficulties with debt, epidemics, and shiftless hired help. She speaks of blacks as livestock to be reared like coveys of game hens:

> I have sixteen little Negroes a raising, the oldest of the sixteen, a little turned of [recently turned] six years old, all very healthy children, excepting my little favorite Isaac. He is subject to a cough, but seldom sick enough to lay up. The poor little fellow is laying at my feet sound asleep. (Gallay 1994, 363)

As though describing a favorite hunting hound, O'Connor regrets that she loves Isaac. Likewise valuable to commentary on the early South is a pair of journalists, Elizabeth Timothy and her daughter-in-law, Ann Donovan Timothy, who published the *South Carolina Gazette* from 1738 to 1740 and from 1782 to 1792, and the religious career of Jane Fenn Hoskens, a London-born Quaker evangelist who accepted a calling to Pennsylvania and was indentured as a teacher in Plymouth, Massachusetts. She recorded her travels about Pennsylvania, Virginia, and the Carolinas as well as Barbados, Ireland, and England in *The Life and Spiritual Sufferings of That Faithful Servant of Christ, Jane Hoskens* (1771).

Politics, too, spurred concerned women to express themselves in print. The American Revolution inspired a consortium of writers to produce Daughters of Liberty broadsides. On October 25, 1774, a patriotic sisterhood in Edenton, North Carolina, issued a formal protest of the tea tax. In consternation at the Boston Port Act, the 51 participants, led by Penelope Barker, resolved:

> We, the Ladys of Edenton, do hereby solemnly engage not to conform to the Pernicious Custom of Drinking Tea.... We, the aforesaid Ladys will not promote ye wear of any manufacturer from England until such time that all acts which tend to enslave our Native country shall be repealed. ("Edenton" 1995, 1)

Their bonfire of tea canisters brought chuckles from English papers, which ridiculed the act as an isolated insurrection led by a fringe minority. Fourteen years after the Edenton revolt, "sundry seamstresses of the City of Charleston" petitioned the South Carolina General Assembly, some identifying themselves with crude block letters, others with an X. Their statement spoke eloquently of the working woman's plight: "Your petitioners have reason to believe their want of employment is occasioned by the great importation of ready made Clothes such as shirts, and breeches, that your petitioners can make here." (Kerber 1986, 99) Although denied the vote, the workers raised their concerns in appropriate form and tone. They urged legislators to protect them from the competition of cheaper foreign labor by imposing a tariff on imported soft goods.

Likewise patriotic, South Carolina letter writer Eliza Yonge Wilkinson was an eyewitness to the British invasion of the South Carolina low country. In *Letters of Eliza Wilkinson, during the Invasion and Possession of Charlestown, South Carolina, by the British in the Revolutionary War, Arranged from the Original Manuscripts by Caroline Gilman* (1839), Wilkinson narrates events and replicates dialogue extending from 1779 to 1782, including the surrender of Cornwallis. Her editor, Caroline Howard Gilman, was also well known for her children's magazine and a memoir, *Recollections of a Southern Matron* (1837). Wilkinson reports an exchange with British officers who visited her house and asked her to play the guitar:

> "I cannot play, I am very dull."
> "How long do you intend to continue so, Mrs. Wilkinson?"
> "Until my countrymen return, Sir!"
> "Return as what, Madam?—*prisoners* or *subjects?*"
> "As *conquerors!* Sir."
> He affected a laugh. "You will never see that, Madam."
> "I live in hopes, Sir, of seeing the thirteen stripes hoisted, once more hoisted,
> on the bastions of this garrison." (Wilkinson 1905, 57)

A self-educated horticulturist, Martha Daniell Logan, author of *The Gardners Kalender* (1772), established a mail-order exchange of seeds, plants, roots, and herbs. The observations of South Carolina flora that she shared with botanist John Bartram comprise *Letters of Martha Logan to John Bartram, 1760–1763* (1763), which are studded with valuable insights into the life of a self-trained scientist.

Published female authors were rare in the federalist South. The first poet from West Virginia, Margaret Agnew Blennerhassett, an immigrant from England, published *Widow of the Rock and Other Poems by a Lady* (1788). A witty, literary writer of textbooks and a novella entitled *The British Partizan*, Mary Moragné of Abbeville, South Carolina, is better known for her essays and diaries. At age 24, she kept tabs on local happenings. On September 21, 1841, her entry notes the efforts of a slave singing "Come Humble Sinner":

> He has taught himself to read; & though he is considered the worst negro on the plantation, he may be yet a chosen vessel of grace. Every day of my life do I inly [inwardly] weep & mourn that I am able to do nothing for the souls of these poor creatures! (Gallay 1994, 371)

Moragné, of French Huguenot extraction, displays the ambivalence of a Christian of sincere conscience who recognizes the evil of a bicultural society that deliberately enslaves blacks. She concludes that elitist, white-dominated Protestantism is too concerned with the afterlife to consider the miseries of slaves.

A genre dominated by colonial and federalist women is captivity lore, which covers the journals, letters, memoirs, and biographies of people who were kidnapped or enslaved by native tribes and who survived to tell of servitude, torture, flight, rape, and forced marriage to native mates. One autobiographer, Mary Kinnan, was 28 years old when Shawnees captured her. They held and tortured her for three years. She published *A True Narrative of the Sufferings of Mary Kinnan, Who Was Taken Prisoner by the Shawanee Nation of Indians* (1795). Her harrowing experience concludes with the decision to avoid the gossip and social ostracism of friends and kin in Virginia and to resettle in New Jersey, where she died in 1848. Another captive, Virginian Margaret Hanley Haulee, reported on her abduction in "My Three Years as a Shawnee Captive" (1849).

In similar vein to the chronicles of former captives, emancipated slaves produced a body of narratives that form a realistic tableau of the misery of bondage. A cautious writer of slave memoir was Harriet Ann Brent Jacobs, whose knowledge of the psychology of miscegenation has become a significant resource for feminists, historians, and sociologists. Born in 1813 in Edenton, North Carolina, she learned reading and needlework from her first owner, Margaret Horniblow. Jacobs composed newspaper features and a personal reflection of her life as a servant and concubine. In defiance of her last owner, Dr. James Norcom, she produced two mulatto children, Joseph and Louisa Matilda, sired by attorney Samuel Tredwell Sawyer. Her justification of demeaning alliances makes its own cockeyed logic: By choosing the white male who would bed her, the slave mistress maintained a slim hold on dignity and autonomy.

Under the pen name Linda Brent, Jacobs wrote a monumental biography, *Incidents in the Life of a Slave Girl, Written by Herself* (1861), published by polemicist and editor Lydia Maria Francis Child. Jacobs suffers the sexual abuse of Norcom, and harassment and torment from his jealous wife. She reports on advertisements for her capture:

> $300 Reward! Ran away from the subscriber, an intelligent, bright, mulatto girl, named Linda, 21 years of age. Five feet four inches high. Dark eyes, and black hair inclined to curl; but it can be made straight. Has a decayed spot on a front tooth. She can read and write, and in all probability will try to get to the Free States. (Jacobs 1988, 149)

Threatened with the sale of her children, Jacobs escaped through a swamp, declaring she was less afraid of poisonous snakes than of white male pursuers. For seven years, while her owners searched and advertised rewards for her recovery, she hid above a shed belonging to her grandmother, an emancipated black who owned a bakery.

In chapter 31, Jacobs describes how her uncle Phillip built a hiding place that was 3 x 9 x 7 feet. From her vantage point, she saw only darkness, but took comfort from the laughter and chatter of her children below. To lighten the stifling atmosphere, she bored holes with a gimlet. Looking through the holes, she reports a dog attack on her child, observes Christmas festivities, eavesdrops on slave catchers, and glimpses her owner on his way north:

> I peeped at him as he passed on his way to the steamboat. It was a satisfaction to have miles of land and water between us, even for a little while; and it was a still greater satisfaction to know that he believed me to be in the Free States. My little den seemed less dreary than it had done. (Jacobs 1988, 176)

The physical torments of stinging insects, hot shingled roof, and cramp and laryngitis from the cold threatened her life. In 1842, Jacobs fled to the North with her family, whose freedom was purchased by abolitionist Cornelia Grinnell Willis ten years later. Until the twentieth century, Jacobs's narrative was classed as a novel because readers assumed from its command of grammar and syntax that it was written by a white author using the persona of an ex-slave.

Like Frederick Douglass and Sojourner Truth, Jacobs involved herself in the Civil War and the abolitionist movement across the Northeast, and championed women's suffrage and rights to property and their children. The volunteer work she and her daughter Louisa performed as relief aides and tutors among refugees in Alexandria, Virginia, was integral in the establishment of the Jacobs Free School. They replicated their efforts at a resettlement center in Savannah, Georgia, and aided newly freed blacks in learning to read and finding jobs until Ku Klux Klan violence forced Jacobs and her daughter to return north.

Less desperate and more successful at publishing than Harriet Jacobs, Frances Ellen Watkins Harper, who was born free in 1825 and orphaned at age three, attained a basic education at her uncle William's school in Baltimore. A well-known educator, writer, and orator, she taught at Union Seminary in Ohio, joined the Maine Antislavery Society, and supported the Underground Railroad. In 1854, she compiled her early poems in an anthology, *Poems on Miscellaneous Subjects*. Widowed in 1864, she supported a daughter and three stepchildren by launching a series of polemical addresses on varied topics. A versatile, profound speaker known as the "Bronze Muse," she published protest verse, stories, and editorial commentary in the *Liberator, Anti-Slavery Bugle, Christian Recorder, Anglo-African Magazine*, and *National Anti-Slavery Standard*. She boldly denounced subjugation and lynching of blacks, and furthered such liberal causes as Christian stewardship, temperance, women's rights, and equal education and work opportunities for all.

Harper's phenomenal literary output ranged over numerous genres and earned her the sobriquet "Empress of Peace and Poet Laureate." Her most popular poems include "Vashti," "Sowing and Reaping," "Advice to Girls," "Drunkard's Child," "The Slave Mother," and "Ruth and Naomi." In 1869, she wrote a biblical epic in blank verse, *Moses: A Story of the Nile*, a description of

European colonists in the South during the seventeenth and eighteenth centuries—the colonial and federalist eras—wrote descriptive and politically motivated works. On the eve of the Revolutionary War, in 1774, women of Edenton, North Carolina, proclaimed that they would not drink tea or use English-made goods; a British cartoonist of the time ridiculed the women.

leadership in the heroic tradition. Her late works, *Sketches of Southern Life* (1872) and *Iola Leroy: or, Shadows Uplifted* (1892), center on female protagonists. *Sketches of Southern Life*, a verse sequence about the fictional Aunt Chloe, lauds a determined former slave who longs to better herself. In "Learning To Read," the 60-year-old student recalls how Uncle Caldwell put pot liquor on pages of a book and hid them in his hat to mislead whites into believing them worthless, food-stained scrap. Aunt Chloe buys glasses and begins reading hymns and the New Testament. Living alone in her cabin, she revels in the power of literacy, which makes her feel queenly.

Harper's novel, one of the first by a black American writer, also details the determination of a stubborn black woman. It follows Iola, a mixed-blood slave, from emancipation to work as a Civil War nurse. She rejects the opportunity to marry a white suitor and pass into white society, and saves herself for the right mate, a doctor of her own race. Harper's last verse collections include *The Sparrow's Fall and Other Poems* (1894), *Atlanta Offering: Poems* (1895), *Martyr of Alabama and Other Poems* (1895), *Poems* (1900), and *Light beyond the Darkness* (ca. 1910). At her death on February 20, 1911, she was buried in Philadelphia's Eden Cemetery. Her manuscripts and papers are housed in the Moorland-Spingarn Research Center of Howard University.

In contrast to the South's female writers and nonwhite authors of both sexes, the white aristocratic male writer was less hampered by prejudice, stereotyping, and social expectations. His command of slaves to perform drudgeries and pamper him with luxuries enhanced a bountiful leisure that accommodated reading in a variety of antique and modern languages, exchange of news and opinions, attendance at social and artistic events, extensive correspondence, and dabbling in belles lettres. Drawing on the traditions of English literature, religion, government, and philosophy and valuing the classics and scripture, Southerners produced a lengthy canon of imitative fare, much of which was written by Virginians, citizens of the South's most populous state. One example of eighteenth-century literary gentility occurs in Robert Beverley's *Low Character of Immigrants to Virginia* (1705); his chief literary contribution is *History and Present State of Virginia* (1722), an overview of upperclass life. He describes the occupations of the moneyed class, who walk their patterned knot gardens and orchards and welcome travelers with the graciousness for which the South was known. A jollier colonial, Ebenezer Cook, left Maryland for England, where he published a tongue-in-cheek verse memoir, *The Sot-Weed Factor* (1708). Composed in the style of European satires, he tweaks the local farmer, sailor, and religious Quaker, and wishes, "May never Merchant's, trading Sails explore This Cruel, this Inhospitable Shoar; but left abandon'd by the World to starve, May they sustain the Fate they well deserve." (Spiller and Blodgett 1949, 183)

Three sober-minded contemporaries—Mark Catesby, John Clayton, and William Parks—emigrated from England and wrote the mild-mannered, thoughtful works that characterize early Southern nonfiction. Catesby, a Londoner and member of the Royal Society, settled in the South to study the flora and fauna of the southern Atlantic coast and the Caribbean. A master horticulturist and ornithologist, he wrote *The Natural History of Carolina, Florida, and the*

Bahama Islands (1731) and *On Migration* (1747). John Clayton made a similar study of piedmont Virginia, and in the mid-1700s published *Flora Virginica*. Parks, a journalist, established the *Maryland Gazette* and a Williamsburg newspaper, and wrote two unusual leisure works: *The Compleat System of Fencing* (1734) and *The Compleat Housewife* (1742).

More stirring nonfiction works of the early eighteenth century come from native Southerners. A North Carolinian, Reverend John Urmstone, composed a letter on "Self-Reliance on the Frontier" (1711). Late in the era, William Wirt, a respected man of letters and an attorney general of the United States, wrote a personal response to a pulpit address in "An Old Virginia Preacher" (ca. 1770), whose comprehension of Christianity and classic models of declamation produced a resounding blend of passion and enthusiasm. Wirt is better known for rendering court testimony against Aaron Burr's treason.

In the areas of debate and public declamation, several names stand above the rest. History, more than literature, reverences Patrick Henry, a prominent native of Hanover County, Virginia, for his impassioned statesmanship and command of language. At the Virginia Convention of March 1775, he launched his famed first-person call for liberty or death, one of the American government's pinnacles of oratory. A blunt, direct organizer of thought, Henry proceeds briskly to the heart of his message about the menacing Redcoats:

> Are fleets and armies necessary to a work of love and reconciliation? Have we shown ourselves so unwilling to be reconciled that force must be called in to win back our love? Let us not deceive ourselves, sir. These are the implements of war and subjugation—the last arguments to which kings resort. (Henry 1905, 39)

Lacking the facile antitheses and embellishments popularized by Thomas Jefferson, his contemporary and fellow Virginian, Patrick Henry pursues less lofty themes and shares the outlook and concerns of the unlettered commoner. His strident claim that "war is inevitable" precedes a brief discreditation of peace lovers. As his sentences grow shorter, he thunders to his oft-cited declaration: "I know not what course others may take; but as for me, give me liberty or give me death." (Henry 1905, 40)

In contrast to Henry and the average libertarians of the pre–Revolutionary age, the Voltaire of American enlightenment was Thomas Jefferson. His incisive knowledge of world history, classical oratory, and eighteenth-century philosophy amply prepared him for the zeitgeist, the moment when the times demanded the right spokesperson. More voluble than George Washington, broader based than James Madison and pamphleteer Judge William Henry Drayton, a more dedicated patriot than planter and memoirist Henry Laurens, and less pedantic than George Mason, author of *Extracts from the Virginia Charters* (1773), or tractarian and historian David Ramsay, author of *History of the Revolution in South Carolina* (1785), Jefferson was a native Southern planter, inventor, and rhetorician groomed by experience and propelled by the right degree of personal ambition for the job of author of American liberty. The sonorous tone and universal themes of his writings led critic Gore Vidal to claim them as "American scripture." (Burns 1997, n.p.)

Ripe for the hazardous task of declaring a separation from the mother country, at age 33, Jefferson penned his famous introduction to war:

> When in the Course of human events, it becomes necessary for one people to dissolve the political bands which have connected them with another, and to assume among the powers of the earth, the separate and equal station to which the Laws of Nature and of Nature's God entitled them, a decent respect to the opinions of mankind requires that they should declare the causes which impel them to the separation. (Spiller and Blodgett 1949, 385)

Backed by nature, the Almighty, and his fellow citizens, Jefferson carefully builds the integral statement of American democracy: "We hold these truths to be self-evident, that all men are created equal, that they are endowed by their Creator with certain inalienable Rights, that among these are Life, Liberty and the pursuit of Happiness." Restrained, yet imbued with the hopes of colonists for the success of their experiment in self-government, the line offers the basics of a civilized life: a chance to live free and to seek contentment.

Jefferson's summary of 18 complaints against King George III, the Hanoverian who could barely speak English, march down the page in parallel form, beginning with the king's refusal to frame laws and concluding with an accusation that the Crown fomented the Indian wars as a means of manipulating one expendable group against another. Declaring George III a tyrant by virtue of his acts, Jefferson moves to the establishment of a free nation. He absolves his fellow patriots of allegiance to Britain and confers their rights to perform the normal acts of a sovereign state: "to levy War, conclude Peace, contract alliances, establish Commerce, and to do all other Acts and Things which Independent States may of right do." (Spiller and Blodgett 1949, 386) The declaration concludes simply with a commitment of the cosigners, who "pledge to each other our Lives, our Fortunes and our sacred Honor." At his death, his role in the establishment of American sovereignty appeared alongside his concern for scholarship in an eloquent, self-written epitaph:

> Here was buried
> Thomas Jefferson
> Author of the
> Declaration
> of
> American Independence
> of the
> Statute of Virginia
> for
> Religious Freedom
> And Father of the
> University of Virginia.
> (Smith, C. 1967, 96)

In 1941, composer Randall Thompson wrote an oratorio in honor of the two-hundredth anniversary of Jefferson's birth. The stirring four-part work, first presented at the University of Virginia in 1943, sets to music segments of three texts: *A Summary View of the Rights of British America* (1774), *Declaration of Causes and Necessity of Taking of Arms* (1775), and a letter to John Adams dated September 12, 1821. The bold marcato introit prefaces Jefferson's career in statecraft with his profound credo: "The God who gave us life gave us liberty at the same time; the hand of force may destroy but cannot disjoin them." (Jefferson 1944, 2) Section two, grimly martial, speaks in a sober tone,

> We have counted the cost of this contest and find nothing so dreadful as voluntary slavery. Honor, justice, and humanity forbid us tamely to surrender that freedom which we receiv'd from our gallant ancestors and which our innocent posterity have a right to receive from us. (Jefferson 1944, 11–12)

With the force of a self-assured orator intent on convincing wavering hearts and minds, he declares, "Our cause is just. Our union is perfect. Our internal resources are great." (Jefferson 1944, 14–15) The third section continues the military theme with a brisk, controlled staccato. Jefferson reminds his audience, "We fight not for glory or for conquest." Unflinching in the face of war, he announces, "We have taken up arms. We shall lay them down when hostilities shall cease . . . and not before." (Jefferson 1944, 31–36) The text ends in tranquil reflection over his boldness. Returning to the first person, he promises Adams, his longtime rival and friend in old age, "I shall not die without hope that light and liberty are on steady advance." (Jefferson 1944, 37–38) A popular choral work for mixed-voice or all-male choirs, *The Testament of Freedom* makes the most of Jefferson's command of diction, his wielding of choice phrases such as "feeble engines of despotism," "hereditary bondage," and "unabating firmness."

The high point of frontier exploration journals is an offshoot of Jeffersonian policies. Having dispatched to the Northwest two expert surveyors, Virginians William Clark and Meriwether Lewis, the president expected them to explore the Missouri River and its tributaries to determine navigable routes for use in trade and national defense. The culmination of their work, originally recorded as *Message from the President, February 19, 1806*, was published in 1814 as *History of the Expedition under the Command of Captains Lewis and Clark*. An edited version appeared in eight volumes in 1905 as *Original Journals of the Lewis and Clark Expedition*. Alternating entries, Lewis and Clark cover flora, fauna, and waterways along with commentary on indigenous tribes, hunting and fishing expeditions, and mishaps with equipment and canoes. A roster names the expedition's four sergeants, two interpreters, 24 privates, seven soldiers, ten boatmen, and, in a footnote, the Shoshone interpreter Sacajawea, and Clark's slave, York, the first black to travel the western route to the Pacific. Setting out from Mandan territory in North Dakota, they moved west by water, portage, and overland march along the Missouri, Snake, and Columbia Rivers to the Pacific Ocean, where they established a base camp and viewed a beached whale. During their encounters with incredulous natives, Clark unwisely lit his pipe with a magnifying glass. The implied power of this unknown method of producing fire strained relations with the tribe until Sacajawea appeared. The surveyors' journal notes that she "confirmed those people of our friendly intentions, as no woman ever accompanies a war party of Indians in this quarter." (Lavender 1988, 283)

Less serious writers of the pre-Republican age than Jefferson and his surveyors presented a panoply of literary styles and interests. In the generation preceding Thomas Jefferson and the Louisiana Purchase, Colonel William Byrd, a member of the Virginia gentry who returned to the mother country for education, amassed holdings of 180,000 acres and presided over the King's Council. His prestigious state afforded him the leisure to collect over 3,600 books for his sizable library and to reflect on his job as commissioner in charge of setting the border between Virginia and North Carolina. After hard gallops in swamps and pine stands, he returned from the East Coast frontier with an appreciation of Virginia husbandry. In defamation of North Carolina's unruly outback, he described in *History of the Dividing Line* (1728):

> Surely there is no place in the World where the Inhabitants live with less labour than in N. Carolina. It approaches nearer to the Description of Lubberland than any other, by the great felicity of the Climate, the easiness of raising Provisions, and the Slothfulness of the People. (Spiller and Blodgett 1949, 170)

Byrd complains that local farmers allow cattle and hogs to wander marshes and swamps the entire winter, thus wasting milk and manure. In a more affable mood, he comments on his own industry in *The Secret Diary* (1712), meticulously recording an early rising, reading in Hebrew and Greek, prayer, attention to illness among his staff, and the settling of accounts. In his leisure time, he prefers claret and a visit to the Raleigh Tavern. Failing to pray at the close of the evening on October 10, 1710, he adds with Pepysian succinctness that he "had good thoughts, good health, and good humor, thank God Almighty." (Byrd 1952, 13)

An outstanding example of the 6,000 slave narratives to derive from the slave era was written by Gustavus Vassa, a native of Benin on Africa's west coast, the area that most influenced the American South. Composed in 1790, *The Interesting Narrative of the Life of Olaudah Equiano, or Gustavus Vassa, the African; by Himself*, a two-volume exposé of slave sufferings, tells of his capture and sale in 1756. A farmworker on a Virginia plantation, he saved for his manumission after he left the South. Like Frederick Douglass, Sojourner Truth, and other manumitted and escaped blacks, he worked for the abolitionist movement in the eastern United States and Great Britain. The work was successful, requiring eight printings and influencing readers on both sides of the Atlantic.

Hard work and husbandry is a recurrent theme of the era. In the early years of the republic, John Taylor, a Revolutionary War veteran and politician who favored agrarianism, applied his success at farming to newspaper articles, which were collected in *The Arator* (1803). A blend of law, governance, and pragmatism, his bland style reflects the influence of Virgil's *Georgics* and amplifies a steady, judicious development of lands, livestock, and resources. In a treatise on democratic principles, *An Inquiry into the Principles and Policy of the Government of the United States* (1814), Taylor debates on paper with John Adams the existence of a naturally superior aristocracy. Taylor concludes that the granting of land, sovereignty, and title by right of birth is an affront to republicanism, which is based on a belief that all people have a right to compete for the good life.

In the settled years following the American Revolution, the beginnings of creative literature appeared in verse, biography, letters, journalism, and essay, often from immigrants establishing themselves in a new land. Richard Henry Wilde, an Irish poet in the vein of the Scottish plowman/bard Robert Burns, settled in Georgia and wrote blithe nature verse, including "My Life Is like the Summer Rose" and "To the Mocking Bird" (1847). A similar nature poem, "I Sigh for the Land of the Cypress and Pine" (ca. 1850), is all that is left of the poems of Charlestonian Samuel Henry Dickson, but its day-bright lyrics suggest a talented, well-read versifier:

> Oh! I sigh for the land of the cypress and pine,
> Of the laurel, the rose, and the gay woodbine,
> Where the long, gray moss decks the rugged oak tree,—
> That sun-bright land is the land for me. (Parks 1970, 18)

A British immigrant and resident of Maryland, Edward Coote Pinkney, penned graceful lyrics and narratives in the style of Continental poets. His best work, "The Voyager's Song" (1825), resounds with the energy and enthusiasm that buoyed New World settlers. In an apostrophe to Ponce de Leon, seeker of the Fountain of Youth, Pinkney begins:

> Sound trumpets, ho!—weigh anchor—loosen sail—
> The seaward flying banners chide delay;
> As if 'twere heaven that breathes this kindly gale,
> Our lifelike bark beneath it speeds away.
> Flit we, a gliding dream, with troublous motion,
> Across the slumbers of uneasy ocean.
> (Spiller and Blodgett 1949, 690)

A thoughtful Virginia attorney born on the island of Bermuda, St. George Tucker wrote less vigorous, more contemplative verse, particularly his poem "Resignation" (ca. 1795), and corresponded with such distinguished men as George Washington, Patrick Henry, and Thomas Jefferson. A sober essay certain to arouse antipathy among planters was Tucker's "A Dissertation on Slavery: With a Proposal for the Gradual Abolition of It in the State of Virginia" (1796). His son, Nathaniel Beverley Tucker, inherited his father's rhetorical skills and intrepidity, a fact demonstrated by his publication of "A Key to the Disunion Conspiracy" (1862). He also wrote a novel, *George Balcombe* (1836), which impressed Edgar Allan Poe during his tenure as editor of the *Southern Literary Messenger*.

A contemporary of Tucker, jurist and biographer John Marshall defined the qualities of the first American president in a five-volume work, *The Life of George Washington* (1807), which carries the lofty phrase, "First in war, first in peace, and first in the hearts of his countrymen." (Trent 1905, 74) Emphasizing the noble qualities and virtues of the first American president, Marshall concluded that Washington earned public reverence for incorruptible principles, truthfulness, emotional stability, and controlled ambition. Because he evinced both patriotic zeal and discretion, Washington stands high among the distinguished founders of democracy. In another mode, Mason Locke Weems, a Virginia parson, published a less lofty biography, *The Life of Washington, with Curious Anecdotes, Equally Honourable to Himself and Exemplary to His Young Countrymen* (1800). It is Weems who circulated the legend that George Washington chopped down the cherry tree. In a subsequent biography, *The Life of General Francis Marion* (1826), Weems sank to scurrilous rumors of an evening's debauchery in March 1780 that resulted in Marion breaking his ankle by leaping from a second-floor window after drinking too many bumpers of wine.

A more dignified theme derives from the classic verse of Francis Scott Key, author of "Defence of Fort M'Henry" (1814). A Washington attorney born in Maryland, he witnessed the predawn attack and recorded on the back of an envelope an epiphany at first light when he saw the flag still floating. The resulting four verses, known both as "The Star-Spangled Banner" and "The National Anthem," formed a four-stanza poem that stressed "O'er the land of the free, and the home of the brave," a repeated line that envisions the best qualities of the new nation. (Key 1905, 96) In contrast to contemporaries, such as the overblown patriotic puffery of Washington Allston's "America to Great Britain" (1810), Key's vivid details of explosions, rocket trails, and gleaming twilight stress reasons for pride that the flag survived a harrowing night and, like the unity of Americans, remains intact.

Significant to nonfiction and to science are the journals and sketches of naturalist and wildlife artist John James Audubon, a preserver of natural beauty. More than other nature artists of his time, he demonstrated an unusually sensitive, refined talent in his American bird and animal portraits set in natural habitats. A native of Les Cayes, Haiti (although historians also propose New Orleans and Paris as his birthplace), he was named Jean Jacques Fougère Audubon-Rabin at his birth on April 26, 1784. The fourth illegitimate son of John Audubon, a French trader, sugar planter, and former lieutenant in the French navy, and a Creole mother, Jeanne Rabine (or possibly Fougère), who died in 1785, he lived in Nantes, France, where he studied dancing, drawing, music, shooting, and fencing. As avocations, he pursued birds and taxidermy. He served as a cabin boy, but did not flourish at sea.

The threat of being shanghaied into Napoleon's navy forced Audubon to flee the military to his father's holdings in Norristown, Pennsylvania, where he studied under French painter Jacques Louis David. To earn his own way, Audubon abandoned his father's wealth and prestige, and at age 18 settled in Louisville, Kentucky, where he cut ties with the past by anglicizing his name. Because of his lack of experience with mercantile concerns, he and his wife Lucie failed at milling and storekeeping. To absolve debt and earn a meager living, he accepted art students and painted portraits. His immersion in bird lore and nature took him away from daily work and bankrupted the couple by 1819. For a few months, he joined the staff of Cincinnati's Western Museum as a taxidermist, and his wife found a position as a governess.

In October 1820, Audubon traveled the Mississippi River to produce *The Birds of America* (1838), a monumental four-volume set. Praised for its quality and detail of animal behaviors, the costly book preceded a thorough seven-volume text, *American Ornithological Biography* (1841). He extended his observations from Florida to Labrador and west to Montana to complete *The Viviparous Quadrupeds of North America* (1845). One of Audubon's essays, "Hospitality in the Woods," characterizes a gracious frontier family who befriended him while the artist was recovering from yellow fever. He continued his work until the failure of his eyesight in 1847. Its excellence gave his canon cachet among naturalists, biologists, writers, artists, printers, and publishers, who rated him above Francis Parkman, George Catlin, and John Muir for the preservation of American wildlife.

The end of the idyllic federalist era came swiftly and painfully as Southern states' rights enthusiasts faced off against Northern abolitionists in a protracted, regional scrap-turned-serious to preserve both the South's right to maintain a slave economy and the economy itself, which was sure to crumble if the admission of Missouri to statehood shook the balance of slave and free states. The era was also a boost to the liberation of women. Two strong abolitionists, Sarah Moore Grimké and Angelina Grimké Weld, grew up in Charleson and detested their father's ownership of slaves. Both sisters defied expectations for proper Southern women by actively opposing slavery. Angelina Grimké published *Appeal to the Christian Women of the South* (1836) and fought her attackers with a tract, *Letters to Catherine Beecher in Reply to an Essay on Slavery and Abolitionism Addressed to A. A. Grimké* (1837). Sarah Grimké sought egalitarian reforms on a broader scale, and fought for women's rights with lectures and her own pamphlet, *Letters on the Equality of the Sexes and the Condition of Women* (1838).

The two most skillful prewar nonfiction writers, John Pendleton Kennedy and John Esten Cooke, turned from the darkening political skies to brighter times in the Old South. Kennedy, a memoirist from Baltimore, Maryland, produced the era's best regional musings in *Swallow Barn, or A Sojourn in the Old Dominion* (1832) and *Horse-Shoe Robinson* (1835), a graceful romance. In the former work, Kennedy details the genteel lifestyle of a James River plantation owned by the Hazard family. The idyllic vision of a time-honored manse clings to a bounty derived from "the multiplication of negroes, cattle, and poultry," a gentleman's way of expressing his concurrence in the practice of numbering slaves among livestock. (Trent 1905, 142) The genial paragraphs about hospitality, blooded horses, architecture, walnut doors and columns, lombardy poplars, Indian corn, and wormy chestnut fencing skirt the question of human rights with romanticized fragments about laundresses "who are never tired of making somersets, and mischievously pushing each other on the clothes laid down to dry." (Trent 1905, 143) John Esten Cooke, brother to Philip Pendleton Cooke, wrote the era's best humor novel, *The Virginia Comedians, or Old Days in the Old Dominion* (1859), a witty overview of class differences.

Taking a different tack, three authors turned to national history as worthy subjects. Charles Etienne Arthur Gayarré, author of "Histoire de la Louisiane" (1847), "Romance of the History of Louisiana" (1848), "Louisiana: Its Colonial History and Romance" (1852), "Louisiana, Its History as a French Colony" (1852), and "History of the Spanish Domination in Louisiana" (1854), collected his segments into a single work, *History of Louisiana* (1866). During the war years, he continued his perusal of past times with a biography, *Philip II of Spain* (1866). In the former work, Gayarré recorded the rules for playing lacrosse, a New World game invented by Native Americans. Texan Dilue Rose Harris reminded the rest of the South that the Southwest had fought its own war for liberty. Her chronicle, *Reminiscences of Colonial Life in Texas* (1904), is a major compilation of facts and movements dating to 1836. Likewise, Sam Houston freed himself from regional embroilment and pushed for the admission of Texas to the Union. In his history *The Victor's Description of the Battle of San Jacinto* (1836), he looked to the growing West as an answer to the national quandary.

On the negative side of prewar literature, orators such as South Carolinians John C. Calhoun and Robert Young Hayne remained anchored to their region's problems and debated their state's position with able spokesmen from the North. In an eloquent, passion-tinged speech concerning this issue, Calhoun, a determined voice for states' rights, admitted the tenuous nature of the South's political position:

> How can the Union be saved? There is but one way by which it can with any certainty; and that is, by a full and final settlement, on the principle of justice, of all the questions at issue between the two sections. The South asks for justice, simple justice, and less she ought not to take. She has no compromise to offer, but the constitution; and no concession or surrender to make. (Trent 1905, 102)

Certain that his homeland had made too many sacrifices already, Calhoun pressed for an honorable, harmonious settlement of Missouri's statehood. The literature that followed this era looked with an altered point of view at American government and culture and a repositioning of faith that forced writers onto new ground. (Ambrose 1996; Auchincloss 1997; Audubon 1940, 1995; Beatty et al. 1952; Benton 1968; Bradbury 1996; Buck 1992; Burns 1997; Cady 1967; Clinton 1994; Davidson and Wagner-Martin 1995; "Edenton" 1995; Ellis 1997; Faust 1988; Gallay 1994; Gilbert and Gubar 1985; Gross 1971, 1973; Henry 1905; Hibbard 1931; Hine et al. 1993; Jacobs 1988; Jefferson 1944; Johnson and Malone 1930; Kerber 1986; Lavender 1988; Lefler and Powell 1973; Lewis and Clark 1922, 1953; Mullane 1993; Parks 1970; Ploski and Williams 1989; Poe and Poe 1987; Rutherford 1907; Salzman et al. 1996; Sherr and Kazickas 1994; Smith, C. 1967; Snyder 1970; Spiller and Blodgett 1949; Sullivan 1995; Thorp 1955; Urdang 1981; Wilson and Ferris 1989; Witalec 1994)

See also the Civil War era; Douglass, Frederick; the Mississippi River.

THE COLOR PURPLE

Alice Walker's masterwork *The Color Purple* (1982), an epistolary saga told through the heroine's letters to God, is a favorite title on a number of high school and college reading lists for courses in women's and African-American literature, sociology, and creative writing. Not as controversial as Eldridge Cleaver's *Soul on Ice* (1968) or James Baldwin's *The Fire Next Time* (1963), *The Color Purple* weathered suppression in Oakland and Hayward, California, in 1984. The book chronicles the emotional turmoil in an abused, devalued black farm woman from 1909 to 1947. Celie, an illiterate teenager who is unaware of the facts of her parentage, believes herself the victim of incest following the sexual bondage enforced by her mother's husband, Alphonso. After he trades her like a field mule, she becomes the second wife of the mean-spirited Albert—whom she calls Mr. She knows that Mr. prefers her sister Nettie but settles for Celie even though, after giving birth to sons and a daughter, she is spoiled merchandise. Arrival in a filthy farmhouse among Albert's four wayward, disobedient stepchildren nets Celie a wound after her stepson Harpo hits her in the head with a rock.

Walker heightens the misery of Celie's marriage to Albert and motherhood to his tribe with emphasis on the worst of her trials—separation from her beloved sister Nettie. In reveries, Celie recalls the happy girlhood of her comely, intelligent sister, who journeys with a missionary family to an Olinka village in East Africa. Albert retains control over Celie in part by convincing her that German mines sank the boat that carried Nettie toward Gibraltar. The fantasies that supplant the real Nettie wear thin as virtual enslavement to Mr. degrades and demoralizes Celie to the point of total despair. She settles for life as Albert's house drone and handmaiden until the creation of a Memphis clothing boutique to sell her brand of lounging pants releases her from marital bondage. The emergence of a whole, healthy inner person rewards the entire community with the love and oneness of an extended family that cherishes and respects an independent woman. Walker stresses that Celie grows and develops primarily through perseverence and a womanly network that uplifts and affirms her.

The central issue of controversy surrounding *The Color Purple* is the theme of lesbianism. Early in the novel, Celie catches a glimpse of Shug Avery, a glamorous blues singer, in a picture in Albert's billfold. In a letter to God, Celie says:

> The most beautiful woman I ever saw. She more pretty then my mama. She bout ten thousand times more prettier then me. I see her there in furs. Her face rouge. Her hair like somethin tail. She grinning with her foot up on somebody motorcar. Her eyes serious tho. Sad some. (Walker 1982, 7)

The arrival of the scrappy, egocentric "Queen Honeybee" to Albert's household forces Celie into the role of nurse, but she enjoys cooking for Shug, bathing her, and combing her hair. (Walker 1982, 45) Daily intimacy introduces Celie to self-love and same-sex love, both of which lift her from drudgery with epiphanies of delight and passion. A quilt made in the "Sister's Choice" pattern, the symbol of Celie's yearning, takes shape in her frame on the porch, where she works in pieces of yellow from Shug's discarded dress. (Walker 1982, 61) The yearning gives place to confession after Celie informs Shug the reason that Albert beats his wife: "For being me and not you." (Walker 1982, 79)

A key element of Celie's coming-of-age is embodied in the indomitable spirit of Miss Sofia, a loyal daughter-in-law who is tough in the face of Albert's badgering and capable of replacing shingles on her rickety house and intimidating Squeak, her husband's lover. At a low point, Sofia's body and will hover near annihilation during a lengthy stretch in jail for assault. When Celie goes to tend her, she flinches at the brutality Sofia has endured:

The Color Purple, a novel by Alice Walker published in 1982, chronicles the emotional turmoil of Celie, an abused and devalued black farm woman, from 1909 to 1947. Celie (Whoopi Goldberg) reads a letter in Steven Spielberg's 1985 film version of Walker's novel.

> They crack her skull, they crack her ribs. They tear her nose loose on one side. They blind her in one eye. She swole from head to foot. Her tongue the size of my arm, it stick out tween her teef like a piece of rubber. She can't talk. And she just about the color of a eggplant. (Walker 1982, 91–92)

In her rise from oppression, Sofia escapes Millie, her white mistress, and reestablishes herself with family. Celie rewards her with an appropriate pair of pants—one leg red and one purple—and dreams that she sees Sofia wearing them and leaping over the moon.

As jubilant as the bicolored pants, Walker's resolution counters the despair of the opening chapters with a fully orchestrated rescue of her heroine, body and soul. In Celie's affirmation of self, she writes to God, "I'm pore, I'm black, I may be ugly and can't cook, a voice say to everything listening. But I'm here." (Walker 1982, 214) Recast as independent woman and entrepreneur at Folkspants, Unlimited, Celie triumphs and reunites with her children, whom Nettie miraculously returns from Africa. At the death of Alphonso, she clears up her concern about incest with her stepfather and takes possession of her patrimony—a house all her own. When Celie's children arrive from Africa, her spirits soar in a newfound family. In a hymn of gladness, she exults, "Dear God. Dear stars, dear trees, dear sky, dear peoples. Dear Everything. Dear God. Thank you for bringing my sister Nettie and our children home." (Walker 1982, 292)

For Steven Spielberg's screen version of *The Color Purple* (1985), Warner Brothers paid Walker $350,000 for the innovative novel. Directed by Quincy Jones, the film adaptation stars a budding actress, Whoopi Goldberg, as Celie and Danny Glover as Mr., the heartless husband. The supporting cast includes Rae Dawn Chong, Margaret Avery, Willard Pugh, Akosua Busia, and Oprah Winfrey as the mighty Miss Sofia, who goes to jail for striking a white man. The generous placement of gospel songs, soul, blues, and jazz stresses the greater backdrop of black achievement from the same period. The film won a Directors Guild of America Award, a Golden Globe for Goldberg, best picture from the National Board of Review, and multiple Oscar nominations for actress, screenplay, art direction, cinematography, costumes and makeup, original score, and supporting actress for Avery and Winfrey. The song "Miss Celie's Blues" was also nominated for best musical theme. ("Alice Walker" 1996; Bradbury 1996; Brooks 1985; Buck 1992; *Contemporary Authors* 1994; Davidson and Wagner-Martin 1995; Dodds 1968; Dunlap 1996; Foerstel 1994; Hine et al. 1993; Hughes and Meltzer 1968; Inge 1990; Jokinen 1996; Ploski and Williams 1989; Rubin et al. 1985; Smith 1992; Snodgrass 1995; Sterling 1968; Walker 1979, 1982, 1996; Wester 1970; Westling 1985; Wilson and Ferris 1989)

See also Walker, Alice.

CONROY, PAT

One of the late twentieth century's most successful and provocative writers, Pat Conroy is a truly Southern literary marvel. He has produced best-selling titles adored by book club members, thrice reprised by Hollywood filmmakers, and dissected in modern fiction, sociology, psychology, creative writing, and cinema classes. His obsession with emotional upheaval has staked out a personal claim on the twentieth century's tragedies: dysfunctional families, terminal illness, alcoholism, divorces, nervous breakdowns, suicides, and shattered souls who refuse surrender. A fierce individualist, he clings to a professional integrity that demands truth, the central issue of his five novels.

For thematic material, Conroy relives personal battles in fiction. He is the first of seven children born to Colonel Donald N. Conroy, a Chicago-born career fighter pilot in the marines and veteran of three wars and a mission to Cuba, and Frances "Peg" Peek Conroy, an Alabama beauty queen. Acting the role of the proverbial army brat, Conroy is loud, destructive, wayward, and spiritually needy. In the introduction to Mary Edwards Wertsch's *Military Brats: Legacies of Childhood inside the Fortress* (1991), he scrolls an image of the past as deadly as concertina wire, as bleak as the surface of the moon:

> I was born and raised on federal property. America itself paid all the costs for my birth and my mother's long stay at the hospital. I was a military brat—one of America's children in the profoundest sense. . . . The sound of gunfire on rifle ranges strikes an authentic chord of home in me even now. (Conroy 1991, xvii)

He recalls how his father's approach struck a mutual terror that made the Conroy children "quiet as bivalves" and typifies life with an overbearing dad as "desperate and sad." Re-creating himself in the harsh no-man's-land of home, he becomes a body temperature occupying furniture, disembodied by the unspoken fear that one day his father would kill him. Out of respect for his mother, he is one of the family's "unwitnesses of our own history," which he summarizes as "a forced march of blood and tears." (Conroy 1991, xix)

Out of contemplation and vengeance, Conroy re-creates the acrimony and turbulence of his youth in some of his bitterest autobiographical fiction, all haunted by evil fathers and authority figures, and influenced by Southern themes and settings. Thinking back over his scarred childhood, he told an interviewer from Doubleday Books:

> I had been blessed as few writers had ever been blessed: by larger than life parents handed out by some Satanic forces in my life. These were huge characters and because of their hugeness there is a little overdoneness about my books and about my writing. ("Pat Conroy" 1996, 2)

The brutish, verbally aggressive father of *The Great Santini* (1976) displays the lack of control, vicious mood swings, and free-floating hostility that Conroy remembers in his own father, a self-appointed expert on children whom Conroy calls "a Nazi Dr. Spock." (*Contemporary Authors* 1994, 3) On fictional landscapes pocked with emotional claymores, the author relives cruelties that became "the central fact of my art and my life." ("Pat Conroy" 1996, 1) The mindset held until Conroy reached age 30, when he ameliorated his view of the Conroy family hierarchy to acknowledge that his quietly assertive mother had been the stronger parent.

In typical fashion for a military brat, Conroy spent his childhood in 23 locations and grew up primarily in North Carolina. Making few lasting friendships or hometown ties with specific places, he changed schools a dozen times. Fortunately, he came under the mentorship of an innovative teacher, Eugene Norris, who introduced him to Thomas Wolfe's *Look Homeward Angel* and to the boardinghouse in Asheville, North Carolina, where Wolfe's mother earned a living cooking and cleaning for tenants. Conroy received a B.A. degree from the Citadel, a tradition-laden military academy in Beaufort, South Carolina, the city in which his father retired. The move was a blessing to Conroy, who developed strong ties with his classmates and teachers, yet the area's military tone resurrected serious conflicts in personal values when, in adulthood, he tried to cope with his oppressive background and subsequent disenchantment with the Vietnam War. He incubated his emotional backlash into strong character conflict for his latest novel, *Beach Music* (1995), a blend of two favorite landscapes—South Carolina and Rome, Italy—in a wrenching story of Jack McCall, a grieving widower coping with the suicide of his wife, who jumped to her death from a bridge in South Carolina. Escalating his usual level of mayhem, the author juggles multiple themes of violence, war, anti-Semitism, and genocide. For authenticity, he exploits a friendship with a Jewish woman in Georgia and builds on memories of *The Diary of Anne Frank*, which his mother read to her brood as a model of Holocaust racism. Paramount negotiated for the text, paying $5.1 million for movie rights and an additional $1.3 million for *Ex*, a screenplay Conroy coauthored with cartoonist Doug Marlette.

Conroy's first novel, *The Boo* (1970), reflects on the anachronistic education offered at the Citadel, fictionalized as the Carolina Military Institute. The work, which Conroy paid $1,500 to publish, honors Lieutenant Colonel Thomas Nugent "Boo" Courvoisie, a beneficent leader and role model who served the Citadel as assistant commander from 1961 to 1967. The good memories of their friendship followed Conroy to his first job near Beaufort, where he taught high school English and met his future wife, Barbara Bolling, a Vietnam War widow and mother of two daughters, Jessica and Melissa, and of Megan, Conroy's first child. In lieu of a post with the Peace Corps, he signed a second contract that moved him east to Daufuskie Island, which outsiders reach by boat from the mainland. To poor, illiterate children unable to pronounce his last name, he became a local hero.

Conroy's job was an educator's nightmare. To a mixed-age class underexposed to basic competencies and lacking information about where they live and who the national leaders are, he taught all subjects and all grades in a one-room, self-contained school. To relieve their ignorance, he drew on a variety of unusual teaching materials to expose them to a world of information:

> We read poetry together. Most of [them] can now quote passages from Langston Hughes, E. A. Robinson and Alfred Noyes. They know the fifty states, the capitals. They know the continents. . . . They can talk about politics. (White 1992, 20)

Conroy took pride in advancing the children's knowledge about music, film, history, and the media. In an impassioned letter to the school board, he stated his attributes: He loved children and teaching, and he evoked love from his students.

Affection and dedication proved unimportant to the local school board, which fired Conroy for refusing to whip students and for bucking the school's old-fashioned administration. He sued and lost, then retaliated in his characteristically creative style—by writing *The Water Is Wide* (1972), an exposé of the abysmal conditions and low educational standards common to coastal South Carolina. Set on the fictional island of Yamacraw, the action depicts the idiocy of rigid educational hierarchies that make no allowances for what children need to learn. In an early exchange with the principal, Mrs. Brown, the protagonist meets his challenge:

> "The state requires us to hand out these textbooks as soon as possible."
> "Can the kids read these books?" I asked.
> "They are supposed to read them. The state department requires them to read them."
> "What if they can't?"
> "Then we must make them read them." (Conroy 1987, 28)

In exasperation with his Gullah-speaking remedial class, the Conroy character chucks coercive methods and the unrealistic syllabus and teaches what the children need to know—the names of sports figures and national leaders, music and art appreciation, swimming, basic facts of human reproduction, and the rules of health and hygiene. His methods are innovative: a class zoo, trick-or-treating on the mainland, and visits to Washington, D.C., and a Harlem

Globetrotters game. He tailors his choice of subjects and skills to one goal: to prepare island children for the greater world outside their pathetically limited microcosm.

Writing *The Water Is Wide* was a twofold learning experience. The children of Daufuskie built a reservoir of essential information and understanding while affording Conroy a chance to rid himself of the racism he had embraced in his youth. He used the book as a platform from which to rail against segregation of blacks into island schools, which he depicted as "reservations where the sons and daughters of cotton pickers were herded together for the sake of form and convenience." (Conroy 1987, 255) The novel cost him a decent recommendation and ended his chance of locating another teaching post in South Carolina, but it won an Anisfield-Wolf award and set him on an odyssey of unburdening, beginning with a speech among his "military brat" peers at Beaufort Air Station. Two years later, Martin Ritt directed *Conrack*, the Twentieth-Century Fox film adaptation of the novel, starring Jon Voight as the teacher and featuring Paul Winfield, Hume Cronyn, and Madge Sinclair as the island administrator. The movie, which Granville Burgess adapted into a musical in 1987, won the author a National Education Association humanitarian award, a suitably vexing fillip to the Beaufort community, who ostracized his family so blatantly that they moved to Atlanta in 1974.

To his credit as a survivor, Conroy launched a writing career that supplanted his failed career in education. His first blockbuster novel, *The Great Santini* (1976), vivified his wretched childhood, which drew him into an approach-avoidance conflict with a joyless martinet of a father. Writing was a liberating, rejuvenating experience that freed him from the emotional restraints of his past. In his words, the book "was the only way I could take to the skies in the dark-winged jets, move through those competitive ranks of aviators and become, at last, my father's wingman." (Conroy 1991, xxv) The plot, a bildungsroman that centers on a year with a military family, comes close to home with the creation of Colonel Bull Meecham, a virulent, hang-tough marine fighter pilot who degrades and browbeats his children. Conroy's ironies center on Bull's adolescent son Ben, the book's "Pat" figure. Bull's confusion of discipline with repression derives from his failure to achieve career aims and his inability to express love. The public revelation of family dysfunction disrupted Conroy's parents and his own family, generating two divorces. The book was so true to life that it served as legal evidence in his mother's charge against her abusive husband, whom she left the day after his retirement parade. The 1979 Warner Brothers screen version, a sleeper starring Blythe Danner as the mother and Robert Duvall as Bull, earned Oscar nominations for Duvall and Michael O'Keefe, the supporting actor in the "Pat" role. Rereleased to meet growing public acclaim, the film won awards for music director Elmer Bernstein at the Montreal World Film Festival and a best film of the year award from the National Board of Review.

Still seething with unresolved conflicts from his youth, Conroy wrote a protest novel about adolescence and manhood, *The Lords of Discipline* (1980), a grim memoir of school days marred by racism, sexism, and the sadistic discipline he had encountered at home. The suspenseful action hinges on a cadet's private war against an extreme form of hazing aimed at the school's first black cadet, Thomas Pearce. Perpetrators known as the "Ten," a secret body of vigilantes, maintain racial and sexual purity by spying, intimidation, and brutality. The focal character, Will McLean, an idealistic loner and freedom fighter, is freighted with a strong likeness to the author. He speaks the ambivalence that Conroy felt about his alma mater:

> At the Institute the making of men was a kind of grotesque artistry. Yet I am a product of this artistry. And I have need to bear witness to what I saw there. I want to tell you how it was. I want precision. I want a murderous, stunning truthfulness. I want to find my own singular voice for the first time. I want you to understand why I hate the school with all my power and passion. Then I want you to forgive me for loving the school. (Conroy 1980, 6)

Will's heroic egalitarianism provoked much rancor from people Conroy had known during his days at the Citadel, but his protest of murderous coming-of-age rituals and mob psychology earned the author a nomination for the Robert Kennedy Book Award. Filmed by Paramount in 1982, the screen version stars David Keith in the unpleasant role of idealistic rescuer.

During the early years of his second marriage, to Lenore Gurgewitz, Conroy moved to Rome and wrote an ambitious novel, *The Prince of Tides* (1986), a lengthy, flawed masterwork that placed his name among the international literary superstars. The story of the private hell of ex-teacher Tom Wingo, son of a shrimper from Colleton, South Carolina, introduces another well-meaning rescuer. Tom attempts to salvage his twin, Savannah, a suicidal poet recovering from nervous trauma. His odyssey takes him to Savannah's psychiatrist to unravel the intricate family past that looms in their memories and destroys their ambitions. Filmed by Barbra Streisand and scripted by Conroy, the 1991 screen adaptation starred Streisand as the psychologist and Nick Nolte as Tom, the rescuer-turned-patient. The emotional role earned Nolte an Oscar nomination.

In 1988, Conroy's Daufuskie debacle returned in a parallel teacher witch hunt after Judith Fitzgerald, on the English staff at St. Andrews High School in Charleston, stirred controversy by placing *The Prince of Tides* on an eleventh-grade optional reading list. Complaints from a fundamentalist minister, Reverend R. Elton Johnson, Jr., about the savage dual rape scene at the heart of protagonist Tom Wingo's emotional conflict forced the school board to sit through Johnson's reading of four pages, which he claimed was "raw, filthy, raunchy pornography." (White 1992, 18) The *Charleston News and Courier* took a pro-censorship stance against the book, which the editors placed outside the pale of "real literature." On February 21, 1988, outraged that news copy called him a "language cripple," Conroy wrote a detailed letter to the editor stating his philosophy of writing:

> I take the whole family of man as my subject and I leave no one out. I see myself as bearing full witness to the times in which I live and explaining both the pain and beauty of my own life to myself. . . . In my book, there is everything from a high school English teacher, like Judith Fitzgerald, to a fundamentalist preacher, like Rev. Johnson. (White 1992, 19)

Conroy insists that the inclusion of three escaped prisoners who rape Savannah and Tom derives from an experience in his own family in which a relative was assaulted and her arm broken.

In the aftermath of the censorship issue, Conroy lectured to Fitzgerald's class about the writer's duty to express truth regardless of the public's squeamishness. The school board dawdled in formulating its reply. They chose to uphold the teacher's right to select reading material, but implied that she had assaulted public taste by selecting an unsuitable work that constituted an affront to public mores. The compromise dodged the issue, but Conroy chose to praise Fitzgerald and remind South Carolinians that he himself had suffered a reprisal from local constituents in Beaufort, who rejected bold, honest classroom practice. The South Carolina Library Association and the South Carolina Association of School Librarians honored Fitzgerald's courage and dedication to free speech with an Intellectual Freedom award. At the ceremony, presenters read Conroy's warm letter thanking Fitzgerald for facing "her own ayatollah in Charleston, one who wore different clothes and worshipped a different God, but who was every bit as much an enemy of language, of literature, of freedom, and the art of teaching." (White 1992, 21) (Burns 1996; Conroy 1980, 1986; *Contemporary Authors* 1994; "Great Santini" 1987; "Pat Conroy" 1996; White 1992)

DOUGLASS, FREDERICK

The South's renowned expatriate orator Frederick Douglass fled slavery and made a place for himself as an impassioned, articulate polemicist for abolitionism, vigorous campaigner for women's rights, and adviser to five presidents. A sensitive firsthand witness to the slave trade, he debated the opposition aloud and on paper and composed multiple autobiographies, editorials, and speeches filled with personal reflections that stirred listeners to donate money and assault Washington with demands for emancipation. With his natural gift for firebrand oratory, Douglass led an American revolt against bondage that extended to Europe and the Caribbean and launched a Reconstruction-era battle for the ballot. His most popular autobiography, *Narrative of the Life of Frederick Douglass, an American Slave* (1845), is the best-documented personal account of slavery to emerge from the American plantation system.

A slave from infancy to age 20, Frederick Augustus Washington Bailey was born in a cabin on Holmes Hill Farm in Talbot County near Tuckahoe, Maryland, in February 1817 or 1818. His master, Captain Aaron Anthony, was an ambitious man who owned three farms and 30 slaves and managed the property of Colonel Edward Lloyd. Anthony concealed from slaves their exact vital statistics, particularly place and time of birth and parents. Douglass lived apart from his sisters Arianna, Kitty, Sara, and Eliza and his brother Perry in the woods with Isaac and Betsey Bailey, his maternal grandparents, while his mother, a literate slave named Harriet Bailey (or Baily), worked the fields of the Stewart farm 12 miles away. It is probable that the master wanted to distance her from his wife to conceal the fact that he was Douglass's father. Douglass commented on the duality of father and master in his second autobiography, *My Bondage and My Freedom* (1855):

> The order of civilization is reversed here. The name of the child is not expected to be that of its father, and his condition does not necessarily affect that of the child. . . . He may be white, glorying in the purity of his Anglo-Saxon blood; and his child may be ranked with the blackest slaves. Indeed, he *may* be, and often *is*, master and father to the same child. (Douglass 1994, 151)

Douglass expands on the dark secrets of Southern slavery with musings about masters who shirk the role of father and husband and even sell their children as chattel. He downplays rumors that his father was the master or that his grandmother Bailey was part Native American. To Douglass, purity of race was a pointless boast.

Until age six, Douglass lived on the perimeter of the Anthony plantation in Betsey Bailey's cabin, a milieu that he details in chapter 4 of *My Bondage and My Freedom*, a valuable eyewitness account of slave conditions. He learned to despise Anthony's overseer, a brutal drunk named Plummer who subdued male and female slaves with lash and cudgel. Douglass was trained as a houseboy at Wye House, where he and the dog Nep vied for kitchen scraps and huddled for warmth by the kitchen hearth. Of these deplorable conditions, he notes,

> there are certain secluded and out-of-the-way places, even in the state of Maryland, seldom visited by a single ray of healthy public sentiment—where slavery, wrapt in its own congenial, midnight darkness, *can,* and *does*, develop all its malign and shocking characteristics; where it can be indecent without shame, cruel without shuddering, and murderous without apprehension or fear of exposure. (Douglass 1994, 158)

His description of the proliferation of tobacco sheds, smithies, coopers' and wheelwrights' shops, barns, docks, and stables demonstrates the need for intense skilled and semiskilled labor, which fell to black people. The account of the slave Esther crying to her attacker, "Have mercy; Oh! have mercy. . . . I won't do so no more," ring with the verisimilitude of a memoirist who carried within him the anguish of servitude throughout his adult life. (Douglass 1994, 177)

Loss exacerbated Douglass's deprivations. In 1825, Harriet Bailey died, but she was so distant from her son's world that he didn't learn of her passing until years later. Upon transfer to the Fells Point district of Baltimore, he served Captain Hugh and Sophia Auld as house servant, errand boy, and companion to their two-year-old son Tommy. The move was fortuitous because city owners were obligated to treat slaves more humanely to avoid the censure of neighbors. The mistress treated Douglass as a representative of the Auld household and saw that he was well fed and decently dressed. Under a benign master, he jettisoned plantation manners and demeanor by traveling about the neighborhood and environs of the city and familiarizing himself with urban life. In an act of altruism, Sophia Auld breached the law against educating blacks by teaching him the alphabet and simple words until Auld objected that education spoiled a good servant.

The rudiments of learning were enough to set Douglass on the path to a fuller, more meaningful life. In secret, he continued studying as a preparation for freedom. He memorized lessons he overheard in white schoolchildren's recitations. He bribed them to scribble words on chalkboards. On his own, he studied *The Columbian Orator*, a pamphlet of popular oratory he bought for a half dollar. In it he learned of Nat Turner's failed slave rebellion. Douglass's reading taught him about abolitionism and filled him with concern for human rights, the theme of his adult activism. Discontented with the slave's lot, he began to despise his wretched condition and to follow the antislavery movement. He observed carpenters at Durgin and Bailey's shipyard and imitated their writings on lumber so that he could escape when he had the opportunity. He practiced tracing letters with chalk on fences, walls, and pavement and copied into Tommy's copybook selected words from a Webster's spelling book, hymnal, and Bible.

A squabble between the Auld brothers resituated slaves. Douglass passed to Thomas Auld's 150-acre farm in St. Michael's, 40 miles south of Baltimore. On January 1, 1833, Auld placed Douglass under the supervision of Edward Covey, a blatant slave abuser known for starving and whipping slaves to break them of independent ways. Farmed out to a plantation near the Chesapeake Bay, Douglass suffered the lash for poor performance at farm labor. In his most famous autobiography, *Narrative of the Life of Frederick Douglass, an American Slave*, he reports: "I was broken in body, soul, and spirit." (Douglass 1994, 58) His intellect flags, his will withers. Standing along the wharf, he calls plaintively to the ships:

> O that I were free! O, that I were on one of your gallant decks, and under your protecting wing! Alas! betwixt me and you, the turbid waters roll. Go on, go on. O that I could also go! Could I but swim! If I could fly. O, why was I born a man, of whom to make a brute! . . . O God, save me! God, deliver me! Let me be free! (Douglass 1968, 76)

Douglass's collapse from heat exhaustion while fanning wheat led to a bitter clash with Covey, who struck him in the head with a slat. Douglass fled the farm and complained to Thomas Auld, who refused to intercede, kept him overnight, then sent him back to Covey. For two hours, Douglass menaced the overseer and won a minor victory by looming over the lesser man.

Douglass's lot changed on Christmas Day 1834, when he went to work for William Freeland in Talbot County. Under a humane master, Douglass launched a Sabbath school for over 20 slaves and nursed in private his dream of freedom. In 1836, he plotted to lead two of his uncles and two companions in paddling a stolen canoe across the Chesapeake Bay. By posing as fishermen on forged passes to Baltimore for the Easter holiday, the men planned to follow the North Star and escape to free territory in Pennsylvania. On the day of their flight, an unidentified informant notified Freeland. Three constables captured and tied the conspirators. They jailed Douglass in Easton and exhibited him and the others to slave dealers for possible sale to Alabama.

According to his autobiography, the abortive escape changed little in Douglass's condition. Captain Thomas Auld valued him and encouraged him with promises of manumission by age 24 if he learned a trade. Douglass returned to Hugh Auld's Baltimore residence and worked in the shipyard, where William Gardner prepared him to join a carpentry team. Four envious white apprentices ganged up on Douglass and beat him so severely they endangered his left eye. Hugh Auld rescued him from Gardner and apprenticed him to Walter Price to learn caulking. Douglass did so well that he superintended his own freelance caulking business. During meetings with a black debating society, he added to his rising fortunes by courting Anna Murray, a free black housekeeper and his future wife.

A quarrel about rights to wages precipitated Douglass's daring escape from slavery. As a result of his skill at caulking, he earned top wages of $9 a week, which he was forced to turn over to Auld. On September 2, 1838, after a disagreement about the money Auld claimed, Douglass feared he would be sold south. He began planning in earnest to flee Baltimore by collecting $17 and the falsified papers of a free seaman. From a train to Wilmington, Delaware, he boarded a steamer for Philadelphia and changed to a night train to New York City, arriving September 3, 1838. In *Narrative of the Life of Frederick Douglass, an American Slave*, he describes the fearful journey in a lengthy, oratorical recreation of his plight. He pictures himself as a fugitive in an alien land, compares dangerous manhunters to a crocodile stalking its prey, and perceives whites as fearful sea monsters that subsist on smaller fish. Homeless, friendless, and broke, he seeks shelter, food, and pocket money. To any who haven't been in his predicament, he challenges:

> Let him be placed in this most trying situation,—the situation in which I was placed,—then, and not till then, will he fully appreciate the hardships of, and know how to sympathize with, the toil-worn and whip-scarred fugitive slave. (Douglass 1968, 112)

Assisted by David Ruggles, secretary of the Vigilance Committee, Douglass settled in New York City, adopted the surname Johnson, and married his beloved Anna. The pair lived at the home of Nathan Johnson in New Bedford, Massachusetts. They abandoned the name Johnson because it was too common and introduced themselves with the surname Douglass, adopted from the protagonist of Sir Walter Scott's *The Lady of the Lake*. Safe among friends, they began a family with the birth of daughter Rosetta and son Lewis Henry.

In hiding for three years, Douglass served as a dock laborer and foundry worker and Anna as a laundress. He came under the influence of William Lloyd Garrison, publisher of the *Liberator*, an outspoken abolitionist journal. Both Garrison and Douglass shared radical ideals and a mutual disaffection for the "back to Africa" movement that returned blacks to a colony in Liberia. In 1841, Douglass joined the Massachusetts Anti-Slavery Society. Before an audience of 500 in Nantucket, he delivered an extemporaneous talk that established his reputation as a persuasive orator. As an antislavery agent selling subscriptions to the *Liberator* and the *Anti-Slavery Standard*, he accepted John A. Collins's offer to work three months for the abolitionist cause. With his decorum and good looks, lyrical images, and dramatic eye contact and stage presence, Douglass won audiences throughout the Northeast. His stage trial extended to four years and prefaced a lifetime career of public declamation.

At this point in Douglass's autobiography, he receives the encouragement his talents needed to emerge and develop. In the Worcester pulpit formerly commanded by Charles Dickens, Matthew Arnold, Ralph Waldo Emerson, Abraham Lincoln, and Henry David Thoreau, Douglass presented his case for national emancipation. He concealed his identity by drawing on a store of incidents from the lives of numerous slaves on the plantation and in the city and dockyard, yet he chose to recount vivid personal and family experiences: the

Frederick Douglass (c. 1817–1895)

severe beating of his aunt Hester, the abandonment of his grandmother in the woods to starve, young girls he liked and admired used as breeders, and hungry fellow workers dipping oyster-shell scoops into a common feeding trough of cornmeal mush. These stirring eyewitness memoirs of slavery inflamed listeners who had no doubt that Douglass was revealing valuable evidence against the damnable slave trade.

Douglass's fame placed him in direct opposition to pro-slavery factions, who accused abolitionists of trammeling the rights of law-abiding slave owners. A notorious symbol of protest, he suffered a beating in Pendleton, Ohio, where a mob crushed his right hand so badly that it was never fully rehabilitated. Despite danger from hecklers and bullies, in seven years he addressed over 650 gatherings and converted thousands to activism. Some were so moved by his smooth delivery that they doubted he had ever been an illiterate slave. To prove authenticity, he risked reenslavement and issued his first memoir, *Narrative of the Life of Frederick Douglass, an American Slave*, a bestseller that left him liable to recapture under the Fugitive Slave Law by naming owners, dates, and events. By 1850, his autobiography had sold 30,000 copies in the North and in Europe, where it was translated into German and French. Two rewrites, *My Bondage and My Freedom*, containing a fuller account of his early years, and *Life and Times of Frederick Douglass* (1881), were the groundwork of a bolder 1892 version published under the same title, *Life and Times of Frederick Douglass*.

Leaving Anna and their four children at home in Lynn, Massachusetts, Douglass earned a reputation as the greatest black emancipator of the age by traveling aboard the *Cambria* to Great Britain, where slavery had been illegal since 1838. En route, he ducked bounty hunters and was forced to accept a berth in steerage to avoid being tossed overboard by disgruntled white racists. More open-minded English, Irish, and Scottish supporters, many of whom had read his autobiographies, paid his former master $711.66 for his manumission. A two-year tour among the English introduced him to complete acceptance among enlightened liberals who welcomed him fully as a fellow altruist. However, officials of the Cunard line, fearing a backlash from their elite clientele, forced him to dine apart from whites on the *Cambria*'s return voyage.

In 1847, Douglass, a revered international spokesman for abolition, entered the United States as its first black international star. He settled in Rochester, New York, and continued his work as a freedom fighter as well as a champion of temperance, nonviolence, world peace, and women's rights. In 1848, he attended the first women's rights convention and, at the request of women's liberation leader Elizabeth Cady Stanton, urged women to seek full citizenship. With British funds, he founded a long-lived free-black newspaper, the *North Star*, which he renamed the *Frederick Douglass' Paper* in 1851 and *The Douglass Monthly* in 1859. On the masthead, he stated his credo: "Right is of no Sex— Truth is of no Color—God is the Father of us all, and we are all Brethren." (Thomas 1997, n.p.) In the opening editorial, he dedicated the paper to

> the cause of our long oppressed and plundered fellow countrymen. May God bless the offering to your good! It shall fearlessly assert your rights, faithfully proclaim your wrongs, and earnestly demand for you instant and even-handed justice. Giving no quarter to slavery at the South, it will hold no truce with oppressors at the North. (Douglass 1989, 129)

In 1850, his passionate editorial rejected prejudicial thinking by attacking the persistent devaluation of human beings. He concluded that the Negro is human, "possessing an immortal soul, illuminated by intellect, capable of heavenly aspirations, and in all things pertaining to manhood, he is at once self-evidently a man." (Douglass 1992, 197)

In his role as defender of liberty, Douglass delivered his most anthologized speech, a pointed antislavery diatribe entitled "What to the Slave Is the Fourth of July?" (1852), a calculated public rejection of a sanctified American holiday because it did not acknowledge enslavement of blacks. He remarked on the separation of races:

> Your high independence only reveals the immeasurable distance between us. The blessings in which you this day rejoice are not enjoyed in common. The rich inheritance of justice, liberty, prosperity, and independence bequeathed by your fathers is shared by you, not by me. (Douglass 1994, 434)

He denounced Independence Day as a "gross injustice and cruelty," a constant reminder of the vanity and heartlessness of whites. He proclaimed holiday festivities "bombast, fraud, deception, impiety" and concluded that the United States reigned above other nations in "revolting barbarity and shameless hypocrisy." (Douglass 1994, 435) In this same period, he turned to fiction as an alternate weapon against slavery and composed a novella, *The Heroic Slave* (1853), a fictional account of an 1841 slave mutiny led by Madison Washington aboard the ship *Creole*.

As turmoil in the South worsened, Douglass abandoned pacifism. He declared that submissive people who tolerate abuse are the most likely to be whipped. Under the influence of John Brown, he began preaching the right of the oppressed to use whatever means necessary to throw off their oppressors. In *Life and Times of Frederick Douglass*, he expresses the fervor of this change of heart:

> My utterances became more and more tinged by the color of this man's strong impressions. Speaking at an antislavery convention in Salem, Ohio, I expressed this apprehension that slavery could only be destroyed by blood-shed, when I was suddenly and sharply interrupted by my good old friend Sojourner Truth with the question, "Frederick, is God dead?" "No," I answered, "and because God is not dead slavery can only end in blood." (Douglass 1994, 719)

Recommitting themselves to help those still in bondage, Frederick and Anna Douglass personally rescued and aided fugitive slaves, whom he escorted to Canada. He dedicated lecture fees to the Rochester branch of the Underground Railroad, which he superintended and described by name, city, and station in his writings. In October 1859, after John Brown's abortive raid on Harper's Ferry, Virginia, Douglass was named an accomplice because of his fervid support of runaways. To avoid arrest, he fled to Canada and journeyed from there to England for a lecture tour. In retrospect, he acknowledged Brown's courage in implicating no one and accepting all responsibility. As a result of Brown's rabid commitment to the unsuccessful insurrection, government marshals ceased their dragnet for additional instigators and made an example of him at a public hanging.

On returning to Rochester, Douglass took up the candidacy of Abraham Lincoln. After the Southern states formed a separate confederacy, he ignored the issue of states' rights and supported the Union army's fight against slavery. Lincoln's Emancipation Proclamation of 1862 heartened Douglass to press for black regiments. In his speech "Men of Color, to Arms!" (1863), he declared, "A war undertaken and brazenly carried on for the perpetual enslavement of colored men, calls logically and loudly for colored men to help suppress it." (Douglass 1994, 778) On his advice, the War Department armed former slaves and employed them in battle. When the 54th and 55th Massachusetts Colored Regiments were established, he recruited likely soldiers, including his sons, Frederick, Jr., and Lewis Henry. President Lincoln sought Douglass's opinion of the role of Negro soldiers in combat against slaveholders and former masters, who vowed to hang all former slaves who transgressed against the South.

By 1864, as the tide of battle favored Union success, Douglass advised caution about accepting freedom as a quick solution to the problems of black people. In a memorable speech, "What the Black Man Wants," delivered in Boston to the annual meeting of the Massachusetts Anti-Slavery Society, he stated his belief that black people deserved full citizenship:

> Slavery is not abolished until the black man has the ballot. While the Legislatures of the South retain the right to pass laws making any discrimination between black and white, slavery still lives there. . . . While a black man can be turned out of a car in Massachusetts, Massachusetts is a slave state. While a slave can be taken from old Massachusetts, Massachusetts is a slave state. (Douglass 1990, 155)

His insistence on complete justice called for reforms in education, prisons, sexual equality, labor, and temperance as well as suffrage. During Reconstruction, he refused to obey Jim Crow laws, which sanctioned whites-only theaters, hotels, and public transportation. He peppered editorial columns with demands for total equality and undertook a killing schedule of lectures and public appearances. Sure of his role as orator and editor, he declined Andrew Johnson's offer of the presidency of the Freeman's Bureau, which passed to General Oliver Otis Howard.

The postwar years brought no respite to Douglass's full schedule of writing and speaking. In 1871, he built Cedar Hill, his 20-room residence, in Washington, D.C., and edited the *New National Era*. His speech "The Work before Us" warned of the rise of random violence and terrorism plotted and carried out by the Ku Klux Klan, White Camellia, and other secret societies of white supremacists. His forceful words helped secure the Fifteenth Amendment, granting black males the right to vote, but his strong activism cost him the support of suffragists, who denounced any legislation that denied the vote to women, black or white. He accepted the presidency of the Freemen's Bank. Under President Rutherford B. Hayes, he served as U.S. marshal of the District of Columbia and, under James Garfield, as the region's recorder of deeds.

Content with Anna at Cedar Hill, Douglass retired in 1877 at age 60 to enjoy free time with his family, which was enlarged by the births of 20 grandchildren. He journeyed to Maryland to settle old scores with former owner Thomas Auld, who greeted him as an equal. In 1879, he delivered a lecture, "The Negro Exodus from the Gulf States," to the American Social Science Association. Still active at age 66, he rallied the National Convention of Colored Men in Louisville with a call for full citizenship for blacks. Emulating the thought patterns of Jefferson and Lincoln, he proclaimed:

> We hold it to be self-evident that no class or color should be the exclusive rulers of this country. If there is such a ruling class . . . this Government of the people, by the people and for the people will have perished from the earth. (Douglass 1994, 445)

His insistence on federal aid for blacks preceded his adamant denunciation of the Supreme Court for scuttling the Civil Rights Act of 1875, which promised full accommodation for nonwhites on public conveyances. The subject of Jim Crow segregation remained a focus of his thinking in December 1883, when he published "The Condition of the Freedmen" in *Harper's Weekly*.

Depressed after Anna's death from stroke, in 1884, Douglass married his white secretary, Helen Pitts, of Rochester. Their union dismayed both whites and blacks. Douglass ignored the turmoil over miscegenation in the Washington press while touring Canada on their honeymoon and retorted to his critics that his first wife resembled his black mother and his second wife his white father. After an extended stay in England, France, Italy, Greece, and Egypt, he accepted the post of consul general in Haiti, but resigned in 1891—partly in anger at white entrepreneurs who exploited local people, but also because of a decline in his health from the fierce Caribbean sun. After much criticism of his resignation, he published an article in the *North American Review* justifying his role in Haitian politics.

Douglass returned to writing about American racism in 1892 with "Lynch Law in the South" for the July issue of the *North American Review*. After a visit to the Chicago World's Fair, he was so enraged that no part of the exposition honored black achievement that he collaborated with I. Garland Penn, Ida Wells, and Ferdinand Lee Barnett on *The Reason Why the Colored American Is Not in the Columbian Exposition* (1893); spoke on "The Race Problem in America" (1894); and wrote one of his most influential essays, *The Lesson of the Hour: Why Is the Negro Lynched* (1894), about mob violence, the topic of numerous speeches. On February 20, 1895, he collapsed and died from heart failure on the speaker's platform at a women's suffrage rally of the National Council of Women in Washington, D.C., and was buried in Rochester's Mount Hope Cemetery. Schools closed in his honor as thousands, black and white, brought their children to honor him. Among his pallbearers were Supreme Court Justice Marshall Harlan and Senator John Sherman; women's liberation leader Susan B. Anthony delivered a eulogy. Grateful citizens raised a commemorative statue in Highland Park, and the Maryland Historical Society built a monument on Route 328 at the Tuckahoe Bridge. Speaking for the women's rights movement, Elizabeth Cady Stanton honored his devotion to liberty, justice, and equality. In 1926, Carter B. Woodson, originator of Black History Month, chose February as the appropriate time to honor freedom fighters born in that month—Abraham Lincoln and Frederick Douglass. ("Anti-Slavery Society" 1990; Asante and Mattson 1992; Bradbury 1996; Douglass 1968; "Fourth of July" 1990, 1992, 1994; "Frederick Douglass" 1997; "Frederick Douglass and John Brown" 1997; Kunitz and Haycraft 1938; Low and Clift 1981; Miller et al. 1987; Quarles 1968, 1981; Ravitch 1990; Rice 1997; Russell 1988; Stein 1979; Thomas 1997; Wilson and Ferris 1989)

ELLISON, RALPH

Ralph Waldo Ellison, the rare Southern writer to be born in Oklahoma, joined fugitive writers from Dixie to live on Riverside Drive in New York City, far from his family's cultural homeland. A gifted humanist with a flair for music and folklore, he fused blues with tragedy to produce a unique vision of the black experience. In *Shadow and Act* (1964), he expressed gratitude for a childhood environment that let him develop beyond the parochialism of racial identity. He blamed immersion in blackness for limiting some black American artists too fearful "to leave the uneasy sanctuary of race to take their chances in the world of art." (Hall and Emblen 1985, 125) Maintaining his individuality by shunning the politics of civil rights, he produced a unique masterwork, *Invisible Man* (1947), a National Book Award–winning psychological and social novel about the spiritual death of a defeated and disillusioned idealist. Committed to dignified, scholarly pursuits, Ellison throve outside the perpetual discontent and jingoism of the Black Nationalist movement and apart from his African-American contemporaries—Ernest Gaines, James Baldwin, Angela Davis, Claude Brown, Eldridge Cleaver, Maya Angelou, and Zora Neale Hurston. Despite self-exile, at his death on April 17, 1994, from pancreatic cancer, Ellison had attained the stature of a senior statesman among black writers of the preprotest era.

The scion of African slaves of the Savannah River area, Ellison was the grandson of a notable patriarch—Alfred Ellison, born into slavery in 1845 in Abbeville, South Carolina, and elevated to local prominence during Reconstruction as an established citizen, constable, and marshal. Although Ellison was born in Oklahoma City on March 1, 1914, he bore the Southern background of contemporaries Richard Wright and Langston Hughes. The son of Ida Millsap Ellison, a building custodian and socialist organizer, and Spanish-American War hero Lewis Alfred Ellison, a construction worker who operated a coal and ice outlet, Ellison was named for transcendental essayist Ralph Waldo Emerson. He lived on the South's western frontier in a state newly arrived in the Union and free of the taint of slavery or the violence and recriminations of Reconstruction. In *Shadow and Act*, he wrote of his hometown,

> ours was a chaotic community, still characterized by frontier attitudes and by
> that strange mixture of the naive and sophisticated, the benign and malignant,

which makes the American past so puzzling and its present so confusing (Hall and Emblen 1985, 119)

He valued the blend of elements in Oklahoma that gave him a wide choice of possibilities, and opportunities that allowed his imagination to grow, "to range widely and, sometimes, even to soar."

From early childhood Ellison was forced to take responsibility for himself. His mother was widowed in 1917 after her husband died from a work-related fall. She supported two sons, Ralph and Herbert, through domestic labor. Ellison profited from her work among privileged whites by reading discarded magazines and listening to opera recordings that she retrieved from the trash. During his school years he ran an elevator, polished shoes and cars, worked in kitchens and restaurants, sold newspapers, and took other menial work that he hoped would rescue his mother from a hard life. In rare moments of leisure, he studied jazz and harmony and conducted research at the black library. By age 21, he entered Tuskegee Institute in Alabama on scholarship and pursued a career composing symphonic music.

Ending three years of music study in 1936, Ellison, like his protagonist in *Invisible Man*, abruptly left college and the South. The next year, his mother

Ralph Waldo Ellison, left, with fellow National Book Award winners Archibald MacLeish, center, and Bernard DeVoto, right, in New York, January 1953

died and his grandfather's South Carolina land was reclaimed for tax default. He and Herbert lived in Dayton, Ohio, where they hunted rabbits and game birds for the table until Ellison emigrated to Harlem. Virtually penniless, he slept on park benches until he could earn enough money to pay for better lodgings. He studied sculpture and photography, but altered his focus after meeting novelist Richard Wright. Under the aegis of the Federal Writers' Project, Ellison began writing for the *Masses, Tomorrow, Negro Quarterly*, and *New Challenge* a series of remarkably mature scholarly essays, radical political views, short stories, and literary critiques, including "The Birthmark" (1940), "Recent Negro Fiction" (1941), "Mr. Toussan" (1941), and "The Way It Is" (1942). His work demonstrates a humanistic grasp of a panoply of literature—Benjamin Franklin's essays, the Gettysburg Address, Ecclesiastes, Henry David Thoreau's nonfiction, T. S. Eliot's *The Waste Land*, Fyodor Dostoyevsky's *Notes from the Underground*, and the novels of André Malraux, Joseph Conrad, Mark Twain, Herman Melville, William Faulkner, Stendhal, and Henry James. Two of Ellison's early published articles—"Creative and Cultural Lag" in *New Challenge* and "They Found Terror in Harlem" in the *Negro World Digest*—prefigure themes and issues of *Invisible Man;* a third, "Richard Wright's Blues" (1945), analyzes the roots of his mentor's vision and artistry.

After service in the merchant marine during World War II, Ellison devoted himself to education and literature. From 1942 to 1943, he edited the *Negro Quarterly*. Four years later, he married businesswoman Fanny McConnell, established himself as a full-time freelance writer, and began publishing regularly in *Noble Savage, Iowa Review, Time, Partisan Review, Cross Section, Washington Post Book World, American Scholar, Reporter*, and the *New York Times Book Review*. Through these outlets he achieved quality fiction in "That I Had the Wings" (1944), "Flying Home" (1944), "In a Strange Country" (1944), and "King of the Bingo Game" (1944).

On the strength of short fiction and polemical writings, he received a Rosenwald Fellowship, which enabled him to work seven years on a psychological novel, *Invisible Man*, a fictive odyssey tinged by surreal, neogothic touches. A pivotal, innovative work that has been proclaimed one of the twentieth century's significant works of world literature, it earned an astonishing amount of praise for a first novel, including a National Book Award for skillful narrative technique and perceptive psychology of the victim. In 1963, Tuskegee conferred an honorary doctorate on Ellison. He published a second work, *Shadow and Act*, a collection of 20 essays on art, folklore, music, and life. Three years later, he lost the incomplete manuscript of a second novel in a fire. In 1986, he published a second collection of short works, *Going to the Territory*, followed by *Flying Home and Other Stories* (1997), his last and most mature stories, which examine questions of racism from a restrained, objective point of view.

Although Ellison's philosophy was out of step with later generations of militant blacks, his sensitive first novel is a portrait of the unnamed invisible man's loss of self during the second semester and summer of his junior year in college. The work opens with a poignant manifesto of self-abnegation easily recognized by students of Southern literature:

I am an invisible man. No, I am not a spook like those who haunted Edgar Allan Poe; nor am I one of your Hollywood-movie ectoplasms. I am a man of substance, of flesh and bone, fiber and liquids—and I might even be said to possess a mind. (Ellison 1952, 3)

Labeled a satire, gothic fiction, and an autobiographical novel, Ellison's masterpiece outdistances the work of his hero, Richard Wright, in skill, vision, and emotional power. Ellison's grim view of festering racism prefigures the Watts and Attica prison riots, Rodney King's martyrdom, and the malcontent of the inner cities during the 1970s. His stories and essays appear in more than 30 collections. As visiting lecturer, creative-writer-in-residence, and expert on black culture, American literature, and Russian literature, he found receptive audiences and classes at Bard, Bennington, Princeton, Columbia, Fisk, Antioch, Yale, Rutgers, University of California, University of Chicago, and New York University, and before European audiences in Austria, Italy, and Germany. He served the Library of Congress as consultant and lecturer, and studied on a Prix de Rome award from the American Academy of Arts and Letters.

Retired to his New York home in 1958, Ellison served on the Carnegie Commission on Educational Television. In 1969, he received the Medal of Freedom from President Richard Nixon. The next year, he was chosen as the Albert Schweitzer humanities professor at New York University, and he advised the committee designing the John F. Kennedy Center for the Performing Arts. Late in life he garnered honoraria from Harvard, Wesleyan, and Brown Universities and received the National Medal of Arts, Chevalier de l'Ordre Arts et Lettres, and Langston Hughes Medallion. In 1975, Oklahoma City honored Ellison with a bronze portrait bust at the Ralph Ellison Branch Library. (Bradbury 1963; Bradbury 1996; *Contemporary Authors* 1994; Corliss 1994; Daniels 1994; Ehrlich and Carruth 1982; Ellison 1952; Farley 1997; Girson 1953; Gross 1971; Hall and Emblen 1985; Harper and Wright 1980; Hill 1966; Low and Clift 1981; Lyons 1994; "Ralph Ellison Profile" 1976; Redding 1951; Reilly 1970; Rubin et al. 1985; Schor 1993; Warren 1965; Warren 1997; Watts 1994)

See also Invisible Man.

FAULKNER, WILLIAM

If Southern literature were to declare a patriarch, the title would go to William Faulkner. In a verbal epitaph, as though chiseling his thoughts in marble, John Fitzgerald Kennedy declared:

> A Mississippian by birth, an American by virtue of those forces and loyalties which guided his work, a guiding citizen of our civilization by virtue of his art, William Faulkner now rests, the search done, his place secure among the great creators of this age. ("Faulkner's Legacy" 1962, 4)

Not everyone shared Kennedy's enthusiasm. A raw genius, Faulkner rejected egregious displays of learning and the trappings of scholasticism for sheer, honest human figures. He infuriated critics, who alternately extolled and degraded him, depending on the issue of the moment or the status of desegregation. Against a backdrop of quibbling and hair-splitting, Faulkner—the distinguished, silver-haired Southerner dressed in tweed jacket with leather elbow patches— gripped his pipe more tightly in his teeth, flashed his dark eyes, and retreated to his home study. Alone with his thoughts, he sipped from a demijohn of Old Crow and continued typing the 19 novels and 80 short stories that locked the literary world's attention on Southern themes and mindsets.

Essential to an understanding of Faulkner's art is a recognition of his sense of place. Born William Cuthbert Faulkner on September 25, 1897, in New Albany, Mississippi, he lived and anchored a career in fiction, essays, criticism, screenplays, and poetry in Oxford, Mississippi, seat of Lafayette County and home of the University of Mississippi. His parents, Maud Butler and Murray Faulkner, settled near the college campus in 1901. The people and environs of Oxford are the meat and savor of his novels and short stories. Of their importance, he declared, "I discovered that my own little postage stamp of native soil was worth writing about and that I would never live long enough to exhaust it." ("The Curse" 1964, 44) The spirit of his work, which he derived from his love of the South and a broader appreciation of all humanity, was delineated in a speech at the University of Virginia in 1958. Faulkner challenged the audience to accept the writer's dilemma of rescuing humankind "from being desouled as the stallion or boar or bull is gelded; to save the individual from anonymity before it is too late and humanity has vanished from the animal called man." (Faulkner 1969, 4) His reasoned opposition to regimentation echoes the humanist creed: to preserve humanity, the stuff from which the artist creates.

Faulkner had reason to be proud of his Southernness. He was the third of four brothers and a great-grandson of Colonel William Clark Falkner, lawyer, politician, Confederate war hero, railroad builder, and author of *The White Rose of Memphis* (1880). (Faulkner altered his surname in 1926 by adding the *u*.) Faulkner maintained the family penchant for literature, as did his older brother John, who wrote two novels and a memoir, *My Brother Bill* (1963). Decades of legends, hunting tales, pervasive rumors, and family lore interwove family history, which extended over the Mexican War, Civil War, Reconstruction era, and construction of the local railroad. An immense sum of background material set Faulkner on a literary odyssey of the antebellum South, emancipation, and the decline of the wilderness with the coming of mechanization.

Never an enthusiastic student, Faulkner left school after the tenth grade and educated himself through reading. He took considerable interest in Sir Walter Scott's novels, French romances and verse, Lew Wallace's *Ben Hur*, Daniel Defoe's *Robinson Crusoe*, the poems of Algernon Swinburne and A. E. Housman, and the family sagas of the Old Testament. Rejected for military service during World War I, he moved to Canada and joined the Royal Air Force. He entered the School of Military Aeronautics in Toronto, but saw little frontline action. In 1918, he accepted an honorary commission as second lieutenant. Against his will, he completed two terms at the University of Mississippi, where he studied French, English, and Spanish; published stories and poems in school literary journals; and wrote for the school paper, the *Mississippian*, and the *Oxford Eagle*. Faulkner chose to write among the literati of the North. Like others of his era, he settled in New York City with a boyhood friend, Mississippi novelist and critic Stark Young, author of *So Red the Rose* (1934) and editor of *Southern Treasury of Art and Literature* (1937). Faulkner clerked in a bookshop and published a poem, "L'Après-Midi du Faune" (1919) in *Nation*. Returning to Oxford in 1922, he worked his way through various low-paying jobs, including carpenter, house painter, and a two-year stint as the university postmaster.

After the publication of *The Marble Faun* (1924), a lengthy imitation of English pastoral verse financed by friend and mentor Phil Stone, Faulkner tried living in New Orleans, an agricultural milieu more conducive to the Southern writer. He contributed works to the *Times-Picayune* and a poem to a noteworthy experimental "little magazine," the *Double Dealer*. Sherwood Anderson, a friend and colleague, encouraged him to publish *Soldier's Pay* (1926), but the novel sold only a few volumes. After completing a satiric novel, *Mosquitoes* (1927), during an extended visit to Pascagoula, Louisiana, he journeyed home to Oxford. In 1927, he married Estelle Oldham Franklin, welcomed her daughter and son as a ready-made family, and established a homestead, Rowan Oak, an antebellum mansion built by a Mississippi pioneer in 1840. To support his family, in 1929 he sought work at the university power plant. He fathered a daughter, Alabama, who died in 1931 nine days after her birth, and in 1933 a second child, Jill Faulkner Summers, who survived him and fostered definitive editions of his works.

Family and area history became Faulkner's delight and burden. He internalized its romance and re-created its idiosyncratic drive and passion at the same time that he distanced himself from the belles lettres arrogance, frothy confections, and grandiose embroidery that had supplanted the South's reality. With a third novel, *Sartoris* (1929), based on his great-grandfather's turbulent feud and murder on the courthouse grounds, Faulkner evolved a trademark style and settled on his homeland as a lifelong literary challenge. Of Colonel Sartoris, modeled after Great-grandfather Falkner, he wrote:

> He stood on a stone pedestal, in his frock coat and bareheaded, one leg slightly advanced and one hand resting lightly on the stone pylon beside him. His head was lifted a little in that gesture of haughty pride which repeated itself generation after generation with a fateful fidelity, his back to the world and his carven eyes gazing out across the valley where his railroad ran, and the blue changeless hills beyond and beyond that, the ramparts of infinity itself. (Faulkner 1964, 299)

Faulkner achieved little of his enormous success in tangible form. Standing worlds apart from his best work are his moneymakers: He composed *Sanctuary* (1931), a horrific rape story, with an eye toward the rewards of titillating scandal, and traveled to Hollywood to earn a living by scripting for the "flickers." As a screenwriter with MGM in 1932 and later, Warner Brothers, Universal Studios, and RKO, he contributed to two World War I commemoratives—*Today We Live* (1933) and *The Road to Glory* (1936)—as well as *Slave Ship* (1937), *Citizen Kane* (1941), *The Magnificent Ambersons* (1942), *Air Force* (1943), *Background to Danger* (1943), *Mildred Pierce* (1945), *The Southerner* (1945), and *The Land of the Pharaohs* (1955). He helped script Rudyard Kipling's Indian adventure *Gunga Din* (1939); an Errol Flynn swashbuckler, *The Adventures of Don Juan* (1949); two Humphrey Bogart–Lauren Bacall vehicles, *To Have and Have Not* (1944) and *The Big Sleep* (1946); and a three-Oscar western classic, *High Noon* (1952). Filming of his own works was never successful, the best being *Intruder in the Dust* (1949), which MGM shot on location in Oxford, with Will Geer playing the role of sheriff.

Faulkner incorporates in his novels the public assemblage of "rag-tag and bob-ends" of rumor and speculation, snippets of family events, and courthouse records in an intense probe of the rise and fall of northern Mississippi families. (Faulkner 1990, 335) *Absalom, Absalom!* (1936), a complex, uneven novel derived from stories he had developed for 15 years, introduced his version of the narrator-historian, who details the life of a pathfinder and faux aristocrat, Thomas Sutpen. In chapter 1, Faulkner introduces Rosa Coldfield, one of many points of view on the subject of Sutpen and his elusive, shadowed origin:

> He wasn't a gentleman. He wasn't even a gentleman. He came here with a horse and two pistols and a name which nobody ever heard before, knew for certain was his own anymore than the horse was his own or even the pistols, seeking some place to hide himself, and Yoknapatawpha County supplied him with it. (Faulkner 1990, 9)

A ruthless slave driver and would-be dynast, he wrests a baronial estate, Sutpen's Hundred, from the wilderness, but fails to hang onto his pioneer beginning or to populate his family with Caucasian namesakes.

William Faulkner (1897–1962) on the grounds of the University of Virginia, founded by colonial and federalist era writer, Thomas Jefferson

During a casual fictional conversation in section two of *Absalom, Absalom!* Faulkner expresses the scope and purpose of his life's work. As Quentin talks about his homeland with Shreve McCannon, his Canadian roommate, Shreve demands to know, "What's it like there? . . . What do they do there? Why do they live there? Why do they live at all?" (Faulkner 1990, 142) At first, Quentin replies that only natives can understand the paradox of Southern gentility and Southern violence. His brief narration of Yoknapatawpha County history—the story of Thomas Sutpen, who uses slave labor to build a vast compound, then loses it and is shot by a peasant for seducing the man's granddaughter—enflames Shreve's imagination. "Jesus, the South is fine, isn't it," Shreve McCannon says. "It's better than the theatre, isn't it. It's better than Ben Hur, isn't it. No wonder you have to come away now and then, isn't it." To readers of Faulkner's fiction, Shreve is the typical outsider who must hear the rich, seamy, passionate tales of Southerners to piece together even a shred of the region's uniqueness. (Faulkner 1990, 176)

Faulkner restates the story of Sutpen through repeated tellings until he has produced a complex net of local accounts, each bandying the ridicule and public humiliation to suit the teller. Sutpen's inability to control destiny derives not so much from physical weakness as from ethical bankruptcy. Ironically, the vigor of the Sutpen genes thrives in his illegitimate son, Charles Bon, offspring of a Haitian octoroon mother. Sutpen's nemesis is sordid and appropriate. He succumbs to his own depravity after he is shot by Wash Jones, an illiterate cracker itching to settle a slight to Milly, Wash's granddaughter, whom Sutpen had impregnated and abandoned. Faulkner published the vengeance plot separately as "Wash," a reworked version appearing in *Collected Stories of William Faulkner* (1950). Wash's death in the cabin he torches with lamp oil follows a measured confrontation with the law:

> "I'm here," Wash said quietly from the window. "That you, Major?"
> "Come out."
> "Sho," he said quietly. "I just want to see to my grand-daughter."
> "We'll see to her. Come on out."
> "Sho, Major. Just a minute."
> "Show a light. Light your lamp."
> "Sho. In just a minute." (Faulkner 1977, 549)

Like one of the avenging Erinyes from Greek mythology, Wash leaps out of the roar and gleam of conflagration, flashing a scythe that "bore down upon them, upon the wild glaring eyes of the horses and the swinging glints of gun barrels, without any cry, any sound." In retrospect of the critical furor that arose over *Absalom, Absalom!* Faulkner was galled that the bravura novel sold so poorly while its melodramatic contemporary, Margaret Mitchell's *Gone with the Wind*, became an instant best-seller.

Influenced by the innovations of James Joyce, Faulkner persevered according to his private literary ideals. He maintained a densely interwoven style, which Clifton Fadiman dubbed "Anti-narrative, a set of complex devices used to keep the story from being told." ("Faulkner's Legacy" 1962, 4) Although seized upon by the scholarly community and honored by the National Institute of Arts and Literature in 1939, Faulkner remained largely ignored by the general reader until his receipt of the American Academy's Howells Medal and a Nobel Prize for Literature, which King Gustav VI bestowed in Stockholm, Sweden, on December 10, 1950. Faulkner's acceptance speech earned its own special niche in literature as the writer's personal creed. In four succinct paragraphs, he reminds young writers that there will always be a place for "courage and honor and hope and pride and compassion and pity and sacrifice which have been the glory of [the] past." (Beatty et al. 1952, 1,060) He also earned a National Book Award in 1951, and the Pulitzer Prize in 1955 for *A Fable* (1954) and posthumously in 1963 for *The Reivers* (1962).

In his last years, from 1957 to 1961, Faulkner served the University of Virginia as writer-in-residence, primarily to remain close to Jill, who lived in Charlottesville. In a lecture, he debunked much of the pseudointellectual criticism of his work with a single denial:

> I don't know anything about style. . . . I think a writer with a lot . . . pushing inside him to get out hasn't got time to bother with style. If he just likes to write and hasn't got anything urging him, then he can become a stylist, but the ones with a great deal pushing to get out don't have time to be anything but clumsy. (Lockerbie 1969, 3)

He affirmed young listeners in Virginia and other university audiences with trust in the individual conscience that voluntarily chooses good over evil. His candid delivery so delighted cadets at West Point that the school established a Faulkner collection of first editions.

Following falls from his horse in January and June 1962, Faulkner suffered a heart attack at his home. He died at the Oxford hospital on July 6, 1962, and was interred at St. Peter's Cemetery in Oxford. Town residents, as well as much of the South and the literary world, mourned his passing. Local friends sought out the home-dug grave and left memorials. University officials purchased Rowan Oak from Faulkner's daughter, established a Faulkner museum, and opened the residence and grounds for tours. The mid-1960s saw the lionizing of his work and a consuming critical interest in Yoknapatawpha, his imaginary county, and the overlay of generations of fictional Sartorises, Snopeses, Sutpens, McCaslins, Carothers, Coldfields, Bundrens, and Compsons who founded and populated the region. Chief among rediscovered treasures was Faulkner's stream-of-consciousness masterwork *The Sound and the Fury* (1929), which preceded a companion piece, *As I Lay Dying* (1930), the latter describing the enduring agricultural class and the former the degenerate white landowners of a circumscribed fictional microcosm of Mississippi. As Americans began implementing desegregation in communities and schools, critics returned to Faulkner's novels to study the onus of poverty and elitist greed on the poor and working-class whites and blacks. Liberal academic circles lauded *Light in August* (1932) for its depiction of miscegenation, fundamentalism, ignorance, superstition, and hate-stoked violence. The work, a virtuoso circular narrative, introduced Joe Christmas, one of Faulkner's most poignant protagonists. Joe's tragedy and tribute are imbedded in the so-called "Faulkner South," a land of unsung heroes whom the author ennobles.

The coda of Faulkner's canon suggests an act of completion. After publishing *Requiem for a Nun* (1950), he drew together the ends and scraps of Yoknapatawpha history for an episodic trilogy: *The Hamlet* (1957), *The Town* (1957), and *The Mansion* (1959). A double helix, the downward spiral follows the plummeting morals and fortunes of Southern patricians as the upward curl boosts the seriocomic Snopes clan to their own peculiar triumph—a self-important redneck risen to the presidency of the local bank. Faulkner's montage of events and episodes mentioned throughout previous stories and novels jells into a full folk album detailing the region's advance and decline. At times heroic, at others markedly grotesque or absurd, the trio relentlessly restates Mississippi social history as an outgrowth of white opportunism, dating from the gentry's oppression of Native Americans through slavery and emancipation.

Faulkner's characters move into an era uneasy with its racial past, yet bound to play out the interracial drama begun in the colonial era—when interlopers uprooted old Ikkemotubbe, a Chickasaw chief—and carried through generations of planters, sharecroppers, survivors of war and destruction, entrepreneurs, and land barons. A film version of *The Hamlet* appeared as *The Long Hot Summer* (1958), starring Paul Newman, Joanne Woodward, Lee Remick, Anthony Franciosa, Orson Welles, and Angela Lansbury. A four-hour made-for-television remake was aired October 6–7, 1985, on NBC, starring Don Johnson, Cybill Shepherd, Jason Robards, Jr., and Ava Gardner. A mishmash screen version of *Sanctuary* appeared in 1960, starring Lee Remick, Yves Montand, Odetta, and Bradford Dillman. Director Irving Ravetch turned out a moderately successful filming of *The Reivers* (1969), starring Steve McQueen and Will Geer.

Beyond Hollywood's unsuccessful attempts to adapt his novels for film, Faulkner's appeal remains one of Southern literature's constants. The Humanities Research Center of the University of Texas Library houses a collection of his papers alongside works by poets T. S. Eliot and e. e. cummings, novelist Ernest Hemingway, and critic H. L. Mencken. On the streets of Oxford, Mississippi's unofficial literary shrine, pilgrims still seek out old-timers to recount local jests at the expense of "Count No-Count," the ne'er-do-well local boy who brought worldwide fame to the delta and Ole Miss. On September 25, 1997, sculptor Bill Beckwith unveiled his life-size statue of Faulkner seated on a bench in a casual pose to honor the centenary of the author's birth. Scholars and fans tour antebellum mansions steeped in tradition and search out landmarks from Yoknapatawpha as though it possessed a discernible longitude and latitude. At the Faulkner manor, visitors roam the garden, peer in the smokehouse door, and marvel at an Underwood portable on which the country's prominent Southern author pecked out the profound parable of his homeland. (Auchmutey 1997; Barger 1989; Barth 1989; Beatty et al. 1952; Bloom 1986; Blotner 1978; Bradbury 1963; Bradbury 1996; Cunliffe 1987; "The Curse" 1964; Ehrlich and Carruth 1982; Faulkner 1957, 1959, 1964, 1967, 1969, 1972, 1977, 1984, 1985, 1987, 1990, 1991, 1996; "Faulkner's Legacy" 1962; Hamilton 1952; Hicks 1968;

Howe 1952; King 1980; Lockerbie 1969; Minter 1982; Morris 1989; O'Connor 1989; Rubin 1974, 1982; Rubin and Jacobs 1961; Rubin et al. 1985; Simonini 1964; Snead 1986; Stein 1979; Stephens 1995; Styron 1962; Sundquist 1985; Wadlington 1987; Walker 1996; Wells 1980; Whitt 1994; Williams, Joan 1980; Wilson and Ferris 1989)

See also short fiction in Southern literature; *The Sound and the Fury*; women in Southern literature.

THE FRONTIER TRADITION

In a restless era of trailblazing, pioneering, and settlement, Southerners, like citizens from the East Coast and immigrants from all parts, left their home states and made new homes in the mountains, far from the settled climes they had known in the sandhills and piedmont. The overblown tales of mountain expeditions color the woods lore of Virginian David H. Coyner's *The Lost Trappers* (1847), merging history with fancy in a classic study of the pursuit of beaver pelts, which were much in demand at the beginning of the nineteenth century for the making of fashionable high-top hats. Partially derived from the journal of Ezekiel Williams, Coyner's text claims that, out of 20 trappers departing up the Missouri River in 1807, only three survived. Williams paddled south on the Arkansas River and returned to Missouri in 1809; the other two went west. Coyner also claims that Williams, settling in the Mississippi Valley, survived off the meat of trapped beaver, the tail of which he considered a "great dainty":

> He separates it from the body of the beaver, thrusts a stick in one end of it, and places it before the fire with the scales on it. When the heat of the fire strikes through so as to roast it, large blisters rise on the surface, which are very easily removed. The tail is then perfectly white, and very delicious. (Coyner 1995, 75)

Williams notes that the trapper recycles much of his prey, saving the scrotum for bait. To mask human scent, he bottles semen and musk to sprinkle over carcasses he has handled. While setting a trap, he steadies the jaws with a scented stick, which protrudes a few inches above the water. Placement is crucial, for the beaver must sink to the bottom and drown. Williams claims that, if the beaver struggles ashore, he may bite off his manacled leg and flee.

A century after Coyner, the lure of mountaineering remained strong in western legendary heroes Kit Carson, John Fremont, Jim Beckwourth, and Jim Bridger. Captain William F. Drannan, who claimed to know them all, published *Thirty-One Years on the Plains and in the Mountains or, The Last Voice from the Plains* (1900). Paralleling the autobiographies of his predecessors, he recounts a wilderness career beginning when he fled Tennessee at age 15 to seek his fortune. With a pal, Johnnie West, he hunts wild turkey and buffalo and visits an Arapaho chief. The duo journeys south to Mexico City, north to Carson's wedding in Taos, and west among notorious gamblers in San Francisco. A chapter on Drannan's appointment to the lead of a wagon train contains the instructions he passes to greenhorns who are unused to circling wagons in Indian country:

> By having each wagon numbered every man knew his place in the train, and when it was necessary to correll [sic], one-half of the teams would turn to the right and the other half to the left. Each would swing out a little distance from the road and the two front teams—numbers one and two—would drive up facing each other. (Drannan 1900, 314)

With the teams turn toward the center and the wagon backs point outside, passengers and livestock are safer from attack and stampede than if they allow the animals too free a range. Drannan completes the preliminaries by appointing scouts and guards and superintending the election of a sergeant. When the wagon train reaches the South Platte River, Drannan is forced to kill nine Sioux and scalp them. To a squeamish female, he justifies his barbarism: "I told her that the Indians did not fear death, but hated the idea of being scalped." (Drannan 1900, 322) Such overdrawn trail techniques heighten the adventure of much of his writing and explain how he survived numerous close calls with death.

Virginian James Clyman, a contemporary of Kit Carson and William Drannan, recorded his observations of William Ashley's second expedition in *Journal of a Mountain Man* (1840). He claims to have read Shakespeare, saved fur trader William Sublette from a blizzard, discovered the South Pass through the Rockies, and advised the ill-fated Donner party not to get caught in the wintry passes of the Sierra Nevadas. In semiliterate English, Clyman tells how he sewed up Jedediah Smith's ear after a grizzly clawed it:

> Grissly did not hesitate a moment but sprung on the capt taking him by the head first pitc[h]ing sprawling on the earth he gave him a grab by the middle fortunately cat[c]hing by the ball pouch and Butcher K[n]ife which he broke out but breaking several of his ribs and cutting his head badly none of us having any su[r]gical Knowledge what was to be done one Said come take hold and he wuld say why not you so it went around. (Clyman 1984, 22)

Although unfamiliar with the rules of grammar and rhetoric, Clyman proves equal to trail first aid. He stanches the bleeding along Smith's left eye and ear where the bear had "laid the skull bare to near the crown of the head leaving a white streak whare his teeth passed."

Novelist Elizabeth Madox Roberts, a respected female regionalist, turned to a strong sense of place for *The Great Meadow* (1930), a historical novel about her Kentucky forebears. A gripping story told in the frontier tradition, the text describes the hardships of Indian raids and fortress exigencies on a staunch pioneer family: Diony Jarvis, her husband Berk, and Berk's mother, Elvira Jarvis. The murder and scalping of Elvira in 1778 sends Berk on a three-year trek in search of the killers. Unsettled by the mayhem that has disrupted her homelife, Diony sits at the distaff to spin flax. To herself she murmurs distractedly:

> See, your mishap. . . . Elvira . . . she came here . . . and thus . . . see. . . . He forgot me when the year was only half done. . . . He went off after revenge, to kill Indians to satisfy the death of his mother. (Roberts 1930, 271)

Roberts focuses on the emotional burden wrought by fear, trauma, and isolation. Left at the fort to fend for herself and the infant Tom, Diony judges the wilderness to be a frightening place and feels herself threatened in every owl hoot and stir of leaves.

Heightening the emotions of her characters, Roberts exaggerates the menace of frontier life with the vigorous hunting song "Bangum Went to a Wild Boar's Den," sung by woodsman Evan Muir. Spun out in chivalric tradition, the five verses recount the carnage of the hunt:

> Bangum drew his trusty knife,
>   Cut 'im down, cut 'im down.
> And he stabbed that wild boar outen his life,
>   Cut 'im down, cut 'im down.
> (Roberts 1930, 281)

The final stanza pictures Bangum inside the den, where the skeletons of a thousand men litter the floor. The even-numbered lines repeat their trochaic insistance on violence. With no hope of locating Berk, and fearful of additional attacks on her family, Diony chooses marriage to Muir as the only way to cope with insecurity and the loss of a male protector and hunter. Roberts cuts the hurried ceremony to Squire Boone's final three words, "Man and wife." (Roberts 1930, 292) The nuptial scene concludes with Diony and the other women slicing and distributing slices of melon, an evocative image of delicate fruit hacked apart for an impromptu celebration.

After a three-year hiatus of emotional trauma, Roberts places an additional onus on Diony. In 1781, her poignant reunion with her first husband tests the prevailing wilderness pragmatism. Diony runs to welcome Berk, now wearied and scarred from three years of fighting Shawnee. He steps awkwardly toward the Muir family hearth and spies Diony and Evan's son Michael in the cradle. Uncertain how to tell of his trials, Berk speaks a strained monologue as though justifying his abandonment of his loved ones:

> Whilst you run the gauntlet their drummer stands at the end and beats the drum, and council-house is down beyond the long line of the clubs. Once they got me down on the ground . . . halfway down the line, my head so numb with the blows I thought a hailstorm had come up. But I flung two off and dodged past the clubs and broke free. (Roberts 1930, 309–310)

The truncated bits and episodes spin out as Berk and Evan eye each other as warily as two fighting cocks, yet with the honesty and friendship that once bound them. A neighbor declares that the law of the frontier allows Diony to pick which of her husbands she will have and which must go. With a courtesy born of necessity in rustic surroundings, she sets out skins for Evan to sleep on and selects Berk once more as her mate. Her home secure and ready for night, Diony sits at the table, muddling over the end of an age, "a new order dawning out of the chaos that had beat through the house during the early part of the night." She recalls the image of Squire Boone, the empire builder, "[moving] securely among the chaotic things of the woods and the rivers." (Roberts 1930,

337–338) Resolute that she has done what is just and proper, she lays her child in the cradle and sinks gratefully into sleep.

Written a quarter century after Roberts's stark novel, Arkansan Janice Holt Giles's *Hannah Fowler* (1956) depicts the same set of problems faced by lone women on the frontier. Her protagonist, Hannah Moore, is long-legged, stout, and eligible, three worthy attributes of a woodsman's mate. Because of her father's sudden death on the trail, she arrives at Fort Pitt with little choice but to marry a local man. After selecting Tice Fowler, she manages well at their crude forest homestead with a small daughter and another child expected within weeks. After Indians nab Hannah, slaughter the livestock, and torch her house, she recalls Tice relating Daniel Boone's advice to captives, "act as natural as you kin, like you wan't botherin' none at all about bein' took. Jist go on like they was folks you was used to, do the best you kin, be cheerful-like, don't be stubborn or sulky." (Giles 1956, 181) Despite advice from a knowledgeable frontiersman, Hannah imagines her husband riding down her captors and setting her free. On her return, she exults: "Tice, she thought, with a rush of choking, fierce emotion, was the *best* man. Oh, she would have died had that Cherokee laid a hand to her!" (Giles 1956, 214) Forced to admit her fear of rape, Giles's heroine has reason to dread the one violation that could have cut off sympathy from the white community, leaving Hannah an untouchable among "decent" women.

Also published in 1956, Texan Fred Gipson's *Old Yeller* reiterates the hardships of the frontier wife. A rancher who studied journalism at the University of Texas, Gipson reported for the *Corpus Christi Caller* and the *San Angelo Times* and produced a series of Southwest works—*The Fabulous Empire: Colonel Zack Miller's Story* (1946), *Hound-Dog Man* (1949), *Big Bend: A Homesteader's Story* (1952), and *The Trail-Driving Rooster* (1955)—before composing his two popular works on the Coates family, *Old Yeller* and *Little Arliss* (1978). The first achieved a steady popularity among young-adult readers and succeeded as the 1963 Walt Disney film adaptation, for which Gipson coauthored the screenplay. Starring Dorothy McGuire as the laboring pioneer mother, the movie contrasted her reactions and bravery against that of four strong male figures—Fess Parker, Tommy Kirk, Kevin Corcoran, and Chuck Connors.

Gipson's first-person narrative, the bildungsroman of Travis Coates, a 14-year-old farm boy, covers action during the late 1860s, when Travis's father drives cattle from Salt Licks, Texas, to market at Abilene to earn "cash money." Left with man-size chores, Travis plows with Jumper the mule and shoots game for his mother and little brother Arliss while contemplating his father's parting words:

> Now, there's cows to milk and wood to cut and young pigs to mark and fresh meat to shoot. But mainly there's the corn patch. If you don't work it right or if you let the varmints eat up the roasting ears, we'll be without bread corn for the winter. (Gipson 1956, 3)

From dealings with "loafer wolves, bears, panthers, and raiding Indians" common to wild frontier settlements, Travis concludes that local cattlemen have no choice but to depart from home and leave their wives and children in charge:

"They needed money, and they realized that whatever a man does, he's bound to take some risks." (Gipson 1956, 4, 2)

Gipson's blend of nature's savagery and bounty forms a realistic, enduring tapestry of farm life on the Texas frontier. Travis's comic run-ins with the "big ugly slick-haired yeller [stray]" grow from grudging acceptance to adoration after Old Yeller saves little Arliss from a bear. Perhaps unintentionally, Gipson also moves Travis to admire the pragmatic mother figure. The author honors the frontier helpmeet as equal to a variety of challenges to home, livestock, sons, and self. As Travis's backup, she displays strength, guts, and a cool head for emergencies and on-the-scene decisions. Far from settlements offering medical care, she threads her needle with a strand from the mule's tail and patches up Old Yeller's wounds after he is gored by a wild range hog. Because the livestock are slaughtered too close to the house and water supply to leave to vultures, she drags the carcasses onto a distant bonfire. When a mad wolf threatens, she knocks it away from Old Yeller with a chinaberry pole and offers to shoot Old Yeller when she and Travis realize that the dog is contaminated with rabies. During her intense labors, Travis comments on her expertise at frontier cures:

> Mama nearly ran herself to death, packing fresh cold water from the spring, which she used to bathe me all over, trying to run my fever down. When she wasn't packing water, she was out digging prickly-pear roots and hammering them to mush in a sack, then binding the mush to my leg for a poultice. (Gipson 1956, 90)

Losing sleep while tending a wounded dog, willful mule, crippled teenager, and nettlesome small son, she is forced to improvise, as demonstrated by the drag that she ties to Jumper to impede him from devouring the corn. In Travis's words, "Altogether, Mama sure had her hands full." (Gipson 1956, 91)

In his father's absence, Travis adopts the tough female as his role model. From her he accepts direction, advice, and soothing words about wilderness terrors. In the end, however, Gipson reverts to the father for the sage commentary of the falling action. Papa's gift of a "cat-stepping blue roan" is welcome, yet not wonderful enough to counter the execution of Old Yeller. Papa remarks on the cruelty of life, then adds:

> But it isn't the only way life is. A part of the time, it's mighty good. And a man can't afford to waste all the good part, worrying about the bad parts. That makes it all bad. . . . You understand? (Gipson 1956, 116)

The lesson sinks in. Gipson balances the warmth of the boy-dog relationship with the harsh truth of plains life. Death is ever-present, whether an outgrowth of the hunt for food or protection of territory, in predatory wolves or vultures that devour animal carcasses, from pea vine or hydrophobia that can madden cattle and dogs, or the grisly demise of the cow-dog Bell from the snapping fangs of a disembodied rattlesnake head. When Papa evaluates the events that have pressed his family to the ends of energy, resources, and courage, he affirms Travis's maturity. In a week or so, Travis lets humor override his funk after little Arliss once more strips naked and frolics in Birdsong Creek, source of the family's drinking water. Along with him is the "bread-stealing speckled pup," the image of its sire, Old Yeller.

Described from the perspective of the early twentieth century, frontiers-woman Elinore Pruitt Stewart, a native of Fort Smith, Arkansas, lived the adventures that Roberts and Giles wrote about. Stewart collected and published *Letters of a Woman Homesteader* (1914) and *Letters on an Elk Hunt* (1915), a series of first-person anecdotes about her life on the Utah border in Burnt Fork, Wyoming. A *Wall Street Journal* book reviewer describes her lavishly detailed letters as "a warmly delightful, vigorously affirmative chronicle." (Stewart 1988, flap) Although isolated on a cattle ranch in 1909, she joys in prairie beauty: "It was too beautiful a night to sleep, so I put my head out to look and to think." (Stewart 1988, 11) Stewart's contemplative nature enhances the lyricism of her style, yet she avoids gushiness with a balance of realism and humor. Her catalog of Christmas treats proves the frontier to be heartier of menu than drier sources claim: She names a spread of geese, hams, hens, doughnuts, rye bread, coffee cake, fruitcake, seeds, nuts, fruit, and jelly. In a droll scene in which locals tweak a Yankee tenderfoot, she cites their dialogue:

> The punchers hurriedly made their beds, as they did so twitting N'Yawk about making his between our tent and the fire. "You're dead right, pard," I heard one of them say, "to make your bed there, fer if them outlaws comes this way they'll think you air one of the women and they won't shoot you. Just us *men* air in danger." (Stewart 1988, 168–169)

These lighthearted scenarios suggest that Stewart's wit and good nature sustained her during a long, lonely residence on the northwestern frontier. A passage from *Letters on an Elk Hunt* displays another side of her observations with opinions about "bunch shooting." After she finds an elk cow bled to death and the tracks of a wandering calf, she is nauseated by evidence that the young stays near the mother until starvation or predators put an end to its misery. She and her husband denounce the style of hunting that haphazardly wounds an animal and leaves it writhing. To Stewart, the method is indecent.

In contrast with Stewart's home-centered narrative, Nat Love migrated west from Tennessee and, as a professional rodeo rider, stayed on the move. The fact that he left a memoir of frontier life is of prime importance to African-American history, for he was one of the few to leave a written record. His informative if inflated autobiography, *The Life and Adventures of Nat Love, Better Known in the Cattle Country as Deadwood Dick* (1907), claims to give a true account of slavery days and to report life on the cattle ranges and plains of the "wild and woolly" West. Born into slavery in June 1854 in Davidson County, Tennessee, he and his siblings, Jordan and Sally, grew up on Robert Love's plantation outside Nashville and lived in a log cabin, which he pictured in a pen-and-ink drawing. He has little to say about his father, a plantation foreman and Union army carpenter, or his mother, a kitchen domestic and weaver. Emancipation left the Love family poor and eager for education.

After hiring out as spare labor on neighboring plantations, Love worked his father's tobacco fields. Following his father's death, he took charge of the family and walked six miles to a job that paid $1.50 per month. An after-hours job breaking colts initiated his career as a horseman and ranch hand. When his uncle began supporting the family, Love headed for the fabled Dodge City, Kansas. His boss supplied "a saddle, bridle and spurs, chaps, a pair of blankets and a fine .45 Colt revolver," the basics for a ranch hand. (Love 1988, 41) The first expedition toward the Texas panhandle put Love's party in jeopardy from a hundred plains Indians, who stampeded their herd. While working at the Duval Ranch in Texas and later at the Gillinger Ranch in Arizona, he learned the rudiments of the lariat, branding iron, rifle, and pistol, and took part in shootouts with bandits. As a necessary adjunct to his work with *vaqueros*, he learned Spanish. During calving and branding sessions, he and other cowboys "lived, ate and often slept in the saddle, as they covered many hundreds of miles in a very short space of time." (Love 1988, 47) Their chores took them to Montana, Wyoming, the Dakotas, and Nebraska, where Love fought horse thieves, rustlers, and more Indians.

The height of Love's career came on July 4, 1876, at a rodeo in Deadwood, South Dakota, where he earned the nickname "Deadwood Dick." He describes his win with straightforward boast:

> I roped, threw, tied, bridled, saddled and mounted my mustang in exactly nine minutes from the crack of the gun. The time of the next nearest competitor was twelve minutes and thirty seconds. This gave me the record and championship of the West, which I held up to the time I quit the business in 1890, and my record has never been beaten. (Love 1988, 93)

Simultaneous with Love's victory in the arena came the news of General George Armstrong Custer's defeat, which caused local authorities to prepare for widespread Indian revolt. The return trip took Love through hostile territory, but he declares that his party was fearless in "Redskin" territory.

Love's insouciance proved his undoing in October 1876, when an unidentified group of Indians in Yellow Horse Canyon shot him in the leg and captured him after he used up his ammunition. His captors dressed the wound and offered membership in the tribe. Love took part in the medicine dance and married a native princess, whose dowry enriched him by a hundred ponies. After a daring nighttime departure, he returned to work in Dodge City, then rode northeast to Junction City, Kansas, over the Haze and Elsworth Trail. His memoir describes an acquaintance with William H. Bonney, alias Billy the Kid, who drank with Love in a saloon in Antonshico, New Mexico. Love confirms Billy's excuse for shooting men who worked for John Chisholm (Chisum), an employer who cheated Billy of his wages. Love claims to have witnessed Billy's death after lawman Pat Garret ambushed him at Pete Maxwell's ranch in Lincoln County, New Mexico.

Love's autobiography concludes with success and optimism. While working 20 years as a drover and wrangler throughout the American Southwest and Mexico, he acquired a reputation for recognizing cattle brands, hunting buffalo for ranch meat, and performing fancy lariat and riding tricks. At age 46, he fell in love in Mexico:

> I saw a handsome young Spanish girl standing in the yard and I suppose I fell

in love with her at first sight, anyway I pretended to be very thirsty and rode up and asked her for a drink. (Love 1988, 125)

After she followed him on the trail, he married her, and in 1890 settled in Colorado and took a job on the Denver and Rio Grande Railroad at $15 per month as a Pullman porter, one of the professions that offered upward mobility to black males. At age 54, he completed his autobiography, which he dedicated to his mother and his wife Alice.

Much of Love's autobiography appears to draw on the frontier convention of the tall tale. He claims that horses were shot out from under him and that his body survived numerous bullets, one of which passed through him and killed his mount. In the final chapter, he boasts that he knew Buffalo Bill, Kit Carson, Frank and Jesse James, Kiowa Bill, and Yellowstone Kelley. Love's moralizing, astonishing deeds, and bold assertions of on-the-scene knowledge of much of the West's history suggests that he had a failing for romance, a standard feature of frontier literature.

A popular Texas folklore collector and writer of frontier life and history, James Frank Dobie—"The Story Teller of the Southwest"—used his western experience for literary purposes. A career newspaper reporter for the *Galveston Tribune* and the *San Antonio Express*, he completed a Ph.D. at Southwestern, Columbia, and the University of Texas and served as a gunnery officer in World War I. After a lengthy career in education, he pursued Southwest lore, a will-o'-the-wisp topic that carried no academic cachet. Dobie ignored trends and turned himself into an expert at unwritten southwestern literature. He published articles on the Old West in *Country Gentleman*, *New Mexico*, *Arizona Highways*, *Southwest Review*, *Natural History*, *Outdoor Life*, *Vogue*, *Saturday Evening Post*, *New York Herald Tribune*, *Magazine of the South*, *Frontier Times*, *American Gun*, and *Texas Game and Fish*. Before it was fashionable to champion the fragile ecology of the open range, Dobie challenged federal programs encouraging the extermination of the prairie dog, coyote, and other predatory animals, and wrote knowledgeably about rattlers, jackrabbits, whitetails, grizzlies, coyotes, panthers, wolves, skunks, and roadrunners. Fired from his role as maverick professor of the University of Texas, he settled on Paisano Ranch outside Austin and continued to write a newspaper column on frontier tradition and pursue his political agenda while publishing *A Vaquero of the Brush Country* (1930), *Coronado's Children* (1930), *The Longhorns* (1941), *Guide to Life and Literature of the Southwest* (1943), *Tales of Old-Time Texas* (1955), *Cow People* (1964), and *Some Part of Myself* (1967), a posthumous memoir of his teaching days. He worked as a consultant on American history for the Library of Congress and promoter of the Texas Folklore Society. Dobie accepted an honorary doctorate from Cambridge, and a few days before his death in Austin in 1964, received from Lyndon Johnson the Presidential Medal of Freedom.

Steeped in frontier lore, Dobie earned his reputation for meticulous scholarship offset by colorful frontier exaggeration. His love of a romantic yarn is evident in *Apache Gold and Yaqui Silver* (1928), a collection of stories about prospectors and lost mines culled from long interviews with Nat Straw, an elderly retired prospector eager to share his stories of mining folklore. Dobie's salute to the western horse, *The Mustang* (1934), is studded with anecdotes such as his picture of the Spanish equestrian: "In contrast to Arabian warriors, *caballeros* preferred riding stallions to mares as more powerful and proud. In battle some of their war stallions bit and kicked the barbarous Indians." (Dobie 1952, 22) In *The Ben Lilly Legend* (1950), Dobie re-creates the legendary career of a famed Alabama tracker and bear and panther hunter who stalked game over Mississippi, Louisiana, Texas, and Mexico, at one time serving Teddy Roosevelt as chief huntsman. The dash of Dobie's stories includes a night that Lilly, wearied by quarrying a female bear, sleeps by its carcass. He awakens to a curious muzzle and growl and empties his rifle in the dark. Unperturbed, Lilly goes back to sleep. The next day, he locates the well-drilled corpse of the male, which had come in search of its mate.

A gutsy hunter, Dobie details scenes of the kill not meant for the fainthearted. In *The Ben Lilly Legend*, he typifies Southern hunters like Lilly as "Big Knives," wielders of the Bowie knife, "the bloodiest instrument ever utilized in American bloodletting," rather than the standard western six-gun. (Dobie 1978, 57) Alongside pictures of Lilly's knives, Dobie corroborates tales of the huntsmen's curiosity about smithy shops, where they reshaped files, rasps, springs, and other steel objects into knives. Dobie compares utilitarian hunting weapons to the Mexican machete and gentleman's hunting knife. He tempered the blades of his killing and skinning knives to break rather than bend and cooled them in panther oil to a "drake-neck" color, then hafted them with buckhorn. Meticulous about its shape, Lilly claimed to need a knife that gouged rather than plunged in. He wanted a two-edged blade so sharp from tip to haft "that if he got it inside a bear it would cut in any direction he pulled or twisted it." (Dobie 1978, 61)

Three serious recorders of frontier life—Willa Cather, John Ehle, and Dee Brown—depart from the southwestern tall tale for the social and historical slant on pioneering. A keen observer of the Midwest, Virginian Willa Cather established her position among the outstanding writers of frontier tradition, which include Mary Hunter Austin, Ambrose Bierce, James Fenimore Cooper, Bret Harte, Francis Parkman, and Mark Twain. In her greatest works— *O Pioneers!* (1913) and *My Ántonia* (1918)—she focuses on the character-building events that bolster families and communities for the hardships that come from pulling up stakes and moving to the swaying savannah covering much of the Midwestern plains. One of the country's premiere prairie realists, Cather devoted much of her serene pastoral writing to diverse reflections of agrarian life, religious outreach, and immigrant culture of the Midwest and Southwest. Her canon of Americana is rooted in the prairie and graced with the spectacle of desert crag and rugged arroyo. She adorns human scenarios with the commonplace faith and good works of rural people. Partially because of the feminist movement, biographies and critiques of her works have undergone late-twentieth-century reexamination, and have found broader influence on college and university reading lists.

A native of Winchester, Virginia, Cather and her family moved west in 1884, in the final decade of true pioneer settlement. At age 11 she experienced the cultural mix of French-Canadian, Bohemian, German, Swiss, and Scandinavian immigrants. The open range with its vastness and grandeur changed her from a sheltered Southern child into a tough, self-possessed plainswoman. Her affection for Red Cloud, Nebraska, a railroad and marketing center of 2,500 residents, provided her with details for a fictional setting, alternately named Black Hawk, Frankfort, Sweetwater, and Moonstone. Her nostalgic reminiscence pictures the spare existence in the backwoods of the Nebraska Divide where she rode her pony to visit Scandinavian, French Catholic, German, Russian, or Central European neighbors, or to frequent the grave of Chief Red Cloud's daughter.

A newspaper columnist and drama critic for the *Lincoln State Journal* her junior year, Cather settled in Pittsburgh, then returned to Nebraska to refresh her memory of the vigor and promise of the plains. The refocusing of creativity on sense impressions gelled into clear pictures of Midwest settings in which her characters came to life. Her second novel, *O Pioneers!* exalts the beauty of the plains, which up to that time had received little notice in fiction. Five years later, she produced a masterwork, *My Ántonia*, a nostalgic piece that lauds compassion, charity, and acceptance of outsiders, three virtues that eased the hard, isolated immigrant life. In addition to novels, Cather contributed short fiction and poetry to *Cosmopolitan, Youth's Companion, Harper's, Collier's, Woman's Home Companion, Smart Set, Atlantic, Ladies' Home Journal, Commonweal,* and *Scholastic.* Her canon received favorable commentary from critics H. L. Mencken, Maxwell Geismar, Lionel Trilling, and Edmund Wilson as well as author Katherine Anne Porter, and garnered the 1930 Pulitzer Prize.

A gifted historian, North Carolinian John Ehle was similarly drawn to the human side of pioneering. His major work, *The Trail of Tears: The Rise and Fall of the Cherokee Nation* (1988), cites journals, government documents, speeches, and other untapped sources in a stirring study of the removal of the Cherokee from the East Coast to Indian territory. Embedded in the diaspora are the stories of Sequoyah, inventor of the Cherokee alphabet; Tsali, a martyr who surrendered to executioners to save his people from displacement; Elias Boudinot, editor of the *Cherokee Phoenix;* Stand Watie, a military leader; and two Cherokee peacemakers, Major Ridge and John Ross. Corroborative information tells of Cherokee ball games, the establishment of the tribe's printing press, burial customs, migrations, and child rearing. Ehle concludes that displacement of the preponderance of five Eastern tribes—notably the Cherokee Nation—disoriented and disrupted family and town life and resulted in the deaths of 4,000 Native Americans.

Ehle's method of research and reportage also served archivist and historian Dee Brown, one of the most distinguished authorities on the West. A renowned storyteller and author of 30 adult and juvenile works of fiction, history, and chronicle, Arkansan Brown focuses on the Civil War, Native Americans, and the American frontier. As he explains in his autobiographical *When the Century Was Young* (1993), he feels a greater kinship with the nineteenth century, the time of Buffalo Bill Cody, Teddy Roosevelt, "Mrs. George Armstrong Custer, and real cowboys and Indians, including Hollow-Horn Bear, the Sioux chief whose face appeared on a postage stamp after his death." (Brown 1993, 9) Brown's ability to resituate his spirit in the past has proved a blessing to history, sociology, and literature because his patient, reflective studies of significant moments in the white settlement of the plains has produced some of the most influential commentary on Native American and cavalry history.

Brown's first historical novel sprang from stories his grandmother told about Davy Crockett. He crafted the unpublished episodes into a novel, *Wave High the Banner* (1942), a deliberately cheerful, patriotic work. During a stint in the military at Camp Forrest, Tennessee, Brown teamed with Martin Schmitt, a librarian, editor, and curator, to coauthor three books on the frontier—*The Fighting Indians of the West* (1948), *Trail Driving Days* (1952), and *The Settlers West* (1955). After World War II, Brown edited *Agriculture History* and assembled research data for two westerns—*Yellowhorse* (1957) and *Galvanized Yankees* (1963)—and articles on frontier themes published in *American History Illustrated, Esquire, Christian Science Monitor, Civil War Times, Southern Magazine,* and *Hinterland.* He collected data on women for *The Gentle Tamers: Women of the Old Wild West* (1958), a tribute to familiar and obscure frontierswomen, including rodeo rider Tillie Baldwin, temperance activist Carry Nation, gunfighter Rose of Cimarron, teamster Arizona Mary, teacher Martha Summerhayes, Ute captive Josephine Meeker, suffragist Clarina Irene Nichols, Wyoming justice of the peace Esther McQuigg Morris, Virginia City madame Julia Bulette, cross-dressing soldier Loretta Valasquez, actresses Lola Montez and Lotta Crabtree, memoirist Elizabeth Custer, Donner party victim Virginia Reed, and one victim commemorated on her headstone only as "Woman." (Brown 1958, 17)

In 1962, Brown returned to male-oriented western history with *The Fetterman Massacre* (originally titled *Fort Phil Kearney: An American Saga*). A grueling recreation of events leading up to the second major American military wipeout, the history details the elements of the 1866 disaster after Sioux, Cheyenne, and Arapaho braves annihilated all 80 cavalrymen under the command of Lieutenant Colonel William J. Fetterman. Brown probed untapped sources—letters, eyewitnesses, and court testimony from a congressional investigation of Colonel Henry B. Carrington's role in the debacle. Critics lauded Brown for fairness and objectivity, two traits that mark his best-seller *Bury My Heart at Wounded Knee* (1970), a bracing critique of racism and genocide. An iconoclast, he departs from the accepted notions about the country's past for his most impressive chronicle, which challenges established notions of manifest destiny and condemns a favorite era of American lore as rampant imperialism and the cause of displacement and manifold miseries suffered by a targeted population of native tribes. The book has earned prominence among multicultural classics as a reputable reference source and the first of a deluge of retrospectives on American plains settlement from a nonwhite point of view.

Contemplating the westering movement, Brown surmised that writers were centered on white immigrants in the West to the exclusion of an equal number of Native Americans who were making the same move, although under duress rather than by choice. After intense research using speeches, maps, duty rosters, treaties, and memoirs on both sides, Brown concluded that an American epic needed to be written. He added that his perusal of military reports discloses falsification of the number and significance of army victories over Native Americans. To frame his themes, he takes the title from the last line of Stephen Vincent Benét's poem "American Names," a reminder of white America's grievous past. An adept spokesman for Native Americans, Brown exposed a reprehensible motif of opportunism and treachery by Indian agents and the self-serving Bureau of Indian Affairs. He disclosed unpunished acts of desecration, arson, rape, infanticide, murder, and theft committed by settlers against tribes inhabiting prime grazing land. In an overview, Brown described the westering movement as catastrophic for the Native Americans—an extreme misapplication of the white reverence for personal freedom. Stripping the era of glamour, he condemned white plains heroes for violence and greed, and upbraided historians for romanticism and rationalization of wrongful acts.

Public reaction was swift and intense. Media interest in Brown's muckraking forced a nationwide reexamination of the settlement of the American West, which he depicts as a blatant land grab and unprecedented genocide. Scores of journals and newspapers published heated arguments about patriotic bias, racial superiority, and revisionism, a blanket accusation against any historical research that turns up new evidence to dispute old claims. Individuals accused Brown of exonerating savagery by belittling such western heroes as General George Armstrong Custer, General William T. Sherman, and Colonel John Chivington, and questioning the governance of Presidents Abraham Lincoln and Ulysses S. Grant.

Brown's supporters countered that his evenhanded study of the Native American point of view is a necessary correction of an era of chauvinism, missionary zeal, jingoism, and double-talk regarding Native American rights. His inclusion of interviews, oral biography, and pictorial evidence gleaned from 270 unpublished photographs of cavalry brutality encouraged historians to reevaluate pompous texts that heap honor on some of the country's most duplicitous, genocidal military leaders. He also calls to account unscrupulous newspaper hacks intent on satisfying reader demand for bloody sagas of the Old West. Overall, reviewers admit that his study of native attitudes toward frontiersmen and cavalry set a precedent for historical analysis.

Brown followed *Bury My Heart* with a less severe chronicle, *Hear That Lonesome Whistle Blow: Railroads in the West* (1977), an exposé of railroad corruption. A repetition of Brown's traditional themes, the chronicle cites multiple examples of white entrepreneurs discounting and overriding Native American rights to valuable land. He justifies Sitting Bull's angry backlash after work crews overran the Yellowstone Valley:

> The reason the surveyors had come into this area was that the owners of the Northern Pacific Railroad had decided to change its route, abandoning the line through previously ceded lands and invading unceded lands without any consultation with the Indians. (Brown 1977, 205)

These and other unflattering comments about arrogant rail owners and self-serving public policy so enraged the Association of American Railroads and

Union Pacific that officials refused Brown access to their private library.

Late in Brown's career, *Bury My Heart* continued to draw the most critical attention. It began to appear on reading lists for high school and college courses in American history and was reissued in 1990, the centennial of the Wounded Knee massacre. An eloquent blend of history and philosophy, Brown's famed reassessment of the Old West remains his masterwork. Now in his late eighties, he still writes about the frontier and challenges illusions of western glory, which he characterizes as an attempt to rid North America of its aboriginal population. (Auchincloss 1965; Blain et al. 1990; Bradbury 1996; Brown 1945, 1958, 1962, 1970, 1977, 1993; Buck 1992; Carmony 1992; Cather 1977, 1991; Clyman 1984; Coyner 1995; Davidson and Wagner-Martin 1995; *DISCovering Authors* 1993; Dobie 1952, 1978, 1990, 1996; Drannan 1900; Ehle 1988; Ehrlich and Carruth 1982; Estell 1993; Fuller 1961; Giles 1956; Kunitz 1942; Lamar 1977; Love 1988; Low and Clift 1981; McVoy 1940; Portis 1968; Roberts 1930; Sherr and Kazickas 1994; Stewart 1979, 1988; Stewart and Ponce 1986)

See also Boone, Daniel; humor, Southern; Lomax, John; Rawlings, Marjorie Kinnan; short fiction in Southern literature; Simms, William Gilmore.

FUGITIVE AGRARIANS

The phenomenon of the Fugitive Agrarians arises from a period of self-consciousness and ferment within a coterie of conservative literary colleagues and students at Vanderbilt University and among interested townspeople in Nashville, Tennessee, during the 1920s. An elitist group composed of white males and formed at the end of World War I, the Fugitive Agrarians were jokingly lampooned as antiprogressives, Luddites, and neo-Confederates. As such, they defied national trends, particularly inclusion of minority races and religions, one-sided prosperity that omitted the South, and a false progress that threatened the social structure that made their homeland unique. They withdrew allegiance from American literature as a whole to the confines of the South as a viable cultural entity—one worth examining, cultivating, upgrading, and shielding from trends and other intrusions not suited to its needs. A circle of modern Southern literati interested in artistic and literary theory, they focused on styles of expression and writing indigenous to the South, and sought to supplant with a rigorous verse style and content the post–Civil War nature lore of Sidney Lanier and the confections and sighings of Paul Hamilton Hayne and other fussy and pretentious authors whom outsiders viewed as the region's only contribution to poetry.

As individual writers, the Fugitive Agrarians—led by Robert Penn Warren, John Crowe Ransom, Merrill Moore, Allen Tate, and Donald Davidson and later joined by John Gould Fletcher, Cleanth Brooks, Randall Jarrell, Stark Young, Andrew Lytle, and John Donald Wade—nurtured their vision of Southern culture. They sought to maintain its integrity in a geographic area threatened by the media, the soullessness of science, the empty promises of modern advertising and hucksterism, industrial pollution, and a plutocracy intent on building

In the 1920s, some writers and poets among Vanderbilt University, Nashville, Tennessee, faculty and students, as well as citizens chose to resist changes in American literature. Known as Fugitive Agrarians, they exalted order and decorum and urged compassion for those Southerners who yearned for a return to the old rural life. Some of the Fugitive Agrarians met again in 1956; left to right: Allen Tate, Merrill Moore, Robert Penn Warren (standing), John Crowe Ransom, and Donald Davidson.

money markets to the detriment of integrity and the value of the individual. Primarily, the Fugitive Agrarians targeted the burgeoning industrialization of the post-Reconstruction era as an insidious threat to agrarian values, which extend to region, family, dynasty, religious faith, local history, and the Southern code of honor. Central to their theory was an exaltation of order and decorum and a compassion for the industrialized Southerner whose heart and spirit yearned beyond the throb and hum of factories and mills to the furrowed cornfields, stands of longleaf pine, unsullied mountain streams, and oyster bays of the traditional homeland.

Deeply rooted in the South and suspicious of progress for its own sake, poet Donald Davidson delineated regional goals and warned that change was not necessarily progressive or beneficial, especially to the only Americans up to that time to have been defeated in war. He produced "The Artist as Southerner" for the May 1926 issue of *Saturday Review,* an essay setting the parameters of Southernism and pinpointing the dangers of modernism to writers and artists of a unique area. A veteran of World War I steeped in Southern history, he inculcated rigidly parochial tenets and aims in his classrooms at Vanderbilt and the Bread Loaf School of English and in his work as literary editor of the *Tennessean.* His outstanding volumes of verse—*An Outland Piper* (1924), *The Tall Men* (1927), and *Lee in the Mountains and Other Poems* (1927)—preceded *The Attack on Leviathan* (1938), a jeremiad that opposes the political, educational, and economic mongrelizing of the United States, and a two-volume work, *The Tennessee* (1948), a classic segment of the Rivers of America Series. An unreconstructed Southerner, he was famous for rebutting Abraham Lincoln's call for national unity with an exaltation of sectionalism, which he described as the basis of democracy. In *Still Rebels, Still Yankees* (1957), he plotted a new course for the South that was high in moral convictions and intent on a regional artistry second to none.

Like Davidson and his peers at Vanderbilt, Allen Tate turned his creative energies and exacting analysis toward illuminating the threat of modernity to the traditions that gave the Old South strength and identity. A noted teacher, biographer, novelist, commentator, poet, and editor of the *Sewanee Review,* he pursued a varied career that took him to the English departments at seven universities. He published two biographies, *Stonewall Jackson: The Good Soldier* (1928) and *Jefferson Davis: His Rise and Fall* (1929), and *The Fathers* (1938), his only novel. Tate's poetry and criticism appear in *Reactionary Essays on Poetry and Ideas* (1936), *Reason in Madness* (1941), and *The Limits of Poetry* (1949). His war poem "Ode to the Confederate Dead" (1922) holds a respectable position in the American canon of battlefield verse for its reflection of Southern classicism drawn from Greek models.

Similarly talented in several disciplines, Tennessean John Crowe Ransom, a Rhodes scholar, was a prolific writer, critic, and commentator who taught for a quarter century at Vanderbilt and influenced a second generation of Fugitive Agrarians. A skilled imagist and ironist with a gift for concreteness, he served as the movement's facile spokesman while writing for the *American Review* and editing the *Kenyon Review,* an influential critical quarterly in American and international circles. Publication of his *Poems about God* (1919), *Chills and Fever* (1921), *Two Gentlemen in Bonds* (1926), and *Selected Poems* (1945) provided some of the early twentieth century's best poetry. His essays, compiled in *God without Thunder* (1930), set forth the opposing fields of humanism and science and forced the student of literature to contemplate technology's fearful challenge to human endeavors. His clarification of the Fugitive Agrarians' intent appears in *The World's Body* (1938) and *The New Criticism* (1941). Speaking personally yet forcefully of the era's shift toward dense, contemplative verse, Ransom proclaims obscurity a necessary adjunct of the serious modern poet: "Apostate, illaureate, and doomed to outlawry the modern poets may be. I have the feeling that modernism is an unfortunate road for them to have taken. But it was an inevitable one." (Beatty et al. 1952, 760) Calling for precision and technical mastery, he declares the complexity of modern art a predictable outgrowth of the 1920s and applauds figurative expression that conveys the dilemmas and challenges of an exacting, often puzzling age.

Robert Penn Warren, a prolific member of the Fugitive Agrarians and winner of a Pulitzer Prize in both verse and fiction, contributed to the group's intense dedication to writing, criticism, and teaching. A distinguished Rhodes scholar, he edited the *Southern Review* and was anthologized in innovative English textbooks. Deeply committed to psychological fiction, Warren produced a heroic poem, *Brother to Dragons* (1953), and a classic literary essay, "Pure and Impure Poetry" (1942). His historical novel *Night Rider* (1939) amplifies the local issues of a late-nineteenth-century tobacco war. Similarly concerned with political upheaval, *Band of Angels* (1955), a romance set in the Civil War era, details the personal sufferings of Amantha Starr, a pampered Kentucky plantation belle who learns at her father's funeral that she is a mulatto. Filmed in 1957, the screen adaptation pairs Yvonne de Carlo with Clark Gable, who plays the buccaneer who purchases her from the slave block. Key to the drama are the roles of Efrem Zimbalist, Jr., and Sidney Poitier, the black foster son drawn to defend both his white father and the emerging black rebellion in New Orleans.

In themes and settings drawn from the twentieth century, Warren achieved popularity with his powerful social novel *All the King's Men* (1946), a study of the dynamic populism of Willie Stark, a fictional character resembling Huey P. "Kingfish" Long, an idolized rabble-rouser and governor of Arkansas. The novel's perceptive account of the rise and fall of a demagogue won Warren recognition as novelist and moralist. The emergence of Stark as golden-tongued reformer for the people conceals *sub rosa* his scheming, bullying, and blackmail, which require compromise and deal-making with the seamy political machines of his predecessors. In a typical stump speech, he leans into the crowd as though singling out one potential voter for an intimate confidence:

> Folks, there's going to be a leetle mite of trouble back in town. Between me and that Legislature-ful of hyena-headed, feist-faced, belly-dragging sons of slack-gutted she-wolves. If you know what I mean. Well, I been looking at them and their kind so long, I just figured I'd take me a little trip and see what human folks look like in the face before I clean forgot. (Warren 1974, 145–146)

He demands that the people look into their own hearts for truth before judging him. He adds, "Not in a book. Not in a lawyer's book. Not on any scrap of paper. In your heart." The animal response roars and swells to a ritual soul-cleansing. To his supporters he yells, "O Lord, and I have seen a sign!" Warren concludes with confidence in Willie's control of the crowd: "He could do it, too. For he had the goods." (Warren 1974, 147)

Like the response to a revival altar call, the cheap sentiment and phony camaraderie works, for Warren's novel, the Mercury Theater radio script, and the resulting screenplay. Filmed in 1949 by Columbia, the cinema version focuses on similar crowd-pleasing antics and posturing that win local support. The movie stars Broderick Crawford as the wily politico Willie Stark, and features John Ireland, Mercedes McCambridge, Joanne Dru, and John Derek. A graphic screen creation of American-style corruption, betrayal, and cunning, it earned Oscars for best picture and Crawford and McCambridge's roles; it was nominated by the Academy for writing, editing, and direction and the supporting role of John Ireland. Later in Warren's career he wrote *World Enough and Time* (1950), *The Cave* (1959), and *A Place To Come To* (1977), none of which approached the taut plotting, scope, and psychological intensity of *All the King's Men*.

During the blossoming of these individual careers, the Fugitive Agrarians throve in a rare example of Southern literary symbiosis. The publication of *Fugitive* magazine in 19 issues from 1922 to 1925 gave voice to the entire Vanderbilt circle and formally initiated a period of American aestheticism known as the Southern Renaissance. The aim of the magazine was the preservation of the best in Southern qualities: love of land, respect for nature, spirituality, commitment to family, and the rugged individualism that sustained the South during the Civil War and Reconstruction. Simultaneously, the Renaissance school of writers, who prefigured the dislocation of World War II, countered the dehumanization of urbanism and rampant growth of the factory system. The ferment of the Fugitive Agrarians paralleled a simultaneous burst of cultural and artistic enthusiasm in the Harlem Renaissance, a black artistic rebirth characterized by the literary agility and taste of Southerners James Weldon Johnson and Arna Bontemps, both activists intent on legitimizing the black experience as material worthy of high artistic aims.

The first formal publication of the Fugitive Agrarians' unified objectives took shape in an aggressive literary manifesto, *I'll Take My Stand* (1930), the outspoken declaration of a symposium of 12 critics—Donald Davidson, John Gould Fletcher, Henry Blue Kline, Lyle H. Lanier, Andrew Nelson Lytle, Herman Clarence Nixon, Frank Lawrence Owsley, John Crow Ransom, Allen Tate, John Donald Wade, Robert Penn Warren, and Stark Young. The text establishes the domain of literature and a demarcation between humanism and the rise of science. A second symposium, *Who Owns America?* (1936), resituated the tenets of agrarianism among small landowners and businesses. A defiance of big business and encroaching liberal views, the symposium attempted to shore up the crumbling facade of the Vanderbilt cabal, but made its stand too late in the group's evolution to stem dissent, self-destruction, and media ridicule. The *Yale Review* taunted the Agrarians' reactionary mode in witty needling: "In Dixie Land twelve take their stand and shed their ink for Dixie." (Karanikas 1966, 175) The Agrarian leadership acknowledged the movement's inability to generalize beyond a limited economic premise and its failure to stir a true renaissance distinctive enough to build on the momentum of the 1920s, but the central committee remained mum on the hegemony of a closed circle of 12 white males.

Despite the movement's dissolution, individual products of the Vanderbilt experiment were manifold and steadily gained influence in national literary criticism, creative research, and teaching. Ransom nurtured a point of reference in a book called *The New Criticism* (1941), which focuses on literature rather than on the author or the circumstances of its creation. Another branch of learning influenced by the hybridized Fugitive Agrarianism was the textbook authorship of Cleanth Brooks and Robert Penn Warren. They produced three influential and enduring overviews: *Understanding Poetry* (1938), *Understand-*

ing Fiction (1943), and *Understanding Drama* (1945). Brooks, a Rhodes scholar, taught at Louisiana State University and edited the *Southern Review*. His innovative classroom technique energized the teaching of explication and appreciation by holding meaning at the forefront of literary study and decentralizing the importance of metrics and literary devices such as metaphor, simile, alliteration, and other technical terms that often stymie and alienate students of literature. Brooks revolutionized the study of Southern dialect with *The Relation of the Alabama-Georgia Dialect to the Provincial Dialects of Great Britain* (1935) and *A Southern Treasury of Life and Literature* (1937), both essential to the pedagogy and literary history unique to the South. In his critical editions, *Modern Poetry and the Tradition* (1939) and *The Well Wrought Urn* (1947), he applied the distinctive New Criticism method to classic English poets from past generations.

To the consternation of devout Fugitive Agrarians, Social historian Wilbur Joseph "Jack" Cash published *The Mind of the South* (1941), the upshot of research into the basis and structure of Southern values. Less literary than his contemporaries, he spoke harsh truths about the shift in values and outlook that permeated Southern fiction, particularly the realism of Erskine Caldwell, Thomas Wolfe, Lillian Hellman, and William Faulkner:

> However much the new Southern authors might differ in their approach to their material, and regardless of what faults they might still display, nearly all of them had decisively escaped from the old Southern urge to turn the country into Never-Never Land, that nearly all of them stood, intellectually at least, pretty decisively outside the legend: and so were able to contribute to the region its first literature of any bulk and importance. (Cash 1941, 379)

Denounced by Richmond Beatty and Donald Davidson, the most dogged of the Vanderbilt faithful, *The Mind of the South* outlasted the dicta of the Fugitive Agrarians and made an indelible mark on Southern history and culture, remaining on college and graduate school reading lists under the headings of history, literature, journalism, sociology, and psychology. Of its incisive commentary, C. Vann Woodward declared, "It would be impossible to prove, but I would venture to guess that no other book on Southern history rivals Cash's in influence among laymen and few among professional historians." (McKnight and Romine 1977, 1C)

Succeeding generations of writers, teachers, journalists, and critics who took the New Critics as their point of departure produced their own distinctive marks on Southern literature, particularly essayist Tom Wolfe, journalist Hodding Carter, literary historian Louis D. Rubin, Jr., and critic C. Hugh Holman, author of *A Handbook to Literature*, a standard work on the shelves of writers, editors, teachers, and librarians, now in its seventh edition. The creative writing to emerge from the Southern Renaissance includes plays by Kermit Turner, Lula Vollmer, and Paul Green; Truman Capote and Flannery O'Connor's short fiction and novellas; Fred Chappell's fiction and poetry; Harper Lee, Ralph Ellison, Walker Percy, and William Styron's unique novels; and the energetic individualism of Shelby Foote, Caroline Gordon, Ernest J. Gaines, John A. Williams, Shirley Ann Grau, Reynolds Price, Elizabeth Spencer, Peter Taylor, Katherine

Anne Porter, Calder Willingham, Ellen Glasgow, Frank Yerby, and Margaret Walker. (Beatty et al. 1952; Blotner 1997; Bradbury 1993; Bradbury 1996; Brooks and Warren 1976; Brooks et al. 1973; Cash 1941; Cunliffe 1987; Gross 1971; Johnson, Greg 1997; Karanikas 1966; Koppelman 1995; Kunitz 1942, 1955; McKnight and Romine 1977; Parsons 1969; Rubin and Jacobs 1961; Rubin et al. 1985; Stewart 1962, 1965; Warren 1974, 1980; Wilson and Ferris 1989)

See also Capote, Truman; Ellison, Ralph; Lee, Harper; Lee, Robert E.; the Mississippi River; O'Connor, Flannery; poetry of the South; Styron, William; theater in the South; Walker, Margaret.

GAINES, ERNEST J.

One of the South's revered Creole novelists, Ernest James Gaines has been called a bayou griot. He can reflect on a time when he had to hide in the bathroom of the insurance agency where he worked part-time to compose on paper towels. Now an established star claimed by the South and the world, he eludes tags that once categorized his work as dialect, regional, and African American. A purposeful writer given to passion and daring, he concentrates on uplifting youth, especially Southerners who lack a full grasp of their history. Of his six novels, Gaines is best known for verisimilitude in a family saga, *The Autobiography of Miss Jane Pittman* (1971), and for sustained drama in *A Gathering of Old Men* (1983). In the former, he created so truth-bearing a portrait of robust Southern black womanhood that, in the minds of readers, his title character has taken a place alongside historical figures Sojourner Truth, Harriet Tubman, and Rosa Parks. The blurring of lines between real and fictional led New York governor Hugh Carey to name Miss Jane in a speech about historical black heroes. Similarly moved by her lifelike words and actions, Jesse Jackson compared Miss Jane's fictional reflections to slave-era stories told by his grandmother.

The source of Gaines's realism is the sight, smell, and taste of his Louisiana homeland; the impetus for his cadence is the bayou dialect. A sensitive, cerebral loner of Anglo-African–Native American lineage, he claims ancestry with sugar plantation slaves. The oldest son of Adrienne J. Colar and Manuel Gaines, a black tenant farmer, he was born January 15, 1933, on River Lake Plantation near New Roads, Pointe Coupée Parish. Along with a sister and two brothers, he spent his childhood in Cherie Quarters, a block of slave-built cabins, and harvested potatoes and tilled the land like a grownup. A handicapped great-aunt, Augusteen "Aunt Teen" Jefferson, reared the Gaines children, not only tending the foursome but operating a treadle sewing machine and cultivating a garden on her hands and knees. Early on, Gaines developed a humanistic touch: From his aunt he learned determination and humility; from visitors he garnered the folk stories and ghost tales that intrigued his imagination. In an interview, Gaines recalled:

> [Aunt Teen] was a cripple and could not go visiting, so people came to visit her.
> I'd be there to serve them ice water, or coffee. There was no radio, no television,

so people *talked* about everything, even things that had happened seventy years earlier. I learned about storytelling by listening to these people talk. (Desruisseaux 1978, 45)

He completed his education at an informal black academy held five months each year in a church in New Rose, the setting he later renamed Bayonne. Known locally for neat penmanship, he became the area scribe and reader for illiterates.

After his parents' separation in 1941, Gaines moved to Vallejo, California, to further his studies. The change cost him the loving Aunt Teen, but reunited him with his mother. Her remarriage brought him a stepfather, Raphael Norbert Colar, a merchant seaman and father of seven children. Colar forced Gaines to abandon street hangouts and make the most of the Vallejo Public Library, which, unlike segregated facilities in Louisiana, was open to patrons of all races. Lonesome and homesick for the Creole South, Gaines searched the stacks for stories set in places like Cherie Quarters and with the lifestyle of the people he yearned for. As he describes his pining for home in "Miss Jane and I" in *Callaloo:*

> I wanted to smell that Louisiana earth, feel that Louisiana sun, sit under the shade of one of those Louisiana oaks, search for pecans in that Louisiana grass in one of those Louisiana yards next to one of those Louisiana bayous, not far from a Louisiana river. . . . And I wanted to hear that Louisiana dialect—that combination of English, creole, cajun, Black. For me there's no more beautiful sound anywhere. (Gaines 1978, 28)

When he found nothing of the real Louisiana in print, he resolved to re-create his homeland in fiction. In 1949, he rented a typewriter and composed a first novel, *A Little Stream*, an unsuccessful derivative work he later burned after its rejection by a New York publishing house.

At Vallejo Junior College and during a stint in the army from 1953 to 1955, Gaines won writing contests and published in *Transfer*, a San Francisco college literary review, his first short fiction, "The Turtles" (1956), a story about sexual coming-of-age. Although he was successful, the unworthiness of his first novel inhibited him from starting a second. While attending San Francisco State College on the GI bill, he bolstered his skills with course work in creative writing. A Wallace Stegner Creative Writing Fellowship underwrote his graduate study at Stanford University. During this period, Gaines profited from the guidance of critic Malcolm Cowley.

Gaines gave himself ten years to succeed as a professional writer. The break in his career occurred in 1956 after agent Dorothea Oppenheimer read "The Turtles" and determined that he had talent worth pursuing. He extracted *Catherine Carmier* (1964) from the shreds of his first novel and published a second novel, *Of Love and Dust* (1967), and *Bloodline* (1968), a collection of short fiction. Keeping himself afloat by washing dishes, working as a printer's devil, and sorting and delivering mail at an insurance firm, he lived on the rim of poverty while completing his masterwork, *The Autobiography of Miss Jane Pittman*. His folk autobiography evolved from the motifs, themes, and character of the protagonist Aunt Fe of "Just like a Tree" (1962), a short story published in *Sewanee Review* in 1968. Critics note the influence of William Faulkner's circular narrative technique and of the obdurate women of Cherie Quarters, whom he compressed into the doughty, hard-edged Miss Jane.

A best-seller-turned-classic, *The Autobiography of Miss Jane Pittman* relies on Gaines's straightforward first-person voice and her ease among the stratified Southerners in largely outdoor settings, ranging from a Civil War–era plantation to a bronco-busting Texas ranch on the eastern edge of the frontier and into the watery Louisiana bayou country. A protester during the civil rights movement who defies authority by drinking from a whites-only fountain, Jane becomes real enough to seem like a historical figure. While still a feisty slave child named Ticey, she challenges the false sense of power and authority by which "secesh" whites hold onto chattel blacks with one hand and a crumbling antebellum gentility with the other. Jane's forthright march from slavery epitomizes the experience of a culture formerly intimidated by a corrupt ruling class. Her pragmatic insistence on freedom seems unquestionably right; her modest but admirable self-actualization calls into question a nation that would allow itself to profit from slave pens no better than hog lots.

Unlike the lifelong power struggle in Miss Jane's life, racial vengeance and a potential lynching in *A Gathering of Old Men* fuel a single power play more Faulknerian in tone and atmosphere than Gaines's other works. The tearing suspense arises in the milieu Gaines knows best: fictional Bayonne, the sugar plantation of his childhood, among the calloused, semiliterate workers who risk late-in-life peace to challenge racial oppression. The grisly introit to a Southern tableau spills out in chapter 1 from a breathless runner yelling "Oh, Aunt Glo; oh, Aunt Glo; oh, Aunt Glo." (Gaines 1983, 4) The messenger warns of the unthinkable: "Beau laying on his back in Mathu's yard. And Mathu squatting there with that shotgun." (Gaines 1983, 8) Like the two sides of the chorus in Greek tragedy, the sheriff faces off against a band of shotgun-toting elders who muddy an investigation by separate claims of guilt. More for himself than for the authorities, suspect Big Charlie sums up the group's resolution: "They comes a day. . . . They comes a day." (Gaines 1983, 189)

Gaines's characteristic blend of mayhem with regional humor and surefire backwoods topics—rebel yells, the Klan, ax-swinging, nigger, pussy, ass, son of a bitch, and Jack Daniels on the rocks—colors the plot in measured dollops as the required legalities spool out to judgment. Battered but unbending, the aged testators appear in court smelling of mothballs and Lifebuoy soap. For the occasion, they deck themselves in the dignity and notoriety of the self-righteous, yet each remains candid and loose enough on the stand to "use all nicknames for his compatriots—Clabber, Dirty Red, Coot, Chimley, Rooster." (Gaines 1983, 212) Titters from the audience rise to roars because Sheriff Mapes is forced to admit that he was sitting on his rear during the fight. After the jury deliberates three hours, Gaines quickly winds down the face-off with a compromise: In view of the fact that the obvious perpetrators are dead, Judge Reynolds places the elderly obstructors of justice on probation for five years and suspends their rights to bear arms—"any kind of firing arm, rifle, shotgun, or pistol, or being within ten feet of anyone else with such weapons. (That was like telling a Louisianian never to say Mardi Gras or Huey Long.)" (Gaines 1983, 213)

Ernest James Gaines in 1993

After the surprise success of *A Gathering of Old Men* and Gaines's appearances as writer-in-residence at Denison and Stanford Universities, his career burgeoned with an invitation to teach at the University of Southwestern Louisiana in Lafayette. Settled and successful, he began a sixth novel, *A Lesson before Dying* (1993). Set in 1948, the book particularizes a strained gentility that masks the black South's outrage at yet another youthful black offender wrongfully marked for the electric chair. Speaking through Grant Wiggins, a compassionate teacher at a plantation school, Gaines interweaves the cadences and commonalities of a devalued people with the race-tinged issues that threaten their existence—miscegenation, disenfranchisement, and racial atrocity. The choice of Jefferson for the protagonist's name sets high expectations.

As Gaines moves toward the boy's 6-x-10-foot cell, he tells the universal story of prison isolation, self-abnegation, and despair. The accused dwells apart from other prisoners and passes his dwindling days among

> a metal bunk covered by a thin mattress and a woolen army blanket; a toilet without seat or toilet paper; a washbowl, brownish from residue and grime; a small metal shelf upon which was a pan, a tin cup, and tablespoon. A single light bulb hung over the center of the cell, and at the end opposite the door was a barred window, which looked out onto a sycamore tree behind the courthouse. (Gaines 1993, 71)

The setting is as bleak as the rescuer's conversations with the prisoner. Repeatedly rejected and insulted, Wiggins insists that Jefferson shake free of his torpor and assert the tenets of civilized society—honor, dignity, respect for family and self.

Gaines strains the mask of the professor with a sermon on myth. As Wiggins moves out of earshot of others, he speaks to Jefferson the words that summarize the creed that has kept him going. Wiggins attacks the myth that white people are better than any other race on earth. He challenges the condemned youth to think beyond his own misery:

> The last thing they ever want is to see a black man stand, and think, and show that common humanity that is in us all. It would destroy their myth. They would no longer have justification for having made us slaves and keeping us in the condition we are in. As long as none of us stand, they're safe. (Gaines 1993, 192)

Like the brown bags of chicken and baked potatoes cooked by loving hands, the words soothe Jefferson at a vulnerable point and ease the hunger for something to believe in.

Gaines crafts chapter 28, "Jefferson's Diary," the testimony to Jefferson's humanity, to fill the few pages of a fitting denouement. The prisoner's painful candor pours out in semiliterate strings of words:

> it look like the lord just work for wite folks cause ever sens I wasn nothin but a litle boy i been on my own haulin water . . . so i can git the people they food an they water on time. . . . (Gaines 1993, 227)

Words made eloquent by time and plight capture Jefferson's tender feelings, previously concealed by bouts of silence, glumness, and discourtesy. Bereft of his mask, he admits to tears and sleeplessness and cries, "lord have merce sweet jesus mr wigin." (Gaines 1993, 220)

Gaines insists on following the victim in the final moments before the execution. In his parting words, Jefferson acknowledges prophetically "its late," a comment on society's backwardness in race relations and his approaching execution. Sparse images dot the pages of his journal like haiku:

day breakin
sun comin up
the bird in the tre soun like a blu bird
sky blu blu mr wigin.
(Gaines 1993, 234)

Gaines justifies the sacrifice of Jefferson in Professor Wiggins's renewal. His own being affirmed by the task of teacher to the condemned, he returns to the lectern baptized in tears.

Profiting from mentors James Joyce, Willa Cather, John Steinbeck, Mark Twain, Ernest Hemingway, Gustave Flaubert, and Guy de Maupassant as well as the peasant-based writings of Nikolai Gogol, Ivan Turgenev, and Anton Chekhov, Gaines re-creates with control and grace the traditions and rhythms of agrarian folk culture. To critics and fans who applauded *A Lesson before Dying*, it is obvious that Gaines has earned a place among folk authors in tune with the rural South. He possesses both the storyteller's gift for control, the historian's insistence on accuracy, and the insider's feel for the region's individuality and idiom. He has noted to interviewers his disdain for critics' tendency to stereotype twentieth-century blacks in urban ghettos, and chooses a more inclusive *dramatis personae* for his fiction.

For poignant portrayals of the American underclass, Gaines has earned worthy honors: a MacArthur Foundation "genius grant" of $355,000, the Joseph Henry Jackson award for "Comeback," a Rockefeller grant, Guggenheim fellowship, Wallace Stegner award, National Endowment of the Arts stipend, two awards from the Commonwealth Club of California, Louisiana Library Association award, San Francisco Arts Commission award, and honoraria from the American Academy and Institute of Arts and Letters and the Black Academy of Arts and Letters. He holds honorary degrees from Denison University, Brown University, Bard College, Whittier College, and Louisiana State University. Book-of-the-Month Club has listed his work as an alternate; in addition to *The Autobiography of Miss Jane Pittman*, two of his titles have been filmed: *A Gathering of Old Men* was featured on CBS-TV on May 10, 1987, starring Lou Gossett, Jr., and Richard Widmark; in 1993, *The Sky Is Gray* (1963) appeared on WHMM-TV as part of a series entitled *The Humanities American Short Story*.

In 1994, Gaines achieved two important milestones: the National Book Critic's Circle Award for *A Lesson before Dying* and an end to bachelorhood with his marriage to Miamian Dianne Saulney, an assistant district attorney in Dade County, Florida. Gaines balances work with writing and part-time residence in Miami and San Francisco, and lives his double life as college professor and black Creole returning to rejuvenating roots in Lafayette and the agrarian suburb in which he grew up. In addition to literary studies of Louisiana, Gaines has also published photo portraits of his homeland. (Babb 1991; "Black and White" 1997; Bradbury 1996; Briggs 1997; Bruck 1977; Bryant 1972, 1974; *Contemporary Authors* 1994; *Dictionary of Literary Biography* 1978, 1984; Gaines 1971, 1978, 1983, 1993, Video 1993; Gaudet and Wooten 1990; Gayle 1975; Gerber 1971; Hicks 1981; Hudson 1985; Laney 1994; Maddocks 1971; Magnier 1995; Martin 1973; Martin and Porter 1995; O'Brien 1973; "Our Culture" 1997; Peterson 1993;

Ploski and Williams 1989; Sheppard 1993; Snodgrass 1995; "Southern Cross" 1973; Stephens 1995; Stoelting 1971; Summer 1993; *Video Hound's* 1994; Wilson and Ferris 1989; Wolff 1969)
    See also *The Autobiography of Miss Jane Pittman*.

THE GLASS MENAGERIE

A gauze-draped threnody to the stunted victims of Southern families, Tennessee Williams's autobiographical *The Glass Menagerie* (1945) has become an American classic of stage, film, television, drama anthology, and textbook. A lyric, impressionistic re-creation of emotion based on Williams's short story "Portrait of a Girl in Glass," the play has been classed as both a drama of mood and a memory play. To achieve concreteness, Williams makes considerable demand of set, special effects, and music. He filters reality through a phosphorescent glow, a physical re-creation of speaker Tom Wingfield's nostalgia and longing. The plot, punctuated by extensive stage directions, forces into conflict Tom, the lone wanderer, against his defiant, opportunistic mother, symbol of the post–World War I era's declining gentlewoman. The family's wretched tenancy of a colorless city apartment eventually drives Tom into the merchant marines. He leaves behind a pathologically withdrawn sister who hides a halting gait while avoiding the social terrors that her mother thrusts in her path.

Sketched on a smoky blue stage amid skeletal backdrops, the play's theme is itself blue and skeletal as the author reflects on disappointments and dislocation in his own childhood. Coarsened by adversity, Amanda Wingfield shreds her children's integrity, forcing them to posture and pretend to cover their slide into a grubby working-class purgatory. Her glib bromides of "Rise and shine!" and "Spartan endurance," and her thin mask of optimism depress both children, impelling Tom into all-night movie houses and Laura into walking the streets to avoid facing her inability to pass a typing test at Rubicam's Business College. Reflecting on the Wingfield family's losses and the evanescence of happy moments, Williams has a phrase flashed on the stage backdrop: "Ou sont les neiges d'antan? [Where are the snows of yesteryear?]," a poignantly romantic scrap from the oft-quoted French poet François Villon.

Williams initiated the stage version of *The Glass Menagerie* in 1943 with a script for MGM entitled *The Gentleman Caller*. Like the wisps of glass that Laura collects, the framework of the finished play is a tenuous, gossamer web of memory and self-doubt. The speaker battles loneliness and despair as he salves with sarcasm and rebellion the unhealable hurt inflicted daily by his mother. Her seriocomic domination and perpetual emasculation balance Tom's wistful visions of Laura, the most unlikely family member to survive the Wingfield fall from gentility. To drown out Amanda's verbal forays, Tom turns his attention to his fragile sister, cranking up records on the old Victrola, cradling the broken glass unicorn from her collection, and blowing out candles. In his farewell, he proclaims, "Oh, Laura, Laura, I tried to leave you behind me, but I am more faithful than I intended to be!" (Williams 1949, 115)

Tennessee Williams rewrote his short story "Portrait of a Girl in Glass" as *The Glass Menagerie,* a play that opened on Broadway in 1945. Laurette Taylor played the Mother and Anthony Ross the Gentleman Caller in this 1946 performance.

The playwright enforces an unflinching inspection of family brutality. Love is the least palpable memory that Tom recalls. His mother, ironically named for the Latin "ought to be loved," uses him as a replacement provider for her absent husband. Her expressions of love for Tom amount to advice about health and sermonettes on hard work and success. Amanda saves for Laura her most fearful predictions of failure:

> I've seen such pitiful cases in the South—barely tolerated spinsters living upon the grudging patronage of sister's husband or brother's wife!—stuck away in some little mousetrap of a room—encouraged by one in-law to visit another— little birdlike women without any nest—eating the crust of humility all their life! (Williams 1949, 34)

Against the blare of Amanda's daily dicta, Laura lives in dreamland. She endures the visit of a sham gentleman caller and receives a rare compliment from Tom's friend Jim, who declares that other girls are "common as—weeds, but— you—well, you're—*Blue Roses!*," a gentle pun on a mispronunciation of the disease pleurosis, which sidelined Laura in high school. (Williams 1949, 105) Despite Amanda's advice on dressing to please gentlemen or Tom's loyal behind-the-hand jokes and misguided invitation to a gentleman caller, Laura remains the family tragedy. She slips away, too elusive and guileless for either Tom or Amanda to save. (Anderson 1971; Bradbury 1963; Bradbury 1996; Cunliffe 1987; Gassner and Quinn 1969; Miller 1971; Parker 1983; Prideaux 1953; Rubin et al. 1985; Spoto 1985; Tischler 1969; Weales 1965; Williams 1949; Wilson and Ferris 1989)

See also *A Streetcar Named Desire;* Williams, Tennessee.

GONE WITH THE WIND

An enduring classic war saga and feminist novel that outdistanced its Southern rival, Stark Young's *So Red the Rose* (1934), Margaret Mitchell's *Gone with the Wind* (1936) remains on sale in variety stores and grocery paperback racks, a palpable testimony to an international literary legend. The novel showcases a legendary list of characters, but turns on the whims and petulant outbursts of its central figure, Katie Scarlett O'Hara, a fetching teenager of French-Irish background. Given to flounces of her hoopskirt and green-eyed flashes of temper at the mention of the imminent Confederate war against the Union army, she sulks over events that spoil her place at the heart of county socials. Mitchell's deft resurrection of womanhood from the tempestuous, daredevil deb continues to win readers, who have kept the book in publication for over six decades and maintained the demand for memorabilia, videos, laserdiscs, dolls, and books about the author and the filming of her novel.

Set in the craggy Blue Ridge Mountains of Georgia's outback, the story opens on the 16-year-old heroine; her younger sisters, Suellen and Carreen; and their mismated parents, Gerald O'Hara, a lowborn Irishman endowed with luck and an eye for fine horseflesh, and Ellen Robillard O'Hara, a pious matriarch whose soft-spoken command runs their mansion and plantation, called Tara after the royal hall of Ireland. Forever separated from the gentility and social graces of her beloved coastal milieu, she enters north Georgia with trepidation:

> Ellen never would, or could, quite become one of them—she had left too much of herself in Savannah—but she respected them and, in time, learned to admire the frankness and forthrightness of these people, who had few reticences and who valued a man for what he was. (Mitchell 1964, 59)

Early on, Mitchell stresses the social and moral impact of plantation woman-hood. Ellen easily controls her girls with a glance, lift of her rosary, and call to prayers. After hearing that Scarlett has flouted widowhood by dancing with Captain Butler at a charity cotillion, she posts a sharp note to Atlanta chastising her eldest for public impropriety as though Scarlett were still a rebellious preteen.

The movie version of *Gone with the Wind* captures the Southern charm of the Wilkeses, Melanie and Ashley and their son Beau, who follow Scarlett from the ruins of Tara to a family resurgence in Atlanta. Key moments express the will-ful rule of Mammy, the flibbertigibbet witlessness of Prissy, the faithfulness of Big Sam, and the somber restraint of Pork, the O'Hara's majordomo. Of Southern blacks, Mitchell has much good to say:

> Not trust a darky! Scarlett trusted them far more than most white people, certainly more than she trusted any Yankee. There were qualities of loyalty and tirelessness and love in them that no strain could break, no money could buy. (Mitchell 1964, 666)

In reflection over her childhood on the plantation and wartime privations as she bolstered Tara to keep the family and its retainers from starving, Scarlett ponders the "faithful few" who remained behind after emancipation—of Dilcey hoeing cotton and Pork dropping his butler's manners to raid henhouses. Dearest is Mammy, the surrogate mother who follows her to Atlanta to chaperone her amid prostitutes, the war's stragglers, occupation forces, and no-good Yankee profiteers.

The 1939 screen version lacks the full story of Scarlett's three children, each born in a separate marriage. Wade is the son of Charles Hamilton, and Ella Lorena is the daughter of Frank Kennedy, the storekeeper whom Scarlett inveigles into matrimony after the notorious blockade-runner, Rhett Butler, spurns her urgent request for marriage and funds to reclaim Tara from the tax collector. The final marriage to Rhett, the black sheep of a prominent Charleston family, and the birth of their spoiled daughter, "Bonnie Blue" Butler, rates the most screen coverage. The film turns from the war and Reconstruction issues to the crumbling facade of the Butlers' marriage, which Scarlett undermines with schoolgirl fantasies of Ashley Wilkes. Her overlong teenage crush on a stale, idealistic remnant of the cavalier South holds fast to the past, like Mrs. Meriweather and Dolly Meade boosting the "Cause" and collecting volunteers to decorate the tombs of the "glorious dead." Multiple losses return Scarlett to reality. She tumbles downstairs while greeting Rhett after their separation, during which he took Bonnie to London. The resultant miscarriage costs the couple the child Scarlett had concealed from her hard-drinking, hardhanded husband.

Gone with the Wind, Margaret Mitchell's 1936 novel of a Georgia family during the Civil War and Reconstruction era, became a popular, though abbreviated movie of her story. The 1939 film starred British actress Vivian Leigh as Scarlett O'Hara and American actor Clark Gable as Rhett Butler.

After Bonnie lurches from her pony in a difficult jump and dies of a broken neck, Rhett and Scarlett's marriage is irrevocably pulled asunder. They separate permanently following Melanie's death from an ill-planned pregnancy that compromises her frail constitution.

Mitchell incorporates much of the Southern milieu and sustains the plot with a universal theme, the will to survive sweeping economic upheaval and the resultant social change. Her depiction of a seedy overseer and womanizer who impregnates the white-trash Slattery girl and of a similar ogre, Johnny Gallagher, who overworks and mistreats convicts, suggests the disparate economic and social levels that exacerbate wartime conflict. Ku Klux Klan violence to rid polite society of riffraff and unemployed ex-slaves costs Scarlett her second husband during a raid on black shanties along the Decatur Road. The debacle that widows her a second time is a minor loss to her, but a prevalent cause of tension and sporadic outbursts of whippings and lynchings during the Reconstruction era. Minor characters, particularly Archie, a CSE veteran and postwar drifter, heighten the drama of Atlanta's slow climb from post-siege deterioration to economic self-sufficiency.

Overall, Mitchell poses the city of Atlanta as a parallel protagonist to Scarlett, the fictional composite of real characters whom the author heard described in local oral stories and saw in family picture albums and cameos. In despair in the grim twentieth chapter, Scarlett grieves for the ominous changes that siege brings to the city: "Atlanta was no longer the gay, the desperately gay place she had loved. It was a hideous place like a plague-stricken city so quiet, so dreadfully quiet after the din of the siege." (Mitchell 1964, 341) With abundant relief in chapter 37, she welcomes boom times, when the town roared

> wide open like a frontier village, making no effort to cover its vices and sins. Saloons blossomed overnight, two and sometimes three in a block, and after nightfall the streets were full of drunken men, black and white, reeling from wall to curb and back again. (Mitchell 1964, 649)

Jubilant in the mix of thugs, cutpurses, gamblers, and streetwalkers, Scarlett herself blooms in the New South as the epitome of its New Woman, who puts behind her the threadbare existence at Tara to welcome commerce. The thriving metropolis of the South woos her with its jangling pianos, rowdies singing and firing pistols, and the ching of money in the till. Pragmatism remains her ally, even after Rhett strides out the grand front hall one last time. Mitchell undergirds her heroine with enough spunk to rethink her immature dependence on men and to find the steel in her spine that kept her going when the rest of Georgia sank before its conquerors. (Blain et al. 1990; Bradbury 1963; Buck 1992; *Contemporary Authors* 1994; Cunliffe 1987; Davidson and Wagner-Martin 1995; Ehrlich and Carruth 1982; Kunitz 1942, 1955; McHenry 1980; Romine 1986; Rubin et al. 1985; Sherr and Kazickas 1994; Stein 1979; Wilson and Ferris 1989)

See also the Civil War era; Lee, Robert E.; Mitchell, Margaret.

THE GRANDISSIMES

The Grandissimes (1880), a rich Southern colonial saga set in 1803–1804, the era of the Louisiana Purchase, remains author George Washington Cable's most revered work. Serialized in *Scribner's* magazine, the novel received strong critical response for his use of a single family as symbols of Louisiana history. Weakened by convoluted structure, the action involves the Grandissimes' feud with the DeGrapions. The central patriarch, a worthy merchant named Honoré Grandissime, contrasts the legendary Bras-Coupé. The ruined slave prince, six feet five and massively built, once presided over his own compound of slaves in the Jaloff nation in Africa, but cut off his arm rather than serve a Louisiana master. As Cable describes the handicap:

> The arm which might no longer shake the spear or swing the wooden sword, was no better than a useless stump never to be lifted for aught else. But whether easy to allow or not, that was his meaning. He made himself a type of all Slavery, turning into flesh and blood the truth that all Slavery is maiming. (Cable 1957, 171)

The slave king embodies a living curse on elite families like the Grandissimes, doomed grandees who battle the ineluctable sins of their fathers for importing and selling black Africans.

Begun in chapter 28, the story-within-a-story of Bras-Coupé's arrival in America to La Renaissance, Don José Martinez's Delta plantation, is an intriguing history. Immured in the hold of the *Egalité*, a symbolic vessel involved in the Golden Triangle's slave trade, Mioko-koanga (renamed Bras-Coupé) arrives at the plantation. Rid of the foul ship's hold, he is grateful for clean food and garments and a whitewashed slave hut, which surpasses his African residence. The event that triggers a lifetime of rebellion is his introduction to the foreman, who forces the unbroken African into the role of field hand. The frenzy that fuels the foreman's assault and murder of two fellow blacks sends Bras-Coupé on an uncharted flight from bondage. His short-lived escape ends with the firing of a pistol ball that pierces his cranium and bounces back, a bizarre symbol of his defiance. Shackled, yoked, and subdued, Bras-Coupé so epitomizes the indomitable courage of the rebel that his owner summons an interpreter, the elegant Palmyre la Philosophe, to acclimate him to his new life.

The love story of Bras-Coupé and Palmyre, an octoroon voodoo priestess, builds on irony, one of Cable's rhetorical strengths. The brazen prince, entranced by an equally courageous female, prostrates himself before the near-white womanly vision and, on the strength of her request, accepts the job of overseer in exchange for betrothal to the priestess. Advancing to the position of gamekeeper, he works out his trial period of six months, then arrives at the bridal scene:

> On the great black piazza, which had been inclosed [*sic*] with sail-cloth and lighted with lanterns, was Palmyre, robed in costly garments to whose beauty was added the charm of their having been worn once, and once only, by her beloved Mademoiselle. (Cable 1957, 177)

Thus, in sullied grandeur, he is wed to Palmyre, a reluctant bride as independent and self-willed as the groom. Overlaid with impending doom, the nuptials conclude in disaster after Bras-Coupé strikes Don José for refusing to refill the prince's wine bumper for the eleventh time. Forced into flight by the *Code Noir*, a body of Southern folk laws that enforce mandatory execution of any black who assaults a white, Bras-Coupé, reborn in strength and defiance, curses the estate ironically known as La Renaissance. He escapes by canoe into the wetlands. His potent malediction brings the plagues of Job—worms to Don José's indigo fields, fever in the black quarters, and devastating illness to the master. On Bras-Coupé's reappearance, he lifts a hand to curse all males of the house, an event that Cable describes with the majesty and severity of Ecclesiasticus:

> The plantation became an invalid camp. The words of the voudou found fulfilment on every side. The plough went not out; the herds wandered through broken hedges from field to field and came up with staring bones and shrunken sides; a frenzied mob of weeds and thorns wrestled and throttled each other in a struggle for standing-room—rag-weed, smart-weed, sneeze-weed, bind-weed, iron-weed—until the burning skies of mid-summer checked their growth and crowned their unshorn tops with rank and dingy flowers. (Cable 1957, 187)

Lassoed by Spanish police, the giant slave is returned to the plantation to be flogged, hamstrung, and branded, and his ears lopped like a hunting hound. After

Don José's death, the mistress, with babe in arms, begs Bras-Coupé's forgiveness. The silent slave, limp yet still magisterial, rescinds the curse with a wave of the hand over the child's forehead, then dies with "Africa" on his lips.

Cable's insistence on romantic touches overloads the novel with additional conventions rampant in Jim Crow–era plantation fiction. The elegant, refined Honoré Grandissime is half brother to Honoré Grandissime, F.M.C., the period's abbreviation for "free man of color." The doppelgänger motif, a common occurrence among families in which the master fathers siblings by his wife and his black concubines, produces the odd pairing of two men with the same name and equal education at a French academy. A social pariah to the prestigious Grandissimes, the quadroon resides on the outskirts of respectability, even after his younger brother welcomes him into the family business and seeks to lessen the ostracism that forms a wall between the white plantation milieu and its tarnished, declassé underside. The worst of the quadroon's fate is the allotment of inherited land, which passes entirely to the white brother. Even though the quadroon successfully parlays his portion of cash into a substantial fortune in real estate, he dreams in vain of acceptance and stands on the brink of suicide in the swollen Mississippi River, where his brother restrains him.

Intent on irony, Cable carries his story to a melodramatic conclusion. The falling action depicts the quadroon as the victim of an attack by his uncle, Agricola Fusilier, who from the opening chapter spews the racist venom that infects Louisiana society. Vexed that his nephew has "gone over to the enemy," Agricola elaborates:

> It implies affiliation with *Américains* in matters of business and of government! It implies the exchange of social amenities with a race of upstarts! It implies a craven consent to submit the sacredest prejudices of our fathers to the new-fangled measuring-rods of pert, imported theories upon moral and political progress! (Cable 1957, 302)

In a subversion of the *Code Noir*, the black Honoré Grandissime stabs Agricola thrice in the back for striking him with a cane. After the quadroon's flight to France aboard the *Américain*, the free man of color arrives at Bordeaux, then leaps from the brig and drowns in the ocean, leaving behind his will, marked in French *M. Honoré Grandissime, Nouvelle Orleans, Etats Unis, Amérique*. (Bradbury 1963; Bradbury 1996; Cable 1890, 1957, 1969; Cunliffe 1987; Ehrlich and Carruth 1982; "George W. Cable" 1994; Gross 1971; Guilds 1970; Kunitz and Haycraft 1938; Petry 1988; Quinn 1936; Rasmussen 1995; Rubin 1969; Rubin et al. 1985; Stein 1979; Stephens 1995; Trent et al. 1946; Twain 1990; Wilson and Ferris 1989)

See also Cable, George Washington.

HALEY, ALEX

A reclaimed Southerner like Edgar Allan Poe and Ralph Ellison, New Yorker Alexander Murray Palmer Haley has contributed the beginnings of a groundswell of interest in black genealogy. Born August 11, 1921, in Ithaca while his parents pursued graduate degrees, he and two younger brothers lived primarily in Henning, Tennessee. His mother, musician Bertha George Palmer, and his father, Professor Simon Alexander Haley, nurtured his talents and insisted on high achievement. Fittingly, he completed high school in Normal, Alabama, and matriculated at Alcorn A&M College in Mississippi and Elizabeth City State Teachers College in North Carolina. At age 19 he halted his education to serve as a waiter on a cargo-ammunition ship in the U.S. Coast Guard. His military career took him to the Pacific, where the undemanding task of mess boy left him time to read, reflect, and write fiction and letters. Ten years after his enlistment, he undertook the post of chief journalist for the coast guard until his retirement in 1959.

While living the writer's nightmare of penury and hunger in a basement apartment in Greenwich Village, New York, Haley sold short works to the *New York Times* magazine, *Harper's*, and *Atlantic*, but earned too little to thrive. Freelancing first paid off in the early 1960s, when he initiated interviews for *Reader's Digest* and *Playboy*, beginning with jazz trumpeter Miles Davis. Haley's meeting with Malcolm X—a controversial figure formerly known as Malcolm Little who was influenced by the Black Power drive of the Student Nonviolent Coordinating Committee—carried the reporter farther than he expected the collaboration to go. The first piece, "Mr. Muhammad Speaks," appeared in the March 1960 issue of *Reader's Digest;* the second, *"Playboy* Interview: Malcolm X," was published in the May 1963 issue.

Haley requested the privilege of writing a biography of the famed street-thug-turned-evangelist, which Elijah Muhammad, leader of the Black Muslims, granted. After Malcolm attacked the Islamic spokesman for corrupting young female members of the sect, the orthodox Nation of Islam stalked and harried Malcolm's family, whom he placed under tight security. Haley began writing and interviewing, although Malcolm harbored suspicion and withheld personal data to shield his family from the media and potential attackers. The assassination of Malcolm X on February 21, 1965, at a meeting of the Organization of

Alex Haley (1921–1992) relaxes at his boyhood home in Henning, Tennessee, 1977.

Afro-American Unity at the Audubon Ballroom in Harlem, New York, left Haley with the beginnings of *The Autobiography of Malcolm X* (1965), which Malcolm had kept in good order. Haley picked up the narrative strands to describe the approach of three assassins, 16 bullets pumped into Malcolm's body, and his collapse at the lectern. The final scenes cover the arrest and conviction of Talmadge Thayer and two Black Muslims, Norman 3X Butler and Thomas 15X Johnson, for conspiracy and murder. Haley includes Malcolm's orthodox Muslim funeral rites, for which actor Ossie Davis delivered the eulogy, and ends with a stirring admission that Malcolm X "was the most electric personality" Haley had ever known. The book sold millions of copies and was translated into eight languages.

Established by the best-seller in the sweeping civil rights movement of the 1970s, Haley undertook a 12-year investigation of the Palmer side of his family. He based his research on slender evidence—stories his grandmother told him about her great-grandparents and their forebear, "the African," who lived in a place he identified as the Kamby Bolongo in West Africa. Searching minute bits of evidence in Gambia, Haley documented five generations dating to Kunta Kinte, his forebear. The African was a sturdy 16-year-old Mandingo warrior when slavers captured him in the village of Juffure in 1767 while he was chopping a tree trunk to make a drum. Four white men bore him to the cargo hold of the *Lord Ligonier* and thence to a slave market in Annapolis, Maryland, on September 29, 1767. Haley traces the African's hardships and joys to a peak in chapter 68, when he introduces Kizzy, Kunta Kinte's firstborn, to the universe:

> Kunta felt Africa pumping in his veins—and flowing from him into the child, the flesh of him and Bell. . . . Lifting a small corner of the blanket he bared the infant's small black face to the heavens, and this time he spoke aloud to her in Mandinka: "Behold the only thing greater than yourself!" (Haley 1976, 290)

The completed genealogical novel, *Roots: The Saga of an American Family* (1976), follows Haley's ancestry over a panoply of laborers, farmers, blacksmiths, lumbermen, Pullman porters, an attorney, a music teacher, and an architect to Alex, the family's historian.

Roots developed into a full-scale business for Haley. A monumental addition to documentation of the African diaspora, the novel was serialized in the *New York Post* and the *Long Island Press*. It coincided with the 200th anniversary of American democracy, a momentous time to rouse black readers to pride in their history. An immediate best-seller, the work earned millions in royalties and won Haley multiple university honoraria, a National Book Award, Spingarn Medal, and Pulitzer Prize. Subsequent lectures, articles, and works spawned by *Roots* include an eight-part ABC-TV series in 1977 for which Quincy Jones provided music. Heading a strong cast are LeVar Burton playing the young Kunta Kinte and John Amos as his adult persona, renamed Toby. The cast includes Ed Asner, Lloyd Bridges, Chuck Connors, Lynda Day George, Lorne Greene, Burl Ives, O. J. Simpson, Cicely Tyson, Ben Vereen, Sandy Duncan, and Maya Angelou as Kunta Kinte's African grandmother in the 570-minute production. The second of Haley's historical fiction, *Roots: The Next Generation* (1979), details the growth of Palmerstown, Tennessee. Scripted by Haley, the sequel appeared on ABC-TV in February 1979; a subsequent television play, *Roots: The Gift*, aired in December 1988. Haley's success was marred by lawsuits charging him with plagiarism from Margaret Walker's *Jubilee* and Harold Courlander's *The African*. Haley won the first court case. He settled the latter suit with a sizable monetary award to the plaintiff.

Retiring to his farm in Knoxville, Tennessee, Haley turned to a pared-down story, *A Different Kind of Xmas* (1988), before undertaking the genealogy of his father's lineage. The resulting novel, *Queen* (1993), is a compelling parallel saga of family history centering on a strong and courageous materfamilias, Queen Jackson, Haley's grandmother, whose odyssey from slavery contrasts the Afrocentrism of Kunta Kinte's story. A mixed-blood slave sired by a white master on an African-Cherokee slave named Easter at the Forks of Cypress, an Alabama plantation, Queen leaves the rural South at the end of the Civil War. Because of her appeal to white men, she toys with the possibility of passing for white. When her sham credentials in the white world fail, she embraces Negro ancestry, bears a son named Abner, who is sired by a drifter named Micah, and marries Alec Haley, a ferryman on the Tennessee River. The novel ends with British coauthor David Stevens's explanation of the loose body of data that substantiate family stories. Composed after the author's death, the afterword cites Haley's vision: "This book will convey visceral America. For our land of immigrants is a testimonial to the merging of the cultures of the world, and of their bloodlines." (Haley 1993, 670) The six-hour CBS-TV miniseries, starring Halle Berry as the title character opposite Danny Glover as her husband and featuring Tim Daly, Martin Sheen, Ann-Margaret, Paul Winfield, Ossie Davis, Madge Sinclair, Jasmine Guy, and Sada Thompson, aired in May 1993. Until his death from cardiac arrest on February 10, 1992, in Seattle, Washington, Haley was still puzzled at the daily mobs of readers, letter writers, and watchers of his televised family history who turned him into a beloved celebrity. ("Alex Haley's Epic Drama" 1993; Breitman 1965; Carson 1991; Chapman 1968; *Contemporary Authors* 1994; Haley 1964, 1976, 1988, 1993; Low and Clift 1981; Ploski and Williams 1989; Wilson and Ferris 1989)

HARRIS, JOEL CHANDLER

Foremost Georgian editor and peacemaker during the troubled Reconstruction era, Joel Chandler Harris, a white journalist and raconteur, is better known as Uncle Remus, a blackface persona endowed with Old World charm and sincerity. Wise to the subtleties of human relations, Harris throve during the unstable, vengeful postwar era, when his whimsical beast allegories eased the disaffection between races and conferred honor on rural, earth-based stories and songs. An unforeseen benefit, the interest of children in his Uncle Remus tales, made him a world-famous aphorist, humorist, and teller of animal fables. Critics carry praise of his winsome animal characters to more scholarly heights by crediting Harris with ennobling the American underclass, validating Negro folklore, authenticating primitive English, and perpetuating a civilization.

From unpromising origins, the author profited from serendipity. Harris, a native of Eatonton, a rural Georgia crossroads, was born December 9, 1848, the offspring of seamstress Mary Harris and an unnamed Irish laborer who courted, seduced, and abandoned her before the birth of their son. The outlook for the education of the bastard child of a transient Irishman was limited to a subscription school. His mother paid the dollar-a-month tuition with a donation from her sympathetic landlord, who also provided them a cottage rent-free. To supplement her son's education, she read aloud to him each night from Oliver Goldsmith's *The Vicar of Wakefield*.

At age 13, Joe Harris, a shy, stuttering, inquisitive lad, encountered Joseph Addison Turner. A kindly mentor, Turner was the editor of the *Countryman*, a weekly literary journal established March 4, 1862. Written in the refined style of British satirists Joseph Addison, Richard Steele, and Oliver Goldsmith, Turner's periodical boasted a circulation of 2,000. The paper's prospectus was ambitious for a four-pager:

> This paper is a complete cyclopedia of the History of the Times—The War News—Agriculture, Stock-raising—Field—Sports—Wit—Humor—Anecdote—Tales—Philosophy—Morals—Poetry—Politics—Art—Science—Useful Recipes—Money and Market Matters—Literature—Gen'l Miscellany. (Harlow 1941, 83)

Harris's literary contribution was the selection of filler from volumes of Rochefoucauld's maxims and *The Percy Anecdotes* (1820). Turner allowed the

Joel Chandler Harris (1848–1908) in 1900

boy's hesitant submission of two- and three-line items of his own composition. In time, Harris came to value the apprenticeship as a poor man's introduction to the liberal arts.

Boarding nine miles from home at Turnwold Plantation, Harris served as printer's devil, using his spare time to read the South's best news sources on events of the Civil War. Turner satisfied the boy's voracious yen for books with volumes from the manor's ample library, and taught him the basics of editing and composition. Harris published regularly, choosing "Marlowe" and "Tellmenow Isitsoornot" as pseudonyms. Equally hungry for acceptance and parenting, he formed a lifelong love for three slaves, Uncle George Terrell, Uncle Bob Capers, and Old Harbert. In their company, Harris enjoyed yams baked in hearth ashes, fresh gingersnaps, and—the best part—beast stories and morality tales told in the grandfatherly style of West African griots of Kaffir, Rhodesian, and Hottentot origin. In adulthood, he reflected on the value of storytelling sessions, which he characterized as "unadulterated human nature," richly grounded on a universal humanity and logic. ("Joel Chandler Harris" 1996, n.p.)

In May 1866, Turner lost his fortune and his paper in the financial upheaval following General William T. Sherman's destructive march to the sea. Displaced from his former job, Harris typeset for the *Macon Telegraph*, then accepted an assistant's post on the *New Orleans Crescent Monthly*. Among the coterie of writers who clustered among Louisiana artists, he came under the influence of humorist Mark Twain and Louisiana local-colorist Lafcadio Hearn. Described in chapter 47 of Twain's *Life on the Mississippi*, Harris becomes a recognizable figure:

> He was said to be undersized, red-haired, and somewhat freckled. He was the only man in the party whose outside tallied with his bill of particulars. He was said to be very shy. He is a shy man. Of this there is no doubt. It may not show on the surface, but the shyness is there. After days of intimacy one wonders to see that it is still in about as strong force as ever. (Twain 1990, 306)

Twain admires the "fine and beautiful nature" in Harris, whom he labels a genius and the only national master of black dialect. Twain got a chuckle from a flock of children who approached the embodiment of Uncle Remus; they were shocked that he was white. To ease their dismay, Harris conquered his shyness and read them the Tarbaby story.

Later career moves put Harris in Forsythe, Georgia, where he edited the *Monroe Advertiser* from 1867 to 1870, and in Savannah, where, under the mentorship of William Tappan Thompson, he covered the Georgia legislature for the *Morning News.* During his sojourn on the coast, he married Esther "Essie" LaRose, the daughter of a steamboat captain of French-Canadian ancestry. Harris's final move was sheer kismet. An outbreak of yellow fever in the summer of 1876 forced him to flee the coast with his wife and two sons, Julian and Lucien. They settled inland in Atlanta, the city most intimately connected with his development as essayist, polemicist, and teller of the Uncle Remus stories. As editor and adviser to Henry W. Grady, proponent of the New South, Harris helped shape the conciliatory policies of the *Atlanta Constitution*, for which he wrote columns and editorials for the next quarter century. In a permanent situation at last, he built a country home named Wren's Nest in token of luck and felicity. In deprecation to his rise to fame, he lovingly referred to himself as a farmer and his home as Snap Bean Farm. Now a museum and garden on Atlanta's outer edge, the property has become a literary shrine on a par with William Faulkner's Rowan Oak and Thomas Wolfe's boardinghouse.

A chance reading of an inaccurate article—William Owens's "Folklore of Southern Negroes" in *Lippincott's* magazine (December 1877)—impelled Harris to pen a rebuttal, "Negro Folklore: The Story of Mr. Rabbit and Mr. Fox, as Told by Uncle Remus," published July 20, 1879. The event coincided with the withdrawal of federal troops from Atlanta, a test of the shaky reunification that bound black and white in the beginnings of an egalitarian society. Because Harris reverenced the black dialect and West African slave narratives that he had absorbed on Turnwold Plantation, he pursued an avocation—compiling, ordering, and preserving beast fables, some of which he located among Daufuskie Island storytellers living near Hilton Head, Georgia. A subsequent serendipity brought Uncle Remus to the world: In 1879, Harris had to substitute for a columnist who had been supplying the paper with dialect vignettes. In his mid-fifties, Harris turned his writing from state politics and economic news to the lore he had heard from the genial old slaves he loved in childhood. The stories were an immediate hit and were reprised in numerous papers, especially the *New York Evening Post*, to which Harris expressed thanks for spreading an underappreciated segment of Americana.

Rather than serve as objective ethnographer of the Uncle Remus stories, Harris chose the role of the aged African griot addressing a young audience, whom he acknowledged as a fictive version of the real Joel Chandler Harris in childhood. The premiere newspaper column, about Br'er Fox's invitation to dine with Br'er Rabbit, introduced characters and situations that became a *modus scribendi* for the remaining quarter century of Harris's career. In a separate venture, he added to American myth with two compilations of stories, *Uncle Remus: His Songs and His Sayings* (1880) and *Nights with Uncle Remus* (1883). The latter introduced Daddy Jack, a Gullah narrator whose complex dialect inhibited the popularity of the work.

Much critical surmise and rebuttal derive from arguments over Harris's purpose. Some declare him an altruist and archivist eager to preserve Afro-American lore. Others insist that he lacked ethnographic and philological fervor and hoped only to entertain and enlighten with some refurbished Aesopic tales. In the introduction to the 1880 volume, Harris's own modest commentary casts light on his academic status:

> It would be presumptuous in me to offer an opinion as to the origin of these curious myth-stories; but, if ethnologists should discover that they did not originate with the African, the proof to that effect should be accompanied with a good deal of persuasive eloquence. (O'Shea 1996, 4)

Thus, it seems safe to assume that Harris had scholarly intent and competence in regional folklore, but that, for whatever personal or professional reason, he opted to retain amateur status, well outside academic wrangles. Indeed, in a

Joel Chandler Harris recounted tales of a clever rabbit and sly fox in dialect through the persona of black storyteller Uncle Remus. Walt Disney combined live action and animation in *Song of the South* in 1946 to bring the stories to life. Uncle Remus (James Baskett) and children (actors Bobby Driscoll and Luana Patten) top a hill with Br'er (Brother) Rabbit, Br'er Bear, and Br'er Fox.

letter to Ambrose Bierce dated July 16, 1896, Harris substantiated his position in the literary community by declaring himself merely a "cornfield journalist." (O'Shea 1996, 3)

An underrated by-product of Harris's first compendium is the wealth of Southern tradition that derives from the black slave's syncretism of Christianity with survival smarts. The author's preface draws attention to the rhythm of a revival hymn, derived from what storyteller Richard Chase termed "the sundown voices of the Negroes . . . singing their sacred songs." ("Joel Chandler Harris" 1996, n.p.) The eight-line stanza rejoices in the comeuppance of Judgment Day:

> Oh, what shill we do w'en de great day comes,
> Wid de blowin' er de trunpits en de bangin' er de drums?
> How many po' sinners'll be kotched out late
> En fine no latch ter de goldin gate.
> > No use fer ter wait twel ter-morror!
> > De sun must n't set on yo' sorror,
> > Sin's ez sharp ez a bamboo-brier—
> > Oh, Lord! fetch de mo'ners up higher! (Harris 1982, 161)

The smugness of fundamentalism, when couched in an underclass patois, seems an appropriate mask for a slave who is otherwise prevented from displaying hatred and contempt for a supercilious master. The nuance of "De wheels er distruckshun is a hummin'" reflects a plausible reversal of roles for dominator and subordinate. By looking to the end of race, class, and social status, the revival singer—like the resourceful, undersized Br'er Rabbit of Uncle Remus's tales—can chortle in private at the discomfiture of white enslavers who find themselves outside the pale of heaven.

Harris was not limited to the Remus format. His familiarity with a variety of character types, social milieus, and dialects is obvious in stories published in *Harper's*, *Saturday Evening Post*, and *Century*, and became the basis for *Mingo and Other Sketches in Black and White* (1884), *Free Joe and Other Georgian Sketches* (1887), and *Daddy Jack the Runaway, and Other Stories Told after Dark* (1889). In addition to the Uncle Remus canon, Harris published 20 volumes, including *Gabriel Tolliver* (1902), a contemplative review of the Reconstruction era; novels, *The Romance of Rockville* (1878) and *Sister Jane, Her Friends and Acquaintances* (1896); short-story collections, *Tales of Home Folks in Peace and War* (1896) and *On the Wing of Occasions* (1900); *The Story of Aaron* (1895), *Mr. Rabbit at Home* (1895), and *Told by Uncle Remus* (1905) for children; and a fictional autobiography, *On the Plantation* (1892), which he serialized and syndicated in national newspapers for $2,500. His ease of phrase resulted in these and other additions to compendia of didactic sayings:

- Why not offer a prize for the man who can graft asparagus on the artichoke so as to make it eatable at both ends?

- Culture is a very fine thing, indeed, but it is never of much account either in life or in literature unless it is used as a cat uses a mouse—as a source of mirth and luxury. (O'Shea 1996, n.p.)

- Small men were trying to play instruments much too large for them, while others were fiddling away with futile earnestness on one string. ("Joel Chandler Harris" 1996, n.p.)

- De vittles wat's kumerlated widout enny sweatin' mos' allers gener'lly b'longs ter some yuther man by rights. (Harris 1982, 221)

- Hit look lak sparrer-grass, hit feel lak sparrer-grass, hit tas'e lak sparrer-grass, en I bless ef 'taint sparrer-grass.

- Ez soshubble ez a baskit er kittens.

- Lazy fokes' stummicks don't git tired. (Snodgrass 1990, *passim*)

- Licker talks mighty loud w'en it gits loose fum de jug.

- Hongry rooster don't cackle w'en he fine a wum.

- Youk'n hide de fier, but w'at you gwine do wid de smoke?

- Watch out w'en youer gittin' all you want. Fatten' hogs ain't in luck. (Bartlett 1992, 536)

With numerous offers of contracts and editorships, Harris resigned from the newspaper in 1900 and devoted his time to freelance writing. The final editions of his folklore—*Uncle Remus and the Little Boy* (1910), *Uncle Remus Returns* (1918), and *Seven Tales of Uncle Remus* (1948)—were published posthumously, complete with original drawings by Harris's illustrator and friend, A. B. Frost. With the help of Harris's son Julian and editor Don Marquis, in his last year Harris issued the tales in *Uncle Remus's Magazine* (1907), which attained a circulation of 200,000. The journal merged with *Home* magazine after the author's death from nephritis on July 3, 1908.

Harris's passing was marked with simple ceremony and a family burial plot in Westview Cemetery, where he, his wife, mother, and children are interred near Joel's friend and colleague, Henry Grady. Alongside the grave is a marker of Georgia granite with this inscription:

> I seem to see before me the smiling faces of thousands of children—some young and fresh and some wearing the friendly marks of age, but all children at heart—and not an unfriendly face among them. And while I am trying hard to speak the right word, I seem to hear a voice lifted above the rest, saying, "You have made some of us happy." And so I feel my heart fluttering and my lips trembling and I have to bow silently, and turn away and hurry back into the obscurity that suits me best. (Harlow 1941, 276)

The sentiment reflects the times and regional experience that Harris embodies and the demeanor of a genuinely unassuming Southern storyteller. He is honored in the lobby of the *Atlanta Journal-Constitution* along with a tribute to author Margaret Mitchell and columnist Don Marquis, creator of a cockroach named "archy." A scholarly collection of Harris's private papers, correspondence, and manuscripts is housed at Emory University.

Critical studies of Harris's stories and their African beginnings indicate that he did more than transmit folklore: His inventive style and perception of slave duplicity broadened the pithy trickster tales into recognizable story-length plots and provided a valuable insight into the slave's worldview. Walt Disney invigorated the stories with color visuals in the double Oscar-winning *Song of the South* (1946). The first film to blend human and animated characters, it grossed millions on successive showings, halted only briefly during the race-conscious

1960s. In the cartoon segment, the mischievous, fleet-footed meddler Br'er Rabbit and his animal pals accompany Uncle Remus down a country road, sing "Zip-a-Dee-Do-Dah," and act out the famous Tarbaby story, initiated by the voice and wide eyes of James Baskett, who plays the lovable Negro narrator. The story follows a Harris original, "Br'er Rabbit, Br'er Fox, and the Tar Baby," published November 16, 1879. After the screen version of Uncle Remus educates his young listener about the rabbit's self-sufficiency, he spins out the humorous Tarbaby incident, in which the rabbit's curiosity and stubbornness nearly costs him his life. Stalked by Br'er Fox, the rabbit is unaware of the snare and comes "pacin' down de road—lippity-clippity, clippity-lippity—dez ez sassy ez a jay-bird." (Harris 1952, 548)

The plot of Harris's most anthologized story demonstrates an amalgam of universal beast lore and traditions of a captive people. A proponent of plantation manners—one of the coping mechanisms that made bondage bearable—Br'er Rabbit insists that the silent Tarbaby reply to his greeting. Further refusal ignites the rabbit's temper. Blows to the Tarbaby's body stick the rabbit, forepaw and hind foot, to the unblinking figure. To the boy's questions about how Br'er Rabbit eludes the fox, Uncle Remus replies, "He mout, en den agin he moutent. Some say Jedge B'ar come 'long en loosed 'im—some say he didn't." Suspense is the hallmark of the plot, which turns on a constant tension between large carnivores and their smaller, wiser quarry, who flourish from a blend of impudence and cunning. The surface story entertains, but the complex strategy of Br'er Rabbit's plots satisfies by reshuffling a plantation hierarchy that relegates the bottom layer to blacks. As the bard explains in *Nights with Uncle Remus*, "Well, I tell you dis, ef deze yer tales wuz des fun, fun, fun, en giggle, giggle, giggle, I let you know I'd a-done drapt um long ago." (Harris 1982, 25) (Bartlett 1992; Bradbury 1996; Davis et al. 1970; Dorson 1959; Ehrlich and Carruth 1982; Harlow 1941; Harris 1952, 1982; "Joel Chandler Harris" 1996; O'Shea 1996; Perkins et al. 1991; Smith, C. 1967; Snodgrass 1990; Twain 1990; Wilson and Ferris 1989)

See also Twain, Mark.

HELLMAN, LILLIAN

A worthy contributor to American drama and to the emancipation of women in drama and in person, Lillian Hellman holds a place alongside Tennessee Williams as the best of Southern playwrights. Confrontations with greed and malice invigorate her dramas, which are moral and psychological sketches of the darker side of human ambition. In a 1997 review of *The Little Foxes* (1939), critic Louis Auchincloss credited her "stinging bite" and declares, "Lillian Hellman lives on because the villains she hated live on. In fact, today they're worse. In her day, at least, they might have felt shame." (Auchincloss 1997, 6H) Her deft clashes between people bankrupt of ethics has reclassed the "little foxes" in the title of her enduring play from a biblical citation to a literary image of insidious viciousness credited solely to Hellman.

Twice the winner of the New York Drama Critics' Circle Award, recipient of the National Book Award and Gold Medal for Drama from the National Institute of Arts and Letters, and a member of the American Academy of Arts and Letters, Hellman penned a succession of memorable dramas, directed two of her plays in New York, and conducted drama workshops during the 1960s at Yale, Harvard, and the Massachusetts Institute of Technology. Along with many of Hollywood's victims of McCarthyism, she earned a reputation for toughness during the mid-1940s when questioned by the House Committee on Un-American Activities, which based its investigation on her support for Spain during its civil war and on friendships with Dashiell Hammett, Richard Wright, and Clifford Odets. She managed to elude and lambaste her tormentors in a glorified memoir, *Scoundrel Time* (1976). The imposition of name-calling, blacklisting, and innuendo and the resulting 307-page FBI dossier inspired her retaliation, which she initiated out of spite. Peripherally, the work helped to establish the Committee for Public Justice to defend artists from government infringement of First Amendment rights.

Hellman claimed both her aunt's boardinghouse in New Orleans and an apartment in Manhattan as home, and returned at six-month intervals to the South, where she felt more relaxed among people she admired and understood. Born in New Orleans on June 20, 1905, the only child of traveling shoe salesman Max B. Hellman and Julia Newhouse Hellman, she recalls the shabbiness of her childhood offset by the love of Sophronia Mason, a black nanny to whom Hellman referred repeatedly in adulthood as though speaking of a beloved relative. In Hellman's autobiography, *An Unfinished Woman* (1969), there is a scene in which a new employee finds a photo of Sophronia in Hellman's library:

> I said, "My nurse, my friend. Handsome woman, wasn't she?"
> "You look like a nice little girl."
> "Maybe I was, but nobody thought so. I was trouble."
> "She didn't think so."
> Hellman takes the picture and, after forty years of ownership, perceives in the pose the affection that Sophronia had had for her as a child. Hellman murmurs, "It takes me too long to know things." (Hellman 1969, 241)

In *Scoundrel Time*, Hellman describes her bonding with Sophronia as a useful entree into understanding and appreciating all people:

> My own liking for black people maybe came a few days after I was born when I was put into the arms of a wet-nurse, Sophronia, an extraordinary woman who stayed on with us for years after. It was she who taught me to have feelings for the black poor, and when she was sure I did, she grew sharp and said it wasn't enough to cry about black people, what about the miseries of poor whites. (Hellman 1976, 43)

Hellman concludes that Sophronia's anger at the unfair distribution of wealth became Hellman's anger, "an uncomfortable, dangerous, and often useful gift." The reflection casts light on the playwright's clever use of human disaffection for social and moral evil.

Playwright Lillian Hellman (1905–1984) arrives in California in 1935.

Of the dual lives she lived in the North and South, Hellman describes at length in *An Unifinished Woman* her educational predicament—being behind the class in New York and ahead in Louisiana. Her solution was admirably practical: During her tenure in New Orleans, she skipped class several times a week, hoisted a sling full of books, bottle of cream soda, and lunch basket into a tree along with

> a fishing pole and a smelly little bag of elderly bait, a pillow embroidered with a picture of Henry Clay on a horse that I had stolen . . . and a proper nail to hold my dress and shoes to keep them neat for the return to the house. (Hellman 1969, 11)

Freed from the earthly demands of home and educational system, she read contentedly as a means of escaping adults, among whom she often felt puzzled and ill at ease.

After two years at New York University and a semester at Columbia, Hellman traveled with her mother before beginning a literary career. She found work with publisher Horace Liveright, served the *New York Herald-Tribune* as literary reviewer, and worked as a play reader for Harold Shulman. Her brief marriage to press agent and playwright Arthur Kober took her to Europe during the rise of fascism, where she first began writing short stories. Poorly matched and bored with her mate, she ended the marriage; once more free and sassy, she adopted the bohemian affectations of the New York theatrical crowd. She lived with novelist Dashiell Hammett until his death in 1961 and shared Hardscrabble Farm, a 200-acre estate in Pleasantville, New York, where they raised poodles. Hammett, author of best-selling detective fiction, drew on her wit and style for Nora Charles, the heroine of his Thin Man mystery series.

Influenced by the writings of Fyodor Dostoyevsky, Mark Twain, Henry James, and Theodore Dreiser, Hellman made a career as a journalist, freelance writer, editor, and playwright. Hammett encouraged her to write drama and suggested that she adapt a Scottish trial as the foundation for her first play. In 1934, she achieved a first-timer's success with *The Children's Hour*, an ironic, daring treatment of gossip and lesbianism. The play—which ran for 691 performances on Broadway and is frequently revived and studied in drama and feminist courses—was banned in Boston, Chicago, and London, and spurred a public perception of her as a rebel. The initiator of slander is a pampered rich student at the Wright-Dobie School named Mary Tilford, whose malicious exploitation of a vulnerable female teacher soon reaches the ears of two more gossips. The irony at the drama's heart is Martha Dobie's realization that the accusation has disclosed a hidden fact about herself that she has denied. To Karen Wright, Martha admits, "It's there. I don't know how. I don't know why. But I did love you. I do love you. I resented your marriage; maybe because I wanted you; maybe because I wanted you all along." (Hellman 1971, 63) Unable to call her feelings by the name *lesbianism*, Martha weakens as she struggles to express her desire:

> There's something in you, and you don't know it and you don't do anything about it. Suddenly a child gets bored and lies—and there you are, seeing it for the first time. . . . In some way I've ruined your life. I've ruined my own. (Hellman 1971, 63)

The taut moments of the stage play disappeared from Universal Pictures's 1961 screen version because Hellman's adaptation quells the suspense that buoys the titillating subject of sexual perversion. Starring a well-matched cast—Audrey Hepburn, Shirley MacLaine, Miriam Hopkins, and James Garner—the film earned two Oscar nominations for art direction and cinematography. Nonetheless, it lacks the emotional electricity and audience appeal of the original.

Succeeding plays elevated Hellman's status with more hits on stage and as vehicles for film. *The Little Foxes*, a tightly constructed family drama, focuses on a scheming manipulator, Regina Hubbard Giddens, an avaricious Southern Lady Macbeth who plots with a Chicago financier to gain 51 percent of the stock of a local cotton mill that will exploit cheap Southern labor. The maid Addie perceives how management, like Regina, is willing to drain the life from others if the act promises enrichment:

> Yeah, they got mighty well-off cheating niggers. Well, there are people who eat the earth and eat all the people on it like in the Bible with the locusts. And other people who stand around and watch them eat it. Sometimes I think it ain't right to stand and watch them do it. (Hellman 1971, 182)

The extent of Regina's guile alarms and disillusions her daughter Alexandra, who loves two of her mother's victims—her dispirited Aunt Birdie and ailing father, Horace Giddens.

Hellman's breaking point for the Hubbard-Giddens cabal is the emergence of Alexandra. A sheltered innocent in childhood, she reaches maturity by realizing that her mother is capable of tormenting Horace past endurance. Regina easily outwits two conniving brothers and gloats at her supremacy over their power struggle:

> Well, they'll convict you. But I won't care much if they don't. Because by that time you'll be ruined. I shall also tell my story to Mr. Marshall, who likes me, I think, and who will not want to be involved in your scandal. A respectable firm like Marshall and Company. The deal would be off in an hour. And you know it. Now I don't want to hear any more from any of you. *You'll do no more bargaining in this house.* (Hellman 1971, 196–197)

Hellman's crisp, efficient dialogue suits Regina by revealing a blend of self-control with careful character study of her brothers' weakness. Her murder of Horace by pressuring him toward a heart attack and withholding his medication is the climactic point at which Alexandra shifts loyalties and prepares to escape the deadly family undertow.

Hellman's drama succeeded on stage and screen. The Broadway play, which opened at the National Theater on February 15, 1939, starred Tallulah Bankhead and Frank Conroy as Regina and Horace Giddens. Bankhead made the most of Regina's complex evil, particularly the crass twisting of her daughter in the resolution:

> Somewhere there has to be what I want, too. Life goes too fast. Do what you want; think what you want; go where you want. I'd like to keep you with me, but I won't make you stay. Too many people used to make me do too many things. No, I won't make you stay. (Hellman 1971, 199)

The play was a stunning success that has been frequently revived and twice filmed, boosting the careers of Elizabeth Taylor, Bette Davis, and Stockard Channing, all former Reginas. Davis starred in Samuel Goldwyn's 1941 film adaptation, with Herbert Marshall as her debilitated husband. Supporting roles

Georgia-born actress Tallulah Bankhead starred as Regina Hubbard Giddens, a scheming manipulator, in Lillian Hellman's *The Little Foxes*, which opened on Broadway in 1939.

played by Teresa Wright, Richard Carlson, and Dan Duryea profited from the direction of William Wyler, whose talents earned Hellman an Oscar nomination along with Academy praise of Wyler, Davis, and Wright.

As the United States became embroiled in World War II, Hellman turned from Southern themes and settings to the rise of fascism for *Watch on the Rhine* (1941) and *The Searching Wind* (1944), then revived her Southern characters in *Another Part of the Forest* (1947), which again treats the Hubbard family of *Little Foxes*. Set in 1880, the play discloses the break with Southern civility during the prime of the family forebear, Marcus Hubbard, a prominent man who rose from working-class origins. The sensibilities and compassion of Marcus and his wife Lavinia contrast with their children, Oscar and Regina, an amoral pair who lack the late-nineteenth-century polish and altruism. In its Broadway debut on November 20, 1946, the play starred Patricia Neal as the young Regina opposite Mildred Dunnock and Percy Waram as the elder Hubbards.

During the 1930s and 1940s, Hellman scripted films from her own works and those of others for Samuel Goldwyn—*The Dark Angel* (1935), *These Three* (1936), *The Children's Hour* (1937), *Dead End* (1937), *The North Star* (1943), and *The Searching Wind* (1946)—and collaborated with Ernest Hemingway on a documentary, *The Spanish Earth* (1937). After adapting the works of Jean Anouilh, Burt Blechman, Voltaire, and others to the American stage, she produced a major theatrical achievement with *Toys in the Attic* (1960). Ever controversial in her memories and fantasies, Hellman's turn to memoir bolstered her popularity and stoked conjecture about her vivid, often conjectural self-portraits. The first, *An Unfinished Woman*, provides background about her youth, emergence as a screenwriter, involvement in the preliminaries to the Spanish civil war, sympathy with fellow Jews persecuted by Nazis, and associations with Hammett and humorist Dorothy Parker.

In 1973, Hellman published *Pentimento: A Book of Portraits*, which contains "Julia," named for a childhood friend who was studying medicine in Vienna when Hellman toured Europe. A convoluted spy thriller, the story depicts the author in complicity with the exotic Julia, a mysterious socialist who winds in and out of the author's clouded war memories. The title heroine is well suited to film. In 1977, the screen role went to Vanessa Redgrave, who, along with Jason Robards, won an Oscar for her performance. The resurgence of notoriety for Hellman preceded by seven years her death on June 30, 1984, from cardiac arrest. In retrospect, she was better known for the company she kept and the witty *bons mots* she tossed at the media than for the dramas and autobiographies she published. Less scrupulous than the social and moral ethos of her plays, the autobiographical works diverted public attention from the strengths of her Depression-era plays to a pushy, hard-edged woman eager for attention. (Auchincloss 1997; Blain et al. 1990; Bradbury 1963; Buck 1992; *Contemporary Authors* 1994; Cunliffe 1987; Davidson and Wagner-Martin 1995; Ehrlich and Carruth 1982; Gassner and Quinn 1969; Hellman 1969, 1971, 1973, 1976, 1997; Hughes 1951; Kunitz 1942, 1955; Lederer 1979; McHenry 1980; Mitgang 1996; Rollyson 1988; Rubin et al. 1985; Sherr and Kazickas 1994; Stein 1979; Wilson and Ferris 1989)

HENLEY, BETH

Beth Henley, an actress, teacher, and playwright, is often judged alongside Calder Willingham, Robert Harling, and Marsha Norman, the best satiric Southern dramatists to emerge from the late twentieth century. She achieved a place among contemporary comedy writers with *The Miss Firecracker Contest* (1980), the dizzy life and times of four misfits in search of acceptance, and *Crimes of the Heart* (1981), a touching, raffish masterpiece of black humor. The latter won the Great American Play Contest sponsored by Louisville's Actors Theatre.

Henley is well suited to Southern theater. Born on May 8, 1952, in Jackson, Mississippi, the locale of much of her writing, Elizabeth Becker Henley is the daughter of attorney Charles Boyce and actor Elizabeth Josephine "Lydy" Becker. Henley's mother starred in Jackson Community Theater productions, and involved her in learning lines and watching rehearsals. The experience prepared her for an introduction to her first love, the plays of Anton Chekhov, whose powerful character dramas became a written mentor. After completing a B.F.A. from Southern Methodist University (SMU) in 1974 and a year's graduate study in acting at the University of Illinois, Henley acted at Dallas's Theatre Three, taught at SMU, and directed for the Dallas Minority Repertory Theatre. In 1975, she joined the drama department at the University of Illinois.

After Henley gave up the stage, she directed past experience on both sides of the apron toward original drama and screenwriting. Searching in vain for appropriate contemporary roles depicting Southern females, Henley—like Richard Wright, Truman Capote, and Jesse Stuart—discovered that the only way to supply the characters she sought was to create her own. Beginning with *Am I Blue?* (1973), a one-act play composed for a class assignment, she established a system of prewriting; then, daily from 11:00 A.M. to 4:00 P.M., she composed in longhand in a spiral notebook, and finally typed each page on an IBM Selectric. She showed her finished work first to well-meaning friends, then to the more critical. Her efforts produced a flurry of spunky, dark, and nonstop funny plays for stage, television, and cinema, including *Morgan's Daughters* (1979), *The Debutante Ball* (1985), *The Lucky Spot* (1986), *True Stories* (1986), *Abundance* (1990), *Signature* (1990), *Control Freaks* (1992), and *L-Play* (1995), as well as a compendium of scenarios entitled *Beth Henley: Monologues for Women* (1992).

Critical response to her plays has been guarded but enthusiastic. *The Wake of Jamey Foster* (1982), a situational comedy, and *Nobody's Fool* (1986), a romantic comedy filmed in the same year, won few kudos because of their bland, low-key humor and a lack of compassion and honesty, two qualities of her stage and cinema masterpiece, *Crimes of the Heart*. A similar judgment assailed *Miss Firecracker*, a seriocomic study of Carnelle Scott (a pint-sized adult orphan from Brookhaven, Mississippi), which premiered at the Manhattan Theatre Club in 1984. Carnelle, a classic overachiever, is a misguided aspirant in a local Fourth of July beauty and talent competition. She recalls falling in love with the image when she saw her cousin, Elain Rutledge, as Miss Firecracker: "She was a vision of beauty riding on that float with a crown on her head waving to everyone. I thought I'd drop dead when she passed by me." (Henley *Monologues*

1992, 82) Observing a Fourth of July motif, Carnelle dyes her hair, dresses in sequins and tap shoes, holds sputtering sparklers in her front teeth, executes splits and somersaults, and twirls a baton to "The Star-Spangled Banner." She immerses herself in the sound and sight of Roman candles and fantasizes her act: "And the rockets' red glare—Boom!—the bombs bursting in air—Boom!—gave proof through the night—that our flag was—Boom!—there!" (Henley *Monologues* 1992, 91) Ably acted by Holly Hunter, Tim Robbins, and Mary Steenburgen, the 1989 movie version bemuses rather than entertains by over-shooting audience expectations with its emphasis on insecurity and bathos.

Henley, who has a natural flair for gothic whimsy—a blend of black humor and Southern gothic—learned the art of depicting lost souls from predecessors Carson McCullers, Eudora Welty, Tennessee Williams, and Flannery O'Connor. In an interview in *Back Stage*, she accounted for the savagery in *Control Freaks:*

> The darker side of life has always appealed to me. I like to have a big perspective on things: The reason things can be so funny is that they can be so sad; the reason they can be so beautiful is that they can be so ugly. If all there was to life was anguish, it wouldn't be so bad. (Collum 1995, 23)

Henley expresses her own psychic wrestlings through original drama, which offers a personal catharsis at the same time it channels her "uncensored out-pouring of feelings and obsessions." (Collum 1995, 23)

Henley's funniest study of life's darker side, *Crimes of the Heart*, taps the offbeat eccentricities of the three orphaned McGrath sisters—Babe, Meg, and Lenny—childhood residents of Hazlehurst, Mississippi. In the opening scene, set "five years after Hurricane Camille," the reunited daughters muddle through multiple failures of marriage, career, and male-female relationships. (Henley 1981, n.p.) Lenny, a dowdy, waning spinster, lives in the family homestead with Granddaddy; her sister, Babe Botrelle, has married well; Meg, still single, has gone to Hollywood in search of stardom. A defining moment before the trio gets together cameos Lenny alone in the kitchen, where she attempts to affix candles to cookies while she sings "Happy Birthday" to herself. Gathered to discuss a family crisis, the girls hug, catch up on each other's lives, bicker, and rehash resentment of their father—whom they recall had nice teeth—for deserting the family when they were young. Their mother's depression and suicide give a clue to the family's extremes of behavior: She hanged her cat along with herself so that she wouldn't have to die alone.

The crux of *Crimes of the Heart* is Babe's misguided attempt to shoot her husband Zackery, a corrupt state senator from Copiah County and patriarchal tyrant who discovers her fling with Willie Jay, a local black youth. The satiric caricature of the next-door meddler and family malcontent, Cousin Chick Boyle, inflicts the community's cynical judgment that Babe must be "in-the-head sick" to attempt to murder her husband. Chick overstates the botched shooting as "this heinous crime" and "manslaughter with intent to commit murder" and high-handedly orders Babe to cooperate with the attorney, "that nice-looking young Lloyd boy." (Henley 1981, 113) Babe defies Chick's melodramatic demand for an explanation of her deed with a double insult, "I just didn't like his stinking looks! And I don't like yours much, either, Chick the Stick!" (Henley 1981, 27)

At the play's periphery, Henley reveals the loveless marriage of Babe and Zackery through seriocomic glimpses. Babe admits that their antipathy grew out of her dislike for Zackery's jokes. Rather than shoot herself, she aims for his heart, but hits his stomach instead. The marital chasm coalesces in a single piercing image—the lemonade Babe laces with sugar to kill the sour taste before she calls for emergency aid for Zackery, who lies bleeding in the living room. In act II, in Babe's first confrontation with an angry, overbearing husband, she carries on an intentionally becalmed, one-sided phone call that dawdles along with "Hello, Zackery? How are you doing? . . . Uh huh . . . uh huh. . . . Oh, I'm sorry. . . . Please don't scream." (Henley 1981, 60) Defiant in the face of jail time for attempted murder, she looks forward to solitude and a respite from her domineering mate and his spying sister Lucille. Quirkily optimistic, Babe relishes an opportunity to learn to play her new sax.

Like Tennessee Williams and William Faulkner, Henley re-creates a Southern specialty—the dotty, off-center, small-town "family with a past." She hammers away at unresolved kinship problems, which overhang the action like dusty valances. The sisters relive their mother's sorrow and inertia—her daylong withdrawals to the back-porch steps, where she smoked and flung ashes at bugs and ants. Refuting claims that Babe should be "put away" for acting as erratically as her mother, Babe retorts that their mother wasn't crazy, only the victim of "a very bad day." (Henley 1981, 31) The sisters' sibling rivalries sound picayunish, particularly Lenny's contention that Grandmama sewed "twelve golden jingle bells" on Meg's skirt when the other girls got only three each, but the McGrath unity in hard times holds steady, proving that their mother's death brought them together against a callous community and private troubles.

As the play winds down to a satisfying denouement, Henley turns from satire to comedy. Babe and Lenny discuss Zackery's condition, Granddaddy's stroke, and the death of Billy Boy, an aged horse struck by lightning. With little insight Babe concludes, "Life sure can be miserable." (Henley 1981, 97) The attorney discovers that Zackery's attempt to blackmail Babe has crumbled in the welter of scandal that threatens his public show of stable family dignity. Chick's diatribe against "you trashy McGraths and your trashy ways: hanging yourselves in cellars; carrying on with married men; shooting your own husbands" ignites Lenny's dormant anger. She grabs a broom and runs Chick up a mimosa tree. (Henley 1981, 112) The play concludes with birthday cake for breakfast and the sisters at last freed of regrets and guilt.

Crimes of the Heart, which won the New York Drama Critics Award, a Tony, and a Pulitzer Prize, got a trial run at the Actors Theatre of Louisville in February 1979 before its New York debut at the Manhattan Theatre Club in 1980, followed by presentation at New York's John Golden Theatre on November 4, 1981. The play worked well in Bruce Beresford's 1986 film adaptation, scripted by Henley and starring Sam Shepard and Tess Harper, with Jessica Lange, Diane Keaton, and Sissy Spacek playing Meg, Lenny, and Babe McGrath. The film won Golden Globe and New York Critics awards for Spacek. Henley, Spacek, and Harper earned Oscar nominations. (Buck 1992; Collum 1995; *Contemporary Authors* 1994; Davidson and Wagner-Martin 1995; *Dictionary of Literary Biography* 1987; Hargrove 1984; Henley 1981, 1986; Henley *Monologues* 1992; Jones 1982; Laughlin 1986; Nemy 1984; Rich 1984; Roberston 1984; Schickel 1984)

HENRY, O.

See Porter, W. S.

HUMOR, SOUTHERN

Southern humor is a useful source of social commentary on regional foibles, from the pervasive themes of political corruption and religious extremism to particular idiosyncrasies of dialect, isolationism, and rural backwoods quirks. The region has produced a broad span of comic literature in a variety of genres—cartoon, critical review, column, memoir, biography, autobiography, folklore, storytelling, essay, editorial, verse, novel, and drama. Tops in their fields are cartoonist Doug Marlette; novelists Mark Twain, Allan Gurganous, Ferrol Sams, and Charles Portis; dramatists Robert Harling, Alfred Uhry, and Beth Henley; memoirist Florence King; autobiographer Maya Angelou; poets Richard Capel Beckett and Irwin Russell; columnists H. L. Mencken, Harry Golden, and Molly Ivins; storytellers Ray Hicks and Jackie Torrence; fablists Gayle Ross and J. J. Reneaux; and folklorists John Lomax, Zora Neale Hurston, and Davy Crockett, the first Southerner to profit from publishing regional tall tales.

A significant link between regional lore and the frontier tradition comes from Tennessean David "Davy" Crockett, noted pathfinder, scrapper, and folksy teller of tall tales. At the height of his political career, the growing legend of his woods exploits prompted primitive penny broadsides and newspaper features; a smash-hit stage parody, James Kirke Paulding's *The Lion of the West* (1831), about Kentucky colonel Nimrod Wildfire, a cardboard image of Crockett; and Mathew St. Clair Clarke's biography, *The Life and Adventures of Colonel David Crockett of West Tennessee* (1833), retitled *Sketches and Eccentricities of Col. David Crockett* in its second printing. Dismayed by scurrilous media caricatures and by Clarke's inaccuracies, Crockett journeyed to Washington, D.C., to hire Thomas Chilton to ghostwrite a dialect memoir, *Narrative of the Life of David Crockett of the State of Tennessee* (1834), one of the era's most popular autobiographies. Within months, Crockett produced two more works—*An Account of Colonel Crockett's Tour to the North and Down East* (1835) and *The Life of Martin Van Buren, Heir-Apparent to the "Government," and the Appointed Successor of General Jackson* (1835), a derisive biography.

Crockett's writings provide a few definitive details of his life. Claiming a North Carolina pioneer as his grandfather, Crockett was born August 17, 1786, in Limestone, Greene County, Tennessee, the fifth of nine children of Rebecca Hawkins and John Crockett, a veteran of the Battle of Kings Mountain. Among his prolix stretchers in *Go Ahead Almanack* (1838) is a humorous account of his infancy:

> I was born in a cane brake, cradled in a sap trough, and clouted with coon skins; without being choked by the weeds of education which do not grow *spontinaciously*—for all the time that I was troubled with *youngness*, my cornstealers were *nat'rally* used for other purposes than holding a pen; and *rayly* when I try to write my elbow keeps coming round lika swingle-tree, and it is easier for me to tree a varmint . . . than to write. (Hudson 1936, 304)

After crossing the Smoky Mountains from Virginia, the family moved to Rogersville, Tennessee. In 1796, they established an inn on the Abingdon-Knoxville road, where Crockett hauled wood and water for wash pots and cultivated vegetables in the family patch. A lackluster student with no taste for agriculture, he ran away from home to accept a job as wagoneer.

After marrying Mary "Polly" Finley in 1806, Crockett tried farming in earnest, supplementing his diminished income by selling wild game and hides. In 1812, he tried changing places to improve his luck. Wanderlust took him to new farmsteads in Lincoln County and on to Franklin, Tennessee. During the Creek Indian War of 1813–1814, he briefly served Andrew Jackson as a scout and gained military experience by enlisting with Major Russell's mounted sharpshooters, who ventured as far south as Alabama and Florida in search of hostile natives. After Polly died giving birth to a daughter, Crockett married Elizabeth Patton, a well-dowered widow, and added her son and three daughters to his family.

Exasperated with farming, the Crocketts searched Lawrence County for a suitable homestead, where Davy established a mill and distillery. Alone, he traversed Alabama and came down with malaria before returning to Tennessee, where he contented himself for a time in overlapping roles as local magistrate, town commissioner, and colonel of the local militia. Only semiliterate, he declared himself unfamiliar with the rules of spelling and grammar. He reports:

> I improved my handwriting in such manner as to be able to prepare my warrants, and keep my record book, without much difficulty. My judgments were never appealed from, and if they had been they would have stuck like wax, as I gave my decisions on the principles of common justice and honesty between man and man, and relied on natural born sense, and not on law, learning to guide me; for I had never read a page in a law book in all my life. (Crockett 1834, 135)

Crockett added oratory to his emerging skills during a campaign for state legislature when he ran against Dr. William E. Butler. He reports that he "choked up as bad as if my mouth had been jam'd and cram'd chock full of dry mush." (Crockett 1834, 141) By overglorifying Butler with stump mockery, Crockett applied reverse psychology that cast him as an ordinary backwoods farmer. The ploy won Crockett a term as a Tennessee state legislator and established his reputation as "the bear hunter, the man from the cane." (Crockett 1834, 167) His homespun grammar, idiom, and choice Crockettisms, such as "bodyaciously," "helliferocious," "riproarious," "fairation," "tetotaciously," and "obflisticated," endeared him to voters who functioned at a parallel level of semiliteracy.

A growing popularity among voters boosted Crockett's political career. Elected to the U.S. House of Representatives at age 41, he supported the Democratic platform and stumped for Jackson until his former commander became too domineering. In typical Crockett style, he denounced Jackson's autocracy and severed all ties, declaring, "I wouldn't take a collar around my neck with the letters engraved on it, MY DOG. Andrew Jackson." (Crockett 1834, 171–172) Crockett's strong individualism and irrepressible witticisms produced a low-key strategy to "work Uncle Sam's farm, till I restore it to its natural state o' cultivation, and shake off these state caterpillars o' corruption." ("David 'Davy' Crockett" 1996, 1)

At a lull in his rise to political power, Crockett launched one of his most popular publications: a series of seven *Crockett Almanacks* (1835–1838), in which he departs from simple narrative to pose as the naive backwoods dupe. Following a hillbilly model of humor, he features fellow congressman Ben Harding as a sidekick and coconspirator in stunts, cliff-hangers, outrageous buffoonery, homely jest, teasing, and rambunctious tall tales. A self-styled hero and rustic prodigy, Crockett inflates his adventures from the level of exaggerated truth to humor. Their episodic adventures extend dangers, hoaxes, and exploits to a parallel of François Rabelais's *Gargantua and Pantagruel* and the mythic Paul Bunyan tales. Crockett claims to have been an infant giant fed on whiskey and rattlesnake eggs. He claims to "run faster,—jump higher,—squat lower,—dive deeper,—stay under longer,—and come out drier, than any man in the whole country." (Crockett 1987, xxix) To potential voters he vaunts that he is "half-horse, half-alligator, a little touched with the snapping-turtle." (Derr 1993, 19) In a marathon bluster, he boasts,

> I can outlook a panther and outstare a flash of lightning: tote a steamboat on my back and play at rough and tumble with a lion, and an occasional kick from a *Zebra*. Goliath was a pretty hard colt but I could choke him.—I can take the rag off—frighten the old folks—astonish the natives—and beat the Dutch all to smash—make nothing of sleeping under a blanket of snow—and don't mind being frozen more than a rotten apple. (Crockett 1987, xxviii)

His stretchers reach epic heights—the prettiest wife, ugliest hound, roughest horse, keenest blade, truest friend, and most dependable rifle, which he named Killdevil. The publication of these "ring-tailed roarers" caused ill-humored detractors to spread rumors that Crockett was more gambler, philanderer, and coward than superhero.

The Crockett canon demonstrates the frontier version of the trickster motif. Boisterous and calculating, he outsmarts "mud turkles," pirates, and Indians and tells of the courtship of Zipporina, who climbs into a bearskin to lure her love into a hugging match with a grizzly. In one story, Crockett describes a ruse he pulls on Job, a barkeep, who refuses him credit for rum, which Crockett buys for rowdy supporters before an election. Crockett trades Job a coon skin, which the barkeep accepts "as legal tender for a quart in the West":

I was not slow in raising it to the counter, the rum followed, of course, and I wish I may be shot if I didn't, before the day was over, get ten quarts for the same identical skin, and from a fellow, too, who in those parts was considered as sharp as a steel trap and as bright as a pewter button. (Beatty et al. 1952, 349)

Careful to separate the tricks from more serious deception, Crockett concludes the episode by claiming to have repaid Job for the rum, but adds, "[He] refused the money, and sent me word that it did him good to be taken in occasionally, as it served to brighten his ideas." (Beatty et al. 1952, 350) Crockett is pleased to learn that Job charged the opposing candidate for the rum, a man too self-important to examine a bar tab for evidence of overcharging.

In 1835, Crockett, the inveterate malcontent, joined pals William Patton, Lindsey Tinkle, and Abner Burgin and set out for San Antonio, Texas, in search of better land farther west. To his detractors at the bar, Crockett tossed a parting shot: "Since you have chosen to elect a man with a timber toe to succeed me, you may all go to hell and I will go to Texas." (Crockett 1987, xxiii) Eight weeks before his death at the siege of the Alamo, he extolled Texas as "the garden spot of the world" and hoped for a seat on its constitutional committee. He concluded, "I am rejoiced at my fate. I had rather be in my present situation than to be elected to a seat in Congress for life. I am in hopes of making a fortune yet for myself and family, bad as my prospect has been." (Crockett 1987, xxiv) According to the diary of eyewitness José Enrique de la Peña, Santa Anna and his Mexican siege troops tortured, bayonetted, then shot Crockett and five or six others on March 6, 1836. A romanticized chronicle, Richard Penn Smith's *Colonel Crockett's Exploits and Adventures in Texas* (1836), sold well in the ensuing months, when public sympathies increased the demand for his humorous lore.

Actor Frank Mayo rode the crest of Crockettmania to stardom in 1872 in Frank Hitchcock Murdoch's five-act melodrama *Davy Crockett*, a romance that depicts Davy in fringed leggings, buckskin tunic, and coonskin cap. The long-barreled flintlock, powder horn, and knife belt common to the era complete the standard attire for the Tennessee pioneer and hunter. A twentieth-century version of the Crockett legend surfaced in 1942, when Arkansas archivist-historian Dee Brown published *Wave High the Banner*, a novel shaped from primary research, legend, biography, superstition, folklore, songs like "Who Will Shoe Your Pretty Little Foot," and the stories Brown's grandmother told him. Walt Disney's idealized frontier television series *Davy Crockett, King of the Wild Frontier* (1954–1955) crystallized for its family audience a sanitized version of Crockett, starring Fess Parker, an endearingly frank portrayer of the famed woodsman's best qualities. The role and its multiverse musical ballad embroiders history with extreme adulation for a backwoods defender of democracy.

The South's resourceful humor is not limited to the semiliterate witticisms of backwoodsmen like Crockett. Thomas Chandler Haliburton, a noted jurist who migrated south from Nova Scotia, preceded the era of dialect humor with a series of newspaper sketches, collected as *The Americans at Home; or, Byeways, Backwoods, and Prairies* (1854). Haliburton's works display a restraint not found in native works, particularly those of Alabaman Francis Bartow Lloyd, author of *Sketches of Country Life* (1898); Mississippian John Mills Allen; Tennesseean

John Sharp Williams; Kentuckians John Allen Wyeth and H. S. Fulkerson; and Georgian Augustus Baldwin Longstreet. The best of the lot, Longstreet, a Yale graduate ably prepared for the state legislature and a judgeship, altered careers by accepting a Methodist ministry, publishing the *Augusta Sentinel*, and serving as president of Emory College, Centenary College, and the University of Mississippi. While writing newspaper sketches, he collected a group of vignettes titled *Georgia Scenes* (1834), a popular success in its expanded form published six years later. The work, featuring "The Horse Swap," stayed in circulation for several decades, but his prestigious professional status forced him to disavow authorship.

In a more straightforward and refined style than his ribald Southern predecessors, Virginian Joseph Glover Baldwin wrote his masterwork *The Flush Times of Alabama and Mississippi: A Series of Sketches* (1853), a jolly parody of local idiosyncrasies, and *Party Leaders* (1855), a political takeoff that poked fun at Thomas Jefferson, Alexander Hamilton, Andrew Jackson, Henry Clay, and John Randolph. The focus of Baldwin's humor is the patent chauvinism that inclines the Virginian to contemplation and adoration of the home state. In reference to local heroes, Baldwin claims, "Great is the Virginian's reverence of great men, that is to say, of great Virginians. This reverence is not Unitarian. He is a Polytheist. He believes in a multitude of Virginia Gods." (Beatty et al. 1952, 385)

In characterizing regional politics, Baldwin is in rare form. He ridicules his fictional victim, Old Major Willie Wormley, with appropriately benign amiability:

> The Major—for a wonder, being a Virginian—had no partisan politics. He could not have. His heart could not hold any thing that implied a warfare upon the thoughts or feelings of others. He voted all the time for his friend, that is, the candidate living nearest to him, regretting, generally, that he did not have another vote for the other man. (Davis et al. 1970, 465)

Moving to the issue of abolitionism, Baldwin declares that the major's slaves welcome him in a rush and passes out "a piece of calico here, a plug of tobacco there, or a card of *town* ginger-bread to the little snow-balls that grinned around him." For all its pointed gibes and racism, Baldwin's rambling, discursive wit aimed at no serious challenge of Southern lifestyle.

Reprising his successful style, Baldwin wrote *The Flush Times of California*, a tongue-in-cheek epistle published in the *Southern Literary Messenger* in November 1853. The work details rambles in San Francisco, where he ultimately was elected to the California Supreme Court. Composed in the style of the sophisticated essays of Washington Irving's *Knickerbocker's History of New York*, Baldwin touches up hyperbole with Rabelaisian high spirits. In a description of Phil Steptoe's overspending following a rich strike, Baldwin exploits the outer reaches of the tall tale:

> I saw him the other day driving a dozen Chinamen tandem through Red-River Street. You know their hair hangs in a long queue to the ground: he hitched them to each other by the tails, and sat back in an old sulkey, with head one side and his heels over the foot-board, smoking a cigar, driving them along in a trot. (Baldwin 1966, 24)

With a deft shift, Baldwin understates in his conclusion, "I am afraid he will turn out badly." He concludes that California's boom times have dwindled to dullness with a few disasters and no more than one hanging a week. In a postscript, he promises to send "a few pounds of bracelets and trinkets by the next steamer." (Baldwin 1966, 24)

Much subdued in the aftermath of the California gold rush, Baldwin wrote *Ebb Tide* (1864), a sober social commentary on the effects of gold on California. In his opinion, the discovery of nuggets at Sutter's Mill "opened a new page in the history of the world." (Baldwin 1966, 44) Recently disbanded soldiers leave the war with Mexico in search of adventure, and Baldwin satirizes the dreams of these neophyte prospectors by repeating the type of hearsay that draws thousands from the East:

> The mountain torrents were dammed up by boulders of auriferous rock, and swept nuggets of gold, like oranges, down the tide—while the hills groaned and their huge sides swelled out, pregnant with crude "yellow-boys," only awaiting some Yankee accoucher safely to deliver them of their precious burden. (Baldwin 1966, 45–46)

To grab their share, swarms of "strong-limbed hoosiers and the adventurous backwoods-men" precede a second tide of European gold seekers, who are loosened by the news "as a quart of molasses loosens [the bowels] of a botts-afflicted horse." (Baldwin 1966, 46–47)

Baldwin's contemporary, George Washington Harris, also derived lowbrow humor from a working man's perspective. A writer of homely sketches and yarns, he drew on his careers as steamboat captain and railroad engineer, both of which put him in close daily contact with undereducated laborers. Told in tedious dialect spelling, his first ventures in publishing were submissions to the *Spirit of the Times*. His collection of newspaper anecdotes, *Sut Lovingood: Yarns Spun by a "Nat'ral Born Durn'd Fool"* (1867), a vigorous trickster's miscellany, contains such idioms as "ontil the merlenium [until the millennium]," "every suckit rider [circuit rider] outen jail," "es restless es a cockroach in a hot skillit," "es quiet es a greased waggin," and "ontil thar's enuf white fros' in hell tu kill snap-beans." (Davis et al. 1970, 469, 474, 475) He followed with *Sut Lovingood's Travels with Old Abe Linkhorn* (1868), an episodic gambit serialized in the *Nashville American*.

A third funster of the era, North Carolinian Johnson Jones Hooper, made his reputation while editing the *East Alabamian* and other newspapers in the area around Montgomery, Alabama. He concealed his dignified position as circuit solicitor and secretary of the Confederate Congress under the persona of a fictional picaro and cardsharp in *Some Adventures of Captain Simon Suggs, Late of the Tallapoosa Volunteers* (1846). A slapstick farceur, Suggs figures in "Taking the Census," "Capt. M'Spaddan," "Polly Peaseblossom's Wedding," and "Widow Rugby's Husband." Hooper pictures Suggs as a harmless booby who decks himself in homemade uniform complete with pincushions for epaulets, hat with oversized cockade, and a silk handkerchief for a sash. A Quixotic knight, he goes forth with hoe handle armed with a rusty bayonet and perches on a barrel top to write a deposition in pokeberry juice on a dirty scrap of paper. Such popular short pieces were reprinted in newspapers in New York, St. Louis, and New Orleans.

In *The Widow Rugby's Husband, A Night at the Uly Man's, and Other Tales of Alabama* (1851) and *Tales of Alabama* (1851), Hooper pursues a broad base of comic encounters that equals the japes of *Some Adventures of Captain Simon Suggs, Late of the Tallapoosa Volunteers*. One of his excursions, "The Captain Is Arraigned before a Jury," takes him to court for playing poker for money. When the charge is read as an affront to "the peace and dignity of the State of Alabama," Suggs mutters, "Humph! . . . *that's* a derned lie as ever Jim Belcher writ! Thar never were a *peaceabler* or more *gentlemanlier* game o' short cards played in Datesville—which thar's a dozen men here is knowin' to it!" (Hooper 1921, 2491) By producing a note from a doctor claiming that Suggs's sons are ill, the defendant obtains his freedom, but makes the error of standing on the street corner to crow over his trickery. The solicitor, outraged at the ruse, rails, "Thar . . . goes as clever a feller as ever toted a ugly head! He's smart, too, d—d smart. . . ." (Hooper 1921, 2495)

In contrast to the unrefined humor of the nineteenth century, the twentieth century produced four notably scrappy, sophisticated humorists—Harry Golden, Fannie Flagg, Florence King, and Molly Ivins. Golden, a Russian Jewish immigrant who grew up on New York's Lower East Side, is often mistaken for a New York native. Having served 18 months for mail fraud and stock manipulation after allying with a shady partner, he changed his name from Goldhirsch to Golden and left New York. He resituated himself, his wife, and four sons in the South in 1941 when he accepted a reporting job for the *Charlotte (NC) Labor Journal*. To fill a gap in Southern journalism, that same year he established the *Carolina Israelite*, an anomaly in the Bible Belt but appreciated for the variety offered by a Yankee Jewish radical. Back-to-back best-sellers—*Only in America* (1958) and *For Two Cents Plain* (1959)—established his reputation for a light touch and universal wit.

A famed friend maker, Golden was a confidant of notables Bertrand Russell, Ernest Hemingway, William Faulkner, Harry Truman, John F. Kennedy, Adlai Stevenson, and the entire family of Carl Sandburg, to whom he dedicated *Enjoy, Enjoy* (1971). The compendium contains some of his best writing, including "Governor Faubus and Little Rock," "The Negro D.A.R.," "What Is a Liberal?," and "The Negro Voter," all lightly tipped with Golden's amiable quips but founded on a hardheaded Yankee outrage that racism and anti-Semitism still sprouted on Dixie's fertile soil. In 1974, he published *Our Southern Landsman*, a collection of mordant, thought-provoking essays on Judaism in the South that holds up the example of famous Southern Jews: Charleston's free-marketer, Benjamin Mordecai; Atlanta's noted humanist, Rabbi David Marx; Eugenia Phillips and Adah Menken, both Confederate spies; Herman, Moses, and Caesar Cone, founders of Cone Mills in Greensboro, North Carolina; and Rabbi Gershon Mendes Seixas, a board member at Columbia University in South Carolina. Concerning black anti-Semitism, he declares that the hatred of blacks for Jews is rare:

> The two luxuries of Western civilization, anti-Semitism and Negrophobia, are denied us. But we have had some advantages, the chief of which is that the struggle of the NAACP and Martin Luther King and Jim Farmer to advance black equality has made the Constitution of the United States a living document. (Golden 1974, 225–226)

Golden lauds the civil rights movement for confirming equal rights to everyone, particularly other fringe groups who profit from the martyrdom of black leaders. He expresses his gratitude for a groundswell that "has strengthened my security and the security of my grandchildren."

Golden was not limited to such controversial subjects as unions, integration, and bigotry. He wrote about food, manners, dress, culture, education—whatever topics seemed most in need of commentary. Carl Sandburg said of him, "Whatever is human interests Harry Golden. Honest men, crooks, knuckleheads, particularly anybody out of the ordinary if even a half-wit, any of them is in his line. He writes about them." (Romine 1978, 1B) The most frequently cited of his essays is "The Vertical Negro Plan" (1944), a wry satire on Southern racism. Basing his logic on the whites' discomfort while sitting with blacks at lunch counters and in schools, Golden proposed that all seats be removed so that whites and blacks would have to stand. His satiric plan turns up regularly in anthologies of humor and in textbook examples of satire.

More at home with fiction, comedienne and humorist Fannie Flagg has worked as a television producer, nightclub stand-up comic, bit actress, and novelist. A veteran of *Wonder Woman*, *The Best Little Whorehouse in Texas*, *Sex and the Married Woman*, *The Jackie Gleason Show*, *The Match Game*, and *Love Boat* as well as Tennessee Williams's drama *Cat on a Hot Tin Roof*, she is adept at offsetting potential tragedy with comedy. Her hard-charging blend of humor and pathos, glimpsed in *Daisy Fay and the Miracle Man* (1981) came to full flower in *Fried Green Tomatoes at the Whistle Stop Cafe* (1987), filmed in 1991 with an experienced cast including Jessica Tandy, Kathy Bates, Mary Stuart Masterson, Cicely Tyson, and Mary-Louise Parker. The film won Oscar nominations for Tandy, and for Flagg and Carol Sobieski, who wrote the screenplay.

Flagg overlays the plot of a heavily suppressed lesbian relationship with the energized friendship of Evelyn Couch, an overweight, unfulfilled visitor to Mrs. Cleo "Ninny" Threadgoode, the "good thread" that ties together dismembered scenes from the past. Ninny's story of Idgie and Ruth, childhood friends and owners of a railside restaurant in rural Alabama, is zany and eccentric on the surface, but a-bubble with drama in the life of a child bride fleeing an abusive marriage. Flagg's narrative stitchery pieces together bits of news and court testimony into a full dramatic tapestry of the interconnected lives of women intent on surviving and securing a bit of joy. At an intense moment in Ruth's sufferings with "that terrible cancer in her female organs," her nurse, Onzell, sits by her bed, clasping her "little skeleton of a hand" and singing "In the Sweet By and By." (Flagg 1987, 285, 288) The scene closes on strong sunlight and Onzell weeping with relief that Ruth's agony has ended. Obeying local rituals, "As she covered the mirror and stopped the clock by the bed, she thanked her sweet Jesus for taking Miss Ruth home." In an epilogue consistent with a down-home tent revival and an Alabama murder trial, Flagg appends genuine recipes for buttermilk biscuits, skillet cornbread, red-eye gravy, and fried green tomatoes with milk gravy.

A more acerbic wit known to draw blood rather than laughs, Florence King is a true Southern hybrid—the daughter of British jazz trombonist Herbert Frederick King and Louise Ruding King, a cigarette-wielding baseball fan from Washington, D.C., where Florence was born on January 5, 1936. According to the droll comedy of *Confessions of a Failed Southern Lady* (1985), King's youth placed her among a trio of misaligned adults living on Park Road after the news of Louise's pregnancy brought her grandmother to the scene to supervise. Granny's allegiance to the United Daughters of the Confederacy and the code of the South failed to gentrify Florence. A closing quatrain in *Reflections in a Jaundiced Eye* (1989) poses Florence's counterpoint to Granny's patriotic obsession:

> Regarding our Democrazy
> And all of those who love it,
> I'll quote my angel mother now
> And end by saying "Shove it."
> (King 1989, 198)

Growing up a family anomaly, King acquired Herb's crisp British enunciation, Louise's prickly demeanor, and Granny's stubborn monomania.

Acerbic wit Florence King makes fellow humorist Fannie Flagg laugh during a 1987 symposium on women and humor in Austin, Texas.

Writing channeled King's trenchant wit into a salable product. After earning a B.A. from American University in 1957 and completing a year's graduate work at the University of Mississippi, she taught history in Suitland, Maryland, then wrote for the *Raleigh News and Observer*, for which she earned a North Carolina Press award. She enjoyed reviewing books for *Newsday* and the *New York Times;* writing a column for *National Review* and articles for *Cosmo, Ms., Playgirl, Southern Magazine*, and *Penthouse;* and writing erotic romances for *Uncensored Confessions*, which she signed with assorted pen names—Cynthia, Emmett X Ree, Niko Stavros, Veronica King, and Mike Winston. Not altogether proud of the latter segment of her résumé, King admits that the discipline of steady composition in a limited genre was not wasted, for it taught her the rudiments of fiction.

In the past two decades, King has thrived among Southern satirists with a steady output of hilarious, readable commentary in a distinctive, aggressive style. Fiercely conservative, antidemocratic, and pro-individual, she has been described as an "unreconstructed Southerner, gun-toting right-wing feminist, high-church Episcopal atheist, postmenopausal misanthropic monarchist." (King 1995, flap copy) Her "legit" satire began with *Southern Ladies and Gentlemen* (1975), a spin-off of her years as a bridal page reporter. Looking over social change in gushy local reporting of lingerie showers, subdeb soirees, and mother-and-daughter tea parties, she concludes that

> Debutanting is the South's way of hanging onto the old image of the belle. There are debutantes everywhere in Dixie, and a profusion of balls both large and small. This is another reason why Woman's Department writers are so nervous; the word "balls" is always cropping up in headlines, along with the expression "coming out." (King 1993, 119)

Experienced with the pushiest of social communities, she claims that two Carolina cities—Shelby to the north and Charleston to the south—lead the "crème de la crème" in pretentious public display. Selecting Miss Royal Stuart Montgomery as a hypothetically overdone belle, King admires the type for gall: "There are plenty of sluts, tramps, and whores around now, but how many hoyden minxes? Many of the Seventies swingers merely fantasize what they would like to do; Royal went out and did it." (King 1993, 126)

In an appended afterword of the 1993 edition, King adds to her list of good ole boys, prom trotters, daddy's girls, gracious do-gooders, invalids with pelvic disorders, and dowagers with hot flashes the latest regional outrage—the homogenized South, vitiated by waves of insipid Northern climbers:

> If Oakland has no *there*, Damnyuppies have no *from*. Whatever ethnic background they once possessed has faded with the geographical and psychological distance they have put between themselves and their origins. Most of them seem to have no distinctive traits, habits, or accents—just master's degrees. (King 1993, 218)

Her later titles—*WASP, Where Is Thy Sting* (1976), *He: An Irreverent Look at the American Male* (1978), and *When Sisterhood Was in Flower* (1982)—move beyond the South to spotlight inconsistencies in American behaviors, particularly those springing from religious fervor or political prejudice. In *WASP*, she leaps to conclusions about uppity women whose shopping list reads like a post-Victorian shaped-verse apologia:

> Alpo
> 9-Lives
> Harper's
> tomato juice
> Worcestershire
> Tabasco
> vodka
> food.
> (King 1995, 24)

The third, *Sisterhood*, opens with a parody of *Moby-Dick* ("Call me Isabel") and lampoons half-baked realms of radical feminism.

On a personal note, King assesses the milieu of home and family traditions with *Confessions of a Failed Southern Lady*, a pseudoautobiographical memoir of the King family. Her jests about mismated parents, precocity, and a tyrannical grandmother sparkle with enough audacity and drollery to suggest actual memories rather than blatant exaggeration. The melange of a mother reading the sports page and chain-smoking Lucky Strikes, Granny counseling women who suffer from tilted womb, and Herb quietly suffering in an out-of-sync household supply verisimilitude and justification for pity. The turn to out-of-the-closet college confessional in the last quarter of the book provides insight into the solitude and diffidence that plagued King's childhood and teen years.

Returning to seriocomic essays in her next three works, King attacks the American penchant for crisis hot lines and ACLU causes and a national reputation for professorial wimps in *Reflections in a Jaundiced Eye*. With a pathologist's glee, she flaunts wickedly raw, Swiftian flayings of American values and a personal vendetta against feminist polemicist Andrea Dworkin in *Lump It or Leave It* (1991) and uncompromising studies of human character in *With Charity for None* (1992). In *Lump It*, King opines: "An America without -ists is like an egg without salt, so defenders of the environment and animal-rights advocates are doing their bit to smoke out and hunt down new villains." (King 1990, 126) In 1995, she reprised earlier essays in *The Florence King Reader*, a collection of her sassiest and least restrained caricatures, including a seventies flower child and a harebrained medievalist.

In one of the inevitable clashes between contemporaries of comparable wit and verve, Florence King attacked Molly Ivins, political satirist for the *Fort Worth Star-Telegram*. In August 1995, King published "Molly Ivins, Plagiarist" in *American Entertainment;* Ivins had little choice but to apologize for withholding credit for significant citations. Ivins, who labels her point of view as populist, shares little of the harsher tones and broad-scale themes of King, self-described as "slightly to the right of Vlad the Impaler." The dustup arose from King's critique of Ivins's 1991 collection *Molly Ivins Can't Say Those Things, Can She?* Four years after the successful volume appeared in print, King saw segments in Ivins's chapter "Magnolias and Moonshine" that derived from King's *Southern Ladies and Gentlemen*, published 20 years earlier.

Although Molly Ivins is not high on Florence King's must-read list, she is a perennial favorite among American political editors. As political columnist three days a week for the *Fort Worth Star-Telegram,* she plies folksy populist put-downs against the idiocies of national politics and ribs Texas's anointed nincompoops who inhabit the legislature, which she dubs "the lege." An Ivins election-year quip appeared in the *Lincoln (NE) Star* on September 27, 1995, in which she pricks the hopeful bubbles that floated General Colin Powell's name among the growing list of potential candidates. To the wishful flock who named Powell, of Jamaican parentage, as proof that the United States is no longer racist, Ivins trounces their hopes: "I hate to point out the obvious again, but Powell is not a very black man. I speak only of hue: He is what is known in some circles as light 'n bright." (Ivins 1995, n.p.) Ivins's ready wit draws blood as surely as a rawhide whip and flicks torment to right and left, and particularly to the fringe. Of the unpredictable sloganeering of candidate wannabe Ross Perot, she deflates his overblown oratory with quips about his "chihuahua voice." Her brief sojourn on the staff of *60 Minutes* wilted with audiences more accustomed to reading her humor in print. Unfazed by the failure of her television appearances, she returned to the job she does best—needling the people who make laws. (Baldwin 1966; "Ballad of Davy Crockett" 1996; Beatty et al. 1952; Blair 1944; Blankenship 1931; Botkin 1944; Bradbury 1996; Brown 1987; Brown 1945; Brunvand 1996; Coad and Mims 1929; *Contemporary Authors* 1994; Crockett 1834, 1987, 1996; "David 'Davy' Crockett" 1996; Davis et al. 1970; Derr 1993; Doar 1969; Ehrlich and Carruth 1982; Flagg 1981, 1987; Gary 1972; Golden 1961, 1974; Groer 1995; Guilds 1970; Hewitt 1959; Hudson 1936; Ivins 1991, 1995; King 1989, 1990, 1993, 1995; "Molly Ivins on American Politics" 1996; "Molly Ivins's Biography" 1996; Neuendorf 1995; Patterson and Snodgrass 1994; Romine 1978; Trent 1905)

See also Harris, Joel Chandler; Mencken, H. L.; Twain, Mark.

HURSTON, ZORA NEALE

A prominent, controversial literary figure from the 1920s, Zora Neale Hurston has earned so enviable a position as foremother of black female novelists that the name Zora suffices to identify her. Along with such designations as ethnologist, spiritualist, essayist, folklorist, novelist, short-story writer, playwright, autobiographer, and Florida regionalist, she is known as the author of the first American feminist novel. Like Margaret Sanger, Dorothy Day, and Emma Goldman, Hurston lacked name recognition until the surge of interest in feminism in the 1970s. Like author Marjorie Kinnan Rawlings, she made so deep a study of southern Florida dialect, customs, and social structure that she enriched and legitimized a segment of Southern fiction often passed over in regional collections that favor Tidewater Virginia, Charleston's Gullah-speaking population, Southern mountains, Creole country on the Mississippi Delta, and the broad span of territory marked by the Uncle Remus dialect.

Born on January 7, 1891, in Notasulga, Alabama, Hurston spent her life clouding the facts. To appear a decade younger than she was and to hide the shame of completing a high school diploma at age 26, she claimed to have been born in 1901 in Eatonville, a minuscule community on Highway 4 only a few miles north of Orlando between Maitland and Winter Park, Florida. Hurston commemorates her homeland in her autobiography, *Dust Tracks on a Road* (1942) with an impromptu paean to Polk County:

> Black men from tree to tree among the lordly pines, a swift, slanting stroke to bleed the trees for gum. Paint, explosives, marine stores, flavors, perfumes, tone for a violin bow, and many other things which the black men who bleed the trees never heard about. (Hurston 1973, 2713)

She was the daughter of seamstress and teacher Lucy Ann Potts and John Hurston, a semiliterate mulatto sharecropper from Alabama. Her father, the poorly paid minister of Zion Hope Baptist Church, eked out cash money as a carpenter.

In her deliberately vague biography, Hurston recalls living on ample farmland dotted with a barn, vegetable patch, citrus and guava trees, chickens, and Cape jasmine, which she later learned by its New York name, gardenia. She finished six years at Hungerford School. Always second to her compliant sister Sarah, Zora demanded attention as the fifth of a family of eight and reports playing "hide and whoop, chick-mah-chick, hide and seek, and other boisterous games" with village children. (Hurston *Dust* 1991, 12) She recalls home lessons from her mother in parsing and long division, and cherishes her mother's exhortation to her brood to "jump at de sun." (Hurston *Dust* 1991, 13)

In "How It Feels To Be Colored Me" (1928), Hurston recalls how white Northern snowbirds slowed down on their drive to sunny Orlando and gawked at black behaviors. A voluble, exuberant exhibitionist, she claims to have put on a "welcome-to-our-state" show:

> They liked to hear me "speak pieces" and sing and wanted to see me dance the parse-me-la, and gave me generously of their small silver for doing these things, which seemed strange to me for I wanted to do them so much that I needed bribing to stop. Only they didn't know it. The colored people gave no dimes. They deplored any joyful tendencies in me, but I was their Zora nevertheless. I belonged to them, to the nearby hotels, to the county—everybody's Zora. (Hurston "How It Feels" 1985, 1650)

The giving nature that pushed Hurston to center stage in childhood presaged a greater display in early womanhood. Unlike the self-pitying, mad-at-the-world childhood of Richard Wright, she claimed not to mind being black, preferred pride to the pose of "tragically colored," and disdained "the sobbing school of Negrohood." (Lyons 1990, 102)

Hurston's formal education was sketchy, but her immersion in community lore was as complete as a college degree. She left school at age 13 to tend the three children of her brother Bob, a Memphis physician. Despite gaps in education, her family boasted a proud lineage that included an alderman and three-term mayor of Eatonville, the first incorporated, self-governing black town in the United States. Local communication emanated from the porch of Joe Clarke's neighborhood store, where idlers swapped stretchers, boasted, teased, sang, recited tales about High John the Conqueror (or John de Conker), and dotted their exchanges with such weary-gay wisdom as "I have been in sorrow's kitchen and licked out all de pots." (Maggio 1992, 302)

Hurston never recovered from the insecurity brought on by her mother's sudden death from a lung ailment in 1904 and by her father's subsequent marriage to Mattie, a woman Zora despised enough to fight with a hatchet. In her autobiography, she describes her mother's abrupt departure in metaphoric terms reminiscent of Emily Dickinson's poem "Because I Could Not Stop for Death":

> Just then, Death finished his prowling through the house on his padded feet and entered the room. He bowed to Mama in his way, and she made her manners and left us to act out our ceremonies over unimportant things. (Maggio 1992, 76)

Like the dismal scenarios of Richard Wright's *Black Boy*, in which young Richard is shuttled among relatives, Hurston lost a sense of belonging in her early teens after her father dispatched her to a Jacksonville boarding school and sent siblings to other families. He was so put out with her impudence that he wrote the school to suggest that the administration adopt Zora.

At age 14, Hurston joined an itinerant Gilbert and Sullivan troupe, earning $10 per week as maid and seamstress. While the company performed British light opera in Baltimore, she worked part-time as barbershop manicurist and waitress in a nightclub. She lived with her sister, Sarah Hurston Mack, entered the Morgan Academy, and earned a high school diploma in 1918. The next year she spent at Howard Prep School preparatory to enrolling in Howard University, the "Negro Harvard," in Washington, D.C. Until 1924, she studied literature under critic Alain Locke, linguist Lorenzo Dow Turner, and poet George Douglas Johnson. While battling an undiagnosed chronic intestinal complaint, she earned an associate degree and published her first fiction, "John Redding Goes to Sea" (1921) in *Stylus*, the university literary magazine.

Emulating flamboyant flappers and developing a persona as a budding artiste, Hurston came into her own in Harlem, New York, center of the buoyant black renaissance of the 1920s, and claimed that she could saunter down Seventh Avenue feeling completely unfettered by prejudice. She wrote in 1928,

> [In Harlem] the cosmic Zora emerges. I belong to no race nor time. I am the eternal feminine with its string of beads. I have no separate feeling about being an American citizen and colored. I am merely a fragment of the Great Soul that surges within the boundaries. (Hurston "How It Feels" 1985, 1652)

Hurston took as mentors the era's singers, painters, sculptors, writers, and revolutionaries and served as research assistant and companion to author Fannie Hurst. At poet Georgia Johnson's S Street Saloon, she maintained her Southern dialect and mannerisms while cultivating friendships with intellectuals such as novelists Jessie Redmon Fauset and Margaret Walker, critic and anthologist Arna Bontemps, painter Aaron Douglas, sociologist Charles S. Johnson, actors with the Krigwa Players, and poets Claude McKay, Sterling S. Brown, Jean Toomer, and Langston Hughes. She published two stories: "Drenched in Light" (1924) in *Opportunity*, and "Spunk" (1925) in Alain Locke's anthology *The New Negro*. The next year saw the publication of more South-based stories— "Sweat," "The Gilded Six-Bits," "Muttsy," "Possum or Pig," and "The Eatonville Anthology"—and three plays, *First One, Spear,* and *Color Struck*. The last two plays won a drama contest sponsored jointly by *Crisis* and *Opportunity* magazines. Her elaborate revue, *The Great Day*, was a melange of work songs, revival sermon, spirituals, and dancing and blues set at a jook joint. It ran on Broadway only one day, January 10, 1932. Hurston recast it at Rollins College the next January under the title *From Sun to Sun*.

Hurston won a scholarship to Barnard College, where she was the first black female to enroll and to earn a B.A. degree, and received a Negro Historical Society Fellowship to research the historic *Clothilde,* the last slave galley bearing Africans to the United States. In 1930, a promising opportunity in Hurston's career was her collaboration with noted poet Langston Hughes on a short-lived fledgling literary quarterly called *Fire!!*, an outlet for black writers coedited by Wallace Thurman. The pair worked on a three-act comedy, *Mule Bone,* which is an adaptation of Hurston's "The Bone of Contention," a tale derived from life in Eatonville, Florida. Hurston and Hughes completed only the third act. It was not performed until February 1991, when a resurgence of interest in Hurston's part in the Harlem Renaissance brought it to the stage at Lincoln Center in New York. Hughes and Hurston abruptly ended their friendship and their collaboration after he accused her of reissuing *Mule Bone* under her name and retitling it *De Turkey and De Law.* Marriage proved no more satisfactory than her ill-fated work with Hughes. While pursuing a graduate degree from Columbia University, she divorced musician Herbert Sheen, a medical student at Howard University, after only seven months of marriage because he demanded an all-or-nothing loyalty.

Hurston profited from an alliance with anthropologists Ruth Benedict and Franz Boas, who guided her fieldwork in Harlem and encouraged her to return to Eatonville to study the black settlement of St. Augustine, Florida. In field notes, she remarked on her delight in folklore as the "pot-likker of human living." (Maggio 1992, 261) Supported by patron Charlotte Osgood "Godmother" Mason, a white heiress, Hurston spent the early Depression era driving Mason's car to backwoods locales. She collected and systematized articles on black lore, six of which appeared in Nancy Cunard's *Negro: Anthology* (1934). Folklorist Alan Lomax called her "probably the best-informed person today on Western Negro folklore." (Lyons 1990, 66)

Posing as "Zora, Queen of the Niggerati," Hurston produced spectacles of folk song, spirituals, and griot lore at black colleges and New York's Harold Golden Theatre. The only female folklorist studying her homeland, she overturned the prevailing theory that the ethnologist should peruse foreign cultures. A contribution to the era's Pan-African movement, the resulting treatise traces the amalgamation of American, Caribbean, and African traditions. Her articles appeared in the *Journal of Negro History* and the *Journal of American*

Folklore. During this fertile period, she helped establish a drama department at Bethune-Cookman College in Daytona Beach and produced a play, *Singing Steel* (1934), and a novel, *Jonah's Gourd Vine* (1934), based on her parents' lives. Her incredible productivity extended into the late 1930s with more stories; two volumes of Southern and Caribbean games, hoodoo, and folklore titled *Mules and Men* (1935) and *Tell My Horse* (1938); and two novels, *Moses, Man of the Mountain* (1939) and *Their Eyes Were Watching God* (1937), a reclaimed treasure that rose to prominence in the 1970s.

During her sojourn among practitioners of Louisiana-style gris-gris, Reverend Father Joe Watson, familiarly known as the Frizzly Rooster, installed Hurston as a voodoo priestess, a theatrical public role that required her to dress in outlandish ritual regalia. The far-fetched nature of *Mules and Men* includes particulars of the initiation:

> I lay naked for three days and nights on a couch, with my navel to a rattlesnake skin which had been dressed and dedicated to the ceremony. I ate no food in all that time. Only a pitcher of water was on a little table at the head of the couch so that my soul would not wander off in search of water and be attacked by evil influences and not return to me. On the second day, I began to dream strange exalted dreams. On the third night, I had dreams that seemed real for weeks. In one, I strode across the heavens with lightning flashing from under my feet and grumbling thunder following in my wake. (Hurston 1973, 2718)

Although Sterling Brown, Richard Wright, Alain Locke, and other vocal critics accused Hurston of coarseness, caricature, and naïveté, other contemporaries lauded her masterwork of dialect, primitivism, arcana, conjure plants and herbal medicine, games, and human sexuality. In particular, they admired a talented female's struggle to override academe's patriarchy and establish her authority on a subject she had obviously mastered.

From Haiti, Hurston migrated to Jamaica in 1936 to document African and Bahamian obeah practice, a search underwritten by two Guggenheim fellowships. Over a period of seven weeks in 1937, while recovering from a soured love match, Hurston sheltered once more in Haiti to write her most famous fiction, *Their Eyes Were Watching God*, a fount of black English and universal themes interweaving patriarchy, racism, sexism, and ageism into a satisfying novel of self-actualization. A contemporary of Margaret Mitchell's *Gone with the Wind* (1936), Hurston's Janie fought similar rounds with patriarchy, paralleling Scarlet O'Hara's allure and slow-forming freedom from dependence on men. At the end of the 1930s, Hurston wed Albert Price III, a graduate student at Columbia University 25 years her junior, but departed from him to tour Florida with Alan Lomax in search of music for a Library of Congress collection and to write *The Florida Negro* for the WPA and the Federal Theater Project. In the summer of 1939, she taught drama at North Carolina Negro College in Durham and returned home to a rocky domestic scene. The marriage foundered in 1940 after Price forced her to choose between research and home. On a Rosenwald Fellowship, she rebounded from divorce while combing South Carolina, Louisiana, Alabama, Haiti, the British West Indies, and Jamaica for novel material. At home in anthropology, she collected anecdotes and songs that elucidated her target—racial delineations among quadroons, octoroons, high yellows, and full-blooded blacks.

The early 1940s saw the divergence of Hurston's career from pure research to more creative writing and reflection. In 1941, she lived in California with friend Katherine Mershon while writing an autobiography, *Dust Tracks on a Road.* Her evocative memoir races along in snatches of conversation, song, and verse marking rhythmic work, snacks of parched peanuts and meals of fried rabbit, and volatile exchanges:

> The pay night [that] rocks on with music and gambling and laughter and dancing and fights. The big pile of cross-ties burning out in front simmers down to low ashes before sun-up, so then it is time to throw up all the likker you can't keep down and go somewhere and sleep the rest off, whether your knife has blood on it or not. (Hurston 1973, 2714)

Pulsating with reckless, primeval life, the work rounds up a panorama of native epithets and terms—store-bought, coolin' board, straw-boss, pushee and pullee, barracoon, jook, grass-gut cow, and "git my switchblade and go round de ham-bone looking for meat." (Hurston 1973, 2715)

Parts of *Dust Tracks on a Road* are marred by Hurston's emotional turmoil as the United States entered World War II, but it won her an Anisfield-Wolf award. In the mid-1940s to early 1950s, she published a failed novel about poor whites, *Seraph on the Suwanee* (1948), as well as stories, articles, and profiles for the *American Mercury*, *Saturday Evening Post*, *Negro Digest*, and *American Legion* magazine, and she reviewed for the *New York Herald Tribune*. A major coup was a cover story about Hurston in the February 1943 *Saturday Review* followed by paired treats: recognition from Howard University as a distinguished alumna and several weeks researching black neighborhoods in British Honduras. Nearing retirement, she abandoned the big-city scene, where educated blacks tended toward elitism, self-promotion, and snobbery, and moved to Belle Glade, Florida, which reminded her of the gentler, less competitive South of her childhood.

Depleted by poverty, obesity, ulcer, and gall bladder attacks, and, in 1948, public vilification from a false accusation of abusing a retarded boy, a fiasco sensationalized by the *Baltimore Afro-American*, Hurston worked on *Life of Herod the Great*. She had supported herself with a string of challenging jobs before a downturn in her affairs ended her career: She failed to sell her fiction, was evicted from her Eau Gallie, Florida, residence, and hit financial bottom. The spiral took her from story consultant for Paramount Pictures, scriptwriter for a Cincinnati radio station, freelance journalist for the *Pittsburgh Courier*, writer for the *Encyclopedia Americana*, librarian at Patrick Air Force Base, columnist for the *Fort Pierce Chronicle,* and substitute teacher in Fort Pierce, Florida. She roused an uproar in 1954 for vocal denunciations of Northern liberalism's push for desegregation. Hurston countered that the closing of all-black schools would demoralize Negro students by divesting them of black teachers and a pro-African curriculum. Virtually unemployable, Hurston sank to housemaid in Rivo Alto, near Miami, and lived on welfare. Late in October 1959, she entered the Saint Lucie County Welfare Home in Fort Pierce to recuperate from a stroke, and died there of heart disease on January 28, 1960. Her unclaimed remains were ignobly interred in an unmarked plot in a black graveyard, the Garden of the Heavenly Rest.

Hurston's work returned to prominence in the 1970s during a revival of interest in storytelling and in black feminism, particularly the works of the Harlem Renaissance. Unself-conscious in their re-creation of black lore, her stories and essays, which began to appear in textbooks and anthologies, energized more polemical black writings with a coarse, often bawdy delight in human society. Her novels and plays were reissued, and her papers were collected at the University of Florida. In August 1973, novelist Alice Walker, author of *The Color Purple*, located Hurston's grave and placed a marker honoring the extraordinary female pathfinder as "A genius of the South." With the assistance of writer Toni Cade Bambara, critic Helen Hunt Washington, biographer Robert E. Hemenway, and historian Henry Louis Gates, Jr., Walker introduced Hurston to a new generation of readers with "In Search of Zora Neale Hurston" (1974), published in *Ms.*, and the foreword to Robert E. Hemenway's *Zora Neale Hurston: A Literary Biography*. Walker's most influential memorial is a collection, *I Love Myself: When I Am Laughing . . . and Then Again When I Am Looking Mean and Impressive: A Zora Neale Hurston Reader* (1979). Other posthumous publications include *The Sanctified Church: The Folklore Writings of Zora Neale Hurston* (1981), *Spunk: The Selected Short Stories of Zora Neale Hurston* (1985), and *Mule Bone: A Comedy of Negro Life* (1990). In 1990, PBS's *American Playhouse* featured a 90-minute biography, *Zora Is My Name*, starring Ruby Dee and Louis Gossett, Jr. In February 1991, 60 years after its composition, *Mule Bone* was produced on Broadway. In 1993, a book collector found among sorority memorabilia from Howard University a lost Hurston play, "Spear," and an essay, "The Ten Commandments of Charm," along with a story, "Under the Bridge." Added to these valuable segments of the Hurston canon, Toni Morrison, Maya Angelou, Susan Straight, Ntozake Shange, and other late-twentieth-century authors have proclaimed their debt to her scholarship, collected lore and wisdom, and sparkling Southern vernacular. (Asante and Mattson 1992; Blain et al. 1990; Bloom 1987; Boas 1978; Bontemps 1942; Bradbury 1996; Buck 1992; *Contemporary Authors* 1994; Davidson and Wagner-Martin 1995; Haskins 1996; Hemenway 1977; Hine et al., 1993; Holloway 1987; Hooks 1997; Howard 1980; Hurston 1973, "How It Feels" 1985, 1990, *Dust* 1991, 1991, 1995; Lewis 1981; Low and Clift 1981; Lyons 1990; Meckler 1996; Nathiri 1991; Pierpont 1997; Ploski and Williams 1989; Porter 1992; Rampersad 1986; Rubin et al. 1985; Sheffey 1992; Sherr and Kazickas 1994; "Voices" 1997; Walker 1975, 1979, 1983; Wall 1995; Washington 1987; Wilson and Ferris 1989; Witcover 1991; Yates 1991; Zora [www.ceth] 1997; Zora [www.detroit] 1997)

See also Their Eyes Were Watching God; Wright, Richard.

I KNOW WHY THE CAGED BIRD SINGS

An exuberant blend of wit, wisdom, and reflection, Maya Angelou's autobiography, *I Know Why the Caged Bird Sings* (1970), demonstrates the spunk of first-person reportage with more than a hint of oral tradition. The premiere volume of the author's six memoirs, the story of the Maya character covers her earliest childhood memories of Stamps, Arkansas, observing "powhitetrash," reunion with divorced parents, rape by her mother's hangdog lover, and the grandmotherly tenderness and discipline that revive Maya, the mute central figure who punishes herself for causing the death of a pedophile. Interspersed are reflections on the Great Depression, threats of Klan-style violence, and the irrepressible high jinks of Maya's adored brother, Bailey "Ju" Junior, whom Angelou's joyful metaphor ennobles as "my Kingdom Come." (Angelou 1970, 19)

A coming-of-age masterpiece, the book opens on a winning portrait—a preschool view of Marguerite "Maya" Johnson, ruffled in Easter-bright lavender taffeta and posed on a bench in the children's section of the Colored Methodist Episcopal Church. She flashes back to age three after her parents' divorce and her arrival by train from Long Beach, California, to Stamps, Arkansas. Living with her grandmother, Mrs. Annie "Momma" Henderson, and Momma's crippled son Willie is potentially dreary, but sharing kinship with a scamp of a brother and reading the English classics enliven otherwise dull days of chores, school, Bible study, and scrubbing to Momma's rigid standard of cleanliness. The precarious balance of good days with bad jostles Angelou's memories of the kinds of shenanigans that endear rather than dismay.

Residing 25 miles southeast of Texarkana on the Texas-Arkansas border, Maya recalls the strictures that separate the cleanest, most respected blacks from any whites, no matter how slovenly, ill-bred, or amoral. Momma is an early 1930s example of black female entrepreneurial daring with her lunch service, which provides lemonade and fried meat pies to cotton gin and sawmill workers. To counter the cashless Depression era, she instructs her grandchildren to make a sign announcing a trading system that awards credit in goods for welfare parcels of powdered milk, eggs, and canned mackerel. Against the gray-tinged horizons of the Hoover-era South, Maya contrasts the surprise arrival of Daddy Bailey, a cynical, citified gent driving a flashy De Soto. She recalls that "his voice rang like a metal dipper hitting a bucket and he spoke English. Proper

English, like the school principal, and even better." (Angelou 1970, 45) Before Bailey Senior drives the children to St. Louis to live with their mother, Momma Henderson sews jumpers and skirts for Maya. Incapable of overt affection, she reminds Maya that "God is love. Just worry about whether you're being a good girl, then He will love you." (Angelou 1970, 47) The numerous close-ups of Momma at counter, sewing machine, and woodstove follow a pattern in Southern literature that honors the rural, Bible-enhanced women who rear and socialize the South's children.

Angelou lambastes Arkansas most effectively by depicting what it lacks. Among her Baxter kin in the sin-rich city of St. Louis, Maya and Bailey Junior depart from the ignorance and superstition of Southern peasant culture. They learn to respect Grandmother Baxter, a light-skinned family matriarch of German heritage who wields political clout as a city precinct leader. Offset by Momma Henderson's puritanism and biblical starchiness, Mother, Vivian "Bibbie" Baxter, glows like a Hollywood creation. Angelou recalls an on-the-scene cognition: "I knew immediately why she had sent me away. She was too beautiful to have children. I had never seen a woman as pretty as she who was called 'Mother.'" (Angelou 1970, 50) Bibbie delights the impressionable pair by cakewalking, shuffling, and showing off her "darling babies." At Louie's tavern, the winsome, safe atmosphere shimmers as Bibbie treats Maya and Bailey Junior to shrimp and sodas and instructs them in the Time Step. Outside, three hulking Baxter brothers—Tutti, Tom, and Ira—manhandle street toughs who threaten the Baxter hegemony. The contrast to the Klan-dominated South turns Maya's world topsy-turvy, this time with her side winning.

Introduction of the villain, the ominously quiet, persuasive Mr. Freeman, a foreman for the Southern Pacific Railroad, allows Angelou a perusal of innocence's last days. At first, she regrets that Bibbie neglects him. Long in need of a cuddly daddy, she remembers her own affection for him:

> He held me so softly that I wished he wouldn't ever let me go. I felt at home. From the way he was holding me I knew he'd never let me go or let anything bad ever happen to me. This was probably my real father and we had found each other at last. (Angelou 1970, 61)

After Freeman masturbates against eight-year-old Maya, then rapes her, the cloud of guilt and remorse that silence her threaten to undo the goodness of her growing-up years. In withdrawal, she recalls, "My belly and behind were as heavy as cold iron, but it seemed my head had gone away and pure air had replaced it on my shoulders." (Angelou 1970, 67) Angelou awards the hero's role to Bailey, who weeps for his sister and informs the family of Mr. Freeman's monstrous intrusion on Maya's virginity. The Bible Belt mentality drags her down as she imagines the recording angel denying her a place in heaven. She experiences a trickle of evil through her body and clamps her jaws together to hold in the wrongdoing that had cost Mr. Freeman his life after the Baxter brothers kicked him lifeless in the backyard of a slaughterhouse.

Maya's resurgence from self-imposed wordlessness and self-abnegation form the remainder of the rising action, which carries the Maya character back to the safe moorings of Momma's guidance and rewards her with Mrs. Bertha Flowers's tutelage in the finer things of life. Maya is in awe of Mrs. Flowers's refinement:

> Her skin was a rich black that would have peeled like a plum if snagged, but then no one would have thought of getting close enough to Mrs. Flowers to ruffle her dress, let along snag her skin. She didn't encourage familiarity. She wore gloves too. (Angelou 1970, 78)

By memorizing verse, Maya absorbs the humanism of literary classics and reconstructs her self-esteem. Angelou portrays the rejuvenated Maya character as overcompensating by smashing heritage china from Virginia in the kitchen of an employer, bluffing her way into the uniformed position of streetcar conductor, and tempting a young male friend into a brief sexual encounter to prove that Maya is not a lesbian.

Among the chronological developments, Angelou inserts timely social commentary. The Maya character satirizes 1930s revivalism, compares secular and religious escapism, extols a 1935 radio broadcast of the Joe "The Brown Bomber" Louis–Primo Carnera fight for its uplift to Southern sharecroppers, and discounts the patronizing racist who devalues the achievements of the class of 1940. The eighth-grade graduates languish in his vision: "We were maids and farmers, handymen and washerwomen, and anything higher that we aspired to was farcical and presumptuous." (Angelou 1970, 152) Momentarily returned to the zero level, Maya declares it terrible to be black and lack control over her destiny.

At a pinnacle of Maya's reminiscence, Henry Reed, the class valedictorian, restores pride by leading the class in the Negro National Anthem, "Lift Ev'ry Voice and Sing," James Weldon Johnson's joyful call to unity and determination, set to music by his brother, John Rosamond Johnson. The spontaneous group-sing reminds that "We have come over a way that with tears has been watered,/We have come, treading our path through the blood of the slaughtered." Maya exults, "Oh, Black known and unknown poets, how often have your auctioned pains sustained us? Who will compute the lonely nights made less lonely by your songs, or the empty pots made less tragic by your tales?" (Angelou 1970, 156)

In one of the many scenes of Dixie's overt prejudice, Angelou employs fantasy to free the Maya character from victimization. She depicts Momma taking Maya to Dr. Lincoln, a white dentist who owes Momma a favor for lending him money. The scenario places Maya's grandmother in a humiliating position at the back entrance, where Lincoln snorts, "Annie, you know I don't treat nigra, colored people. . . . I'd rather stick my hand in a dog's mouth than in a nigger's." (Angelou 1970, 159) When Momma withdraws to negotiate in private on the issue of dental treatment for her granddaughter, Maya envisions a heroic confrontation in which Momma overpowers Dr. Lincoln and berates his sassy nurse. On their return from a bus ride to Texarkana to consult a more compliant dentist, Maya tells her brother about Momma vanquishing the "peckerwood dentist." Momma's version claims that she forced Lincoln to pay $10 in back interest on his debt. Her coda resonates like biblical prophecy: "I figger, he gonna be that kind of nasty, he gonna have to pay for it." (Angelou 1970, 163–164)

Like Mark Twain, Angelou is most obviously a Southern writer when dealing with the themes and settings of the region and speaking such idiosyncratic terms as clabbered milk, cater-cornered, mourners' bench, play pretties, siditty, hants, juju, and cracker. The concluding chapters of *I Know Why the Caged Bird Sings*, which recede from Stamps to cover Maya's departure from the South and her growing-up years in California, lack the generous memories that recount her connection with the rural South. The visit to Mexico with Daddy Bailey, running away from home, and getting a job as streetcar conductor depart from the warmth and humor of the tent revival, ironing cat's faces on shirts, playing mumbledy-peg around the chinaberry tree, hiding Uncle Willie in the onion bin to keep him out of the grasp of Klansmen, wearing makeover clothes that Momma cuts from adult discards, and empathizing with cotton pickers who stop by Henderson's store to buy sardines, cheese, soda crackers, and peanut patties. Like Mark Twain's *The Adventures of Huckleberry Finn* and Harper Lee's *To Kill a Mockingbird*, Angelou's *I Know Why the Caged Bird Sings* holds a place of honor among frequently banned books. Her work was distinguished in 1983 when the Alabama state textbook commission suppressed it for classroom use. In the 1990s, challenges came from schools and homes outside the South—Bremerton, Washington; Benning and Pleasanton, California; and Charles County, Maryland.

Angelou's tour de force first autobiography translates moderately well to the screen. The movie version of *I Know Why the Caged Bird Sings*, which appeared on CBS-TV as the *Saturday Night Movie* on April 28, 1979, starred Constance Good as the pubescent Marguerite. Her performance complemented the work of Esther Rolle as Grandmother Henderson, John Driver as Bailey Junior, Diahann Carroll as Vivian "Mother Dear" Bailey, Roger Mosely as Daddy Bailey, and Ruby Dee as Grandmother Baxter. (*Afro-American* 1985; Angelou 1970; Bailey 1984; Banerjee 1990; Bloom, Lynn 1985; Bogle 1988; Bradbury 1996; Dunlap 1996; Elliott 1989; Foerstel 1994; Hine et al. 1993; Houtchens 1993; Lewis 1981; McPherson 1990; Oliver 1983; Shapiro 1993; Shuker 1990; Smith, Sidonie 1973; Stepto 1979)

See also Angelou, Maya.

INVISIBLE MAN

A major achievement in African-American fiction, Ralph Ellison's *Invisible Man* (1947) demonstrates the author's ambivalence toward blacks in American society. In a 1967 interview published in *Harper's,* he stated his complex view of working-class blacks:

> If I cannot look at the most brutalized Negro on the street, even when he irritates me and makes me want to bash his head in because he's goofing off, I must still say within myself, "Well, that's you too, Ellison." And I'm not talking about guilt, but of an identification which goes beyond race. (Gross 1971, 160)

For Ellison, the refutation of the myth of the American Dream was a necessary step in assessing the Negro's progress in a racist society bent on exploiting, subjugating, and ultimately destroying evidence of black creativity. By creating a nameless lost soul as protagonist, the author reconfigures in fiction the social malaise that reduces a promising black man—a potential Booker T. Washington—from naïveté and idealism to a spiritually catatonic withdrawal.

To illustrate the negativism that deflates and cripples youthful energy, Ellison hypothesizes an unnamed, semiautobiographical narrator, a 20-year-old college dropout from the South who is a ginger-hued grandson of slaves. In manhood, the speaker looks back over his coming-of-age and declares that he lives unseen because white people have chosen to ignore his very existence. Holed up rent-free on the outskirts of Harlem in the cellar of a whites-only building, he wars against the Monopolated Light & Power Company and flees Ras the Destroyer. He illuminates his ceiling with 1,369 illegally wired incandescent lightbulbs and affirms himself in their light and in the soul-satisfying query of Louis Armstrong's blues ballad "What Did I Do To Be So Black and Blue." For dessert, he feasts on vanilla ice cream and sloe gin.

Ellison infests his protagonist's memory with assorted horrors and humiliations. The narrator recalls hazing at his high school graduation, when he and others are forced to spar blindfolded in a boxing ring, a symbol of his continued clash with unseen forces. The match ends after contenders scramble on an electrically charged rug for fake coins and bills, emblematic of the rigged award system that punishes black go-getters. Initially, the narrator anticipates a bright future. During his junior year at an all-black Southern school, he chauffeurs his employer, Mr. Norton, a benefactor from Boston. One outing takes Norton to the old Slave Quarters, where Jim Trueblood divulges that he has impregnated both his wife Kate and his daughter Matty Lou. The shock of Trueblood's heinous crime kayos Norton. The narrator ferries his employer to the Golden Day to revive him with whiskey. Upon their return to campus, the president, Dr. A. Hebert Bledsoe, an obvious lackey to the white moneyed class, upbraids the narrator for showing a white philanthropist around the quarters and sends the narrator away with sealed letters to potential employers that mark him for failure.

Paralleling the author's departure to the North, the protagonist migrates to New York, where he attempts to rid himself of his drawl, yet is unable to reply in kind to the jingling spiel of Peter Wheatstraw, a messenger who engages him in harmless big-city jive talk. Contrasting the lighter moments of the narrator's odyssey are the fearful polemics of Ras, a West Indian street orator. At a Long Island paint factory, the narrator botches his job by putting the wrong additive in buckets of white paint. As a result of a fight with a white worker, the narrator fails to control the pressure in a tank, which explodes and engulfs him in white paint. Ellison's deft handling of names like Wheatstraw, the adulteration of white paint, and the explosion that overlays the narrator's black skin prefigure the spiritual breakdown that ultimately suppresses his negroid identity and drives him underground.

Ellison's novel counters menacing urbanism with an oasis of kindness and generosity in Mary Rambo, a kindly old Negro matron who shelters the narrator and feeds him cabbage on her limited budget until he recovers. That winter he paces the streets of Harlem and returns momentarily to the South in the taste of roasted yams. Witnessing the eviction of Primus Provo, an 87-year-old ex-slave, and his wife from their quarters, the narrator discovers his natural talent for impromptu speech by railing against hirelings and demanding minority rights. Ellison uses this incident as the narrator's introduction to Brother Jack, member of an idealistic organization that helps black people fight oppression. The narrator fails to grasp Jack's marginalization of the elderly victims:

> The old ones, they're agrarian types, you know. Being ground up by industrial conditions. Thrown on the dump heaps and cast aside. . . . They're like dead limbs that must be pruned away so that the tree may bear young fruit or the storms of history will blow them down anyway. (Ellison 1952, 252–253)

At a Lenox Avenue address, Jack hires the narrator and tells him why things must change for blacks. He advises the narrator to relocate and shun his past by adopting a new identity. To a loner like the narrator, the appeal of better quarters on the Upper East Side, a salary of $60 a week, and $300 for food, back rent, and new clothes overcomes any hesitancy about giving up his true self to join a social reform movement about which he knows nothing. The leap from unemployed drifter to orator is not as easy as the narrator's first spontaneous demonstration of talent. He listens to the members' criticisms and accepts Brother Jack's compliments and a job attracting members to the movement.

Ellison stresses the narrator's idealism by surrounding him with hints of disasters ahead. Still riding the crest of his new popularity, he ignores an unstamped, unsigned note that warns against rampant ambition. His rival, Brother Wrestrum, accuses him of opportunism. An initial betrayal by the movement's inner circle reassigns him downtown to handle the "woman question." After the dissolution of the Brotherhood, the narrator searches for them and locates Brother Clifton selling paper dolls on a street corner, but arrives too late to stop a police officer from shooting Clifton. The symbolism of the execution of a doll seller escapes the narrator, who is himself a frail, malleable toy to the Brothers.

The beginning of the narrator's retreat from reality occurs on his return to Harlem in a near-dream state. Distraught with grief and confusion, he returns to his office and ponders one of Clifton's dolls, at last confronting face-to-face a marionette like himself. Still loyal to the cause, he organizes an elaborate procession and funeral for Clifton at Mount Morris Park and delivers a moving, despairing eulogy. Alarmed by the narrator's autonomous action, the committee breaks down into squabbling and sniping. Ellison enhances the confrontation between the narrator and the movement's leadership after the narrator dislodges Jack's glass eye. The narrator is drawn into a sidewalk confrontation with Ras the Exhorter, a mythic figure drawn from Abyssinian lore, who leads a violent faction of black nationalists who reject any alliance with white leadership.

The author guides the narrator into the preliminary stages of invisibility as he dons dark glasses and accepts greetings intended for "Rever'n B. P. Rinehart," a symbolic name for a cynical exploiter, numbers runner, and phony cleric that envisions the narrator's fragile self as a shell or rind. By August, the loss of leadership sends the black community into free fall. At Morningside, the narrator is drawn toward street fighting. Gunshots sound in the distance and looters prowl the sidewalks. Voices blame Ras for fomenting the uproar. Ras's call for a lynching sets the narrator on a dangerous mission against a growing street force. He maneuvers through chaos back to Mary and looks for Brother Jack. His mind toys with his shoddy treatment and discovers it "was all a swindle, an obscene swindle! They had set themselves up to describe the world. What did they know of us, except that we numbered so many." (Ellison 1952, 438) Police seal the narrator's fate by confiscating his papers and shutting him in an underground cell. Safely incarcerated in an urban womb, the narrator yields to darkness and invisibility. He lights a symbolic fire by igniting first his high school diploma, then a doll from Clifton's sales kit, an anonymous letter that warns him of danger from the Brotherhood, and finally the slip of paper containing his new identity as a member of the Brotherhood. Mentally, he witnesses his castration by Jack, Bledsoe, Norton, Ras, and the school superintendent. A subterranean anomaly, the narrator grows into total estrangement. (Bradbury 1963; Bradbury 1996; *Contemporary Authors* 1994; Corliss 1994; Daniels 1994; Ehrlich and Carruth 1982; Ellison 1952; Girson 1953; Gross 1971; Harper and Wright 1980; Hill 1966; Low and Clift 1981; "Ralph Ellison Profile" 1976; Redding 1951; Reilly 1970; Rubin et al. 1985; Schor 1993; Warren 1965; Watts 1994)

See also Ellison, Ralph.

LATE-TWENTIETH-CENTURY WRITERS

From the beginning a fertile ground for storytelling, eloquent speech and essay, humor, aphorism, and evocative verse, the South retains its place as a national center for artists. Among the potters, masons, carpenters, dancers, preachers, and sculptors stands the current crop of writers on a par with some of the past masters. Current criticism lauds the fiction of Jill McCorkle, Sylvia Wilkinson, Bobbie Ann Mason, Kaye Gibbons, and Jerry Bledsoe, and anticipates a greater literary return from the early originality of Ferrol Sams, Will Campbell, and William Price Fox. The oratory of Billy Graham, Jesse Jackson, Andrew Young, Martin Luther King, and Barbara Jordan has set Southern polemics apart from other national voices; the storytelling of Jackie Torrence, J. J. Reneaux, Gayle Ross, and Ray Hicks is rated among the best. The acumen of literary historian Louis D. Rubin, Jr., columnists Harry Golden and Molly Ivins, satirist Florence King, and the second generation of teachers and critics sprung from the Fugitive Agrarians has turned an internal eye on the foundations from which regional strengths have grown.

A distinguished moralist among mid- to late-twentieth-century writers and critics, Walker Percy examined the modern dilemmas with attention to existential themes of rootlessness and confusion. A battler of the despair that arises from modern technology, he brought to light the bête noir the Fugitive Agrarians had warned of decades earlier. The existential strands of his best fiction— *Love in the Ruins: The Adventures of a Bad Catholic at a Time Near the End of the World* (1971), *The Second Coming* (1980), and *The Thanatos Syndrome* (1987)— exemplify the focus of his concern about the pervasive melancholia of the twentieth century. The sadness he pondered was a personal onus, begun in his youth when his father killed himself and his mother perished in a car wreck. His battle with pulmonary tuberculosis, contracted from his work as a pathologist at Bellevue Hospital in New York, slowed his body and enlivened his mind to debate the age-old humanistic questions of alienation and amorphous values, which he found in the classic works of French and Russian authors.

Southern drama has profited from the candid and compassionate playwright Alice Childress, author of the Obie-winning play *Trouble in Mind* (1955). She topped her first work with an American Library Association Best Young Adult Book, *A Hero Ain't Nothin' but a Sandwich* (1973), a heart-touching ghetto piece also selected by the Lewis Carroll Shelf Award and the Jane Addams Children's Book committees and *New York Times Book Review* as distinctive young-adult fiction. After scripting it for the New World Pictures adaptation to screen in 1977, starring Cicely Tyson and Paul Winfield, Childress won additional kudos, including a Paul Robeson Award for Outstanding Contributions to the Performing Arts and Black Filmmakers Hall of Fame. A Southern expatriate who grew up in Harlem, Childress gained vision and experience from the American Negro Theatre and the Radcliffe Institute. In her multivoiced examination of the delinquency of Benjie Johnson, she gives his patter a natural, genial flow, as in his explanation of school entanglements:

> The real trouble is school and a jive-ass Black teacher name Nigeria. He pretend to be a Black Nationalist, but done turn Uncle Tom and got together with Mista Cohen, who is a Jew. The two of them did me in. Nigeria got the nerve to wear a black, red, and green button on his jacket. (Childress 1973, 14)

The funky charm and grace of her protagonist contrasts the idiosyncratic voicing of the other commentators, including the insouciant Jimmy-Lee Powell, teacher Bernard Cohen, mother Rose Johnson Craig, and Walter, a sleazy spokesman for the pusher's right to sell to buyers stupid enough to take dope.

Formed out of the interweaving of potentially explosive issues, Childress's appealing story backs off for such moments of wisdom, pathos, and humor as Benjie's grandmother's singing "Precious Lord Take My Hand" and proclaiming, "If I gotta love white, make mine Jesus!" (Childress 1973, 119) The author concludes her slim didactic novel with the commentaries of Benjie's stepfather and a streetwise corner philosopher who hurls cynical lines at passersby about children doomed by narcotics. Determined to change some attitudes, the anonymous street preacher declares himself a scion of Nat Turner and offers a muted hope in his call to action: "Freeeeeeeedom now! Freeeeeeeeeeeeeeeedom now!" (Childress 1973, 123) Banned along with the works of Langston Hughes and Kurt Vonnegut, Jr., in Long Island, New York, during the mid-1970s, the novel remains in demand on school reading lists and as reading theater up to the time of Childress's death in 1994 and beyond.

Similarly at home with harsh, fearful topics, poet and playwright Sonia Sanchez, currently the Laura Carnell Professor of English and Women's Studies, developed her poetic persona during the 1960s, taking for mentors the stridence of the day as spoken by Angela Davis, Stokely Carmichael, and Malcolm X. Educated organically in the civil rights movement and at San Francisco State, she spoke her own concerns through a richly epigrammatic style of verse. Not as lyric as Maya Angelou nor as serrated as Nikki Giovanni, Sanchez remains fixed on an autobiographical realism and embraces a broad panoply of human events and commonalities as the basis for her works, including activism for women's rights as well as black-centered civil rights. In addition to *Homecoming* (1969) and *We a BadddDDD People* (1977), she published *It's a New Day* (1971), a collection of hopeful poems that anticipates the spirituality of *A Blues Book for Blue Black Magical Women* (1974). Moving toward an imagist truth, she produced *Homegirls and Handgrenades* (1984) and *Under a Soprano Sky* (1987), which contains "An Anthem (for the ANC and Brandywine Peace Community)." The poem pieces together snatches of history, dating to "madmen [who] goosestep in tune to Guernica." (Sanchez 1997, 82) Inflamed with the sufferings of Soweto, her vows of retaliation shred the death talk and courageously spread her zeal to end South Africa's wrenching racial gulag.

In 1997, Sanchez published a painfully personal poetry cycle entitled *Does Your House Have Lions?*, a verse tribute to her brother, who suffered the alienation and private hell of AIDS. She samples the voices of immediate family and ancestors as the extended kinship group talks its way through hardship and disapproval of the victim's homosexuality. The brother's voice caresses the mother, calling her "my living saint" for thriving in his head in angelic smiles that accepted him in childhood and gave him strength. (Sanchez 1997, 15) The segment marked "Father's Voice" contrasts the gentle ways of the mother with fragmented memories of his dad's callousness. Cadence picks up from tortured sentences to the quickened antiphony between the ancestral voice and its audience. A female asks, "have you prepared a place of honor for me?" In reply, the suffering brother asks the nature and cause of his cough, a snake rattling in his throat and embalming his chest. The ancestor speaks again of bitter tea; the family coddles and cajoles the dying son, speaking their love with "i [sic] am here my baby in your hospital room." (Sanchez 1997, 59) Sanchez shapes the rhapsodic departure of the brother's spirit as he prepares for the ritual dressing in white. Leaving his family redeemed, whole in their sorrow, he slips away on a current of air.

Also a realist from the white perspective, poet and novelist Fred Chappell, a native of North Carolina, made a poignant passage when he took the classroom duties of Randall Jarrell at UNC-Greensboro after Jarrell's unexpected death in 1964. Already the author of an autobiographical novel, *It Is Time, Lord* (1963), Chappell developed both prose and verse strands of his talent with contrasting novels, *The Inkling* (1965), a gentle, home-centered fiction, and *Dagon* (1968), a terrifying sketch of pagan ritual and sadism that won the French Academy's Prix de Meilleur des Lettres Etrangers. A poet at heart like contemporary James Dickey, Chappell turned to multiple verse collections, beginning with *The World between the Eyes* (1971). He is completing a land-based novel cycle: *I Am One of You Forever* (1985), *Brighten the Corner Where You Are* (1989), and *Farewell, I'm Bound To Leave You* (1997), with a fourth, tentatively titled *Look Back All the Green Valley*. His intent is to express the sociological and political changes that have wrenched his home state from rural complacency to an industry-fueled urbanism. For his dynamic celebrations of the enduring Southern people in story, novel, and verse, he has won the T. S. Eliot Award, Bollingen Prize, and O. Max Gardner Award.

Another skilled, dramatic contemporary writer, Gail Godwin lives among her created scenarios as though they were home folks, and speaks of characters and their loves and hates with the assurance of an insider. A native of Alabama, she learned the groundwork of narration at the University of North Carolina at Chapel Hill and as a reporter for the *Miami Herald*. After completing a doctorate at the University of Iowa, she began writing Southern novels, succeeding with memorable home-and-hearth works: *A Mother and Two Daughters* (1982), *A Southern Family* (1987), and *The Good Husband* (1994). In an interview, she explained that writing spiritual fiction fills a gap in her life left by her negation of organized religion.

An accomplished plotter of action and motivation, Godwin is comfortable writing about the love and treachery of the modern family, as in *A Southern Family*, a dense, emotional novel detailing the Quick family's individual reactions to a suicide. Her familiarity with the cadence of Southerners lends validity to perceptive passages, for example, this commentary on blacks and the law from a North Carolina sheriff:

> Didn't you know we don't allow no niggers in Graham County? . . . Lord, God, I can't believe you boys was up here for a whole week fishing and not knowing about that law. We had to pass it for their own good. A nigger's life isn't worth diddley-squat once he crosses our county line. (Godwin 1987, 155)

At home in the beauties and vulgarity of the South, Godwin's contented sense of place allows her to move across social strata and among people of varying degrees of education and background without making awkward attempts to adjust the social elements that separate and alienate individual characters.

Another knowledgeable native, Reynolds Price, an affable writer, speaker, and educator, has maintained an extensive career since his days as a Rhodes scholar, which preceded his membership on the English staff of Duke University. The publication of a first novel, *A Long and Happy Life* (1962), established him among regional voices injecting spunk and scope into Southern fiction. In a memoir of his favorite novel, author Jerry Bledsoe recalls being drawn into the book's opening scene, which pictures motorcyclist Wesley Beavers journeying toward Mount Moriah. The story of an unlikely romance between Beavers and Rosacoke Mustian, a pensive girl-woman, the novel draws on a fatherless teen who regrets the swiftness with which life ends, taking her father as though he had been "swept away by the Holy Ghost, bag and baggage, in a pillar of fire instead of drunk and taken at dusk by a pickup truck he never saw but walked straight into as if it was a place to rest." (Price 1961, 33) Price jogs relentlessly over Southern terrain to the climax, Rosacoke's decision concerning an unplanned pregnancy. In the telling of her story, the author salts in the Appalachian idiom that has given the language such phrases as "was studying something [pondering]," "see what ails him," "swelled up and biggity [proud]," and "rocked back on his heels," a description of the conclusion of a native tête-à-tête or commercial exchange familiarly known as "hunkering down."

The tender telling of Rosacoke's dilemma prefigures later strengths in Price's female characters, notably the title character of *Kate Vaiden* (1986), a subtle, forgiving portrait of an unwise middle-aged protagonist who acts on an internal compulsion similar to Rosacoke's. In retrospect of his adventurous female characters, Price displays a fondness for both Rosacoke and Kate, and remarks, "I've always been interested in the kind of revolutionary woman that my mother was, the woman who would absolutely not buy the harem-wife-mother stereotype that was forced upon all women in my early life." (Humphries 1991, 210) He implies that an intense radical freedom in women is the necessary balance to the destructiveness of families. Price's admiration for the "moral outlaw" is the source of the passion and independence that drive his novels.

A more recent voice for women comes from that rare first novel, Kaye Gibbons's *Ellen Foster* (1987), winner of the Sue Kaufman Prize from the American Academy and Institute of Arts and Letters, followed by more solid fiction—*A Virtuous Woman* (1989), *A Cure for Dreams* (1991), and *Charms for the Easy Life* (1993). Much praised in literary circles, by critic and teacher Louis Rubin, and by authors Eudora Welty and Walker Percy, *Ellen Foster* is the moving monologue of a neglected, abused ten-year-old. She expresses not only family dysfunction but also the insensitivity of relatives, court judges, school companions, and community members who look past the misery of an orphan to criticize her white trash origins and her unequivocal adoration of a black friend. The true-to-childhood thoughts of the protagonist, Ellen, who names herself Foster after joining a foster family, cut to the tender nerve endings. Of the death of her foul-tempered, alcoholic dad, she shudders

> They put her [mother] in a box too and him in a box oh shut the lid down hard on this one and nail it, nail it with the strongest nails. Do all you can to keep it shut and him in it always, Time would make him meaner to me if he could get out and grab me again. (Gibbons 1990, 70)

Canny to a world that ladles out hurts with bold indifference, Ellen sizes up all alterations in her life plan, making do on a pitifully small bounty and reaching for whatever relationships offer bits of compassion, decency, and family camaraderie.

In the frontier tradition, Pulitzer Prize–winning author Larry McMurtry, latest master of the western saga, has rejuvenated an American classic. In *Lonesome Dove* (1985)—a smash novel that spawned a 1989 CBS-TV miniseries, popular video, and sequel, *The Streets of Laredo* (1993)—he adopts a pragmatic attitude toward law and order. To restructure the standoff between Texas rustlers and Mexican herders along the Rio Grande, he lessens the distance between justice and opportunism. The resulting plot takes shape around two endearingly rough-cut characters, Augustus "Gus" McCrae and Captain Woodrow F. Call, former Texas Rangers turned quasi-respectable livestock agents. Living an easy distance north of likely pickings, the two ride out of their rough adobe on Hat Creek by night to raid Pedro Flores's herd, tended by *vaqueros*. McMurtry examines border thievery through the eyes of the innocent—Newt, the youngest and least-tried member of the rustling party, who ponders the vagaries of respect for rights and property:

> It was puzzling that such a muddy little river like the Rio Grande should make such a difference in terms of what was lawful and what not. On the Texas side, horse stealing was a hanging crime, and many of those hung for it were Mexican cowboys who came across the river to do pretty much what they themselves were doing. (McMurtry 1985, 125)

Larry McMurtry, a master of the western saga and representative of late-twentieth-century Southern writers, photographed in 1993

Further muddying the issue is Newt's hero worship of the Captain, a stern proponent of retribution for horse thieves. That Call and his crew can heist a whole herd is incomprehensible to the boy. Newt's deduction sums up much of the appeal of shoot-'em-up lore: "If you crossed the river to do it, it stopped being a crime and became a game."

Like Louis L'Amour, McMurtry smudges the line between law-abiding and lawless. An easy hand with plains conventions, he builds on the affability of his protagonists before testing them with a more perplexing legal question: the culpability of their ex-associate, Jake Spoon, who allied with the Suggses, a low-life bunch with a yen to torment nesters. The enormity of their crime of murdering, then hanging and burning the corpses of guileless sodbusters gnaws at Jake, but not enough to separate him from his companions. In judgment of his former pal, Gus speaks the lawman's ready quip: "Ride with an outlaw, die with him." (McMurtry 1985, 572) The code of on-the-scene apprehension and punishment turns momentarily light with Jake's acceptance of a lynching: "I'd a damn sight rather be hung by my friends than by a bunch of strangers." (McMurtry 1985, 575) With cavalier grace, Jake spurs his horse and swings slack in the noose before Gus can order his execution. The self-administered hanging strikes Gus as admirable. He remarks, "He died fine." (McMurtry 1985, 576)

Also on the boundary between lawful and unlawful choices lies the heroic return from war of Inman, protagonist of Charles Frazier's historical novel *Cold Mountain* (1997). A surprising best-seller, the Civil War narrative, Frazier's first published fiction, measures the day-by-day survival of the wounded rebel soldier and the parallel struggles of his pampered love, Ada Monroe, who must distance herself from a polite Charleston upbringing to earn a living on a mountain farm. Encouraged by fellow North Carolinian Kaye Gibbons, Frazier researched the dogged trek of his great-great-uncle, W. P. Inman, casting him in an epic struggle no less daunting than that of the wanderer Odysseus. Frazier painstakingly touched up the text with the calls of night birds, the color of creek water in winter, and the textures, smells, and tastes of the protagonist's Appalachian homeland. Central to Frazier's Homeric themes lies the indifference of home folk to Civil War issues as the exigencies of the wartime economy occupy their attention, demanding frugality and mental and physical dexterity if they intend to survive. The menace of cold, hunger, despair, and brutal pursuers matches the determination of Inman to return alive to declare in person his love for Ada. The irony of their brief reunion fits the period, when the hazards of the times limited the normal parameters of happiness. (Chappell 1985; Childress 1973; *Contemporary Authors* 1994; Davidson and Wagner-Martin 1995; Frazier 1997; Gibbons 1990; Giles 1997; Godwin 1987; Gossett 1997; Hill 1992; Hine et al. 1993; Humphries 1991; Inge 1990; McMurtry 1985; Perkins 1997; Powell 1994; Price 1961, 1986; Sanchez 1993, 1997; Singleton 1996; Walsh 1990)

See also Fugitive Agrarians; Henley, Beth; poetry of the South; short fiction in Southern literature; theater in the South; women in Southern literature.

LEE, HARPER

An intriguingly reclusive author, Nelle Harper Lee, like Margaret Mitchell, said her say with one superb novel. *To Kill a Mockingbird* (1960), a frank examination of small-town bigotry, is set in a fictional milieu that mirrors Lee's home in Monroeville, Alabama. A distant relative of Robert E. Lee and the third daughter and last child of attorney and newspaper publisher Amasa Coleman

Lee and pianist Frances Finch Lee's four children, Lee remains strongly Southern. She claims the Confederate commander and Virginian Thomas Jefferson as her heroes. Born April 28, 1926, she grew up next door to author Truman Capote's Aunt Sook Faulk, also Lee relatives, and became Capote's lifelong confidante through annual summer visits. His memories of her bloomed into the tomboyish character Idabel Thompkins in Capote's *Other Voices, Other Rooms* (1948).

Lee is a lifetime reader and favors Jane Austen, Charles Lamb, Mark Twain, Samuel Butler, Henry Fielding, Marcel Proust, and Robert Louis Stevenson. Her education followed the family pattern—public school in Monroeville and a year at Huntington College in Montgomery prefatory to the University of Alabama, where she concentrated on journalism, history, and literature. Her school activities included editing the newspaper, the *Rammer Jammer*. She obtained a B.A. and worked one year toward a law degree, which she later claimed is a worthy adjunct to professional writing. In 1950, after a year as an exchange student at Oxford University, she ended her formal education and moved to New York City. She wrote by night and worked days as a reservations clerk for Eastern Air Lines and British Overseas Airways.

Determined to succeed as a professional writer, Lee lived in a cramped cold-water flat and worked at fiction, breaking the rhythm for trips home to tend her ailing father, who died in 1962. In a rare one-page essay, "Christmas to Me," published in *McCall's* magazine in December 1961, she reflects on missing home for the holidays: "an old memory of people long since gone, of my grandparents' house bursting with cousins, smilax, and holly." (Lee "Christmas" 1961, 63) Still an unknown in a city renowned for sheltering would-be novelists, she spent Christmas Day with a young well-to-do family who surprised her with an envelope on the tree. Inside was their gift: "You have one year off from your job to write whatever you please. Merry Christmas." Lee's gently reflective piece summarizes the unexpected largesse as faith in her ability. The giver described the risk as "a sure thing." (Lee "Christmas" 1961, 63)

To her unidentified benefactors and to the reading public, Harper Lee fulfilled her promise. Writing from noon to early evening, she completed a few pages per day, each of which she revised two times. She claims that she worked out dialogue orally while golfing. She shaped three short fictional sketches, and in 1957 submitted them to an agent. On his suggestion, she lengthened the story, applying legal training and deductive logic to its plot. Her editor insisted on tighter construction, which required another two and a half years of work. The text completed, Lee submitted it for publication and traveled with Capote to Kansas to help him research a journalistic novel, *In Cold Blood* (1965).

Lee's masterwork, *To Kill a Mockingbird*, reflects the racial and political tenor of the era. During this period, Autherine Lucy, a black student, attempted to enroll at the University of Alabama graduate school. More important to the civil rights struggle, Alabama was embroiled in the Montgomery bus boycott, the event that catapulted freedom fighter Dr. Martin Luther King, Jr., to international attention. Lee's fictional events take place in the town of Maycomb, a Southern microcosm of the Jim Crow era and the site of a rape trial and near-lynching. Other details derive from her life: Truman Capote became the inquisitive Dill; the tree where Scout and Jem leave gifts for Boo stood behind the town elementary school until felled by disease; the old Hodge place became the Radleys' residence; Atticus Finch evolved from Lee's father; and Monroeville's courtroom became the crucible in which Atticus is tested and that local preservationists restored. She dedicated *To Kill a Mockingbird* to her father and sister Alice, formerly partners in a family law firm, "in consideration of Love & Affection." Still dividing her activities between Monroeville and New York City, she has published reflective essays for *Vogue* and *McCall's* magazines, but no more novels.

To Kill a Mockingbird remained on the best-seller list for 73 weeks. It won honors from the Alabama Library Association, Literary Guild, Book-of-the-Month Club, British Book Society, *Reader's Digest* Condensed Books, the Brotherhood Award from the National Conference of Christians and Jews, *Bestsellers'* paperback of the year for 1962, and $500 for the 1961 Pulitzer Prize, followed by dinner with a clutch of artists at the White House hosted by President John F. Kennedy. Five years later, President Lyndon Johnson named Lee to the National Council of Arts. A compassionate view of childhood, the book was translated into 30 languages, sold 11 million copies in 15 years, and become an American and European classic of young-adult literature.

Harper Lee, in 1962, on the set of *To Kill a Mockingbird*, with actor Gregory Peck dressed as Atticus

Various adaptations of print make *To Kill a Mockingbird* accessible to students: Popular Library produced a large print edition in 1962; Miller-Brody publishes an audiocassette narrated by Maureen Stapleton; in 1970, Christopher Sergel wrote a stage version for Dramatic Publications. The 1962 black-and-white film, narrated by Kim Stanley and starring Gregory Peck as Atticus, Philip Alford as Jem, and nine-year-old Birmingham native Mary Badham as Scout, was scripted by Texas playwright Horton Foote, author of *Tender Mercies* (1983). In her assessment of his effort, Harper Lee concluded, "If the integrity of a film adaptation is measured by the degree to which the novelist's intent is preserved, Mr. Foote's screenplay should be studied as a classic." (Johnson, Claudia, et al. 1997, 8) The movie, which Lee claims initiates "a new era of responsibility in Hollywood," maintains its position among the best in literary viewing for classroom study. It earned humanitarian awards and garnered Oscars for Peck's acting and Foote's screenplay, and nominations for best picture, director, photography, music, and Badham's starring role as central intelligence and chief mischief maker. To honor Peck's performance and his resemblance to her father, Lee gave him Amasa Lee's gold pocket watch inscribed "To Gregory from Harper, 1962." (Buck 1992; *Current Biography* 1961; Davidson and Wagner-Martin 1995; Ehrlich and Carruth 1982; "First Novel" 1961; Hart 1983; Hecimovich 1997; Inge 1990; Johnson, Claudia "Christmas" 1997; Lee 1960, 1961; "Literary Laurels" 1961; Moates 1989; "Mockingbird Website" 1997; Price 1996; Skube 1997; Smykowski 1997; *Something about the Author* 1977; Stein 1979; Stuckey 1966; Whitt 1994; Wilson and Ferris 1989)

See also Capote, Truman; *To Kill a Mockingbird*.

LEE, ROBERT E.

No figure so captured the South's imagination during the Civil War era than Robert Edward Lee. The straight-backed, soft-spoken son of Virginia planters, he embodied the best of Southern manhood. Born in Stratford, Virginia, on January 19, 1807, he inherited the aristocratic tastes and mystique of his father, Henry "Light-Horse Harry" Lee, author of *Memoirs of the War in the Southern Department of the United States* (1812). Like the patricians of Republican Rome, Robert E. Lee ascended the prescribed ladder of civic and personal honor: salutatorian of his class at West Point in 1829, marriage to heiress Mary Randolph Custis of Arlington two years later, engineering aideship in a Washington war bureau until 1837, promotion to Fort Hamilton in 1841, and hero of the Mexican War, where he served under General Winfield Scott. The last half of Lee's career was no less distinguished. He fought Indians in Texas and assisted in the suppression of John Brown's attack on Harper's Ferry, Virginia, on October 16, 1859.

As the Civil War loomed, Lee left his post in Texas to answer President Abraham Lincoln's call to lead the First Cavalry of the Union army. The crisis that threatened an idyllic career forced Lee into a choice between loyalty to the nation and allegiance to the South. Although he was not a secessionist, he rejected supervision of troops that were certain to invade his homeland and chose instead to command the Confederate military. In a letter to his son dated January 23, 1861, Lee justified his decision:

> The South, in my opinion, has been aggrieved by the acts of the North. . . . I feel the aggression and am willing to take every proper step for redress. It is the principle I contend for, not individual or private benefit. As an American citizen, I take great pride in my country, her prosperity and institutions, and would defend any state if her rights were invaded. But I can anticipate no greater calamity for the country than a dissolution of the Union. (Bowler et al. 1996, 379)

Lee defines secession as blatant revolt and mourns that the cohesion established by the framers of the Constitution had been fractured. He prepares to return to Virginia and "share the miseries of my people; and, save in defense, will draw my sword on none."

Lee's immediate task required establishment and organization of a Southern army. By June 1, 1862, he led the Army of Northern Virginia, a command for which he was trained and psychologically suited. Battles in Richmond, Sharpsburg, and Fredericksburg proved him a world-class strategist. The inevitable defeat of his troops began with the accidental shooting and death of his best adviser and friend, Stonewall Jackson, and the crushing defeat at Gettysburg, Pennsylvania, July 1–3, 1863. The climax at Appomattox Courthouse on April 9, 1865, which ended the slow decimation of Confederate forces and the destruction of a wide swath of public and private property, summoned Lee's courtesy, judgment, and forebearance. The next day he issued a brief commentary known as "Lee's Farewell Address to His Soldiers," a lovingly calm, reassuring piece that has become a favorite recitation in the style of the chivalric South. In his parting sentiments, he rejects more sacrifice of valiant soldiers and offers them "the satisfaction that proceeds from the consciousness of duty faithfully performed." (Trent 1905, 199) He concludes by wishing God's blessing and protection on all.

After the South's collapse as an independent republic, Lee incurred the inchoate wrath of many staunch Confederates, especially those who were homeless, displaced, and too overcome by injury, hunger, and trauma to start their lives anew. A man of character and composure, he stood before his humbled fellow Southerners as a model of nobility and courage in the face of regional disaster. Declared an outlaw, with all lands confiscated by the federal government, he maintained equanimity, visited the wounded, surveyed the damage that General William T. Sherman's march had wrought, and attempted to restore regional faith in the Union. By August 1865, Lee had established a new direction for his life by accepting the presidency of Washington College in Lexington, Virginia. For his commitment to the school's liberal arts program, it was renamed Washington and Lee in his honor.

During the dismal postwar period, creative people turned their amorphous sorrow and suffering into art. Writers, stonemasons, sculptors, and painters focused on Lee for numerous portraits and tributes. A Virginia poet, James Barron Hope, composed "Washington and Lee," the close of *The Lee Memorial*

Commander of Confederate forces during the Civil War, Robert E. Lee (1807–1870) on his gray horse Traveller, gazes from a hill with his generals and staff.

Ode, recited at the completion of the Lee monument in Richmond and published in *A Wreath of Virginia Bay Leaves* (1895). Hope declares that the general's name is deathless because his men continue to honor him and Southerners revere his memory. Connecting Lee to Virginia's noble past, Hope writes:

> Our past is full of glories,
> It is a shut-in sea,
> The pillars overlooking it
> Are Washington and Lee:
> And a future spreads before us,
> Not unworthy of the free.
> (Trent 1905, 301)

Georgia poet Will Henry Thompson visualizes a similar nobility in "The High Tide at Gettysburg." Written with insight into the smoke, noise, and momentary heroism of so telling a loss, Thompson pictures the chain of command, with Lee preceding "matchless infantry" and Pickett leading with a rush that breached the walls of destiny. Thompson closes with a poignant blend of defeat, pride, and "the cheers of Christendom." (Fulton 1917, 439)

Fellow Virginian John Reuben Thompson, editor of the *Southern Literary Messenger*, chose a dramatic moment in Lee's life to envision in verse. Thompson defined a memorable cry from the men in "Lee to the Rear," the call of forces plunging into an unpromising conflict in the Wilderness. Lee, "a grey-bearded man in a black slouched hat," seized the battle flag of a Texas regiment and tried to lead the charge against a nearly impregnable stronghold. Realizing that the general was risking himself to gallop before them, his troops forced him back. Their colonel promised that, if the general remained safe, the men would act as his agents:

> Turning his bridle, Robert Lee
> Rode to the rear. Like the waves of the sea,
> Bursting the dikes in their overflow,
> Madly his veterans dashed on the foe.
> (Parks 1970, 150)

Thompson reports that at sunset, the field and brook were red with the gore from 10,000 fallen Union soldiers, but that fate decreed ruin for the Wilderness victors. Thompson holds to the veteran's adoration of Lee, whose nobility and courage were couched in memorable gestures of defiance as examples for his followers.

Virginian Daniel Bedinger Lucas, a handicapped attorney who was released from military duty because of a spinal malformation, was on a mission to Montreal, Canada, when he learned of Lee's surrender. Lucas's ornate verse, "The Land Where We Were Dreaming," invokes classic images, particularly his memory of Lee:

> As while great Jove, in bronze, a warder god,
> Gazed eastward from the Forum where he stood,
>   Rome felt herself secure and free—
>   So Richmond, we, on guard for thee,
>   Beheld a bronzèd hero, god-like Lee,
>   In the land where we were dreaming!
> (Parks 1970, 161)

In verse as in life, Lucas remained steadfast to the cause like so many other disillusioned Southerners, who wondered how a noble philosophy could be so thoroughly vanquished by an invading army.

Other Civil War poets, including Virginian Abram Joseph Ryan and Dr. Francis Orrery Ticknor of Baldwin County, Georgia, intensify the link to the chivalric tradition. Ryan's "The Sword of Robert Lee" (1880) exalts the leader's stainless honor, valor, and pride:

> Out of its scabbard! Never hand
>   Waved sword from stain as free,
> Nor purer sword led braver band,
> Nor braver bled for a brighter land,
> Nor brighter land had a cause so grand
>   Nor cause a chief like Lee!
> (Wann 1933, 155)

In like manner and tone, Ticknor's "The Virginians of the Valley," "Virginia," and "Lee," all of which date to a posthumous 1879 collection, resound with an epic fire and majesty. The latter verse, a tribute both sentimental and inspirational, elevates the hero to godlike proportions. Margaret Junkin Preston, a lyric poet of the post–Civil War era, produced similar historical and religious verse. A favorite, "Gone Forward," published in *Cartoons* (1875), builds on Lee's final words: "Let the tent be struck." (Trent 1905, 339) In medieval Christian tradition, she commits him to heaven among the Red Cross knights of the Crusades.

Not all anti-Union sentiment appeared in sober lines. Virginian Innes Randolph produced a feisty, anti-Recontruction ballad, "I'm a Good Old Rebel," filled with the defiance and scorn that the losing side was forced to endure:

I hate the Constitution,
    This great republic too;
I hate the freedman's buro,
    In uniforms of blue.
I hate the nasty eagle,
    With all his brags and fuss;
The lyin' thievin' Yankees,
    I hate 'em wuss and wuss.
(Parks 1970, 144)

In his recollections of battles, Randolph refers to Lee as "Marse Robert," the affectionate plantation name that soldiers used in private to characterize their loyalty. Randolph's speaker concludes with a sorehead's anguish: He can't take back the South's defeat, but he asks for no pardon and refuses to be reconstructed.

A memorable voice of the Reconstruction era, local-colorist and dialect author Thomas Nelson Page, author of *In Ole Virginia* (1887), came under Lee's influence at Washington College, where Page edited the college magazine. Page's well-honed sketches and vignettes appeared in *The Old South, Essays Social and Political* (1892), in which he described the fervor of men enlisting for battle to preserve their property and families. He characterizes Lee in defeat as a trustworthy hero still beloved by Southerners, both military and noncombatant. Confederate soldiers, shrunk to a handful of worn, starved veterans, maintain the indomitable spirit that Page glorified in verse. To him, Lee's remnants comprised "the crystallization of Southern courage." (Trent 1905, 465)

The twentieth century continues to redefine the qualities that Lee embodied. Stephen Vincent Benét cameos Lee in a lyric dramatic monologue, a segment of his Pulitzer Prize–winning epic ballad *John Brown's Body* (1929). In an aide-de-camp's view of the general, Lee sits in his tent, revealing a black-on-white outline, as stark as the idolatry that lifts him from the ordinary:

His hands are lying there
Quiet as stones or shadows in his lap.
But there is nothing ruined in his face,
And nothing beaten in those steady eyes.
If he's grown old, it isn't like a man,
It's more the way a river might grow old.
(Loban et al. 1958, 221)

Benét's contemporary, Donald Davidson, produced a collection, *Lee in the Mountains and Other Poems* (1927), that delineates the war era's trust in Lee. In "Sanctuary," Davidson, a staunch Fugitive Agrarian, sequences the mounting pride of place and ancestry that dates to settlers of the Appalachians. To mountain folk hunted by a faceless, nameless troop imbued with a pillage-and-burn lust, the speaker urges endurance:

> Do not look back. You can see your roof afire
> When you reach high ground. Yet do not look.
> Do not turn. Do not look back.
> Go further on. Go high. Go deep.
> (Beatty et al. 1952, 771)

In the title work "Lee in the Mountains," the poet expresses the South's difficulty in shaking off the terrible loss of surrender by picturing General Lee as "Robert Lee in a dark civilian suit who walks, an outlaw fumbling for the latch, a voice commanding in a dream where no flag flies." (Beatty et al. 1952, 767) In the forgiving, uplifting vision, the speaker removes the Confederate hero from a military milieu by supplanting the gray uniform with mufti and stripping the Confederate battle flag from the sky. He flashes back to the April day when Lee's soldiers gathered at Appomattox to stack their weapons, admit defeat, and interrogate one another for signs of betrayal. In this emotional aftermath of conflict and disillusion, Lee continues to lead young men who come to the Virginia college in search of knowledge. Ambivalent yet sturdy, and bereft of citizenship, the former general feels isolated, trapped, yet bound to educate the student body on issues of faith and valor.

A contemporary of Virginia novelist Ellen Glasgow and other regionalists of the Southern Renaissance, James Branch Cabell, an aristocrat and scholar from Richmond, taught French and Greek and wrote for the *Richmond Times* before emigrating to Harlem for two years to write for the *New York Herald*. On his return to Richmond in 1901, he began contributing short stories to *Harper's Monthly Magazine* and the *Saturday Evening Post*, in which he serialized a novel, *The Eagle's Shadow* (1904). Slow to gain attention, Cabell published short stories, criticism and reviews, drama, medieval romance, editorials, verse, allegory, and memoirs, but is best known for his essays on Virginia. In a contemplative sketch on the post–Civil War South in *Let Me Lie* (1947), Cabell remarks on the atmosphere that prevailed in the wake of defeat:

> The Confederacy had fallen, which was bad enough in all conscience; and, which appeared to have been far more horrible, Reconstruction had followed. Herewith one employs the word "horrible" on account of the backwardness of the English language, which, as yet, has not produced any adjective better qualified to express the more lenient aspects of Reconstruction, as your elders viewed Reconstruction. (Beatty et al. 1952, 834)

He reflects on hearing the details of war and destruction. To exalt the leaders of the vanquished, he compares survivors to venerable graybeards from the Bible, and Robert E. Lee to "divinity, because a god, or at any rate a demigod, had come forth from the Northern Neck of Virginia to dwell in the Confederate states of America." (Beatty et al. 1952, 835) Remarking on the general's "serene glory," Cabell pictures him in statuesque grandeur: seated on Traveller, his heroic steed, "like King Arthur returned from out of Avalon, attended by the resplendent Launcelots and Tristrams and Gareths and Galahads, who, once upon a time, had been the other Confederate generals." The picture reprises the romanticism that deterred Southerners from releasing their dreams of a sovereign Camelot in favor of a realistic grasp of their role as recovering rebel states. (Beatty et al. 1952; Benét 1982; Bowler et al. 1996; Bradbury 1963; Fulton 1917; Gross 1971; "James Branch Cabell" 1996; Kunitz 1942; Kunitz and Haycraft 1938; Loban et al. 1958; Parks 1970; Quinn 1936; Rubin et al. 1985; Trent 1905; Wann 1933; Wilson and Ferris 1989)

See also the Civil War era; Fugitive Agrarians.

LOMAX, JOHN

A collector of verse and musical Americana, John Avery Lomax spurned those elements of national culture that imitated European style and content and rejected the American experience as worthy of appreciation or study. He pioneered efforts to preserve native folk songs and lore by rescuing from oblivion 10,000 songs, including crude saloon ditties, Negro spirituals, washboard and field songs, moody ballads of flirtation and unrequited love, chanteys of boaters and wagoneers, tragic reveries of levee builders and track layers, worldly gospel songs, tawdry prison plaints and rotgut blues, drovers' jingles, mountain fiddlers' tunes, and chain-gang chants indigenous to the South and Southwest. For maximum authenticity, he championed the creative impetus of slave and underclass experiences in shanties and lumber and rail camps, on barges and overland mail wagons, at harvest reels and card games, and among soldiers, seducers, dicers, outcasts, tie tampers, hoboes, moonshiners, and loafers. His anthologies have influenced compilers of a national literature, providing them with titles, verse, and metaphors as familiar as "Irene, Good Night," "Rock Island Line," "John Henry," "Midnight Special," "The Arkansas Traveler," "Take This Hammer," and "Casey Jones," a familiar narrative song about a Memphis railroad engineer killed outside Canton, Mississippi.

Lomax's experience derives from the South's unrefined frontier border, a cultural milieu that springs from a mix of pioneer experiences. The son of Susan Frances Copper and farmer James Avery Lomax, he was born in Goodman, Mississippi, on September 23, 1867. In 1869, his family traveled 500 miles west by mule and ox-wagon to settle in northwest Texas. A treasured narrative by his mother tells how the family made a new start on the Bosque River along the Chisholm Trial, over which drovers moved herds from San Antonio to Wichita and Abilene, Kansas. Envigorated by the era's optimism and drive, he befriended ranch hands and cowboys, and memorized the melodies and verses of their jovial workday songs. After studying for a year at Granbury College, he taught at Weatherford College for six years before entering graduate studies at the University of Texas. As an avocation, he continued searching out the unusual and true among the wry and witty expressions of Southwest folk music.

While teaching at Texas Agricultural and Mechanical College, Lomax impressed the college president, who insisted that he seek more training in recognizing and evaluating folklore. With additional course work in linguistics, he became more discerning about dialect, reflected in the regional pronunciations and makeshift spellings of idiom, for example, goin', gwine, gwinter, gonna, gon', and gonter. In 1907, Lomax completed an M.A. in English at Harvard and received from scholarly folklorists the impetus and funds to turn his hobby into a career. He returned to Texas to organize the impersonal narrative airs and melodies of no specific date or author that circulate orally through such homogeneous groups as stevedores, herders, prisoners, lumbermen, housemaids, rodeo hands, and migrant fruit pickers. Doleful songs punctuate stanzas with the eerie yodel of the cowboy riding guard late at night and crooning animal lullabies to settle milling longhorns. Lomax's impressive portfolio served as the basis for a best-seller, *Cowboy Songs and Other Frontier Ballads* (1910), a classic compendium that highlights the interconnected frontier themes of independence and individuality. Response was so favorable that he published a second compilation, *Songs of the Cattle Trail and Cow Camp* (1917).

Many of Lomax's choice discoveries bear the lack of refinement, piquance, easy sociability, racial stereotyping, and outback ribaldry found in the writings of Southern humorists Mark Twain, Davy Crockett, and Augustus Longstreet Baldwin. A favorite of blues singers is "De Midnight Special," a varied ballad that adapts easily to appended verses. Most likely of Caucasian origin, the song begins with complaints about the sameness of prison food. The mention of actual jailers, transfer agents, and wardens places the stanzas in select locales, as with this version from a Texas lockup:

> Ef you go to Houston,
> You better walk right,
> You better not stagger,
> You better not fight.
> Or Sheriff Benson
> Will arrest you,
> He will carry you down.
> Ef de juris [*sic*] find you guilty,
> You'll be penitentiary bound.
> (Lomax and Lomax 1934, 73)

Other lines from the musical melange thrum with comic situations and scurrilous references replete with miscegenation, profligacy, sexism, addiction, violence, and sacrilege, as found in "Yella Gal," "Dirty Mistreatin' Women," "Rye Whiskey," "Frankie and Johnny," "Lulu," and "Drink That Rot Gut." Less rambunctious songs like "Little Liza Jane," "De Ballit of de Boll Weevil," "Old Cottonfields at Home," "Down in the Valley," "Shortenin' Bread," "Pick a Bale of Cotton," and "Alabama-Bound" reflect a nostalgia for past times in the South when cotton was profitable and the Negro provided the labor that enriched the boss.

Integral to Lomax's folk research is his replication of dirt-level English, as spoken by Tom Hight in "Starving to Death on a Government Claim." Tom, an "old bach'lor" sodbusting in Greer County, speaks honestly of his situation:

> My clothes are all ragged, as my language is rough,
> My bread is corndodgers, both solid and tough;

> But yet I am happy and live at my ease
> On sorghum molasses, bacon, and cheese.
> (Lomax 1965, 261–262)

Unwittingly enticed from the rural South by the Homestead Act of 1862, Tom Hight sees himself as a victim of the westering lure and resolves to abandon his claim, escape the prairie's extremes of weather, and "travel to Texas and marry me a wife/And quit corndodgers the rest of my life." Less mournful is a preface to American ragtime, "At a Georgia Camp Meeting," a nostalgic memory of "many a happy face . . . people happy and free." The song recounts how worshippers depart church to dance, kiss, and sway to a brass band. The jolly memory ends with "Yes indeed the rhythm was sure O.K. Soon your worry left in a hurry, down at the Georgia camp meeting holiday." (Gamse 1961, 122)

After the death of his wife and a physical and financial breakdown, Lomax quit his bank job and spent the 1930s collaborating with his elder son, John Lomax, Jr., who drove the Ford and helped his father search the Southwest for isolated examples of Americana. Funded by Macmillan Press, Lomax made a second fact-finding foray about the South with his teenaged son Alan. The duo took on a monumental project—cataloging the heartfelt ballads and rhythmic chants of poor white sharecroppers, camp meeting revivalists, chain-gang escapees, penitentiary inmates, levee stevedores, saloonkeeps, lumberjacks, cardsharps, wagoneers and buffalo skinners, well diggers, and native blues singers, all of whom he identifies with easy familiarity by their nicknames—Ike, Jumpin' Judy, Benny, Ida Red, Shaddy, Mohee, Black Betty, L'l Alex, and Cap'n George. These recordings he and his son collected in *American Ballads and Folk Songs* (1934). During their tour, they discovered Huddie "Leadbelly" Ledbetter, a fresh, innovative bass who was serving a sentence for armed assault at the Angola Prison Farm in Louisiana. Their recording of Leadbelly's rich lyrics so impressed Governor O. K. Allen that he pardoned the singer so that he could accompany the Lomaxes on their 6,000-mile journey across the South.

While serving the Federal Writers' Project as national folklore acquisitions editor, Lomax disdained the contrived, government-controlled effort because it compromised his gut instincts about the underpinnings of national songs. For the remainder of his professional life, he managed the Archive of Folk Music of the Library of Congress and added his 10,000 recordings to its collection. His last three works—*Negro Folk Songs as Sung by Lead Belly* (1936), *Our Singing Country* (1941), and *Folk Song U.S.A.* (1947)—preceded a renaissance of blues and native folk tunes. Lomax insisted that American balladeers spoke the commonalities of the South and West, which reflect the challenge of bad luck and random violence, joy in camaraderie and kinship, and a reverence for liberty and the land. His exacting vocabulary popularized such local terminology as dogies, chitlins, hoecake, bandy-shanked, rukus, high-steppin', cotton-eyed, breakdown, and weevily. Shortly before his death from cerebral hemorrhage in Greenville, Mississippi, on January 26, 1948, he published an autobiography, *Adventures of a Ballad Hunter* (1947), a salute to the vigor, diversity, and distinctive flavor of Southern and Southwestern Americana.

At the end of the twentieth century, Alan Lomax continued the crusade to identify and catalog national treasures. A Southern author, recording editor, and preservationist like his father, he has captured the low-down jests, bawdy tales, tuneful grievances, joyous game chants, holy-roller shouts, and songs of love and travail that characterize the patois and dynamics of the working-class experience. Among his additions to the canon of Lomax and Lomax are "I Be's Troubled," "Old Rattler," "Ma Rainey's Black Bottom," and versions of "Stagolee" and "Shake, Rattle an' Roll," a rock classic revived in the 1950s by Bill Haley and the Comets and by Elvis Presley. In *The Land Where the Blues Began* (1993), his precise recounting of folk spirit and yearnings honor the work of John Lomax, who taught him the trade. (Botkin 1944; Brunvand 1996; Dobie 1996; Gamse 1961; Hazard 1927; Lamar 1977; Lomax 1947, 1965; Lomax and Lomax 1934; Rubin et al. 1985; Trent et al. 1946; Wexler 1995; Wilson and Ferris 1989)

See also the Mississippi River.

McCULLERS, CARSON

A student of pain, loneliness, and alienation, Carson McCullers shaped novels, plays, and short stories around forlorn, spiritually isolated characters caught in harsh, often grotesque situations as well as in the normal angst of adolescence, widowhood, and social stigma. In a reflective moment, she declared, "I become the characters I write about and I bless the Latin poet Terence who said, 'Nothing human is alien to me.'" (Cook 1975, 18) An expatriate and pillar of the Southern Literary Renaissance, she was embraced by the New York literati, who proclaimed her canon a literary touchstone. For a quarter century, she endured debilitating respiratory illness, paralysis, homesickness, and despair far from her roots while she wrote of Southern decadence. Drawn to pathetic characters occupying a limited landscape, she revealed a strangely morbid obsession with, but nevertheless genuine compassion for, motherless teenagers, cripples, misfits, freaks, alienated drifters, and moral isolates.

McCullers's point of view mirrors her hometown, Columbus, once a Georgia mill village. She was born Lula Carson Smith, the first child of Marguerite Waters and Lamar Smith, a watch repairman, on February 19, 1917. Her father and mother kept a jewelry store and lived with Marguerite's mother, Lula Carolina Carson Waters, for whom their oldest was named. Carson, known as "Tartie," led the childhood revels of her brother Lamar, Jr., and sister Margarita "Rita" Gachet, who later edited fiction for *Mademoiselle*. Carson enjoyed rowdy activities, but caromed from emotional highs to pensive lows. She grew more introspective in solitude, an emotional exile she describes in the popular story "Sucker" (1971):

> He used to talk to himself a lot when he'd think he was alone—all about him fighting gangsters and being on ranches and that sort of kids' stuff. He'd get in the bathroom and stay as long as an hour and sometimes his voice would go up high and excited and you could hear him all over the house. Usually, though, he was very quiet. (McCullers 1986, 240)

Critics have noted that McCullers, a restrained bisexual, mulled over personal matters and frequently recast her reminiscences from a male perspective such as Sucker's or from characters with masculine names and nicknames, particularly Frankie Addams and Mick Kelly.

McCullers lived the stereotypical Southern tradition, including baptism in the Baptist faith and envelopment by a pushy mother who wanted to fend off the world from her "Little Precious." McCullers attended kindergarten and the Sixteenth Street School until 1925, when the family moved from her grandmother's residence to their own place. Childhood expeditions about their backyard and around the streets of Columbus furnished visions of the stifling atmosphere of a Southern small town. Like the characters in her fiction, she studied piano and foresaw a career as a concert soloist. A local dance club invited her to join because she was the only pianist their age. Her activities centered on home after she suffered a lung ailment in 1932, originally diagnosed as tuberculosis but later attributed to rheumatic fever. Writing was a second choice to music after she was confined to bed and could no longer sit long hours at the keyboard. She completed Columbus High School at age 16 and read from American, British, French, and Russian classics. She admired the keen details in Marcel Proust's *Remembrance of Things Past*. The dramas of Eugene O'Neill influenced a work of juvenilia, *The Faucet*, her first home-acted play, in which her brother and sister assumed major roles.

After her piano teacher, Mary Tucker, moved away, McCullers arranged to sell an heirloom ring to pay her way by rail to Savannah and by steamship to New York to study at the Juilliard School of Music. She intended to serve both the literary and music muses by dividing her time between piano and creative writing classes at night from New York and Columbia Universities. Reflecting on the bold journey from her familiar Southern hometown, she recalled in adulthood the safety pin that fastened $500 in cash to her underclothes. She was a neophyte at city life and boarded at a modest house that bustled with late traffic. After discovering that the house was a brothel and the frequent visitors were clients calling on prostitutes, she took rooms at the more sedate Parnassus Club.

During early training, McCullers acquired the discipline demanded by her career. She had the writer's flair for soaking up atmosphere, motivation, and dialogue. On free days, she roamed the dock area or took the subway into the city. On one of her jaunts, she lost the remainder of her school money and had to work part-time as a typist, waitress, dog attendant, accompanist for ballet classes, and bookkeeper to pay tuition at Columbia. In her sophomore year, she returned to Georgia and wrote without salary for the *Columbus Ledger* to learn more about journalistic style. That summer she met her future husband, James Reeves McCullers, Jr., a 22-year-old soldier from Alabama stationed at Fort Benning, Georgia.

In New York the next year during the dismal end of the Depression, McCullers enrolled at Washington Square College while Reeves studied journalism at Columbia. The first of a series of his future wife's life-threatening bouts with rheumatic fever forced him to arrange emergency retreats to Georgia, where she spent the winter with her parents and wrote two stories, "Wunderkind" and "Like That," which she sold to *Story* magazine. Still relatively young and inexperienced, she composed most of *The Mute*, the original title of *The Heart Is a Lonely Hunter* (1940), a complex social novel blending themes of unionism, civil rights, rootlessness, and violence with her signature interest in adolescence and wounded, misaligned families. At a pivotal time in her career, continued frail health influenced her to marry Reeves. Their impromptu home wedding on September 20, 1937, preceded temporary settlement in Charlotte, North Carolina, where Reeves worked as credit investigator for a small loan company. A subsequent move took them to Fayetteville near Fort Bragg, North Carolina, where she completed *The Heart Is a Lonely Hunter*. The novel won a Houghton Mifflin Fiction Fellowship competition prize of $1,500 and was published in 1940.

McCullers earned instant fame from the publication of *The Heart Is a Lonely Hunter*, an eloquent, densely plotted circular narrative. Set in a Southern mill town like Columbus in the 1930s, the action orchestrates the chance acquaintance of five characters in small-town America. In a balanced counterpoint, she allies the unlikely gathering of soulful seekers around John Singer, a lonely, gentle-eyed deaf-mute who works as a silver engraver and spends free time with a fellow mute, Spiros Antonapoulos, whom he has restrained in an institution for the retarded. Like the pair of mutes talking in hand signals, the frustrated attempts of McCullers's cast to communicate moved her to write empathetic, regret-filled passages that acknowledge the spaces that divide and hamper relationships. The awkward friendship between her adolescent protagonist, Mick Kelly, and Singer, the boarder who rents Mick's former bedroom, expresses the yearning for face-to-face communication:

> She talked to him more than she had ever talked to a person before. And if he could have talked he would have told her many things. It was like he was some kind of a great teacher, only because he was a mute he did not teach. (McCullers 1967, 207)

After Singer's suicide, Mick finds his body. Her mind recoils with terror at so much blood, and at his funeral, she disdains the absurdity of the rouge and lipstick the undertaker applies to Singer's corpse to make him look natural. To Mick, there are no plastic skills that can transform death into something more palatable or less final.

When the novel first began generating waves of commentary, critics proclaimed McCullers a young Southern prodigy and lauded her depth and skill at shaping human responses. Writing for the *New Republic*, Southern critic and novelist Richard Wright characterized her insights into mood and attitude as a variety of naturalism. Attracted to both sexes, McCullers had made a meticulous study of androgyny by stressing masculine and feminine traits in major characters, particularly Biff Brannon, the heavily bearded owner of the New York Café, who wears perfume and his mother's wedding ring and longs for motherhood. In a protracted examination of Biff's duality, she discloses the price Biff pays for hiding his alter ego from his wife Alice:

> He stood before the mirror and rubbed his cheek meditatively. He was sorry he had talked to Alice. With her, silence was better. Being around that woman always made him different from his real self. It made him tough and small and common as she was. (McCullers 1967, 11)

Analyzing the cause of her disinterest, Biff declares that Alice lacks the sort of kindness that he admires. Without an inborn curiosity about people, she is incapable of perusing the personal quirks and traits that he so loves to notice in his café clientele. When Biff makes a new discovery about someone he observes, he has no one—least of all a mate—with whom to share his insight.

Much critical conjecture centers on one of Biff's acquaintances, Dr. Benedict Mady Copeland, a brooding Negro general practitioner in late midlife who reads Spinoza and Marx. John Singer writes of Copeland in a letter:

> The black man is sick with consumption but there is not a good hospital for him to go to here because he is black. He is a doctor and he works more than anyone I have ever seen. . . . This black man frightens me sometimes. His eyes are hot and bright. (McCullers 1967, 183)

Fearful as death looms, Copeland fights with his daughter Portia about her marriage to Willie, a shiftless carouser who is beneath her worth. Of all his shattered hopes, he regrets most her failure to live up to her intellectual potential. McCullers empathizes with Copeland because he is too idealistic to survive the upheavals of the black community or even tiffs with Portia. Among the novel's circle of lonely hearts, he stands out as a wasted martyr to the cause of human relations.

McCullers's skillful characterization and deft plotting cinched her place among American realists. Her friend, Southern playwright Tennessee Williams, proclaimed her the master prose writer of her time and the best the South had produced. The success of *The Heart Is a Lonely Hunter* and McCullers's departure from the seedy landscape around Fayetteville rekindled her hopes for a stable marriage with Reeves. Enjoying financial security for the first time, he squired her about Greenwich Village, where they settled into a pleasant colony of writers and artists. McCullers summered at Bread Loaf, a writers' colony outside Middlebury, Vermont, and learned from an impressive number of professional writers—critics Louis Untermeyer and Bernard De Voto and poets W. H. Auden, Robert Frost, and John Ciardi—and two fellow Southern fiction writers, Eudora Welty and Katherine Anne Porter.

McCullers had no intention of remaining in the South, but she used her brief tenure near Fayetteville and its military surroundings as the setting for *Reflections in a Golden Eye* (1941), a poignant but quirky novella about sexual perversion and self-mutilation. The work, suggested by her husband's chance remark about a voyeur apprehended for spying on married couples at Fort Bragg, served as writer's therapy, a literary exercise to relieve tedium and depression. McCullers seems to luxuriate in the physicality of the voyeur's escapades as he rides naked on a horse:

> With the soldier a marvelous change came over the animal; he cantered or single-footed with proud, stiff elegance. The soldier's body was of a pale golden brown and he held himself erect. Without his clothes he was so slim that the pure, curved lines of his ribs could be seen. As he cantered about in the sunlight, there was a sensual, savage smile on his lips that would have surprised his barrack mates. (McCullers 1941, 37)

Carson McCullers (1917–1967), at her Columbus, Georgia, home in 1941

Originally titled *Army Post*, the bizarre story went fast and sure and brought McCullers $500 from *Harper's Bazaar*, in which it was serialized.

By the time McCullers mapped out a third novel, tentatively titled *The Bride and Her Brother*, her mood had changed, perhaps because she had wearied of marriage to a rescuer. Engulfed in regret and apprehension, she jeopardized her health with heavy drinking and smoking, both symbols of newfound independence. Living apart from Reeves, she shared February House, a large Victorian brownstone in Brooklyn Heights, with Auden, dancer Gypsy Rose Lee, novelists Richard Wright and Christopher Isherwood, and composer Benjamin Britten. Their artistic fraternization paralleled the heady atmosphere of Bread Loaf. Late-night impromptu gatherings brought McCullers in conversation with painter Salvador Dali, diarist Anais Nin, and composers Leonard Bernstein and Aaron Copland. Within three months, McCullers had to summon her mother to nurse her through a renewed bout of respiratory illness, which forced a return to Georgia. Her work progressed with the submission of short stories to *Vogue* and the publication of *Reflections in a Golden Eye*. A cerebral stroke threatened her concentration because of migraine headaches and impaired sight in her left eye. Her disposition altered to manic periods of intense writing as though she were driven to complete a life's work before her body failed altogether. As a test of concentration, she completed "A Tree, a Rock, a Cloud" (1942), which was published in *Harper's Bazaar* and anthologized in the *O. Henry Memorial Prize Stories of 1942.*

Out of need for a companion, McCullers reunited with Reeves and returned to New York in a tentative relationship. She sipped at codeine-laced cough syrup and sherry to suppress coughing. Reeves, too, lapsed into heavy drinking and illicit liaisons. While attending a six-week workshop at the Yaddo Artists' Colony in Saratoga Springs, New York, McCullers halted work on *The Member of the Wedding* to complete the framework of a novella, *The Ballad of the Sad Café* (1951). The novel details a Southern gothic romance between a gawky spinster and her cousin, an eccentric hunchback homunculus, whom McCullers relishes in lavish description:

> He did not wear trousers such as ordinary men are meant to wear, but a pair of tight-fitting little knee-length breeches. On his skinny legs he wore black stockings, and his shoes were of a special kind, being queerly shaped, laced up over the ankles, and newly cleaned and polished with wax. Around his neck, so that his large, pale ears were almost completely covered, he wore a shawl of lime-green wool, the fringes of which almost touched the floor. (McCullers 1951, 18)

The unusual novella added to McCullers's considerable fame. Heartened by the bevy of essays, reviews, and stories sold to *Decision, Vogue, Saturday Review, New Yorker,* and *Harper's Bazaar,* she enjoyed the fleeting respite and once more journeyed south to Georgia when her strength ebbed from anemia, pneumonia, and pleurisy.

McCullers remained a prisoner of lung distress throughout her divorce. Once free of Reeves and buoyed by a Guggenheim Fellowship, in 1942 she established a pattern of healing, publishing new works, writing at Yaddo, and fleeing to Columbus for recuperation from annual setbacks. The American Academy of Arts and Letters awarded her a $1,000 grant. Instead of exulting, she sank once more into self-doubt and allied tentatively with Reeves, who reported for active duty in Europe, where he participated in the D-Day landing at Normandy and the Battle of Brest. After the death of her father, McCullers invited her mother and sister to share an apartment and later a house in Nyack, New York, on the Hudson River. Reeves, a veteran of 15 months of combat and recovering from a serious arm wound, arrived in New York in 1945 to marry Carson a second time.

That summer at Yaddo, after five years of intense writing and revision, McCullers finished *The Member of the Wedding* (1946), a funny-tender adolescent debacle caused by a teenaged girl's insistence on being included in her brother's wedding. Loved for its sensitivity to childhood's end, the book preceded a second Guggenheim Fellowship. She and Reeves used the money for a fling in postwar Paris, where McCullers was swamped by fans. In August 1946, she suffered a paralytic stroke and was hospitalized in an American hospital for rehabilitation. Evacuated on a litter, she returned to the United States and fought to strengthen the weakened left side of her body. In a show of independence, she once more separated from Reeves, whose alcoholism eclipsed his role as rescuer.

Encouraged by kudos from *Mademoiselle* and *Quick* magazines, McCullers collaborated with playwright Tennessee Williams on a stage adaptation of *The Member of the Wedding*. She wrote alongside him at his Key West cottage while he fine-tuned *Summer and Smoke*. Her distillation of the original trio—Berenice Sadie Brown, John Henry, and Frankie Addams—intensifies relationships and themes with bittersweet exchanges. As Frankie thrusts into new territory, McCullers reveals the price of maturity:

> Berenice: All my life I've been wantin' things that I ain't been gettin'. Anyhow those club girls is fully two years older than you.
> Frankie: I think they have been spreading it all over town that I smell bad. . . . Oh, I could shoot every one of them with a pistol.
> John Henry: I don't think you smell so bad. You smell sweet, like a hundred flowers.
> Frankie: The son-of-a-bitches. (McCullers 1960, 385–386)

Berenice's maternal intuition and humanity and John Henry's childish tag echo counter moments when no amount of wisdom or innocence can calm Frankie. In a private purgatory, she mourns, "I feel just exactly like somebody has peeled all the skin off me. I wish I had some good cold peach ice cream." (McCullers 1960, 398)

In 1950, McCullers's play opened at Philadelphia's Empire Theatre and ran for 501 performances. On Broadway, the brilliant pacing and on-target emotion of *The Member of the Wedding* won the New York Drama Critic's Circle Award and the Donaldson Award. Columbia filmed the play in 1952; Julie Harris, Ethel Waters, and Brandon de Wilde starred as the triad who occupy a Southern kitchen and discuss the sufferings of Frankie Addams, not quite a woman but too lanky for childhood. Harris won an Oscar nomination for her role, an autobiographical re-creation of McCullers's own coming-of-age.

Content at the three-story house in Nyack, McCullers succeeded at poems, essays, and short fiction. In the best health of her adult life, she vacationed in Ireland, England, and France, and made friends with novelist Elizabeth Bowen and poet and critic Edith Sitwell. Dismayed by paralysis in her left arm, in 1951 she traveled to New Orleans with Reeves, where pneumonia again swamped her energy. She retreated to her mother's care in Nyack. The next year, McCullers and Reeves sailed to Italy on the *Constitution*. They bought their first home, an old vicarage in Bachvillers on the outskirts of Paris on the Oise River. While working in Rome on an omnibus collection, *The Ballad of the Sad Café and Collected Short Stories*, and a screenplay, McCullers sank once more into depression from her fears of another stroke and from coping with Reeves's dementia and chronic alcoholism. Fogged by her own consumption of alcohol, she was alarmed by his intent to commit suicide and fled to the United States before he killed himself in a Paris hotel room in November 1953.

A widowed invalid, McCullers returned to early texts to produce works for stage and ballet. She teamed with Tennessee Williams for a lecture tour that included Goucher College, Columbia University, and the Philadelphia Fine Arts Association. Temporarily, she worked and rested at his Key West home, a productive holiday that ended because of her mother's death. McCullers continued arranging stage productions of her works and submitted fiction and poems to *Mademoiselle, Literary Cavalcade,* and *Botteghe Oscure.* The failure of the Broadway opening of a play, *The Square Root of Wonderful* (1958), exacerbated worry about her paralyzed arm. Psychoanalysis once more strengthened her confidence.

In her declining years, McCullers worked as often and as hard as tenuous health allowed. She appeared at the American Academy of Arts and Letters with Danish writer Isak Dinesen to champion the arts. While planning a musical version of *The Ballad of the Sad Café*, McCullers underwent orthopedic surgery and retired to a wheelchair. Without grasp in her left hand, she typed one-handed in bed to finish her most troubled work, *Clock without Hands* (1961), a novel ten years in the making, and collaborated with playwright Edward Albee on a dramatic stage adaptation of *The Ballad of the Sad Café*. In 1964, a broken hip and crushed elbow ended her hope for restored mobility. After a third stroke on August 15, 1967, she suffered a brain hemorrhage and lay comatose at Nyack Hospital, where she died on September 29, 1967. She was buried nearby at Oak Hill Cemetery.

McCullers centered her work in Southern settings and mastered regional themes, especially eccentricities, racism, and gothic touches. European critics admired her sympathy for lonely, isolated, and estranged characters. *Time* magazine ranked her as one of the 12 notable authors of the era; emerging Southern writers Joan Williams and Gail Godwin named her as a major influence on their fiction. The Fugitive Agrarians embraced her as a stalwart of the movement's second wave. From *Die Welt* she won the Prize of the Younger Generation. Warner Seven Arts filmed the darkly perverse *Reflections in a Golden Eye* (1967), starring Marlon Brando, Elizabeth Taylor, Brian Keith, and Julie Harris. The year after McCullers's death, Warner filmed *The Heart Is a Lonely Hunter* (1968), a compassionate, heavily autobiographical reflection on the South and its society, divided rich and poor, black and white. Sondra Locke and Alan Arkin won Oscar nominations for their perceptive interaction as Mick Kelly, the teenage malcontent, and Mr. Singer, the deaf-mute who boards at the Kelly home and exposes her to symphonic music. McCullers's children's verse was published in *Sweet as a Pickle and Clean as a Pig: Poems* (1964). Her sister, editor Margarita Smith, collected 20 early short stories, essays, and poems for a posthumous collection, *The Mortgaged Heart* (1971), containing "Sucker," a classroom favorite describing a worrisome orphaned child who acts up to gain attention, and "The Haunted Boy," about the residual guilt and horror of a mother's suicide. In 1990, a lackluster Merchant-Ivory cinema of Albee's stage version of *The Ballad of the Sad Café* featured an odd pairing of Vanessa Redgrave and Cork Hubbert as Miss Amelia, the mannish store owner, and her peculiar, petulant cousin Lymon. (Auchincloss 1961; Bradbury 1963; Bradbury 1996; Buck 1992; Carr 1975; Cook 1975; Davidson and Wagner-Martin 1995; Ehrlich and Carruth 1982; Inge 1990; Kelly 1982; King 1980; Kohler 1951; Kunitz 1942; McCullers 1941, 1951, 1967, 1968, 1973, 1983, 1986; Rubin 1982; Rubin et al. 1985; Sherr and Kazickas 1994; Stein 1979; Whitt 1994; Wilson and Ferris 1989)

See also Fugitive Agrarians; *The Member of the Wedding;* Williams, Tennessee.

THE MEMBER OF THE WEDDING

A memory novel recording the prepubescent insecurities of a 12-year-old girl, *The Member of the Wedding* (1946) is a widely acclaimed childhood reverie on the search for belonging and peace with self. The story employs motifs common to Southern fiction—the sounding of the mill whistle at noon, meals of peas and rice with pot liquor, and a motherless family's dependence on a black housekeeper and cook as surrogate mother, an essential device in Margaret Mitchell's *Gone with the Wind* and Harper Lee's *To Kill a Mockingbird*. At the request of her employer, Frankie Addams's nanny, Berenice Sadie Brown, thinks up activities to occupy both her charge and John Henry West, a pesky, whimsical neighbor child who demands attention. Their three-way dialogue moves unevenly over varied interests—John Henry's reasons for cutting the pictures from the face cards they use for games of three-handed bridge, Berenice's advice to Frankie about getting along with Frankie's widowed father, and Frankie's obsession with her brother Jarvis's betrothal to Janice and their impending marriage at Winter Hill.

McCullers's genius for humor and pathos interweaves a series of images for the jangled, out-of-sync world of the preadult. On the street, a drunken soldier offers $100 for the monkey-man's monkey. In the distance, a piano tuner bangs at a misaligned string. Among local girls, Frankie knocks on unyielding doors and imagines persecutors saying nasty things behind her back. Like the author, Frankie "belonged to no club and was a member of nothing in the world." (McCullers 1973, 1) Whereas Janice and Jarvis sounded like an ideal pair, Frankie, renamed F. Jasmine, mated with no supportive name or role. In an extended fantasy, she grasps a butcher knife to punctuate her prediction that the wedding will open a new era for her:

> We will be walking down a dark road and see a lighted house and knock on the door and strangers will rush to meet us and say: Come in! Come in! . . . We will have thousands and thousands of friends. We will belong to so many clubs that we can't even keep track of them. We will be members of the whole world. Boyoman! Manoboy! (McCullers 1973, 112)

Intent on fleeing the confines of the sultry kitchen in a too-familiar hometown, she foresees the wedding as the end of teenage ennui and her entree into an exciting adult society.

McCullers applies gentle humor to Frankie's out-of-kilter summer. The yearning for inclusion leads the protagonist awry as she applies little-girl logic to mature situations. She follows the reeling soldier into a beer hall and, innocent of the preliminaries to seduction, accepts his invitation for a grown-up date, a near-disaster that she is too young and inexperienced to understand. After Mr. Addams gives her permission to charge an outfit for the wedding at MacDougal's, she returns from shopping with silver slippers to accessorize a bargain-basement treasure, a womanly orange satin evening dress. Berenice turns her head from the gaudy "human Christmas [tree] in August" and comments succinctly, "It don't do." (McCullers 1973, 84) Frankie shies from Berenice's "candy opinion," but agrees to stand still for a fitting as Berenice restyles the dress into more appropriate wedding attire. (McCullers 1973, 86)

Ethel Waters, left, and Julie Harris, right, reprise their stage roles of Berenice Sadie Brown and Frankie Addams in the 1952 movie *The Member of the Wedding* by Carson McCullers.

The dissolution of the fragile threesome—Berenice, Frankie, and John Henry—consumes the falling action, quickly shifting Frankie into a new cosmos. Because she aches for a "we of me," she misbehaves at the ceremony by insisting on going along on Janice and Jarvis's honeymoon, and sinks into self-induced despair, "[wishing] the whole world to die." (McCullers 1973, 135) In an ugly humor on the bus ride home from the wedding,

> Her shoulders were hunched over her swollen heart. . . . She was sitting next to Berenice, back with the colored people, and when she thought of it she used the mean word she had never used before, nigger—for now she hated everyone and wanted only to spite and shame. (McCullers 1973, 137)

Immured in a me-first crusade, Frankie changes her name from the exotic F. Jasmine to the more practical Frances and courts friendship with Mary Littlejohn. On new trails, Frankie ignores the anguish of John Henry, whose eyes roll into a distorted grimace as the excruciating pain of meningitis kills him. She is oblivious to the departure of Berenice, the family bulwark, whose wayward son is sentenced to a chain gang and who won't be needed after the Addams family moves in with Frankie's aunt and uncle. At 13, Frances Addams has moved beyond weddings and exclusion to new friends and new obsessions. (Bradbury 1963, 1996; Buck 1992; Carr 1975; Cook 1975; Davidson and Wagner-Martin 1995;

Ehrlich and Carruth 1982; Inge 1990; Kelly 1982; King 1980; Kohler 1951; Kunitz 1942; McCullers 1967, 1968, 1973, 1983; Rubin 1982; Rubin et al. 1985; Sherr and Kazickas 1994; Stein 1979; Westling 1985; Wilson and Ferris 1989)
See also McCullers, Carson.

MENCKEN, H. L.

A confirmed cynic and severe derider of the South, Henry Louis Mencken—a literary gadfly known as the "Sage of Baltimore" and the city's acid tongue—earned a reputation for being a conscientious stylist. In his day, he rose to acclamations as the nation's foremost aphorist, humorist, and critic of popular culture. Better versed in negatives than positives, he evenhandedly satirized more than his homeland in sharp-barbed invective, review, essay, and diatribe. Mencken, a writer of admirable prose models, lambasted proud politicians, seedy rogues and mountebanks, provincial no-nothings, and sentimental, mawkish fools, as in *Last Words* (1926), a denunciation of the extremes tolerated by a democracy:

> I enjoy democracy immensely. It is incomparably idiotic, and hence incomparably amusing. Does it exalt dunderheads, cowards, trimmers, frauds, cads? Then the pain of seeing them go up is balanced and obliterated by the joy of seeing them come down. Is it inordinately wasteful, extravagant, dishonest? Then so is every other form of government: all alike are enemies to laborious and virtuous men. (Mencken, "Last Words" 1996, 2)

For such personal glee at the fate of fools, Mencken satisfied himself with similar well-honed generalizations. He earned a select coterie of fans and a sizable army of enemies, led by victims of his gibes. Literary historians of the ebullient post–World War I era compare Mencken to Sinclair Lewis for despising the era's smug parochialism and self-delusion. In the introduction to *The Vintage Mencken*, Alastair Cooke notes that Mencken emulated Friedrich Nietzsche and George Bernard Shaw, and set his goal

> to be the native American Voltaire, the enemy of all puritans, the heretic in the Sunday School, the one-man demolition crew of the genteel tradition, the unregenerate neighborhood brat who stretches a string in the alley to trip the bourgeoisie on its pious homeward journey. (Mencken 1983, ix)

Mencken's one-of-a-kind wit has endeared his name and style to would-be Menckens who lack the color, control, and chutzpah to reprise a master satirist.

Mencken was a descendant of self-satisfied German burghers, a mold that prefigured his place in American culture. The eldest of manufacturer August Mencken and Anna Abhou's four children, he was born September 12, 1880, in Baltimore, Maryland. His paternal grandfather settled in Baltimore and opened a cigar factory. Likewise inspired by the Puritan work ethic, his father and uncle flourished in the tobacco business. Mencken was required to function as office boy, cigar seller, and assistant bookkeeper in the family trade, but he hated the job. In his teens, he prepared himself for a journalistic career by operating a home printing press and studying news writing through correspondence courses. He attended Friedrich Knapp's Institute and earned a superb record at Baltimore Polytechnic, from which he graduated in 1896. The day after his father's death in January 1899, Mencken began a daily job hunt at the *Baltimore Herald* and refused the editor's rejection. Working gratis, he typed up obituaries. Judged competent to handle small stories, he eventually netted a beginner's beat—the police desk. His first published contribution to journalism was a five-line blip about a horse thief. The power of the press sparked a glint of mischief that remained his beacon for a half century.

A staff writer, editor, and columnist under the heading "The Free Lance," Mencken worked for the *Baltimore Sun* most of his career, and earned a reputation as antiacademic, libertarian, iconoclast, skeptic, and subjective critic of artsy writing, particularly professorial rantings and sentimental verse, both of which he abominated. A year after he published a poetry collection, *Ventures into Verse* (1903), he advanced to editor of the *Evening Herald*, for which he covered political conventions, circulated essays to most of the journals of his day, and produced serious criticism of his idols, George Bernard Shaw and Friedrich Nietzsche. When news reporting began to bore him in 1906, Mencken departed permanently from the newsroom and stuck to criticism and commentary, even during periods when he longed to reenlist in the frenetic army of news gatherers.

With drama critic George Jean Nathan, Mencken shared the editorial role for *Smart Set: A Magazine of Cleverness* (1914) and collaborated on two plays, *The Artist* (1912) and *Heliogabalus* (1920). Alone, Mencken wrote *A Book of Burlesques* (1916) and *A Book of Prefaces* (1917), a model of terse style that novelist Richard Wright adopted as a writing text. The partnership of Nathan and Mencken survived to serve an intellectual audience with *The American Mercury* from 1924 to 1933, covering the boom years of realists Willa Cather and Eugene O'Neill; poet Ezra Pound; naturalists Theodore Dreiser, Sinclair Lewis, James Branch Cabell, and Sherwood Anderson; utopist Aldous Huxley; and novelists James Joyce, F. Scott Fitzgerald, Joseph Conrad, D. H. Lawrence, and Somerset Maugham. Because prejudice against Germans deprived Mencken of a forum in the popular press during World War I, over three decades he produced *The American Language* (1919–1948), a six-volume best-seller and impetus to scholarly research into American linguistic contributions, from baseball and railroad slang to immigrant phrases, radio patter, and energetic vulgarisms. To rib the man-in-the-street vernacular, he freely translated the Declaration of Independence into gutter English. During these supercharged years, frequent trips to Chicago and New York found him grousing over the latter city as "a third-rate Babylon" and rejoicing in Baltimore, his unpretentious hometown.

Mencken made an issue of the South's diminished educational and literary expectations and frequently tweaked its cherished institutions and pretensions. In *Prejudices, Second Series* (1920), he christened the region the "Sahara of the Bozart [beaux arts]," a judgment shared by a trio of noted Southerners—playwright Paul Green, novelist Thomas Wolfe, and essayist Wilbur J. Cash, author of *The Mind of the South* (1941). (Dolmetsch 1969, 27) On the issue of Southern violence and bigotry, Mencken once noted:

H. L. Mencken (1880–1956) returns to the United States following a European vacation in 1930.

> The Klan is actually as thoroughly American as Rotary or the Moose. Its child-
> ish mummery is American, its highfalutin bombast is American, and its fun-
> damental philosophy is American. The very essence of Americanism is the
> doctrine that the other fellow, if he happens to be in a minority, has abso-
> lutely no rights—that enough is done for him when he is allowed to live at all.
> (Webb 1995, 2)

From the era of the Scopes Monkey Trial came some of Mencken's brightest
literary pyrotechnics. The issue was the teaching of evolution in public schools,
a practice banned in Tennessee, Oklahoma, Florida, and Mississippi. The American Civil Liberties Union chose a Tennessee challenge of free speech as their
test case. Libertarians found a willing adversary in George W. Rappelyea, an
enemy of First Amendment protections who had deliberately singled out 24-
year-old biologist John T. Scopes as a scapegoat. The trial was held in Dayton,
Tennessee, July 10–25, 1925. The atmosphere suggested a traveling carnival with
its hawkers of Bibles and religious tracts, sellers of roasted peanuts and lemonade, and vendors of souvenirs, including paper fans imprinted with Bible verses
and a postcard of a human male with the features and posture of an orangutan.
Reporters from around the world lounged in small dollops of shade while awaiting a verdict. Among them was H. L. Mencken.

Banking on a firsthand view of "the ninth-rate country town," Mencken
milked the scenario for some of his finest caustic editorials. In a July 25, 1925,
dispatch to the *Evening Sun*, he belittled the "Dayton illuminati" as "Homo
Neanderthalensis," drinkers of "the favorite tipple of the Cumberland Range:
half corn liquor and half Coca-Cola." (Mencken, "Hills of Zion" 1996, 1) He
ridiculed Freemasons, Ku Kluxers, glossolalia, and fundamentalists, adherents
to a literal interpretation of scripture. Of the latter, he chortles:

> So far the exegetes who roar and snuffle in the town have found . . . only blaz-
> ing ratifications and reinforcements of Genesis. Darwin is the devil with seven
> tails and nine horns. Scopes, though he is disguised by flannel pantaloons and
> a Beta Theta Pi haircut, is the harlot of Babylon. Darrow is Beelzebub in person.
> (Mencken 1991, 577)

With financing wheedled from the *Sun*, Mencken hired Clarence Darrow, a
revered criminal lawyer whom Seventh-Day Adventists had typified as "the
beast with seven heads and ten horns" described in Revelations 12, a monster whose apparition prefaced the end of the world. The scene ranged out
of touch with reality as torchlit singers bellowed apocalyptic hymns, "an
evangelist made up like Andy Gump" predicted dire punishments for the
disbeliever, and a young mother, rapt with fear, sat agog, oblivious to her
suckling infant during a late-night testimonial. (Mencken, "Hills of Zion"
1996, 3)

According to Mencken's narrative, Darrow faced one of his longtime favorite objects of verbal abuse, William Jennings Bryan, a former secretary of state
known as the Great Commoner. Mencken concluded his day-by-day series with
a tribute to Darrow: "On the one side was bigotry, ignorance, hatred, superstition, every sort of blackness that the human mind is capable of. On the other

side was sense." (Mencken 1991, 611) The verbal combat ended in a draw: Scopes lost the case. Mencken finagled an additional $100 from his employer to pay the fine, which Judge Raulston had set at a minimum. In ensuing months, the state supreme court of Tennessee struck down Raulston's ruling on a technicality that a judge is not allowed to set a fine above $50. Bryan, who was seriously sapped by the heat and the emotion-charged proceedings, died in his sleep five days after the trial.

Mencken's public letdown came during the Roosevelt years, when the bombing of Pearl Harbor on December 7, 1941, and the resultant declaration of war against Japan the next day turned readers away from persistent disrespect toward a president the nation loved and revered. Anti-egalitarianism readers disdained cheap shots at the New Deal and Mencken's claim that he constituted a one-man political party. Mencken remained alone at a rowhouse on Hollins Street until age 50, when he married writer Sarah Powell Haardt. Saddened at her death five years later, he returned to his bachelor flat. Six years before a stroke paralyzed and silenced him, he completed *A New Dictionary of Quotations, on Historical Principles* (1942) and *Heathen Days, 1890–1936* (1943), a three-volume comic memoir. His invalidism required the daily tending of his brother and a few friends. At his death from heart failure on January 29, 1956, he was cremated and interred next to Sarah in Baltimore's Loudon Park Cemetery. His desk and portable typewriter, which he pounded two-fingered style, reside at the Enoch Pratt Library; personal correspondence on literary criticism was published in 1961.

Laden with jubilant hyperboles and impudent, often aggressive *mots justes*, Mencken's quotable lines resound with honesty and disgust, which he leveled at varied targets ranging from Christian Scientists, antievolutionists, and chiropractors to prudes, the FBI, Holy Rollers, and censorship, as well as the self-promoting British, whom he suspected of operating American politics like a long-distance organ-grinder. His parodies emulate traditions dating from Horatian satire to Samuel Johnson's dictionary. For his years of travel and thumping out splenetic commentary two-fingered style on a portable typewriter, Mencken earned his star as an individualist and defender of the underdog, whether the badgered agnostic, friendly German Jew, or beleaguered bootlegger. In 1932, he won an award from the *Nation* for honest reportage. His obdurate, at times self-aggrandizing, satiric style often swamped the victim in a single stroke, especially the idols of mass culture—Rudolph Valentino; President Woodrow Wilson, who led the United States into World War I; and FDR, who repeated the action nearly a quarter century later.

A clever wordsmith who invented wherever he found a dearth of appropriate terminology, Mencken coined the terms "Homo boobiensis," "booboisie," and the "Bible Belt," after experimenting with "the *Hookworm Belt*, the *Hog-and-Hominy Belt*, the *Total Immersion Belt*, and so on." (Mencken 1991, 483) His wildcatter's style influenced radio newscasters and columnists, particularly Menckenesque humorist Florence King. (Bradbury 1996; Clark 1931; *Contemporary Authors* 1994; Cunliffe 1975; Dolmetsch 1969; Ehrlich and Carruth 1982; Grigson 1963; Hart 1983; Hicks "The Critic" 1968; Kunitz 1942;

McArthur 1992; Mencken 1983, 1991, "Hills of Zion" 1996, "Last Words" 1996; Webb 1995; Wilson and Ferris 1989; Young 1937)

See also humor, Southern.

THE MISSISSIPPI RIVER

Southern literature has an affinity for water. Edgar Allan Poe's "The City in the Sea" (1831), Matthew Fontaine Maury's essay "The Amazon and the Atlantic Slopes of South America" (1853), Francis Lister Hawks's observations of colonial piracy in *History of North Carolina* (1858), Sidney Lanier's ode "Song of the Chattahoochee" (1877), Marjory Stoneman Douglass's treatise *The Everglades: River of Grass* (1947), James Dickey's Cahulawassee in the novel *Deliverance* (1970), and others denote a reverence for bodies of water as images of replenishment and spirituality as well as commerce, natural wonder, and escapism. In a bit of juvenilia scribbled in grade school, Jesse Stuart wrote:

> Muddy waters, how I loved your crying
> Night and day—forever past my open door,
> Down through the reckless channel breaks along the shore
> Where winter wind in ankle-sedge is sighing.
> (Richardson 1984, 104)

Of the Mississippi in particular, there is no paucity of description and glorification, from the early explorations of Daniel Boone and naturalist/watercolorist John James Audubon, author of *The Birds of America*, in the Mississippi Valley to the frontier annals of David H. Coyner's *The Lost Trappers*, the plantation background of George Washington Cable's *The Grandissimes*, and a voyage north by steamer from Mississippi to Memphis, Tennessee, in Richard Wright's autobiography *Black Boy*. De Soto's men wrote journals about the river, where De Soto himself was interred in a late-night water burial. In 1704, Andre Pénicaut, a French explorer and carpenter, wrote *Fleur de Lys and Calumet: Being the Pénicaut Narrative of French Adventure in Louisiana*, in which he describes living among the Natchez and hunting buffalo on the "Missicipy River." His generous description lauds the beauties and abundance of fruit, game, nut trees, fragrant grass, and berries, and the welcome of a handsome race of Native Americans. A generation later, Father Le Petit, a Jesuit missionary among the Natchez of the lower Mississippi Valley, penned a bitter rebuttal of Pénicaut's opinions in letters collected in *The Jesuit Relations and Allied Documents: Travel and Explorations of the Jesuit Missionaries in New France, 1610–1791* (1900). The priest, in complaining about his hard lot as a proselytizer among indigenous peoples he labels savages, provides a description of native religious practices. His commentary inadvertently captures the vigor and harmony of tribes celebrating a thanksgiving of first fruits, at which they carry to their temple the best of fruits, corn, and harvest vegetables.

Throughout the New World's precolonial history and beyond, journalists and letter writers provided substantial commentary on the development of the Mississippi Valley as a vigorous region of the emerging nation. Harriet Martineau, an English gentlewoman and author in a range of fields, vacationed along the Mississippi Valley for six months and published two memoirs: *Society in America* (1837) and *Retrospect of Western Travel* (1838). In the latter volume, she remarks on coming ashore in "incredible" woodlands and on the fetching shore villages. At Adams Fort, Mississippi, she recalls "White houses nestled in the clumps; goats, black and white, browsed on the points of many hills; and a perfect harmony of colouring dissolved the whole into something like a dream." (Hudson 1936, 68) Planter Bennet H. Barrow, a contemporary of Martineau, kept a diary, *Plantation Life in the Florida Parishes of Louisiana, 1836–1846* (1943), which details the system by which he oversaw slaves. Among his rules are strict orders that slaves remain on the land and that they never marry or conduct business beyond the premises. A free black barber, William Johnson, composed daily musings on his life in Natchez, one of Mississippi's oldest white settlements. From 1841 to 1844, he observed the dichotomy of a society that boasted of refined tastes while a sleazy underworld of crime emerged from the riverboat society, replete with gamblers, hustlers, and itinerant riffraff. Attorney Reuben Davis, author of *Recollections of Mississippi and Mississippians* (1889), gives a less critical account of the shore inhabitants, whom he calls sober and industrious out of respect for the hardships of their pioneering venture. He generalizes the Southern stereotype—that Mississippians are God-fearing, respectful to women, loving and merry with friends, and ardently political during elections.

Peripatetic Europeans came to the Mississippi for exploration and scientific study. Alexander Wilson, a Scottish naturalist who compiled *American Ornithology; or, The Natural History of the Birds of the United States* (1875), was overpowered by thick canes in the Mississippi bottomlands, where a profusion of wildflowers dotted the landscape and hawks scoured the sky for prey. On his first journey to the river, Viscomte de Chateaubriand, author of *A Tour through the Southern and Western Territories of the United States of North-America; the Spanish Dominions on the River Mississippi, and the Florida; the Countries of the Creek Nations; and Many Uninhabited Parts* (1792), admired the colors and variety of the swamps hung with trumpet vine, redolent with jasmine, and edged with tulip trees, cypress, and magnolia. His word pictures reflect the same delight in riverside nature that details myriad notebooks, journals, and letters from pioneers, river travelers, and soldiers quartered along the shore.

One Southern author found a life's work in art and literature depicting nature along the Mississippi River. Intrigued by the wildlife he captured on the river's shores, John James Audubon traveled by flatboat as far south as the bayous, canebrakes, and tributaries around New Orleans to collect specimens of wildlife and paint migratory waterfowl, blossoms, creepers, fruit and seed pods, ferns, and leaves. His reflections on the locale in "Early Settlers along the Mississippi" attest to a widespread frontier optimism: "Who is he of the settlers on the Mississippi that cannot realize some profit? Truly none who is industrious." (Fulton 1917, 17) He names the plentiful resources—food, timber, vines, vegetables, ample pasturage, all essential to the fruitful farmstead. In a utopic vision, he looks to the future, "when the great valley of the Mississippi, still covered with primeval forests interspersed with swamps, will smile with corn-fields and orchards." (Fulton 1917, 19)

Until his death on January 27, 1851, Audubon devoted his talents to capturing natural poses of animals and birds. Leaving his family in 1827, he packed a portfolio of sketches and journeyed from Bayou Sara, Louisiana, to England to collaborate with engraver William Home Lizars of Edinburgh. The duo published *The Birds of America* (1838), a monumental four-volume set that extols the beauties of flora and fauna found in the Mississippi Valley. The collection sold for $1,050 and earned applause for its quality and detail of animal behaviors. It comprises 435 aquatinted plates of 1,055 life-size birds in their natural surroundings. To underwrite the expensive prints, Audubon sought subscribers, including the kings of France and England, the duke of Orleans, Daniel Webster, and the Library of Congress. To lessen the cost of the etched-copper plates and to increase circulation, Audubon hired J. T. Bowen, a Philadelphia lithographer, to reduce, print, and hand-paint the plates. In 1838, before returning home to Louisiana, Audubon published a subsidiary work, *Synopsis of the Birds of America*. A thorough text appeared in 1841 in seven volumes as *American Ornithological Biography*, cowritten by Scottish anatomist and naturalist William MacGillivray, who eased Audubon's difficulties with English composition.

In the late nineteenth century, Mark Twain, the nation's strongest proponent of the "Father of Waters," wrote frequent descriptions of life on the river in his travelogues, including chapters in *Innocents Abroad* (1869), *The Gilded Age* (1873), and *A Tramp Abroad* (1880), composed when he was far from home. In *The Gilded Age*, Twain fills chapter 4 with the sounds and bustle of deckhands aboard a small river steamer. The leadsman's call to the pilot contains the origin of the pseudonym "Mark Twain":

> "Seven feet!"
> "Sev-six and a *half!*"
> "Six feet! Six f-"
> Bang! She hit the bottom! George shouted through the tube: "Spread her wide open! *Whale it to her!*"
> Pow-wow-chow! The escape-pipes belched snowy pillars of steam aloft, the boat ground and surged and trembled—and slid over into—
> "M-a-r-k twain!" (Twain n.d., 28)

The implied safety of the leadsman's measure prefaces a moment's breather from a close call with grounding and potential disaster, which later occurs. In *A Tramp Abroad*, Twain recalls similar fear on his first riverboat passage when he was ten. Asleep in a berth, he had a dream of impending doom from snagging, explosion, or other catastrophe. He awoke at 10 P.M. shrieking "Fire, fire! *jump and run, the boat's afire and there ain't a minute to lose!*" (Twain 1906, 76) A clutch of sweet ladies remained unstirred and teased him for bursting into the saloon in his nightshirt.

Even a passing commentary of the Mississippi's qualities, such as the following passage from Twain's *Pudd'nhead Wilson* (1894), results in a protracted literary caress:

> [Liners] came out of a dozen rivers—the Illinois, the Missouri, the Upper Mississippi, the Ohio, the Monongahela, the Tennessee, the Red River, the White River, and so on—and were bound every whither and stocked with every imaginable comfort or necessity, which the Mississippi's communities could want, from the frosty Falls of St. Anthony down through nine climates to torrid New Orleans. (Twain 1964, 22–23)

Washed by ample waters, Twain's riverscape stretches like a languid jungle cat, "sleepy and comfortable and contented." His protagonist, a manumitted ex-slave named Roxy, works eight years as a chambermaid on the river aboard a steamer, the *Grand Mogul*, on which she thrives and rises to a supervisory position. At her retirement, she looks forward to spending her savings of $400 for a serene rest in New Orleans near the river.

Unlike earlier glimpses of riverside life, Twain's Mississippi trio—*The Adventures of Tom Sawyer* (1876), *Life on the Mississippi* (1883), and *The Adventures of Huckleberry Finn* (1884)—comprise his Mississippi period, which develops memory with vivid detail. While following Tom Sawyer and his pirate gang on a jaunt in *The Adventures of Tom Sawyer*, Twain depicts them running away from home to lodge in the unpopulated forest of Jackson's Island, three miles below the mythical St. Petersburg. A boy's-eye-view of utopia, the haven requires little more than hooks and fish line and the log raft that takes the trio—Tom, Huck Finn, and Joe Harper—away from town at a point where the river looms a mile wide. Tom arrives with a boiled ham, his part of the supplies, and climbs a bluff to overlook the gang's meeting place. Twain tinges the after-midnight departure with childhood magic: "It was starlight, and very still. The mighty river lay like an ocean at rest." (Twain, *Tom Sawyer* 1962, 93) At Tom's whistle, the other two boys assemble—Finn the Red-Handed and the Black Avenger of the Spanish Main alongside Tom, the Terror of the Seas. With appropriate imaginings of a full-rigged three-master, the three shove off into the current and pole past the town, which "lay peacefully sleeping, beyond the vague vast sweep of star-gemmed water." (Twain, *Tom Sawyer* 1962, 95)

Unlike a fictional episode, Twain's childhood idyll bears the pictorial markings of an escapist adventure relived. Wearied of Injun Joe's trial in St. Petersburg, the boys withdraw from civilization and look their last "with a broken and satisfied heart." (Twain, *Tom Sawyer* 1962, 95) By 2:00 A.M., they are pitching their tent on uninhabited land and looking forward to a night in the open air. The next morning finds them content that the current has carried the raft away; its unforeseen departure seems "like burning the bridge between them and civilization." (Twain, *Tom Sawyer* 1962, 100) For the moment, they are happy to strip their clothes at a sandbar and splash in the river, then return to camp to discover the treat of fresh-caught catfish fried in bacon drippings.

For a more detailed reminiscence on his youthful romance with the Big Muddy, Twain journeyed south in the spring of 1882 on a steamboat cruise from St. Louis to New Orleans and returned to merge fresh impressions with a series of seven reflective articles entitled "Old Times on the Mississippi" (1875) that he had published in *Atlantic*. The embellished memoir, *Life on the Mississippi* became one of the more enduring Southern reflections and a discursive source of Twain's attitudes, expectations, and experiences. Begun with an un-Twainlike history and analysis, *Life on the Mississippi* presents two chapters filled with formal description, including geology, quotations from historian Francis Parkman, and the expeditions of La Salle and De Soto. Twain can't resist boasting that the Mississippi's drainage basin "is as great as the combined areas of England, Wales, Scotland, Ireland, France, Spain, Portugal, Germany, Austria, Italy, and Turkey." (Twain 1990, 1) He relieves the stiffness of his introduction with a pastiche of digressions, joshing and tall tales, youthful indiscretions, and two mock-serious verses of a keelboatman's version of "Barbara Allen."

Complex for all his downhome charm, Twain sees the river from two overlapping points of view: The Mississippi is his boyhood homeland and a vehicle of escape, which eventually takes him far, yet returns him to the familiar sandbars and landings of Hannibal. Chapter 4 of *Life on the Mississippi* contains a frequently anthologized memory of childhood, a resurrected ambition to become a riverboat pilot, a step up from his status as a village lad in outback Missouri. Months after running away from home at age 15, he recalls a trip on the *Paul Jones*, a paddlewheeler bound from the Ohio River in Cincinnati down the Mississippi to New Orleans: "When we presently got under way and went poking down the broad Ohio, I became a new being, and the subject of my own admiration. I was a traveller!" (Twain 1990, 33) Intent on journeying to the Amazon, he soon learns a truth about travel: It requires more money than his paltry savings.

A true American pragmatist, Twain segues from escape to commerce. A jovial character, Horace Bixby, agrees to mentor the boy for $500, most of which Twain will receive on credit until he can earn his license. At this point in the memoir, Twain (who is still the unpublished young Samuel Clemens) has already begun studying and analyzing cat's-paws, bluffs, deep-water crossings, and currents like Holy Writ to protect the delicate underside of the sternwheeler from snagging, rupturing, or running aground. The mass of detail required to navigate a 1,200-mile river at first threatens to swamp him. Intent on success, he concentrates on the task of memorizing the shoreline up and down, and on August 30, 1852, receives the gilt-edged certificate that proclaims him "a suitable and safe person to be intrusted [sic] with the power and duties of Pilot of Steam Boats, and to license him to act as such for one year." (Welland 1991, 77) As the memoir indicates, Twain possessed the quickness and cool accuracy needed to steer the majestic waters in all weathers.

Twain's encyclopedic knowledge of Mississippi River travel cannot stave off the fearful disasters common to shallow-draft steamboats. In chapter 20, he turns to the death of the *Pennsylvania*, which he observed from the deck of the *A. T. Lacey* near Ship Island in the vicinity of Memphis, Tennessee. Sketchy details about the explosion of half the steamer's eight boilers at first report 150 deaths. Twain reports that victims were blown into the river or enveloped in steam. Ironically, water itself is the chief danger, as all who breathe steam die of scalded lungs:

> Shrieks and groans filled the air. A great many persons had been scalded, a great many crippled; the explosion had driven an iron crowbar through one man's body—I think they said he was a priest. He did not die at once, and his sufferings were very dreadful. (Twain 1990, 148)

Twain's unembellished reportage follows the explosion and resulting fire through rescuers' pitiful attempts to save the ship, crew, and passengers. His brother Henry, an unsalaried "mud clerk" on the steamer and the prototype of Sid in *The Adventures of Tom Sawyer*, is listed among the casualties.

The next day, Twain records how survivors lie unprotected from the sun on Ship Island. Lacking food, bedding, sanitary facilities, and medication, they await the next steamer, which carries them to Memphis. He learns that Henry is among the 40 treated in a public hall, and lauds the attentions of physicians, medical students, and local ladies, who bring "flowers, fruits, and dainties and delicacies of all kinds." Twain declares that

> Memphis knew how to do all these things well; for many a disaster like the *Pennsylvania*'s had happened near her doors, and she was experienced, above all other cities on the river, in the gracious office of the Good Samaritan. (Twain 1990, 150)

The sight of gruesomely burned heads swathed in linseed oil and raw cotton overwhelms his imagination. He is particularly moved by the "dead room," where the moribund, desensitized by morphine, are carried for their final struggles. Henry, too, dies. Wracked with guilt and regret, Twain leaves the death of his brother to his autobiography, written 23 years later, in which he describes how inexperienced medical students overdosed Henry with morphine.

At the height of his career, Twain turned once more to the Mississippi River for the setting of his most beloved work, *The Adventures of Huckleberry Finn*. The river is the escape route for one of world literature's most famous pairs—Huck Finn and Jim, the disgruntled slave of Miss Watson, one of Huck's two old-maid benefactors and foster mothers. Both travelers depart with a mission: Jim fears being sold "down to Orleans" and Huck flees Pap, his abusive, alcoholic father. Huck decides that helping Jim elude captors is the honorable thing to do. He declares to Jim, "People would call me a low-down Abolitionist and despise me for keeping mum—but that don't make no difference. I ain't a-going to tell, and I ain't a-going back there, anyways." (Twain, *Huck Finn* 1962, 55)

Chapter 12 contains Twain's idealized picture of the lazy glide during which Huck gets to know Jim like a brother. The two fish and talk and take an occasional swim to ward off drowsiness. Huck comments:

> It was kind of solemn, drifting down the big, still river, laying on our backs looking up at the stars, and we didn't ever feel like talking loud, and it warn't often that we laughed—only a little kind of a low chuckle. We had mighty

good weather as a general thing, and nothing ever happened to us at all—that night, nor the next, nor the next. (Twain, *Huck Finn* 1962, 77–78)

The serene, even quality of their days and nights lulls them into a dreamy acquiescence to the river's will. Night skies light up in a flourish as they float by small towns, then pass the gaudily lit outskirts of St. Louis at 2:00 A.M. When they need food, Huck slips ashore to buy bread and bacon or steal corn, persimmons, crabapples, or a chicken. He rationalizes petty larceny with some of Pap's skewed logic.

On the way to Cairo, Illinois, at the confluence of the Mississippi and Ohio Rivers, Twain heightens expectations as Huck and Jim look forward to their arrival in free territory, where Jim can throw off slavery. In chapter 16, the two discuss how they will know Cairo when they pass it. After several false alarms with "jack-o'-lanterns or lightning bugs," Jim grows twitchy with anticipation. (Twain, *Huck Finn* 1962, 101) The shift in behaviors emphasizes the disparate nature of their journeys. Huck, a runaway child, ponders the implications of helping a runaway slave, who exacerbates the crime against his owner by plotting to return and liberate his children from bondage. Without a twinge at his own creation of a murder scene to implicate Pap in a bogus crime, Huck's conscience pinches him with thoughts of cheating Miss Watson of her rightful property.

Interspersed with Huck and Jim's episodic adventures on land and water are returns to the raft and attempts to reestablish the duo's original contentment and purpose. In chapter 19, they dangle their legs in the water and smoke their pipes while enjoying the feeling of autonomy and safety. One of Twain's lyric passages describes life on a raft: "We had the sky up there, all speckled with stars, and we used to lay on our backs and look up at them, and discuss about whether they was made or only just happened." (Twain, *Huck Finn* 1962, 135) The overlay of light against dark is replicated in showers of sparks from a steamboat's stacks and the early morning stoking of chimneys, which became the duo's alarm clock to remind them to tie up and sleep away the day out of sight of paterollers and bounty hunters seeking slaves to return in exchange for a fat purse.

In chapter 16 of a restored version of *The Adventures of Huckleberry Finn*, published in 1996, Twain presents an intimate portrait of 13 rafters during an after-dark tale swapping highlighted with fiddle music and break dancing. Mixed in their tall tales is river lore:

> They talked about how Ohio water didn't like to mix with Mississippi water. Ed said if you take the Mississippi on a rise when the Ohio is low, you'll find a wide band of clear water all the way down the east side of the Mississippi for a hundred miles or more, and the minute you get out a quarter of a mile from shore and pass the line, it is all thick and yaller the rest of the way across. (Twain 1996, 119)

Unusual in comparison to the more familiar scenes from the standard version, this episode places Huck naked in the water like a bare-bottomed infant baptized in a stream. He is able to pull aboard the passing raft and sit unclothed and unobtrusive to absorb oral lore before the men chastise him for his boldness and send him back to the river with threats of rawhiding him for eavesdropping. Restored to the raft, Huck welcomes it as his peripatetic home.

Twain's friend and colleague, Louisianan George Washington Cable, settled in New England, yet returned throughout most of his career to the scenes of the Mississippi Delta for his best fiction. One of his late romances, *Gideon's Band* (1914), captures the commercial rivalries of the mighty antebellum steamship companies in the feud between the Courtenay and Hayle lines. Set in 1852, the novel focuses on an outbreak of cholera, which sweeps through doomed lower-class passengers in the hot, close-packed steerage before threatening the breezier cabins of elite passengers above the waterline. Heavily laden with Cable's hatred of plantation-era racism, the novel clings to the romance of river travel while assaulting the reader with strong diatribes against the South's old evil, slavery.

The twentieth century brims with tributes and musings on the Mississippi River. John A. Lomax and his son, Alan Lomax, collected and popularized Mississippi river songs in their collection *American Ballads and Folk Songs* (1934). In "Stagolee," the songwriter narrates the downfall of Stack Lee, a roustabout on the Lee family steam line, which plied the Mississippi from Memphis, Tennessee, to ports north and south, from Cairo, Illinois, to the Gulf of Mexico. A virulent no-good, Lee was the focus of barrelhouse blues, stevedore chants, and honky-tonk ballads throughout Louisiana and Texas. In one version, Lee shoots Billy Lyons in a barroom quarrel on Christmas morning. The procession of advisers and witnesses through the courtroom includes Billy's wife, Stagolee's friend, a police officer, and defense and prosecution attorneys. The latter disputes Stagolee's claims to an aged mother with a witty stanza: "Gentlemen of this jury, wipe away your tears, for Stagolee's aged mammy has been dead these 'leven years." (Lomax and Lomax 1934, 96)

In 1942, Eudora Welty echoed the vigor and scurrilous wit of "Stagolee" by reframing a European dream narrative in the Mississippi River milieu of her childhood. *The Robber Bridegroom*, a spirited, rambunctious fairy tale of a stolen bride, opens on Rodney's Landing, an isolated spot on the Mississippi River, where planter Clement Musgrove intends spending the night at a country inn before continuing homeward over a dark path through the wilderness. For background, Welty ruffles the waters:

> The river was covered with foam, and against the landing the boats strained in the waves and strained again. River and bluff gave off alike a leaf-green light, and from the water's edge the red torches lining the Landing-under-the-Hill and climbing the bluff to the town stirred and flew to the left and right. (Welty 1942, 2)

Like the piano player who supplies mood music for a silent movie, Welty shapes and varies the river milieu, blending hurrying carriages, the bellows of flatboatmen, and rushing, flying sounds with the harsh breath of the wind. By the end of the story, Musgrove reunites with his daughter Rosamond at a more civilized point on the river—the docks in New Orleans. Uncertain whether to believe Rosamond's tale of a transformation in the behavior of wild, flaxen-haired, woman-grabbing Jamie Lockhart, Musgrove checks out her story. Satisfied at last, he parts from his dear girl with a "Good-by. . . . God bless you" and sets sail for home. (Welty 1942, 185) (Baldanza 1961; Bloom *Mark Twain* 1986; Boorstin 1965; Bradbury 1996; Crystal 1987, 1995; Davis and Beidler 1984; Dobie 1996; Douglass 1947; Ehrlich and Carruth 1982; Emerson 1985; Fulton 1917; Gallay 1994; Griswold 1992; Hazard 1927; Hutchinson n.d.; Kaplan 1966; Levine 1984; Lomax and Lomax 1934; Lyttle 1994; McArthur 1992; O'Connor 1966; Quinn 1936; Rasmussen 1995; Richardson 1984; Shalit 1987; Thomas and Thomas 1943; Twain 1906, 1959, *Huck Finn* 1962, *Letters* 1962, *Tom Sawyer* 1962, 1996, n.d.; Welland 1991; Welty 1942)

See also Twain, Mark; Welty, Eudora.

MITCHELL, MARGARET

The source of a Southern growth industry, Margaret Mitchell could not have guessed how the public would respond to her epic romance *Gone with the Wind* (1936), the world's most popular novel, which is still climbing beyond 25 million copies. Neither classic fiction nor a true literary feat by contemporary standards, the novel has evolved into a touchstone of Southernness, a fount of wisdom on the life and times of the quintessential Georgia belle, and a prequel to the feminist movement. Played onscreen by British actress Vivien Leigh, the green-eyed minx of the Civil War era was one of Hollywood's most sought-after roles. In its contrived sequel, *Scarlett* (1991), South Carolinian Alexandra Ripley, romance writer and author of *Charleston* (1981) and *New Orleans Legacy* (1987), multiplied the story's original settings with moves to Savannah, Boston, and Ireland, where the reprised heroine reunites with her ex-husband, Rhett Butler, gives birth to a second child sired by him, and defeats a murder charge.

The original Scarlett O'Hara owes her birth and lineage to reporter Margaret Munnerlyn "Peggy" Mitchell, a member of the inner circle of society in Atlanta, Georgia, who dared smoke, drink, dress, and swear in defiance of local conventions. Born on November 8, 1900, the second child and first daughter of attorney Eugene Muse Mitchell, president of the Atlanta Historical Society and the Atlanta Bar Association, and suffragist Mary Isabelle "Maybelle" Stephens Mitchell, the author boasted a lineage combining the Irish Catholics of her mother's side with a blend of Scotch-Irish and French Huguenots on the Mitchell side. She claimed five generations of prominent Atlantans, comprising a long association with the city's history and growth. Mitchell attended Woodberry School and Washington Seminary, and gained a reputation among her peers for playing one beau against another. Shortly after the death of a serious suitor, Lt. Clifford Henry, in World War I, she entered a premed program at Smith College in Northampton, Massachusetts, but ended her public education abruptly at age 19 after her mother's death during a flu epidemic.

On her return to Atlanta, Mitchell kept house for her brother Stephens, attended their ailing father, and prepared for formal presentation to society. She ruined her chances at membership in the Junior League by wearing a whimsical, revealing Arabian getup to a debutante cotillion and by supporting black charities. In 1922, she was married for three months to a congenial scapegrace, Berrien Kinnard "Red" Upshaw, a bootlegger who was rumored to have roughed her up in humiliating bouts of marital rape. To supplement his chancy earnings, she took a $25-a-week job reporting and writing features for the *Atlanta Journal Sunday Magazine*, for which she interviewed Hollywood heartthrob Rudolph Valentino. She idolized *Baltimore Sun* critic H. L. Mencken and satirist Ring Lardner, and began composing stories, autobiography, a 1920s flapper novel, and *Ropa Carmagin,* an unfinished novella about miscegenation. She rejected these beginnings in favor of domesticity, begun in 1925 with marriage to John Robert Marsh, a public relations executive with the Georgia Power Company and the best man at her first wedding.

In 1926, Mitchell quit the paper after falling from a horse and severely wrenching her ankle. At her husband's suggestion, she compensated for limited mobility by writing a novel. She began working organically in daily sessions at the Atlanta Public Library, setting plantation-era memories of her grandmother and the Jonesboro aunts into a historical romance, a project the author preferred to cloak with secrecy. In 1935, she hesitated to show her manuscript to Harold S. Latham, a visiting publisher from Macmillan whom she had

Margaret Mitchell (1900–1949) reads congratulatory mail following announcement of the Pulitzer Prize for her novel *Gone with the Wind* in 1937.

met while chauffeuring friends to Rich's Department Store. He bought the book on first perusal and published the thousand-page hardback novel to an astounding demand, even at the jacked-up price of $3 per copy. Moviemakers fought over rights before the much-touted work had gone to press.

Gone with the Wind, originally titled "Tomorrow Is Another Day," takes its title from Ernest Dowson's lyric poem "Cynara," which contains the line "I have forgot much, Cynara! gone with the wind." (Romine 1986, F1) The novel was immediately presented as the July 1936 Book-of-the-Month Club selection and earned plaudits for characterization from some quarters as well as accusations of trite diction and weak structure. Despite mixed reviews, the novel sold 500,000 copies in three months. It earned a Pulitzer Prize and was named book of the year by the American Booksellers Association. One squib claims that Hitler banned the novel in Germany because it uplifted people whom his Nazi band intended to suppress. The book remained on the best-seller list through 1937. A Depression-era spirit-lifter dubbed *GWTW* by the cognoscenti, the novel lifted spirits during hard times as Scarlett, unaccustomed to suffering, ponders how to feed her family and skeletal house staff:

> Nothing her mother had taught her was of any value whatsoever now and Scarlett's heart was sore and puzzled. It did not occur to her that Ellen could not have foreseen the collapse of the civilization in which she raised her daughters, could not have anticipated the disappearings of the places in society for which she trained them so well. (Mitchell 1964, 427)

A surviver of the rag-end of the Civil War, Scarlett brightens the novel's mid-text low and the hearts of readers by grasping a hoe and working like a field hand. The film version worked up to the indelible scene in which Scarlet lifts a fist to heaven and proclaims, "As God as my witness, I'll never be hungry again."

The 1939 MGM/Selznick-International film version—which netted Mitchell an unprecedented $50,000 on speculation for a first novel—is a Technicolor extravaganza that broke movie house attendance records. Mitchell attended the Atlanta premiere at Loew's Grand Theater on December 15, 1939. Starring Clark Gable as Rhett Butler, the film pares to a minimum the complex story line, which follows the fortunes of a full cast of characters from the Civil War through Reconstruction. The action, which is 220 minutes long, features the high points of Mitchell's description of General William T. Sherman's march on Atlanta and the fire that consumed antebellum mansions along with the heart of the city. It won ten Oscars for best picture, Sidney Howard's adapted screenplay (assisted by David O. Selznick and F. Scott Fitzgerald), Victor Fleming's direction, Lyle Wheeler's art direction, cinematography and film editing, production designer William Cameron Menzies, and actresses Vivien Leigh and Hattie McDaniel, portrayer of Mammy and the first black actress to receive an Academy Award. Oscar nominations went to special effects for the train depot scene, a stunningly realistic display of hundreds of extras and mannequins posed as war victims, and for actor Clark Gable's role as Scarlett's husband, Olivia de Havilland for portraying Melanie Wilkes, and music director Max Steiner for "Tara's Theme," set to lyrics by Mack David in 1954 and retitled "My Own True Love." Reset for wide screen in the 1960s, the film continues to air in theaters and on television.

Mitchell's post-*GWTW* career disappointed readers who anticipated a sequel. She shunned the demanding followers who gave her no rest while she nursed an aged father and invalid husband. She came out of hiding to raise money for the Red Cross and to post Care packages during World War II, and was instrumental in building a Civil War reference collection in the Margaret Mitchell Public Library in Fayetteville, Georgia. She died August 16, 1949, of brain injury, resulting from a tragic accident while crossing the street with her husband three blocks from home. Struck by an errant taxicab on Peachtree Street, she lingered four days in an Atlanta hospital, where nurses closed windows in the sweltering heat to dampen the calls of mobs of well-wishers. After a private service broadcast to throngs outside the church, she was buried in Oakland Cemetery. In keeping with her wishes, her husband directed the destruction of her manuscripts and private correspondence.

Fans idolized Mitchell and turned her apartment and Underground Atlanta, the center of Civil War destruction, into literary shrines. A Gray Line Tour takes tourists on a "Gone with the Wind Pilgrimage," featuring Mitchell's childhood homes and mansions that suggest the classic lines of Tara and Twelve Oaks. The Atlanta Public Library displays its Margaret Mitchell Collection, featuring the few remaining notes. A cluster of buildings in Stone Mountain Park suggests the ambience of the plantation era. Carriage tours circle the remains of "the Dump," a historic monument that was Mitchell's residence on the first floor of the Windsor House Apartments on Crescent Street, which a blaze destroyed in 1994. A cyclorama in Grant Park offers a three-dimensional reprise of the Siege of Atlanta, enhanced by sound and light artistry. The Turner television station reprises the film annually and merchandises *GWTW* memorabilia and collectors' copies of the video. In the 1970s, a musical version composed by Harold Rome launched a world tour. In 1985, the fiftieth anniversary of the book's publication, the U.S. Post Office issued a stamp featuring Mitchell as an icon of American culture. Mitchell's publisher attempted to milk *GWTW* nostalgia in 1996 with the publication of *The Lost Laysen*, a bit of juvenilia that was best left unpublished. (Blain et al. 1990; Bradbury 1963; Buck 1992; *Contemporary Authors* 1994; Davidson and Wagner-Martin 1995; Ehrlich and Carruth 1982; Gage 1997; "Historian's Gallery" 1997; Kunitz 1942, 1955; McHenry 1980; "Margaret Mitchell House" 1996; Mitchell 1964; Pyron 1991; Romine 1986; "Scarlett" 1996; Sherr and Kazickas 1994; Stein 1979; Wilson and Ferris 1989)

See also *Gone with the Wind*.

NATIVE SON

An internationally revered literary lion and spokesman for oppressed blacks, Richard Wright set standards for African-American realism and candor in his controversial novel *Native Son* (1940), a dark bildungsroman that renounces the American ideal of equality for all. An astute portrait of bigotry, cruelty, and dehumanization, the novel took shape in an astonishing four months, leaving the author much restructuring and additional dialogues and scenes to compose to express his lofty theme and purpose. At heart, the unflinching portrait of a black criminal attacks racism's long-lived myth: the purported sex mania that black males are accused of harboring for white females. The publication of *Native Son* stirred decades of wrangling and encouraged a generation of black writers to address directly this and other issues inherent in centuries of racial prejudice.

Wright opens on an unpromising scenario: a Depression-era Chicago ghetto, the milieu of 20-year-old Bigger Thomas, a moody, volatile, unemployed street tough whom his mother foresees as bound for the gallows. In a reflective essay, "How 'Bigger' Was Born" (1940), Wright characterizes his protagonist as an explosive paranoid:

> resentful toward whites, sullen, angry, ignorant, emotionally unstable, depressed and unaccountably elated at times, and unable even, because of his own lack of inner organization which American oppression has fostered in him, to unite with the members of his own race. (Wright 1991, 523)

In the first episode, Bigger prefigures his ignoble demise by squashing a rat with a frying pan. Moody and temperamental, he battles free-floating discontent while playing at crime in Doc's poolroom with buddies whose recreation is, in Wright's words, "utterly inadequate to fill up the centuries-long chasms of emptiness which American civilization had created in these Biggers." (Wright 1991, 530)

Wright draws on pre–World War II tension to create cogent scenes that provide a microscopic view of twisted thinking. Childlike in his ignorance, Bigger displays low self-esteem, inarticulate ambitions, and yearning for power in jumbled thoughts about world events:

> He liked to hear of how Japan was conquering China; of how Hitler was running the Jews to the ground; of how Mussolini was invading Spain. He was not

concerned with whether these acts were right or wrong; they simply appealed to him as possible avenues of escape. (Wright 1991, 130)

Fantasizing about a similar liberation of blacks, he anchors his hopes on an unidentified external force capable of quelling racism. In contrast to his lethal dreams of vanquishing oppressors, Bigger vents his frustration by slashing the felt lining of a table in Doc's pool hall and threatening his friend Gus with an exposed blade.

Overall, Wright depicts an impotent youth who has served a three-month stretch in reform school for stealing tires, but who is unlikely to commit a weightier crime that requires bold premeditation. Rather than engage in a felony with his peers, Bigger turns from them to obey his mother and seek a job at the Hyde Park residence of his nemesis, Henry Dalton, the wealthy owner of South Side Real Estate, and Mrs. Dalton, a blind society matron known for charitable gestures toward blacks. The Daltons are parents of Mary, a silly, spoiled University of Illinois coed who deliberately nettles her conservative father by asserting independence and bad-mouthing his capitalistic values. Coincidentally, Bigger's friends had ogled Mary during a movie newsreel that depicts her as the naughty rich girl who actualizes late-teen rebellion by dating a leftist.

Early on, Wright indicates that the juxtaposition of Bigger and Mary precipitates an unintended murder. To earn $8 a week and room and board, he begins driving Mary to school, where he encounters her boyfriend, Jan Erlone, an idealistic communist. The couple's offer of friendship confuses and terrifies Bigger, who shares their meal at Ernie's Kitchen Shack and ignores Bessie, his weak-willed lover, in favor of more fashionable and prestigious friends. At the couple's insistence, Bigger, who is uncomfortable amidst pointed stares, dribbles out the details of a lamentable autobiography: He was born in Mississippi and resituated in Chicago at age 15, where he quit school in the eighth grade. His father was killed in a riot in the South. Mary's plan for Bigger to deposit her trunk at the train station precedes casual driving around and sipping liquor with the couple, who joke and openly neck in front of him. Control of the powerful car and absorption of alcohol dissociate Bigger from the racial strictures of South Side Chicago that require distance between races. As he justifies his violation of racial taboos, "He was not driving; he was simply sitting and floating along smoothly through darkness." (Wright 1991, 89)

The potential for tragedy occurs in the Dalton home, where Bigger again violates society's rule that prohibits black males from fraternizing with white females. After Mary grows liquor-loose and lolls out of control, he propels her to her bedroom. He yields to temptation and nestles Mary as she buries her face in his shoulder. The pseudosurrender goads him on:

> Her face turned slowly and he held his face still, waiting for her face to come round in front of his. Then her head leaned backward, slowly, gently; it was as though she had given up . . . he eased his hand, the fingers spread wide, up the center of her back and her face came toward his and her lips touched his, like something he had imagined. (Wright 1991, 96)

The surreal embrace restates in the flesh Bigger's response to the figure in the newsreel. When Mrs. Dalton intervenes, Bigger stands quietly and muzzles Mary with a pillow until her mother leaves. Wright indicates that Mary's suffocation is accidental.

Wright revs up the action as outsiders challenge Bigger's muddled thinking. The crime mounts as Bigger plots to implicate Jan and dismember Mary's remains to force them into the Dalton's furnace. Investigation, stirred by Mary's unexplained absence, begins with the Daltons' detective, Mr. Britten, who examines the trunk that Bigger was to have ferried to the station. He follows the false lead to Jan, who is suspect more for connections with Marxism than for dating Mary. Naively believing he is free of suspicion, Bigger further entangles himself in crime by penning a ransom note demanding $10,000, a mishandled ploy that he copies from the Loeb and Leopold extortion plot of 1924. Fed by romantic crime schemes, Bigger scribbles directions for the transfer of money and signs the note with "Red," followed by a hammer and curving knife meant to represent the gold emblem on red background of the communist flag. The media exploit Jan's involvement by linking him to foreigners and Jews. Bigger foils his own scheme by inadvertently leading reporters to the overflowing furnace hopper, from which they retrieve Mary's earring and bone fragments, examples of Wright's naturalistic examination of details.

Wright sends his protagonist on a haphazard odyssey that elucidates Bigger's aimlessness and irrationality. A mounting list of crimes grows to premeditated murder after he flees to an abandoned shell in the Black Belt—"a tall, snow-covered building whose many windows gaped blackly, like the eyesockets of empty skulls." (Wright 1991, 266) Bessie, a poorly defined character who hovers on Bigger's horizon, weeps with fear as he releases his frustrations with hasty intercourse. Devoid of regret, he contemplates his choices, then bashes Bessie's head with a brick because she knows too much. At the same time that an armed manhunt pursues the purported sex criminal about Chicago, Bigger tosses Bessie's corpse down an air shaft. Almost immediately, Bigger's insouciance reverts to terror and guilt. Wright indicates that his protagonist's fantasies had often portrayed him in the role of killer.

In a steadily growing counterpoint, Wright contrasts Bigger's savagery with the howling whites who seek vengeance for Mary's death. Local hysteria concludes with Bigger's entrapment. Like a tormented beast, he watches from the roof of an abandoned building, his stomach roiling with hunger:

> He felt like dropping to his knees and lifting his face to the sky and saying: "I'm hungry!" He wanted to pull off his clothes and roll in the snow until something nourishing seeped into his body through the pores of his skin. (Wright 1991, 286)

Bigger's double violation of innocence forbids the clean snow from restoring him to health. As though chilled by guilt, he feels the saliva at the corners of his lips turn to ice. In a continuation of water imagery, he meets his end from tear gas and icy streams from a fire hose. Dragged like a sack upside down, his head bumping the stair treads, he hears a growing mob calling "Kill that black ape!" (Wright 1991, 314)

Wright focuses book III on a quieter setting in Bigger's cell, where he awaits judgment and punishment. Grisly details surface after authorities take him to

In 1942 Canada Lee played Bigger Thomas to Anne Burr's Mary Dalton in the stage adaptation of Richard Wright's 1940 novel *Native Son*. Wright and playwright Paul Green collaborated on the adaptation.

the Cook County Morgue for an inquest into Mary's death. Edward Robertson, the editor of the *Jackson (MS) Daily Star*, exacerbates fears of black males assaulting white women. With a bit of self-serving choplogic to salve Southern consciences, he opines:

> We of the South believe that the North encourages Negroes to get more education than they are organically capable of absorbing, with the result that northern Negroes are generally more unhappy and restless than those of the South. (Wright 1991, 324)

Robertson salts his editorial with stereotypical epithets: "dead-black complexion," "mixed blood," "criminal and intractable nature," "depraved types," "sneak thief and liar," and "poor darky family of a shiftless and immoral variety." He moves directly to the death penalty as the only method of preventing future Biggers from committing outrages against white women. Wright's emphasis on racist publicity challenges an era when Southern conservatism diminished the chance that a black defendant could expect a fair trial.

Marshaling an implausible number of visitors within Bigger's cell, Wright creates a tableau of possible solutions to black crime. He chooses as his first spokesman Reverend Hammond, Mrs. Thomas's pompous minister, who represents the religious fundamentalism that Southern congregations embrace as their sole bulwark against oppression and hardship. Hammond presses Bigger to repent and accept religion, turning to the afterlife as an antidote to the inequities of earthly life. Bigger has little reason to believe the assertion that "Gawd gives eternal life th'u the love of Jesus." (Wright 1991, 329) More stopgap answers appear: Jan offers a more practical source of aid in the assistance of Boris A. Max, whose name suggests his role as attorney for the local Communist party. The parade continues with a visit from David A. Buckley, the prosecutor and a candidate for office, plus Mary's liberal family, Bigger's mother and siblings, and Al, Gus, and Jack, the three pals from Doc's poolroom who had shared dreams of greatness through crime.

The travesty of justice that arraigns Bigger makes little use of evidence. After an emotional hearing, six male members of the grand jury vote unanimously to try Bigger for murder. A cross-burning and an insane cellmate who rails against society and the U.S. president for perpetuating ill-treatment of blacks precede more out-of-proportion newspaper accounts of Governor H. M. O'Dorsey's summons to two regiments of the Illinois National Guard to protect Bigger from mob violence. Another article invokes psychologists from the University of Chicago on the subject of the black male's innate lust for white women. Their erudition echoes Klan mentality: "White women have an unusual fascination for Negro men." (Wright 1991, 424)

The author compounds the elements that doom and damn Bigger. After witnesses declare him "mean and bad, but sane," the trial proceeds with an unsettling list of items:

> the knife and purse Bigger had hidden in the garbage pail . . . the brick he had used to strike Bessie with was shown; then came the flashlight, the Communist pamphlets, the gun, the blackened earring, the hatchet blade, the signed

confession, the kidnap note, Bessie's bloody clothes, the stained pillows and quilts, the trunk, and the empty rum bottle. (Wright 1991, 441)

With dramatic overstatement, the prosecution reconstructs the Daltons' furnace to demonstrate how Bigger forced Mary's dismembered corpse into the flames. Max attempts to help Bigger by claiming that he is among many blacks awaiting justice and by begging for life imprisonment. In retort against Max's sympathy for a black felon, Buckley implies that Bigger is a murderer and rapist. He represents the lawful side of society and typifies Bigger as a woolly-headed black lizard whom white males would destroy underfoot like vermin. The image replicates the scene in book I in which Bigger views the film *Trader Horn*, a melodramatic talkie filmed in Africa in 1930 that won an Oscar for its sensationalized depiction of cannibalism, tribalism, bestiality, and near-naked white women. Buckley shreds Bigger's character with examples of his rejection of family, work, religion, education, and the white ethos, and opens the courtroom window to the shouts of the mob outside.

The author's summation of compelling evidence leaves no out for Bigger. Inevitably, the Honorable Chief Justice Alvin C. Hanley and the grand jury arrive at a judgment. Speaking through Max, Wright makes a useless plea blaming society:

> We planned the murder of Mary Dalton, and today we come to court and say: "We had nothing to do with it!" But every school teacher knows that this is not so, for every school teacher knows the restrictions which have been placed upon Negro education. The authorities know that it is not so, for they have made it plain in their every act that they mean to keep Bigger Thomas and his kind within rigid limits. (Wright 1991, 459)

The pronouncement of guilt precedes a sentence of death on March 3. The doom-laden resolution depicts Bigger as sleepless, isolated, and, except for Max, friendless. Further misunderstanding of Bigger's search for meaning and self-worth concludes his last days.

In his reflection on the phenomenon of Bigger Thomas in a first-person epilogue, Richard Wright connects the fictional criminal to the milieu of Jackson, Mississippi, as he recalls it in the 1910s and 1920s. Bigger, he claims, "goes back to my childhood, and there was not just one Bigger, but many of them, more than I could count and more than you suspect." (Wright 1991, 506) An incipient Bigger, the swaggering bully who stalked Wright, found joy in cornering the small and weak as a means of imparting meaning to a squalid existence. Wright acknowledged that his own interest in trade unions and communism sprang from the chasms that separate whites and blacks. After comparing the discontent of Southern blacks to the peasants who overthrew Czar Nicholas II in 1917, Wright adds,

> I am not saying that I heard any talk of revolution in the South when I was a kid there. But I did hear the lispings, the whispers, the mutters which some day, under one stimulus or another, will surely grow into open revolt unless the conditions which produce Bigger Thomases are changed. (Wright 1991, 518)

He concludes that the world's Bigger Thomases are capable of either communism or fascism—whichever overthrow will topple the class that flaunts a disproportionate share of power. (Bain et al. 1979; Baker 1972; Barksdale and Kinnamon 1972; Bloom 1987, 1988; Boger 1968; Bradbury 1996; Butler 1991; Chapman 1968; *Contemporary Authors* 1994; Fabre 1990; Gayle 1980; Low and Clift 1981; Ploski and Williams 1989; Popkin 1978; Rubin et al. 1985; Salzman et al. 1996; Trotman 1989; Walker 1988; Webb 1968; Williams 1970; Wilson and Ferris 1989; Wright 1991)

See also *Black Boy*; Wright, Richard.

NORMAN, MARSHA

A screenwriter, novelist, and Pulitzer Prize–winning playwright, Kentuckian Marsha Norman is a student of naturalistic, nonverbal human behaviors with a gift for revealing the dark moments in the lives of everyday people. She has applied innovation and experience with disturbed patients to her best works: *Getting Out* (1977), the transformation of Arlie the crazy into Arlene the recovering schizophrenic prostitute, and her masterpiece, *'night, Mother* (1982). The former, which casts separate actresses to play two sides of a damaged personality, prefigures *'night, Mother*, a verbal duel between a cold, lacerating mother and her daughter, a rational, integrated self that longs for release from a landslide of trivial, everyday defeats. The success of *'night, Mother* typifies Norman's can-do attitude toward on-the-job training. It followed two critical failures: *Third and Oak: The Laundromat and the Pool Hall* (1978) and *Circus Valentine* (1979), written while she was playwright-in-residence at Louisville's Actors Theatre. Norman credits herself with surviving the onslaught of critical pessimism and continuing to write. *'night, Mother*, which was written in New York and first presented in December 1982 at the American Repertory Theatre in Cambridge, Massachusetts, has circulated among 32 foreign countries, traveling as far from the American experience as New Guinea.

Norman has reason to understand the internal free-for-alls that erode the average person. A native of Louisville, Kentucky, and the daughter of realtor Billie Lee and Bertha Mae Conley Williams, Norman grew up in the confines of fanatical Christian fundamentalism, a debilitating force that stifled and isolated her in childhood. Like Carson McCullers, Norman took refuge in listening to her Aunt Bubbie read aloud and in piano lessons. Norman graduated from Agnes Scott with a B.A. in philosophy in 1969, and received a Master of Arts in Teaching degree from the University of Louisville in 1971.

A useful adjunct to her career as a playwright was teaching for the Kentucky Department of Health and in Jefferson County Schools, where she superintended gifted students. After a job with the Kentucky Arts Commission in 1974 and editing and reviewing for the *Louisville Times* from 1974 to 1979, she worked with emotionally disturbed children at the Kentucky Central State Hospital, the source of her empathy for tormented people. She has produced a steady output of dramas: *It's the Willingness* (1978), *The Holdup* (1980), *In Trouble at Fifteen* (1980), and *The Fortune Teller* (1987). She also composed unproduced screenplays for Joseph E. Levine and United Artists, and is represented in *The Best Plays of 1978–1979: The Burns Mantle Yearbook of the Theatre* (1980).

Frequently compared to novelist Carson McCullers and Beth Henley, a fellow Southerner and author of *Crimes of the Heart*, Norman focuses on stunted relationships. Less regional than Henley, Norman chooses a universality of language and setting to place her characters at large among humankind, and gives them free rein over an enveloping black humor. The pared-down one-liners of *'night, Mother* pit mother Thelma Cates against daughter Jessie in a farewell wrangle over Jessie's impending suicide, which seems like the sensible conclusion to the daughter's dead-end life of giving without getting, trying and not succeeding, and planning for no attainable aims. In Jessie's view, death is preferable to a lifetime of not having a very good time. The mother of a sneak thief, wife of an errant husband, and daughter of a self-indulgent, badgering harpy, Jessie is balancing too many balls in the air when catastrophe looms ahead in the form of dismissal from her job of clerking in a hospital gift shop. The 1986 Universal film version, starring Sissy Spacek and Anne Bancroft, preserves a two-character dialogue that rehashes old griefs, yet discloses too little hope to lure Jessie from her intended suicide.

Norman's explicit instructions for characters and setting depict Jessie as in control to the point of making peace with death more easily than making peace with her mother. Thelma, an aging manipulator who lives on a rural lane and expects her daughter's daily attentions, realizes that the cluttered emotional baggage of Jessie's life parallels the clutter of their living quarters. Outwardly, their milieu offers a modicum of feminine niceties but nurtures no growth in the emotionally arid pair. The portentous humor in Thelma's retorts to Jessie's dead-serious admission opens the way to an evening of prickly give-and-take:

Jessie: I'm through talking, Mama . . .
Thelma: You'll miss. You'll just wind up a vegetable. How would you like that?
    Shoot your ear off? (Norman 1983, 17)

The sterile, kitchen-based dialogue satirizes the failed lives of two women centered in such temporal concerns as cupcakes, dish detergent, Christmas lists, and teenage escapades with drugs.

A grim humor plays through the clash like arced lightning, occasionally illuminating a memorable image. To Jessie, ending a fruitless existence is an opportunity to get off the bus when she wishes. Thelma inanely suggests buying a dog, then retorts sarcastically, "You're not having a good time!" (Norman 1983, 33) To make her case about eccentricities, she cites Agnes Fletcher, a pyromaniac who wears whistles around her neck and buys expensive birds. Thelma claims, "It's that okra she eats. You can't just willy-nilly eat okra two meals a day and expect to get away with it. Made her crazy." (Norman 1983, 40) The stark conclusion of the play leaves no ifs in Norman's plotting. Black humor gives way to a dismal finality as the shot ends Jessie's arguments with son, mother, and self.

Norman has won a fair sprinkling of honors. After succeeding with *Getting Out*, she received a National Endowment for the Arts grant in 1978 as well as the John Gassner New Playwright's Medallion, a George Oppenheimer-Newsday award, and the Outer Critics Circle award. Her most successful play, *'night, Mother*, earned both the Pulitzer and a Tony. Continuing to turn out quality stage and screenplays, Norman published *Traveler in the Dark* (1984), *Sarah and Abraham* (1988), and *D. Boone* (1992). Her apt blend of music and dialogue earned a second Tony for the Broadway production of *The Secret Garden* (1991), a reworking of the Frances Hodgson Burnett children's classic. (Blain et al. 1990; Buck 1992; *Contemporary Authors* 1994; Davidson and Wagner-Martin 1995; *Dictionary of Literary Biography* 1985; Norman 1983; Schroeder 1989; Spencer 1987)

O'CONNOR, FLANNERY

A rare Roman Catholic lay theologian and innovative symbolist from the Bible Belt, Mary Flannery O'Connor is sometimes described as a Christian realist. She was a tough-minded, unsentimental spokeswoman for the relentless seeker and an unapologetic explicator of the doctrine of human limitation. She disdained such narrow classifications as regionalist or writer of Southern gothic. In "The Fiction Writer & His Country," a peevish riposte to commentary on writers of the Southern school, she quibbled that no authority had defined the Southern school or named the writers who belong to it. She adds:

> Sometimes, when it is most respectable, it seems to mean the little group of agrarians that flourished at Vanderbilt in the twenties; but more often the term conjures up an image of Gothic monstrosities and the idea of a preoccupation with everything deformed and grotesque. Most of us are considered, I believe, to be unhappy combinations of Poe and Erskine Caldwell. (O'Connor 1969, 28)

O'Connor's wry humor is typically self-directed. Herself a purveyor of ugliness, grim retribution, and unforeseen epiphanies, she achieved a remarkably high position among authors of psychological fiction and black humor. She was a visionary of the fragmented family, sullied Southern gentility, and destabilized society that preceded integration.

To demonstrate her concept of wickedness and grace, O'Connor produced jangled communities, misaligned family loyalties, false religious extremists, and loners who yearn for the unnamed antidote to inner strife. Her quirky antihero, Hazel "Haze" Motes, protagonist of *Wise Blood* (1952), epitomizes the out-of-kilter sensibilities and ill-founded motivations that waylay O'Connor's entire cast of doomed and erring souls. Of her protagonist, she wrote in 1962:

> The book was written with zest and, if possible, it should be read that way. It is a comic novel about a Christian *malgré lui*, and as such, very serious, for all coming novels that are any good must be about matters of life and death. (O'Connor 1983, 2)

In further commentary, O'Connor appends tongue-in-cheek description of Motes's integrity as dependent on his inability to free himself from religion, which skulks in his background "from tree to tree in the back of his mind."

Destiny and determination prepared O'Connor for a short but brilliant artistry. The only child of Regina Cline and Edward Francis O'Connor, a government real estate appraiser, O'Connor was born in Savannah, Georgia, on March 25, 1925. Reared in the Catholic faith, she made religion a focus of her life and read Old Testament prophecy, St. Augustine, Thomas Aquinas, and Teilhard de Chardin as well as philosophers Martin Buber and Martin Heidegger and the early church mystics. Educated until age 13 at local Catholic schools—St. Vincent's Grammar School and Sacred Heart Parochial School—she moved to a historic manse in Milledgeville, Georgia, near her mother's family, where her father was treated for systemic lupus erythematosus, a hereditary degenerative malady that causes inflammation of connective tissue, swollen joints, fatigue, and degeneration of the kidneys, lungs, and heart. The disease crippled his daughter at age 25.

Before her illness, O'Connor earned a B.A. in sociology from Georgia State College for Women, where she drew cartoons for the campus newspaper. On a fellowship at the School for Writers at the State University of Iowa, she mastered the technical deftness of Joseph Conrad and Henry James. Intent on assembling details, images, and sensations with precision, she published her first short fiction, "The Geranium" (1946), in *Accent*. She completed an M.F.A. in 1947 and worked briefly with poets Elizabeth Hardwick and Robert Lowell and critic Alfred Kazin at the Yaddo writers colony in Saratoga Springs, New York. FBI surveillance of a do-nothing writer caused a colony uprising, which forced O'Connor and her colleagues to decamp. She moved to New York City, then to Ridgefield, Connecticut, to live with friends Robert and Sally Fitzgerald, who comprised her literary family.

Severely disabled by lupus and hospitalized in Atlanta from 1950 to 1959, O'Connor recovered after cortisone treatment and blood transfusions. She settled at Andalusia, a dairy and poultry farm outside Milledgeville, where she lived under her mother's care and raised pet peafowl and ducks. O'Connor compensated for poor health by corresponding with a broad spectrum of friends and well-wishers and by writing idiosyncratic fiction, often categorized as the height of Southern gothic. Annoyed with comparison of her stories to those of Faulkner, she fired off one of her typical crusty retorts: "Nobody wants his mule and wagon stalled on the same track the Dixie Limited is roaring down." (O'Connor 1969, 45) The toughness she displayed with this and other witty repartee belied the frailty of her constitution, which failed her at age 39.

A three-time winner of the O. Henry award for short stories and recipient of the Rinehart-Iowa Fiction Award, O'Connor published in *Kenyon Review*, *Harper's Bazaar*, *New World Writing*, the *Critic*, and *Sewanee Review*. She wrote enthusiastically and did not think of herself as a cripple, but she did profess the power of redemptive suffering, which she regularly inflicted on her characters. She managed limited mobility on crutches and made infrequent appearances at universities. In one college lecture, she explained her philosophy of literature: "It is the business of fiction to embody mystery in manners, and mystery is a great embarrassment to the modern mind." (Hicks 1969, 30) No doubt her belief in mystical power impelled her on a mission to Lourdes, France, which

Flannery O'Connor (1925–1964) in 1962

failed to alter the death sentence under which she lived. Anemia, fainting spells, and surgery to remove a benign fibroid tumor in 1964 precipitated a rapid decline of her kidneys and multiple infection, which caused her to cancel lectures in Texas and Massachusetts. Before her death from lupus on August 3, 1964, she received extreme unction and asked her friends for prayers.

O'Connor's first strong move into mainstream literature occurred with "A Good Man Is Hard To Find" (1953), featuring Red Sammy Butts, the first of many psychopaths in her fiction. The story anticipates one of her frequently anthologized pieces, "The Displaced Person" (1954), a masterpiece of alienation, which contrasts the unfounded fears of Mrs. Shortley with the innocence of hardworking immigrants, the Guizacs, who have escaped a Nazi death camp. O'Connor's two novellas—*Wise Blood* and *The Violent Bear It Away* (1960)—and her collected stories, *A Good Man Is Hard To Find and Other Stories* (1955), were the sum of her lifetime publication. *Everything That Rises Must Converge* (1965), published the year after her death, and her collected essays and lectures in *Mystery and Manners* (1969) and *The Habit of Being* (1979) attest to the increasing demand for her intuitive style. Additional collections include *The Presence of Grace and Other Book Reviews* (1983) and *Conversations with Flannery O'Connor* (1987), a series of interviews. The 1979 MCA film of *Wise Blood*, directed by John Huston, stars Brad Dourif as the ill-fated drifter, Hazel Motes, a Tennessee army veteran-turned-preacher who lines his shoes with pebbles and wraps his torso in barbed wire in his search for a new religion, called the Church without Christ. (Blain et al. 1990; Bradbury 1963; Bradbury 1996; Buck 1992; Collum 1997; Davidson and Wagner-Martin 1995; Ehrlich and Carruth 1982; Ketchin 1994; McGloughlin 1997; Mitchell 1995; O'Connor 1969, 1979, 1983; Polter 1997; Sherr and Kazickas 1994; Walker, John 1996)

POE, EDGAR ALLAN

Usually described as a tormented, frenzied, but impeccable literary genius, Edgar Allan Poe, master of a broad span of genres and exalter of the neurotic persona, has survived the lurid distortions and bizarre rumors that bedeviled his personal reputation. A fertile creator of exacting criticism, ethereal verse, lacy arabesques, doppelgänger motifs, black comedy, satire and journalistic hoax, as well as intuitive, emotive fiction, he was the soul of the American romantic movement, whom critic Alphonse Smith dubbed "necromancer of American literature." (Smith, C. 1967, 120) In a brief but fervid 16-year career, Poe pioneered American-style criticism, ratiocinative fiction, gothic romance, tales of dual personality and premature burial, scenes of nervous agitation and unworldly compulsions, outré science fiction, revenge plots, brooding verse, and the psychological thriller. His deftly limned Inspector C. Auguste Dupin influenced a following of imitations, the most notable being Sir Arthur Conan Doyle's Sherlock Holmes. Poe's command of imagery, rococo detail, and poetic device thrilled and delighted loyal fans on both sides of the Atlantic, especially in France, where he ranks as a major literary influence on poets Charles Baudelaire, Stephané Mallarme, Paul Valery, and Arthur Rimbaud. The Mystery Writers of America honored Poe by awarding Edgars for the best works in their genre.

Poe's many-sided career languished from his dire penury, the result of happenstance, inexperience, and mishandling of funds. He earned first place and $100 in prize money from the *Philadelphia Dollar Newspaper* for "The Gold Bug" (1843) and sold "The Raven" (1846), his masterpiece poem, for $9. From admirers such as poet William Butler Yeats and playwright George Bernard Shaw he received critical acclaim, but others discounted his artful works, including Ralph Waldo Emerson, who dismissed him as a "jingle man," and James Russell Lowell, who evaluated his worth as "three-fifths genius and two-fifths sheer fudge." Perhaps a greater measure of his influence as poet and critic lies in the long list of disciples, including Ambrose Bierce, Hart Crane, Dante Gabriel Rossetti, Algernon Swinburne, Ernest Dowson, Robert Louis Stevenson, and Wallace Stevens.

Poe was not a true Southerner. His birth parents, British actress Elizabeth Arnold and former attorney David Poe, Jr., were players with Mr. Placide's Theatre Company, which toured the East Coast. They were engaged at a Boston theater on January 19, 1809, when he was born. After his father, suffering from tuberculosis and alcoholism, disappeared and died in 1810, his mother, a teenager twice widowed, found a stage job in Richmond, Virginia, the city that claims Poe. Within months, she too died of tuberculosis, leaving three children: two-year-old Edgar, his six-year-old brother Henry, and their sister, Rosalie, age one. The children dispersed to foster homes. Edgar's godfather, John Allan, a punctilious and opinionated partner of Ellis & Allan, tobacco exporter, and his barren wife, Frances Valentine "Fanny" Allan, offered the boy a home. His new mother loved him, but Allan merely tolerated Edgar because he was attractive and intelligent. Poe adopted Allan's last name as a middle name, but rejected the family's stolid, predictable, bourgeois attitudes. Preferring solitude, he once swam six miles up the James River against the current.

When Allan's work took him to Great Britain from 1815 to 1820, Edgar attended Irvine Grammar School in Irvine, Scotland, residing in a grim English boarding school, Manor House at Stoke-Newington outside London. Poe later employed its spooky buildings as a setting for an autobiographical story, "William Wilson" (1838). Upon the family's return to Virginia, 11-year-old Poe entered private school. When he reached his teens, his profligacy with money alienated John Allan and forced Poe to leave home. In 1826, Allan paid Poe's tuition to the University of Virginia in Charlottesville, where he achieved high marks in law, Latin, and French. Because Allan scrimped on Poe's allowance, the boy earned living expenses from the gaming table and eked out a few luxuries on pocket money Frances Allan sent him. Erratic and emotionally unstable after his fiancée, Sarah Elmira Royster, married someone else at her parents' urging, Poe forced university officials to expel him in December 1826 for gambling and tippling. Less the aristocratic Southern rakehell than a deeply disturbed youth, he seemed to court trouble as a means of communicating with his distant father. Allan deepened Poe's hostility by forcing him to work in the family counting house to pay the $2,500 Poe owed his creditors.

On his own in March 1827, Poe settled in Boston, where he published *Tamerlane and Other Poems* (1827) at his own expense and signed his pamphlet "By a Bostonian." The sentimental verse sequence, an emulation of Byron, weaves a dazzling filigree saturated with Islamic imagery and facts about a fierce fourteenth-century Mongol conqueror. The work has merit, but Poe earned nothing from the venture. Under the alias Edgar A. Perry, he joined the army and served on Sullivan's Island, South Carolina, milieu of "The Gold Bug." Attached to Battery H of the First Artillery at Fort Independence in Boston Harbor, Fort Moultrie in Charleston, and Fort Monroe, Virginia, he rose to the rank of regimental sergeant major by his second year. Bored with military tedium, before gaining his discharge he published *Al Aaraaf, Tamerlane, and Minor Poems* (1829), source of "Israfel," another of Poe's Islamic poems. A kind lieutenant helped him reconcile with Allan; however, the brief period of peace ended after Frances Allan died and her husband remarried and sired an heir who ousted Poe from hopes of an inheritance. At Allan's insistence, Poe entered West Point, but he despised the rigid militarism and pointless drills. After deliberately refusing to participate in army routine or attend classes, he was court-martialed and ousted in 1831 and returned to poetry, publishing *Poems by E. A. Poe: A Second Edition*, which contains "To Helen," a model of his ideal woman, who existed apart from the mundane and permanently out of reach. In a romantic ecstasy, the speaker envisions her from afar:

> Lo! in yon brilliant window-niche
> > How statue-like I see thee stand,
> > The agate lamp within thy hand!
> Ah, Psyche, from the regions which
> > Are Holy Land!
> (Parks 1970, 64)

Artistically decorative and dotted with visual accoutrements, his vision is as rich as the gilt-hued paintings of the pre-Raphaelites. Ironically, three years later, at Allan's death, Poe found himself disinherited and penniless. His daily squalor bore no resemblance to his verse dreams, and the jolt forced him for the first time to abandon poetic reverie and support himself without outside help. In "To One in Paradise," he creates a beguiling setting for poetry:

> A green isle in the sea, love,
> > A fountain and a shrine
> All wreathed with fairy fruits and flowers,
> > And all the flowers were mine.
> (Parks 1970, 67)

Significantly, the dream world dissolves into smoke, leaving the speaker to cry, "Alas! alas! with me/The life of Life is o'er!" Perhaps on the outskirts of a discovery about the real world, the poet vows distractedly, "No more—no more—no more—," and declares his day as all trances and his night dreams filled with footsteps, "In what ethereal dances,/By what eternal streams." (Parks 1970, 68)

The mid-1830s were kinder to Poe as his essays, poems, and stories began to attract critical acclaim. He published five stories in the *Philadelphia Saturday Courier* and earned $50 for "Ms. Found in a Bottle" (1833) from a contest sponsored by the *Baltimore Saturday Visitor.* A contest judge gave him entree to a monthly magazine, the *Southern Literary Messenger,* where he earned his first living wage as associate editor and enlarged its circulation from 500 to 3,500. This brief period of stability saw the publication of "Morella," "Berenice," and "Hans Pfaal," all marked by his selectivity with language and apt feel for rhythm and tone. Loss of the job from alcoholism prefaced a downward spiral of Poe's fortunes. Permanently shut out of the Allan household, he formed a lasting family unit with his brother and aunt, Maria Poe Clemm, a seamstress who later opened a boardinghouse to help support "dear Eddie." In a secret Episcopal ceremony on September 22, 1835, he married 13-year-old Virginia Clemm, Maria's frail, simple-witted daughter. The mismatched pair repeated their vows publicly on May 16, 1836, in Richmond. Poe idealized his bride in "To Helen" and other poems. His renowned series of alluring, enervated young women modeled on Virginia were usually marked for death, yet fetchingly wreathed in pathos and a childlike delicacy that kept them tantalizingly close, yet unattainable.

Edgar Allan Poe (1809–1849)

Poe's career foundered after he returned to the *Messenger* in December, but again declined to act responsibly. He was fired within two years for the failure of his only novel, *The Narrative of Arthur Gordon Pym* (1838), an adolescent autobiography that was published in the *Messenger* in two installments. He left unfinished his drama, *Politian*. Cheated of his investment after *Harper's* bought the *Messenger*, Poe moved to Philadelphia, a center of publishing, where he attempted to rehabilitate Virginia's failing health in a series of five rented residences. He coedited *Burton's Gentleman's Magazine* and published some of his most important fiction in the *Philadelphia Saturday Courier* and *Godey's Lady's Book*. In 1840, he ventured another collection, *Tales of the Grotesque and Arabesque*, containing "The Fall of the House of Usher," one of his most theatrical works. Cited as an example of Poe's penchant for exotica, the story contains many arcane allusions and foreign phrases:

> His chief delight, however, was found in the perusal of an exceedingly rare and curious book in quarto Gothic—the manual of a forgotten church—the Vigiliae Mortuorum Secundum Chorum Ecclesiae Maguntinae [Watches of the Dead According to the Choir of the Maguntian Church]. (Poe 1962, 92–93)

Recognized for mastery of language and structure, Poe edited *Graham's* magazine, which featured his reviews of Nathaniel Hawthorne's *Twice-Told Tales* and Henry Wadsworth Longfellow's *Ballads*. Poe produced skillfully plotted short stories—"The Murders in the Rue Morgue" (1841), "The Masque of the Red Death" (1842), and "The Pit and the Pendulum" (1842). The quality of his mature composition indicates a newfound seriousness in his work, but he earned less than $100 per story. The next year saw the height of his horror fiction, "The Tell-Tale Heart" and "The Black Cat."

Resettled in a Bronx tenement in 1844 after months of freelancing, Poe purchased his own publication, the *Broadway Journal*, but he lacked the business acumen to prosper, and had to move the family to Fordham. After his journal folded in 1846, he lost his investment and joined the staff of the *New York Evening Mirror* as literary critic, published "The Raven," and took up new subjects for "The Balloon Hoax," "The Cask of Amontillado," "The Oblong Box," and his influential critical essay "The Philosophy of Composition," in which he uses "The Raven" as a model of literary structure. Making demands on the artist to seek reality, he declares:

> With as deep a reverence for the True as ever inspired the bosom of man, I would, nevertheless, limit, in some measure its modes of inculcation. I would limit to enforce them. I would not enfeeble them by dissipation. The demands of Truth are severe. She has no sympathy with the myrtles. (Parks 1970, 335)

The advice to remain "cool, calm, unimpassioned" and to be "simple, precise, terse" sounds strange coming from the pen of this renowned romancer, who often was unequal to his principles, both literary and financial.

Within a year, Poe's quarrelsome, litigious nature cost him the esteem of colleagues and critics. While living on a pittance, he escorted Virginia to a party, where she suffered a throat hemorrhage and collapsed while singing. On January 30, 1847, she died in their unheated cottage clutching Catterina, their tortoiseshell cat, to keep warm. Melancholic and suicidal, Poe composed "Ulalume" (1847) in her memory, verse fantasy that enlivens his dead bride as a mythic goddess:

> She is warmer than Dian:
> 　She rolls through an ether of sighs,
> 　She revels in a region of sighs:
> She has seen that the tears are not dry on
> 　These cheeks, where the worm never dies.
> (Parks 1970, 79)

He published the verse eulogy to Virginia Clemm in *Colton's American Review* under a pseudonym, N. P. Willis. Jolted by loss, he struggled to remain clean of liquor, opium, and laudanum so that he could write for the *Sunday Times*. He flirted with numerous women and actively pursued poet Sarah Helen Whitman of Providence, Rhode Island, in an attempt to rebuild his fortunes by marrying into wealth and prestige.

Deranged and suffering from a brain lesion, Poe survived only two more years. His readable works dwindled to a handful of poems: "Annabel Lee" (1849), "For Annie" (1849), "The Bells" (1849), and "Eldorado" (1849). "Eureka" (1848), a hodgepodge of science and pseudointellectualism, was unpublishable. "Annabel Lee," one of his oft-quoted salutes to idealized womanhood, became a standard recitation piece for its mythic evocation of lost love:

> And the stars never rise, but I feel the bright eyes
> 　Of the beautiful Annabel Lee;
> And so, all the night-tide, I lie down by the side
> Of my darling—my darling—my life and my bride,
> 　In her sepulchre there by the sea,
> 　In her tomb by the sounding sea.
> (Parks 1970, 82)

Unlike the ethereal women in verse, the mates Poe courted were real and less than willing to live with a mad poet. On a journey to Richmond, ostensibly to gain backing for a new project and to court Sarah Royster after she was widowed, he took a train bound for New York. When he became too ill to continue, he departed in Baltimore, where ward heelers dragged him about to pad the polls. On October 3, 1849, he sheltered in a street drain outside a tavern. Rescuers took him to Washington College Hospital, where he called out "Lord, help my poor soul" and died of a brain hemorrhage on October 7. He was buried in Baltimore's Westminster Presbyterian Church Cemetery in a family plot where his aunt and wife's remains were reinterred.

East Coast journals and newspapers noted his brief life and considerable contribution to journalism and literature. In an encomium, the *Saturday Evening Post*, which had published "The Black Cat" and "A Succession of Sundays," reported:

> Edgar Allan Poe is dead. This announcement will startle many, but few will be grieved by it. The poet was known, personally or by reputation, in all this country, but he had few friends; and the regrets for his death will be suggested

principally by the consideration that in him literary art has lost one of its more brilliant but erratic stars. (Poe 1976, 89)

The editors countered some of the more scurrilous tales that confused the tics and manias of his characters with the author himself. They claimed that he spoke eloquently and punctuated his well-modulated tones with expressive eyes. Primarily a dreamer and a mystic, he was known for fitfully walking the streets engrossed in a private conversation with self, "always to bear the memory of some controlling sorrow." (Poe 1976, 89)

Reverend Rufus Wilmot Griswold, executor of Poe's considerable literary legacy, muddled the poet's seamy reputation with inaccuracies and forged letters. Biographer Arthur Hobson Quinn, author of *Edgar Allan Poe: A Critical Biography* (1941), launched a campaign to undo Griswold's multiple dishonors and to laud Poe's skill as critic, wordsmith, romantic poet, and founder of the American school of terror, psychological thriller, and science fiction. A posthumous work, *The Poetic Principle* (1850), established Poe's reputation for aesthetic grace. Primarily from his faithful French readers, he earned an international following, and American audiences were quick to embrace his works as national treasures. The Lamar Library at the University of Texas in Austin began collecting his works; Philadelphia's Free Library endowed a display of Poe's papers and manuscripts, including the only handwritten copy of "The Raven." A Poe Foundation opened in Richmond, and Baltimore displayed a seated statue inscribed with a line from "The Raven": "Dreaming dreams no mortal ever dared to dream before." (Ehrlich and Carruth 1982) Late in 1996, a New York cardiologist reassessed postmortem details and published in the *Maryland Medical Journal* his surmise that Poe did not die a derelict but a victim of rabies. (Anderson 1993; Bloom, Harold 1985; Bradbury 1996; Budd and Cady 1993; Clarke 1991; Crenson 1996; Cunliffe 1987; Davis et al. 1970; "Edgar Allan Poe" (www.iptweb) 1997; "Edgar Allan Poe" (www.parec) 1997; "Edgar Allan Poe National Historic Site" 1997; Ehrlich and Carruth 1982; Guilds 1970; "Keeping Posted" 1976; Krutch 1992; Kunitz and Haycraft 1938; Lockerbie 1969; Meyers 1992; Parks 1970; Poe 1962; Quinn 1936; Rubin et al. 1985; Sheldon 1995; Silverman 1991; Simonini 1964; Smith, C. 1967; Stein 1979; Sullivan 1986; Whitt 1994; Wilson and Ferris 1989)

See also poetry of the South; short fiction in Southern literature.

POETRY OF THE SOUTH

The first Southern belletrists to depart from political oratory, documents, and business letters were poets. Their themes, versification, and diction lacked confidence in Southern language, so New World poets turned to the European models studied and admired as the epitome of literary grace. Georgian Mirabeau Buonaparte Lamar, a war hero from the Battle of San Jacinto, followed the cavalier traditions of effusive love poetry for "The Daughter of Mendoza," published in his *Verse Memorials* (1857). Another imitator of European verse, Edward

Coote (or Coate) Pinkney produced *Rodolph, and Other Poems* (1825), a slender volume containing "A Serenade," a Byronic piece that honors his wife, and "A Health," a toast to the ideal beauty, a gently feminine woman who elevates her admirer's life to an idyllic state that is "all poetry." (Spiller and Blodgett 1949, 692) Far removed from the reality of American colonial life, these examples demonstrate a hesitance to accept the American language and aesthetic impulse as worthy.

The South was the first region to produce writers interested in the philosophies, governance, and natural beauty of their native land. Less attuned to Continental verse style, Alabama poet Samuel Minturn Peck belongs to the generation of New South poets who find beauty and inspiration in their surroundings. A lilting love note, "A Southern Girl," depicts the type of belle who uses grace and coquetry to draw beaux to her balcony. A more rural setting in "The Grapevine Swing" anticipates the joyous young manhood of Robert Frost's "Birches." Other nature poets include Madison Julius Cawein, author of "The Whippoorwill," and Frank Lebby Stanton, writer for the *Atlanta Constitution*, who muses on "The Graveyard Rabbit" and on the owl in "A Plantation Ditty." A North Carolina poet and newspaperman who penned some frolicsome outdoor images, John Charles McNeill is best remembered for "Away Down Home," a jolly piece that echoes the frog's bass belch of "knee-deep."

Racial consciousness, a minority theme in poetry, inspired numerous minor Southern writers. Two devout Jewish female poets—Penina Moise and Adah Isaacs Menken—studied the early-nineteenth-century milieu for subjects of their verse. Moise, a blind teacher and muse, produced "Man of the World" and "The Exalted Theme of Human Praise" for her collection *Hymns Written for the Use of Hebrew Congregations* (1856). Menken, an actress and writer, penned "One Year Ago" and "Hear, O Israel!," a compelling religious poem based on the stately call to worship: "Hear, O Israel, the Lord our god is one." Georgia's Cherokee poet John Rollin Ridge, grandson of Native American orator Georgian Major Ridge and son of Tennessean John Ridge, wrote verse under his tribal name, Yellow Bird. Known primarily for writing *Life and Adventures of Joaquin Murieta, the Celebrated California Bandit* (1854), Ridge turned to verse in 1868 for *Poems*, a collection celebrating his native roots. In "The Harp of Broken Strings," he describes himself as "a wanderer from my distant home, from those who blest me with their love." (Witalec 1994, 541) Living in California forces him to revisualize his Georgia home and the wanderings of other displaced Cherokee in stories and sketches for West Coast newspapers.

No Western poet compares with Edgar Allan Poe for musical imagery. His genius for blending alliteration, cacophony, euphony, and sibilance complements far-flung settings and mythic allusions and outdistances other antebellum Southern poets—his rival, Georgian Thomas Holley Chivers, and numerous secondary figures, including South Carolinians Alexander Beaufort Meek and William Gilmore Simms and Virginia brothers John Esten Cooke and Philip Pendleton Cooke. Poe's whimsical diction moves about a mental landscape named by musical designations: Mount Yaanek, Auber, Weir, Eldorado, Aidenn, and an ethereal undersea castle. In "The Fall of the House of Usher" (1840), he inserts "The Haunted Palace," a seraphic kingdom decked with ruby and pearl and set in a green valley where evil fantastic forms rush outdoors "and laugh—but smile no more." (Davis et al. 1970) In "Ulalume" (1847), a lugubrious verse honoring his dead wife, Poe pictures Psyche "[rolling] through an ether of sighs"; her wings trail mournfully on the earth. The picture he embroiders with tragedy and otherworldly grace honors Virginia Clemm at the same time that it alleviates Poe of too firm a tie to reality.

The twentieth century provided an appreciative ear for the poetry of black writers. In the early decades, writers of the quality of Countee Cullen, Sterling Brown, Jean Toomer, Georgia Douglas Johnson, and Anne Spencer blossomed into first-rate versifiers during the fertile collaborative effort known as the Harlem Renaissance. Cullen, labeled a young wonder, began publishing verse in high school and produced *Copper Sun* (1927), *Caroling Dusk* (1928), and *The Black Christ, and Other Poems* (1929) in his twenties. The familiar lines of "Heritage" (1925) are his most popular strains: "What is Africa to me: copper sun or scarlet sea." (Mullane 1993, 517) His contemporary, Sterling Brown, is known primarily as an editor and critic, but produced one volume of poetry, *Southern Road* (1932), which refers to black mythic heroes Casey Jones, John Henry, and Stagolee. Among fellow blacks of the Renaissance, Toomer completed his best-received work, *Cane* (1923), an experimental melange of poetry, scenarios, and sketches interlaced with Southern references, themes, and concerns. The scarcity of his verse and plays is symptomatic of the repression and neglect common to writers of the era, who often went unpublished until rediscovery in the 1960s. Much of Toomer's fiction and memoir remained unpublished at his death. He is best known for complex imagery in "Brown River, Smile," a pulsating call for action and creativity. Turgid and brimming with historical references, the poem incorporates pueblo ritual and prairie traditions in its concept of a new America. Johnson, an Atlanta-born poet and playwright, wrote *The Heart of a Woman and Other Poems* (1918), an emotive collection on themes of frustration and passion, and *Bronze: A Book of Verse* (1922), which deals with racism and ambition. Her verse anthology, *An Autumn Love Cycle* (1928), favors romantic, womanly motifs, a strong current that yearns for "Lovelight" and charges "I Want to Die While You Love Me." Four years before her death, she produced *Share My World* (1962), a compendium of sage advice and reflection written in her eighties. A quieter, more pensive muse, Virginian Annie Bethel Bannister wrote under the pen name of Anne Spencer. She produced soulful verse, beginning with "Before the Feast of Shushan" (1920). Her work is collected in anthologies by Robert T. Kerlin, Louis Untermeyer, Alain Locke, Arna Bontemps, Langston Hughes, and Countee Cullen.

The versatile poet who stands out among black authors of the early twentieth century is Floridian James Weldon Johnson, composer of "The Negro National Anthem" (1900), which he wrote with his brother John Rosamund Johnson, and *The Autobiography of an Ex-Coloured Man* (1912), a painful memoir that circulated anonymously until Johnson claimed authorship in 1927. An activist, attorney, professor at Fisk University, Broadway songwriter, and diplomat, Johnson was trained at Atlanta University. He became one of the early proponents of the

National Association for the Advancement of Colored People, which he served as field secretary; his government career includes consular posts in Venezuela and Nicaragua. He published classic poetry collections—*The Book of American Negro Poetry* (1922) and his lyric oratory, *God's Trombones: Seven Negro Sermons in Verse* (1927)—and collaborated with his brother Rosamund on *The Book of American Negro Spirituals* (1925) and its sequel, *The Second Book of Negro Spirituals* (1926).

A scholarly amateur writer, Johnson drew on folklore and black religious traditions in a style later perfected by Zora Neale Hurston. In "O Black and Unknown Bards," he asks how the black poet discovered lyricism. Surprised that verse could spring from bondage, the speaker asks how "Steal Away to Jesus," "Jordan Roll," "Swing Low," "Go Down, Moses," and "Nobody Knows de Trouble I See" could emerge from the soul of a "captive thing." (Bontemps 1974, 1) In tribute to the unnamed spiritual composer, the speaker declares, "You—you alone, of all the long, long line of those who've sung untaught, unknown, unnamed, have stretched out upward, seeking the divine." (Bontemps 1974, 2) In the frenetic, rapturous soul sermon "Go Down Death," Johnson applies his compassion for Sister Caroline, a black sufferer, whom Death, like a medieval knight, sweeps out of her torment and deposits in glory and peace on Christ's bosom.

The pinnacle of Johnson's verse, "The Creation" (1927), was published in *God's Trombones*, a collection of seven sermons that demonstrate in verse the powerful pulpit oratory that shaped Frederick Douglass, Barbara Jordan, Dr. Martin Luther King, Jr., Adam Clayton Powell, and Reverend Jesse Jackson. Based on the first chapter of Genesis, the poem depicts an anthropomorphic deity standing in space and is driven by loneliness to create the world. His mighty sweep slices light from dark; his agile hands create sun, moon, and stars. Told in dramatic parallelism and simple diction, the lines maintain the view of God as a deity longing for company. The melodramatic conclusion pictures him as a "mammy bending over her baby" when he shapes amorphous clay into a divine image. In the final lines, Johnson simplifies the complex work of creating human life, ending with the first man inhaling God's breath, the epitome of the human soul. Awed at the moment's wonder, the speaker concludes, "Amen. Amen." (Chapman 1968, 366)

After the devastation of the post–Civil War era, a reemergence of the white male poet occurred at Vanderbilt University in the 1920s among a group that named itself the Fugitive Agrarians. A highly touted literary phenomenon calling for elevated standards in the arts, the group rallied under the leadership of master teacher John Crowe Ransom, one of the era's facile imagists. Ransom maintains his place in poetry anthologies and texts primarily on the strength of poems on the subject of mortality—"Piazza Piece" (1924), "Bells for John Whiteside's Daughter" (1924), "Spectral Lovers" (1924), "Necrological" (1924), "Janet Waking" (1927), and "Dead Boy" (1927). The second is a study in contrast between the usual energy of a young girl and her stillness in death. A country girl, she harries the geese, who cry an inarticulate "Alas" for "the little lady with rod," now propped for viewing in a fixed expression the poet describes as a "brown study." (Beatty et al. 1952, 752) In a reversal of animal with child, "Janet Waking," a gently humorous poem, pictures the innocence of Janet, who searches out her hen Chucky and finds it dead from bee sting. Ransom swells the tone and diction to a mature reminder that death is a "forgetful kingdom" from which none return. (Beatty et al. 1952, 753) The last of the poems departs from strong sentiment and sees the male child in bestial realism, a "pig with a pasty face . . . squealing for cookies." (Beatty et al. 1952, 754) Like a scion of the patriarchal tree, he has been wrenched from his moorings, leaving the family sad and shaken.

Female poets also thrive in the twentieth century. The versatility of Sara Teasdale, Maya Angelou, Diane Glancy, and Nikki Giovanni has enlarged the Southern canon beyond its traditional themes to broader issues, not the least of which is a demand that the female poet be recognized as a Southern artist. An early lyricist, Sara Teasdale published *Rivers to the Sea* (1915) and *Flame and Shadow* (1920), both resonant with the lithe grace and beauties of poems such as "I Shall Not Care" and "There Will Come Soft Rains," a title that Ray Bradbury reprised for a chilling science fiction short story. A victim of idealized American womanhood, Teasdale fought for self-actualization through innovative verse inspired by her love of the classic lyricism of Sappho and the outspoken voice of Christina Rossetti, one of England's pre-Raphaelites. Teasdale's reward was the first Pulitzer Prize for poetry, but it failed to offset her dismay at the social and traditional roles that threatened her creative being. In shock after the death of her lover, poet Vachel Lindsay, she killed herself.

More successful at combating debilitating traditions, autobiographer, playwright, and poet Maya Angelou excels at multiple forms of expression. In *I Know Why the Caged Bird Sings* (1970), a memoir of her childhood, she honors Johnson's richly emotional anthem "Lift Every Voice and Sing." At a low moment in a middle school graduation following a bureaucrat's limited expectations for black children, she and others join their student leader in the affirming lines of Johnson's anthem. In the second of its three stanzas, they sing of a stony road, bitter punishment, tears, slaughter, and dying hopes before moving to a stirring symbol, the "white gleam of our bright star." (Ploski and Williams 1989, 183) The last stanza concludes with a humble, heartfelt prayer for guidance and righteousness as black people continue their striving for liberty and justice. The poem maintains its control of emotion in part from the dignified cadence and simple eloquence of poet Johnson. Once sung or read aloud by protest marchers, school groups, congregations, and soloists, the anthem is now denigrated as sentimental and passé.

An exceptional paean to womanhood comes from *Now Sheba Sings the Song* (1987), the product of poet Maya Angelou and artist Tom Feelings. Fluid, primal, and rhythmic against the sepias and browns of interspersed drawings, the lines depict women as nurturing powers, as diverse and complex as individuality can make them. The song begins with the speaker's memory of life in the womb and pursues an open embrace of life, "ripe with expectancy." (Angelou 1987, 15) The images return to the Limpopo, Kilimanjaro, and Nile, but the swaying, finger-popping, flirtatious female replicates the character of Vivian "Bibbie" Baxter, Angelou's mother, in *I Know Why the Caged Bird Sings*. Angelou's praise of the strength and endurance of black women implies that eons of black history equip them for the trials of American racism and prepare them for better times.

A contemporary of Maya Angelou, Cherokee poet, playwright, and essayist Diane Glancy has earned the title of Cherokee poet laureate for her collections: *Traveling On* (1982), *Brown Wolf Leaves the Res* (1984), *One Age in a Dream* (1986), *Offering* (1988), *Iron Woman* (1990), and *Lone Dog's Winter Count* (1991). Critics admire her close ties to nature, as demonstrated in "Letters to My Father," in which the speaker remains on the family farm and looks out toward the city. The speaker perceives omens of destruction in the urban area: "The wild turnips I pull are small white clouds with roots of heat-lightning in the distance." (Witalec 1994, 299) In honor of her grandmother, who died when Glancy was a teenager, the poet grasps and wields language as a ritual power tool, for which she has received the National Federation of State Poetry Societies award and an American Indian Theater Company prize.

A scholarly poet, children's author, and critic, Tennessean Randall Jarrell succeeded the original Fugitive Agrarians of Vanderbilt as the facile Southern poet of the mid-1900s. The early works, *Blood for a Stranger* (1942), *Little Friend, Little Friend* (1945), and *Losses* (1948), predict an artistry and sensitivity that grows out of a scholarly background. His "Death of the Ball Turret Gunner" from *Selected Poems* (1955), a five-line war protest poem written from the point of view of a dead soldier mutilated by gunfire through the Plexiglas shield on the underside of a World War II bomber, attests to the poet's gifted wordcraft. Jarrell was a professor of modern poetry at the University of North Carolina at Greensboro, a beloved teacher and reader of poetry until his sudden death in a traffic accident in 1965. He regularly recited his published works to spellbound campus gatherings. Favorites were "Lady Bates" (1955), the gentle apostrophe to a black child drowned in a river baptism, and the title poem from *The Woman at the Washington Zoo* (1960), a fearful, sensually charged meeting of two caged beings. The blue-uniformed office worker, facing cages of shiny-eyed beasts, recognizes the terror in her spirit and pleads, "Oh, bars of my own body, open, open!" Repressed and wretched, she acknowledges her emptiness and begs the "wild brother": "You know what I was, you see what I am: change me, change me!" (Jarrell 1969, 215–216)

Better known in the 1990s, poet and novelist James Dickey receives a mixed reception from critics, who admire his sturdy images and experimentive wizardry but question or reject his peculiar blend of animism with Southern ritual, mysticism, and fundamentalism. Decidedly unartsy in appearance and behavior, Dickey the man stands apart from the intensely candid visionary who is Dickey the poet. His studious concern for regional eccentricities reverberates with the oddities of Southern religious practice. An early work, "The Heaven of Animals" (1962), prefigures his obsession with imagination and violence, a dichotomy that requires bloodletting in the presence of the divine. A rhapsodic trance, the poem interweaves fervid flashes of insight with the musty exudations of the barnyard beast. In "May Day Sermon to the Women of Gilmer County, Georgia, by a Woman Preacher Leaving the Baptist Church" (1967), he

James Dickey (1923–1997) at the University of South Carolina, Columbia, South Carolina, 1990

muses on the rural obsession with fundamentalism and describes the violence of a father determined to beat religion into his wayward daughter. The screaming father, shouting and flailing with a willow limb, contrasts with the family livestock, which prance and shy at the strangely apocalyptic ritual torture. The father believes that religion will "pull down the walls of the barn like Dagon's temple set the Ark of the Lord in its place change all things for good, by pain [stet]." (Bottoms 1997, B1) The juxtaposition of beast with bestial father is Dickey's idiosyncratic touch, a reckoning of the ignorance and zeal that mars Southern biblical literalism with the perverse urge to abuse and tyrannize. An autonomous poet, Dickey answers to no strictures of school or form but opens himself to the muse that inspires his seraphic visions.

The failure of labels to capture Dickey's multifaceted inventions is demonstrated in "Angina," a physical and emotional study derived from the illness of his own mother. Tense and deliberately restrained, the poem depicts a woman who ponders her physical limitations, her four children, and the hints of mortality in tingling, stultifying angina. Enfeebled by disease and forced into invalidism like Katherine Anne Porter's Granny Weatherall or William Faulkner's Addie Bundren, she awaits death. Her becalmed spirit speaks the finality of her days: "I must be still and not worry, not worry, not worry, to hold my peace, my poor place, my own." (Dickey 1965, 65) The collection in which "Angina" appears won the National Book Award the year that Dickey was appointed poetry consultant to the Library of Congress. Subsequent verse collections include *Jericho: The South Beheld* (1974) and *Puella* (1982). (Angelou 1970, 1987, 1993; Bloom 1987; Bontemps 1974; Bottoms 1997; Bradbury 1996; Calhoun and Hill 1983; Chapman 1968; Davidson and Wagner-Martin 1995; Davis et al. 1970; Dickey 1965, *Deliverance* 1970; Ehrlich and Carruth 1982; Jarrell 1969; Kunitz 1942; Low and Clift 1981; Moore 1987; Morrow 1997; Payne 1981; Ploski and Williams 1989; Poe 1962; Price 1997; Pritchard 1990; Rubin et al. 1985; Sherr and Kazickas 1994; Wilson and Ferris 1989; Witalec 1994)

See also Angelou, Maya; the Civil War era; the colonial and federalist eras; Fugitive Agrarians; Lee, Robert E.; Poe, Edgar Allan; Simms, William Gilmore.

PORGY AND BESS

A story that outranks its original tellers in fame, *Porgy and Bess* (1935) evolved into the nation's first folk opera. As an American musical institution, the opera is far better known than the kernel works or their originator, Dubose Heyward, who was dropped from the credits of the Broadway production. The story of the Charleston beggar began with Heyward's tragic dialect novel *Porgy* (1925). Founder of the Poetry Society of South Carolina, Heyward wrote under the influence of South Carolina regionalist Julia Peterkin, a local novelist who was the first to feature coastal blacks in serious fiction. Personally annoyed with Baltimore critic H. L. Mencken's assessment of the South as a cultural Sahara, Heyward determined to prove him wrong and published a local-color verse collection, *Carolina Chansons* (1922), before turning to drama. In "Dusk," an evocation of Charleston's urban beauty, he remarks,

> But I—I who have known
> Her tenderness, her courage, and her pity;
> Have felt her forces mold me, mind and bone,

Life after life, up from her first beginning—
How can I think of her in wood and stone!
(Parks 1970, 235)

His caressing lines call attention to church chimes from St. Michael's steeple, lissome afternoon reveries by the harbor, and a lifestyle that Heyward calls "brave and splendid." Rejoicing in belonging, the speaker exults, "And these my songs, my all, belong to her." (Parks 1970, 236)

Heyward and his collaborator wife, playwright Dorothy Hartzell Kuhns Heyward, adapted *Porgy* into a play enlivened with spiritual music in 1927. Despite the Heywards' origination and development, *Porgy and Bess* is often identified as the work of lyricist Ira Gershwin and his brother, composer George Gershwin, the father of American jazz, who wrote *American in Paris* (1928) and the immortal jazz anthem *Rhapsody in Blue* (1924). As a result of the Gershwins' coauthorship with Dubose and Dorothy Heyward, the original grew upbeat, soulful, and luminous with the addition of Gullah street libretti, gospel, and fervent jazz lyrics and music. In 1935, the stage musical was a hit on Broadway, on tour in the United States and in London, and in subsequent appearances around the world, including Soviet Russia and Africa.

Heyward's story of Porgy re-creates the street culture of Charleston in the early 1900s. It derives from the author's experience among dock workers in the coastal city's deep harbor at the confluence of the Ashley and Cooper Rivers, a central clearinghouse for newly arrived African slaves prior to the Civil War. Catfish Row, drawn from Cabbage Row, a real cul-de-sac much smaller than the fictional setting implies, is the home of Porgy, the legless black beggar whom Heyward created from a living model named Goat Cart Sam. The text rhapsodizes his handicap:

> For, as the artist is born with the vision of beauty, and the tradesman with an eye for barter, so was Porgy equipped by a beneficent providence for a career of mendicancy. Instead of the sturdy legs that would have predestined him for the life of a stevedore on one of the great cotton wharves, he had, when he entered the world, totally inadequate nether extremities, quick to catch the eye, and touch the ready sympathy of the passerby. (Heyward 1929, 12)

A somber mystic with "Congo blood," Porgy dwells apart from the intimacy shared by other residents because he is too disabled and saddened to join in the lively activities of the ghetto.

In Heyward's vision, violence as well as pleasure springs from daily doings in Catfish Row. During a lamplit crap game, the attack of Crown, a burly, animalistic longshoreman, concludes a cheery Saturday-night gathering of local men drinking corn whiskey and bubbling with good wishes. Shortly before Crown stabs Robbins, the likable family man, Robbins outlines his wife Serena's connection with quality whites:

> "Dat lady ob mine is a born white-folks nigger," he boasted. "She fambly belong tuh Gob'ner Rutledge. Ain't yer see Miss Rutledge sheself come tuh visit she when she sick! An' dem chillen ob mine, dem is raise wid *ways*." (Heyward 1929, 17)

Anne Brown as Bess and Todd Duncan as Porgy played their original 1935 roles in a 1942 revival of *Porgy and Bess*, based on *Porgy*, a novel adapted as a play written by Dubose and Dorothy Heyward and published in 1927.

Heyward contrasts the effects of liquor on the benign Robbins and on Crown, a malignant malcontent, who rages and accuses his opponent. The mounting tension, offset by street sounds and distant plucks on guitar strings, flashes into strife. A rangy monster with splayed claws, the surly and foul-mouthed Crown menaces Robbins. The two clash and slide "down, down, down the centuries" into a clench that ends with a vicious swing of a cottonhook. Heyward notes, "Robbins was dead: horribly dead." (Heyward 1929, 19–20)

Just as he deplores Robbins's brutal slaying, Heyward's compassion for the maimed beggar energizes part II of *Porgy*. The haphazard police investigation of black-on-black murder results in the unnecessary arrest of Peter, an innocent bystander who is Porgy's daily guide to King Charles Street and Meeting House Road, his prime begging spot. Left without an assistant for the ten days of Peter's incarceration, Porgy hammers together a wobbly cart and expands his horizons by traveling over the city behind his evil-smelling goat. On arrival at the back gates of elegant homes, he is greeted with pity, coins, and morsels of food and thrust back into the alleyways. Elevated into a favorite Charleston street anomaly, he thrives on attention and generosity while rival beggars gnash their teeth in vain at his popularity.

Heyward smoothly segues into the major conflict with the appearance of Bess, who alters the scenario like the bright-skinned serpent to Eden. An alluring alcoholic and heroin addict and Crown's mistress, she arouses suspicion and distrust among the residents of Catfish Row. The cook Maria serves her a meal, but only Porgy offers shelter and a bed. While Bess tosses in the throes of cocaine-fed demons, Serena prays in a literary model of an antiphonal group plea to the Almighty:

> "Oh, Jedus, who done trouble de wateh in de sea ob Gallerie—"
> "Amen!" came the chorus, led by Porgy.
> "An' likewise who done cas' de Debbil out ob de afflicted, time an' time agin—"
> "Oh, Jedus!"
> "Wut mek yu ain't lay yo' han' on dis sister' head?"
> (Heyward 1929, 99)

Serena's intercession effects the change; Bess recovers. The addition of Bess to Porgy's celibate life softens his disposition, just as a steady, nonviolent mate helps Bess rid herself of paranoia, drug addiction, and drink. After a hurricane orphans an infant, the couple adopts him, forming a ready-made family.

At the story's climax, Heyward sets the action at a community picnic on nearby Kittiwah Island, a windward wilderness locale where Crown reveals to Bess that he is still alive and has been on the lam to avoid arrest for murder. Although Porgy remains out of earshot onboard the ferry, he perceives the carnal grappling of Bess and Crown in the rough. At her return, he questions her. She is surprised at his intuitive powers:

> "How yuh known?"
> "Gawd gib cripple many t'ings he ain't gib strong men." Then again, patiently, "War it Crown?" . . .

"He comin' fuh me when de cotton come tuh town."
"Yuh goin'?"
"I tell um—yes."
(Heyward 1929, 124)

To retain his new happiness, Porgy apparently stabs Crown to death in a confrontation that Heyward chooses not to portray. Porgy flees the police, who search for him merely to identify the body. On his return home after five days in jail for fleeing the authorities, he finds the baby gone and Bess departed with a drifter to Savannah. Heywood leaves him defeated, bowed with age, and sunk into despair.

In 1935, the author collaborated with the Gershwin brothers to produce *Porgy and Bess*, an ambitious, spirited, three-act folk melodrama that would be forever attached to George Gershwin's list of smash hits. In Heyward's memories of working with Gershwin, he tells a humorous anecdote about Gershwin's trip to Charleston to soak up atmosphere among poor blacks. At a gospel "shouting," Gershwin was so taken with the clapping, stamping worship ritual that he outshouted the natives. The absorption of regional events, dialect, and lifestyle apparently inspired the composer, for his vigor and style transformed Heyward's novel into a stage spectacle. The fast-paced opera stresses drama and the immediacy of community ritual, as with act I, scene ii, which opens on the wake for Serena's man, Robbins, whose remains lie uncovered on the bed. Mourners pass by and drop coins into a saucer on the corpse's chest to pay for his funeral. Serena envisions widowhood in the vital, mournful ballad "My Man's Gone Now." The scene ends with a spiritual.

Working as a team, Gershwin and Heyward excelled at varying motifs and rhythms. In act II, they contrast the hardships of domestic life in the subculture of Catfish Row with fishermen repairing nets, hurricane warnings, and "The Buzzard Song," an evil omen that terrifies Porgy. A high point in the second act is the duet "Bess, You Is My Woman Now," a bluesy serenade that establishes Bess's sexual and spiritual alliance with Porgy. The picnic at Kittiwah Island rouses all to jubilation. Sportin' Life, who jostles the community's fundamentalist fervor, touts skepticism by stealing the preacher's verve and thunder to mock Bible truths. The meeting between Bess and Crown revives their lustful attraction while picnickers board the boat for return to the mainland. At the end of the act, the authors juxtapose life with sudden and unforeseeable death as Bess lies delirious in Porgy's room two days later while Gullah street vendors hawk their strawberries, honey, and crabs outside the window. The act ends with fisherman Jake's drowning in a storm and survivors crying, "Oh, Doctor Jesus."

The collaborators stir Catfish Row into an intense turmoil of emotion, fear, and menacing weather as the search for a murderer churns act III. Bess creates a musical lull in the action while crooning "Summertime," Gershwin's famed lullaby, to the orphaned infant of Clara and Jake. The scene concludes as Crown grapples with Porgy. Fearful portents terrorize the cripple, whom police pick up to identify Crown's body. Sportin' Life heightens Porgy's superstitious fears with a claim that the dead man's corpse will ooze blood when the killer comes near it. In Porgy's absence, Bess gives way to a jolt of happy dust, the narcotic powder that calms her for the long journey north to New York, the city that symbolizes illicit love, easy pleasures, and the decadence that accompanies the high life. When Porgy returns happy and enriched by successful crapshooting with jail inmates, he is startled to find his home empty. He recovers from loss to sing "I'm on My Way," a jubilant affirmation of his optimism and love for Bess.

The rambunctious musical rocked New York's Alvin Theater with the fortuitous pairing of Anne Brown and Todd Duncan in the title roles, and with supporting parts acted and sung by John W. Bubbles, Warren Coleman, and the Eva Jessye Choir. Local theatricals have revived the opera throughout the twentieth century for its singable show tunes—"There's a Boat Dat's Leavin' for New York," "Good Mornin', Sistuh," "I Got Plenty of Nuttin'," and "It Ain't Necessarily So," a taunting, street-smart solo popularized by Cab Calloway and reprised by Sammy Davis, Jr. The familiarity of lyrics and tunes established Dubose Heyward locally as a literary authority on South Carolina's Gullah dialect, which thrives in the low country and the adjacent sea islands, now a coastal resort. To the north, however, black critics James Weldon Johnson, Sterling Brown, and W. E. B. Du Bois contested the exoticism of *Porgy and Bess* for making Gullah blacks seem mechanical, simple-witted, and ruled by instinct, ignorance, and superstition.

The Heywards spent the last 15 years of their careers in Charleston and at their shore retreat at Folly Island, and produced *Mamba's Daughters* (1929), a novel that ventures from the black microcosm to feature interaction between the races. Their work influenced the Harlem Renaissance and helped legitimize the depiction of African Americans in serious art. Apart from their collaboration, Dorothy Heyward succeeded with a screen adaptation of James Michener's *South Pacific*. On his own, Heyward published *Angel* (1926), *The Half Pint Flask* (1929), *The Brass Ankle* (1931), and *Star-Spangled Virgin* (1939). In 1959, Samuel Goldwyn filmed *Porgy and Bess* for Columbia Pictures. Directed by Otto Preminger, the cinema featured an all-star cast—Pearl Bailey and Diahann Carroll, with Sidney Poitier as Porgy, Dorothy Dandridge as Bess, and Sammy Davis, Jr., as the meretricious pimp and drug pusher Sportin' Life, who seduces Bess with wondrous, wicked visions of New York City. The movie won Oscars for musical directors André Previn and Ken Darby and an Academy Award nomination for photographer Leon Shamroy. (Bradbury 1963; Clark 1931; Ehrlich and Carruth 1982; Erb 1996; "Goat Cart" 1996; Gross 1971; Heyward 1929; Kunitz 1942; Parks 1970; Rubin et al. 1985; Stein 1979)

See also Mencken, H. L.; regionalism.

PORTER, W. S.

Once celebrated as the most popular American short-fiction writer and creator of the surprise ending, William Sydney "Will" Porter, who wrote under the pseudonym O. Henry, seemed an unlikely candidate for the honor. He was a native of Greensboro, North Carolina, the grandson of a North Carolina newspaper publisher. His parents were Mary Jane Virginia Swaim and Dr. Algernon Sidney Porter, an unsuccessful general practitioner who succumbed to alcoholism. Motherless at age 3 and a school dropout by age 15, Porter depended on his maiden aunt for sustenance and security. He won a college scholarship but had to turn it down because his aunt was unable to pay for books and supplies.

With no hope of further education, Porter earned pocket money at the counter in the W. C. Porter Drugstore, owned by his uncle. In 1882, while recuperating from chronic lung weakness and a suspicious cough, he moved to a Texas ranch in La Salle County run by a peace officer and former Texas Ranger, Captain Lee Hall. Hall and other old hands shaped Porter into a dude westerner, throwing in the ritual razzing of the tenderfoot. After clerking in a land office and in the First National Bank of Austin, Porter turned to journalism and produced a column for the *Houston Post*, "Tales of the Town," which were compiled and published posthumously in 1939.

In 1895, Porter was convicted—and later exonerated—of embezzling $4,702.94. He was accused of spending the stolen cash on his foundering magazine *Rolling Stone*, which he purchased in 1894 for $250 and filled with original witticisms, stories, and illustrations. He skipped town and worked as a stevedore on the Mississippi Gulf and temporarily for the *New Orleans Picayune*, then fled to Honduras and South America to live for three months on the largesse of an amiable bandit. Porter returned to serve his time when he learned that his wife, Athol Estes Porter, was near death from tuberculosis. For three years and three months, Porter bore the number 30664 on his shirt in the Ohio State Penitentiary in Columbus. With the aid of a compassionate prison physician, he worked in the dispensary.

From his cell, Porter published the first 14 of his career total of 600 clever, episodic short stories and vignettes. The first two, "The Miracle of Lava Cañon" (1898) and "Whistling Dick's Christmas Stocking" (1899), appeared in *McClure's* magazine. He wrote under the pseudonym of O. Henry, perhaps adapted from the name of guard Orrin Henry or from frequent calls to a prison cat named Henry. The best of the lot, "A Retrieved Reformation" (1903), which he modeled on the life of safecracker and fellow prisoner Jimmy Conners, spawned Paul Armstrong's stage melodrama *Alias Jimmy Valentine* (1909), a popular tune, and a 1928 film by the same name, the first that MGM made with sound.

In the last decade before his death from tuberculosis, diabetes, and cirrhosis of the liver at the Polyclinic Hospital on June 5, 1910, Porter moved to New York, married Sara Coleman, and lived on the run from his former identity. He remained close to his daughter Margaret, but primarily stayed to himself, perhaps out of fear that his prison record would end his writing career. In search of inspiration, he lived in Washington Square and explored the streets around Madison Square in New York City, his "Baghdad-on-the-Hudson." (Ehrlich and Carruth 1982, 131) He wrote for the *New York World* and *McClure's* his signature tragicomic sketches filled with fragmented caricatures of rakes, con artists, blackmailers, vagrants, shysters, thieves, and underdogs. His forte was tender nobodies such as Jim and Della, the penniless couple in "The Gift of the Magi"

(1905), a beloved Christmas story that employs his usual big scene and flash of recognition at the end. He published nine collections, including *The Four Millions* (1906) and *Hearts of the West* (1907), source of his famous creation, the Cisco Kid. Porter completed one play, *Lo* (1909), in collaboration with Franklin P. Adams. At his death, Porter's work suddenly came into vogue, spawning a demand for three more story collections and his 12-volume *Collected Works*, published in 1913. In 1918, the Society of Arts and Letters established in his honor an annual memorial award for the best American short story. Doughboys in the trenches during World War I embraced his Americanism and his stoicism, which critic Alphonse Smith reports as "cheerful acceptance of 'The Things That Are To Be.'" (Smith, C. 1967, 166)

Porter cultivated populist plots that celebrate the oral anecdote. His characters, even the most villainous, are a likable lot whose shortcomings lead to an unforeseen zinger, the quick catch in the last lines that reveals a tidy change of heart or comeuppance. The device concludes one of his most famous Southern stories, "A Municipal Report," in *Strictly Business* (1910), which he wrote in rebuttal of Frank Norris's claims that only three U.S. cities are "'story cities'— New York, of course, New Orleans, and, best of the lot, San Francisco." (Henry 1953, 597) Opening with a rambling discourse about Nashville, Tennessee, the narrator introduces a studied juxtaposition: Major Wentworth Caswell, a strut-

William Sydney Porter (1862–1910), known as O. Henry

ting, pretentious no-good of whom the author says, "A rat has no geographical habitat," and King Cettiwayo, the antique Negro carriage driver whose favorite sales pitch promises "The seats is clean—jes' got back from a funeral, suh." (Henry 1953, 599, 601) The author carries the story of Azalea Adair beyond his usual sketch with a genial study of Southern womanhood:

> She was a product of the old South, gently nurtured in the sheltered life. Her learning was not broad, but was deep and of splendid originality in its somewhat narrow scope. She had been educated at home, and her knowledge of the world was derived from inference and by inspiration. (Henry 1953, 603)

The speaker builds interest in Azalea's plight by establishing her relationship to the cad, who robs her, and the aged servant, Cettiwayo, who promises, "She ain't gwine to starve, suh, . . . she has reso'ces, suh; she has reso'ces." (Henry 1953, 605) Realizing that the old retainer killed the major to rid Azalea of a leech, the speaker departs Nashville, pausing at the Cumberland River to toss in a coat button, a solid piece of evidence that proves King Cettiwayo guilty of murder. ("Heart of the West" 1993; Henry 1953, 1993; Hurston 1995; "Inspirational Short Stories" 1996; "Katherine Anne Porter" 1995; Kennedy 1988; Kunitz 1942; Laskin 1994; Lyons 1985; Myers 1985; "Pardon" 1958; Poe 1962; Porter 1952, 1985; Quinn 1936; Rubin et al. 1985; Smith, C. 1967; "Southerner Ellen Gilchrist" 1985; Stein 1979; Trent et al. 1946; Watson 1997)

See also short fiction in Southern literature.

PROTEST LITERATURE

The Southern writer's use of polemic, drama, novel, and poetry as a means to express discontent or vent outrage dates to early times and encompasses the documents written by revolutionaries of the stature of Thomas Jefferson and Thomas Paine, the speeches of Patrick Henry, slave narratives of William Wells Brown and Harriet E. Wilson, and the declaration of a group of North Carolina women later known as the Edenton Tea Party. An anomaly in linguistic history, Sequoyah, a self-made scholar born in Taskigi (Tuskegee), Tennessee, created "talking leaves," writings spelled out in his original phonetic Cherokee alphabet, which could be learned in a few days. In the first half of the nineteenth century, his brilliant answer to the problem of Native American preliteracy lifted the Cherokee from restriction to spoken language to reading, writing, and the first Native American mail system. Sequoyah served in the Cherokee cavalry regiment of the U.S. Army during the Creek War of 1813–1814. Crippled by a knee injury while trapping and hunting, he was limited to home chores. He developed his talents as painter and silversmith in the years preceding his tribe's forced removal to Arkansas. In 1821, he completed the Cherokee alphabet of 200 characters and returned to Tennessee to launch a literacy program and mail service between Arkansas and Tennessee, the separated halves of the Cherokee Nation.

In conjunction with editor Elias Boudinot, a Cherokee educated in a Moravian academy in Salem, North Carolina, and his assistant, missionary and Bible translator Stephen Foreman, Sequoyah set up a printing press in New Echota, Georgia, in 1827 and began publishing the *Cherokee Phoenix* and the *Cherokee Advocate*, a four-page newspaper written in Cherokee and English to elicit readership among whites and Native Americans. An outspoken platform defending native rights and advancing general knowledge about tribal law, these works were landmarks in the uniting of the races in the southern Appalachians. Sequoyah influenced opinion through journalistic essays that lauded the work of the Bureau of Indian Affairs and the reorganization of the Cherokee Indian territory. During the harsh aftermath of the Trail of Tears—Andrew Jackson's forced exile of the Cherokee, Choctaw, and Creek to Indian territory—Boudinot supported the move as an inevitable separation of races. Angry tribe members murdered him and other dignitaries who signed the Treaty of 1835, which ceded Cherokee lands to the U.S. government.

After the departure of much of the South's indigenous population during the Trail of Tears removal, Southern protest writing and oratory concerned itself primarily with the plight of blacks. In 1864, West Virginian Martin Delany published the *Declaration of the Principles of the National Emigration Convention*, a resetting of Jeffersonian principles and style to declare unjust the oppression and sale of human beings. The next year, former slave and Presbyterian minister Henry Highland Garnet, a contemporary of Frederick Douglass and an outspoken proponent of abolitionism, delivered his Memorial Discourse, later known as his "Call to Rebellion," before the U.S. House of Representatives. With suitable rises of passion and exhortation, he pressed his hearers to end human bondage:

> SLAVERY! How much misery is comprehended in that single word? What mind is there that does not shrink from the soul, all men cherish the love of Liberty. . . . To such degradation it is sinful in the extreme for you to make voluntary submission. (Mullane 1993, 117)

In a twist on the usual format of antislavery orations, Garnet proclaims the congressmen themselves slaves to a rigid social system founded on racism. As he builds to his conclusion, he urges, "It is in your power so to torment the God-cursed slaveholders that they will be glad to let you go free." (Mullane 1993, 120)

In a post–Civil War effort to assuage hostilities, Georgian Henry Grady, North Carolinian Walter Hines Page, Floridian Philip Randolph, and Virginian Booker T. Washington were eager for the South to heal and move beyond the divisive issues that spawned the Civil War. Grady, a journalist and publisher of the *Atlanta Daily Herald* and the *Atlanta Constitution*, became a spokesman for peace during the post–Civil War era. A proponent for the New South, he crusaded in editorials and oratory for an end to bitterness and wrangling over the fall of the Confederacy, and urged investment in industry to quicken the moribund Southern economy. Grady had no patience with crepehangers and romantics who devoted their energies to vengeance and the stoking of old griefs and animosities.

In "The New South," a speech before the New England Society on December 21, 1886, he began by quoting an energetic declaration of Benjamin Hill: "There was a South of slavery and secession—that South is dead. There is a South of union and freedom—that South, thank God, is living, breathing, growing every hour." (Beatty et al. 1952, 488)

Grady's optimism derives from an appreciation of American history. He does not abandon the maimed population of the South, whom he pictures with the hypothetical case of "the footsore Confederate soldier." He describes the march south after the surrender at Appomattox:

> He finds his house in ruins, his farm devastated, his slaves free, his stock killed, his barns empty, his trade destroyed, his money worthless, his social system, feudal in its magnificence, swept away; his people without law or legal status; his comrades slain, and the burdens of others heavy on his shoulders. Crushed by defeat, his very traditions are gone. (Beatty et al. 1952, 490)

Grady lays out a vigorous plan of rehabilitation for the recovering region. He encourages hiring free Negroes, assisting education, and developing jobs through cooperative efforts with Northern entrepreneurs. He declares that the South has profited from the collapse of the plantation system by developing a true democracy. Unable to denounce the war years as wasted, he lauds Confederate efforts during the war but champions the rise of a Union free of slavery.

His contemporary, Walter Hines Page, cultivated a career similar to Grady's. While editing the *Raleigh Chronicle* and the *Atlantic Monthly*, Page conducted a parallel crusade for civic convalescence in his most cogent essays—"The Forgotten Man," "The School That Built a Town," and "The Rebuilding of Old Commonwealths," published together in 1904. Less versatile than Grady, Page spoke with authority and force on the needs of farm families, epitomized as "the forgotten man." An advocate of free education, he fought tentative retrogressive moves toward antebellum elitism and decried the joylessness and complacency of the laboring class. Noted for his evenhandedness toward women and children, he demanded a school tax to raise women along with men to a high standard of competency and urged cities to establish free libraries. Page concluded with a stirring prophecy for national health: "The neglected people will rise and with them will rise all the people." (Beatty et al. 1952, 506)

Unlike Page and Grady, Philip Randolph and Booker T. Washington chose publishing and education as the best outlet for their talents. Randolph is best known for leading marches and strikes of janitors, laborers, and maintenance workers. In 1942, he composed "Program of the March on Washington," a straightforward declamation protesting unfair laws, unequal representation, a segregated military, and lax enforcement of the Fifth and Fourteenth Amendments to the Constitution. Washington produced two significant autobiographies: *Up from Slavery* (1901) and *My Larger Education* (1911), both cherished first-person recollections of the black struggle for self-fulfillment and an expanded role in civic life and prosperity. In the first title, he describes the immediate needs of newly freed slaves, recalling that few migrated very far from the plantation. His own family settled in Malden, West Virginia, where they lived in a cabin no better than the one they left. Like his stepfather, he worked at a salt furnace and used every resource to educate himself. When his teacher asked his name, he created for himself the combination of Booker Taliaferro Washington. Although lacking in identifiable ancestry, he claims:

> From any point of view, I had rather be what I am, a member of the Negro race, than be able to claim membership with the most favored of any other race. I have always been made sad when I have heard members of any race claiming rights and privileges, or certain badges of distinction, on the ground simply that they were members of this or that race, regardless of their own individual worth or attainments. . . . Every persecuted individual and race should get much consolation out of the great human law, which is universal and eternal, that merit, no matter under what skin found, is in the long run, recognized and rewarded. (Slater 1996, 410)

In *Up from Slavery*, he amplified his universalism by publishing the Atlanta Exposition Address, which demands attention toward the needs of the Negro race. Forming a third of the South's population, the 8 million blacks whom the government sought to ignore needed just laws, an end to violence, and encouragement to embrace education and jobs as a way out of ignorance and squalor. Washington urged his listeners to cast their buckets in local waters. To set the example, he established a profitable career at Tuskegee Institute, which he endowed with buildings, acreage, and programs to teach science, domestic skills, and agriculture to unlettered blacks.

These and other protest writings and oratory of the nineteenth and early twentieth centuries differed in tone and content from the mid-1900s. As whites continued to profit from industrialization, education, and just laws, minorities realized that dreams of equality would remain out of their grasp unless they demanded their share. Novelist Richard Wright spoke to the issue of lynching in his impassioned protest poem "Between the World and Me," which he published in *Partisan Review* in 1935. Speaking in first person, he composed a grim encounter between his poetic persona and a recently murdered black. Set in the woods by a scorched sliver of a hanging tree pointing at the sky like a charred, accusing finger, the poem reverently examines the victim's shoe, hat, shirt, and trousers, meaningfully stiffened with black blood. Aghast at the meatless skeleton, the speaker reincarnates himself as the quarry and hears the gin-loud racists laughing, fondling whores, passing the communal bottle, and eating peanuts as though the execution were an evening's entertainment. The torment of tar, feathers, and cooling gasoline ignites into a blaze, forcing the speaker to leap heavenward and clutch at death as a refuge from agony. The encounter strips the speaker of innocence. Unable to dissociate from the lynched victim, the speaker concludes, "Now I am dry bones and my face a stony skull staring in yellow surprise at the sun." (Chapman 1968, 438)

Wright's eloquent but graphic accusation contrasts the grandeur and scriptural gravity of Dr. Martin Luther King, Jr., the twentieth century's passionate peacemaker and freedom fighter. The recipient of a Nobel peace prize, King developed in stature and outreach from minister of Birmingham's Dexter Avenue Baptist Church and regional leader of a boycott of the city bus system and protest marches to an international spokesman for nonviolence and racial inclusiveness. His followers locked arms, prayed, and sang "We Shall Overcome" and "O Freedom," spirituals that date to slave times. While confined in Alabama for protesting a racist local government, he composed "Letter from a Birmingham Jail" (1963). In its soulful lines, he expresses the hard truth of social change: "We know through painful experience that freedom is never voluntarily given by the oppressor; it must be demanded by the oppressed." (Mullane 1993, 636) He cites the examples of James Meredith and Rosa Parks, both dignified but adamant citizens who rejected the status quo and insisted on full participation in democracy.

On August 28, 1963, King's march on Washington, D.C., climaxed at a mass gathering before the Lincoln Memorial for his elegaic "I Have a Dream" speech, the era's stirring rallying cry. A masterpiece of parallelism and the gospel delivery indigenous to black Protestantism, the text demands that America honor its "promissory note" by ending police brutality, segregation of public facilities and business, voting restrictions, and the shabby treatment that confined Negroes to perpetual poverty. Leaning into his "I have a dream" segment, he looked to the future of his own children and cried out with joy, "Free at last! Free at last! Thank God Almighty, we are free at last!" (Mullane 1993, 650) Marked for martyrdom, King realized that counterforces plotted his doom; nevertheless, he led the Poor People's March on Washington in 1968. Murdered by a fanatic on April 4 of that year, he was eulogized around the world and honored beyond the adulation accorded royalty and elected officials.

A legend within months of his demise, King influenced the style and cadence of a generation of gifted Southern black orators, particularly Andrew Young, a former U.S. representative to the United Nations; Reverend Jesse Jackson; and U.S. congresswoman Barbara Jordan. Young is an energetic speaker, but prefers straight oratory to the lyricism of Jackson and Jordan. Jackson, a peripatetic goodwill ambassador, president of the National Rainbow Coalition, and sometime candidate for public office, is a quasi-official spokesman for black interests. On October 26, 1995, he expounded in Indianapolis on the worsening race relations that are producing a structural crisis in American cities. The focus of his text protests economic downsizing and diminished quality of life in black America at the same time that it corroborates the finding of the Million Man March, led by black Muslim leader Louis Farrakhan. Jackson's ethos calls for commitment to marriage and the family and a renewed push for affirmative action, which congressional conservatives threaten. He concludes that the U.S. citizenry deserves action to end stereotypes depicting blacks as welfare cheats and criminals who undermine national morals. Before the 1996 Democratic National Convention, held in Chicago, Jackson invoked Dr. Martin Luther King's healing vision of peace and equality. Reiterating the issues outlined in the Indianapolis speech, Jackson demanded more respect for citizens and an energetic reinvestment in America. He concluded that the liberal agenda is a mission worth struggling for.

Unlike Young and Jackson, Barbara Jordan—popularized as a member of the House Judiciary Committee weighing articles of impeachment against Presi-

An orator in the tradition of Martin Luther King, U.S. Congresswoman Barbara Jordan (1936–1996) of Texas acknowledges applause following her keynote address "Who Then Will Speak for the Common Good?" at the July 1976 Democratic National Convention in New York.

dent Richard Nixon—avoided dry political harangue and returned to the pulpit mannerisms that won King a national parish. In 1974, while deliberating the fate of the corrupt Nixon presidency, she galvanized the panel with a passionate affirmation of American constitutional law:

> My faith in the Constitution is whole, it is complete, it is total. I am not going to sit here and be an idle spectator to the diminution, the subversion, the destruction of the Constitution. If the impeachment provision in the Constitution of the United States will not reach the offenses charged here, then perhaps that 18th-century Constitution should be abandoned to the 20th-century paper shredder. (Hines 1996, 2)

In 1976, Jordan gained her own national platform at the Democratic convention with "Who Then Will Speak for the Common Good?" An inspiring, uplifting rally, the cadences and phrasing ignited a fervent response from the audience, who cheered her statement: "First we believe in equality for all and privileges for none." (Jordan 1996, 1) The core issue—the disparate demands that disjoined her party—threatened the common good. As though challenging each listener, Jordan exerted a personal tone and leaned into the crowd to admit that forming a national community is a difficult task. In conclusion, she reminded her listeners that the haves and have-nots are equally deficient, a point made by Abraham Lincoln when he declared, "As I would not be a slave, so I would not be a master."

On March 16, 1993, Jordan presented the Nancy Hanks lecture at the Kennedy Center on the subject of "The Arts and the American Dream." Her protest against public apathy during a widespread deletion of the arts from public life calls for expression of human dreams. Her reasons validate the 1990s trend toward cultural inclusion:

> Assimilation was never the goal of the diverse ethnic groups in America. Inclusion without discomfort is now and ever will be the goal. Maybe one day we will be comfortable enough with each other to drop the hyphens. There should be no hyphenated Americans. (Jordan 1993, 114–115)

She reminds her audience that art is powerful. Its message inspires hope and communication, which are the themes of Maya Angelou's inaugural poem "On the Pulse of the Morning," delivered in Washington, D.C., on January 20, 1993. To that verse, Jordan exults, "I listened; I heard; I believed." (Jordan 1993, 117)

During the intense ferment of the battle for civil rights, oratory dwelled alongside fiction and first-person narrative as the prime literary forces that initiated an end to Jim Crow and segregation. In 1959, Texan John Howard Griffin produced a singular first-person protest against racism by darkening his skin with chemicals and collecting data in the South from a black man's point of view. His best-seller *Black Like Me* (1960) speaks directly to the rot at the heart of human relations:

> The Negro. The South. These are details. The real story is the universal one of men who destroy the souls and bodies of other men (and in the process destroy themselves) for reasons neither really understands. It is the story of the persecuted, the defrauded, the feared and detested. (Griffin 1976, 5)

In an epilogue appended 16 years later, Griffin reasserted his findings. He added that during his discussions with Dr. King, Dick Gregory, Roy Wilkins, Stokely Carmichael, Whitney Young, and other champions of equality, they attested to the ominous truth that "these principles were worth dying for, and that there were plenty of people who were willing to see us disappear." (Griffin 1976, 167)

Black orators and authors not only refused to disappear, they grew more vocal in the second half of the twentieth century, as evidenced by H. Rap Brown's *Die Nigger Die!* (1969), playwright Alice Childress's *Trouble in Mind* (1955), Eldridge Cleaver's prison journal, *Soul on Ice* (1968), and Frank Yerby's *Judas, My Brother* (1968). Missourian Julius Lester, author of *Look Out Whitey! Black Power's Gon' Get Your Mama!* (1968), gained new respect for slave narratives with *To Be a Slave* (1968), a Newbery Honor book that coordinates first-person memoir along with Lester's comments. A powerful, moving testimony to the evils of slavery, the text extracts from forgotten history the eyewitness accounts of individuals who suffered racial degradations. According to first-person testimony by Dick Gregory in his protest volumes—*No More Lies: The Myth and Reality of American History* (1976) and his witty autobiography, *Nigger* (1964)—the task of educating the majority on the deadly divisiveness of prejudice against minorities requires deeds as well as words. Strong words came from Mississippian Anne E. Moody, CORE activist and author of *Coming of Age in Mississippi*

(1968), an articulate on-the-scene account of sit-ins and demonstrations. Her skillful combination of memoir and protest produced cogent commentary on times fraught with danger and corresponding apathy:

> Yes, Saturday night is Nigger Night all over Mississippi. . . . Some Negroes would come to town on Saturday night just to pick a fight with another Negro. Once the fight was over, they were satisfied. They beat their frustrations and discontent out on each other. I had often thought that if some of that Saturday night energy was used constructively or even directed at the right objects, it would make a tremendous difference in the life of Negroes in Mississippi. (Moody 1968, 291)

In a blend of pride and nostalgia, she recaptures the vigor of her fellow activists, who helped her withstand the terror, humiliation, and pain of racial turmoil. Before joining a Freedom Day celebration, she weeps in anticipation of "singing, suffering, and Soul," the outgrowths of a camaraderie deeper and more committed than mere friendship. With her fellows, she sings a familiar line from Southern spirituals: "And before I'll be a slave I'll be buried in my grave and go home to my Lord and be free." (Moody 1968, 370)

At the end of the twentieth century, civil rights mutated with the addition of a public outcry against the black warrior's role in an unjust war. West Virginia novelist Walter Dean Myers drew on the tradition of the black griot to write *Fallen Angels* (1988), the story of the black experience during the Vietnam War. Dedicating his battlefield narration to his brother Sonny, who was killed in the fighting, Myers relates the accidental drafting of a fictional soldier, Richard Perry, a victim of a bureaucratic foul-up, and his role in the 22nd Replacement Company assigned to Tan Son Nhut in 1968. The misery of sector patrol duty, diarrhea from malaria pills, shrapnel wounds, death from friendly fire, and news from home of war resisters burning draft cards jostle his equanimity, leaving him vulnerable and fearful. Dehumanization looms near as Richard's nerves snap and he pours round after round from his M-16 into the face of a thin Vietnamese man. Violence escalates as Vietcong approach with hands lifted in a sign of submission. Battlefield slang lessens the savagery that becomes a way of surviving: "A woman from the village went over and stabbed one in the side. He tried to get her knife away from her, and two guys lit him up. His body jerked around like a rag puppet being dragged by a dog." (Myers 1988, 182) In retrospect, Richard reminds himself that he too has killed a human being. "I thought how he looked how I had felt. . . . I remembered looking down at him and feeling my own face torn apart."

Myers overlays the night reconnaissance, whir of choppers, and squabbles over body count with the humanity of a positive influence. Richard looks up to Lieutenant Carroll, "a quiet guy, with dark hair and dark, calm eyes and an uneasy smile." (Myers 1988, 44) In the aftermath of Private Jenkins's death, Carroll removes his helmet and bows his head. He prays without artifice: "Lord, let us feel pity for Private Jenkins, and sorrow for ourselves, and all the angel warriors that fall. Let us fear death, but let it not live within us. Protect us, O Lord, and be merciful unto us." As Richard recovers from a leg wound, he is relieved of duty when a doctor studies his paperwork and locates a medical deferral. Safe from war, Richard flies to Osaka, then home. To himself, he prays for God's intervention in the lives of platoon mates. With the earnest magnanimity of a victim, Richard reminds himself, "I just wanted God to care for them, to keep them whole." (Myers 1988, 309)

Steeped in the era's absorption in violence, Tennessean Nikki Giovanni raises a militant voice protesting continued racial prejudice. Often graphically retaliatory and driven to thoughts of torture and murder, her verse, once excused as precocious examples of adolescent rebellion, fills a lengthy canon of dynamic, hate-tinged poetry: *Black Feeling, Black Talk* (1967), *Black Judgement* (1970), *Recreation* (1971), *Gemini: An Extended Autobiographical Statement on My First Twenty-five Years of Being a Black Poet* (1971), *Spin a Soft Black Song* (1971), *Cotton Candy on a Rainy Day* (1978), *Those Who Ride the Night Winds* (1982), and *Sacred Cows and Other Edibles* (1988). A favorite discussion topic among critics is the overt venom of Giovanni's "The True Import of Present Dialogue: Black vs. Negro" (1968), often referred to by its pointed opener "Nigger can you kill." Laden with images of arguing, suffering, and truncating limbs and lives, the harsh vernacular phrases jog and jolt, halting for frequent rhetorical questions before taking off again toward one of Giovanni's uncompromising conclusions. Less confrontational are her essays in *Racism 101* (1994), which mull over the duty of the writer and the best of her contemporaries. To the next generation, she declares that meatloaf is as worthy a subject as heroism. Terse in prose as well as verse, she declares: "Poems are dreams. Dream. But dreams are conceived in reality. Meatloaf is real. Write that poem." (Giovanni 1994, 177) (Beatty et al. 1952; Chapman 1968; Cwiklik and Lewis 1990; Dockstader 1977; Foreman 1938; Foster 1981; Fowler, *Conversations* 1992, *Nikki Giovanni* 1992; Giovanni 1978, 1994; Griffin 1976; Hine et al. 1993; Hines 1996; "After the Million Man March" 1996, "Speech to the 1996 Democratic National Convention" 1996; Jordan 1993, 1996; Lester 1968; Low and Clift 1981; Moody 1968; Mullane 1993; Patterson and Snodgrass 1994; Perkins 1996; Ploski and Williams 1989; Ravitch 1990; Slater 1996; Snodgrass 1993; Traveller Bird 1971; Waldman 1990; "Where an Alphabet Was Born" 1988; Wilkins 1970)

See also Black Boy; Invisible Man; Native Son.

RAWLINGS, MARJORIE KINNAN

Marjorie Kinnan Rawlings is a rarity among Southern authors. Frequently listed as a female Florida regionalist, she defied the confining categorization of regionalist with substantial achievements in conservation, feminism, local history, and young-adult fiction. Choosing to live and work among humble central Florida folk, she enriched her writing with an understanding of the demands of marshland agriculture and an instinctive respect for families isolated and marginalized by swamp and wilderness. Multiple strands of Southern tradition course her works, melding frontier themes with love of land and family, patriotism, respect for nature, and faith in the individual.

The daughter of patent attorney Arthur F. Kinnan and Ida May Traphagen Kinnan, Rawlings was born August 8, 1896, among the urban rhythms of Washington, D.C. She attended local schools, won her first writing award from *McCall's* magazine at age 16, and earned a Phi Beta Kappa key at the University of Wisconsin. For a decade, she worked as publicist for the YMCA and assistant editor of *Home Sector*, wrote ad copy and features for the *Louisville Courier-Journal*, and served the *Rochester Journal-American* as reporter and personal-advice columnist. Citified until midlife, she left her home in Rochester, New York, to move light-years away from urban clutter to the primal pine woods and palmetto scrubs of central Florida. For the remainder of her life, she maintained a home at Cross Creek, a tin-roofed rural retreat with screened-in porch overlooking swamp. In the distance, herons stood guard and deer gathered on Lochloosa Lake near Hawthorne, Florida, a part of the Ocala National Forest.

On a fishing trip in 1928, Rawlings and her first husband, newspaper reporter Charles A. Rawlings, first encountered the untamed beauty of Florida. Within a few months, the couple sold their New York holdings and bought the farm with its 72-acre orange grove, a hot, steamy setting thick with mosquitoes, rattlers, opossums, and alligators. As though born to the frontier, Rawlings made a home in the rugged marshland. Years later, she reflected, "For myself, the Creek satisfies a thing that had gone hungry and unfed since childhood days. I am often lonely. Who is not? But I should be lonelier in the heart of a city." (Rawlings 1953, 5) On the advice of agent Maxwell Perkins, she began writing regional fiction. For eight hours each day, she pecked at a bedside Royal typewriter or on a Smith-Corona on the veranda. She averaged three pages a day, about half her intended output.

Unsuccessful attempts at publication left Rawlings near despair when she began using impressions of Florida as a milieu. An avid cook, hunter, and friend maker, she mastered the local dialect, diet, and customs for *When a Whippoor-will* (1930), a story collection marked by the commonalities of the piney woods: catfish fries and sweet potato peddlers, kerosene lamplight and moonshiners, palpable heat waves and fresh, airy daybreaks. Her sketches present more than surface detail, as demonstrated in a scene from a square dance:

> The dancers sashayed. The individual couples concentrated on each other, shoulders pressed together like wrestlers. The whole dance was violent, earnest, without levity.
> *"Sluf-sluf! Shuffle-shuffle! Sluf-sluf!"*
> The music stopped as abruptly as though the instrument had been struck from the fiddler's hands. The dancers fell away from one another wherever the end of the set found them. (Rawlings 1940, 42)

Living at Cross Creek had proved a worthy investment. Unlike local colorists who glide over the surface like a spreading knife over icing, Rawlings sought the inner flavor—the deep-buried insights into the semitropics that only a resident could know. Her stories served as the kernel of two films: *The Sun Comes Up* (1949), starring Jeanette MacDonald, Claude Jarmon, Jr., and Lloyd Nolan, and *Gal Young 'Un* (1979), a humorous romance between a refined middle-aged woman and a Florida moonshiner, winner of the 1981 Grand Jury Prize at the Sundance Film Festival.

Encouraged by a spate of successes, Rawlings submitted other short fiction to *Scribner's* magazine, including "Cracker Chidlings" (1931) and "Jacob's Ladder" (1931). The latter, which pits human strivings against nature, is a study of contrasts:

> The occasional hammocks were dried up except in the lowest swamps and along the edges of lakes and streams. The creeks were withered down to the brown beds, cracking wide with thirst. The frogs, who had sung all spring in the good damp, were silent under the ooze where they had burrowed. Across the roads the moccasins and king snakes moved all day in search of water. (Rawlings 1950, 110)

Published as a novella, *Jacob's Ladder* won a Scribner's writing contest and earned Rawlings $750, enough to install indoor plumbing at Cross Creek.

After a divorce, Rawlings retired to Big Scrub to research a first novel, *South Moon Under* (1933), a mature reflection on swamp folk. Enriched with exchanges in dialect, the novel moves effortlessly among the private nuances that Rawlings knew from firsthand experience with neighbors, as depicted in this exchange between a family of moonshiners about federal agents:

> "I'm carryin' bad news, Aunt Py-tee. Hit concern you as much as Lant."
> "Well, set down, anyway."
> "Lant, Cleve's turned you up to the Prohis."
> Piety said sharply, "He ain't done no sich thing."

"I know what I'm sayin'. Ain't I tried to ask him out of it, until it was me keep still or him to knock me down for it?" (Rawlings 1933, 308)

For its faithful re-creation of the Florida wild, *South Moon Under* was nominated for a Pulitzer Prize and featured by Book-of-the-Month Club. Rawlings won the 1933 O. Henry Memorial Short Story Contest with "Gal Young 'Un," one of numerous feminist works, which depicts a female protagonist's flight from a domineering patriarchal male.

In seclusion from well-wishers and other distractions, Rawlings retreated to Banner Elk, North Carolina, near the Cherokee reservation. Apart from the tropics and denizens of the swamps, she applied a similar sensitivity to people in remote settings with "A Mother in Manville" (1936), the story of a visiting author who befriends a local boy. While chopping and stacking firewood and admiring laurel blooms, he gives clues to his background and the beloved mother who spoils him with treats. The speaker comments on his courtesy:

He did for me the unnecessary thing, the gracious thing, that we find done only by the great of heart. Things no training can teach, for they are done on the instant, with no predicated experience. He found a cubbyhole beside the fireplace that I had not noticed. There of his own accord, he put kindling and "medium" wood, so that I might always have dry fire material ready in case of sudden wet weather. (Rawlings 1940, 221)

Marjorie Kinnan Rawlings (1896–1953) in 1939

At the nearby orphanage, the unnamed author learns that the stories of the doting mother are fantasies. As the title suggests, the boy perches on the edge of manhood bereft of the parental backing he needs as he approaches maturity.

Rawlings's empathy for the motherless woodcutter prefigures a greater concern for coming-of-age in her masterwork, *The Yearling* (1938), winner of a Lewis Carroll Shelf Award. She began her third novel before leaving North Carolina, pulling her imagination back to Cross Creek and the resilient residents who lived in tenuous harmony with nature. Composed in the frontier tradition, *The Yearling* won a Pulitzer Prize and assured her place in the National Academy of Arts and Letters. A sensitive young-adult classic set in a harsh outback homestead, the novel recounts the late childhood of 12-year-old Jody Baxter, the "betwixt and between" man-child of Ora, a demanding mother, and Penny, the lenient father who has just returned from service in the Civil War. Set on the Florida frontier in the late 1860s, the story reveals the cracker dialect, husbandry, and hardscrabble existence of isolated settlers like Penny on a harsh, yet reassuringly stable landscape:

> The peace of the vast aloof scrub had drawn him with the beneficence of its silence. Something in him was raw and tender. The touch of men was hurtful upon it, but the touch of the pines was healing. Making a living came harder there, distances were troublesome in the buying of supplies and the marketing of crops. But the clearing was peculiarly his own. The wild animals seemed less predatory to him than people he had known. The forays of bear and wolf and wildcat and panther on stock were understandable, which was more than he could say of human cruelties. (Rawlings 1970, 18)

Like other returning war veterans, Penny embraces the frontier for its raw, clean expanse, which is free of the taint of slavery and the national conflict that killed too many on both sides of the issue.

Rawlings's story focuses on Jody's attachment to an orphaned fawn, which he and his father raise. Jody names the fawn Flag for the white scut of a tail that flirts and bobbles as the fawn noses about the sawgrass. Roaming the scrub trees, fetter bush, and sparkleberry, Jody and Flag become inseparable. Central to the plot is a prevalent frontier theme—the survival of the strong and the winnowing out of the weak of all species, human and animal. Nature's short-term gifts are a given for women like Ora, who had buried her previous children soon after their births. Unlike the Baxter infants, Jody's friend Fodderwing Forrester, "born peculiar—from the second settin'," survives but lives out his days a cripple. (Rawlings 1970, 137) Misshapen and sickly, he dies suddenly, leaving his parents and brothers to share the unforeseen loss with Jody. Jody realizes, "This was Death. Death was a silence that gave back no answer." (Rawlings 1970, 204) Fodderwing's passing presages the annual caprices of nature in the Florida marshes—the flooding of Lake George, scarcity of game, and desperation among predatory animals, especially a bear named Old Slewfoot, Rawlings's symbol of the bestial, untamed forces of the wild. Persistently stalking the bear, Penny triumphs with a doubly fortuitous kill, ending night raids on the corncrib and at the same time supplying his family with meat. During the sharing of Slewfoot's ample haunches with neighbors, the feud that erupts epitomizes the latent, smoldering animosities that precipitate violence among independent backwoods homesteaders.

The crux of Rawlings's novel pits Jody's love for Flag against his obedience and respect for Penny and Ora. Wiser heads instruct the boy to return Flag to the wild before he tramples the corn patch and jeopardizes the winter grain supply. Earlier, Penny had warned his son, "A creetur's only doin' the same as me when I go huntin' us meat. . . . Huntin' him where he lives and beds and raises his young uns. Hit's a hard law, but it's the law. Kill or go hongry." (Rawlings 1970, 43) Ora had long "been sparin'" to make the most of kitchen staples, medicine, water, meat, cow peas, "'baccy," berries, and wild greens. To assure their survival, she shoots the deer. Like the pet execution in Fred Gipson's *Old Yeller*, Flag's death breaks the boy's heart. The emotional trauma unsettles Jody, sending him fleeing from his parents to seek comfort elsewhere. After a brief sojourn among friends in Volusia, he returns to the clearing by mailboat. No longer a child, Jody accepts the ways of the Florida wild and reenters his family as its third adult. MGM's 1946 technicolor film version, starring Gregory Peck, Jane Wyman, Chill Wills, and Forrest Tucker, won audiences to its pure, unspoiled vision of love between footloose child and pet. The movie earned Oscars for the child star, Claude Jarman, Jr., and for photography and art direction. It also received Academy Award nominations in five categories—editing, direction, male and female leads, and best picture. The title won such respect from educators, librarians, and parents that it is still popular in play form as well as video, large print, and audiocassette.

The success of *The Yearling* ended the first phase of Rawlings's career. In 1941, Rawlings moved with her second husband, restaurateur Norton Sanford Baskin, to the penthouse of his hotel, the Castle Warden, in St. Augustine. She shifted creative emphasis from novel to verse, memoir, and nonfiction, much of which she sold to *New Yorker, Scribner's, Harper's, Atlantic Monthly, Collier's,* and *Saturday Evening Post.* Most successful of the nonfiction titles is *Cross Creek* (1942), an anecdotal autobiography, and its sequel, *Cross Creek Cookery* (1942), a collection of local recipes. These first-person publications brought her years of grief because of a protracted suit for libel and breach of privacy brought by a woman she named without permission. After a second divorce, bouts of heavy drinking, and the death of her agent, Maxwell Perkins, Rawlings's health suffered. She slowed her pace, publishing *The Secret River* (1956), a Newbery runner-up, and *The Marjorie Kinnan Rawlings Reader* (1956), and researching a biography of Richmond regionalist Ellen Glasgow. The biography was left in note form at the time of Rawlings's death from brain hemorrhage in a St. Augustine hospital on December 14, 1953. She is buried in Antioch Cemetery near her home, which is one of Florida's historic sites.

A feminist before the term was invented, Rawlings rose above the limitations of regionalism in part through her sympathetic, affirmative glimpses of stoic frontier women. She earned honorary doctorates from Rollins College and the universities of Tampa and Florida. She willed Cross Creek to the University of Florida, which also houses her collected manuscripts and considerable correspondence in the library's rare book room. Among the sheaf of personal letters collected for publication in 1983 are missives written by fans Mary McLeod Bethune, N. C. Wyeth, Pearl Primus, Robert Herrick, Mary Margaret McBride, Thornton Wilder, Eleanor Roosevelt, Carl Van Vechten, Sigrid Undset, and John Steinbeck; their accolades attest to Rawlings's skill in depicting poor white Florida crackers. Colleagues Zora Neale Hurston, Charles Scribner, Margaret Mitchell, Esther Forbes, Jesse Stuart, James Branch Cabell, and A. J. Cronin applauded her accurate depictions of rustic life and regard for human values. A periodical, the *Marjorie Kinnan Rawlings Journal of Florida Literature*, publishes criticism of her works. (Bigelow 1966; Blain et al. 1990; Bradbury 1963; Buck 1992; Chapman 1974; *Contemporary Authors* 1994; Davidson and Wagner-Martin 1995; Ehrlich and Carruth 1982; Hart 1983; Kleinberg 1990; Kunitz 1942; Lieb 1996; Magill 1958; "Marjorie Kinnan Rawlings" 1996; "Marjorie Kinnan Rawlings Society" 1996; Rawlings 1933, 1940, 1942, 1950, 1953, 1970; Rubin et al. 1985; Sackett 1996; Sherr and Kazickas 1994; Stein 1979; Stuckey 1966; Wagenknecht 1952; Walker, John 1996; Wigginton 1970; Wilson and Ferris 1989)

REGIONALISM

In various contexts, the term *regionalist* has been leveled at would-be authors, dabblers, and poetasters as a mildly sneering pejorative. In the case of local colorists of the Southern canon, the term carries distinction, for the genre offers an appropriate niche for solid writing that isolates the sound, cadence, natural settings, and themes of particular areas of the American South. Southern qualities enrich a wide spectrum of fiction, from the ripsnorting good time of Guy Owen's picaresque tale *The Ballad of the Flim-Flam Man* (1965) to Shirley Ann Grau's bitter novel *The Keepers of the House* (1964), from the slow buildup of drama in Elizabeth Spencer's *The Voice at the Back Door* (1956) to the seamy white-trash ineptitudes depicted in Erskine Caldwell's *Tobacco Road* (1932) and *God's Little Acre* (1933) or the graceful homage to a farmer's life in Wendell Berry's *The Memory of Old Jack* (1974). The region's best include notable women— Tennesseean Catherine Marshall, author of *Christy* (1967), Floridian Marjorie Kinnan Rawlings, who wrote *The Yearling* (1938), and Julia Mood Peterkin, whose immersion in plantation lore permeates her fiction. The list includes an outlander from Ionia, Greece, Lafcadio Hearn, author of *Chita: A Memory of Last Island* (1889), which is set in the same Creole milieu as Kate Chopin's *The Awakening* (1899).

One musical voice endowed with the beauties of his homeland belonged to poet Sidney Lanier. Born in Macon, Georgia, in the generation that came of age in Civil War times, he scrapped his dream of graduate study in Germany after completing a degree from Oglethorpe University and joined the Macon volunteers. His service with the signal corps ended in 1864 with capture and imprisonment in Fort Lookout, Maryland, where he made the best of his predicament by entertaining fellow inmates with a flute he kept in his sleeve and with recitations of favorite poems. The four months he spent behind bars jeopardized his life with tuberculosis, which killed him in 1881 at age 39. From these difficult times came three children's books, *The Boy's King Arthur* (1880), *The Boy's Mabinogion* (1881), and *The Boy's Percy* (1882); works of prose criticism, *The Science of English Verse* (1880), *The English Novel* (1883), *Music and Poetry* (1898), and *Shakespeare and His Forerunners* (1902); and his prison novel, *Tiger Lilies* (1867). In hindsight at upbeat, optimistic prewar chauvinism, he remarks on the false hopes generated by the coming conflict:

> [War] offered test to all allegiances and loyalties; of church, of state; of private loves, of public devotion; of personal consanguinity; of social ties. To obscurity it held out eminence; poverty, wealth; to greed, a gorged maw; to speculation, legalized gambling; to patriotism, a country; to statesmanship, a government; to virtue, purity; to love, what all love most desires—a field wherein to assert itself by action. (Wann 1933, 193)

Following the extended parallelism, he exonerates President Jefferson Davis, "termed the ring-leader of the rebellion," for acquiescing to the will of Southerners, and declares the fate of warriors and noncombatants alike fair and just.

With an unusually cheerful disposition and a genius for regional poetry, Lanier shored up his compromised health and personal fortunes by playing the flute with Baltimore's Peabody Orchestra and writing some of the most popular lyrics of the postwar era. He published in *Lippincott's* magazine, *Harper's*, *Scribner's Monthly*, and other journals, catching incipient critical attention with "Corn" (1875), a genial, Thoreauesque nature lyric that makes undemanding symphonic music of waving green branches of beech, oak, and pine. The poet's appreciation for respite in solitude compares with the pastoral art of Henry Wadsworth Longfellow's *Evangeline*. In unself-conscious musing, Lanier pictures himself in lush settings:

> I wander to the zigzag-cornered fence
> Where sassafras, intrenched in brambles dense,
> Contests with stolid vehemence
> The march of culture, setting limb and thorn
> As pikes against the army of the corn.
> (Wann 1933, 170)

In addition to elegiac pieces, he mastered a jolly dialect for "The Power of Prayer: or, The First Steamboat Up the Alabama" (1875). The grandeur of his verse matured in "The Symphony" (1875), "Sunrise" (1880), and "The Marshes of Glynn" (1878), often cited as his best work. The beneficent beauties of the sea marsh come to life as he immerses himself in sensual imagery:

> Affable live oak, bending low—
> Thus—with your favor—soft, with a reverent hand,
> (Not lightly touching your person, Lord of the land!)
> Bending your beauty aside, with a step I stand
> On the firm-packed sand,
>   Free
> By a world of marsh that borders a world of sea.
> (Marshall 1979, 159)

Critics differ on their response to his luxuriant tone poems, which escape deeper into nature and repose than the usual surface treatments. The poet, canny of the unusual life-forms that flourish at the point where seawater inundates the biota of fresh streams and rivers, indicates his immersion with exultation:

> How still the plains of the waters be!
> The tide is in his ecstasy;
> The tide is at his highest height;
> And it is night.
> (Marshall 1979, 161)

His spirit seeks "the Vast of the Lord," but, like Hamlet, fears "the shapes that creep under the waters of sleep," a likely reference to a fitful contemplation of his looming demise.

In nonfiction, an unusual literary cycle derives from Eliot Wigginton, an energetic teacher and editor who guided his students in Rabun Gap, Georgia, in a project popularly known as Foxfire. Wigginton, a self-deprecating idea man, directed a magazine, compendia, and other spinoffs of his original title, *The Foxfire Book* (1969), which contains a melange of rural Americana from recipes and ghost stories to interviews with country cooks, healers, banjo makers, moonshiners, and tent preachers. Wigginton's first collection, originally pub-

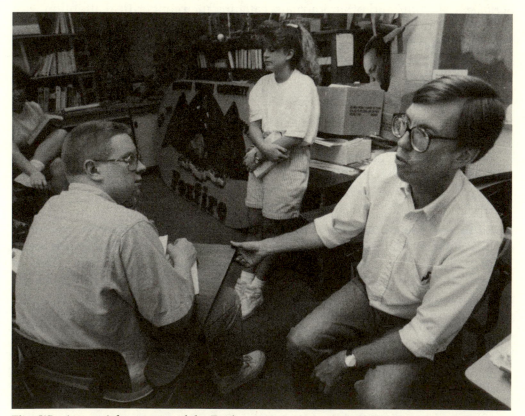

Eliot Wigginton, right, creator of the Foxfire project, meets with Rabun County, Georgia, high school students in 1991.

lished in *Foxfire* magazine, begins with photos and testimony of Aunt Arie, a mountain woman living alone in the style of her mountain forebears. An enthusiast of hillbilly ways, she avows, "We made a good life here, but we put in lots'a' time. Many an' many a night I've been workin' when two o'clock come in th' mornin' cardin'n'spinnin'n'sewin'." In defiance of change, she adds, "They want me t'sell an' move away from here, but I won't do it. It's just home—'at's all. I spent my happiest days here." (Wigginton 1970, 30)

A respected example of regionalism among African-American males is the fiction of dialect author Charles Waddell Chesnutt, a revered author of the Reconstruction South. A forerunner of the Harlem Renaissance, he wrote in difficult times, when wooing a publisher meant catering to racists. He was an admirer of Joel Chandler Harris, whose Uncle Remus character he emulated in style and ingratiating tone. A native of Cleveland, Ohio, Chesnutt followed his freeborn family in 1866 to Fayetteville, North Carolina, where he was educated by the local agency of the Freedman's Bureau. He set up a normal school to train black teachers and wrote for newspapers before returning to Cleveland to read and practice law. With the help of Creole regionalist George Washington Cable, he published *The Conjure Woman* (1899) and *The Wife of His Youth and Other Stories of the Color Line* (1899). Chesnutt is also remembered for three novels and a biography of orator and abolitionist Frederick Douglass.

The complexity of Chesnutt's dense, nongrammatical dialect humor is a stumbling block to readers of regional prose. An example from "Mars Jeems's Nightmare" demonstrates the difficulties of comprehending thick heartland dialogue:

> Mars Jeems did n' 'low no co'tin' er juneseyin' roun' his plantation.—said he wanted his niggers ter put dey min's on dey wuk, en not be wastin' dey time wid no sech foolis'ness. En he would n' let his han's git married,—said he wun n' raisin' niggers, but wuz raisin' cotton. (Rubin 1969, 381)

Chesnutt continues his accommodatingly humorous comment on slave management with Jeems's method of discouraging romance: At the beginning of a dalliance, he sold one of the parties "way down in Robeson County ter his yuther plantation, whar dey could n' nebber see one ernudder." Despite the thickness of the patois, Chesnutt published short fiction in *Atlantic Monthly* and the *Cleveland News and Herald,* and wrote on such controversial themes as passing for white, the focus of *The House behind the Cedars* (1900).

One of Chesnutt's stronger stories, "A Matter of Principle" (1899), turns on the irony of racism in the home of Cicero Clayton, a snobbish mulatto member of the Blue Vein Society, who inadvertently scares away a likely beau for his daughter Alice. In the confusion of their guest, Congressman Hamilton M. Brown, with a black African, Clayton sends his dark-skinned houseboy Jack with a false note declaring that Alice has diphtheria. The double irony occurs O. Henry–style in the final lines, in which Jack makes the most of the debacle to romance Alice for himself. Unaware that his almost-white daughter allows affectionate gestures from a black man, Cicero continues prating about his sententious philosophy, "What the white people of the United States need most, in dealing with this problem, is a higher conception of the brotherhood of man." (Guilds 1970, 292)

Unlike Chesnutt and his open defiance of Southern bigotry, Mary Noailles Murfree overcame a different type of prejudice with deception. A famed local-color writer from late-nineteenth-century Tennessee, she eased her own publication problems by taking male pseudonyms, originally R. Emmett Dembry, then Charles Egbert Craddock, under which she became famous. Murfree needed no assistance in learning her trade. The daughter of an established Tennessee family, she became an invalid in childhood from a fever. Hampered by lameness on one side of her body, she compensated with literary interests, receiving refinement and cultural stimulus at home before entering a Philadelphia finishing school. She remained unmarried and lived at home, putting her energies into submissions for *Lippincott's* magazine and *Atlantic Monthly* until blindness ended her work about 1920. A posthumous novel, *The Erskine Honeymoon*, appeared in installments in the *Nashville Banner*.

A beloved local colorist and author of 20 volumes, Murfree was accepted under her male persona because of a robust style, an irony in view of the paralysis that crippled one side of her body. She was successful with numerous genres, including social protest, historical romance, supernatural, dialect fiction, novella, and short stories. The first story, "The Dancin' Party at Harrison's Cove," appeared in *Atlantic Monthly* in May 1878. Her best-seller *In the Mountains of Tennessee* (1884) earned national fame and won Theodore Roosevelt as a fan. In the spring of 1885, with a strong following to back her decision, Murfree revealed her identity to publisher Thomas Bailey Aldrich and began to write under her real name. Largely because the demand for regionalism had waned, Murfree was never again as successful as she had been while writing mountain yarns.

Murfree's frequently anthologized story, "The 'Harnt' That Walks Chilhowee" (1884), told in the Southern mountain dialect of isolated whites, focuses on the qualities of Clarsie Giles, an overworked mountaineer girl who touches the heart of Simon Burney for being merciful to creatures in need:

> She air mighty savin' of the feelin's of everything, from the cow an' the mare down ter the dogs, an' pigs, an' chickens; always a-feedin' of 'em jes' ter the time, an' never draggin', an' clawin', an' beatin' of 'em. Why, that thar Clarsie can't put her foot out 'n the door, that every dumb beastis on this hyar place ain't a-runnin' ter git nigh her. (Wann 1933, 630)

A convoluted tale about a man running from the law, the story depicts the goodness of the tenderhearted Clarsie, who saves bites of food from her own plate and carries them in a bucket to feed the restless "ghost." This and other stories pleased readers of *Lippincott's* and *Atlantic Monthly*. Murfree lost her audience appeal after turning to longer fiction.

Three female regionalists from Tennessee took their example from Murfree. Already blessed with an ambiguous name, Will Allen Dromgoole produced 14 novels and articles for the *Nashville Banner*. Her poetry earned her the designation of Poet Laureate of Tennessee and Poet Laureate of the Poetry Society of the South. Less well known, Sarah Barnwell Elliott, a native of Georgia, settled in Tennessee and produced novels, including *Jerry* (1891) and *The Durket Sperret* (1898). In contrast to the other writers of Appalachian local color, Emma Belle Miles wrote of isolation and poverty from her experiences living in a cabin on Walden's Ridge, which she described in *The Spirit of the Mountains* (1905).

Regional literature from the East Coast outdistanced Murfree and her followers in fame, readership, and influence. A robust voice from the Gullah-rich county of Laurens, South Carolina, Julia Mood Peterkin absorbed the West African patois of her nanny, Mauma. Peterkin replicated local idiom and conversational style in vignettes and short fiction for *Smart Set*, *Poetry*, *American Mercury*, and the *Reviewer*, which published her first sketch, "From Lang Syne Plantation" (1921). Her titles grew more playful: "The Merry-Go-Round" in 1921 and five more in 1922: "Cat-Fish," "Cooch's Premium," "The Plat-Eye," "The Ortymobile," and "Betsy." After earning an M.A. degree from Converse College and marrying planter William Peterkin, she took Carl Sandburg's advice and eluded stifling domestication as well as inflated belletrism by retreating to private quarters to write about what interested her: the semibarbarism of plantation life. Cut off from literary companionship, she complained to the staff at the *Review:*

> I am trying hard to get a good medium for my stuff. There is much here to be written and I want it to be intelligible and attractive. There's nobody here to discuss it with me. I cannot develop unless I have criticism, and while I'm not looking for blows at all, I do want the reaction of somebody who is interested in my doing things right. (Clark 1931, 222)

In solitude, she created fictional escapades for her novels—*Green Thursday* (1924), *Black April* (1927), and *Scarlet Sister Mary* (1928), a Pulitzer Prize winner.

Perhaps isolation benefited Peterkin's work by freeing her from society's rigorous rules about what the Southern author was allowed to mention in the outside world. Her best work, *Scarlet Sister Mary*, was so disconcerting to local tastes that the public library in Gaffney, South Carolina, banned it from the stacks, and aristocrats refrained from mentioning Peterkin's name. The reasons are obvious: The protagonist, Sister Mary, is a lively, sexually uninhibited fieldworker who weds July, a rounder and wife abuser, but languishes in his absence. With the advice of midwife Maum Hannah to Mary about retrieving strayed husbands, Peterkin captures both the Southern affinity for spiritualism and the music of the low-country dialect:

> You take my advice an' go see Daddy Cudjoe an' get em to fix you a charm to keep July home. Daddy is a wise man. E knows black magic as well as white. E could gi you a charm so strong July never could leave you no more. Not long as e lives. Daddy's wise. (Peterkin 1928, 114)

Less cumbersome than the patois of Chesnutt and Harris, Peterkin's dropped consonants and smooth elisions re-create the low-country sound without hampering cadence.

In a scene reminiscent of Dubose Heyward's *Porgy* (1925), source of George and Ira Gershwin's folk opera *Porgy and Bess* (1935), Peterkin thickens the Gullah sounds of a hearty evangelistic prayer session during high winds. Sister Mary, an amoral pariah, struggles to save her home from impending destruction by risking a return to a church prayer service, from which she has been ousted for sexual impropriety. A fellow evangelical asks, "You want to go up to de mourner's bench, Si May-e [Sister Mary]?" Still the lusty, unrepentant picaro, Mary shouts, "No, Jedus! I want to go home! Fo Gawd's sake, take me home." (Peterkin 1928, 273) Peterkin concludes Mary's reaffirmation in the church with the contrite sinner meekly awaiting a second baptism. A fillip of humor ends the novel as Daddy Cudjoe requests her conjure rag, since Scarlet Sister Mary is "gwine to quit wid mens now." Mary smiles seductively, "I couldn' gi way my love-charm. E's all I got now to keep me young." (Peterkin 1928, 345)

In *Bright Skin* (1932), a novel of unrequited love and longing, Peterkin's insistence on telling the truth about plantation society reveals an unpleasant fact—the existence of color prejudice among blacks. Less sanguine and idyllic than her earlier works, the story of Blue depicts harsh episodes in the life of his wife Cricket, a pretty, curly-haired girl-woman whose skin is too light to suit cruel Africa-black neighbors. Aunt Fan warns her nephew Blue about marrying Cricket, whom she predicts will be as wild as Cricket's mother, a free spirit who mated with a white man. Blue, who has adored Cricket from his youth, insists on marriage, even though Cricket is set on having Man Jay, a no-good local who has run off to New York. Her actions prove Aunt Fan's prediction that Cricket, as heedless of good sense as her mother, is rushing toward disaster.

Against the intertwinings of jealousy and mating, Peterkin depicts intense, vocal gospel meetings in which the black community rids itself of sin and guilt. Sequential Sundays offer baptism, testimony of dreams and religious conversion, the Lord's supper, and the "right hand of fellowship" extended while worshippers march past the pulpit of Heaven's Gate Church singing:

Religion is a powerful chain,
Every link spells Jesus' name.
All you sin been taken away,
Glory, Hallelujah.
(Peterkin 1973, 215)

The revival season ends with a circle dance to the spiritual "I Shall Not Be Moved," sung while the righteous wash one another's feet and weep for joy. Among the cries of exaltation, Cricket shrieks when Big Pa falls dead. Sunday quiet gives way to the sawing of boards for a coffin "so Big Pa need not sleep his last sleep in a store-bought box." (Peterkin 1973, 218) At the burial the next day, Cricket, the too-light outcast, places a symbolic bouquet of "white snow on the mountain" near Big Pa's head marker.

The popularity of regional writing buoyed the career of Virginian Ellen Glasgow, a contemporary of Peterkin, Murfree, and Dromgoole. Reared like one of Richmond's patrician belles and presented to society at the obligatory St. Cecilia Ball, Glasgow grew up among the FFV—an insider's reference to the First Families of Virginia. Because of delicate health, she was educated at home, where she read from the Victorian era's rebel philosophers: Charles Darwin, Arthur Schopenhauer, Thomas Malthus, John Stuart Mill, Thomas Henry Huxley, and Friedrich Nietzsche. At the University of Virginia, which refused to admit women, she insisted on taking the honors exam in political economy and passed it. An iconoclast who refused the persona of the simpering debutante, she rebelled against cloying nineteenth-century strictures and embraced liberation in the New South, which abandoned what Glasgow termed "expiring gestures of chivalry" and outworn notions of decorous femininity in favor of the vigorous intellectual curiosity of the technological age. (Glasgow 1929, ix) Of her intent to create a true picture of the Tidewater's evolving character, events, and themes, she commented sensibly on the treasure at hand:

> The race that inherits a heroic legend must have accumulated an inexhaustible resource of joy, beauty, and tragic passion. To discard this rich inheritance in the pursuit of the standard utilitarian style is for the Southern novelist, pure folly. (Gross 1971, 117)

Glasgow's first novel, *The Descendant* (1897), was published anonymously. A naturalistic tale of post–Civil War class restructuring, it initiated a lengthy career that concluded with an autobiography, *A Woman Within* (1954), written after a near-fatal heart attack and published posthumously. The work resounds with loving remembrances of her friends among the literary South, especially James Branch Cabell and Marjorie Kinnan Rawlings.

Glasgow's determination to devote her talents to Virginia's social history resulted in a respected body of fiction and a literary reputation that outclassed other writers of her age. The author's abandonment of the region's lofty self-image and elegiac self-pity produced a stir among Southerners still clinging to the antebellum mindset. In *Deliverance* (1904), she describes a childlike female who awakens to the postwar South:

> She dwelt upon some undiscovered planet—a world peopled with shades and governed by an ideal group of abstract laws. She lived upon lies . . . and thrived upon the sweetness she extracted from them. For her the Confederacy had never fallen, the quiet of her dreamland had been disturbed by no invading army, and the three hundred slaves, who had in reality scattered like chaff before the wind, she still saw in her cheerful visions tilling her familiar fields. It was as if she had fallen asleep . . . and had dreamed on steadily through the years. (Rubin 1969, 423)

Not readily acclaimed by Richmond's elite, Glasgow ignored local critics and created an egalitarian cast of characters more in keeping with the ideals of democracy, as with the poor farm laborers and sturdy working class in *The Voice of the People* (1900), *The Romance of a Plain Man* (1909), and *The Miller of Old Church* (1911). Her female protagonists in *Virginia* (1913), *Life and Gabriella: The Story of a Woman's Courage* (1916), *Barren Ground* (1925), and *The Battle-Ground* (1929) attack constraints on women, whether they derive from belittling, patronizing, or idealizing. As Betty, an assertive, pre–Scarlett O'Hara heroine in *The Battle-Ground*, addresses Dan, her weak-willed love, she speaks with the self-assurance of the liberated female: "We will begin again . . . and this time, my dear, we will begin together." (Glasgow 1929, 444) Glasgow's bittersweet Queensborough satires, an urban cycle composed of *The Romantic Comedian* (1926), *They Stooped*

Ellen Glasgow (1873–1945)

to Folly (1929), and *The Sheltered Life* (1932), have an Austenesque quality. They reprise her defiance of Southern patriarchy, as do *Barren Ground* and *Vein of Iron* (1935), both titles from her Old Dominion cycle.

Although sheltered by parents and a long-suffering black nurse because of headaches and a hearing impairment, Glasgow shook off debilitating parental expectations to travel in Europe, live for five years in New York City's Upper West Side, and conduct a discreet affair with a married man, the mysterious Gerald B. Independent by nature, she flourished in her chosen field, enjoyed the celebrity of a best-selling author, and cultivated friendships with Joseph Conrad and Henry James. She expressed support for women's rights by helping to found the Equal Suffrage League of Virginia, and she encouraged fellow authors by organizing the Conference of Southern Writers at the University of Virginia. She reached a height of achievement in 1942 with *In This Our Life*, a Pulitzer Prize-winning novel followed by a sequel, *Beyond Defeat* (1966). A transitional author and forerunner of twentieth-century realism, she displayed a competence with historical saga and established a place among the Southern moderns who emerged from an era of syrupy sentimentality to a truer vision of heroic standards.

Unlike Glasgow, Virginian Earl Hamner, Jr., freelance radio scriptwriter and author of *Spencer's Mountain* (1961) and its sequel, *The Homecoming* (1970), earned a prized place in Southern literature for a return to sentiment. His rural family vignettes, which preceded popular film versions and a family-oriented television series, "The Waltons," are set in the Virginia mountains. Episodes in the life of Clay-Boy Spencer intertwine his coming-of-age with the mores and values of parents and forebears. His father and mother, Clay and Olivia Spencer, protect the mountain that bears the family surname so that their children can enjoy a heritage of pristine woods, maple groves, and the profusion of wildflowers that brighten the Virginia hill country. The counterpoint of rusticity and urge for modern conveniences thrusts Clay into moments of guilt. He frees himself from doubts about preserving the Spencer heritage with sporadic promises to build Olivia a house on the mountain. Hamner notes that Olivia expects "Clay to go to his grave waiting for that magical day when the money, the time and the materials would appear with which to build the house." (Hamner 1961, 235) The 1963 Universal Studios movie version of *Spencer's Mountain* stars Henry Fonda and Maureen O'Hara as the parents and James MacArthur as Clay-Boy.

In *The Homecoming*, Hamner resets the family's lifetime of quiet satisfaction against the unease of the Depression. The elder Clay, who is late to arrive home on Christmas Eve 1933, leaves Olivia and their eight children to cope with a mounting anxiety that borders on despair. The story concludes with a last-minute resolution: Clay returns from his job at the Du Pont Company in Waynesboro, 40 miles away, after hitchhiking through deep snow to Hickory Creek. He lightens the family's mood with gifts from Santa Claus, whom he claims to have seen fly across the sky and land on the Spencers' roof. The crowning gift is a pot of hyacinths, a spot of spring to reaffirm Olivia's hope. The 1971 movie version stars Richard Thomas as Clay-Boy and Patricia Neal as his mother in a taut relationship; the television series replaced Neal with Michael Learned, a good balance of love, grace, and discipline against the lusty, hardworking father and family sage, played by Ralph Waite. The compelling quality of the television series comes from the Walton grandparents, a beloved pair played by Ellen Corby and Will Geer. Their near-mythic additions of morality and heritage create a feeling of Southern tradition rich in love, faith, and promise.

A fleeting voice in the canon of Southern humor comes from the Georgia-based novels of Olive Ann Burns, a journalist for the *Atlanta Constitution-Journal*. A local humorist endowed with humanistic vision, she wrote *Cold Sassy Tree* (1984) and its sequel, *Leaving Cold Sassy* (1992), left unfinished after her death from lymphoma in 1990. Drawing on family memories of Commerce, Georgia, for Southern customs, history, and eccentricities, she reset a family event—the death of her great-grandmother Power and her great-grandfather's remarriage three weeks after the funeral. Squibs of data resonate with such Southern trivia as the first steam fire engine in "aught-one or aught-two," "Mr. Henry W. New-South Grady," and reflections on the snobbish town folk, whose fraternization with mill-hill children threatens embarrassment for anyone seen with a worker "sweaty and lintheaded from the factory or, Lord forbid, . . . coming out of a privy." (Burns 1984, 83, 108)

A framework novel told in 1914 by 22-year-old Hoyt Willis "Will" Tweedy, *Cold Sassy Tree* focuses on the outrage of Grandpa Rucker's family after violating three fixed taboos: Don't marry too soon, don't marry too young, and don't marry a carpetbagger. Miss Love, a strong-minded Baltimore suffragist, earns her keep as hatmaker at Rucker's store and agrees to a union of convenience that exists only on a marriage certificate. The family's consternation batters in vain against Grandpa's decision:

> Aunt Loma was bout to burst. "Think, Pa!" she ordered, tears streaming down her face. "Just think. Ma hasn't been d-dead but three w-w-weeks!"
> "Well, good gosh a'mighty!" he thundered. "She's dead as she'll ever be, ain't she? Well, ain't she?" (Burns 1984, 6)

The Blakeslees' love match blossoms on Valentine's Day, when he buys his new bride a "graphophone" and lively disks to play. In return, she teaches him the turkey trot. Burns's sentiment grows heavy as Rucker nears death from a beating after he tries to nab a robber. He dies without knowing about the second Mrs. Blakeslee's pregnancy.

Burns's contrast of Rucker's first wife, Mattie Lou, with Miss Love reflects the change in Southern mores. The first Mrs. Blakeslee was the dutiful wife, mother, and grandmother. In ornate euphemistic style, the local paper mourns, "Asleep in Jesus, blessed sleep from which none ever wake to weep . . . a sacred mother of Israel, has gone to receive the cross of righteousness which God has promised to all those who love His appearing." (Burns 1984, 59) The exuberant second wife, named Love for her birth on February 14, violates Georgia stereotypes by staying home on Sunday with the windows uncurtained and pounding out Ta-Ra-Ra-Boom-de-Ay on the piano. A tender nostalgia piece, the novel made the Book-of-the-Month Club list, was reproduced by Bantam Audio and Books on Tape, and was featured in 1990 as TNT's made-for-television movie, starring Richard Widmark as Grandpa Rucker Blakeslee and Faye Dunaway as Love Simpson Blakeslee, his loving milliner-turned-owner's wife. Neill Patrick Harris plays the central intelligence, Will Tweedy. (Auchincloss 1965; Beatty et al. 1952; Berry 1974; Blain et al. 1990; Buck 1992; Burns 1984, 1992; Caldwell 1933, 1940; Chapman 1974; Clark 1931; *Contemporary Authors* 1994; Davidson and Wagner-Martin 1995; Ehrlich and Carruth 1982; Gabbert 1991; Giles 1956; Glasgow 1929, 1939, 1954, 1963; Grau 1964; Gross 1971; Guilds 1970; Hamner 1961, 1970; Hibbard 1931; Inge 1990; Johns 1996; Kunitz and Haycraft 1938; Low and Clift 1981; Marshall 1979; Owen 1965; Payne 1981; Peterkin 1928, 1940, 1973; Quinn 1936; Rouse 1962; Rubin 1969; Rubin et al. 1985; Sherr and Kazickas 1994; *Something about the Author* 1991; Spencer 1956; Stein 1979; Steinberg 1984; Stithem 1994; Summer 1984, 1992; Trent et al. 1946; *Video Hound's* 1994; Wann 1933; Wilson and Ferris 1989)

See also the Civil War era; the colonial and federalist eras; the Mississippi River; *Porgy and Bess*.

RELIGIOUS FUNDAMENTALISM

Because an enthusiastic religious fundamentalism is indigenous to Southern life, religious motifs, lyrics of spirituals and gospel hymns, and biblical themes are standard elements of Southern literature. Among fundamentalists, worship is an active, pervasive facet of family life and a driving force in community activities, particularly during controversy over such divisive social issues as desegregation and miscegenation. Despite messages of love, acceptance, and inclusion of outsiders in the New Testament, Southern fundamentalism evolved in separate racial camps, each with its own tenets, rituals, and hymnology. In a 1915 evaluation of a Ku Klux Klan rally in Stone Mountain, Georgia, journalist Harry Golden connects fervid fundamentalism to white supremacy, a perverted offshoot. Tongue in cheek, he exults, "Southern white, Protestant womanhood henceforth would be protected from being forced into concubinage to the Negro, into the brothels maintained by Catholic monks, and into the factory harems of the Jews." (Golden 1959, 260) His witty rejoinder masks a real weakness of fundamentalism: the dispersion of half-truths and ignorance, a product of the fertile imaginations of a religious group skeptical of rival faiths, alternate interpretations of the Bible, racial mixing, and liberal education.

Unlike other areas that accommodate a variety of philosophies and styles of worship, the South tends toward the Baptist faith and a bedrock conservatism that insists on a personal relationship with Jesus Christ, a public acknowledgment of being "saved" by the Almighty rather than earning salvation through good works, baptism by whole immersion before a body of witnesses, and—the keystone of faith—acceptance of a literal interpretation of scripture. Of the Southern fundamentalist, Golden remarks upon the insistence of white zealots on proselytizing Jews. In *Only in America* (1958), he warns that assimilation into Protestant communities endangers the fragile Jewish community. He concludes, "The fear involves those who have always considered themselves the *most* assimilated, the *most* successful, and the *most* integrated; and most scared of all is the fellow who had a Confederate grandfather." (Golden 1958, 140) The influence of fundamentalism on politics and social issues encourages a narrow interpretation of morals and public and private behavior. Fundamentalists generally abhor and repudiate homosexuality, divorce, adultery, premarital intercourse, and abortion. Their tenets discourage displays of affection and sexuality, revealing clothing and ostentatious makeup, and closed-couple dancing.

Southern literature is rife with the fervor and extremism that fundamentalism encourages. Mark Twain, a master satirist, isolates the vocal cadences and poses of the evangelist, whose mastery of group psychology is inherent in the oratory of noted Southern preachers, particularly Dr. Billy Graham, Reverend Jesse Jackson, and Dr. Martin Luther King, Jr. Twain lampoons the use of group coercion by unscrupulous tent revivalists in chapters 19–20 of *The Adventures of Huckleberry Finn*. The duke and king, a pair of rapscallions who manipulate Jim and Huck and commandeer their raft on its journey north, define religion as an open field to be worked for profit. The older of the two hucksters claims to make his living at a number of trades, including patent medicine, acting, mesmerism, phrenology, teaching at a singing-geography school, lecturing, laying on of hands, telling fortunes, and missionizing. In a scene revealing the idiosyncrasies of the latter profession, the duo drops in at a crude tent revival in Pokeville, set in sheds fitted out with log-slab benches where rural people collect in search of divine grace. In standard charismatic form, the preacher raises his Bible and shouts, "It's the brazen serpent in the wilderness! Look upon it and live!" to which the congregation replies, "Glory!—A-a-*men!*" (Twain 1962, 148) An altar call to the mourners' bench brings the mentally and emotionally ailing and the shame-ridden. The extoller welcomes hesitant stragglers with "come with a broken spirit! come with a contrite heart! come in your rags and sin and dirt! the waters that cleanse is free, the door of heaven stands open—oh, enter in and be at rest!"

With no hidden agenda of derision or consternation at the practice of saving souls, Huck, Twain's naïf, describes the proceedings of the altar call. He comments that the shouting and crying obscure the preacher's words, but the people continue pouring down the aisles with tears wetting their faces. At the front benches, they "sung and shouted and flung themselves down on the straw, just crazy and wild." (Twain 1962, 148) The inclusion of the scene in Twain's introduction of his two con artists derides the bilking of the unsuspecting of donations put to illicit purposes after the king confesses to piracy on the Indian Ocean and promises to reform his life by returning to his fellow freebooters to rescue them from perdition. The joyous reclamation of a former sinner reveals the good-hearted generosity of rural Southerners. Twain depicts them as likable rubes who are easily tricked into thanks, praise, kisses and displays of joy, and invitations for the king to visit their homes. With a deft return to his real persona, the king filches a three-gallon jug of whiskey and reflects on the ill-gotten profits: "Take it all around, it laid over any day he'd ever put in in the missionarying line." In his opinion, "It warn't no use talking, heathens don't amount to shucks alongside of pirates to work a camp meeting with." (Twain 1962, 150)

A realistic treatment of a similar community of believers occurs in Richard Wright's *Black Boy* (1945), an autobiography that details the punitive aspect of a closed religious group on an adamant unbeliever. While living with his devout maternal grandmother, the Richard character develops an individuality that appalls his family. Stress from kin and friends forces Richard to defend his opinions and rebut their stringent proselytizing. At length, to please his invalid mother, he relents and is baptized. Wright characterizes the rite as a symbol of group solidarity rather than a private testament of faith. Of the rampant emotionalism that accompanies the ritual, the author says:

> A low, soft hymn began. *This may be the last time, I don't know . . .*
> They sang it, hummed it, crooned it, moaned it, implying in sweet, frightening tones that if we did not join the church then and there we might die in our sleep that very night and go straight to hell. (Wright 1966, 168)

Because the family uses baptism as a symbol of submission, Richard must fight for self-sufficiency. Against the shallow religiosity of his uncle, Richard denounces baptism and salvation with a cursory "To hell with that." To his uncle's remonstrances, Richard retorts, "You are not an example to me; you could never be. . . . You're a *warning*. Your life isn't so hot that you can tell me what to do." (Wright 1966, 176)

Similarly disillusioned with the concept of salvation through acceptance of Christ and baptism is Ruth Anne "Bone" Boatwright, protagonist of Dorothy Allison's *Bastard Out of Carolina* (1992). Following acceptance into a local church and baptism at Bushy Creek, Bone is unmoved by the experience, which occurs under a hackneyed motif—a painting of Jesus at the Jordan River:

> When my head went under, my throat closed up and my ears went deaf. With cloudy water soaking my dress and my eyes tight shut, I couldn't hear the choir or feel the preacher's bruising grip. Whatever magic Jesus' grace promised, I didn't feel it. (Allison 1992, 152)

Bone's creek immersion results in chills, sweating, and fever from a dunking in polluted water. As assertive as Richard Wright, she retreats from a public show to a private, self-made faith comprised of reading from the Book of Revelation. In its fiery directives and visions of damnation, she takes comfort in the hope of a promised apocalypse, "God's retribution on the wicked." Because of the sexual abuse Bone suffers from her stepfather, she welcomes the message of Revelation: "It struck me like gospel music, it promised vindication."

Melissa Fay Greene, a contemporary of Dorothy Allison and the author of *Praying for Sheetrock* (1991), acknowledges the juxtaposition of religiosity with seamier aspects of the Southern working-class psyche. In an evaluation of the good and bad that coexist in standard down-home scenarios, she remarks:

> The secret life of the black people of McIntosh County unfolded inside closed cabins; and within the humble little Holiness churches, where perspiring worshipers in radiant clothing jumped and chanted in unison; and inside the weedy roadside juke joints, where moonshine and marijuana changed pockets by the light of neon beer signs. (Greene 1991, 79)

Within the confines of an ostensibly godly community, Greene finds evidence of a world of sin in shrimpers who gather on board their boats by night to drink whiskey and play cards by the light of swinging kerosene lamps. A greater arena of wrongdoing, however, is the white majority that circumscribes the Negro ghetto and tyrannizes nonwhites with segregation, rejection, and oppressive social dicta. Greene characterizes such racism as "the intentional betrayal of the black community," enforced by poverty, joblessness, and subtle forms of coercion.

Control is a significant factor in the success of religious fundamentalism. In a stage satire showcased at the Spoleto festival in Charleston, South Carolina, Larry Larson, Levi Lee, and Rebecca Wackler's *Tent Meeting* (1987) delighted audiences with their caricature of the stereotypical Southern street preacher. The playwrights overdo the audacity of Reverend Ed, an overbearing revivalist and child abuser, to create a figure known to followers of twentieth-century scandals among indiscreet televangelists, sonorous expounders of gospel, and religious charlatans. A failed father and devious shyster, Reverend Ed avoids truth by raving, "God's on his highway and all is right with the world." (Larson et al. 1987, 7) By implication, he leads his dim-witted son Darrell in an attempt to drown the freakish infant Reverend Ed sired on his daughter Becky Ann. Act III, a stage re-creation of a fundamentalist baptism, depicts the frenzied sin-bashing, breath-sucking style of the pulpit ecstasy:

> Sweet Jesus . . . you have shown us that . . . even in death . . . there is resurrection. And let it be known . . . that . . . in the second coming of our Lord . . . sweet Jesus became a man. (Larson et al. 1987, 47)

The chaotic, yet predictable spiel jerks on in disconnected cadence toward a lengthy, supercharged emotional jolt, "and was resurrected . . . as an eggplant." The skill of Reverend Ed to move people with his rambling, emotive sermon contributes to rising hilarity. Unwitting viewers get caught up in the hypnotic images and find themselves snookered by a disreputable, jake-leg Bible-thumper. The character, by nature deserving of ridicule, seems to stand in front of a tomato-hurling mob with defiant nose uplifted in delicious anticipation of his just merits. In this pose, caricature suits satire as a broad stroke of candor encircling the figure in the spotlight for the world's delight and edification. (Allison 1992; Golden 1958, 1959; Greene 1991; Larson et al. 1987; Twain 1962; Wilson and Ferris 1989; Wright 1966)

See also Mencken, H. L.; O'Connor, Flannery.

SHORT FICTION IN SOUTHERN LITERATURE

Short fiction is a Southern specialty, as demonstrated by the works of Shirley Ann Grau, Flannery O'Connor, Richard Wright, Allan Gurganus, and others. The master creator of the American short story, Edgar Allan Poe, a contemporary of Honoré de Balzac and Nathaniel Hawthorne, deserves the preponderance of fame for innovation in Southern short stories. His 68 titles extend over a variety of genres: arabesque, grotesque, science fiction, ratiocination, literary hoax, treasure hunt, and psychological thriller. In critical essays he declared that short stories should strive for a unity of effect. In his review of Hawthorne's *Twice Told Tales* in *Graham's* magazine, April–May 1842, he stated:

> In the whole composition there should be no word written of which the tendency, direct or indirect, is not to the one pre-established design. And by such means, with such care and skill, a picture is at length painted which leaves in the mind of him who contemplates it with a kindred art, a sense of the fullest satisfaction. The idea of the tale, its thesis, has been presented unblemished. (Quinn 1936, 91)

It was a goal he attained in "Metzengerstein" (1832), "A Descent into the Maelstrom" (1841), "The Masque of the Red Death" (1842), "The Mystery of Marie Rogêt" (1842), "The Premature Burial" (1844), "The Purloined Letter" (1844), and "The System of Dr. Tarr and Prof. Fether" (1845).

Poe set his cornucopia of short stories over a broad, imaginative literary map: the sea near Java for "Ms. Found in a Bottle," a cell in Spain in "The Pit and the Pendulum," "The Cask of Amontillado" in a crypt, classical Greece for "Shadow—A Parable," "Hop-Frog" in a medieval royal court, "The Assignation" on the Ponte di Sospiri (Bridge of Sighs) in Venice, "The Murders in the Rue Morgue" in the Quartier St. Roch of Paris, a London coffeehouse for "The Man of the Crowd," and the Hudson River for his witty hoax story "The Sphinx." Out of the 68, his most Southern settings occur in "The Oblong Box," "The Balloon Hoax," and "The Gold Bug." In the latter, Poe depicts William Legrand and his manumitted servant Jupiter using a scarab to work out Captain Kidd's cryptograph to locate a treasure chest on Sullivan's Island near Charleston, South Carolina.

Within Poe's study of the Gullah dialect and an offshore Atlantic island, he pursues arcane details, such as the scarabaeus, the mythic beetle held sacred in classical Egypt as a talisman of Ra, the sun god, and carved on amulets and jewelry to protect owners from disease, loss, and misfortune. Jupiter sums up the qualities of the "goole-bug" in dialect replete with West African influence:

> Claws enuff, massa, and mouff too. I nebber did see sich a deuced bug—he kick and he bite ebery ting what cum near him. Massa Will cotch him fuss, but had for to let him go 'gin mighty quick, I tell you—den was de time he must ha' got de bite. I didn't like de look ob de bug mouff, myself, nohow, so I wouldn't take hold ob him wid my finger, but I cotch him wid a piece ob paper dat I found. I rap him up in de paper and stuff a piece of it in he mouff—dat was de way. (Poe 1962, 174)

The shift of *th* to *f* and *d*, pronunciation of "first" as "fuss," the pronoun *he* for *his*, and the creation of verb forms such as cotch (caught) and rap (wrapped) particularizes not only the place but the race of the speaker and the era of linguistic development in which the story takes place. Once the treasure is recovered, Jupiter leaps and frolics in the gold as though luxuriating in a bath. Energizing the story with an authenticated black point of view, he exclaims, "And dis all cum ob de goole-bug! de putty goole-bug! the poor little goole-bug, what I boxed in dat sabage kind ob style! Aint you shamed ob yourself, nigger?—answer me dat!" (Poe 1962, 188)

The source of the lost-treasure motif is the legendary Carolina coast, an in-and-out nightmare of coves and backwaters frequented by pirates and freebooters. Captain Kidd (1645–1701), a notorious privateer, supposedly wrecked a longboat on Sullivan's Island, where the parchment was found. The cryptograph, concealed in invisible ink, appears when subjected to hot water. Composed of numbers, ciphers, and punctuation marks, the lengthy coded message reads like computerese. Using ratiocination, Poe's term for deductive logic, the hero, William Legrand, unscrambles the mystery and discloses the site of the bishop's hotel, the devil's seat, and the spot where Kidd buried his accumulation of rings, chains, crucifixes, censers, punch bowls, sword hilts, and European coins, totaling "three hundred and fifty pounds avoirdupois," worth a million and a half dollars. (Poe 1962, 190) Poe's skill at blending detail with suspense makes "The Gold Bug" a popular example of short fiction in textbooks and collections.

Sharing the title of the best author of Southern short works is writer and reporter William Sydney Porter, the North Carolinian who moved to Texas and renamed himself O. Henry. One of his best humorous stories, "The Ransom of Red Chief," published in *Whirligigs* (1910), places a tale of kidnap and comeuppance in Alabama. The first-person narrator comments drily, "There was a town down there, as flat as a flannel-cake, and called Summit, of course." (Henry 1953, 1144) Proceeding on that note, the story unveils how the speaker and Bill Driscoll pooled their "joint capital of about six hundred dollars" and knocked together a plan to milk "philoprogenitoveness," a parental love of offspring that, they declare, "is strong in semi-rural communities." Selecting the only child of Ebenezer Dorset, a "mortgage financier and a stern, upright collection-plate passer and forecloser," they snatch a likely child victim and hide him in a cave on a mountain two miles from town. (Henry 1953, 1144)

Porter spoofs the kidnappers' difficulties with Johnny Dorset, self-christened Red Chief, who talks them to distraction; asks long, disjointed strings of questions; and smacks Bill in the eye with a piece of brick. From the outset, Red Chief declares that abduction is a lot more fun than living with his parents. At daybreak, the narrator intervenes as the chief sits on Bill's chest and uses a case knife to remove his scalp. Bill, who delivers an unholy string of "indecent, terrifying, humiliating screams," considers using his gun after the chief compounds the morning's insults by dropping a hot boiled potato down Bill's back and squashing it. (Henry 1953, 1146) The reply to their ransom note makes clear the father's delight in a respite from Red Chief. To end the kidnappers' misery, Dorset offers a counterproposal: "You bring Johnny home and pay me two hundred and fifty dollars in cash, and I agree to take him off your hands." (Henry 1953, 1151) O. Henry brings the unwise abduction of the Alabama brat to a painless conclusion. Lest he require "a bed in Bedlam," Bill makes the trade, holding Dorset to a promise to subdue Red Chief while Bill crosses the "Central, Southern, and Middle Western States, and be legging it trippling for the Canadian border." (Henry 1953, 1152)

In a less jocular vein, Porter writes of Colonel Aquila Telfair, protagonist of "The Rose of Dixie" from *Options* (1909), set in the fanciful Toombs City, Georgia. A stereotypical Southern aristocrat, Telfair is studying Burton's *Anatomy of Melancholy* as a deputation arrives, finding him eager and financially ripe for an offer to edit the *Rose of Dixie* magazine, whose watchword is "Of, For, and By the South." (Henry 1953, 683) After orating for 40 minutes on "English literature from Chaucer to Macaulay" and the battle of Chancellorsville, Telfair accepts. (Henry 1953, 681) With a staff that O. Henry describes as "a whole crate of Georgia peaches," Telfair thrives, building business to five times its original bottom line, yet failing to expand the world's awareness of his "Rose."

Porter swells his enjoyment of spoofing mossbacked sons of the South with the introduction of the advertising manager Beauregard Fitzhugh Banks, "a young man in a lavender necktie, whose grandfather had been the Exalted High Pillow-slip of the Kuklux [*sic*] Klan." (Henry 1953, 682) After the magazine picks up speed by publishing a view of Andrew Jackson's home, engravings of the "battle of Manasses [*sic*]," a biography of Confederate spy Belle Boyd, an article on the Hatfield-McCoy feud, and poems by Leonina Vashti Haricot, a New York promoter named T. T. Thacker labels Telfair's "Rose" a "Southern parlor organ." (Henry 1953, 684) Telfair rebuts Thacker's diatribe against the journal's editorial policy with a literary coup. He publishes:

Second Message to Congress
Written for
THE ROSE OF DIXIE
BY
A Member of the Well-Known
BULLOCK FAMILY, OF GEORGIA
T. Roosevelt.
(Henry 1953, 689)

In similar tongue-in-cheek joshing of self-important Southerners, Porter's "The Duplicity of Hargraves" from *Sixes and Sevens* (1911) ridicules Major Pendleton Talbot, a distinguished scion of Mobile, who has suffered a reversal of fortunes. He and his daughter Lydia take a room in Washington. Talbot strikes up a friendship with fellow boarder Henry Hopkins Hargraves, a vaudevillian who thrives on anecdotes from Dixie. Seated over the ingredients for mint juleps, the two discuss the South's beloved pastimes:

> The fox hunts, the 'possum suppers, the hoe downs and jubilees in the Negro quarters, the banquets in the plantation-house hall, when invitations went for fifty miles around; the occasional feuds with the neighboring gentry; the major's duel with Rathbone Culbertson about Kitty Chalmers, who afterward married a Thwaite of South Carolina. (Henry 1953, 873)

On visiting an evening performance of Hargraves's stage act, entitled "A Magnolia Flower," Talbot discovers that the enterprising actor has isolated the old gentleman's idiosyncracies and produced a made-up persona "as nearly resembling Major Talbot as one pea does another." (Henry 1953, 875)

To Lydia's chagrin, the popular stage performance leaves Talbot fuming, muttering, "This is an abominable desecration." (Henry 1953, 876) Hargraves, however, is unaware of the deep insult, and the next morning reads aloud to Talbot from the *Post*'s critique of his "first nighter":

> His conception and portrayal of the old-time Southern colonel, with his absurd grandiloquence, his eccentric garb, his quaint idioms and phrases, his moth-eaten pride of family, and his really kind heart, fastidious sense of honor, and lovable simplicity, is the best delineation of a character rôle on the boards today. (Henry 1953, 876)

Hargraves compounds the humiliation by offering Talbot several hundred dollars to salve the hurt, thus corroborating Talbot's belief that Northerners are dishonorable shysters who will pass up no opportunity to turn a fast buck. Hargraves gets his share of revenge by playing Uncle Mose Mitchell, a former slave who supposedly returns to pay Talbot $300 he owed for selling some mules. Lydia, who is unbound by her father's extremes of honor, conceals Hargraves's duplicity.

O. Henry's ragbag cast of lovable rascals, grifters, and criminals contrasts the rugged Granny Weatherall, a memorably crusty figure in the canon of Porter's second cousin, Katherine Anne Porter. A Pulitzer Prize–winning realist, Porter wrote delicate, precisely worded short stories and novellas set in Texas and Mexico. Born May 15, 1890, in Indian Creek outside San Antonio, Texas, Porter lived in poverty in childhood. She was reared by a paternal grandmother, Aunt Cat, on whom she reflects in "Portrait: Old South" (1940). As soon as Porter freed herself from Our Lady of the Lake convent school and ended an unpromising youthful marriage, she established a pattern of pursuing personal interests and being on the scene at significant world upheavals, including the Mexican Revolution and the European battlegrounds of World War II. Following stints reporting for the *Fort Worth Critic* and Denver's *Rocky Mountain News*, Porter launched a career in short fiction, notably *Flowering Ju-*

das (1930), *Pale Horse, Pale Rider* (1939), *The Old Order: Stories of the South* (1944), and *The Leaning Tower and Other Stories* (1944).

In *Flowering Judas*, the first collection, she published "The Jilting of Granny Weatherall" (1930), a classic stream-of-consciousness story and textbook example of symbolic realism. Told through the flickering consciousness of the title character, the narrative moves in and out of Granny's memory, returning to her deathbed and the ministrations of Doctor Harry, a young country physician who patronizes and cajoles as though soothing a fretful child. The story compresses and interchanges segments of Granny's life, recounting a deep humiliation that accompanied the jilting in her girlhood and her intent to destroy love letters to George and John lest the children discover that she was abandoned at the altar. Jilted a second time on her deathbed, she looks back regretfully, "Oh, no, oh, God, no, there was something else besides the house and the man and the children. Oh, surely they were not all? What was it? Something not given back." (Porter 1985, 350)

The irony of Granny's passage is the gathering of daughters, priest, and doctor who patronize and whisper their concerns to ease her fears. In interior musings, the old pioneer musters the strength on which she has always relied. At the heart of the story, she mulls over marriage to John, a time of stout endurance when she dug postholes to fence in a hundred acres and rode over wintry roads to tend "sick horses and sick Negroes and sick children." (Porter 1985, 349) The woman who has truly weathered all, Granny pothers over the loose ends of her life—the six bottles of wine she wants to send Sister Borgia and the hurtful link to George, an unfinished business that gives her no peace. In her last moments, "taken by surprise," she stretches toward the dimming light. Disappointed that God gives no sign of relieving her angst-ridden soul, she blows a final puff of breath to release her struggling spirit and extinguish the corporeal remains that hold it captive. (Porter 1985, 352)

A central factor binds Porter to regional traditions: images of the redoubtable old Southern woman. This recurrent fictive persona, amply identified in Granny Weatherall, sprouts in Miranda, a semiautobiographical protagonist of "Old Mortality" (1930), a novella about a modern girl's attempt to understand her Aunt Amy, a willful belle who lived hard and died young. The details of Aunt Amy's life are so immured in the conventions of the Old South that Miranda is at a loss to understand her relative's penchant for caprice. After leaving the security of a convent school to marry, Miranda—bearing a strong autobiographical likeness to the author—senses that she is covering some of the same territory that Amy encountered on her way to full emancipation.

Unlike Porter, who lived a vagabond expatriate existence dotted with four husbands and numerous lovers, Kentuckian Caroline Gordon was rooted to home and made a fruitful alliance with the "South first" philosophy of the Fugitive Agrarian movement. Well educated at home by her father and at Bethany College in West Virginia, she welcomed the assistance of Ford Madox Ford, in whose office she had worked during her thirties. She wrote in the Southern agrarian tradition and published *Penhally* (1931), *Aleck Maury, Sportsman* (1934), and *None Shall Look Back* (1937), a reflective fictional biography on the life of Klan founder General Nathan Bedford Forrest, before reaching farther back to the pioneer tradition with *Green Centuries* (1941) and forward to the contemporary era in *The Garden of Adonis* (1937) and *The Women on the Porch* (1944). Her career encompassed teaching at Woman's College (now the University of North Carolina at Greensboro) and the College of St. Catherine in St. Paul, Minnesota, as well as publication of two critical works, *The House of Fiction* (1950), a textbook of short works, and *How To Read a Novel* (1957), both collaborations with her husband, Allen Tate.

Gordon's well-plotted thriller "The Captive" depicts the multiple problems of Jinny Sellards Wiley, a lone woman in Prestonburg, Kentucky, who was abducted by Cherokee and Shawnee after they murdered her family. Collected in *The Forest of the South* (1945), the story allies stream-of-consciousness with the captivity motif, a staple in frontier literature. Drawing on naturalistic Jungian notions about memory and myth, the story is a sexually charged first-person narrative that details the kidnap and return of a real pioneer mother. After Cherokee attackers Mad Dog and Crowmocker set her cabin on fire and bash her children with tomahawks, they hustle Jinny Wiley, the protagonist, onto a trail leading far from white settlements. She struggles to keep up, fashioning a sling to snuggle Dinny, her suckling infant, close to her breast. To facilitate rapid travel, an annoyed brave deliberately grabs Dinny by the feet, yanks him free from his mother's hold, and smashes his skull against a tree. During the Cherokees' rapid-paced flight, Jinny straggles behind, hampered by bloodied feet, fatigue, trauma, and sorrow for her family. Gordon emphasizes the savagery of Jinny's experience with the ghoulish vision of her daughter Sadie's fair-haired scalp, which swings from a captor's belt. The impact of so much violence over a stretch of a few days reminds Jinny that she too faces a grisly death at the hands of barbarians.

Gordon's breathless pacing hurtles the story toward some unknown rendezvous deeper in the Kentucky woods. Balanced against the kind attentions of Crowmocker, an elderly chief, are intimidating shouts and leers from Mad Dog, a vigorous, spiteful brave. After the column pushes its way uphill through dense bracken, it arrives at "the biggest rockhouse ever I seen," a dialect reference to a cave. (Gordon 1952, 874) Before the Cherokee depart to a nearby mine to dig up balls of lead, Mad Dog ties Jinny with thongs and leaves her by a dying fire. She takes her mind off the abductors by singing folk songs and thinking about two suitors who courted her in girlhood, but the approach of Mad Dog rekindles fear of the young, sexually active male whom she imagines as "A devil. A devil come straight from hell to burn and murder." Gordon describes his face in the colors of passion and death:

> His eyes was black in the circles of paint. His tongue showed bright between his painted lips. The red lines ran from his forehead down the sides of his cheeks to make gouts of blood on his chin. (Gordon 1952, 881)

A flagrant phallic symbol echoes his fierce masculinity, foreboding, and ritual paint: Near a barren rises a large elm peeled and painted to resemble a monster rattlesnake coiled about it. These grotesque details heighten the terrors that push Jinny to the ends of courage.

Evanescence, a characteristic of Gordon's fiction, intensifies the ebb and flow of hope, a struggle that occupied the real Jinny Wiley for over a year before her escape. The fictional Jinny clings to the faint chance of rescue by frontiersman Tice Harmon or through the intervention of Crowmocker. She sinks into desperation as the older Indian sweeps a handful of silver brooches into his buckskin bag and accepts the trade: loot for the woman. Brusquely, he turns from her, retorting, "A promise . . . to a white coward! Go to your work." (Gordon 1952, 882) Dreams of a white boy the Cherokees torture and burn, and fantasies of Lance Rayburn, Jinny's former suitor, disturb her sleep. Gordon's feminist theme takes hold of the falling action after Jinny accepts responsibility for her reclamation, rolls into the rain to soak and stretch the bindings on her hands, and flees on foot down the creek toward a settlement.

Gordon elongates the suspenseful flight from pursuing Indians, which takes Jinny to a blockhouse. In sight of safety, she must scream her name over the roar of water and beg to be helped across the stream and into the gates. An elderly white man strings logs with grapevine and begins poling Jinny across the stream to safety. To her faltering rescuer, Jinny snorts, "Go on and pray, you old fool, . . . I'm a-going to git across this river." (Gordon 1952, 889) In the final sentence, Jinny thanks luck for her rescue. Gordon concludes the story with a wry touch of humor and anticlimax in Jinny's parting words, which remind the reader that chance played no part in her salvation.

In contrast to the fame of other twentieth-century short-fiction writers from the South, Zora Neale Hurston possessed a considerable talent not widely appreciated in its time. Her stories cover a 34-year span, beginning with "John Redding Goes to Sea" (1921) in *Stylus*, Howard University's literary magazine. Hurston's range extends over a wide field of interests, but her strength lies in a command of black vernacular and experience with the all-black community of Eatonville, Florida. The canon of 19 published stories and seven extant works recovered after her death include "Book of Harlem," a Bible parody, and "Harlem Slanguage," a glossary of such folk dialect and idiom as "I'm cracking but I'm facking," and a seven-stage color scale that ranks Negro skin tones from "yaller" through "yaller, high brown, vaseline brown, seal brown, and low brown," down to dark black. (Hurston 1995, 232)

Familiar themes in Hurston's writing are sexism, wife abuse, and male dominance, all found in her novel *Their Eyes Were Watching God* (1937). In "Spunk" (1925), she presents front-porch society sitting in judgment of Spunk Banks, a self-satisfied local who flaunts his liaison with Lena, the wife of storekeeper Joe Kanty. Like a Greek chorus, the gathering hoots and catcalls while Joe tests the edge of his razor and goes to the palmetto thicket to retrieve Lena. Hurston depicts Joe's timidity with a quip about his Adam's apple, which "was galloping up and down his neck like a race horse." (Hurston 1995, 28) The plot moves over familiar territory: Spunk kills Joe, is judged not guilty, and moves in with Lena. The falling action depicts Joe's ghost in the form of a black bobcat stalking Spunk. Before his death from an accident with a saw in a lumber mill, Spunk declares that Joe's ghost pushed him. Hurston's familiarity with rural Florida mores pursues the story back to front-porch gossip. As Spunk's remains lie on a makeshift cooling board, locals muse over the next man to court Lena.

The touchstone of Southern fiction, William Faulkner, devised a vast set of characters who populate his stories and novels. He worked and reworked the personae of his scenarios through numerous incarnations and published them in seven collections: *These 13* (1931), *Doctor Martino and Other Stories* (1934), *The Unvanquished* (1938), *The Wild Palms* (1939), *Go Down, Moses* (1942), *Collected Stories of William Faulkner* (1950), and *Big Woods* (1955). Critics often reflect on Faulkner's short stories as they influenced or derived from more thorough plots, for example, Caddy, Quentin, and Jason Compson and their father, who are a young family in "That Evening Sun" (1931) and were major figures in Faulkner's signature family saga, *The Sound and the Fury* (1929). Likewise, "An Odor of Verbena" (1938) returns to the flawed ambitions of Colonel Thomas Sutpen, the dynasty maker and protagonist of *Absalom, Absalom!* (1936), the author's famed Southern saga.

Faulkner's most studied story is "The Bear," first published in the *Saturday Evening Post* on May 9, 1942, and revamped in *Go Down, Moses* later that year. An enigmatic, nostalgic melange of local history and legend, the narrative is a complex treatment of personal and family responsibility. In the short version, Faulkner traces the maturation of Ike McCaslin through his boyhood passion for the annual bear hunt with his elders, General Compson and Major de Spain. An animistic evaluation of untrammeled wilderness, the story spans six years, taking Ike deeper into the mysteries of the woods as he follows the tutelage of Sam Fathers and learns to track an enormous bear named Old Ben. The elusive, oversized Ben carries a burden of legend for the corncribs he has ravaged and the pigs and calves he has devoured. The bear has become so treasured a quarry that Ike devotes every hunt to searching for the one set of ruined claw marks that indicates Old Ben's presence.

A restatement of Henry David Thoreau's philosophy of simple living at Walden Pond, Faulkner's plunge into the wild requires less technological assistance as it demands more intuitive awareness. Ben becomes a totemic figure, the incarnation of pure nature before human interlopers breached his territory. He teases Ike by getting closer with each encounter, yet withholding their inevitable confrontation. In the lengthy tutelage in woods lore that precedes meeting Ben, Sam advises:

> Be scared. You can't help that. But don't be afraid. Ain't nothing in the woods going to hurt you if you don't corner it or it don't smell that you are afraid. A bear or a deer has got to be scared of a coward the same as a brave man has got to be. (Faulkner 1977, 211)

The coaching and drilling pay off in the boy's skill at tracking, analyzing, and applying logic to the hunt. Finally, he sights his quarry, "immobile, fixed in the green and windless noon's hot dappling, not as big as he had dreamed it but as big as he had expected, bigger, dimensionless against the dappled obscurity, looking at him." (Faulkner 1985, 213) Like an impalpable legend of the primeval forest, Old Ben disappears, sinking like a bass into a pool without movement or stir of its surroundings.

Faulkner imposes on the story a distaste for the technology that threatened the primitivism of his homeland. In the shorter version of "The Bear," he compresses the meeting into a precipitate, thrill-choked moment. When Ike locates the right dog, a minuscule "fyce" overburdened with boldness, and is able to discard watch, compass, and gun, he receives nature's stamp of manhood: Old Ben allows himself to be tracked and rears up so close that the boy spots a tick on the animal's right inner thigh:

> Sprawling, he looked up to where it loomed and towered over him like a cloudburst and colored like a thunderclap, quite familiar, peacefully and even lucidly familiar, until he remembered: This was the way he had used to dream about it. Then it was gone. (Faulkner 1985, 380)

In the moment's aftermath, the boy realizes that he didn't fire a shot. Discussing the abortive hunt with his father, Ike tries to account for his failure to shoot Old Ben. The philosophic father presents the boy with a heavy burden of abstraction: "Courage, and honor, and pride," his father said, "and pity, and love of justice and of liberty. They all touch the heart, and what the heart holds to becomes truth, as far as we know the truth. Do you see now?" (Faulkner 1985, 282) From the bear, Ike learns the difference between foolhardiness and courage, between savagery and appreciation of the sanctity of the wild.

Southern stories as satisfying as Faulkner's "The Bear" are rare classics that hold a place unequaled within or outside the region. More familiar to readers are the humor-washed satire of local idiosyncrasies. A popular Southern novelist, poet, scriptwriter, and radio essayist, and winner of the 1984 American Book Award for Fiction, Ellen Gilchrist captures the unique idiocies of her homeland. A down-home philosopher and savant, she maintains close ties with her Southern forebears from Vicksburg, Mississippi. She grew up at Hopedale Plantation in Issaquena County near Greenville, Mississippi, close to the smell of humid earth and the companionship of farm livestock. A significant factor in her rearing was the attendance of black caregivers, for whom she developed an abiding affection, and a helpful lineup of eccentric relatives. In the autobiographical *Falling through Space* (1987), she follows a Southern tradition of intergenerational relations and names the kinfolk who influenced her—a grandfather from England, a cousin who is a cheerleader, an uncle who was a country physician, an aunt who raised angora rabbits, and her mother, who encouraged a belief in fairies that dance in the moonlight.

A past editor of the *New Orleans Vieux Carré Courier*, Gilchrist turned to short stories and poems with a Louisiana flavor. She studied at the University of Arkansas in Fayetteville, a remarkably open society lacking the social restrictions that had smothered her in her hometown. Since beginning a career as a writer of short fiction and novels, she has published in *Atlantic Monthly*, *Mademoiselle*, *Cosmopolitan*, *New York Quarterly*, and *Southern Living* in addition to her volume of verse *The Land Surveyor's Daughter* (1979), novels and novellas, and rambunctious story collections—*In the Land of Dreamy Dreams* (1981),

Victory over Japan (1983), *Drunk with Love* (1986), *Light Can Be Both Wave and Particle* (1989), *The Age of Miracles* (1995), and *Rhoda: A Life in Stories* (1995).

A master at short fiction, Gilchrist, like Faulkner, focuses on the downward spiral of the Southern aristocrat. Choosing the lush Mississippi Delta or the indolence of New Orleans, she pursues comic incongruity by following blue-blooded heroines on tawdry escapades often sparked by her own adventures. Her characters, nurtured in Dixie's fundamentalist horror of sin, grow familiar with pangs of conscience, as Gilchrist explains in "Anna, Part I":

> Adultery. Pandora's box. You open it and all the Furies come flying out, jealousy, rage, pain and sorrow, all the shades and Furies of the world. They flew out now, lit upon the dresser, laughed down at her from the sconces and the chandelier. (Gilchrist 1986, 236)

Some of her characters grow so adept at rationalizing their peccadilloes that they emerge as caricatures. A typically vibrant funster, Nora Jane Whittington, buys a stage pistol, dresses in nun's wimple and robe, and robs a bar, then flees New Orleans to reunite in California with a feckless lover. After a liaison with a second lover, she seeks amniocentesis to determine which bedmate fathered her twins.

Critics find the source of the resilient Rhoda and other of Gilchrist's hoydens and gilded social matrons among the eccentrics created by Flannery O'Connor and Eudora Welty, the touchstones of the modern Southern short story. Gilchrist's female survivors include Traceleen, maid of the amoral Miss Crystal, whose shenanigans take a literary jab at the tarnished underside of refined Southern society; and Rhoda Manning, a wisecracking teen who annoys her father by smoking Lucky Strikes and departing in a stolen, unlicensed jeep to a tryst with a pool shark. In a series of letters to Blue Cross, Blue Shield dated from August 1993 to April 1994, Rhoda states confidently that she has become so accustomed to relying on herself that she is no longer willing to pay a company for health insurance. She hedges, "I'll let you know what I decide." (Gilchrist, *Rhoda* 1995, 214) In her introduction to *Rhoda: A Life in Stories*, Gilchrist accounts for her character's originality and boundless spunk:

> There are no shadows in Rhoda. Rhoda is passion, energy, light. If germs get inside her, her blood boils up and devours them. If she loses a pearl ring, it's proof there is no God. If it's necessary to drop an atomic bomb to save Western Civilization, she's ready. (Gilchrist, *Rhoda* 1995, x)

Laced with gutter talk, comic-strip dialogue, and chaotic uproar, Gilchrist's stories read like tawdry but titillating gossip, a sure selling point to readers, who remain dedicated fans. (Auchincloss 1961; Becker 1966; Bradbury 1963; Bradbury 1996; "Celebrated Writer" 1985; *Contemporary Authors* 1994; Doar 1975; Ehrlich and Carruth 1982; Faulkner 1969, 1977, 1984, 1985, 1990, 1991; Fraistat 1984; Gilchrist 1981, 1983, 1986, 1987, 1990, *Age* 1995, *Rhoda* 1995; Goldsmith, 1988; Hammons 1984; "Heart of the West" 1993; Henry 1952, 1953, 1993; "Pardon" 1958; Hurston 1995; "Inspirational Short Stories" 1996; "Katherine Anne Porter" 1995; Kennedy 1988; Kunitz 1942; Laskin 1994; Lyons 1985; Myers 1985; Poe 1962; Porter 1985; Quinn 1936; Rubin et al. 1985; Sherr and Kazickas

1994; "Southerner Ellen Gilchrist 1985; Stein 1979; Trent et al. 1946; Whitt 1994; Young 1986)

See also Faulkner, William; Hurston, Zora Neale; McCullers, Carson; Poe, Edgar Allan; Stuart, Jesse; Walker, Alice.

SIMMS, WILLIAM GILMORE

The South's first true literary genius and interpreter of his era, William Gilmore Simms, a first-generation American, made his mark on literature with two innovations: an emphasis on regional literature as a serious study and the inclusion of Native American characters. The first fiction writer to treat Native Americans as realistic characters, he fleshed out *The Yemassee: A Romance of Carolina* (1835) with believable tribe members. The creation of a multiracial Southern milieu was an easy task because Simms knew well the Carolina frontier, tidewater, and lowlands, which he depicted in lush chivalric romance, picaresque thrillers, and swashbuckling pirate tales. He was a restless, energetic intellectual well versed in the Greek and Roman classics, Shakespeare, and Milton. Of Scotch-Irish ancestry, he was born in Charleston, South Carolina, on April 17, 1806, to Harriet Ann Augusta Singleton and storekeeper William Gilmore Simms, an Irish immigrant. After his mother's death in 1808 and the bankruptcy of the family mercantile trade, Simms's father joined General Andrew Jackson's volunteers in Mississippi and left the boy with his maternal grandmother, Mrs. Jacob Gates. The abandonment resulted in a court battle, which sealed Simms's fate to remain in Charleston.

Simms struggled all his life to fit in with local snobs who considered him a snot-nosed Mick upstart unfit for their signal honor: membership in the St. Cecilia Society. In childhood he received scant education but was drawn to poetry, which he wrote assiduously, copying the forms and style of European masters. Apprenticed in an apothecary shop, he left the pharmaceutical trade to study law in 1824. During a journey to join his father, he composed an ambitious poem, *Monody, on the Death of General Charles Cotesworth Pinckney* (1825). He helped found the *Album*, a short-lived vehicle for regional poetry, and wrote for the *Southern Literary Gazette*, another short-lived effort. He turned from the failed venture to journalism and used his family's money to finance the *Charleston City Gazette*, a pro-Union newspaper. The uproar that followed his published opinions drove him out of the South.

While living in Hingham, Massachusetts, Simms determined to write professionally. He composed a stirring chivalric romance, "The Swamp Fox" (1832), a boots-and-saddles tale of night maneuvers, blitzkrieg strikes, and rapid, last-minute retreats. Written at a steady clip of iambic tetrameter pierced with frequent caesura, the eight-line verses vivify the romance of chargers and sabers, gallant steeds, and a hasty fording of the Santee River:

Now stir the fire and lie at ease—
    The scouts are gone, and on the brush
I see the Colonel bend his knees,

> To take his slumbers too. But hush!
> He's praying, comrades; 'tis not strange;
>   The man that's fighting day by day
> May well, when night comes, take a change,
>   And down upon his knees to pray.
> (Young 1937, 285)

Prefiguring the urgency and patriotic fervor of Henry Wadsworth Longfellow's "Paul Revere's Ride" (1872) and John Greenleaf Whittier's "Barbara Frietchie" (1864), "The Swamp Fox" conceals the identities of Marion, his men, and their Tory victims, led by Sir Banastre Tarleton. In place of military details, Simms stresses nature in "turfy hammock," red deer, owls, alligators, and cooters, the Southern dialect term for turtles.

In addition to war poetry, Simms composed an extensive narrative poem, *Atalantis, a Story of the Sea* (1832), a fantasy love match between a sea sprite and a demon; a novella, *The Book of My Lady* (1833); and a psychological novel, *Martin Faber, the Story of a Criminal* (1833). Under the influence of New England poet William Cullen Bryant, Simms resettled in New Haven, Connecticut, and began writing longer works of fiction, a five-volume series known as the "Border Romances." He set *Guy Rivers* (1834) in Georgia's goldfields. The remaining volumes dot the map of Dixie—*Richard Hurdis: or, The Avenger of Blood, a Tale of Alabama* (1838), *Border Beagles: A Tale of Mississippi* (1840), *Beauchampe, or The Kentucky Tragedy, a Tale of Passion* (1842), *Helen Halsey: or, The Swamp State of Conelachita* (1845), and *Charlemont* (1856).

The second of Simms's novel series, a colonial-era romance called *The Yemassee*, earned critical respect for its depiction of a Native American family in the capital of Pocata-ligo. The story features Chief Sanutee, his wife Matiwan, and Occonestoga, their son, during the inevitable clash of cultures that kills the braves and dooms the bucolic lifestyle of a South Carolina tribe. A readable frontier novel, the book opens in 1715 as the worried couple discuss their incorrigible son. Sanutee, a friend and ally of Tory settlers, interrupts Matiwan's hesitant beginning with a list of the youth's errors in judgment:

> Occonestoga is a dog, Matiwan; he hunts the slaves of the English in the swamps for strong drink. He is a slave himself—he has ears for their lies—he believes in their forked tongues, and he has two voices for his own people. Let him not look into the lodge of Sanutee. Is not Sanutee the chief of the Yemassee? (Simms 1964, 36)

This domestic exchange accents a major complaint against colonial whites— their dissemination of alcohol, which was unknown to the Yemassee before the coming of settlers. Overriding her obdurate husband, Matiwan states that she has shared her husband's bed, cooked venison for guests, and borne a son. Sanutee grows so distraught with Occonestoga that he refuses to let Matiwan claim to be the boy's mother.

In chapter III, Simms develops the character of Sanutee, father and native chieftain whose personal, ancestral, and civic duties force him to evaluate realistically the quandary of a tribe facing an "intrusive race." From the beginning of Simms's romance, Sanutee acknowledges that the stakes are high for his people, who must yield to the insurgent whites if they succeed at overrunning Yemassee land. The author credits him with philosophical foresight and pragmatism in forecasting the destiny that awaits his people. Sanutee "knew that the superior must necessarily be the ruin of the race which is inferior—that the one must either sink its existence in with that of the other, or it must perish." (Simms 1964, 39) Wise to the duplicity of the intruder, he acknowledges that the "Christian (so called) civilization" held both the sword and the sacrament over his people. At first impressed by the English, he had come to the conclusion that they were the source of "the degradation which was fast dogging their footsteps." (Simms 1964, 40) Strongly defending native sovereignty, Sanutee clings to religious and ancestral ideals that require the Yemassee to guard their patrimony as a gift to emerging generations.

At the heart of Simms's novel, insidious whites undermine native unity. The chief's burden of his profligate son's spying pulls the proud, uncompromising Sanutee from Matiwan, who refuses to abandon Occonestoga. In a pivotal scene, the son confronts the father. With tomahawk raised in defiance, he sings the scalp song and prepares for the one-sided slaughter of the older man when Matiwan screams. Tribesmen rush in and arrest her son, causing her to fall at Sanutee's feet. Sanutee attends a formal hearing with other dignitaries and sternly rejects pleas to rescue his son from the humiliation of the removal of his arrow-shaped clan tattoo and banishment from the tribe on earth and in the hereafter. In a dramatic tableau, women sing the exile's doom: "They know thee no more—they know thee no more." (Simms 1964, 209) Unable to bear her son's protracted agony and the humiliation of having his tribal mark sliced from his skin, Matiwan strikes him with a hatchet concealed in her dress. The novel concludes in three-way tragedy: The family's grief and shame is revealed for all to judge as Matiwan collapses in Sanutee's arms.

Simms believed that the South held a distinctive place in world history, and he strove to capture the Carolina mindset and immortalize its heroes. Seven additions to his romance series highlight themes and settings of the South's involvement during the Revolutionary War. *The Partisan* (1835), set during the days of Francis Marion, the "Swamp Fox," preceded a rise in the author's fortunes. A widower in his early twenties, he married a wealthy bride, Chevilette Eliza Roach, and returned permanently to South Carolina, where he sired 14 children. At Woodlands, his wife's 7,000-acre plantation on the Edisto River near Barnwell, he prospered in the role of hospitable Southern gentleman farmer and pursued writing as a career. His prodigious canon over the next quarter century includes volumes of verse, newspaper submissions, and novels, including *Mellichampe* (1837) and *The Kinsmen* (1841), later retitled *The Scout*. A short-story collection, *The Wigwam and Cabin: Life in America* (1848), and an anthology of lyrical poems, *Areytos: or, Songs of the South* (1846), preceded a nonfiction anthology of sketches, reviews, travelogues, political tracts, and critical commentary along with biographies of four Southern military heroes—Francis Marion, Captain John Smith, Chevalier Bayard, and General Nathanael Greene. Simms's two comedies—*Charleston, and Her Satirists* (1848) and *Father Abbot*

(1849)—skewer the extravagances of fops and belles. A Southern apologist, he supported local journals such as the *Magnolia* and *Southern and Western*, and in 1849 began a six-year stint as editor of the *Southern Quarterly Review*, a pulpit for the pro-slavery aristocrat. In a position of authority, he groomed writers such as novelist Nathaniel Beverley Tucker, humorists Johnson Jones Hooper and William Tappan Thompson, and sports writer William Elliot, author of *Carolina Sports by Land and Water* (1846). As a result of Simms's influence on Southern readers, his literary reputation spread, rivaling the popularity of Edgar Allan Poe.

By 1850, after the publication of two volumes of his collected works, Simms slackened his rapid pace. He turned to a new sketch of the colonial era in *Godey's Lady's Book*. Subtitled "A Tale of the Revolution," his spy thriller *Katherine Walton: or, The Rebel's Daughter* appeared in installments from November to April and was published in novel form in 1851. Additions to the Revolutionary romances include *The Sword and the Distaff* (1852), *The Forayers* (1855), and *Eutaw* (1856). Three years later, he assembled ample historical data on colonial-era piracy for *The Cassique of Kiawah* (1859). His mastery of descriptive verse is evident in *The Edge of the Swamp* (1853), a lowlands tone poem richly studded with South Carolina's abundant flora and fauna—"cypresses, each a great ghastly giant, eld and gray" and "the whooping crane, gaunt fisher in these realms." (Beatty et al. 1952, 286–287) In the decade preceding his death from cancer on June 11, 1870, he groomed two promising authors, South Carolina poets Paul Hamilton Hayne and Henry Timrod, dubbed the poet laureate of the Confederacy. Known as the Charleston school, the trio was featured in *Russell's* magazine, a quality antebellum periodical that succumbed during the Civil War.

The war years were brutal to Simms and his protégés, all of whom were staunch supporters of the Confederacy and entrenched romantics clinging to the refinement and leisure of the antebellum South. The challenge to state sovereignty quickened his pride in the South and heightened his defense of slavery and secession, which he championed in prominent editorials and media articles. Woodlands was twice burned, the second time by General Sherman's marauders. Simms's valuable 10,000-volume library was destroyed. His outlook darkened after the deaths of friends, children, and wife.

When his lands were confiscated, Simms left Charleston and reestablished himself in Columbia. Overwrought and desperate for cash, he continued writing to support six underage children and grew defensive and pettish when his Confederate loyalties were challenged. He believed that Southern sensibilities surpassed those of other regions. As he explains in "The Morals of Slavery":

> Their grace of manner, courteous bearing, gentleness of deportment, studious forbearance and unobtrusiveness—their social characteristics, in general—all assumed to spring from the peculiar institution of Negro Slavery, as affording superior time, as well as leisure, to the controlling race—are usually admitted without question. (Gross 1971, 104)

In an age of bitter realism, the demand for his idealistic romances waned. A few faithful readers were amused by the comedy of *Paddy McGann* (1863); a North Carolina legend, *The Cub of the Panther* (1869); and a humorous domestic sketch,

"How Sharp Snaffles Got His Capital and Wife" (1870), which lampoons the abject penury and ignorance of rural whites. The verbal lambasting of the uppity Sam Sharp comes painfully close to the condescension that the Simms family had known:

> You hedn't a stalk of corn growing, and when I scratched at your turnip-bed I found nothing bigger than a chestnut. Then, Sam, I begun to ask about your fairm, and I found that you was nothing but a squatter on land of Columbus Mills, who let you have an old nigger pole-house, and an acre or two of land. Says I to myself, says I, "This poor fellow got *no capital;* and he hasn't the head to git *capital;*" and from that moment, Sam Snaffles, the more I obzarved you, the more sartin 'twas that you never could be a man, ef you war to live a thousand years. (Guilds 1970, 200)

Simms concludes the riotous tale with Sam declaring his 36 children as his earthly estate, and offering his tormentor *"going shar's* in my 'capital.'" (Guilds 1970, 227)

At his passing, Simms finally received his due from Charleston's social cream, the people he had courted most of his career. He was buried in the prestigious Magnolia Cemetery and merited praise for over 70 titles in a host of genres—historical romance, mannered regional novels, crime and spy thrillers, supernatural fiction, magazine serials, farce and tall tales, satire, biography, chauvinistic history, short-fiction anthology, novella, drama, narrative verse, nature poem, sonnet, ballad, criticism, editorial, letters, travelogue, geography, lecture, and oratory. His commitment to a comprehensive Southern canon earned him the sobriquets the "Southern Cooper," the "American Scott," and the "Dr. Johnson of Charleston." (Beatty et al. 1952; Cady 1967; Ehrlich and Carruth 1982; Gross 1971; Guilds 1970; Kunitz and Haycraft 1938; Quinn 1936; Rubin et al. 1985; Simms 1964, 1995; Stein 1979; Trent 1905; Wilson and Ferris 1989; Young 1937)

See also theater in the South.

THE SOUND AND THE FURY

William Faulkner's masterpiece, *The Sound and the Fury* (1929), details the South's corruption and vitiation through the fall of the Compson family, a dying dynasty that represents in miniature the whole of the South's social strata. In an interview for *Paris Review*, he detailed the image that initiated the novel:

> It began with a mental picture. I didn't realize at the time it was symbolical. The picture was of the muddy seat of a little girl's drawers in a pear tree, where she could see through a window where her grandmother's funeral was taking place and report what was happening to her brothers on the ground below. (Cunliffe 1987, 188)

The explosion of the image carried Faulkner far beyond the scope of short fiction and into the minds of unusual characters, whose points of view shape and interpret events in a piecemeal re-creation of what Faulkner termed "the tragedy of two lost women." The work held his attention, giving him no peace until 15 years after the book was published.

A four-part saga covering about 35 years from the 1890s to 1928, *The Sound and the Fury* takes its title from a line in *Macbeth* where the tragic hero reacts to the death of the queen, referring to "a tale told by an idiot full of sound and fury signifying nothing" (V, v, 29). Fittingly, Faulkner's story begins with the inchoate musings of 33-year-old Benjy Compson, an inarticulate moron tended by house servants and by his sister Candace. To substantiate the denunciation of the crumbling Compson dynasty, Faulkner moves to a second narrator, Benjy's idealistic brother Quentin, a Harvard undergraduate obsessed with guilt and an urge to kill himself for an imagined act of incest. The third segment turns to another speaker—Jason, the proud, manipulative family pragmatist, who tries to hold together a semblance of order on the basis of money, intimidation, and coercion. The fourth section completes the study of family depravity with its characterization of the outsider Dilsey Gibson, the family maid and mother *in absentia*. A faithful servant, she runs the household, tends Mrs. Compson, and parcels out acceptance, love, faith, and compassion for the children.

In *The Sound and the Fury*, Faulkner pioneered his unique version of the stream-of-consciousness technique by experimenting with deliberate complexities signaled to the reader by text cues. For example, in the Benjy segment the author presents an incident in which Benjy requires help crawling through a fence that separates Compson land from land they had sold to developers of a golf course:

> "Wait a minute." Luster said. "You snagged on that nail again. Cant you never crawl through here without snaggin on that nail."
> *Caddy uncaught me and we crawled through. Uncle Maury said to not let anybody see us, so we better stoop over, Caddy said. Stoop over, Benjy. Like this, see.*
> (Faulkner 1984, 4–5)

As Faulkner indicates with his shift away from standard English, the verbally impaired Benjy is unacquainted with a normal mode of discourse. His difficulty in maneuvering through the fence recalls to him an earlier incident when he and his sister Caddy had gone over the same route. To inform the reader that Benjy has jumped back to another event, Faulkner drops quotation marks and recounts the memory in italics.

In the novel's second part, Faulkner introduces another variation in standard English expression. To relate Quentin's obsessive, presuicidal frame of mind, the author creates a stream of words without explicit beginning and point of reference as though they are flowing without inhibition through the narrator's mind. In obvious psychic pain, Quentin begins in the middle:

> *told me the bone would have to be broken again and inside me it began to say Ah Ah Ah and I began to sweat. What do I care I know what a broken leg is all it is it wont be anything I'll just have to stay in the house a little longer that's all and my jaw-muscles getting numb and my mouth saying Wait Wait just a minute through the sweat ah ah ah behind my teeth and Father damn that horse damn that horse. Wait it's my fault.*
> (Faulkner 1984, 129–130)

The conventional mechanisms of writing—orderly thought, capital letters, spacing, and punctuation—give way to a rush of insanity blending so completely with fragmented language that the meaning transcends conventional denotation. Thus, the grammar of madness supplants normal speech and thought patterns. With this technique, Faulkner provides the reader a keener awareness of Quentin's inability to let go of hurtful memories or to focus on the present. Unable to halt a consuming fear that he has violated the Compson honor by failing to govern his promiscuous sister, he annihilates himself to stop the pain.

The Sound and the Fury stirred up widespread critical furor that continues to spawn learned interpretation and surmise. One evaluation suggests that, if the order of sections were reversed, readers would have a clearer understanding of Faulkner's focus, which is the moral collapse of the family and, by extension, the fall of the South and the death of American society. The events would reveal more lucidly how the father, Jason Compson III, a dilettante attorney and lover of belles lettres, seeks refuge in drink and cynicism, and the neurotic mother, Caroline Compson, takes to her bed in a shade-darkened room and resorts to whining and hypochondria as a means of shifting domestic and parental responsibilities to servants. On the other hand, the implied chaos builds from Benjy's confusion and ultimate castration, introduced in part 1; through Quentin's suicide at Harvard on his sister's wedding day in part 2; Caddy's marriage to banker Sydney Herbert Head, her daughter Quentin's theft of Jason's strongbox, and her elopement with a carnival barker and Jason IV's emergence as childless head of the family in part 3.

By moving the story toward treachery and betrayal in part 4, Faulkner exalts Dilsey's position of strong parent, ethical model, and symbol of redemption. Although she is incapable of staving off certain ruin for the aristocratic Compsons, her love encompasses the family in the only positive emotion they are ever to feel. The conclusion of *The Sound and the Fury* occurs on the bleak, chill morning of April 8, 1928. Dilsey takes Benjy to an Easter Sunday service, where Reverend Shegog hammers out an Old Testament–based sermon. As though recounting the Compson tragedy, he proclaims:

> I see de light en I sees de word, po sinner! Dey passed away in Egypt, de swingin chariots; de generations passed away. Wus a rich man: whar he now, O breddren? Wus a po man: whar he now, O sistuhn? Oh I tells you, ef you aint got de milk en de dew of de old salvation when de long, cold years rolls away! (Faulkner 1984, 341)

Enlightenment yanks Dilsey bolt upright. On her exodus from church, she exclaims her epiphany: "I've seed de first en de last," a parallel to the alpha and omega of Revelation. The vision summarizes the Compson fortunes and Faulkner's celebration of her dignity and abiding faith. (Faulkner 1984, 344)

The Sound and the Fury is a masterpiece of motif and meaning. Faulkner replays images of time, fire, water, mud, and green grass and trees as he accounts for Benjy's perception of security in the outdoors and Caddy's muddy drawers and ultimate loss of virginity, the beginning of the end for the remaining four Compson children. The overlay of family memories with the hopeless future that lies ahead follows the saga inexorably to catastrophe. In the falling action, Caddy and her daughter dissociate themselves from the Compson fate; Quentin loses touch with reality and drowns himself in the Charles River; and Jason, the embezzler whose niece steals his ill-gotten stash of money, is left to cope with a sickly mother and imbecile brother. Benjy's tenuous position in his brother's hands highlights the novel's conclusion: A minor mishap in the horse-drawn buggy sets Benjy to howling for the limited realm in which he feels at home. Faulkner indicates that the Compsons, like Luster at the reins of the buggy, have lost control of a household because no family member is competent to take charge. A film version of *The Sound and the Fury* aired in 1959. Starring Yul Brynner as Jason Compson, the supporting cast featured Joanne Woodward, Jack Warden, and Ethel Waters as Dilsey. (Beatty et al. 1952; Bradbury 1996; Faulkner 1984; Howe 1952; Lockerbie 1969; Rubin and Jacobs 1961; Rubin et al. 1985; Whitt 1994)

See also Faulkner, William; short fiction in Southern literature.

A STREETCAR NAMED DESIRE

One of the strongest pairings of opposite siblings in American stage history, Tennessee Williams's *A Streetcar Named Desire* (1947) showcases Blanche Dubois, the long-wilted Southern blossom who cheapens and coarsens her life with lies and illusion after she flees to her sister Stella, her sole protector. The worst of Blanche's mendacity is the self-deception that precipitates emotional decline. Lost in the dreamy labyrinth of former suitors, an effete husband, and memories of rounds of luncheons, excursions among the elite, jewelry, and summer furs, Blanche speaks the famed shibboleth of failures: "I have always depended on the kindness of strangers." (Williams 1947, 142) Her flight into madness overrides nymphomania, the deaths of her parents, and a brutal rape by her brother-in-law, the hulking Stanley Kowalski.

Set in New Orleans's garden district, *A Streetcar Named Desire* laces the text with proper nouns that are both evocative and symbolic. Eunice, from the Greek for kindly, expresses compassion toward neighbors. Stanley Kowalski, the patriarchal Pole who demands a husband's rights under the Napoleonic code, reflects his heritage from Central Europe. Blanche, who flaunts a French background by translating her first name, leaves unstated the meaning of Belle Reve, her "beautiful dream" home that once provided refuge from the deteriorating South. Transferred from the streetcar named Desire to one named Cemeteries, she reaches Elysian fields, the Roman land of the dead. Repeated images of death occur in the name of Allan Grey, Blanche's doomed husband, whose last name is the color of death and his first the name of Edgar Allan Poe, the South's master of the macabre. Likewise, foreshadowings overwhelm Blanche in the ominous surname of the superintendent, Mr. Graves, and the newsboy collecting for the *Evening Star*. Picturing herself as "la Dame aux Camellias," the tragic consumptive, Blanche plays out the imagined scene from Alexandre Dumas with Stanley, her Armand.

A 1949 Broadway production of *A Streetcar Named Desire* by Tennessee Williams includes actors Marlon Brando as Stanley Kowalski, seated, left, Nick Dennis as Pablo Gonzales, and Rick Bond as Steve Hubbel; Kim Hunter, standing, left, was Stella Dubois and Jessica Tandy played her sister Blanche.

Against these necrotic images, Blanche demands control of light. A threat to her tattered reputation, light forces her to see the faded beauty and sordid past that ends a potential romance with Mitch. From her arrival, she demands, "And turn that over-light off. Turn that off! I won't be looked at in this merciless glare!" (Williams 1947, 19) While luring Mitch, she asks him to shade the light with a paper lantern, declaring, "I can't stand a naked light bulb, any more than I can a rude remark or a vulgar action." (Williams 1947, 55) To perpetuate an illusion of romance, she places a candle stub in a bottle in a pathetic gesture of Continental joie de vivre. When Mitch unmasks Stella, he finds her to be shopworn merchandise—despairing, aged, and sodden with alcohol. In hysteria she shrieks, "Fire! Fire! Fire!" (Williams 1947, 121) As sanctuary slips away from her grasp, Blanche stands pathetically unprotected before the matron who will lead her away as Stanley rips the paper lantern from the light.

Williams plays out Blanche's demise with dramatic counterpoint. The dissonance of Stella's kindly ministrations against the tamale vendor's cry of "Red-hot!" illuminates an innocence drifted from the maidenly image. Blanche claims that she is a Virgo and sings "It's Only a Paper Moon" from the bathtub, while

Stanley spills out the tidbits he has learned about her lurid reputation. Ironically, Blanche's words rise on "But it wouldn't be make-believe if you believed in me!" The final pairing of images allies her vision of paramours as daisies on the lawn with the call of the blind Mexican vendor selling "Flores para los muertos [Flowers for the dead]." (Williams 1947, 119) Boosting herself to the image of the Holy Virgin, Blanche debates with Stella and Eunice the color of her jacket, which she claims is "Della Robbia blue. The blue of the robe in the old Madonna pictures." (Williams 1947, 135)

Inevitably, the play's psychological realism unmasks Blanche as a victim of the failed moral code that the South had long abandoned. Her mental dissociation mirrors the pull between what was once expected of the refined elite and the menace and crass, honky-tonk blare that penetrates the windows of her sister's apartment. Long parted from Belle Reve, the dream of a plantation Blanche sold to pay debts, she survived seedy years in the Flamingo Hotel, which she recalls as the "Tarantula Arms":

> I think it was panic, just panic, that drove me from one to another, hunting for some protection—here and there, in the most-unlikely places—even, at last, in a seventeen-year-old boy but—somebody wrote the superintendent about it—"This woman is morally unfit for her position." (Williams 1947, 118)

Herself a lurking arachnid fleeing bright lights, she retreats from the foul nest where she once lured men. With no shelter but the apartment of her sister to run to, Blanche flirts with Mitch and distractedly tries to telephone Shep Huntleigh, an old flame from Dallas. Her neurasthenic daintiness gives way to crazed self-absorption and hysteria as, mothlike, she is wafted toward destruction. (Bradbury 1963; Bradbury 1996; Cunliffe 1987; Gassner and Quinn 1969; Miller 1971; Parker 1983; Prideaux 1953; Rubin et al. 1985; Spoto 1985; Stein 1979; Tischler 1969; Weales 1965; Williams 1947; Wilson and Ferris 1989)

See also *The Glass Menagerie;* Williams, Tennessee.

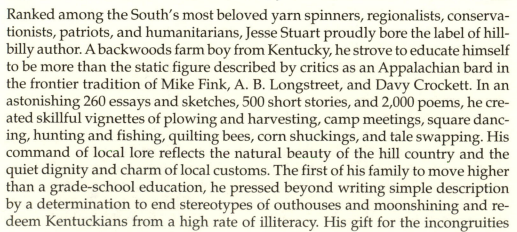

STUART, JESSE

Ranked among the South's most beloved yarn spinners, regionalists, conservationists, patriots, and humanitarians, Jesse Stuart proudly bore the label of hillbilly author. A backwoods farm boy from Kentucky, he strove to educate himself to be more than the static figure described by critics as an Appalachian bard in the frontier tradition of Mike Fink, A. B. Longstreet, and Davy Crockett. In an astonishing 260 essays and sketches, 500 short stories, and 2,000 poems, he created skillful vignettes of plowing and harvesting, camp meetings, square dancing, hunting and fishing, quilting bees, corn shuckings, and tale swapping. His command of local lore reflects the natural beauty of the hill country and the quiet dignity and charm of local customs. The first of his family to move higher than a grade-school education, he pressed beyond writing simple description by a determination to end stereotypes of outhouses and moonshining and redeem Kentuckians from a high rate of illiteracy. His gift for the incongruities and beauties of life in isolated Appalachian farms has been compared to similar folk themes in the works of Joel Chandler Harris, Bret Harte, Elizabeth Madox Roberts, and Isaac Bashevis Singer.

Key to a study of Stuart as author and man is an understanding of his material poverty. Born August 8, 1907, in a one-room rented cabin five miles from Riverton, Kentucky, in W-Hollow, Jesse Hilton Stuart was the second child and first son in a family of seven children and endured from childhood the mental and physical toll of dawn-to-dusk drudgery. Two of his works, "What America Means to Me" and "Clearing in the Sky," describe the hardships of semiliterate tenant farmers like his forebears, whom he once typified as "feudists, killers, drinkers, country preachers, Republicans, and fine soldiers" on his father's side and "schoolteachers, moonshiners, rebels, and Democrats" on his mother's side. (Pearson 1984, B14) His parents, Martha Hilton and Mitchell Stuart, hauled water and tilled a 50-acre plot while holding other jobs. His mother hired out as a domestic; his father, sidelined by a heart condition, found part-time work on the railroad and in mining. Stuart's vigor was also weakened by boyhood bouts with typhoid fever, pneumonia, and tuberculosis, for which he received minimal medical care. Yet, he proved sturdy enough to help his grandfather, Nathan Hilton, with the masonry and carpentry necessary to build the family home.

Stuart's early life is filled with the details that lend validity to his memoirs. While attending Plum Grove Elementary School, he earned 75 cents a day as a water boy as well as irregular windfalls selling pelts from trapped game and herbs and roots collected on his restless rambles about the mountains. At the end of 30 haphazard months of formal education, he was passed to the seventh grade and took a teaching post at Cane Creek Elementery School in 1924. The pre-Depression years were a fertile background for his oddments written on scrap paper and poplar leaves, but bouts of frustration with poverty caused him to fly into a rage and burn his books to spare his siblings the same yearnings for knowledge. After he finished public school in 1926, he found jobs with a carnival, local smithy, and the Auckland Steel Mills, and completed basic training for the army at Camp Knox, where he preferred reading Robert Burns and Edgar Allan Poe to drilling and sharpshooting.

Stuart's higher education was no less stalked by need and hard labor. He worked as a campus menial to pay tuition to Lincoln Memorial University in Harrogate, Tennessee, where he majored in English, and from 1928 to 1929 edited the literary magazine *The Blue and the Gray*. During graduate work at Vanderbilt University and George Peabody College for Teachers, he studied under Robert Penn Warren and poet Donald Davidson, famed Fugitive Agrarians whose poetry page he read in the *Knoxville Journal*. Stuart began work on *Beyond Dark Hills* (1938), an autobiographical project influenced by his readings of poets Carl Sandburg, Rupert Brooke, and Walt Whitman and novelists Thomas Hardy and Thomas Wolfe. Stuart's straightforward lines speak the immediacy of the farm boy's life:

> In paradise I found life first a battle.
> When I was six I worked at thinning corn,
> I went to work before day in the morn.

At four each morn I rose to feed the cattle
Before the chickens flew down off the trees.
And when I found the cow one autumn morn
I drove her up and stood on the warm leaves
Where she had lain, to get my cold feet warm.
(Richardson 1984, 102–103)

Although Stuart followed a disciplined schedule, unforeseen hardships dogged his efforts. He often had to choose between tuition and regular meals, and he struggled to balance study, part-time jobs, and verse writing. He fell short of a master's degree after a dormitory fire consumed his thesis on fellow Kentucky regionalist John Fox, Jr., author of *The Kentuckians* (1897), *The Little Shepherd of Kingdom Come* (1903), and *The Trail of the Lonesome Pine* (1908).

In 1929, Stuart began the dual career of writer and educator in Greenup County, Kentucky. He composed a popular short story for *Esquire*, "Split Cherry Tree" (1939), a poignant reflection on the vast chasm that separated untutored mountaineers from educators, a common motif of his writing. In the story, a gun-toting father threatens a teacher for keeping his son Dave after school to learn what the father considers frivolous subjects. In the end, the father recognizes that his son must inhabit a different world. The father tells Dave:

> You must go on to school. I am as strong a man as ever come out'n th' hills fer my years and th' hard work I've done. But I'm behind, Dave. I'm a little man. Your hands will be softer than mine. Your clothes will be better. You'll allus look cleaner than your old Pap. Jist remember, Dave, to pay your debts and be honest. Jist be kind to animals and don't bother th' snakes. That's all I got agin th' school. Puttin' black snakes to sleep and cuttin' 'em open. (Stuart 1982, 147)

The gist of the story delineates the difference between Stuart's outlook and that of his father's generation, and the father's coming-to-knowledge of his belittlement in the eyes of an educated son.

Reflecting his own trials as an upstart and iconoclast in fictionalized autobiographies, *The Thread That Runs So True* (1949) and *To Teach, To Love* (1970), Stuart narrated the life of a semiautobiographical 17-year-old teacher who attempts to upgrade rural education by lobbying for school consolidation. In 1934, he moved even farther from his parents' expectations for him by publishing a tour de force, a first verse collection, *Man with a Bull-Tongue Plow*, a sonnet sequence of 703 stanzas. After his marriage in 1939 to a teacher and old friend, Naomi Deane Norris, Stuart compromised with his past by settling on the family homestead and harmonizing his remodeling of the old buildings with its rustic surroundings. While farming and herding cattle and sheep, he fathered a daughter, Jessica Jane, whose birth and childhood he later described in *Hold April* (1962). These early works set in the coves of Appalachia earned him the title "the American Robert Burns."

With *Album of Destiny* (1944), an ambitious work 11 years in the making, Stuart speaks about local people and seasonal work through two voices, those of Kathaleen and John. Honoring the pathfinders who settled the mountains and worked the land, he echoed concerns of his literary friends Robert Penn Warren and Allen Tate, central figures among Vanderbilt University's Fugitive

Agrarians, who disdained the withering money hunger of cities as a blight on the South. Stuart's themes eludicate the value systems and traditions that strengthened Scotch-Irish mountaineers from their beginnings. From serving McKell High School as principal and the county newspaper as editor in 1956, he moved on to a new challenge as lecturer and writer-in-residence at the University of Nevada and American University in Cairo, Egypt. In 1962 he assumed posts at the U.S. Bureau of Educational and Cultural Affairs and Eastern Kentucky University.

Overall, Stuart produced a prodigious amount of writing and lectures for *Commonweal, Today's Health, Esquire, Woman's Day, Yale Review, Progressive Farmer, Christian Science Monitor, Audubon*, and *Harper's*, and undertook numerous tours and symposia. A versatile, energetic writer, he kept up a steady outpouring of 30,000 words per day. His chronicle of the elemental good of folk culture pleased and enlightened fans in Europe, Asia, and Africa. For young-adult audiences, Stuart published *Mongrel Mettle* (1944), *The Beatinest Boy* (1953), *Red Mule* (1955), and *Old Ben* (1970). His most popular titles include *Trees of Heaven* (1940), *Taps for Private Tussie* (1943), *Hie to the Hunters* (1950), *Kentucky Is My Land* (1952), *Mr. Gallion's School* (1967), *The Kingdom Within: A Spiritual Autobiography* (1979), *Lost Sandstones and Lonely Skies* (1979), and *If I Were Seventeen Again* (1980). One of his novels, *Daughter of the Legend* (1965), contains his study of the Melungeons, a swarthy mountaineer clan of unknown origin whose presence among Scotch-Irish settlers has provoked generations of fighting, victimization, and ostracism. His dirt-honest musings earned the praise of Malcolm Cowley, William Saroyan, Hal Borland, Edgar Lee Masters, Mark Van Doren, and William Rose Benét, who lauded him as a native ethicist.

Stuart's fictional place names and characters, like William Faulkner's imaginary Yoknapatawpha County, produce an organic whole. His personae blend the humor and verisimilitude of residents ranging from revivalist preacher to neighbor and local grifter. A natural wit, he was named Kentucky's poet laureate in 1954, and his works have been anthologized among the country's best essays, stories, and poems. After a series a heart attacks in 1954, Stuart slowed down briefly for a Caribbean cruise and composed in longhand on two reams of ship's letterhead the novel *Land beyond the River* (1956). He received the Berea College Centennial award, $5,000 from the Academy of American Poets, and honorary degrees from the University of Kentucky, Lincoln Memorial University, Baylor University, and Marietta College, along with the Jeannette Sewal Davis prize, Guggenheim Fellowship, Academy of Arts and Sciences award, Thomas Jefferson Memorial award, Governor's Distinguished Service Medallion, and NEA "best book" citation. More important to the South's literary treasury, he prefigured a generation of mountain-based authors, including Virginian Earl Hamner, Jr., a regional autobiographer who wrote *Spencer's Mountain* (1961) and *The Homecoming* (1970), the nucleus of the television series *The Waltons;* and young-adult fiction writer Cynthia Rylant, the noted Kentucky author of *Missing May* (1992).

A crippling stroke ended Stuart's travels in 1978. The next year, the state of Kentucky dedicated 733 acres in Greenup County as the Jesse Stuart Natural Preserve; also in 1979, the Jesse Stuart Foundation was established to further his beliefs in education. He remained in a coma from May 1982 until his death February 17, 1984 in a nursing home in Ironton, Ohio, and was buried in the Plum Grove Cemetery. Over a crowded lifetime of speaking, teaching, and writing engagements, he had toured 49 states and 94 countries as an ambassador of education and folk culture. His papers and works are collected in the Jesse Stuart Room at Murray State University in Murray, Kentucky. (Blair 1967; Bradbury 1963; Chapman 1974; *Contemporary Authors* 1994; Ehrlich and Carruth 1982; "Jesse Stuart Foundation" 1997; "Jesse Stuart State Natural Preserve" 1997; Kunitz 1942; Pearson 1984; Richardson 1984; Rubin et al. 1985; Snodgrass 1993; *Something about the Author* 1972; Stein 1979; Stuart 1940, 1949, 1950, 1965, 1966, 1982, 1997; Wilson and Ferris 1989)

STYRON, WILLIAM

In the tradition of Carson McCullers and Thomas Wolfe, William Styron is a brilliant novelist and memoirist who returns repeatedly to Southern motifs and settings, yet pursues the expatriate life as though fleeing some part of self. Winner of the American Academy of Arts and Letters Prix de Rome, Edward MacDowell and Howells medals, American Book Award, National Book Critics Circle Award, Ordre des Arts et des Lettres, and a Pulitzer Prize, he has earned a suspect praise clouded by doubts of authenticity from critics who try to force him into the preconceived mold of Southern gothic. His early predilection for violence, romantic excess, guilt, and degeneracy fits the description; on the other hand, his later penchant for existential self-evaluation defies the stereotype, particularly in *Darkness Visible: A Memoir of Madness* (1990), an intuitive, probing memoir about depression and alcoholism completed after his seven-week recovery from a hellish brush with Halcion, a drug that exacerbated his desire to self-destruct. On his way back to mental wholeness he recalls, "For those who have dwelt in depression's dark wood, and known its inexplicable agony, their return from the abyss is not unlike the ascent of the poet, trudging upward and upward out of hell's black depths and at last emerging into what he saw as 'the shining world.'" (Styron 1990, 84)

He was born June 11, 1925, in Newport News, Virginia, where he swam, crabbed, and sailed the James River and Atlantic shoals. He was the only child of shipyard cost engineer and draftsman William Clark and Pauline Abraham Styron. From a warm, sustaining family, Styron blames his downward spiral into mental breakdown as the outgrowth of his mother's death from cancer in 1938 when he was 13. In "A Tidewater Morning" (1993), a fictionalized memoir, he re-creates the confusion and misgivings he felt during her decline. On her last morning, the character screams with anguish:

> It was a shriek that swept up and down my naked body like a flame. It was an alien sound, which is to say unexpectedly beyond my sense of logic and my experience, so that for the barest instant it had the effect of something histrionic, out of the movies, a Frankenstein-Dracula film in which a bad actress emoted implausible terror. But it was real. (Styron 1993, 89)

In adulthood, he retriggered the memory of loss and grief by listening to his mother's favorite vocal recording, Johann Brahms's *An Alto Rhapsody*.

Attuned to literature early in his life, Styron grew up in Middlesex County, worked as an usher at the Village Theatre, and attended Christchurch, an Episcopal boarding school. He completed his education at Davidson College and Duke University. Before receiving a B.A. degree, he launched a career in writing and served as a lieutenant in the marine corps during World War II. He began publishing fiction and essays at a measured pace. Influenced by William Faulkner and Robert Penn Warren, Styron received critical attention for *Lie Down in Darkness* (1951), which he set in a fictional version of the town of Newport News; *The Long March* (1953), a semiautobiographical memoir, situated on a North Carolina marine base; and *Set This House on Fire* (1960), a mundane novel about a Southern expatriate living in Europe. On attending William Faulkner's funeral in 1962, he was pleased to see these titles on Faulkner's shelves.

Styron continued writing fiction worthy of the master's regard. His strongest submission to the Southern canon came in 1967 with *The Confessions of Nat Turner*, a brooding, hellishly angry and violent historical novel detailing the pre–Civil War milieu of Virginia slaves who commit themselves to a doomed flight from bondage. Critics compare the innovative internal monologue to Herman Melville's *Benito Cereno*, a dark, forbidding novella about a slave revolt aboard ship. Styron published his novel during the racial uprisings in Detroit and Newark, which fed the media with film clips of burgeoning rage and rampant disorder. In a succinct introduction, he relates details of the failed 1831 Virginia revolt of 60 slaves. Ironically set on July 4, the uprising—a brisk, murderous black sabbath—overrode the slaves' civility and humanity for a bloody payback to their enslavers. Local authorities suppressed the two-day binge of random killing, which took 55 lives.

Styron follows the historic events to their inevitable end. In the aftermath of arrest and incarceration, Turner and 16 compatriots, whom the Southampton County newspaper depicts as "gloomy [fanatics]" and "ferocious miscreants," died on the gallows. (Styron 1967, xv) In Styron's version, Turner, a skilled insurrectionist, comes of age in a plantation kitchen on the edge of the white world's respect and nurturance. Reared like Samuel Turner's house pet and protégé, he learns carpentry and anticipates manumission until fate ends his master's prosperity. Relocated in the hands of Thomas More, Turner learns the bitter truths of slavery. More overworks and starves him, degrades his self-esteem, and cankers his spirit. The fictional leadership is comprised of a handful of unremarkable black men bent on vengeance: Nelson, driven insane by frequent sale and the dissemination of his children; Henry, the indomitable hatemonger deafened in boyhood after a drunk overseer struck him on the head; Sam, inexplicably driven to kill his owner; Hark, the brooding husband and father whose family had been sold South; and Turner, the sturdy crucible in which black rage was ground, reconstituted, and shaped into blind terrorism.

The Confessions of Nat Turner is at home in the environs of the Dismal Swamp, a physical setting that parallels Turner's toxic mental state. During the slaves' prefatory discussions and plans, he fixes in his mind the miry perimeters of a stronghold suited to "resolute, woods-canny Negroes":

> Large . . . trackless, forbidding, as wild as the dawn of creation, it was still profusely supplied with game and fish and springs of sweet water—all in all hospitable enough a place for a group of adventurous, hardy runaways to live there indefinitely, swallowed up in its green luxuriant fastness beyond the pursuit of white men. (Styron 1967, 335)

Like serpents in Eden, the plotters intend to bide their time in the wetlands, then slither up the coast to Norfolk. Turner, beset with false notions of God's blessing, acknowledges that the cabal is "a heady scheme, beyond doubt, swarming with problems, perils, uncertainties." With a wry touch of gallows humor, he adds that his followers, already the pit bottom of human society, have nothing to lose. His role in the attack ends with a rush toward Mrs. Whitehead, the remaining vulnerable white person. Nat plunges his sword into her side, then ends her suffering with the blow of a fence rail. The symbolism overhangs the oddly understated scenario, countering Nat's absurdly anachronistic phallic weapon with the demountable wooden pen that holds his people on plantations throughout the South. In his final hours before execution, he looks beyond earthly death to ponder the messianic promise, "Then behold I come quickly." (Styron 1967, 426)

Choosing to view slavery from the inflamed psyche of Turner himself, Styron abandons the strictures of historical fiction and sets out to write a "meditation on history." (Styron 1967, ix) He outraged chroniclers and critics by stressing the mad messiah's desire for Miss Anne, a white female. Detractors accuse Styron of perpetuating a stereotype that has fueled a simplistic Ku Klux Klan mentality among racists and given legal authorities cause to suspend constitutional guarantees and justify generations of intimidation, abuse, and murder of black suspects. In *William Styron's Nat Turner: Ten Black Writers Respond* (1968), Mississippi critic and novelist John Williams, author of *The Man Who Cried I Am* (1967), accuses Styron of resorting to a fatal white myopia that discounts black leadership and overlooks the monstrous machinations of plantation owners bent on rationalizing and preserving slavery. Williams and his colleagues verbally arraign Styron for the hijacking of black heroes, the core of the African American's belief system.

In *The Confessions of Nat Turner* and later writings, Styron develops a pictorial quality amply suited to screen adaptation. The aborted plans to film the novel quickened the hopes of actor James Earl Jones, who was cast in the role of Turner. Jones quotes from Styron's article in the October 1992 issue of *American Heritage* the novelist's exasperation with controversy:

> It would have seemed inconceivable to me that within a short time I would experience almost total alienation from black people, be stung by their rage, and finally cast as an archenemy of the race, having unwillingly created one of the first politically incorrect texts of our time. (Jones and Niven 1993, 228)

Styron's only work to succeed on screen is *Sophie's Choice* (1979), an offbeat, semiautobiographical account of the complex love entanglement of Nathan

William Styron in Roxbury, Connecticut, 1984

Landau, a schizophrenic Jewish library worker, with Sophie Zawistowska, a tragic Polish-Catholic survivor of Auschwitz who collapses from malnutrition beside Nathan's desk. The multiple ironies of Sophie's choices keep her alive, but cost her two young children. The dilemma of survival among mad Nazis haunts the beautiful protagonist, who unwisely accepts assistance from a deeply troubled rescuer. Styron uses Nathan's malignant humor to offer snide, usually unflattering digs at the South, homeland of the speaker, Stingo, who falls in love with Sophie. In one serene lull-before-the-cloudburst, Nathan teaches her about the South:

> He infected Sophie with his enthusiasm, imparting to her all sorts of useful and useless information about the South, which he accumulated in gobs and bits like lint; loving Nathan, she loved it all, including such worthless lore as the fact that more peaches are grown in Georgia than in any other state and that the highest point in Mississippi is eight hundred feet. (Styron 1979, 440)

Symptoms of Nathan's mania—checking out novels by George Washington Cable and developing an affected Southern drawl—warn Sophie that he will soon resume beating her and disappearing and reappearing in their boarding-house love nest at odd hours.

Styron's use of the tormented codependency of Sophie and Nathan casts a twisted shadow on the novel's view of Nazi terrorism. Because both characters are incapable of speaking the truth, the narrative moves jerkily over uneven snatches of flashback, describing Sophie's pre–World War II relationship with her father and husband, both intellectuals on the staff of a university in Cracow. Styron temporarily resets the action at a Virginia peanut farm, where Stingo takes Sophie to seclude her from her demonic lover. The gesture is boyish and chivalric in the Southern sense but inadequate. Sophie, who struggles with fearful, guilt-laden memories, is driven to confess the heaviest of her mental burdens—that she chose death for her daughter Eva so that her son Jan could live. She flees from Stingo, leaving a note in a characteristic blend of English and German: "I feel so bad, I must go now. Forgive my poor Englisch. I love Nathan but now feel this Hate of Life and God. FUCK God and all his Hände Werk. And Life too. And even what remain of Love." (Styron 1979, 500) Sophie returns to Nathan and accepts their dual suicide as a solution to mutual emotional impairment. Stingo's voyeurism, originating in a perpetual state of lust, draws him back to Brooklyn to the scene where the couple, dressed in raffish costumes and poisoned with sodium cyanide, lie entwined on the bedspread, where they died while listening to *Jesu, Joy of Man's Desiring*.

Alan Pakula's 1982 film version of *Sophie's Choice* for Universal Pictures stars Kevin Kline, Peter MacNicol, and Meryl Streep as the unlikely trio of Nathan, Stingo, and Sophie. The film intrigued critics with its quality casting and cinematic beauty, but failed to earn equivalent box office respect. Told with voice-over of the naive Southern writer Stingo, the screenplay alternately teases and revolts with its seesaw romance, freighted with bursts of rage, innovative lovemaking, and confession. Meryl Streep, who managed a convincing Eastern European accent, earned an Oscar and awards from the National Board of Review, Los Angeles Film Critics Association, New York Film Critics, National Society of Film Critics, and Golden Globe. Academy Award nominations went to Pakula for screen adaptation and to cinematographer Nestor Almendros as well as the costumer and music director, Marvin Hamlisch. (Clarke 1968; "Confessions" 1967; *Contemporary Authors* 1994; Donaldson 1993; Gross 1971; Hamilton 1968; Jones and Niven 1993; Rubin et al. 1985; Stein 1979; Styron 1960, 1967, 1990, 1993; Wilson and Ferris 1989)

THEATER IN THE SOUTH

From the first arrivals of English settlers to the Virginia and Carolina shores, theatrical centers in colonial Williamsburg, Savannah, and Charleston were endowed with the heritage of Jonson, Marlowe, and Shakespeare. Some colonists had read contemporary dramas and seen them performed at Blackfriar's and Shakespeare's Globe Theater. Like the conservative communities they left behind, colonists carried the puritanic antitheater prejudice: They believed that, by portraying characters onstage, actors tempted viewers into evil. Child rights advocates decried the use of boy actors to play female roles as an insidious corruption in thespian companies in which adult pedophiles had easy access to the unsuspecting young.

To assure the colonies of the best in community morals, some newcomers to the Southern colonies forbade acting troupes, whom the overly pious labeled wanton dregs bent on seducing the audience into lewdness. The most virulent social critics abased all stage folk with a universal charge of sloth, lying, crude jesting, swearing, blasphemy, mockery, lust, whoring, debauchery, idolatry, and sacrilege. On August 27, 1665, magistrates in Accomac County on the James River set an example of propriety by ousting actors William Darby, Cornelius Watkinson, and Philip Howard during their production of Philip Alexander Bruce's *Ye Beare and Ye Cubb*, an amusing interlude performed at Cowle's Tavern near Pungoteague, Virginia. The confrontation between the upright and the frivolous resulted in a verdict of not guilty, but the precedent remained potent as a challenge to future idlers daring to infect the New World with Old World faults.

In the late seventeenth to early eighteenth centuries, a greater deterrent to Southern colonial drama was a matter of priorities. Until frontier hamlets achieved economic stability, peaceful coexistence with natives, and freedom from onerous domestic and agricultural duties, settlers had neither time nor opportunity to build stages, make costumes and props, rehearse scenes, or pause for regularly scheduled entertainment and enlightenment. By the eighteenth century, demand for theater developed among coastal plantation families, many of whom were aristocratic Anglicans educated in the Cavalier tradition, acquainted with the arts, and well traveled in the sophisticated cities of Europe. Money pouring in from lucrative indigo, rice, cane, and cotton markets underwrote the lavish stage entertainments that planters missed at their isolated country estates. Until permanent stages were erected, strolling players entertained outdoors, while local and European troupes set up in schools as well as innyards, courtrooms, meeting halls, market pavilions, and barns. Posters and program notes listed titles of French and English dramatic and musical favorites by Molière, William Shakespeare, John Dryden, Colley Cibber, George Farquhar, Joseph Addison, Thomas Otway, Francis Beaumont and John Fletcher, and William Congreve. A pastoral play produced by the reading theater of William and Mary in 1702 transformed a school building into a temporary stage; the next year, British immigrant Anthony Aston produced *Fool's Opera* in Charleston under deplorably primitive conditions.

Ultimately, the South led the way for American theater by hosting the first play, the first college performance, the first professional actor, and the first permanent playhouse. In 1716, Charles and Mary Stagg's company found a home in the New World's premiere theater, built by William Levingston, a merchant and dancing master, in Williamsburg, Virginia. The structure was a rustic shed with a shingled roof, where a student company produced Susanna Centlivre's *The Busy-Body* in 1736. The Williamsburg theater sufficed for colonial needs, but it was a far cry from Europe's gilded stages. Still, its establishment was a significant moment in colonial city planning. The introduction of an entertainment center to Virginia's colonial capital set a pattern for other communities; for balance, the thriving trade center needed churches, schools, dry goods stores, apothecary shops, livery stables, inns, legal centers, newspapers, and auditoriums. Within two decades, Williamsburg's example influenced a growing trend toward the construction of permanent theaters.

- Inspired by a traveling troupe from New York, in 1736, Charleston, South Carolina, welcomed the Dock Street Theater. The new facility opened with *The Recruiting Officer*, a comedy by Farquhar, which closed with an epilogue composed by South Carolinian Thomas Dale.

- By 1751, popular demand forced Williamsburg's theatrical promoters to construct a new playhouse, paid for by public subscription. The city's second auditorium opened with the Murray Company's production of William Shakespeare's *Richard III*.

- A 1769 map of Halifax, North Carolina, features a "Play House," the state's first, proving the Carolina coast receptive to theatrical entertainment.

Growing interest in drama and other divertissements was not without deterrents. In 1774 conservative elements in the Continental Congress passed a resolution against "horseracing . . . gaming, cockfighting, exhibitions of shews, plays, and other expensive diversions and entertainments." (Dorman 1967, 19) The measure was largely ignored because of difficulties in enforcement, but it made a token gesture toward ridding the colonies of vice. Despite this wave of legislative conservatism, theater continued to thrive in the South, albeit unevenly and at a slow pace.

- The mid-1780s saw a mass growth in theater. Savannah's playgoers pressed into service a rented meeting hall for the traveling troupe of Godwin and Kidd in 1785. The next year, Richmond's Hall of the Academy, built by promoter Alexander Quesnay, opened simultaneously with Charleston's Harmony Hall, which welcomed theater audiences outside the city limits. The out-of-the-way setting was a deliberate evasion of the £100 amusement tax. When business flagged, Harmony Hall welcomed orators and musicians as well as amateur performers, but the remote location proved its undoing. Greater Charleston's playhouse closed within a few years.

- In 1790, Ann Robinson and Susannah Wall acted in English Restoration dramas and comedies at the grand opening of the first theater in Augusta, Georgia. Their premiere season concluded with a visit of newly elected president George Washington, whom they welcomed with a performance followed by a formal banquet.

- In 1791, New Orleans established a French-language theater, the Theatre St. Pierre, which preceded by a matter of months a French theater in Charleston. To lure English-speaking patrons, promoters stressed a varied program of music, pantomime, and dance as well as opera and drama.

- Charleston continued to set the pace for coastal theatricals. South Carolinians and visiting notables enjoyed the Charleston Theatre, which opened with a comic opera, *The Highland Reel*, in August 1792. Displaying three tiers of boxes, columns, glass chandeliers, stonework, venetian blinds, and a palisaded courtyard, the new venture delighted its clientele by the excellence and taste of its architecture and decor.

- As Mobile, Alabama, developed into an important cotton warehousing and shipping center on the Gulf of Mexico, a functional three-doored facade opened on its first stage at the end of the eighteenth century.

- New Orleans continued to set the pace for luxury, comfort, and outstanding appointments. Its St. Pierre Theatre was lavishly decorated in 1808 with parquet and double tiers of loges. The aggrandizement of frontier stages climaxed in such Palladian beauties as New Orleans's First St. Charles and New American Theaters, both architectural ornaments to the city.

- Simultaneous with developments in Mobile and New Orleans, Richmond suffered a major setback in civic offerings after a chandelier spread fire across the stage and destroyed the Richmond Theater, killing 71 of the 600 attendees. Evangelists used the catastrophe as an example of God's punishment of impiety. The public reacted illogically by conferring blame on Alexander Placide and his company, who carried the stigma until they disbanded.

- William Chapman's floating theater stood atop a simple barge fitted with a gangplank. In the 1830s, it traveled the Mississippi and Ohio Rivers as far south as New Orleans; its ports of call included Memphis, St. Louis, and Cincinnati. According to Irish actor Tyrone Power's *Impressions of America; during the Years 1833, 1834, and 1835* (1836), Chapman's water-based theater was an ark-shaped affair that made its way downriver in early fall. Power comments, "At each village or large plantation he hoists banner and blows trumpet, and few who love a play suffer his ark to pass the door, since they know it is to return no more until the next year." (Hudson 1936, 83) At the end of the annual route, Chapman sold his raft for firewood, returned north, and built a new theater, complete with improvements suggested by experience.

- In honor of Chief Justice John Marshall, Richmond's art lovers remodeled the Marshall Theater in 1838, decking it with the crimson, gilt, and damask of classical stage architecture. After the building's demise in a fire in 1862, the same strong demand for drama influenced the city to restore the theater in the waning days of the Civil War.

- Citizens of Raleigh, North Carolina, boasted the opening of Tucker Hall in 1867, a show-class building equipped with 11 painted scenes and 26 wings.

- Lexington, Kentucky, proclaimed its support of theater arts in 1887 with the building of the North Broadway Opera House, a gaslit auditorium that hosted large touring companies. Among the celebrities to act on Lexington's stage were James O'Neil; Helen Hayes; Lillian Russell; Sarah Bernhardt; and John, Ethel, and Lionel Barrymore. By the latter quarter of the eighteenth century, the first dramatic performance west of the Alleghenies helped to establish Lexington as "the Athens of the West." Frontier promoters invited troupes from Montreal, Quebec, and Albany.

The establishment of permanent homes for drama encouraged writers to seek outlets for their creative art. In the years following the Revolutionary War, a buoyant national self-confidence spawned a need for a uniquely American theater. When companies struck out in new directions, playgoers experienced plays set on home ground. Repertories experimented with regional presentations, often laced with local politics and scandals and contemporary themes of agrarian rights, slavery, and state pride. One of the first to cut ties with Europe was Virginia soldier and legislator Robert Munford, who spoofed election corruption with *The Candidates* (1798), a three-act satire that contains the first appearance of a Negro character, Ralpho. Another play in Munford's *A Collection of Plays and Poems* (1798) is *The Patriots*, a pacifist drama that debunks the glories of war.

In addition to dramatic themes, Southern playwrights dramatized inspirational Americana. A major memoirist and playwright of historical subjects, George Washington Parke Custis, foster son of General George Washington, authored *The Indian Prophecy* (1827), a staging of a meeting between Washington and a native clairvoyant who predicts that the general will one day rule a mighty empire. With *Pocahontas, or The Settlers of Virginia* (1836), Custis drew on

Captain John Smith's *Generall Historie of Virginia, New England and the Summer Isles* (1624) to become the first and most famous of many writers and artists to recast the Pocahontas legend. Elaborately produced at its premiere on January 16, 1830, at Philadelphia's Walnut Street Theatre, *Pocahontas* honored George Washington's birthday. Late that same year, a New York production at the Park Theatre initiated a series of revivals in the Northeast.

Custis opens his legendary play on the James River, where natives observe two English ships and a sloop riding at anchor. When Pocahontas receives the news of the landing in scene 2, she admires the English:

> Oh, 't was a rare sight to behold the chiefs as they leap'd on shore, deck'd in all their braveries; their shining arms, their lofty carriage, and air of command, made them seem like beings from a higher world, sent here to amaze us with their glory. (Custis 1938, 175)

Her companion, Mantea, fears the newcomers, but Pocahontas proclaims stoutly, "Come good, come ill, Pocahontas will be the friend of the English." (Custis 1938, 175)

Custis depicts Pocahontas as a model of hospitality and open-mindedness. From the outset, she intends to treat the English seafarers to appropriate amusements. In scene 3, Rolfe, unaware of the princess's nearness, wanders the Virginia woods, admiring the beauties of forest, water, and wildlife in a lengthy soliloquy, and concludes, "Verily, things are on a great scale in this New World." (Custis 1938, 177) Pocahontas graciously welcomes Rolfe, who has already heard of the noble Powhatan princess. When hostilities arise, she takes refuge in the tomb of Madoc, where she overhears her father, who bears the tribal name Powhatan, plotting treachery and massacre against the English. Powhatan intends to betroth her to Matacoran as his reward for valor in the war to drive out white explorers. At the end of act II, she remains true to her original plans and prays that the Good Spirit will strengthen her heart to save Rolfe.

With a motif common to early Native American plays of the early 1800s, Custis busies his main character with noble ambassadorial tasks. At the beginning of act III, Pocahontas has paddled her canoe to the English hunting lodge. She warns Smith of 700 archers who will assault them with poisoned arrows at daybreak. Returned to her father's palace, she finds the chief perturbed that she refuses Matacoran. When braves interrupt their domestic discussion to present Smith, whom they captured in battle, Powhatan insists that Pocahontas take her place on the throne to observe the presentation of war captives. The text avoids anticlimax by saving the rescue scene to the end of act III, when Smith stands tough against Powhatan and refuses even a "rusty nail" as ransom. (Custis 1938, 190)

Custis heightens the drama's resolution with pagan ritual. After executioners place the stone under Smith's head and raise their clubs for the sacrifice, Pocahontas and her friend Omaya intervene and plead for mercy. Her father calls them "silly girls" and places them under guard. Smith accepts imminent death, demands that his banner fly over his grave, and bequeaths to Pocahontas his gold chain, "symbol of the *preux chevalier* [gallant knight]." (Custis 1938,

191) As tension mounts, Powhatan signals the executioners with a wave of his feather fan. When English muskets fire in the distance, Pocahontas uses the distraction as an opportunity to pull free of her captors. She calls on godly power by name: "the Supreme Being, the true Manitou, and the Father of the Universe." (Custis 1938, 191) After Powhatan relents, the English announce victory over his braves. English officers reward Pocahontas with immediate betrothal to Rolfe, a symbolic gesture of alliance between the opposing forces. Trapped by circumstance, Powhatan assents and pledges "friendship to the English, so long as grass grows and water runs." (Custis 1938, 192) He proposes a curiously English tradition of "giving away the bride" and predicts that his daughter's courage will remain a part of stage and literary lore. (Custis 1938, 192)

Custis's role in drama extends beyond Virginia with commentary and plays of national significance. His career had begun with *Conversations with Lafayette* (1824). In the spring of 1830, he produced *The Railroad*, a technical triumph calling for a steam engine on stage. In 1833, he completed *North Point or Baltimore Defended*, followed by *The Eighth of January* (1834) and *The Pawnee Chief*, of which no production information or publication date remains. Four years after her father's death, Mary Custis Lee appended a memoir to *Recollections and Private Memoirs of Washington, by his Adopted Son, George Washington Parke Custis* (1859).

From their debut, stage originals from the colonial South portrayed the emergent individualism of American playwrights, who felt no need to continue emulating European stage plays. Such regional legends and lore as the adventures of pirates prevailed in dramas. In 1767 the first satiric opera, Andrew Barton's *The Disappointment, or The Force of Credulity*, focused on the legends of the English pirate Edward Teach, whose vessels skirted capture in the Atlantic by hiding in the ample coves and sounds east of New Bern, Wilmington, and Oriental, North Carolina. Barton ridiculed a frenzy of searches for Blackbeard's pirate trove, a major portion of which supposedly was hidden on the outer banks and inner recesses of the Pamlico Sound. The trend held firm over half a century later when Congressman Lemuel Sawyer wrote *Blackbeard: A Comedy in Four Acts* (1824), a political farce set on the same legend-rich waters of North Carolina's outer banks. Sawyer's subsequent work, *Wreck of Honor: A Tragedy in Five Acts* (1826), appealed to contemporary tastes, but was only a temporal success. He is better known for *Printz Hall: A Record of New Sweden* (1839), *A Biography of John Randolph of Roanoke: With a Selection of His Speeches* (1844), and *Autobiography of Lemuel Sawyer* (1844).

Theatrical centers supporting local art and artists lay mostly farther south in Charleston, which maintains a centuries-old reputation as an incubator for the most promising of emerging talent with the Spoleto Festival, held annually in late spring. In 1805, William Ioor, a local physician, wrote his first drama, *Independence: or, Which Do You Like Best, the Peer or the Farmer*, a paean to Thomas Jefferson that Ioor adapted from a novel. His second work, *Battle of Eutaw Springs and Evacuation of Charleston* (1807), which honored South Carolina's role in the Revolutionary War, traveled to Philadelphia in 1813 and returned to South Carolina five years later for a revival. A fellow Charlestonian, John Blake White, featured the theme of dueling in *Modern Honor* (1812), an early social drama.

Novelist William Gilmore Simms, also a Charleston native, chose the stage as a political medium, furthering the move to annex Texas with *Michael Bonham, or The Fall of Bexar* (1844). He favored slavery in the divisive question of Missouri's admission to the Union with *Norman Maurice, or The Man of the People* (1851).

American theatrics reached a golden era in the nineteenth century with the stage brilliance of Lotta Crabtree, Edwin Forrest, Charlotte Cushman, Edwin Booth, Ada Rehan, John Drew, Lola Montez, and amateur Sam Houston, secretary of the Nashville Thespian Society and comic in the farce *We Fly by Night*. Vigorous theatricals continued to meet the demand for strongly American themes and settings in drama as well as comedy. In contrast to the serious, divisive topic of abolition of slavery, Louisiana playwright Victor Séjour produced *Diegarias* (1844) for Le Théâtre Français. The play was one of at least 20 titles he wrote for the French stage after he left the United States. North Carolina playwright and drama critic John Augustin Daly's frivolous *Under the Gaslight* (1867) depicted the Easterner's romanticized notion of frontier danger with a truly American stereotype, the victim tied to the railroad tracks and set free by the heroine as a smoke-spouting engine pulls around the bend. By incorporating realistic stage machinery, the producer buoyed to stardom Rose Eytinge, who claimed Abraham Lincoln and Secretary of State William Henry Seward as fans. Daly's creation of another stereotype, the Native American villain, powers *Horizon* (1871), a play stressing the difference between Eastern and Western mentalities, a recurrent theme in frontier literature.

An unexpected failure from the Southwest is that of Missouri humorist Mark Twain, who teamed with New Yorker Bret Harte to produce a memorable flop, *Ah Sin, the Heathen Chinee* (1876), a four-act comedy that failed in Washington, D.C., and New York because of poorly coordinated revision. Joseph Daly skewered the inept play with his witty criticism:

> The construction of this play and the development of the story are the result of great research, and erudition, and genius, and invention—and plagiarism. . . . When our play was finished, we found it was so long, and so broad, and so deep—in places—that it would have taken a week to play it. I thought that was all right; we could put "To be continued" on the curtain, and run it straight along. But the manager said no; it would get us into trouble with the general public, and into trouble with the general government, because the Constitution forbids the infliction of cruel or unusual punishment; so he cut out, and cut out. . . . I believe it would have been one of the very best plays in the world if his strength had held out so that he could cut out the whole of it. (Coad and Mims 1929, 259)

The debacle of *Ah Sin* left Twain disillusioned with his mentor and stung by Harte's abrupt departure for Europe. In his autobiography, Twain blamed Harte for alienating New York critics, and linked his collaborator's name with calumny, idleness, alcoholism, and low character.

The twentieth century has produced a powerhouse of dramatic innovation, particularly the experimental performances originating at the University of North Carolina in Chapel Hill. In the first half of the century, the students of drama instructor Fred Koch turned out stage works with a professional appeal:

Thomas Wolfe's first play, *The Return of Buck Gavin* (1919), about a clan chieftain of the Smoky Mountains; Bernice Kelly Harris's *Ca'line* (1932), in which a character demonstrates how to "clay" a hearth; and Fred Koch, Jr.'s *Wash Carver's Mouse Trap* (1935), a Smoky Mountain version of the trickster, who charges a fee to remove vehicles stuck on his muddy road.

From the same learning experience at UNC, student Paul Green evolved into North Carolina's most prominent playwright and progenitor of local grassroots spectacles. He earned a panoply of honors for himself and the university, the launching platform for the American outdoor drama movement. A native of Harnett County near Lillington, North Carolina, Green grew up in a rich lineage of English and Scots settlers of the Cape Fear region. Reared on a cotton farm and educated by Baptists at Buie's Creek Academy, he learned the agrarian values, dialects, and activities that tinged his work with authenticity. Central to his canon of 30 one-act plays are the religion, traditions, and mores of working-class and rural whites and blacks, including bootleggers, mill workers, tenant farmers, conjurers, and hillbillies. In a statement of purpose, he declared:

> I can't help feeling that [home folks] are experiencing life that no art can compass. . . . There among them I felt at home as I'll never feel at home elsewhere. The smell of their sweaty bodies, the gusto of their indecent jokes, the knowledge of their twisted philosophies, the sight of their feet entangled among the pea-vines and grass, their shouts, grunts and belly-achings, the sun blistering down upon them, and the rim of the sky enclosing them forever, all took me wholly, and I was one of them—neither black nor white, but one of them, children of the moist earth underfoot. (Clark 1931, 268–269)

His skill in crafting realistic action, characterization, and voicing of country folk derives from generous inclusion of folk magic and healing, ha'nt stories, religious beliefs, old saws, and holiday games and traditions, all integral to the regionalist's medium.

While learning his craft, Green experimented with comedy, fantasy, parable, and tragedy. He wrote his first local-color play, *The Last of the Lowries* (1920), in the style of John Millington Synge's mournful tableau *Riders to the Sea*. The dialect drama examines the tragic lives of a noted band of mountain outlaws. Green adapted the plot from a story by Mary C. Norment that appeared in an 1875 edition of the *Wilmington (NC) Daily Journal Print*. The plot recounts the decade-long search for half-breed Croatan outlaws who hid from authorities in the Scuffletown Swamp until their deaths in 1874. In 1924, Green sent to the *Review* "In Aunt Mahaly's Cabin—A Folk Play for the Negro Theatre," which appeared in the April issue. A departure from crime and Scuffletown lowlife, the play incorporates ghosts, superstition, and ballads, each wearing what the author called "North Carolina clothes." (Clark 1931, 262) By December, Green had so endeared himself to the *Review*'s staff that he agreed to serve as its editor.

Green turned to religion for a humorous antifundamentalist comedy, *Quare Medicine* (1925). At the height of the action, Old Man Jernigan aids his son Henry by besting Henry's priggish daughter-in-law Mattie, a pro-missionary, antitobacco meddler. In pity, Old Jernigan looks toward Henry and mutters,

"Poor soul, not at peace in his own household, going about like a man with the mulligrubs, can't sleep, can't eat, worried, worried down to the ground." (Green 1956, 110) Doctor Immanuel delivers his Universal Remedy, which he advertises with a jingle:

> Two dollars a bottle, two dollars,
> Going at two dollars,
> Are you weak and heavy laden,
> Sore distressed, sad distressed?
> It will cleanse of evil passion,
> Restore your bowels of compassion,
> Accidents, diseases chronic—
> The marvelous Egyptian Tonic.
> (Green 1956, 116–117)

After the elixir restores "manly courage" and rids Henry of petticoat tyranny, Jernigan exults with a folksy exclamation, "Well, I be durned if I ever seed the beat!" (Green 1956, 128)

At the peak of his career, Green earned a Pulitzer Prize for his first full-length drama, *In Abraham's Bosom* (1927), an agrarian folk tragedy composed in dialect and produced in New York for a disappointingly short run. Set in the "turpentine woods of eastern North Carolina," the play opens with a mournful work song:

> Oh, my feets wuh wet—wid de sunrise dew,
> De morning star—wuh a witness too.
> 'Way, 'way up in de Rock of Ages,
> In God's bosom gwine be my pillah.
> (Green 1952, 669)

The verse sets the tone for the despairing story of Abe, a misguided idealist who abandons fieldwork to open a school. Agrarian and spiritual themes dominate the work, which critic Stark Young describes as ambitious but profoundly grim, dooming Abe from the start. Green's subsequent works—*The Field God* (1927), *The House of Connelly* (1931), and *The Laughing Pioneer* (1932)—fared better on New York stages. His antiwar drama *Johnny Johnson* (1928), cowritten by Kurt Weill, was produced in Finland; and in Hollywood he wrote for Warner Brothers and MGM the screenplays *Voltaire* (1933), *State Fair* (1933), and *Cabin in the Cotton* (1943), a Dixie melodrama that pits a tenant farmer against a drawling belle, played by Bette Davis.

On a two-year Guggenheim fellowship in Germany, Green studied Alexis Granowsky's Yiddish repertory theater and experimented with a broader definition of people's pageant by blending ballet, dialogue, pantomime, poetry, film, lighting, and music. The genre succeeded in four folk dramas: *Tread the Green Grass* (1932), *Roll, Sweet Chariot* (1934), *Shroud My Body Down* (1934), and *The Enchanted Maze* (1935). In 1941, Green returned to conventional drama to write the stage version of Richard Wright's *Native Son*, a fictional odyssey that takes a hapless youth from his first employment by whites to the commission of a senseless murder.

Playwright Paul Green (1894–1981) with cast members of *The Stephen Foster Story* at Bardstown, Kentucky, in 1959

In 1937, Green produced his classic outdoor drama *The Lost Colony*, which launched a national movement characterized by spectacle and pageantry. A brooding, austere study of the English settlement of the Carolina coast, *The Lost Colony* became the longest-running American outdoor drama. An introspective dramatization of Sir Walter Raleigh's role in England's doomed first colony, the production is held for six weeks each summer on the site of the first landings on Roanoke Island in Manteo, North Carolina. Green composed the text to honor the 350th birthday of Virginia Dare, who had played through his memory alongside "rotting ribs of many a ship, the disappearing records of struggle and death." (Adams 1951, iv) To establish the historical significance of the doomed colony, the author links North Carolina's settlement to England by identifying 118 colonists by familiar English names—Browne, Chapman, Colman, Dare, Harris, Johnson, Jones, Little, Taylor/Tayler, and Wyles.

In the opening scene, set on Roanoke Island in the summer of 1584, colonists sing three stanzas of "O God that madest earth and sky," a praise anthem typical of seventeenth-century hymnody, which precedes the minister's prayer and a salute to settlers:

> O lusty singer, dreamer, pioneer,
> Lord of the wilderness, the unafraid,
> Tamer of darkness, fire and flood,
> Of the soaring spirit winged aloft
> On the plumes of agony and death—
> Hear us, O hear!
> The dream still lives,
> It lives, it lives,
> And shall not die!
> (Green 1937, 4–5)

The unnamed narrator/historian explains that the English-speaking settlers left England in April 1584 to colonize the New World. Led by explorers Phillip Amadas and Arthur Barlow, the company alights from rough passage over the Atlantic onto Roanoke Island three months later, when local tribes are harvesting corn. Contrasting the pious prayers and hymn singing of English Christians, native worshippers take part in incantations, ritual, and prayers led by their medicine man.

Green employs chiaroscuro and contrasting settings in the unfolding events that shape the Carolinas. After the deaths of the original colonists, Raleigh persuades Queen Elizabeth I in May 1587 to send three ships from Plymouth containing 121 replacements. In anticipation of his arrival on the North American coast after sailing for eight weeks in the *Golden Trinity*, Old Tom Harris, an Old World malcontent, mutters:

> What a wilderness and desolation! So this is Roanoke Island in the new world, this is the land of Sir Walter's great visioning. . . . Heave, ship, blow storm, and always the same. We are sailing to the new land of freedom, we are pioneers of a dream, me hearties. (Green 1937, 45)

On July 23, 1587, the next landing party arrives at the barren fort and reclaims it for England. Against Tom's perpetual grousing, they sing contrasting choral works—a chantey about Raleigh and "Adam lay ybounden," a medieval myth about the Garden of Eden.

The events of the Virginia colony form a textured tapestry woven of joy and grief. On August 18, Old Tom and the other settlers welcome Virginia Dare's birth to Ananias and Eleanor White Dare, daughter of Governor White. Funeral hymns counter Eleanor's lullabies at Virginia's cradle after more violence and death assail the colony. The English yearn for home and celebrate Christmas with a yule log, candles, holly, and ivy. During the absence of leaders to fetch supplies from England, hardship depletes the colony. Still waiting for relief from England late in the winter of 1588, leader John Borden ponders their uncertain destiny:

> Rowing the sounds and tramping those endless bogs and wilderness of salt sea grass, my mind worked in a turmoil of fever and fret. Why? Why? Why? I kept asking myself—why has no sign, no word come from the governor and Sir Walter? (Green 1937, 87)

Concealing his dismay, John urges the settlers to behave like soldiers. He and the much-divided survivors depart for the native village of Croatoan, leaving their destination carved on a tree. In the last view of them, they sing, "O God, our mighty Father. . . . We walk this way alone." (Green 1937, 103) Green surmises that the remaining few were killed by Spanish adventurers, died on the journey, or were assimilated by friendly natives.

In subsequent theatrical works, Green followed the trend of adapting Southern history when he wrote *The Highland Call* (1939), a biographic glimpse of Flora MacDonald, legendary rescuer of Bonnie Prince Charlie and settler among North Carolina's tobacco planters. Additional titles return to familiar colonial events: *The Common Glory* (1947), a tribute to Virginian Thomas Jefferson; *Faith of Our Fathers* (1950), a study of George Washington; *Wilderness Road* (1955), an outdoor drama set among the pioneer stock of Berea, Kentucky; and *The Founders* (1957), a retelling of the Pocahontas–John Rolfe story. To acknowledge Green's place in Southern drama, in 1978 the University of North Carolina dedicated the Paul Green Theatre and established the Department of Dramatic Art and the Extension Division, which has aided 55 fledgling folk theaters since 1963.

Similar to Paul Green's *The Last of the Lowries*, William Norment Cox's popular play *The Scuffletown Outlaws: A Tragedy of the Lowrie Gang* (1924) fictionalizes antiwar feelings of Scotch-Croatan (Lumbee) half-breed chief Henry Berry Lowrie. A historical figure who protested forced service in the Confederate army, Lowrie speaks the outsider's distrust of the overclass: "I thought ye my friend, a-workin' to help me and the rest, when every other domn white mon was a-workin' to kill us. Mon, ye ha'e been brave, but the brave mon most times gits shot." (Walser 1956, 52) Cox's re-creation of swamp dialect rings true with local pronunciations of man/mon, creek/crick, and fire/far, as well as folk verb forms (help, helped/hep, holp).

Other Southern dramas appealed to audiences for their re-creation of spiritual, agrarian, historical, and folk themes. In 1923, Lula Vollmer's *Sun-Up* opened on Broadway with a revenge plot about the Cagles, a North Carolina mountain family who shelter in the Appalachians away from involvement in World War I. In an emotional speech at the end of act 2, Rufe Cagle declares his love of the land:

> Out thar on that hill my pap died fer whut he thought wuz right. He's at rest down thar in the valley near to your maw. Some day Mom will lie thar, and you and maybe—me. Hit's ours. . . . We don't own all the land, but hit's ours jest the same, to love and enjoy 'cose God A'mighty give it to us. (Vollmer 1938, 996)

After a letter from the War Department relates Rufe's death in action, his widowed mother, Liza Cagle, hides a deserter under a potato pile when the sheriff trails him through snow to the Cagle cabin. The play concludes with a confrontation between Mrs. Cagle and the stranger whose father wronged the family. In a grim version of an eye for an eye, she intends to kill the deserter, but she halts at the command of her son's spirit, which reminds her "As long as thar air women—thar will be—sons. I ain't no more—to you—than other mothers' sons—air to them." (Vollmer 1938, 1008) *Sun-Up* had a successful 12-month run, followed by a European tour, and a revival in the 1928–1929 season in New York and Paris. Vollmer was less successful with later folk plays, *The Shame Woman* (1923), *The Dunce Boy* (1925), *Trigger* (1927), *The Hills Between* (1938), and *Moonshine and Honeysuckle* (1938).

In the same vein of folkloric drama, South Carolinian Howard Dixon Richardson made an international success of *Dark of the Moon* (1945), an icily evocative drama originally named for Barbara Allen, the doomed lover in a mournful English ballad. A musical legend play about frontier witchcraft, *Dark of the Moon* succeeded in New York, starring Carol Stone and Richard Hart. The play toured stages in the United States, Canada, and Europe in its original form and as a ballet performed by the National Ballet of Canada. It won Richardson the Maxwell Anderson Award and off-Broadway recognition for a 1951 revival. Richardson also achieved recognition for his teleplays for *Cameo Theatre, Alcoa Hour, Goodyear Playhouse, Alfred Hitchcock*, and *Matinee Theatre*.

In the mode of Paul Green's historical outdoor drama based on local events and personalities, West Virginian Kermit Hunter is a second progenitor of the genre. He developed from a regionalist playwright to the most widely performed dramatist in the United States. During the 1950s and 1960s, Hunter supplied 40 communities with historical pageants written for production by grassroots dramatic groups. A poet and piano major trained at the Juilliard School of Music, he developed his blend of talents at the drama school of the University of North Carolina, earning both the Joseph Feldman Playwriting Award and Rockefeller and Guggenheim Fellowships. A founder of the outdoor drama as a theatrical genre, he wrote outdoor spectacles, including these Southern settings: *Walk toward the Sunset*, the story of the swarthy Melungeon clan whose uncertain origin continues to spawn surmise about the settlement of Kentucky Ozark hill country; *Unto These Hills*, a North Carolina pageant of Cherokee history from 1540 to 1842 featuring the story of Tsali, Cherokee martyr; *Voice in the Wind*, a survey of Florida history; and *Chucky Jack*, the story of Revolutionary War hero John Sevier, performed in Gatlinburg, Tennessee.

One of Hunter's most significant contributions to Southern frontier literature is *Horn in the West* (1952), a paean to Daniel Boone that runs annually in summer stock in Boone, North Carolina. Depicting the ideals of piety and freedom, the text departs from Paul Green's prototype of outdoor spectacles by highlighting drama over spectacle. Narrated by a balladeer, the play lauds the North Carolina settlers who defied the regulators of Hillsboro in Alamance County in 1771. Against the backdrop of Blue Ridge mountaineers confronting insurgent Redcoats, an outsider, Dr. Geoffrey Stuart, abandons his Tory allegiance to King George III to support the pioneers. Hunter inserts a cameo of the legendary Daniel Boone, an experienced frontiersman who aids the small mountain band during a tribal uprising.

At a high point in October 1780, John Sevier makes a stand against Gen. Patrick Ferguson's Tory troops at the Battle of King's Mountain. Adopting the spirit of the libertarian Carolinians, Stuart's family rallies. The physician's son Jock joins against British tyranny, and is arrested and condemned to hang. Fearful of losing Jock, Stuart maintains loyalty to the Crown until Redcoats ransack William Morris's home in Morganton. Well schooled in law and history, Stuart realizes the illegality of their act, which violates laws dating to the Magna Carta. In the end, his shift of allegiance costs him his home and son.

Downplaying individual losses, Hunter lifts his play from the personal to the historical by exalting the theme of martyrdom to the cause of independence. Long before feminism revitalized women's roles in significant events, Hunter stressed the part of Nancy Ward, daughter of a British officer and Cherokee mother. Ward's role as peacemaker during troubled times earned her a seat at the council of chiefs and the power to lift the death sentence. A conciliatory look at Southern colonial history, *Unto These Hills* offers a unique blend of action, courage, and unity with bright touches of North Carolina mountain dialect, frontier humor, folk dance, and a Cherokee fire dance.

The national interest in outdoor spectacles and pageantry begun by Paul Green's *The Lost Colony* and Kermit Hunter's *Unto These Hills* and *Horn in the West* continued with Hunter's *The Liberty Tree* (1970), a re-creation of skirmishes between Redcoats and patriots in the turmoil preceding the colonies' separation from England. The presentation, held in Columbia, South Carolina, features high-spirited square dancing as well as confrontations between political factions. Writing in the same genre, Hubert Hayes produced *Thunderland*, a biography of Daniel Boone performed in Asheville, North Carolina, in Biltmore Estate's Forest Amphitheatre. Current outdoor dramas based on historical themes and presented on or near the site of significant events offer a panorama of themes and events from American history:

- *The Aracoma Story*, by Thomas M. Patterson, Logan, West Virginia

- *Christy, the Musical*, by Shirley Dolan, Sandy Kalan, Ken McCaw, Townsend, Tennessee

- *Chucky Jack*, by Kermit Hunter, Gatlinburg, Tennessee

- *The Common Glory*, by Paul Green, Williamsburg, Virginia

- *The Cross and Sword*, by Paul Green, St. Augustine, Florida
- *First for Freedom*, by Max B. Williams, Halifax, North Carolina
- *The Floyd Collins Story*, by Pat Hayes, Brownsville, Kentucky
- *From This Day Forward*, by Fred Cranford, Valdese, North Carolina
- *The Hatfields and McCoys*, by Billy Edd Wheeler, Beckley, West Virginia
- *Honey in the Rock*, by Kermit Hunter, Beckley, West Virginia
- *Horn in the West*, by Kermit Hunter, Boone, North Carolina
- *The Last Hanging in Pike County*, by Janice Kennedy, Lexington, Virginia
- *The Legend of Daniel Boone*, by Jan Hartman, Harrodsburg, Kentucky
- *Listen and Remember*, by Dare Harris Steele, Waxhaw, North Carolina
- *The Long Way Home*, by Earl Hobson Smith, Radford, Virginia
- *Looney's Tavern: The Aftermath and the Legacy*, by Ranny McAlister, Double Springs, Alabama
- *Micajah*, by Fred Burgess, Autryville, North Carolina
- *The Murder of Chief McIntosh*, by Benjamin Griffith, Carrollton, Georgia
- *Pathway to Freedom*, by Mark R. Sumner, Snow Camp, North Carolina
- *Prickett's Fork: An American Frontier Musical*, by Seseen Francis, Fairmont, West Virginia
- *Reflections of Mark Twain*, by Terrell Dempsey and Albert Conrad, Hannibal, Missouri
- *Shadows in the Forest*, by W. C. Mundell, Harrodsburg, Kentucky
- *The Shepherd of the Hills*, adapted from the novel by Harold Bell Wright, Branson, Missouri
- *The Stephen Foster Story*, by Paul Green, Bardstown, Kentucky
- *Stonewall Country*, by Don H. Baker, Lexington, Virginia
- *Strike at the Wind!* Pembroke, North Carolina
- *The Sword of Peace*, by William Harcy, Snow Camp, North Carolina
- *Texas!* by Paul Green, Canyon, Texas
- *The Trail of the Lonesome Pine*, by Earl Hobson Smith, Big Stone Gap, Virginia
- *Turpentine Wine*, by Drue Morris, Destin, Florida
- *Unto These Hills*, by Kermit Hunter, Cherokee, North Carolina
- *The Wataugans*, by Ronnie Day, Elizabethton, Tennessee
- *Young Abe Lincoln*, by Billy Edd Wheeler, Evansville, Tennessee

Apart from the mostly white historic creations, the birth of black theater built a similar pride in genealogy and regional background. A slow evolution dating to the Harlem Renaissance, the phenomenon owes some of its innovation and energy to Southerner Zora Neale Hurston. In 1991, an unusual odyssey brought *Mule Bone*, the collaborative effort of Langston Hughes and Hurston, to Lincoln Theater. Hurston's dream of a glorious experiment in black theater led her to offer Hughes half the project because in her opinion he was more practical. Her contribution was researching black dialect. Begun in 1930 in the creative milieu of the Harlem Renaissance, their three-act play is a broad comedy, rich in courtship ritual, quips, farce, and parody of the Jim Crow South. Scheduled for a performance in Cleveland in mid-February 1931 by the Gilpin Players, the oldest U. S. black theater group, the project languished after the authors sparked a literary quarrel. According to a note from Hughes, "This play was never done because the authors fell out." (Hurston, *Mule Bone* 1991, 5) The apparent cause of their breakup was twofold: Hurston angered Hughes by filing for copyright of the unfinished play, and Hughes infuriated Hurston by a proposal to split the royalties three ways, offering a third to Louise Thompson, their typist. Friends and associates regretted the schism between two bright, established spokespersons for black vernacular. Theater historians surmise that a genuine black folk opera could have stimulated an all-black theater, an art form long supported by critics W. E. B. Du Bois and Alain Locke.

In its current form, *Mule Bone* partially fulfills the expectations of supporters of black playcraft. The plot resembles the impetus for *Their Eyes Were Watching God* (1937), Hurston's novel about front-porch society outside Joe Clarke's store and post office. The focal event, a fight between Clarke and Jim Weston over Daisy Taylor, results in Weston smacking his friend Dave Carter with the hock of a mule. Community involvement results in a set-to between Baptists and Methodists, who take sides during the political fervor brought on by Clarke's candidacy for mayor. Act III, set on the railroad tracks near sunset after citizens run Weston out of town, details the reconciliation of the two scrappers. After swapping boasts about their love for Daisy, they decide that she is not worth their mutual enmity. Dave assures his friend, "if they try to keep you out dat town we'll go out to dat swamp and git us a mule bone a piece and come into town and boil dat stew down to a low gravy." (Hurston, *Mule Bone* 1991, 152) The two dance off down the tracks, with Jim picking his guitar and Dave prancing in time to the music.

In the late 1980s, the blending of whites and blacks in Alfred Uhry's first play, *Driving Miss Daisy* (1986), the longest-running play in Atlanta's history, heralded an era in which the interaction of the races elucidated themes of coping with bigotry, inner-city tensions, anti-Semitism, and random violence. A native of Atlanta, Georgia, and protégé of composer Frank Loesser, Uhry established a reputation as a lyricist and librettist during the previous decade, when he won a Drama Desk Award and Tony nominations and awards from the American Theatre Wing and League of American Theatres for *The Robber Bridegroom* (1975), based on Eudora Welty's folk novella. He had a broad-based background in musicals since adapting John Steinbeck's saga novel *East of Eden* for the musical *Here's Where I Belong* (1968), but returned to teaching before continuing in the light musical genre with *Chapeau* (1977), *Swing* (1980), *Little Johnny Jones* (1982), and *America's Sweetheart* (1985).

The impetus to the character of Miss Daisy surfaced from Uhry's memories of his crusty maternal grandmother, Lena Fox, a hard-edged Jewish teacher who defied family insistence that she let her black chauffeur, Will Coleman, replace her at the wheel. The countertemperaments of 72-year-old Miss Daisy Werthan and her driver, Hoke Coleburn, charmed playgoers, whose applause earned Uhry the Pulitzer Prize for drama and an Oscar for the 1989 film adaptation starring Jessica Tandy, Morgan Freeman, Dan Aykroyd, and Esther Rolle. The film won Oscars for best picture, actress, screenplay, and makeup. The popularity of the movie spawned a 1992 pilot for CBS-TV, pairing Joan Plowright and Robert Guillaume as Miss Daisy and her black driver.

Uhry succeeds with the sparse dialogue of *Driving Miss Daisy* by controlling events, downplaying sentiment and confrontation, and drawing out the benign relationship that ornaments the old age of Hoke and Miss Daisy. In establishing the character of Hoke, Uhry pictures him applying for the job of chauffeur at the office of Miss Daisy's son, Boolie Werthen, who asks how long Hoke drove for Judge Stone, his past employer. In his genial Southern drawl, Hoke replies and takes the opportunity to establish his principles:

> Seven years to the day nearabout. An' I be there still if he din' die, and Miz Stone decide to close up the house and move to her people in Savannah. And she say "Come on down to Savannah wid me, Hoke." 'Cause my wife dead by then and I say "No thank you." I didn't want to leave my grandbabies and I doan' get along with that Geechee trash they got down there. (Uhry 1988, 7)

In her declining years, Miss Daisy relinquishes her hold on autonomy and turns to others for direction. In a brief exchange after she loses touch with reality, she admits to Hoke, "You're my best friend. . . . You are. You are." (Uhry 1988, 47) The gentle, sad vignette in the final scene shows Miss Daisy at a retirement home seated before her Thanksgiving dessert, which Hoke gently feeds her.

Uhry's more recent work includes scripting the films *Mystic Pizza* (1988) and *Rich in Love* (1992). In 1997, he returned to the stage and Southern themes with *The Last Night of Ballyhoo*, a melancholy piece that depicts the isolation of two Georgians of German-Jewish ancestry on the eve of the Nazi invasion of Poland. Uhry sets the action at the Standard Club, a local Jewish hangout where singles meet and dance. Their ambivalence toward their European-Jewish ancestry derives from late-1920s Jew baiting. The Olympics Arts Festival committee showcased *The Last Night of Ballyhoo* at Atlanta's Alliance Theatre, where Uhry is currently playwright-in-residence.

A year after *Driving Miss Daisy* won accolades for stage and film presentations, Louisiania playwright and screenwriter Robert Harling produced *Steel Magnolias* (1987), a solid winner onstage at New York's WPA Theater and in college and theater productions in the United States and Europe. A reprise of the staunch female, Harling's framework of tough Southern women becomes the foundation on which a network of friendship grows and thrives. Written in ten days, Harling's warmly human drama parallels the loss of his sister Susan from severe diabetes and kidney failure two years earlier after the birth of a child. The fictional version of her anguish earned him a National Kidney Foundation Outstanding Achievement Award. The comedy takes place in Chinquapin—a microcosm drawn from Harling's native Natchitoches, Louisiana—where Truvy Jones operates a neighborhood hair parlor. Focusing on the wedding, marriage, motherhood, and death of Shelby, Harling alternately heightens and darkens the events shared by customers of Truvy's Beauty Spot over a four-year period.

Harling maintains an uplifting vision of womanly fortitude with the delightful eccentricities of the beauty shop coterie. The play opens with Truvy's hiring of Annelle Dupuy, a young, inexperienced outsider in need of work. In her welcome to the close-knit community, Truvy spreads a little gossip about the woman who owns the boardinghouse:

> Ruth Robeline . . . now there's a story. She's a twisted, troubled soul. . . . Husband killed in World War II. Her son was killed in Vietnam. I have to tell you, when it comes to suffering, she's right up there with Elizabeth Taylor. (Harling 1988, 9)

The subject of psychic pain, comically introduced, interweaves the story in numerous forms: Clairee's resurgence from widowhood, Annelle's divorce from a small-time criminal, the pessimistic Miss Ouiser's reunion with an old boyfriend, and M'Lynn's fears for her diabetic daughter. Prefatory to Shelby's kidney transplant, M'Lynn discusses the surgical procedure with Truvy:

> Truvy: They have to saw you in half?
> M'Lynn: They do it on Circus of the Stars all the time. . . . It'll make my waist smaller because they take out my bottom ribs to get my kidney out. (Harling 1988, 59)

Like a tangy three-bean salad, alternate layers of humor, wit, and drama surface and submerge, reflecting the tough constitution of Chinquapin's women.

Harling carefully parcels out sentiment, never letting emotion control the plot. In the final scene, the friends ponder Shelby's death following the transplant. Annelle, speaking a fundamentalist philosophy, rejoices that Shelby has become a guardian angel. M'Lynn accepts Annelle's point of view, but admits that she would rather have her daughter alive. In a moment of reflection, she recalls the ease of Shelby's birth and realizes that her daughter also departed life gently:

> There was no noise, no tremble . . . just peace. I realized as a woman how lucky I was. I was there when this wonderful person drifted into my world and I was there when she drifted out. It was the most precious moment of my life thus far. (Harling 1988, 67)

Truvy's enthusiasm for looks stops the emotion from getting out of hand with a compliment to M'Lynn on how well her hair has held up to sorrow. The 1989 Universal film version lacks Harling's commitment to control. Starring Shirley MacLaine, Olympia Dukakis, Sally Fields, Julia Roberts, Tom Skerritt, Daryl Hannah, Sam Shepard, and Dolly Parton (as Truvy), the lush, emotionally over-

Playwright Horton Foote in 1992

ripe movie won a People's Choice Award for best film and nomination for an Oscar, and a Golden Globe award for Roberts.

Texan Horton Foote, a playwright and contemporary of Harling, has a longer string of Southern drama to his credit. Known as "the great eliminator," he prides himself on paring down dialogue and action to the elements of a human conflict. His half century of plays for stage, screen, and television began in 1944 with *Only the Heart* and includes *The Trip to Bountiful* (1953), in which Lillian Gish played the lead. Subsequent works have done well in film, particularly *Tomorrow* (1960), *Baby, the Rain Must Fall* (1965), *Hurry Sundown* (1967), and *Barn Burning* (1980), which he derived from a story by William Faulkner. The winner of an Oscar and Writer's Guild of America Screen Award for the 1962 screen adaptation of Harper Lee's *To Kill a Mockingbird*, Foote has earned subsequent awards for *Tender Mercies* (1983) and the movie adaptation of *The Trip to Bountiful* (1985), as well as honorary degrees from Drew University, Austin College, and the American Film Institute, and a Pulitzer Prize for *The Young Man from Atlanta* (1995). Foote retired to New Hampshire in the 1970s, then returned to screenwriting as a favor to actor Robert Duvall, for whom he wrote *Tender Mercies*, the story of a country singer whose alcoholism robs him of family and stardom. In 1997, *The Death of Papa* proved that the octagenarian can still create theatrical magic. The play—premiering in Chapel Hill, North Carolina, and starring Matthew Broderick, Ellen Burstyn, Polly Holliday, and the playwright's daughter, Hallie Foote—is the last of his nine-part "Orphans' Home Cycle," an autobiographical excursion into the fictional Robedaux family of Harrison, Texas. Its poignant end to a Southern dynasty hinges on Foote's themes of change, destiny, and the hapless people who act out their predestined parts.

In an interview with writer Sheila Benson for *Modern Maturity*, Foote described his writing as "an ongoing saga, a moral and social history of a certain section of the country, specifically this part of Texas." (Benson 1996, 53) The definition fits *The Widow Claire* (1987), a one-act stage play about a widow's decision to remarry. He set the story in his fictional Harrison, Texas, the locale to which he returns in many of his scripts. Typical of his talky, low-key writing, the plot depicts the petty, insidious hometown folk who browbeat Claire, forcing her to accept a lesser man as husband and father to end her loneliness and keep her rambunctious children in line. As Foote indicates, the essence of *The Widow Claire* is a search for place and identity. (Adams 1951; Arner 1985; Banks 1970; Beatty et al. 1952; "Before Jamestown" 1990; Benson 1996; Benton 1968; Blum 1951; Bordsen 1997; Bradbury 1996; Brockett 1968; Brown "Horton" 1997; Clark 1931; *Contemporary Authors* 1994; Correll 1961; Custis 1859, 1938; Dorman 1967; "Driving Miss Daisy" 1996; Foote 1993; Gassner 1967; Gener 1997; Gillett 1952; Green 1937, 1956; Harling 1988; Hart 1956; Hartnoll 1983; "Horn in the West" 1990; Hoyle 1956; Hoyt 1955; Hudson 1936; Hughes 1951; Hunter 1967; Hurston 1973, 1990, *Dust Tracks* 1991, *Mule Bone* 1991, 1995; Jones 1982; Koch 1922; Kunitz and Haycraft 1938; Lewis 1943; "The Lost Colony" 1990; Low and Clift 1981; Mackay 1976; Malone 1933; Moody 1966; *National Cyclopedia* 1967; *North Carolina Authors* 1952; "Outdoor Drama" 1996; Quinn 1938; Rampersad

1986; Rankin 1965; Rasmussen 1995; Roberts 1962; Spearman 1953; Stick 1983; Uhry 1988; Urdang 1981; Walser 1955, 1956; Wilson and Ferris 1989; Wynn 1990)

See also Capote, Truman; Henley, Beth; McCullers, Carson; *To Kill a Mockingbird;* Williams, Tennessee; Wolfe, Thomas.

THEIR EYES WERE WATCHING GOD

Reclaimed four decades after its publication and exalted as prime fruit of the Southern Renaissance, Zora Neale Hurston's *Their Eyes Were Watching God* (1937) is a literary landmark: the first American feminist novel of the twentieth century. It delineates two contrasting groups of African Americans: the settled life of the all-black community of Eatonville, Florida, and a significant part of the unsettled black diaspora—the eastern stream of migrant workers who maintain work rhythms, superstitions, and customs derived from Africa and the Caribbean. A dialect classic of black American fiction, the work demonstrates Hurston's belief that "there is no agony like bearing an untold story inside you." (Maggio 1992, 308) She relieves potential discomfort by interspersing her female bildungsroman with characteristic touches—eastern fables, folk beliefs, wisdom lore, an insult ritual known as playing the dozens, pranks, testifying, proverbs, and witty repartee. An outgrowth of Hurston's scholarship in black idiom, gestures, mannerisms, and mindsets, the novel showcases a compelling heroine, 40-year-old Janie Crawford Woods, forerunner of the liberated woman.

The glory of Hurston's best novel lies in the language. Told as framework confessional, the testimony begins at the end of Janie's lengthy marital odyssey, which she describes to friend Pheoby Watson, a patient, long-suffering listener. Janie, who is newly widowed, is returning to Eatonville, Florida, and shocks the town's front-porch critics by appearing in faded shirt and muddy overalls and flaunting her symbol of emancipated womanhood, the "great rope of black hair swinging to her waist and unraveling in the wind like a plume." (Hurston 1990, 2) Lulu Moss, a drawling gossip, deprecates Janie's marriage to a young male and mutters, "She sits high, but she looks low." (Hurston 1990, 3) Symbolic of Janie's checkered reputation is the heaping plate of "mulatto rice" that Pheoby brings, a humble yet nourishing off-white feast cooked as a coming-home present.

The body of the novel covers nearly a quarter century, 1897–1921, and recounts Janie's coming-to-knowledge through three relationships—Logan Killicks, an old man who comes to bed with dirty feet; Joe "Jody" Starks, a self-absorbed climber with a yen for a trophy wife; and 30-year-old Vergible "Tea Cake" Woods, the only man that Janie mourns. Her background lacks the intimate mothering that might have prepared her for an equitable marriage. Abandoned in infancy by her mother, Leafy Washburn, Janie depends on Nanny Washburn, her maternal grandmother, who fears that Janie will inherit Leafy's penchant for wildness and illicit love. By rushing Janie to marry young, Nanny attempts to unload a burden as troublesome as her sick headache.

Hurston earns her place among the Harlem Renaissance innovators for exalting the humble in black culture. Janie's prenuptial inheritance comes not from stored wealth or casks of heirloom jewels but from the African-American oral tradition. Woman to woman, Nanny recites a parable comprised of her own bitter experience with male domination: "De white man throw down de load and tell de nigger man tuh pick it up. He pick it up because he have to, but he don't tote it. He hand it to his womenfolks." The moral of Nanny's exemplum becomes a self-fulfilling prophecy for the post–Civil War generation: "De nigger woman is de mule uh de world." (Hurston 1990, 14)

Pressing on to new territory, Hurston creates Janie as the Eve of a new generation that must fashion its own Eden. Unlike Nanny and her emotional baggage of white masters, Chickamauga, Atlanta's fall to General Sherman, and a shamefully wayward daughter, Janie works her way up to self-actualization at age 17 by tossing aside her apron and eloping with Starks, whose ambition to become town mayor requires an obedient beauty for the mayor's wife. Like Rapunzel in the tower, Janie is alienated and alone much of the time, her days festering with repression and ill will, while jovial idlers cluster at Jody's store to pass the time, collect gossip and news, and share lively anecdotes about an aged mule.

Hurston draws on traditions as old as St. Paul for the discounting of women. The symbol of Jody's control rests on Janie's head—the required head rag that swathes her lustrous hair just as the possessive husband cocoons his woman to protect her from admirers. In an unprecedented show of autonomy, Janie involves herself in local give-and-take when it applies to Jody. On his behalf, she makes an impromptu encomium comparing him to George Washington and Abraham Lincoln. She concludes, "You have tuh have power tuh free things and dat makes you lak uh king uh something." (Hurston 1990, 55) The gathering applauds her eloquence. Nonplussed, Jody chomps his cigar and keeps still. Later, he retaliates by denying her a part in the mule's funeral and, before a similar clutch of customers, degrades her importance to the level of children and beasts.

A significant aspect of Hurston's feminism is her acknowledgment of women's right to passion and sexual fulfillment. As Jody presses her into submission, her seven-year marriage degenerates into a physical and verbal concentration camp, which she weathers with a growing dormancy:

> She wasn't petal-open anymore with him. She was twenty-four and seven years married when she knew. She found that out one day when he slapped her face in the kitchen. . . . She stood there until something fell off the shelf inside her. (Hurston 1990, 67)

Janie gathers the fallen object and identifies it as her romanticized image of Jody, now smashed in the dust. By age 37, Janie sleeps alone and stores up love for a dream man who will cherish her for herself. Jody suffers a fierce comeuppance through protracted agony and death from an internal anguish more virulent than Janie's hurt. Before announcing his demise to the community, she makes an emblematic gesture—loosening her hair and concealing under her widow's veil the new, free-flowing Janie.

Hurston is careful to avoid rescuing her Rapunzel with one dash of the prince's charger. Mating her heroine a third time, she sets Janie on tenuous marital ground after an alliance with Tea Cake, an unlikely husband for the mayor's widow and the butt of local jokes. Like the fresh-picked strawberries that he presents her, love looks fresh and tasty to Janie. She thrills to a shared game of checkers and fishing in nearby waters. Hurston posts signs of potential disaster after Tea Cake takes her money, leaves unannounced, and returns with an offhand explanation of a chicken and macaroni supper he bought for friends so that he could find out how rich people feel. The misunderstanding hinges on his fear that Janie is too elevated for his friends and their humble entertainments, but she declares herself free of the past and proves her trust by confessing that she has $1,200 in the bank that she acquired from the sale of Jody's store.

The shift in setting from Eatonville to "the muck," an agricultural commune on Lake Okechobee in the Everglades near Clewiston and Belle Glade, resituates the protagonist from the familiar hometown to a rented shack among Bahamian field hands, alligators, and white bosses who superintend seasonal work. Mrs. Turner, a snob, injects another challenge to Janie's felicity by flaunting a light-skinned brother, a pseudointellectual carpenter. Hurston's voice sounds through the narrator's mask when she comments:

> Mrs. Turner, like all other believers, had built an altar to the unattainable—Caucasian characteristics for all. Her god would smite her, would hurl her from pinnacles and lose her in deserts, but she would not forsake his altars. (Hurston 1990, 139)

The contrast with Tea Cake's dark skin and meager learning is insignificant to Janie, who prefers trips with her husband to Palm Beach, Fort Myers, and Fort Lauderdale. Tea Cake's crude method of establishing primacy is to whip Janie in public. The episode ends with a free-for-all that drives Mrs. Turner back to Miami, "where folks is civilized." (Hurston 1990, 145)

Hurston's falling action tests Janie with a realistic version of the biblical famine, fire, and flood. Janie and Tea Cake ignore local Seminoles who warn that a hurricane threatens the Everglades. Possums, rabbits, and snakes depart the quarters, leaving the unwise to fend for themselves. After the dike bursts and 200-mile-per-hour winds lacerate them, the couple battle rising waters and a rabid dog. Tea Cake helps a volunteer crew bury the dead. A month later, he sickens with "hydrophoby." When he hallucinates and threatens Janie with a gun, she shoots him. The episode replicates the menace of a scenario that Hurston wrote in 1926 in her short story, "Sweat," in which an angry woman named Delia waits for her estranged lover to fall prey to a lurking rattlesnake:

> She mused at the tremendous whirr inside, which every woodsman knows, is one of the sound illusions. The rattler is a ventriloquist. His whirr sounds to the right, to the left, straight ahead, behind, close under foot—everywhere but where he is. Woe to him who guesses wrong unless he is prepared to hold up his end of the argument! Sometimes he strikes without rattling at all. (Hurston, "Sweat" 1985, 1648)

In the novel, the passion that impels Janie is fear rather than vengeance. Once Tea Cake is dead and Janie exonerated by the court, her swelling emotions subside like the floodwaters. Her quest fulfilled, she sits at peace with Pheoby and sighs, "Ah done been tuh de horizon and back." (Hurston 1990, 182) A model of an integrated self, Janie the griot confers grace. She informs and prepares Pheoby, who exclaims, "Ah done growed ten feet higher from jus' listenin' tuh you, Janie. Ah ain't satisfied wid mahself no mo'." (Hurston 1990, 182–183)

In passing the torch, Janie can verbalize for herself the two requirements for a settled life: peace with God and a firsthand knowledge of marital compromise. Just as Nanny passed on her twisted bit of man-woman wisdom, Janie returns the favor by sharing the anecdotal history of her three marriages. She becomes the living proof that enlightenment exacts a price, and that woman must learn to love herself first above all temptations to do otherwise. Hurston creates a touchingly female image to conclude the day. As Janie eases into a quiet backwater of memories, she casts a metaphoric net toward the azimuth, tugs it back to her body, and drapes it familiarly over one shoulder. Hurston places a gentle hand on her heroine and allows her a reflective moment to settle back, open the folds of her net, and "[call] in her soul to come and see." (Hurston 1990, 184) (Asante and Mattson 1992; Bloom 1987; Boas 1978; Bontemps 1942; Bradbury 1996; Hemenway 1977; Holloway 1987; Howard 1980; Hurston, "Sweat" 1985, 1990; Low and Clift 1981; Lyons 1990; Nathiri 1991; Pierpont 1997; Ploski and Williams 1989; Sheffey 1992; Walker 1975, 1979, 1983; Washington 1987; Wilson and Ferris 1989; Witcover 1991; Yates 1991)

See also Hurston, Zora Neale.

TO KILL A MOCKINGBIRD

One of America's best-selling books, *To Kill a Mockingbird* (1960) is a Southern literary success story. The volume, which sold over 11 million copies in its first 15 years of publication, has never been out of print. It continues to top high school and college reading lists, and is often cited as students' favorite work. According to critic Claudia Durst Johnson, "The novel challenges our stereotypes—of the Southerner, the African American, the eccentric, the child, the young lady." (Johnson, Claudia 1997, 3) A significant factor in the novel's authenticity is its reflection of the Scottsboro Trials of 1931, in which nine young blacks were sentenced for allegedly raping two white women on a train passing through Paint Rock, Alabama. Similar to Lee's depiction of a courageous lawyer willing to jeopardize his public stature by defying a display of racism, the Scottsboro case is memorable for sentencing eight of the nine defendants to death and for the challenge of Judge James E. Horton, who denounced community opinion and aided poor black men wrongly accused and convicted.

Harper Lee's affectionate but incisive study of small-town bigotry presents a slice of the South. Set in Maycomb, Alabama, in the summer of 1933, nearly four years into the Depression and at the beginning of Adolf Hitler's rise to power, the novel depicts recognizable Southern situations: fond memories of Stonewall "Ol' Blue Light" Jackson, a black factory worker maimed by a cotton gin, respect for both shotguns and songbirds, and a courthouse with a colored balcony. The focus is a protracted confrontation between outraged racists and an attorney, Atticus Finch, who defends a black man accused of raping a white girl, the explosive scenario that remains a Southern shibboleth. Less controversial glimpses of Alabama include the history of First Purchase African M.E. Church, which Lee describes as "in the quarters outside the southern town limits, across the old sawmill tracks," and a despicable character named Robert E. Lee "Bob" Ewell, a shiftless cracker, both ignoramus and wise-mouthed strutter, whose hangdog children receive health department assistance in controlling "diseases indigenous to filthy surroundings." (Lee 1960, 120, 172) The contrast suggests the author's intent to set forth the real South without voicing negative conclusions: between emancipated slaves struggling to provide a steeple and bell and a ne'er-do-well living in a ramshackle abandoned cabin erected on "lumps of limestone" and combing the city dump for tools, food, and oddments.

The crucible in which characters are tested is the Maycomb County courthouse, scene of innuendo, lies, histrionics, and threats during the trial of Tom Robinson for the rape of Mayella Ewell. Scout examines the building's ramshackle architecture and finds it "faintly reminiscent of Arlington in one respect: the concrete pillars supporting its south roof were too heavy for their light burden." (Lee 1960, 164–165) The patchwork additions, attached to a Victorian framework, feature Greek revival columns and an oversized clock tower containing a corrupt timepiece—a "rusty unreliable instrument, a view indicating a people determined to preserve every physical scrap of the past." As though criticizing Maycomb's antebellum attitudes, Lee notes that dim upstairs cubbyholes and their ratlike, officious inhabitants exhibit a rarefied decay composed of changelessness, mold, dust, and the odor of urine. Like much of the ignorant, semiliterate citizenry, the town's justice center wears a false facade—a moral superstructure that is courteous and welcoming to whites but supercilious and inhumane to blacks. Outdoors, safe from the heated exchange between defense and prosecution, Dolphus Raymond, a harmless eccentric, consoles Jem: "Cry about the simple hell people give other people—without even thinking. Cry about the hell white people give colored folks, without even stopping to think that they're people, too." (Lee 1960, 203)

The novel's action, gleaned from the reminiscence of Jean Louise "Scout" Finch, plunges into simmering racial vitriol at a moment of high boil. As Scout, a motherless six-year-old reared by a beloved black surrogate mother, tries to understand her father's role in seeking justice, she and her brother Jem get a stern talking-to from a neighbor, Miss Maudie Atkinson:

> "I simply want to tell you that there are some men in this world who were born to do our unpleasant jobs for us. Your father's one of them. . . . We're the safest folks in the world," said Miss Maudie. "We're so rarely called on to be Christians, but when we are, we've got men like Atticus to go for us." (Lee 1960, 218)

The encomium uplifts the story at a down moment, after the Finch children witness how their father loses his case. Miss Maudie puts in perspective Atticus's slim moral victory—he has made a tentative inroad against prejudice by keeping the jury out longer than expected.

Lee parallels the legal miasma in Maycomb with a charming counterpoint: the Finch children's consuming curiosity about their father's work and about Arthur "Boo" Radley, a reclusive next-door neighbor reputed to be a dangerous lunatic. Breaks from neighborhood play threaten the backyard idyll with harsh moments of realism: Atticus shoots a rabid dog, Jem is punished for destroying a neighbor's snow-on-the-mountain camellias, and Scout wanders into a scruffy, moiling lynch mob. With her characteristic candor, she identifies Walter Cunningham, whom her father has helped with legal advice, and asks, "Hey, Mr. Cunningham. How's your entailment gettin' along?" (Lee 1960, 155) The ingenuous question, posed Southern-style as an entree into genial conversation, breaks the tension. Lee depicts Cunningham as an unlikely vigilante who drops his belligerant mask to grasp Scout and acknowledge a greeting that she asks him to pass along to young Walter.

In the falling action, Lee maintains control by departing the sad perspective of another despairing black man who hangs himself in his cell rather than face a death sentence. Keeping her eye on Scout, the author returns to the realm of children. Accompanied by Dill Harris, a summer visitor, Scout and Jem keep vigil on the Radley house and make touchingly generous offerings of pennies in a hollow tree, the free zone shared by Boo and his unclaimed friends. The collision between innocence and evil derives not from Boo, but from Ewell, who accosts Scout, dressed in a ham costume, on her way home from a school Halloween pageant. In the unlit schoolyard, a shadowy rescuer saves her from certain attack and stabs Ewell under the ribs with a kitchen knife. As Atticus and Sheriff Heck Tate gather details of the crime scene, Boo, like a friendly ghost, materializes at Jem's bedside.

A powerful, frank view of hypocrisy and racial persecution, *To Kill a Mockingbird* evokes strong feelings among critics and readers. The novel has been challenged for use in public classrooms: schools in Eden Valley, Minnesota (1977), Vernon-Verona-Sherill, New York, (1980), Warren, Indiana (1981), Waukegan, Illinois, Casa Grande, Arizona (1985), and Park Hill, Missouri (1986), where it was suppressed in a junior high school classroom. However, the novel has not made the American Library Association's most frequently challenged books and materials, which include Maya Angelou's *I Know Why the Caged Bird Sings* and the perennial favorites of censors, Mark Twain's *The Adventures of Huckleberry Finn* and J. D. Salinger's *The Catcher in the Rye*. An interesting commentary on Lee's forthright study is its apparent acceptance in Southern schools, which have made no overt efforts to ban it. (Bradbury 1996; Dunlap 1996; Foerstel 1994; Hecimovich 1997; Inge 1990; Johnson, Claudia 1997; Lee 1960; "Literary Laurels" 1961; Moates 1989; "Mockingbird Website" 1997; Price 1996; Skube 1997; Smykowski 1996; *Something about the Author* 1977; Stein 1979; Stuckey 1966; Whitt 1994; Wilson and Ferris 1989)

See also Capote, Truman; Lee, Harper.

TWAIN, MARK

The antebellum South's grand old man, Mark Twain of Hannibal and Hartford moved beyond regional humor, local color, and aphorism to become an international star of satire and fiction. *The Adventures of Huckleberry Finn* (1884) and *Pudd'nhead Wilson* (1894) allied him with his childhood in Hannibal, Missouri, which he recast as the fictional St. Petersburg. *Life on the Mississippi* (1883) recaptured his two years as a licensed Mississippi riverboat pilot. In vivid scenes of lower-class whites, runaway slaves, and snooty social-climbing bourgeois, he re-created palpable visions of a South that revered the Mississippi River, tolerated prejudice, and produced wickedly mischievous young boys.

Though Twain lived most of his adult years in the West and New England, he bore a lifelong adoration of the South. Born November 30, 1835, in Florida, a backwoods Missouri hamlet on the banks of the Mississippi River, Twain (originally named Samuel Langhorne Clemens) was the third son of storekeeper, justice of the peace, and judge John Marshall Clemens and Jane Lampton Clemens, a congenial Virginia blueblood who believed in a humanistic education for her six children. Young Twain, a scampish mimic and purveyor of humor and pranks, dreamed of ennobling himself from his backcountry origins by someday piloting a riverboat. In his autobiographical *Life on the Mississippi*, he re-creates boyhood fantasies of greatness:

> I went meekly aboard a few of the boats that lay packed together like sardines at the long St. Louis wharf, and very humbly inquired for the pilots, but got only a cold shoulder and short words from mates and clerks. I had to make the best of this sort of treatment for the time being, but I had comforting daydreams of a future when I should be a great and honored pilot, with plenty of money, and could kill some of these mates and clerks and pay for them. (Twain 1990, 32)

Resettled in Hannibal at the age of 4, he lived in sight of the Mississippi River for most of his youth. He absorbed rural riverside ambience until his father's death ended Twain's education when he was 18.

In lieu of schooling, the obvious trade for Twain was printing, which he practiced journeyman-style in New York, Philadelphia, Cincinnati, and in Mississippi River settings in St. Louis, Missouri; and Muscatine and Keokuk, Iowa. As printer's devil in his late teens for the *Hannibal Journal*, his older brother Orion's newspaper, Twain adopted a series of pseudonyms, including Epaminondas Adrastus Perkins, Josh, and Thomas Jefferson Snodgrass. In 1859, he completed rigorous study of complicated river maps and current charts and secured a river pilot's license. His life's ambition to navigate the Mississippi River on a broad-decked sternwheeler ended in late April 1861 when Mississippi's secession from the Union halted north-to-south river commerce.

The war ended Twain's residency on his beloved Mississippi River. After enlisting with 14 other youths in the Confederate irregulars of Marion County, Missouri, he departed when the others gave up their military calling at the end of two weeks. He made little public comment on their prewar experience until 20 years after Lee's surrender at Appomattox Courthouse, when he published

Samuel Langhorne Clemens, known as Mark Twain (1835–1910)

"The Private History of a Campaign That Failed" (1885). In a tongue-in-cheek description of firsthand Civil War adventures, Twain refers to the militia as Marion Rangers. The boys prefer evening rambles in search of girls; none cottons to discipline or taking orders. Their misspent nights of patrolling and looking for the enemy conclude in a unanimous disbanding after rumors of the approach of General Ulysses S. Grant terrify them. Twain ends his memoir on the wry note that he had become expert in retreating.

For whatever reason, Twain left the war to join Orion, the newly appointed secretary to the governor of Nevada, in Carson City, where Twain mined quartz, prospected for silver, and wrote for the *Virginia City Territorial Enterprise*. In 1867, he published his first serious short work, "The Celebrated Jumping Frog of Calavaras County," under his pseudonym—the river man's cry of "mark twain." The phrase meant two lengths of the measuring line, a safe depth for logy, shallow-keeled steamers, which were easily ruptured by jutting crags, submerged wrecks, or floating debris. In his early period, Twain built a career on a blend of Southern yarns and the tall tales of the Southwest, a literary style enhanced by the influence of humorist Artemus Ward and local-colorist Bret Harte. Twain branched out to comedy, essays, young-adult literature, autobiography, satire, lectures, history, and anecdotes. To this considerable list of genres he added travelogues about his visit to Panama, Nicaragua, the Azores, Gibraltar, Europe, Russia, Turkey, the Holy Land, and Hawaii, where he interviewed and observed in 1866 on assignment for the *Sacramento Union*.

After a three-year epistolary courtship of Olivia "Livy" Langdon, Twain married his best and only girl on February 2, 1870, and settled in Buffalo, where he edited his father-in-law's paper, the *Buffalo Express*. A refined, citified daughter of a wealthy coal merchant of Elmira, New York, Livy had a lasting influence on her husband's themes and subject matter, and has been accused of bowdlerizing his more risqué humor. Despite tuberculosis of the spine, Livy gave birth to son Langdon and survived typhoid fever. The loss of Langdon to diphtheria preceded the births of Susy in 1872, Clara in 1874, and Jean in 1880.

From New York, Twain moved to a blended environment: a self-styled gingerbready Southern riverboat mansion in the New England milieu of Hartford, Connecticut. A comfortable, house-proud family man and international personality, he wrote novels—*Roughing It* (1872) and *The Prince and the Pauper* (1882)—and a misbegotten stage play, *Ah Sin, the Heathen Chinee* (1876), a collaboration with Bret Harte. These titles stretched his imagination far from his Missouri childhood to experiences outside Dixie. In the mid-1880s, he returned to the South for the first time since his move in late youth and reconstructed childhood memories for *Life on the Mississippi* and *The Adventures of Huckleberry Finn*.

The atmosphere of the antebellum South prevails in Twain's Mississippi period. In *The Autobiography of Mark Twain* (1924), he remarks on the subtle line that separates black and white comrades in his childhood. From his allies, he selects Uncle Dan'l, a middle-aged slave, as the prototype for Jim. Twain remarks fondly,

He has served me well these many, many years. I have not seen him for more than half a century and yet spiritually I have had his welcome company a good part of that time and have staged him in books under his own name and as "Jim," and carted him all around—to Hannibal, down the Mississippi on a raft . . . —and he has endured it all with the patience and friendliness and loyalty which were his birthright. (Twain 1959), 6)

Twain's memories of slavery are gauzy and idealized, a fact that has opened his writing to severe castigation from black critics who believe that romanticized pictures of an avuncular relationship between master and slave are an affront to the black race.

At the height of his fame from the best-selling *Adventures of Huckleberry Finn*, Twain turned to fantasy, satire, and history for *A Connecticut Yankee in King Arthur's Court* (1889), a chaotic masterwork about freedom and human rights, endangered abstracts in both medieval England and the antebellum South. He pursued Tom Sawyer, his cheery, boyish scamp, with a sequel, *Tom Sawyer Abroad* (1894), but stopped short of publication to develop new material. While living outside Florence, Italy, in the grandeur of the Villa Viviani, Twain looked more closely into the question of slavery with the writing of *Pudd'nhead Wilson* (1894), a tragedy of murder and misidentity set in a pre–Civil War Southern microcosm in Twain's favorite milieu, the Missouri towns that line the Mississippi River.

Originally planned as "Those Extraordinary Twins," a spoof about Chang and Eng Bunker, the conjoined twin farmers living in North Carolina, *Pudd'nhead Wilson* opens in Dawson's Landing, a river hamlet like Hannibal that lies south of St. Louis. In a genteel atmosphere, a desperate slave mother creates a new Prince and Pauper by switching at birth a pair of infant boys identical in skin tone and racial characteristics. The patrician becomes a slave and the slave, through no effort or quality of character, advances to the aristocracy. The story begins at the boys' birth in 1830. Because the slave mother, Roxana, called "Roxy," has only a trace of black ancestry, she takes charge of the motherless Thomas à Becket "Tom" Driscoll, the rightful heir of his uncle, Judge Driscoll, a member of the FFV, the First Families of Virginia. (Twain 1964, 24) Terrified that she and her infant may be sold down the river because of false charges of theft, Roxy deftly slips into Tom's frilly gown her own child, the flaxen-haired, blue-eyed, illegitimate son of the aristocratic colonel Cecil Burleigh Essex. To justify her act, she mutters, "Tain't no sin—white folks has done it." (Twain 1964, 36) Twain heightens the pathos of her situation with the choice of the boy's name, Valet de Chambre, which she thinks grand-sounding enough to ennoble her boy. To the rest of the world, he is Chambers, a slave undeserving of a surname.

The plot moves rapidly over the boys' upbringing to the crisis and falling action during an intense period in June 1853. Twain skims over their youth with a short paragraph:

Tom got all the petting, Chambers got none. Tom got all the delicacies, Chambers got mush and milk, and clabber without sugar. In consequence Tom was a sickly child and Chambers wasn't. Tom was "fractious," as Roxy called it, and overbearing; Chambers was meek and docile. (Twain 1964, 41)

Contrasting the misidentified boys, Twain exaggerates the repulsive nature of the false Tom, a haughty tippler and scofflaw in manhood, who abuses at will the false Chambers, his valet. The false Tom's drinking and gambling debts drive him to murder his uncle during an attempted robbery. After rheumatism brings unemployment at the lowest ebb of Roxy's fortunes, she informs the haughty, Yale-educated Tom of his real identity and blackmails him for whiskey and half his allowance. In despair at Roxy's power to expose him, Tom mutters melodramatically, "I've struck bottom this time; there's nothing lower." (Twain 1964, 69)

The setting of the murder trial enhances Twain's study of society's separation between black and white, slave and free:

> Tom with a weed on his hat, had seats near Pembroke Howard, the public prosecutor, and back of them sat a great array of friends of the family. . . . In the "nigger corner" sat Chambers; also Roxy, with good clothes on and her bill of sale in her pocket. It was her most precious possession, and she never parted with it, day or night. (Twain 1964, 147–148)

The intrusion of David Wilson, an eccentric ne'er-do-well country lawyer and amateur fingerprinter from New York, introduces late-nineteenth-century forensic analysis in answer to the question of which son is the rightful heir and which the slave.

Speaking Twain's disdain for race prejudice, Wilson creates a situation that rebukes society as a whole: The false Chambers is unprepared in dress, mannerisms, and outward show of gentility and education to assume the heir's position. Twain notes, "Money and fine clothes could not mend these defects or cover them up; they only made them the more glaring and the more pathetic." (Twain 1964, 167) The false Tom, bred to indolence and self-appeasement, faces social and personal debasement as the son of a manumitted slave. His predicament produces a social conundrum—a challenge to the prevailing belief that Negroes are born inferior. Twain abandons the method by which the murderer adapts to his fall in station by having him sold down the river, the traditional punishment for bad slaves. Roxy falls into an emotional decline and takes refuge in her church. After serializing the tale in *Century* magazine in seven installments running from December 1893 to June 1894, Twain published his pensive novel in illustrated book form. Frank Mayo's 1896 stage play of *Pudd'nhead Wilson* preceded a movie version in 1916 and a PBS-TV rendering in 1983, starring Ken Howard as the attorney and Lise Hilboldt as the slave mother.

Twain's later years brought world-famous visitors, including short-story writers George Washington Cable, Rudyard Kipling, Joel Chandler Harris, and Harriet Beecher Stowe, author of *Uncle Tom's Cabin*, one of the forces that created an abolitionist ferment prior to the Civil War. Dressed in a white linen planter's suit, his face framed in silvery locks, he looked the picture of Old South contentment and hospitality, and thrilled English fans when he journeyed to Oxford to receive an honorary doctorate. Never blessed with entrepreneurial instincts, Twain scraped along on his earnings and became a popular after-dinner speaker during times when royalties failed him. Lawsuits, haphazard financial management, and ill-advised investments in the Paige compositor and Kaolatype machine depleted him, forcing him onto the lecture circuit to meet expenses. The deaths of daughter Susy in 1895 from meningitis and wife Olivia in 1904 and the severe epileptic seizures that killed daughter Jean in 1909 saddened and embittered him.

Twain's late satire, irony, and allegory attest to his unhappiness, particularly the allegorical story "The Man Who Corrupted Hadleyburg" (1898) and two posthumous works, the morality novella *The Mysterious Stranger* (1916) and a caustic treatise on religion, "Letters from the Earth" (1963). To clarify public misconceptions about his life and blatant atheism, Twain, who claimed to use "a pen warmed up in hell," began dictating his autobiography to Albert Bigelow Paine in 1906. At Twain's death from heart disease at Stormfield in Redding, Connecticut, on April 21, 1910, the manuscript lay unfinished.

Twain remains the country's best-loved teller of tales and most frequently cited satirist. Both Florida and Hannibal, Missouri, honor him with museums. Florida boasts the preserved cabin in which he was born; Hannibal showcases the home his father built in 1844. On a knoll near Hannibal, a statue of Twain rises above the inscription: "His religion was humanity, and the whole world mourned for him when he died." His skill with humor, local color, and anecdote eased the disdainful message of his damning stories, which hint at a streak of doubt that foolish humanity is worth saving. A controlled-prose artist, Twain often presented satiric monologues to fans who packed lecture halls for evenings of rambling commentary, punctuated by puffs on his pipe or cigar. A vehicle for Hal Holbrook and other imitators, one-man shows in the style of Twain continue to blend witty Southern jest with his decidedly dark view of the human condition. (Baldanza 1961; Bloom 1986; Boorstin 1965; Bradbury 1996; Crystal 1987, 1995; Davis and Beidler 1984; Dobie 1996; Ehrlich and Carruth 1982; Emerson 1985; Hazard 1927; Hutchinson n.d.; Kaplan 1966; Lee 1966; Levine 1984; Lyttle 1994; McArthur 1992; O'Connor 1966; Rasmussen 1995; Shalit 1987; Thomas and Thomas 1943; Twain 1959, *Huck Finn* 1962, *Letters* 1962, *Tom Sawyer* 1962, 1964, 1990, 1991, 1995, 1996; Twain and Harte 1991; Welland 1991)

See also the Mississippi River.

WALKER, ALICE

One of the South's true celebrities in the latter quarter of the twentieth century, Alice Malsenior Walker continues to shed light on feminism, child advocacy, equal rights, and humanism. She credits her homeland with inspiring this claim:

> No one could wish for a more advantageous heritage than that bequeathed to the black writer in the South: a compassion for the earth, a trust in humanity beyond our knowledge of evil, and abiding love of justice. We inherit a great responsibility . . . for we must give voice to centuries not only of silent bitterness and hate but also of neighborly kindness and sustaining love. ("Alice Walker" 1996, 2)

Her most popular work, *The Color Purple* (1982), flourished both as novel and film. Walker's personal interest in Zora Neale Hurston has revived interest in one of the brilliant, colorful writers of the Harlem Renaissance, and her determined magazine articles and novels about female genital mutilation have sparked an international colloquy on a centuries-old ritual that has become a *cause célèbre* for American legislators, world health workers, and the United Nations.

Such a whirlwind of issues and enthusiasms come naturally from Walker. The eighth and last child of part-time domestic worker Minnie Tallulah Grant and Willie Lee Walker, a landless sharecropper and dairyman, she was born of black-Cherokee ancestry in Eatonton, Georgia, on February 9, 1944. In an article for *On the Issues*, she describes her strong matriarchal background:

> My mother, in addition to her other duties as worker, wife, and mother of eight children, was the mother of the church. I realize now that I was kind of a little church mother in training, as I set out for the church with her on Saturday morning. . . . There has never been anyone who amazed and delighted me as consistently as my mother did when I was a child. (Walker 1997, 18)

From early childhood, Walker profited from her mother's storytelling and from the example of the creativity found in her mother's flower bed, from which she selected blossoms to take on their Saturday church cleaning as decoration for the altar.

Walker's irrepressible good nature was dimmed by a childhood accident when her brother fired a BB into her right eye. A Boston surgeon removed disfiguring scar tissue, but she remained blind in one eye and eventually was fitted with a glass eye. The loss of binocular vision plunged her into depression and challenged her to turn to writing as a new means of expression. She reflects on her reclusive recuperation: "I no longer felt like the little girl I was. I felt old, and because I felt I was unpleasant to look at, filled with shame. I retreated into solitude, and read stories, and began to write poems." (Smith 1992, 1178–1179) A natural scholar, she excelled in literature, graduating first in her class. She attended Spelman College in Atlanta on a rehabilitation scholarship for the handicapped. She departed from home with $75 collected from neighbors to pay her bus fare, and carried her mother's gifts of luggage, a sewing machine, and a typewriter. In her junior year, she entered Sarah Lawrence College in New York, where she came under the influence of authors Jane Cooper and Muriel Rukeyser, who passed her poems to an editor at Harcourt, Brace, Jovanovich. Before completing a B.A. degree in English, Walker visited the home of Dr. Martin Luther King, Jr., attended the Youth World Peace Festival in Helsinki, Finland, and traveled to Uganda on an exchange program. She longed to move to Africa, but in the summer of 1963, she joined civil rights demonstrators at the March on Washington for Jobs and Freedom, where King delivered his "I Have a Dream" speech.

With a strong background in classical verse, world literature, history, and activism, Walker was well on her way to a successful career as a poet, novelist, and contributing editor at *Ms.* magazine. She was a case worker for the New York City Department of Social Services, but chose to return to the South to assist in black voter registration and teach history for the Head Start program, both acts of love for her homeland, which she longed to free from racism. She won an American Scholar essay contest and publication for "The Civil Rights Movement; What Good Was It?" In 1967, she worked with Black Studies Friends of the Children of Mississippi as a collector of the oral histories of black women.

Walker's first story, "To Hell with Dying," and her first volume, *Once: Poems* (1968), were published the year of her marriage to civil rights attorney Melvyn Rosenman Leventhal. After the shooting of Dr. King, she suffered a miscarriage before carrying a second pregnancy to term. Her daughter, Rebecca Grant, was born about the time she published her first novel, *The Third Life of Grange Copeland* (1970), the realistic story of the downward spiral of an embittered tenant farmer in the Jim Crow era who abandons his family, then returns home and murders his wife. A depiction of the postslavery brutality of poverty and ignorance, the novel presents an unsettling picture of self-demolition as an outgrowth of the residual slavery mentality. After teaching at Jackson State and the University of Massachusetts and serving as writer-in-residence at Tougaloo College in Mississippi and fellow at the Radcliffe Institute, she introduced a women's studies course at Wellesley and featured the neglected writings of Zora Neale Hurston, noted folklorist and author of *Mule Bone* and *Their Eyes Were Watching God*. Managing home, school, research, and a writing career, Walker received a doctorate from Russell Sage College in 1972 and wrote *In Love and Trouble: Stories of Black Women* and *Revolutionary Petunias and Other Poems*, both published in 1973, and won a National Book Award nomination,

Alice Walker, at a San Francisco, California, press conference on travel in Cuba, October 1993

Lillian Smith Award, and the Rosenthal Award from the National Institute of Arts and Letters. Her next book, *Langston Hughes, American Poet* (1974), was an initial venture into writing for children.

Strongly influenced by the works of Flannery O'Connor and Hurston, Walker edited *I Love Myself When I Am Laughing . . . and Then Again When I Am Looking Mean and Impressive: A Zora Neale Hurston Reader* (1979), and published *Meridian* (1976), a novel about the civil rights movement, about the time of her divorce. The autobiographical novel describes a young woman's assistance to Southern freedom fighters. She continued to thrive in a variety of settings: as associate professor at Yale University and, after winning a Guggenheim Fellowship, at the University of California at Berkeley, where she made a permanent home and began teaching African-American studies. In this fertile period, she collected short works for *You Can't Keep a Good Woman Down: Stories* (1981), which won a Bay Area Book Reviewer's Association Award.

After establishing a loving relationship with Robert Allen, editor of *Black Scholar*, and moving to Mendocino, California, Walker achieved the pinnacle of her writing career with *The Color Purple*, a much-loved and praised novel that has sold over 10 million copies and is available in 22 languages. The novel gave her financial security and won a nomination for the National Book Critics Circle Award and the Pulitzer Prize, making Walker the first black female author to receive it. The following year, she served as consultant for Quincy Jones's screen version of *The Color Purple*. A mixed success, the film's critical backwash forced her to counter carping from blacks that she had further degraded the reputation of

African-American males in the character of Mr., the novel's cruel, abusive husband, who deliberately conceals letters from his wife Celie's sister Nettie during Nettie's sojourn in Africa. The novel earned Walker the Fannie Hurst Professorship of Literature at Brandeis University. The premier of the movie in her hometown was celebrated with a parade and local notoriety.

Still producing at a rapid pace, Walker published essays and verse in *In Search of Our Mother's Gardens: Womanist Prose* (1983), *Horses Make a Landscape Look More Beautiful* (1984), *Good Night Willie Lee, I'll See You in the Morning: Poems* (1984), *Living by the Word: Selected Writings, 1973–1987* (1988), and *The Temple of My Familiar* (1989), a mystical novel that advances the African lore of *The Color Purple* through a character who has lived numerous reincarnations. The novel's first-person commentary on female circumcision preceded *Possessing the Secret of Joy* (1992), the story of Tashi and a stronger statement of Walker's womanist doctrine, which she declares is more sensuous and loving than feminism. To further her understanding of genital mutilation, she traveled to Africa with director Pratibha Parmar to film a documentary, "Warrior Marks: Female Genital Mutilation and the Sexual Blinding of Women," which prefaced her commentary on women's rights in *Warrior Marks* (1990). Walker emphasized the damage to Africa from the crippling of women through removal of the clitoris to reduce sensation, ostensibly as a deterrent to adultery. More traumatic is enfibulation, the suturing of the female labia, or the removal of the entire vulva, an extreme procedure that causes horrendous pain during intercourse, encourages urinary and vaginal odor and infection, and jeopardizes the health of mother and child during delivery.

In the 1990s, Walker completed more poetry for *Her Blue Body Everything We Know: Earthling Poems* (1991) and a child's story, *Finding the Green Stone* (1991). With the publication of *The Same River Twice* (1996), she returned to black outrage at the issue of spousal abuse in *The Color Purple*. She established Wild Trees Press in Navarro, California, a platform for female and black authors, and completed *Anything We Love Can Be Saved: A Writer's Activism* (1997), a collection of polemical writings against nuclear proliferation and endangerment to nature and in support of Native Americans and their cultural heritage.

Although Walker's themes have broadened in vision and number, she makes regular pilgrimages to the abiding issue of male dominance. In "The Only Reason You Want To Go to Heaven" (1997), a speech originally delivered at Auburn Theological Seminary on April 25, 1995, she challenges the absolutism and heartlessness of male leaders of orthodox Christianity, declaring that, like the men of Islam and Judaism, they have enslaved, robbed, and cruelly used women. Walker finds hope and reason for thanksgiving in the rise of feminist scholarship, "a resurgent belief in the sacredness of the feminine, which has been deliberately erased, demonized and disparaged in all major religions." (Walker 1997, 22) She professes her trust that indigenous people have spoken abiding truths in their defense of the earth mother, "the ancient Goddess/God of all pagans and heathens," a deity that transcends the strictures of the white-dominated Christian faith. ("Alice Walker" 1996; Bradbury 1996; Brooks 1985; Buck 1992; *Contemporary Authors* 1994; Davidson and Wagner-Martin 1995;

Dodds 1968; Hine et al. 1993; Hughes and Meltzer 1968; Inge 1990; Jokinen 1996; Ploski and Williams 1989; Rubin et al. 1985; Sherr and Kazickas 1994; Smith 1992; Snodgrass 1995; Sterling 1968; Walker 1979, 1982, 1996, 1997; Wester 1970; Westling 1985; Wilson and Ferris 1989)

See also *The Color Purple;* Hurston, Zora Neale.

WALKER, MARGARET

Margaret Abigail Walker, a poet and novelist very much at home in her native Birmingham, Alabama, has earned a meager share of honors for a lengthy career as educator, poet, critic, and novelist. A skilled narrator, she turned the events of the life of Margaret Duggans, her great-grandmother, into a historical novel titled *Jubilee* (1966), a powerhouse Civil War romance often compared to Margaret Mitchell's *Gone with the Wind*, Alex Haley's *Roots* and *Queen*, and Ernest J. Gaines's *The Autobiography of Miss Jane Pittman*. Composed in partial fulfillment of the University of Iowa's requirements for a Ph.D. in creative writing, the historical fiction depicts the uncertainties of the war era and the dual bursts of hope and despair that accompanied the first years of emancipation for Southern slaves.

Daughter of a music teacher, Marion Dozier, and a Methodist theologian, Rev. Sigismund C. Walker, a Jamaican educated at Tuskegee Institute, Margaret Walker learned to value literature, music, and scholarship from the shelves of books and recordings in her home and from oral reading, which she relished in early childhood. In her earliest memories, she combined the rhythms and melodies of her mother's songs with the emphasis and symbolism of her father's sermons. She grew up among cultivated people and, after her parents moved to Louisiana to take jobs at New Orleans University, began writing poetry by age 11. She recalls,

> My images have always come from the southern landscape of my childhood and adolescence. The meaning or philosophy came from my father, from his books and from his sermons. Most of all, it came from reading the Bible. (Smith 1992, 1194)

She offered her work to Langston Hughes for a critical evaluation and received his encouragement and the advice to leave the South. An overachiever, she completed high school at Gilbert Academy at age 18 and earned a B.A. degree from Northwestern University prefatory to graduate studies, one of her father's aims for her. During her college years, editor and scholar W. E. B. Du Bois published her verse in *Crisis* magazine.

While living in Chicago, Walker, like other struggling artists, took part in the Federal Writers Project and the South Side Writers' Group, where she enjoyed the camaraderie of three of the black literati—critic Arna Bontemps, novelist Richard Wright, and poet Gwendolyn Brooks, the best of the Chicago Renaissance. Walker completed two collections of inspirational verse, *For My People* (1942) and *Ballad of the Free* (1966). The first volume, introduced by Stephen

Vincent Benét, bears the promise of a born image maker. The title poem, obviously influenced by Walker's familiarity with black sermons, rises from the page like the full-voiced organ accompaniment to an oratorio. Like a beneficent spirit, the speaker looks down at the long history of black people who sing dirges and celebrate jubilees, baptize and preach, and migrate to the ghettos of great cities. In "Dark Blood," the speaker hovers over the lands of her ancestors, sighting "sugar sands and islands of fern and pearl, palm jungles and stretches of a never-ending sea." In "Lineage," she summons sturdy, lyrical matriarchs in a procession of black grandmothers who smell of soap, onions, and wet clay. (Gilbert and Gubar 1985, 1825) *For My People* earned her a place among Yale University's Series of Younger Poets, the first black woman to receive the national honor. She also won mention on the New York Public Library's Honor Roll of Race Relations and received fellowships from the Rosenwald and Ford Foundations. The long silence between her two collections denotes time spent in the classroom at Livingstone College, West Virginia State College, and Jackson State College.

The vigor and depth of research that preceded the writing and publication of *Jubilee* created new interest in Walker's work. The novel interweaves a considerable body of black lore, including songs, a sermon, and a prayer. The story of Elvira "Vyry" Dutton Brown, a white-skinned slave, begins in Dawson County, Georgia, where the protagonist learns to cope with the vagaries of whites. Outwardly a dutiful servant to her master and father, John Morris Dutton, she marries a blacksmith, freedman Randall Ware, and lives peaceably with the white hierarchy. She steadfastly rejects hatred until the critical mass of prewar times looms over her. Walker intensifies the era at the hanging of two slave women for murdering a white owner, where irony accompanies the preacher's exhortation to remember that slaves are sacred property, given in trust from God. The preacher turns to the Bible for proof of the moral obligation to teach slaves right from wrong. His voice rises to emphasize:

> The Christianizing of the black heathen is your sacred duty. He was brought to these great shores for a Christian purpose. It is your duty to see that that great and sacred purpose is fulfilled; that the savage becomes a docile, faithful, humble, and obedient servant. (Walker 1966, 101)

The sickening irony forces Vyry to choose a safe direction for her life. After Ware flees, she attempts an escape with their children, Jim and Minna, and is returned to the whip, which lays open her back. The owners, too, suffer through precarious social change, a factor that sets Walker's text apart from less charitable fiction of the 1960s.

The crux of Vyry's later years arises from the absence of Ware, who is reported dead of fever. During the Reconstruction era, she marries Innis Brown, a "meriney-colored man," and migrates to the lowlands outside Abbeville, Alabama, where night riders terrorize them. (Walker 1966, 244) Endowed with a pathfinder's spunk, Vyry refuses to be cowed by "poor buckra." (Walker 1966, 50) She continues to cooperate with whites, selling baskets of greens and eggs door to door and serving as a midwife. After ten years of separation from Ware, the falling action returns him to Vyry. Both husbands misread her emotions until they discover the indelible marks of servitude on her back. Walker's insistent realism fuels Vyry's farewell to Ware:

> You and me didn't have no chance to make a marriage. Slavery killed our chance. I use to dream I would see you coming down the Big Road, I wanted you to come so bad—but you didn't come. (Walker 1966, 408–409)

In an extensive soliloquy, Vyry loosens the resentment she carries for being stripped and sold on an auction block, having urine dumped on her, being denied literacy, and Dutton's admission that he sired her. The novel ends on a note of reconciliation as Vyry opts to remain married to Innis.

The proceeds from *Jubilee* came at a time when Walker's salary and royalties supported two sons, two daughters, and her disabled husband, Firnist James Alexander. The novel has gone through six translations and adaptation as an opera. Public acclaim following *Jubilee* earned Walker a Houghton Mifflin Literary Fellowship, support from the National Endowment for the Humanities, a White House Award for Distinguished Senior Citizens, and honorary doctorates from Northwestern University, Rust College, Dennison University, and Morgan State University. Its critical reception encouraged Walker to generate more poetry. In 1970, she published *Prophets for a New Day*, a reflective collection on racism and civil rights leaders, whom she compares to biblical patriarchs. Two years later, she produced a critical self-analysis, *How I Wrote Jubilee*, followed in 1990 with *Why I Wrote Jubilee and Other Essays on Life and Literature*. In intervening years, she wrote two more poetry anthologies, *October Journey* (1973) and *This Is My Century: New and Collected Poems* (1989), and additional critical works, *A Poetic Equation: Conversations between Nikki Giovanni and Margaret Walker* (1974) and an analytic biography, *Richard Wright, Daemonic Genius: A Portrait of the Man, a Critical Look at His Work* (1985). (Bradbury 1996; Buck 1992; *Contemporary Authors* 1994; Davidson and Wagner-Martin 1995; Dodds 1968; Hine et al. 1993; Hughes and Meltzer 1968; Inge 1990; Jones 1983; Ploski and Williams 1989; Rubin et al. 1985; Smith 1992; Snodgrass 1995; Sterling 1968; Walker 1966; Wester 1970; Westling 1985; Wilson and Ferris 1989)

WELTY, EUDORA

No compendium of Southern literature is complete without ample commentary and works by Eudora Welty. A staple in twentieth-century American literature, she is best known for novels and short stories with the unique flavor, conventions, and dark, absurdist humor of her native Mississippi. Her sure-footed familiarity with ordinary life reads, as Sinclair Lewis declared, "as clear as the Gettysburg Address." ("Shangri-La" 1970, 100) Less grim than Carson McCullers and quicker paced and less ponderous than William Faulkner, Welty is a rarity: a writer who cares nothing for labels and who thrives, secure and contented, in a self-created fictional microcosm. A master of balance, she has a gift for honoring personal triumphs and ennobling all strata of society, whether outcasts, criminals, addlepates, connivers, or rapscallions, all members of her piquant and sassy cast of eccentrics. Overall, she displays what Robert Penn Warren calls a "shining unity"—a oneness with the South and an acute sensitivity to the evanescence in human endeavor, the wilting of dreams and ambitions in the rush of history. (Welty 1972, flap)

A quiet, unassuming homebody who never married and never left the South, Welty has been a professional writer for over a half century. She dwells in the pleasant atmosphere of her hometown and remains "underfoot locally." (Laskin 1994, 200) She attends local theater productions, supports local politics, and maintains the two-story Tudor residence built by her family, which she typifies as "small-town comfortable." (Powell, Dannye 1994, 329) In her autobiography she justified the decision to remain in Jackson by declaring that "a sheltered life can be a daring life as well. For all serious daring starts from within." (Welty 1984, 114) In a personal opinion about life in New York City, she once commented that people never share a whole life. Rather, small wedges of two lives briefly bump together. True continuity, she maintained, came about in the South, "where people don't move about as much, even now, and where they once hardly ever moved at all, the pattern of life was always right there." (Laskin 1994, 195)

The rightness of Welty's life is the rock on which she has built her career. Born April 13, 1909, she is the eldest of three children of insurance company executive Christian Webb and teacher Mary Chestina Andrews Welty. Welty describes them as a Yankee Republican father and a Southern Democrat mother, but exonerates them both as lifelong readers and lovers of stories, songs, and anecdotes. In a gladsome autobiography, *One Writer's Beginnings* (1984), she relates the importance of reading and writing to her childhood:

> You learned the alphabet as you learned to count to ten, as you learned "Now
> I lay me" and the Lord's Prayer and your father's and mother's name and
> address and telephone number, all in case you were lost. (Welty 1984, 14)

Her memoir exalts the value of learning, which she believes "stamps you with its moments." (Welty 1984, 15) For her, the moments produced a dependable pulse that steadied her sensitivity to human joys and anticipations into a lifetime rhythm.

Welty recalls a childhood waylaid by a rapid heartbeat, a syndrome that confined her to bed "like [the speaker in] Robert Louis Stevenson's 'In the Land of Counterpane.'" (Powell, Dannye 1994, 328) The experience nurtured a meditative enjoyment of imagination, one of the bases of her well-structured short stories. A product of Jackson city schools, Mississippi State College for Women, and the University of Wisconsin, she earned a B.A. in 1929 and completed two years of graduate study in advertising at the Columbia University School of Business. Uninspired with advertising, which she described as "sticking pins into people to make them buy things that they didn't need or really much want," she credits contact with New York City as a significant contributor to her education, and singles out the theater and the Metropolitan Museum as favorite haunts. (Kunitz 1942, 1063)

When her father died of leukemia in 1931, Welty returned to Mississippi. To aid her mother and two younger brothers, Edward and Walter, she worked in journalism and at radio station WJDX in the 1930s and traveled the state as a junior publicity agent for the Jackson bureau of the Works Progress Administration. The job taught her of a camera and how to interview and shuffle human data, a skill that undergirds her best fiction. Her works, which became staples in *Prairie Schooner, Hudson Review, Harper's Bazaar, New Yorker, Atlantic Monthly*, and *Sewanee Review,* gained the eye of Robert Penn Warren, Cleanth Brooks, Granville Hicks, and other critics, who marveled at her technical accuracy, ready wit, and sharp imagery. Her earliest stories come to life with the interests, incongruities, and dilemmas of the folk whom Welty met on the road. These encounters produced the clear perspectives of characters in her first story, "Death of a Traveling Salesman," published in *Manuscript* in 1936, and in subsequent short fiction—"Petrified Man," "Powerhouse," "Keela, the Outcast Indian Maiden," and "Clytie." The outstanding title among her first works is "Why I Live at the P.O.," a droll story published in *Southern Review*. The first-person narrator, Sister, reveals the idiosyncrasies of a bizarre clan composed of Papa-Daddy, Uncle Rondo, Mamma, and Stella-Rondo, the invidious, backbiting sibling who engineers the family's alienation of Sister, who packs up her fern and canning jars full of preserves and, in nine trips with the express wagon, takes up residence at the post office, where she can grow butter beans and live in peace.

Welty's prodigious career is so appealing to writers, teachers, and readers that her autobiography, *One Writer's Beginnings*—a collection of lectures delivered at Harvard—made the best-seller list. No longer dismissed as an entertaining Southern regionalist, she has established credence as the champion of the near-tragic, a controlling image of "A Worn Path," a frequently anthologized story collected in her earliest short-fiction anthology, *A Curtain of Green and Other Stories* (1941), with a preface by her friend and colleague Katherine Anne Porter. Set in December, the story of Phoenix Jackson, a decrepit caregiver, presents her internal monologue during a familiar journey to town for medicine to soothe an ailing grandson. Her mind wanders as she imagines a boy offering a slice of marble cake. Failing eyes turn familiar images into false signals, misreading a scarecrow for a ghost. The path makes demands on Phoenix but her name holds true—like the mythic rejuvenating bird, she trusts God and wards off imminent disaster by dint of resolve and a pinch of luck. Arrived in a metropolitan skyscraper, she counters the big-city sneers of a nameless bureaucrat until rescued by a nurse who sums up the task of caring for a child who swallowed lye three years before: "She doesn't come for herself—she has a little grandson. She makes these trips just as regular as clockwork." (Welty 1980, 147)

Welty's humanity commands the telling of Phoenix Jackson's story. The description of "an obstinate case" unites the will of the gasping child with the persistence of his grandmother. As Phoenix perceives their symbiosis, "We is the only two left in the world. He suffer and it don't seem to put him back at all. He got a sweet look. He going to last." (Welty 1980, 148) The duo—one snuggled in a patchwork quilt, the other struggling to remember what she came to town

Eudora Welty in Jackson, Mississippi, 1972

for—epitomizes the precarious state of creatures in nature. On her way out of the doctor's office, Phoenix skillfully cadges a nickel and adds it to the nickel that she cleverly concealed from a white hunter to buy her grandson a paper windmill. The simple bit of technology is a treat meant to enthrall the sick boy and reward his courage. Yet, Welty retrieves the story from sentiment by re-minding the reader that Phoenix still has the return trip to make—down the stairs, out of town, across the ditch, and back along the path to their isolated home on the Natchez Trace. Adept at turning surface simplicity into shrewd, split-second epiphany, Welty ends the story with Phoenix slowly managing the stairs, "going down." (Welty 1980, 149) The image concludes the television version, filmed for Mississippi ETV in 1994.

Compared to modernists James Joyce, Anton Chekhov, William Faulkner, and her idol, Virginia Woolf, Welty earns a place among the world's skilled storytellers. As is true of Faulkner's steadfast Southerners, there is nothing frivolous or contrived about Welty's characters. All validate the Southern experience, colloquial grace, and dialect, a strength of "Where Is the Voice Coming From?" (1963), a surprising story told from the point of view of the murderer of Medgar Evers, civil rights activist in Jackson, Mississippi. She states confidently in the introduction to *The Collected Stories of Eudora Welty* (1980):

> Whoever the murderer is, I know him: not his identity, but his coming about, in this time and place. That is, I ought to have learned by now, from here, what such a man, intent on such a deed, had going on in his mind. (Welty 1980, xi)

She adds, "I could make no mistake" with a hometown story that burst from current events and pushed through her concentration on a novel. At home in the intricate emotional landscape, Welty meticulously dissects motivation and builds her fiction on the minor ironies and commonalities that reflect a sincere intent. Usually isolated, her protagonists tend to demand recognition and social sustenance. Their inner faith and determination outweigh whatever gracelessness, wayward thoughts, and minor sins detract from overall goodness and worth.

Unlike regionalists, who tend to tie themselves to the flagpole on courthouse square, Welty has not remained static or parochial. Her first novella, *The Robber Bridegroom* (1942), merges the tall tale with Southern gossip, legend, fantasy, and folk wisdom for a playful frontier story rich with energy and optimism. In her second collection, *The Wide Net, and Other Stories* (1943), a broad parade of people and situations attests to the author's versatility and curiosity about the intersections between humdrum reality and shimmering moments of magic, myth, and mystery. Drawn from sources close to home, the stories transcend Mississippi in their depth and clarity. They precede a new direction, *Delta Wedding* (1946), a matriarchal saga novel derived from her first perusal of the dynamics of the Southern family, plantation strictures, and oral tradition. More from the male point of view, *The Ponder Heart* (1954) is a comic triumph that anticipates the mismatings and jangled domesticity of Allan Gurganus's *Oldest Living Confederate Widow Tells All* (1984) and Clyde Edgerton's *Raney* (1985).

Impeded from serious work during her mother's illness, Welty wrote little between 1955 and 1970, but incubated *Losing Battles* (1970), a comedy in the vein of *Delta Wedding*, and a Pulitzer Prize winner, *The Optimist's Daughter* (1972), her most autobiographical fiction. Both works resonate with a mature vision and sympathy for human regrets and antipathies. *Losing Battles*, a fictional elongation of a two-day family reunion, celebrates the ninetieth—and last—birthday of Granny Vaughn. In the quiet moments of the final chapter preceding graveside rites for her, Welty displays her ear for the gossip of temporal-minded onlookers as Jack and Gloria advance through rows of tombstones past the fresh-earth smell of the latest Vaughn grave:

> "That boy walking in front of you has brought himself to a funeral without a shirt-tail behind," said a voice at their backs.
> "It's Jack Renfro. I feel like telling his mother," said somebody else.
> "*She's* not much better. Look at *her* collar and cuffs. Look at her skirt."
> (Welty 1970, 428–429)

The gossip distracts Gloria, but Jack, intent on the service, pulls her attention back to it. The fast pacing of the Beecham-Renfro clan's exchanges and squabbles concludes as it began, with the trivial and the mock-serious. Before the singing of "Bringing in the Sheaves," an unidentified voice disdains the Mississippi flag that drapes the bier, complaining that it has been wrapped with march music and has lain unused all summer on top of the piano. The fretful meddler concludes, "Let's hope it didn't sour."

A subsequent collection, *The Eye of the Story: Selected Essays and Reviews* (1978), provides a window on Welty's methods and philosophy of fiction. Her lengthy career and influence on subsequent authors is reflected in her ample list of awards, including a sheaf of honorary degrees, a Guggenheim Fellowship, O. Henry Award, National Institute of Arts and Letters grant, Cleanth Brooks Medal, Chevalier de l'Ordre des Arts et Lettres, William Dean Howells Medal, National Book Award, Brandeis Medal, National Medal for Literature, Presidential Medal of Freedom, and National Medal of Arts, awarded in 1987. Perhaps more to her honor are the careers of Southerners Reynolds Price, Ellen Gilchrist, and Anne Tyler, all Welty protégés. (Bradbury 1963; Bradbury 1996; Buck 1992; *Contemporary Authors* 1994; Cunliffe 1987; Davidson and Wagner-Martin 1995; Ehrlich and Carruth 1982; "Eudora Welty" (www.cssc) 1996, (www.intercall) 1996; Jones 1982; Kakutani 1980; King 1980; Kunitz 1942; Laskin 1994; Powell, Dannye 1994; Ruas 1985; Rubin 1982; Rubin and Jacobs 1961; Rubin et al. 1985; Shaffner 1970; "Shangri-La" 1970; Stein 1979; Stephens 1995; Stone 1983; Welty 1942, 1970, 1972, 1980, 1984; Wilson and Ferris 1989; Zorotovich 1983)

See also the Mississippi River.

WILLIAMS, TENNESSEE

One of the foremost producers of drama in America and a nostalgic spokesman for Old South elegance, Tennessee Williams set all but two of his extensive canon in the Mississippi-to-the-Gulf milieu. He was a bold romanticist who believed in the Arcadian myth of a gracious Southern past. To flesh out themes of loss and tarnished glory, he created models of fragile beauty, inadequacy, and vulnerability on the brink of catastrophe. His characters fall victim to greed, sexual depravity, and violence. His insights into the masked tensions and frustrations of refined white women lie at the heart of notable characters—Amanda

Wingfield, whose absentee husband "fell in love with long distance"; Stella Kowalski, who refuses to acknowledge that her husband is an opportunistic brute; and Maggie the Cat, a sexually abandoned wife who believes that her marriage can be revived. Williams's literary output includes three volumes of poems, essays, 65 plays for stage and screen, eight short-story anthologies, an autobiography, and two novels, *The Roman Spring of Mrs. Stone* (1950) and *Moise and the World of Reason* (1975).

Much of Williams's life parallels the frustrated, hardscrabble existence he delineated in his characters. Born March 26, 1911, Thomas Lanier Williams, a remote kinsman of poet Sidney Lanier and scion of Tennessee pioneer stock, grew up a restive and compulsive soul. His demands on self and talent far outdistanced his ability to fulfill them. The elder son of a gracious Southern matron, Edwina Dakin, and Cornelius Coffin Williams, an alcoholic who made a meager living selling shoes, he was a native of the starchy community of Columbus, Mississippi. Williams despised his father, whom he considered too working class to appreciate his mother's refinement. While his father covered sales routes, Williams and his older sister Rose lived with their mother and maternal grandparents at the rectory of St. Paul's Episcopal Church, where his grandfather, Rev. Walter Edwin Dakin, was minister. Williams adored his grandparents because they coddled him and tried to build up his sickly physical condition and stem his lifelong irrational fear of terminal illness and insanity.

After Williams's father was transferred to headquarters in 1919, the family left the Deep South and relocated in a dim, undistinguished apartment in St. Louis, Missouri, which Williams recalls was "the color of dried blood and mustard." (Kunitz 1942, 1088) The family, which had grown with the birth of second son Dakin, moved frequently and suffered the frayed-at-the-edges penury Williams later immortalized in *The Glass Menagerie*. Like narrator Tom Wingfield, Williams tended to romanticize Southern gentility, but he tinged descriptions of Amanda Wingfield with sarcasm grounded in realism. Similar to the Wingfield family dissolution, Williams's family never recovered the harmony it had enjoyed in the South and relied on "Grand" Dakin to travel north to tend her ailing daughter. Grand's arrival was a momentary touch of sweetness—a return of spending money and loving attention.

Reticent to a fault, Williams retreated from his parents' quarreling and sniping to his typewriter, a gift from his mother, who appreciated his sensitivity and literary leanings. Against the criticisms of his father, who denounced writing as an unmanly profession, Williams persisted in his efforts and won $25 from a ladies club for a sonnet sequence on spring and published in *Smart Set* a contest-winning essay, "Can a Good Wife Be a Good Sport" (1927). Still in his teens, he sold his first story, "The Vengeance of Nitrocris" (1928), to *Weird Tales* for $15. His mother wrote an as-told-to commentary on family dysfunction, *Remember Me to Tom* (1963), which reveals Williams's dedication to his sister Rose, whose schizophrenia locked her into catatonic withdrawal.

One of the Depression era's high school graduates, Williams entered Washington University on a tenuous financial basis but sufficed on gifts of money from Grand. At his father's insistence he studied journalism but revealed his true stripe while writing for a college drama club, the Mummers, earning honorable mention for *Beauty Is the World* (1929). He transferred to the University of Missouri but left because he couldn't afford tuition. For three years, he sold for International Shoe. During this period, he suffered an emotional collapse, quit his selling job, and returned to his grandparents in Memphis to recuperate. During his convalescence, he wrote *Cairo! Shanghai! Bombay!* (1935) for the Memphis Garden players. At last on firm footing, he produced *The Fugitive Kind* (1936) and *Candles to the Sun* (1937), his first full-length dramas. Five years older than most undergraduate seniors, he completed a degree in 1938 at the University of Iowa while supporting himself by waiting tables at the Iowa State Hospital.

It was during Williams's nine-year odyssey to a B.A. degree that his Midwestern fraternity brothers of Alpha Tau Omega dubbed him Tennessee for his rich drawl. He defended his nickname, claiming that

> the Williamses had fought the Indians for Tennessee and I had already discovered that the life of a young writer was going to be something similar to the defense of a stockade against a band of savages. (Ehrlich and Carruth 1982)

A year after graduation, Williams applied his new name to "The Field of Blue Children" (1939), published in *Story* magazine. A long way from professional status, he moved from Chicago to New Orleans to California in search of employment. In Los Angeles, he found a position plucking chickens; other jobs covered the labor spectrum—elevator operator in an apartment-hotel complex, waiter, teletype operator, cashier, usher, and, during his sojourn in New York, a reciter of verse at the Beggar's Bar in Greenwich Village. His health and stamina were so challenged that the draft board stamped his file 4F.

Success came no more easily than Williams's college degree. An early work, *Battle of Angels* (1940), did not survive its debut in Boston because conservative audiences were shocked by the play's questionable religious themes and overt sexuality. As he did throughout his career, Williams proved himself a scrapper by continuing to revamp the play, which won a $1,000 award from the National Institute of Arts and Letters. During a six-month stint for MGM in 1943, he earned a reputation as Hollywood scenarist before gaining notoriety as a stage dramatist. Undependable finances continued until 1945, forcing him into part-time stints while he turned out stories and one-act plays in his off-hours.

Sharing the leadership of post–World War II modernism with Arthur Miller and Eugene O'Neill, Williams became one of the most influential and controversial voices among American dramatists. His haunting characterizations focused on frail, doomed protagonists who flee into illusion. Audiences recognized his skill at dialogue and setting, which tended to place each act at a significant turning point. He received a Group Theatre Prize in 1939 for one-act plays, which were later anthologized as *American Blues* (1948). He made it to Broadway for the first time with *You Touched Me!* (1945), a collaboration with Donald Windham. Williams gained star status from his long-running Broadway success *The Glass Menagerie* (1945), which opened in Chicago on December 26, 1944. The event, along with a Drama Critics Circle Award, Donaldson Award, and Sidney Howard Memorial Prize, clinched Williams's reputation as gifted playwright.

In an essay for the *New York Times*, Williams connects his meteoric fame to a national phenomenon:

> I was snatched out of virtual oblivion and thrust into sudden prominence, and from the precarious tenancy of furnished rooms about the country I was removed to a suite in a first-class Manhattan hotel. My experience was not unique. Success has often come that abruptly into the lives of Americans. (Williams 1947, 7)

In the same essay, he reflected on a reemergence into the comfort of his old life after cataract surgery on his left eye. Readjusted from "spiritual dislocation" inflicted by sudden fame, he fled to a simpler, less pretentious life in Mexico and became his natural self once more. The realignment brought the immediacy and satisfaction necessary for serious work and provided the setting for his last great play, *Night of the Iguana* (1961), filmed three years later by MGM and starring Richard Burton, Deborah Kerr, Ava Gardner, and Sue Lyon. The adaptation won Oscar nominations for photography and supporting actor Grayson Hall, but garnered harsh criticism for uneven drama.

While enjoying Mexico, Williams wrote "The Poker Night," the kernel that developed into his first Pulitzer Prize winner, *A Streetcar Named Desire* (1947).

Tennessee Williams (1911–1983), right, with longtime friend and fellow writer Carson McCullers, center, and Sam Goldwyn, Jr., Key West, Florida, 1957

The play opened on Broadway on December 3, 1947, received 20 curtain calls, and earned him a second Donaldson award and the New York Drama Critics Award. A tragic drama about a frightened, alienated former Southern belle caught in a web of falsehood, fantasy, and moral deterioration, *A Streetcar Named Desire* created the unstable world of Blanche Dubois, one of Dixie's memorable victims. In a personal introit to *Streetcar*, Williams reminds the reader, "time is short and it doesn't return again. It is slipping away while I write this and while you read it, and the monosyllable of the clock is Loss, Loss, Loss, unless you devote your heart to its opposition." (Williams 1947, 10) The poignant removal of 30-year-old Blanche to an asylum in the final scene echoes a personal memory—despair after his sister Rose was lobotomized and placed in an institution in 1938 without his knowledge. In the bluesy, gritty, working-class tenements of New Orleans, Blanche's downfall evokes pity for the vulnerable and defeated. A coveted stage role, the part went first to Jessica Tandy and passed to Vivien Leigh, who won an Oscar for the 1951 Elia Kazan film version.

Williams's second Pulitzer Prize award was for *Cat on a Hot Tin Roof* (1955). Reprised in 1984 on *Showtime* by Jessica Lange and Tommie Lee Jones, the play ripples with the effects of lies on a competitive family whose patriarch is dying of cancer. Paralleling the falsehoods of marriage, the author champions faith and loyalty as the virtues that uphold one flagging union while two other wedded pairs sink under chronic deception. Maggie the Cat, a sensual heroine much more resilient than Blanche Dubois, confirms her belief in her husband, who lives in past glories on the football field and drowns in self-pity, alcoholism, and regret for a ruined friendship. Best known of Williams's other plays are *Summer and Smoke* (1948), which debuted on the Dallas arena stage before opening on Broadway, and *The Rose Tattoo* (1950), winner of a Tony. Less successful were *Camino Real* (1953), *Suddenly Last Summer* (1958), *Sweet Bird of Youth* (1959), *The Fugitive* (1960), *Period of Adjustment* (1960), *The Milk Train Doesn't Stop Here Anymore* (1963), and *Small Craft Warnings* (1972), a late title in Williams's career that sketches the eccentrics who frequent a bar.

In a move toward adult fare in the 1950s–1960s, Hollywood embraced Williams's realistic drama, adding to the stage hits 15 film greats, including *The Wanton Countess* (1954), *Battle of Angels* [retitled *Orpheus Descending* (1957) and filmed as *The Fugitive Kind* (1960)], *Kingdom of Earth: The Seven Descents of Myrtle* (1968) [retitled *Last of the Mobile Hotshots* (1969)], *This Property Is Condemned* (1966), and *Boom* (1968). Williams reprised *Baby Doll* (1956), a reclamation of *Twenty-Seven Wagons Full of Cotton* (1946), as *Tiger Tail* in 1978. The combined influence of Williams's work on stage and screen made him world-famous. President Jimmy Carter awarded him a Medal of Freedom in 1980 to honor contributions to American drama.

Although Williams averaged completing one play per year, was regularly celebrated and revived in theaters worldwide, and garnered more awards than any other figure of his generation, he suffered critical abandonment in the declining years. According to a frank autobiography, *Memoir* (1975), and a subsequent collection of his letters to an old friend, Donald Windham, Williams was battered by neuroses, exhaustion, alcoholism, drug addiction, and unsuccessful retreats to sanitariums. He spent years living near the Vieux Carré in New Orleans but resided primarily in Key West, Florida. Away from the city, he inhabited a beloved refuge, which he had shared with his longtime mate, Frank Merlo, who died in 1962. During these difficult years, gossip columnists and hasty critics claimed that Williams had outlived his talent; others recognized that he had taken a new direction toward social issues, including homosexuality and social corruption.

Fearing that addictions had destroyed his talent, Williams continued a daily schedule of writing plays to a lessening demand. Of his immersion in work, he explained with touching candor, "I'm a compulsive writer because what I am doing is creating imaginary worlds into which I can retreat from the real world because . . . I've never made any kind of adjustment to the real world." (Miller 1971, 54) Despite an honorary degree from Harvard in 1982, insiders witnessed the toll of periods of self-doubt, moodiness, and loneliness, demonstrated by pathetic late-night cruising in gay bars. At his death from choking on a bottle cap in February 24, 1983, he was residing in New York's Hotel Elysée, befogged by prescription drugs and cocaine. Broadway dimmed its marquees to honor his passing; Truman Capote wrote a touching tribute published in *Playboy* in January 1984. The playwright's remains were interred in Calvary Cemetery, St. Louis, far from the warm Southern clime he had loved.

Late in 1994, the death of the executor of Williams's estate brought to light an astonishing number of unpublished works, approximately 30 percent of his extant titles. Among new plays was a musical version of *The Rose Tattoo*, an opera built on *A Streetcar Named Desire*, and the score for a ballet of *Suddenly Last Summer*. In September 1996, *The Notebook of Trigorin* opened in Cincinnati, starring Lynn Redgrave. The event presaged discoveries and rediscoveries of his lesser-known works, rewrites, and fragments, including *The Red Devil Battery Sign* (1975), an innovative study of the Kennedy assassination; a revision of *Summer and Smoke* as *Eccentricities of a Nightingale* (1976); and *Something Cloudy, Something Clear* (1981), an experimental drama that breaches the unity of time to interweave events from different periods. In an era less concerned with Williams's sexual preference, viewers and critics returned to his texts for a fairer interpretation of themes. (Anderson et al. 1971; Bradbury 1963; Bradbury 1996; Capote 1987; Cunliffe 1987; Ehrlich and Carruth 1982; Gassner and Quinn 1969; Grigson 1963; Kunitz 1942; Miller 1971; Mulligan 1990; Parker 1983; Prideaux 1953; Ruas 1985; Rubin et al. 1985; Spoto 1985; Tischler 1969; Weales 1965; Williams 1947, 1949, 1952, 1975, 1977; Wilson and Ferris 1989)

See also The Glass Menagerie; A Streetcar Named Desire; women in Southern literature.

WOLFE, THOMAS

A robust but doomed genius like poet John Keats, Thomas Clayton Wolfe, one of North Carolina's favorite sons, died while still astounding critics with his lyric narratives. Imaginative, intemperate, and egocentric, he produced brash, brocaded writings that influenced the best of subsequent generations. Overlaid with self-pity and an unflattering self-absorption, they resonate with his exuberant word experiments and the vastness of his vision. Critics accuse him of a multitude of sins, the greatest being puerile moods that swung decidedly down and an out-of-control obsession to write about himself; the least, of dying too young to mature. A significant spokesman, Southern literary historian Louis D. Rubin, Jr., summarized his appeal from a writer's perspective:

> That there were limitations to Thomas Wolfe's version of the Good, the True and the Beautiful, that the clamorous rhetorical announcement of a supposedly unique sensibility soon palls without the solidity and sturdiness of human experience to back it up, that there was considerably more both to life and to the practice of letters than the impassioned assertion of unsatisfied appetite—that kind of realization would come in due time. (Perkins 1997, 169)

Although Wolfe's novels and short stories are left largely to the academic world, their scope, eloquence, and originality continue to rank among great American autobiographical fiction of the 1930s.

Wolfe emerged from a jangled, harried childhood. A native of Asheville, North Carolina, Wolfe was born on October 3, 1900, and grew up in the family's multigabled white clapboard boardinghouse, Old Kentucky Home. The last of eight children, he was buffeted by the antagonisms that produced daily emotional spats between his mother, money-minded realtor Julia Elizabeth Westfall Wolfe, and his profligate father, William Oliver Wolfe, a stonecutter with a love of life, literature, and alcohol. According to North Carolina historian LeGette Blythe's reflective piece about the father, Thomas Wolfe describes his burst of anger at his troop of recalcitrant children:

> "Why, you miserable young fiends from hell!" he shouted, "Where have you been? Here it is way in the night and you are just now reporting. Have you no regard for your poor old father! Have you no bowels of mercy? Merciful God, the agony I have endured, not knowing what possibly horrible fate may have befallen you, fearing that maybe you all were lying cold and stiff, your identity not established, upon some mortuary slab!" (Blythe 1964, 1B)

The bombast and self-pity echo large on the page and suggest the source of Wolfe's immense egotism and untrimmed verbiage. Wolfe's mother moved Thomas, his sister, and three brothers to St. Louis during the 1904 World's Fair to operate an inn, the North Carolina. The family sojourn in Missouri cost them Grover, who died of typhoid.

Once apart from home and hometown, Wolfe never returned. While attending the North State Fitting School, a private academy, he profited from a close association with a teacher, Mrs. J. M. Roberts, who encouraged his writing talent. Entering the University of North Carolina at Chapel Hill at age 16, Wolfe emerged as a major literary talent, editing the literary magazine and the newspaper, the *Daily Tar Heel;* he was named class poet of 1920. During the summer of his sophomore year, he worked in the shipyards of Newport News, Virginia, and coped with the death of his brother Ben, Grover's twin, who died of influenza before achieving his dream of becoming a writer. Wolfe displayed a competitive edge in 1919 by winning the Worth Prize for an essay, "The Crisis in Industry." His first play, "The Return of Buck Gavin: The Tragedy of a Mountain Outlaw," derives from the ferment of the drama department, which was led by Professor Fred Koch and produced contemporaries Lula Vollmer, Kermit Hunter, and Paul Green.

Intent on writing for the stage, Wolfe migrated to Harvard, where he studied three years in George P. Baker's 47 Workshop and earned an M.A. in playwriting. The apprenticeship, extended by an additional postgraduate year, prefaced flight to New York, the place he intended to round out a self that never seemed to fit the hillbilly stereotype of the Appalachias. In "The Train and the City," he welcomed the metropolis:

> The city flashed before me like a glorious jewel, blazing with the thousand rich and brilliant facets of a life so good, so bountiful, so strangely and constantly beautiful and interesting that it seemed intolerable that I should miss a moment of it. I saw the streets swarming with the figures of great men and glorious women, and I walked among them like a conqueror, winning fiercely and exultantly by my talent, courage, and merit, the greatest tribute that the city had to offer, the highest prize of power, wealth, and fame, and the great emolument of love. (Wolfe 1987, 13–14)

Marriage to urbanism introduced him to the witty, carefree side of his personality. An exuberant friend maker, he made his way among the learned. Unselfconscious of Southern speech and background, he sampled city fare in all its fullness and diversity, and gave back to acquaintances an innocence, observations, and childlike enjoyment.

Six years of teaching English at the Washington Square College of New York University paralleled private time composing his outstanding autobiographical novel, *Look Homeward Angel: A Story of the Buried Life* (1929), a wistful remembrance of Ben and of the author's departure from Asheville. A thin disguise as the stuttering neophyte, Eugene Gant, takes Wolfe from Altamont (Asheville) to Pulpit Hill (Chapel Hill) aboard a train symbolizing his escape from the wearying entanglements of family. In frequent Whitmanesque digressions, Wolfe remarks on the emotional turmoil of his character:

> O sea! (he thought) I am the hill-born, the prison-pent, the ghost, the stranger, and I walk here at your side. O sea, I am lonely like you, I am strange and far like you, I am sorrowful like you; my brain, my heart, my life, like yours, have touched strange shores. (Wolfe 1957, 522)

A romantic, overblown bildungsroman, the book derives from Wolfe's feeling of otherness among a boisterous, close-knit family. It needled his kin and much of Asheville and the South and raised a storm of local protest about the obvious identity of the fictional setting.

Freed from the need to balance teaching time with writing, Wolfe began a lifetime of journeys about Europe. He kept prodigious notes in journals about people, places, and an emotionally taxing love affair with writer Aline Bernstein. He moved to Brooklyn to write in earnest, publishing "The Angel on the Porch" in *Scribner's* August 1929 issue. On a fifth trip abroad, he ended the affair and

Thomas Wolfe (1900–1938) visits with his mother on the steps of her home in Asheville, North Carolina, in 1937.

returned to publish "A Portrait of Bascom Hawke" in April 1932, winning $5,000 in a novella contest sponsored by *Scribner's*. With the aid of editor Maxwell Perkins, Wolfe completed *Of Time and the River: A Legend of Man's Hunger in His Youth* (1935), a sprawling, episodic satire that ridicules the self-importance of Harvard campus life. A sixth voyage to Europe brought the notoriety due a distinguished author. He toured the West before the publication of *From Death to Morning* (1935) and, five months later, *The Story of a Novel* (1936), a detailed explication of his writing method. On a visit to Canada, he became ill and entered a hospital in Seattle, Washington. He died at age 38 following two unsuccessful surgeries at Johns Hopkins Hospital in Baltimore, which disclosed a fatal tuberculosis covering one side of the brain. His body was returned to Asheville for burial in Riverside Cemetery. His sister Mabel and brother Fred donated their inherited family manse to the city of Asheville. It remains a historic and literary shrine, complete with antiques, memorabilia, family pictures, and furnishings. A glimpse of his topcoat hanging in the closet of the glassed-in porch demonstrates his immense size; he is said to have been six feet six and amply padded.

Like his jovial, verbose father, Wolfe loomed larger than life. He was given to prodigious eating, drinking, and womanizing, and developed a formidable reputation for hot temper, limpid oratory, soured friendships, and undisciplined emotions. He left unpublished a massive amount of writing that was divided into three titles: *The Web and the Rock* (1939), a symbolic novel that details the flight of his persona, George Webber, from the hometown web to the permanence of a metropolis; *You Can't Go Home Again* (1940), a tempered, satiric examination of degeneracy in the 1920s; and *The Hills Beyond* (1941). A mass of letters, journals, scenarios, short stories, and vignettes comprise the William B. Wisdom collection at Harvard's Houghton Library. Additional Wolfeiana reside at the library of the author's alma mater, the University of North Carolina at Chapel Hill. In 1957, Ketti Frings produced a Pulitzer Prize–winning adaptation of *Look Homeward Angel* in three acts, reissued in 1979 by Frings and Peter Udell as a musical comedy. (Beatty et al. 1952; Blythe 1964; *Contemporary Authors* 1994; Hicks 1968; "Home-Grown" 1968; Jones 1974; Lask 1968; "Looking Homeward" 1995; Perkins 1997; "Thomas Wolfe Homepage" 1996; "Thomas Wolfe Memorial" 1997; "Thomas Wolfe Web Site" 1997; Turnbull 1968; Wolfe 1935, 1957, 1987)

See also theater in the South.

WOMEN IN SOUTHERN LITERATURE

An ambivalence toward womanhood holds firm in the Southern psyche. The Southern literary canon frequently reflects a dichotomy of females forever combating the no-man's-land that lies between its poles: the ethereal wraiths of Edgar Allan Poe's "Ligeia" and "To Helen" and the wispy paragons and sea nymphs of William Gilmore Simms's antebellum poetry versus weathered, indomitable women the likes of Marjorie Kinnan Rawlings's Ora Baxter, Ernest

Gaines's Miss Jane Pittman, William Faulkner's Addie Bundren, Eudora Welty's Stella Rondo, and Katherine Anne Porter's Granny Weatherall. Well into the late twentieth century, the roll call of outspoken, self-willed women continues with Charles Frazier's Ada Monroe and Kaye Gibbons's Ellen Foster. Diverging from the idealized lady, these models suggest that Dixie's women come closer to realism when adversity forces them into a multidimensional social and political milieu. Slavery, poverty, and ignorance have no place in the lifestyle of the elite woman, whose choices of behavior are limited by a social order based on cavalier values. When a struggle between the ideal and shifting mores takes place within a single person, as is the case with Margaret Mitchell's Scarlett O'Hara, the character endures doubts about her values and constantly reassesses motivations and the means to attain them, while the active, assertive self tries to make peace with the obedient, docile self. Lacking compromise, the paradigm dooms any hope for balance and wholeness.

Margaret Mitchell is a good example of a Southern author exploring the types of women who confronted collapsing social structures when the Civil War ended their chivalric past. Her cast covers the gamut of feminine roles the Old South demanded—Mammy, Dilcey, and Prissy, the black house servants who take their cues from their mistress, Ellen Robillard O'Hara. Ellen is the epitome of the dainty but tough Charlestonian whose daily round of duties requires decisions about work, workers, livestock, and family. She scolds her recalcitrant husband, a reckless horseman who loves to jump fences, and supervises the Slatterys, an ignorant white farming-class family, and her own three daughters, Scarlett, Suellen, and Carreen, who often fall short of maternal expectations in bouts of competing, tattling, and sniping. Certain of the role of Southern lady, devout Catholic, and matriarch in the plantation tradition, Ellen labors tirelessly for the good of her extended household. Always carefully groomed and polite, she is iron-sure of the chasm that separates her notions of right and wrong behavior, as is evident at family vespers: "Ellen had taught [Scarlett] that at the end of each day it was her duty to examine her conscience thoroughly, to admit her numerous faults and pray to God for forgiveness and strength never to repeat them." (Mitchell 1964, 72) Long after Ellen's death, Scarlett hears her mother's admonitions in her mind and suffers the consequences at every breach of childhood instruction.

From a background as a bred-in-the-bone Atlanta aristocrat, Mitchell maintained the belief that quality is inborn, in horses and slaves as well as bluebloods. Dilcey's arrival as the bride of Pork, the butler, agrees with the tenor of Ellen O'Hara's household: "Dilcey was tall and bore herself erectly. . . . She was self-possessed and walked with a dignity that surpassed even Mammy's for Mammy had acquired her dignity and Dilcey's was in her blood." (Mitchell 1964, 65) However, Mitchell's characters, like fine silver, are not sapped by polite society's demands for an unstained patina of grace and charm. The crucible that pits women against hunger, terror, and siege tatters the edges of their graciousness at the same time that it reveals more precious and valuable inner strengths. The dilemmas of the war years compel the staunchest Old South belles to make choices and temper their behavior with the exigencies of hard times. A serio-

In *Gone with the Wind* (1936), Margaret Mitchell explored the types of women who confronted collapsing social structures when the Civil War ended the South's chivalric past. Characters included Melanie Wilkes and Scarlett O'Hara, portrayed in the 1939 movie by Olivia de Havilland, left, and Vivian Leigh.

comic foil to Ellen, Aunt Pittypat Hamilton is the pampered Atlanta spinster who retreats to feigned collapse and smelling salts when compromise forces her beyond the limits of propriety. While sheltering Scarlett, recently widowed after her husband's death in service to the Confederate army, Aunt Pitty questions the spirited young kinswoman, who retains the verve and social élan of a youthful deb still eager to flirt and enjoy the round of city social events with her rivals, India Wilkes and Maybelle Merriwether. In the aftermath of the message that Ashley is missing in action, his wife Melanie straightens her spine against a shock that brings pallor to her face while Aunt Pitty weeps into her handkerchief and Scarlett slumps into the corner of the carriage. A closeup of Scarlett's reaction finds her stumbling upstairs to her rosary and mouthing words that Ellen would approve, yet tormenting herself in private for the sin of loving Melanie's husband. A complex figure, Scarlett battles willfulness inherited from the O'Haras with the gritty self-control obtained from the Robillards. Throughout, the author stresses the inequality of Scarlett's traits, with the Irish characteristics regularly overriding the Robillard graciousness and probity.

Mitchell's strength as a novelist is deft character development, which requires her to look beyond plantation manners to the evolving urbanism that separates Atlanta from the rural outback. Far at the other end of the social scale, the Hamilton and O'Hara women and their servants inhabit the same city as the working girls, epitomized by Belle Watling, the gold-hearted madame whom Rhett Butler admires for her kindness and generosity. Mitchell remarks on the prewar standard that limits the interaction of Belle with proper women:

> Belle stood out above the rest, due to her flaming hair and the gaudy, overly fashionable dresses she wore. She was seldom seen on Peachtree Street or in any nice neighborhood, but when she did appear respectable women made haste to cross the street to remove themselves from her vicinity. (Mitchell 1964, 246)

War blurs the lines that keep the extremes on opposite sides of the street. The crush of wounded at Atlanta's makeshift hospital summons the Hamilton and O'Hara women to volunteer as nurses. Still upright and dainty, they roll bandages and tend the fallen. In an unforeseen confrontation, Belle arrives on the scene to offer Melanie gold coins tied in a handkerchief. Moral and social issues clash, contrasting proper upperclass manners and good grooming with the avowed Christian act of a pariah who makes a pathetic attempt to look and act like her betters. The beloved "Miss Melly" juggles social dicta with wartime need and accepts Belle's charity, but is appalled that Uncle Peter, the proud manservant of Aunt Pitty's house, scolds her. "Scarlett, he *hollered* at me! Nobody has ever hollered at me before in my whole life." (Mitchell 1964, 247) The humor of the brief contretemps foreshadows a permanent alteration of expectations, a cataclysmic reshuffling of norms and behaviors that dooms to extinction the stereotypical plantation darling.

On the stage, Tennessee Williams broadens Margaret Mitchell's examination of New South demands. His plays offer an ample list of female personae—Amanda Wingfield in *The Glass Menagerie* (1945), Maggie the Cat in *Cat on a Hot Tin Roof* (1955), and Alma Winemiller, the compelling, poignant old maid of *Summer and Smoke* (1948). In the latter example, Williams strikes at the approach-avoidance syndrome of passionate, intense females who cede to the antebellum past their will to embrace twentieth-century liberation. In the oppressively antique niceties of Glorious Hill, Mississippi, Miss Alma's attempts at happiness produce the dramatic ironies for which Williams is known. Still obedient to Papa, she must justify buying a $14 hat and must devote her life to a childishly neurotic mother. Miss Alma's inarticulate yearning hints at sensuality, but overt desire retreats behind chronic palpitations and self-conscious posturing as clubwoman, belletrist, and vocalist for weddings. Beneath the emotional cowl of the prim ladyhood expected of a minister's daughter, she searches for the physical half of her body and, in the final moments before the falling curtain, leads a crass, repellent young blade to Moon Lake Casino, the sin den she has battled as a monument to wickedness. Williams politely withdraws from Alma the gentlewoman at a telling moment, leaving the reader to guess at her reaction and to wonder if she will retreat to the weak-wristed semiself that denies her substance.

Summer and Smoke is one of Williams's frustratingly incomplete dramas. The work's reticence mimics the hesitance of Alma to depart Victorian mores and grasp the intimacy of the full womanhood that threatens to pass her by. Ambivalence toward an old friend, John Buchanan, forces her to mislead him: With winsome smiles she lures and teases, but her criticism of his dissipation conceals a more painful truth—that he is too much the dashing roué to value a virgin. John strikes to the heart of her split image when he comments: "I see something white at the window. Could that be you, Miss Alma? Or, is it your *doppelgänger*, looking out of the window that faces my way?" (Williams 1952, 676) To the playwright's honor, the 1961 screen version of Miss Alma, brilliantly delineated by bright-eyed but reticent Geraldine Page, earned an Oscar nomination.

A master of the American short story, William Faulkner avoided the quivering Almas to center on an easily identifiable Southern brick—the intractable elderly woman whose faith and breeding require a certain adherence to an enduring code of manners and public behavior and a resilience against tests of honor and self-preservation. In 1996, Mark Smirnoff, editor of *The Oxford American*, included in a compendium an unpublished Faulkner manuscript, "Rose of Lebanon." The story features the characteristic Faulkner heroine who dominates "A Rose for Emily" (1931), *Intruder in the Dust* (1948), *As I Lay Dying (1930)*, "An Odor of Verbena" (1938), and his other re-creations of intractable Old South womanhood. The main character, bearing the peculiarly double-male name of Lewis Randolph, reaches a pinnacle of romantic girlhood on the night that Memphis volunteers leave home to enlist in the Confederate army. The narrator recalls, "She was one of the girls that kissed a hundred and four men. Coming all the way up from Mississippi in a muddy carriage paved with hot bricks." (Faulkner 1996, 8) Long separated from the "hothouse rose" upbringing by old age, she joins her 50-year-old millionaire son at a formal dinner. When a guest disparages "the scarecrows without shoes" who menaced defenseless women in the 1860s, she rises at her place, grips a fruit knife, and relives the horror and revulsion she felt toward a Yankee rapist who had dishonored her 65 years earlier in the kitchen where she heated milk for her son's bottle. Faulkner's powerful staging of a dramatic confrontation divulges without dialogue the foul words that stream from the old survivor's mouth, just as she had rebuked her attacker in young womanhood.

Similar to Faulkner's bulwarks, female characters in Harper Lee's *To Kill a Mockingbird* (1960) form a chorus of pros and cons on matters of hypocrisy and moral courage. On the negative side stands unloving Aunt Alexandra, a corseted bulwark of manners who hammers at nine-year-old Scout Finch, a willful tomboy. To Scout, her aunt is "analogous to Mount Everest: Throughout my early life, she was cold and there." (Lee 1960, 82) Scout's brother Jem eyes his own nemesis, Mrs. Dubose, the cantankerous biddy who dislikes little boys trampling her camellia bed, but who dies a heroine by defeating an addiction to painkillers. Less ambiguous is Calpurnia, the housekeeper and mother substitute who welcomes the Finch children to her church and explains to them why she talks "nigger talk" to other blacks, even though she knows standard English. Apart from interaction with the neighbors and kin who influence the Finch children, Scout's positive female voice speaks up in class for the emerging younger generation. When the teacher asks for a definition of democracy, Scout, well schooled by the teachings and example of her noble father Atticus, replies that there should be equal rights for all and special privileges for none. Her statement foretells of a young womanhood that defies pigeonholed roles for varying stations and races and a lifetime of activating her father's egalitarianism.

Unlike the women known to Mitchell, Williams, Faulkner, and Lee but no less doughty and resourceful, the hill woman commands her own place in Southern literature written by Mary Noailles Murfree, Cynthia Rylant, Jesse Stuart, Charles Frazier, and Harriette Arnow. A favorite of feminist critics is Arnow's Gertie Nevels, the displaced mountaineer from Ballew, Kentucky, who adapts to a Detroit worker's ghetto in *The Dollmaker* (1954). A fierce parent, she insists that an anonymous driver give her a ride. In a quiet voice she says, "I'm sorry you're th army; frum Oak Ridge, I reckon, but I'd a stopped you enyhow. . . . You can shoot me now er give me en this youngen a lift to th closest doctor." (Arnow 1972, 11) Adept with a knife, with the command of an Amazon she hacks and loosens the car from entanglement with pine saplings and directs the driver as he frees the wheels. When the terrible ride is interrupted 15 miles from medical help by her four-year-old son's impeded breath, she turns the blue-lipped face toward her and shakes him to loosen mucus. To the amazement of her companions, she slices into her son's throat, digs clotted matter from his trachea with a hairpin, and shapes a tube from wood to fit into the airway to keep pus and blood from reaching his lungs.

Described as a stoic who envisions life as cyclical tragedy, Arnow's Gertie Nevels holds to Christian beliefs and her land-based skills. Confined to a polyglot community sustained by the demonic workings of a factory, she makes a go of her meager livelihood and diminished stature by turning to religion, whittling, and an animal will that refuses to admit defeat. A fellow hillbilly, Mrs. Miller, expresses the author's view of the displaced Kentuckian:

> My people back home . . . they hated Catholics frum away back—an they ain't never heared a commies; but boy, if anybody went around a callen my people commies on account of they don't like Catholics they'd git their heads knocked in, and nobody ud wait to round up bedsheets fer to do th job in—they'd do it onu spot . . . without waiten tu mess around with a lot a KKK's. (Arnow 1972, 540)

Mrs. Miller declares that there are more racists and Klan types in Detroit than in the hills. Along with the pejorative "hillbilly," the compounded threats of strikes, worker riots, unemployment, cultural rivalries, loneliness, loss, and alienation batter Gertie and her sisterhood to near insanity. Focusing on a single challenge—how to whittle a Christ figure from wood—she actualizes an unvoiced philosophy that life must return to divinity for renewal and ultimate salvation. In the controlled flicks of her knife on cherry wood, she shapes the divine form but leaves the face blank. When asked why she fails to complete the icon, she replies, "They was so many would ha done; they's millions an millions a faces plenty fine enough—fer him. . . . Why, some a my neighbors down there in th alley—they would ha done." (Arnow 1972, 599)

An innovative and less intense look at womanly sacrifice and longing comes from Atlantan Calder Willingham, whose satiric Rose, protagonist of his novel *Rambling Rose* (1972), expresses candidly and forthrightly her sexual urge and need for love. Told through the eyes of Buddy Hillyer, an adult admirer, the plot re-creates Rose as seen during his early puberty in 1935. She arrives to fill a domestic post as maid and caretaker for the three Hillyer children—Doll, Waski, and Buddy—yet initiates chaos that her employer, Daddy Hillyer, terms "one hell of a damnable commotion." (Willingham 1972, 13) Rose's naïveté about her friendship with Buddy extends to overt provocation:

> she lay there beside me in complete unselfconsciousness with an arm around me, her skimpy nightgown up almost to her waist and her bare leg against mine, and her soft round breast mashed against my arm and side. (Willingham 1972, 61)

Their brief sexual experimentation precedes her numerous escapades with a string of men and a failed flirtation with Daddy Hillyer, who murmurs tearfully, "Rose, Rose, Rose . . . you poor miserable little child." He reminds her that Mrs. Hillyer defends the downtrodden and that he must remain loyal to his wife while warding off temptations under his own roof. With lofty sentiment, he compares his tenuous position as paterfamilias to the Greek forces at Thermopylae, where "the Persians shall not pass." (Willingham 1972, 38, 39)

Balanced against Daddy Hillyer's fight to maintain composure in the presence of blatant nymphomania is the beneficence of Mother Hillyer, who refuses to label Rose a temptress. In the throes of a severe toothache, Rose attempts to weasel out of trouble for bedding indiscriminately with local men. Mother Hillyer commiserates and refuses to let Daddy fire Rose:

> I will not allow you to cross-examine her, grill her and pick on her! . . . Why, it's completely unjust. It wasn't her fault those men fought over her this time any more than it was when they fought over her the last time. How is she to blame?— men *like* her, that's all. (Willingham 1972, 151)

The 1991 film version, scripted by Willingham and starring Laura Dern as Rose, Lukas Haas as Buddy, and Robert Duvall and Diane Ladd as the Hillyers, conveys the tragicomedy of the oversexed servant teetering on the edge of disaster. Set in a rambling country house on a quiet riverbank, *Rambling Rose* is a rare example of authentic Southern background, complete with the call of katydids and night peepers. It earned Oscar nominations for Dern and Ladd.

Black authors have made equally bold statements about the authenticity and validity of their fictional matriarchs. In "They Came To Stay" (1989), a commemorative introduction to a photographic essay for *National Geographic*, Maya Angelou lauds the strength of her black female ancestors, who "lived through conditions of cruelties so horrible, so bizarre, the women had to reinvent themselves." (Angelou 1989, 208) She declares that their resurrected selves overcame the multiple horrors of slavery, patriarchy, forced breeding, and media stereotyping on a scale ranging from the innocuous Aunt Jemima to the sluts of pulp fiction and the Hollywood screen. Jackie Torrence, a storyteller in the Uncle Remus mode, echoes Angelou's affirmation with memories of a strong North

Carolina grandmother who refused to give in to poverty. In Torrence's brief memoir, *The Importance of Pot Liquor* (1994), a grandmother, Ola Hannah Carson, treats her daughter Ceola with herb tea, root salve, and home remedies to overcome diphtheria. When cash dries up, Grandmother Carson trades butter, eggs, chickens, goat's milk, garden vegetables, and canned goods to the doctor in exchange for medical care.

Fiction of the last decades of the twentieth century continues the tradition of wit, grit, and good humor in Southern protagonists. A good-natured favorite among Southern readers is 78-year-old Mattie Rigsbee, protagonist of Clyde Edgerton's *Walking across Egypt* (1987), an upbeat novel that depicts the familiar Southern old lady who presses visitors with pieces of cake and shares her secret for crisp bacon—stretching out each slice on a cold pan before frying. A regular at the Listre Baptist Church, Mattie befriends Wesley Benfield, a delinquent given to precriminal activities that presage a slide toward hard prison time. In Edgerton's trademark comic repartee, Mattie announces to her childless feminist daughter Elaine a change in the family structure:

> "I'm getting married so I can have my own grandchildren. I'm signing the papers tonight."
> "Mother, that is ridiculous. What papers?"
> "The guardian papers on Wesley Benfield. So he can live here."
> "*Wesley.* The juvenile delinquent? Mother, sit down. Are you sitting down?"
> (Edgerton 1987, 209)

True to her down-home goodness, Mattie quells a family uproar over an adoption she considers the right thing to do for a needy fellow human being. In the final scene, she offers fresh-baked biscuits and butter and says the standard blessing, "Thank you, Lord, for these and the many blessings Thou hast given us." (Edgerton 1987, 214) The words apply equally to the biscuits and to Wesley.

Allan Gurganus's Lucy Marsden, the plucky widow reflecting over her marriage to a lusty veteran in *Oldest Living Confederate Tells All* (1984), contrasts the domestic and political wars of the Marsden household. While her husband battles flashbacks of a fallen comrade, Lucy, a child bride, grows up in quick snatches, mastering motherhood in a loosely run household. Gurganus's command of red-clay dialect strengthens the character with forthright candor:

> Wedding trip clear to Georgia. By train then buggy. Talk about dust. And me in the excellent new dress (it wearing me), dove-gray piping, ankle-length hem, the short bolero-ish jacket, cute. Cap acted real polite. Every ten miles he asked did I want watering, like I was some thirsty filly or had a bladder condition. (Gurganus 1989, 77)

Shoved body and soul from virginity to the blessed state of consummated matrimony, Lucy gives birth in quick succession to Cap's nine offspring and turns to her maid Castalia for solace when good humor thins to steely endurance.

Gurganus balances comedy and tragedy in the mounting discontent that divides Cap and his wearied wife. The long-ago death of baby Archie surges to memory as Lucy tells of the blinding of Ned, whom Cap steals away from his mother's care for an introduction to guns and incipient manhood. Lucy's immediate response is to build a bonfire of Cap's firearms collection—the ivory derringers, cherry-handled dueling pistols, and German revolvers. With a ready quip at the crepehangers who hurry to her house with casseroles: "How could women *bake* them so fast? Or did ladies keep some constantly on hand for any possible maimings of local kids, specifically Captain Marsden's?" (Gurganus 1989, 620) Grimly determined while greeting Cap at the door, she holds him at pistol point and disdains the kill of the misbegotten hunt. In her sorrow and rage, she muses, "it seems I am the duck diving down to bite on something far beneath dim water, a bird who's chose to spare herself through drowning." (Gurganus 1989, 625) Long widowed when she relives the pain for an interlocutor, Lucy re-creates the anguish of the abused wife as though Cap's fierce egotism can still brandish new hurts in her face.

A surprisingly popular depiction of Southern womanhood, *Having Our Say*, the memoir of Sarah and Elizabeth Delany, appeared in print in 1993. The disciplined upbringing of two North Carolinians—economics teacher Sarah "Sadie" Delany and Dr. Elizabeth "Bessie" Delany, a dentist—reflects on Southern family life of the black gentry and historic events and developments after the sisters moved to Harlem. Born in a time when antimacassars on mahogany chair backs and homemade soap cooked up from potash lye and chicken fat were women's work, the sisters elude ties to proper Southern females and live their own lifestyle in Mount Vernon, New York. At first taken for black hired help, they establish themselves through Sadie's sweet talk and Bessie's adamant self-determination. Looking back on the source of their strength, the Delanys credit their father's emphasis on character, cleanliness, and education as the backbone of a prosperous family. Their wisecracking autobiography preceded an audiocassette read by Whoopi Goldberg, *The Delany Sisters' Book of Everyday Wisdom* (1994), and Emily Mann's 1995 stage adaptation. (Adams 1993; Angelou 1989; Arnow 1972; Astor 1994; Baker 1993; Bell-Russel 1995; Bradbury 1996; Brock 1993; Buchanan 1994; "A Century" 1993; Delany and Delany 1993, 1994; Donahue 1994; Dummett 1993; Edgerton 1985, 1987; Faulkner 1996; Franklin 1995; Gaines 1995; Giles 1993; Gurganus 1989; Hearth 1993; Hoffman 1995; Koenig 1993; Lee 1960; Lockerbie 1969; Mitchell 1964; Moore 1993; Nudd 1995; Simon 1995; Stuttaford 1993; Williams 1947, 1949, 1952, 1975; Willingham 1972)

See also *Gone with the Wind*; Poe, Edgar Allan.

WRIGHT, RICHARD

A brilliant iconoclast, realist, and literary touchstone, Richard Nathaniel Wright, the sire of African-American realism, became the United States first internationally acclaimed black man of letters. Known as a forthright essayist, autobiographer, poet, critic, lecturer, and novelist, he produced the standard against which the purpose and candor of other authors are measured. His revealing autobiography, *Black Boy: A Record of Childhood and Youth* (1945), preceded a torrent of black chronicles, verse, oratory, and literary criticism, and influenced

Richard Wright (1908–1960) in 1943

the twentieth century's sterling African-American authors—Ralph Ellison, Ann Petry, James Baldwin, Maya Angelou, Chester Himes, and Toni Morrison. By chronicling personal defiance of Jim Crow, he typifies the brutality and racism that is the impetus to the civil rights struggle. Wright's fierce reflections became a literary touchstone and the scripture that heartened flagging spirits of Southern black leadership.

Wright's life precipitated his grim outlook for the black Southerner. Born September 4, 1908, on a cotton plantation in the village of Roxie, Mississippi, 20 miles east of Natchez, Wright was named for his grandfathers, both former slaves. He came of age in the Jim Crow South and carried the scars of its cruelty throughout his life. He was the first of two sons of teacher Ella Wilson Wright and Nathaniel Wright, an illiterate sawmill hand, tenant farmer, and runner for a Beale Street drugstore that merchandised the products of a bootlegger. Nathan Wright deserted his family for another woman when his eldest was three and Leon Alan only two. The destitute family moved frequently, first to Natchez, then in 1917 to an apartment in a bordello in West Helena, Arkansas. Ella Wright's frail health after a paralytic stroke forced her to leave the boys in an orphanage.

From 1920 to 1925, Wright lived with his maternal grandparents and various relatives in Jackson, a turbulent time exacerbated by the hypercriticism of his grandmother, Margaret Bolden Wilson, a devout religious fundamentalist who earned a living as nurse and midwife. He characterizes much of Southern piety with his depictions of her stiff, overtly hostile Seventh-Day Adventist strictures, which required cleanliness, Saturday church attendance, vegetarianism, abstention from alcohol and tobacco, and frequent whippings for real or imagined misbehavior. A hostile woman by nature, she exploited biblical example as a means of beating her grandson for reading secular works.

Despite his wretchedness at home, Wright excelled academically. He attended Jim Hill School, and in 1925 graduated valedictorian from the Smith-Robertson School. He found employment as delivery boy for the W. J. Farley clothing store, bellhop at Edward House, dishwasher at the Lyle Drugstore, grocery stocker, and ticket seller for the Alamo Theater. He secured a self-directed education from extensive readings of Thomas Mann, Joseph Conrad, and contemporary American authors—Theodore Dreiser, Sinclair Lewis, F. Scott Fitzgerald, Sherwood Anderson, and H. L. Mencken, whose *Book of Prefaces* served Wright as a primer. In 1923, Wright published a three-part story, "The Voodoo of Hell's Half-Acre," in the *Southern Register*. Alarmed by the title and subject matter of his first foray into short fiction, his fanatic grandmother alienated him by labeling his art a sin. In the turmoil of adolescence, Wright seemed to battle not only the family but all society while reaching for self-actualization as both writer and adult male. Financed with cash skimmed from his theater job, he fled to Memphis, saved his earnings, and relocated in Chicago's Black Belt. These events form the action of his autobiography, which ends as the train chugs north from Tennessee.

In 1927, Wright worked alternately as postal employee, porter, hospital attendant, and insurance seller, and accepted government handouts of lard, flour, and molasses while he perfected his craft. By age 29 he had moved in with friends in Brooklyn, New York. During an era of Red-baiting, he served as executive secretary of the John Reed Club and joined the leftist IWW. He found employment editing Harlem news in the *Daily Worker* and contributed articles to *Left Front* and the *New Masses*, both communist journals. His prospects improved after he allied with the 1935 WPA Illinois Writers Project and accepted the job of publicist for the Chicago Negro Theater. He gained recognition for "Between the World and Me," a dramatic monologue about a lynching published in *Partisan Review* in 1935. He wrote an unsuccessful novel, *Cesspool;* most of *Lawd Today*, an apprentice work published posthumously in 1963; and his autobiography in segments, which appeared as *Uncle Tom's Children: Five Long Stories* (1938). The work earned him $500 in prize money from *Story* magazine.

During his rising fortunes, Wright ended a foundered six-month marriage to Dhima Rose Meadman, an extroverted exotic dancer. With a Guggenheim endowment and identification as one of 12 distinguished American blacks, he published a best-seller, *Native Son* (1940), a tragedy of one of American fiction's most complex victims. Revered as the first Book-of-the-Month by a black novelist and as one of the best American social novels, the work reflects the story of Robert Nixon, who was electrocuted in 1938 for killing a white female. *Native Son*, which earned Wright the NAACP's Spingarn Medal, gave him financial security; critical acclaim provided money to buy a home for his invalid mother in Chicago and allowed the author a year's retreat in Cuernavaca, Mexico. During this period of financial and literary advancement, he visited his father, whom he pitied as a peasant forever trapped by racism and ignorance. He comments in *Black Boy* that blood ties and facial similarities make them kin, but "we were forever strangers, speaking a different language, living on vastly distant planes of reality." (Wright 1966, 42)

In 1941, John Houseman and Orson Welles produced a stage version of *Native Son*. The novel was well scripted by North Carolinian Paul Green, winner of the Pulitzer Prize and cofounder of historical outdoor drama, who had befriended Wright while working at the Federal Negro Theater in Chicago. The Broadway production starred Canada Lee as Bigger Thomas, a part he continued to play with a road company. After Wright rejected Harold Hecht's proposal to rewrite Bigger Thomas as a white man for a Hollywood film, Pierre Chenal directed a low-budget 1950 version in Argentina and starred Wright as Bigger and Jean Wallace as Mary Dalton. The film company went bankrupt, but not before the film had toured theaters in Buenos Aires, New York, and Venice. An updated 1986 Cinecom version, featuring Akousuwa Busia, Elizabeth McGovern, Matt Dillon, Geraldine Page, and Carroll Baker, earned acclaim for its grim realism.

At the beginning of World War II, about the time Wright married Ellen Poplar and settled in Brooklyn's Bedford-Stuyvesant district, he began to distance himself from Marxism and edge toward the existentialism of Albert Camus and Jean-Paul Sartre. He published two reflective essays: "I Tried To Be a Communist" in *Atlantic Monthly* and "The Man Who Lived Underground" in *Cross Section*. Frequently walking in Fort Greene Park to gather his thoughts or vacationing at Pigeon Cove near Rockport, Massachusetts, he set to work on *Black*

Boy, which he completed by the end of the war. The work also achieved Book-of-the-Month Club status.

As a guest of the French government, Wright visited France for the first time in 1946. Joining the expatriates clustered about Gertrude Stein's salon and Sartre's *Les Temps Modernes,* in 1947 he settled his wife and daughter Julia in Paris, where his second daughter Rachel was born. In peace at last, he sought a rural atmosphere at a Norman farm in Ailly, France, where he could grow potatoes and corn; as a means of identifying elements of the Black Africa movement, he visited Ghana. He completed *The Outsider* (1943), proclaimed as the first American existential novel, as well as two more novels—*Savage Holiday* (1954) and *The Long Dream* (1958)—and three commentaries about his travels. Still alienated from the United States at the time of his sudden death from a heart attack while undergoing tests at the Clinique Chirugicale Eugéne Gibez in Paris on November 28, 1960, he left unfinished *Eight Men,* a collection of essays, novellas, short fiction, haiku, and radio plays. His ashes and an incinerated copy of *Black Boy* lie together in Pére Lachaise, resting place of such notables as Isadora Duncan, Molière, Father Abelard, and Oscar Wilde. A continuation of *Black Boy* was published posthumously in 1977 as *American Hunger.* In 1991, the Library of America produced a two-volume collection of Wright's works. (Bain et al. 1979; Baker 1972; Barksdale and Kinnamon 1972; Bloom 1987, 1988; Boger 1968; Bradbury 1996; Butler 1991; Chapman 1968; Fabre 1990; Gayle 1980; Low and Clift 1981; Payne 1981; Ploski and Williams 1989; Popkin 1978; Salzman et al. 1996; Trotman 1989; Walker 1988; Webb 1968; Williams 1970; Wilson and Ferris 1989; Wright 1966, 1977, 1991)

See also *Black Boy; Native Son;* poetry of the South.

YOUNG-ADULT LITERATURE

The South has nurtured a fine selection of young-adult writers, ranging from Mark Twain, creator of the river adventures of Huck Finn and Tom Sawyer to Mississippian Mildred Taylor, author of *Roll of Thunder, Hear My Cry* (1976) and Dori Sanders, author of *Clover* (1990). The pinnacle of nineteenth-century writing for youth comes from aphorist and storyteller Joel Chandler Harris, author of the Uncle Remus tales, a collection of native dialect stories that preserve the South's slave heritage. Also from the late 1800s, Martha Farquharson Finley initiated the Elsie Dinsmore books, which met popular demand for girls' adventure stories. Over the nearly three decades between 1876 and 1905, she produced 100 titles, including *An Old Fashioned Boy* (1870), *Our Fred: or, Seminary Life at Thurston* (1874), *The Mildred Books* (1878–1894), and *Twiddletwit: A Fairy Tale* (1898).

In the frontier tradition is Arkansan Charles Portis's delightful young-adult adventure story *True Grit* (1968), an uproarious quest novel that pits a fearless farm girl against brigands, cutthroats, a Texas Ranger, and Reuben "Rooster" Cogburn, a hard-drinking federal marshal. Portis, trained in journalism, turned to fiction full-time in 1964 and applied skillful reportage to three novels: *Norwood* (1966), *True Grit*, and *The Dog of the South* (1979). A master of outback dialects, witty repartee, first-person narration, and the milieu of Indian territory in the days of brazen lawlessness, he achieves a balance of picaresque characterization in *True Grit*, a best-seller that was serialized in the *Saturday Evening Post* beginning May 18, 1968.

Set in the Mississippi Valley at the jumping-off point for the law-abiding East, the action dispatches 14-year-old Mattie Ross, a budding ranch accountant, from her family's farm in Dardanelles County to Fort Smith, Arkansas, where she hunts Tom Chaney, her father's murderer. The unlikely trio of Mattie, Rooster, and the meddler LaBoeuf treks into the Choctaw Nation, a "sink of crime" where brigands flee civilized society and flout the law. Portis depicts Mattie as an obdurate miss from a conservative Presbyterian home who identifies her father's corpse, then joins her chaperone, Yarnell Poindexter, at a triple hanging superintended by Judge Isaac Parker, the notorious "hanging judge" of pulp western fiction. Mattie deals with a devious auctioneer for Little Blackie, a pony she rides through the episodic final chapters. Fast-paced and suspenseful, the plot places Mattie at a shootout outside a dugout in the San

Bois Mountains, accompanying three outlaw corpses to J. J. McAlester's store, galloping toward the Winding Stair Mountains, and tumbling into a pit of hibernating rattlers. Portis speeds the return to Fort Smith by having Rooster gallop back with Mattie fretful and semiconscious on his back. The rescue ennobles Rooster, whom Mattie worships for a quarter century and honors with an appropriate burial under a Confederate tombstone.

The figures and voices of Portis's comic tour de force fit the screen version so completely that, for the most part, the story line remains the same as the novel. Filmed by Paramount in 1969, the screen adaptation of *True Grit* features a well-matched cast: John Wayne as Rooster, Kim Darby as Mattie, and Glen Campbell as the egotistical Texas Ranger LaBoeuf. Robert Duvall and Dennis Hopper play members of Lucky Ned Pepper's mail-robbing gang. The movie earned John Wayne an Academy Award and received an Oscar nomination for the title song. The part of Rooster fit Wayne so handily that he reprised the role in *Rooster Cogburn* (1975) opposite Katherine Hepburn. Warren Oates played the part of Rooster in a 1978 television version.

North Carolinian Theodore Taylor, a contemporary of Portis, sets two related adventure tales in the Caribbean. *The Cay* (1970), winner of the Jane Addams Children's Book award, is a popular work that has suffered from censorship for its inclusion of racism. The story tells of an 11-year-old Virginian, Phillip Enright, who is separated from his family during a Nazi U-boat torpedo raid on the steamer that takes the boy and his mother away from danger near the petroleum refineries in Willemstad, Curaçao. Influenced by his mother's prejudices, he spurns the assistance of his rescuer, Timothy, a 70-year-old West Island deckhand who tends the boy's injury and helps him cope with blindness brought on by a head wound. Timothy's selflessness eases the fears of isolation on an uncharted isle and prepares the boy for the loneliness that envelops him after his savior dies in a hurricane. The screen adaptation, filmed by Richard Crenna for Pendick Productions in 1974, stars James Earl Jones as the dockhand from the Virgin Islands. After 23 years, Taylor acquiesced to pressure from young readers, parents, teachers, and librarians and returned to the pairing of Timothy and Phillip for *Timothy of the Cay* (1993), a prequel that explains how Timothy got from his home in Charlotte Amalie, Saint Thomas, to Curaçao.

From another point of view, young-adult novelist Bette Greene examines the effects of World War II close to her native Tennessee. *Summer of My German Soldier* (1973) tells the bitter story of an unloved Jewish teenager, Patty Bergen, who reaches for affection and maturity in a brief encounter with a German prisoner of war. Set in Jenkinsville, Arkansas, the novel describes Rice County's outrage at the trainload of POWs who pass through town on their way to a prison camp. The contrast with her own life in permanent detention spotlights her one surrogate parent, the maid, Ruth Hughes, who recognizes that unconditional love is the best antidote to neglect and brutality from Patty's parents, Pearl and Harry Bergen, owners of a local mercantile store.

Greene describes Patty's empty heart, which immediately makes room for 22-year-old Anton Reiker as he flees captivity. A former medical student, he comes from English-German ancestry and, unlike Patty, enjoyed a warm family relationship with his mother and father, a history professor at the University of Göttingen. While gossip swirls about a U-boat bringing eight Nazis to U.S. soil, Patty carries food to the backyard garage apartment, where she hides Anton until he can hop a late train out of town. When the truth emerges that a local Jewish girl has sheltered a POW, Harry Bergen lashes out at her for the web of falsehood that concealed her actions. Greene characterizes the Southern community's lurid thoughts about Patty's relationship with Anton. The story quickly recedes from bright, positive notes to doom for Patty.

In the resolution, Greene dislodges her protagonist from her grandparents' care in Memphis to the courtrooms, from which she is remanded to the Jasper E. Conrad Arkansas Reformatory for Girls in Bolton. During the four-to-six-month sentence the Bergens abandon her, and her lawyer, Mr. Kishner, labels her an embarrassment to all Jews. The Christmas season is bleak, smelling of the bleach Patty uses in the reformatory laundry, but a surprise visit from Ruth revives her spirits. Glum that she has no gift for Ruth, Patty responds to the genial good nature of the former family maid, who counters, "Now that don't make no nevermind, Patty Babe, 'cause come next Christmas I'm gonna give you a list more'n six feet long. But right now I got you a little somethin' else." (Greene 1973, 188) She pulls a yellow shoe box tied with red ribbon from a shopping bag and offers a symbolic bit of maternal love—fried chicken breasts wrapped individually in pink napkins. According to Ruth, the absence of love in the Bergen home derives from the same source that stamps labels with "ir-regular" and "seconds": "You've got yourself some irregular seconds folks, and you've been paying more'n top dollar for them. So jest don't go a-wishing for what ain't nevah gonna be." (Greene 1973, 192) The warmth of Patty's relation-ship with Ruth shines in the 1978 NBC-TV adaptation starring Esther Rolle and Kristy McNichol.

A favorite Virginia author, Cynthia Rylant, wins the trust and affection of young readers with her compassionate short stories and novels. Her Newbery Medal–winning novel, *Missing May* (1992), is a blend of realism and mountain humor. One of the few fictional works to set the Appalachian poor in a trailer, the story describes the burden of sorrow borne by Summer, an orphan living with her Aunt May and Uncle Ob. While explaining their interest, May ex-plains to Summer:

> So [Ob] said, "We're taking her today, May," and we just packed you up and took you. Those folks never cared. Those Ohio kin—they're good people mostly, but they're limited, honey. . . . I had me a little girl finally, something I'd wanted all my life. (Rylant 1992, 85)

After her aunt's sudden death from diabetes and heart failure, Summer battles her Uncle Ob's distress by agreeing to accompany him on the search for "Miriam B. Young: Small Medium at Large," a spiritualist whom he hopes can help him communicate with his wife's spirit. (Rylant 1992, 53) The unspoken hurt and grief emerges after Summer is startled by an owl. Rylant describes the incident in existential terms: "The wings were so completely silent and we so unpre-pared." (Rylant 1992, 83) Like the unforeseen death that robs them of May, the flight tears at Summer's tough constitution. After a bout of tears, she and Ob release their hold on May's spirit in an act of grace—they stake Ob's wooden whirligigs in May's empty garden and set the blades awhirl in the wind. (Bernard 1955; De Montreville and Crawford 1978; *DISCovering Authors* 1993; Fuller 1968; Greene 1968; Greene 1973; Lamar 1977; Marquardt and Ward 1979; Portis 1968; Rhodes 1968; Rylant 1984, 1992; Sanders 1990; Sherr and Kazickas 1994; Snodgrass 1991, 1995; Stewart 1979, 1988; Taylor 1984; Taylor 1970, 1993; Wolff 1968)

See also Boone, Daniel; Harris, Joel Chandler; Rawlings, Marjorie Kinnan.

HOME STATES OF SOUTHERN AUTHORS

Alabama
Beckett, Richard Capel (1845–?)
Brown, Dee (1908–)
Flagg, Fannie (1941–)
Godwin, Gail (1937–)
Hurston, Zora Neale [traditionally listed as a Floridian] (1891–1960)
Le Vert, Celeste (*fl.* mid-1800s)
Lee, Harper (1926–)
Lloyd, Francis Bartow (*fl.* late 1800s)
Peck, Samuel Minturn (1854–?)
Percy, Walker (1916–1990)
Sanchez, Sonia (1934–)
Walker, Margaret (1915–)
Wyeth, John Allen (1845–?)

Arkansas
Cleaver, Eldridge (1935–)
Giles, Janice Holt (1909–1979)
Portis, Charles (1934–)
Stewart, Elinore Pruitt (1876–?)

Delaware
Cary, Mary Ann Shadd (1823–1893)

Florida
Johnson, James Weldon (1871–1938)
Johnson, John Rosamund (1873–1954)
Randolph, Philip (1889–1979)

Georgia
Andrews, Eliza Frances "Fanny" (1840–1931)
Boudinot, Elias (ca. 1803–1839)
Burns, Olive Ann (1924–1990)
Chivers, Thomas Holley (1807–1858)
Conroy, Pat (1945–)
de La Coste, Mary Ravenel (*fl.* mid-1800s)
Dickey, James (1923–1997)
Elliott, Sarah Barnwell (1849–1938)
Foreman, Stephen (1807–1881)
Gay, Mary Ann Harris (*fl.* mid-1800s)
Grady, Henry W. (1850–1889)
Greene, Melissa Fay (1952–)
Harris, Joel Chandler (1848–1908)
Johnson, Georgia Douglas (1877–1966)
Johnston, Richard Malcolm (1822–1898)
Jones, Charles Colcock (1831–1893)
King, Dr. Martin Luther, Jr. (1929–1968)
Lamar, Mirabeau Buonaparte (1798–1859)
Lanier, Sidney (1842–1881)
Longstreet, Augustus Baldwin (1790–1870)
McCullers, Carson (1917–1967)
Mitchell, Margaret (1900–1949)
O'Connor, Flannery (1925–1964)
Oliver, Thaddeus (1826–1864)
Ridge, John (1803–1839)
Ridge, John Rollin (1827–1867)
Sams, Ferrol (1922–)
Stephens, Alexander Hamilton (1812–1883)
Thompson, Will Henry (1848–?)
Ticknor, Dr. Francis Orrery (or Orray) (1822–1874)
Turner, Joseph Addison (1826–1868)
Uhry, Alfred (1936–)
Walker, Alice (1944–)
Willingham, Calder (1922–)
Wilson, Augusta Jane Evans (1835–1909)
Yerby, Frank (1916–)

Illinois
Torrence, Jackie (1944–)

Kentucky
Arnow, Harriette (1908–)
Berry, Wendell (1934–)
Brooks, Cleanth (1906–)
Brown, William Wells (1816–1864)
Cawein, Madison Julius (1865–1914)
Cullen, Countee (1903–1946)
Davis, Jefferson (1808–1889)
Fox, John, Jr. (1863–?)
Fulkerson, H. S. (1836–?)
Gordon, Caroline (1895–1981)
Mason, Bobbie Ann (1940–)
Norman, Marsha (1947–)
O'Hara, Theodore (1820–1867)
Roberts, Elizabeth Madox (1886–1941)
Stuart, Jesse (1907–1984)
Tate, Allen (1899–)
Warren, Robert Penn (1905–)

Louisiana
Barrow, Bennet H. (*fl.* 1850s)
Bontemps, Arna (1902–1973)
Brown, Dee (1908–)
Brown, H. Rap (1943–)
Cable, George Washington (1844–1925)
Capote, Truman (1924–1984)
Carter, Hodding (1907–1972)
Gaines, Ernest J. (1933–)
Gayarré, Charles Étienne Arthur
    (1805–1895)
Grau, Shirley Ann (1929–)
Harling, Robert (1951–)
Hellman, Lillian (1905–1984)
King, Grace Elizabeth (1853–1932)
Menken, Adah Isaacs (1835–1868)
Morgan, Sarah (1841–?)
O'Connor, Rachel (1774–1844)
Séjour, Victor (1817–?)
Young, Andrew (1932–)

Maryland
Carroll, Anna Ella (ca. 1820–1893)
Cook, Ebenezer (ca. 1670–ca. 1732)
Custis, George Washington Parke
    (1781–1857)
Douglass, Frederick (1817[?]–1895)
Finley, Martha Farquharson (1828–1909)
Garnet, Henry Highland (1815–1882)

Harper, Frances Ellen Watkins (1825–1911)
Jones, John Beauchamp (1810–1866)
Kennedy, John Pendleton (1795–1870)
Key, Francis Scott (1780–1843)
Mencken, H. L. (1880–1956)
Palmer, John Williamson (1825–1906)
Randall, James Ryder (1839–1886)
Reese, Lizette Woodworth (1856–1935)
Rich, Adrienne (1929–)
Wilson, Harriet E. Adams (ca. 1807–ca. 1870)
Wirt, William (1772–1834)

Massachusetts
Douglas, Marjory Stoneman (1890–)
Gilman, Caroline Howard (1794–1888)
Hentz, Caroline Lee Whiting (1800–1856)
Pike, Albert (1809–1891)
Poe, Edgar Allan (1809–1849)

Mississippi
Allen, John Mills (1846–1917)
Campbell, Will (1924–)
Davis, Varina Howell (1826–1906)
Dorsey, Sarah Anne Ellis (1829–1879)
Faulkner, William (1897–1962)
Foote, Shelby (1916–)
Gilchrist, Ellen (1935–)
Hannah, Barry (1942–)
Henley, Beth (1952–)
Johnson, William (?–1851)
Lomax, John Avery (1867–1948)
Loughborough, Mary Ann (*fl.* 1850s)
McDowell, Katherine Sherwood
    (1849–1883)
Moody, Anne E. (1940–)
Nicholson, Eliza Jane Poitevent
    Holbrook (1849–1896)
Russell, Irwin (1853–1879)
Smedes, Susan Dabney (1840–?)
Spencer, Elizabeth (1921–)
Taylor, Mildred (1935–)
Wells–Barnett, Ida Bell (1862–1931)
Welty, Eudora (1909–)
Williams, John (1925–)
Williams, Tennessee (1911–1983)
Wright, Richard (1908–1960)
Young, Stark (1881–1963)

Missouri
Angelou, Maya (1928–)
Armstrong, Paul (1869–)

Chopin, Kate (1851–1904)
Glancy, Diane (1941–)
Gregory, Dick (1932–)
Lester, Julius (1939–)
Teasdale, Sara (1884–1933)
Twain, Mark [Samuel Langhorne
    Clemens] (1835–1910)

New York
Haley, Alex (1921–1992)

North Carolina
Blythe, LeGette (1900–1996)
Chappell, Fred (1936–)
Cox, William Norment (*fl.* 1920s)
Daly, John Augustin (1838–1899)
Delany, A. Elizabeth (1891–1995)
Delany, Sarah L. (1889–1996)
Edgerton, Clyde (1944–)
Ehle, John (1925–)
Frazier, Charles (1950–)
Gibbons, Kaye (1960–)
Gurganus, Allan (1947–)
Hawks, Francis Lister (1798–1866)
Hayes, Hubert (1901–)
Henry, O. [William Sydney Porter]
    (1862–1910)
Hooper, Johnson Jones (1815–1862)
Jacobs, Harriet Ann (1813–1897)
McCorkle, Jill (1958–)
McNeill, John Charles (1874–1907)
Marlette, Doug (1949–)
Norment, Mary C. (*fl.* 1870s)
Owen, Guy (1925–1981)
Page, Walter Hines (1855–1918)
Price, Reynolds (1933–)
Sawyer, Lemuel (1777–1852)
Spencer, Cornelia Phillips
    (1875–1908)
Taylor, Theodore (1921–)
Urmstone, John (*fl.* 1720s)
Vollmer, Lula (*fl.* 1920s)
Wilkinson, Sylvia (1940–)
Wolfe, Thomas (1900–1938)

Ohio
Chesnutt, Charles Waddell
    (1858–1932)
Flash, Henry Lynden (1835–?)
Heyward, Dorothy (1885–1940)
Thompson, William Tappan (1812–1882)

Oklahoma
Beattie, Richmond (1905–1961)
Ellison, Ralph (1914–1994)

Pennsylvania
Bartram, William (1739–1823)
Boone, Daniel (1734–1820)
Preston, Margaret Junkin (1820–1897)
Ramsay, David (1749–1815)

South Carolina
Allison, Dorothy (1949–)
Allston, Joseph Blyth (1833–1904)
Allston, Washington (1779–1843)
Aston, Anthony (*fl.* 1710s)
Ball, Carolina Augusta (1823–?)
Bruns, John Dickson (1836–1883)
Calhoun, John C. (1782–1850)
Cash, Walter J. (1900–1941)
Chesnut, Mary Boykin (1823–1886)
Childress, Alice (1920–1994)
Dale, Thomas (ca. 1700–1750)
Dickson, Samuel Henry (1798–1872)
Drayton, William Henry (1742–1779)
Elliott, William (1788–1863)
Grant, Caesar (*fl.* 1920s)
Grayson, William John (1788–1863)
Grimké, Sarah Moore (1792–1873)
Hayne, Paul Hamilton (1830–1886)
Hayne, Robert Young (1791–1839)
Heyward, Dubose (1885–1940)
Ioor, Dr. William (*fl.* 1780–1830)
Jackson, Reverend Jesse (1941–)
Laurens, Henry (1724–1792)
Legaré, Hugh Swinton (1797–1843)
Legaré, James Matthews (1823–1859)
Logan, Mary Daniell (1702–1779)
Meek, Alexander Beaufort (1814–1865)
Moise, Penina (1797–?)
Moragné, Mary (1818–?)
Peterkin, Julia (1880–1961)
Pinckney, Eliza Lucas (1739–1762)
Richardson, Howard Dixon (1917–1984)
Ripley, Alexandra (1934–)
Rubin, Louis D., Jr. (1923–)
Simms, William Gilmore (1806–1870)
Stanton, Frank Lebby (1857–?)
Timothy, Ann Donovan (ca. 1725–1792)
Timrod, Henry (1829–1867)
Weld, Angelina Grimké (1805–1879)

White, John Blake (1781–1859)
Wilkinson, Eliza Yonge (*fl.* 1799–1782)

Tennessee
Agee, James (1909–1955)
Crockett, Davy (1786–1836)
Davidson, Donald (1893–1968)
Davis, Reuben (1813–1890)
Drannan, Capt. William F. (*fl.* 1890s)
Dromgoole, Will Allen (1860–1934)
Giovanni, Nikki (1943–)
Greene, Bette (1934–)
Harris, George Washington (1814–1869)
Jarrell, Randall (1914–1965)
Love, Nat (1854–1921)
Marshall, Catherine (1914–)
Miles, Emma Bell (1879–1919)
Murfree, Mary Noailles [*pseud.* Charles
    Egbert Craddock] (1850–1922)
Ransom, John Crowe (1888–1974)
Ridge, Major (ca. 1770–1839)
Sequoyah (ca. 1760–1843)
Taylor, Peter (1917–)
Williams, Joan (1928–)
Williams, John Sharp (1854–1932)

Texas
Dobie, J. Frank (1888–1964)
Foote, Horton (1916–)
Gipson, Fred (1908–1973)
Griffin, John Howard (1920–)
Harris, Dilue Rose (*fl.* 1890s–1910s)
Ivins, Molly (1944–)
Jordan, Barbara (1936–1996)
Lomax, Alan (1915–)
McMurtry, Larry (1936–)
Porter, Katherine Anne (1890–1980)
Reneaux, J. J. (1955–)
Ross, Gayle (1951–)

Virginia
Baldwin, Joseph Glover (1815–1864)
Beverley, Robert (ca. 1670–ca. 1735)
Bledsoe, Jerry (1942–)
Boyd, Belle (1843–1900)
Bryan, Daniel (*fl.* 1810s)
Byrd, Colonel William (1674–1744)
Cabell, James Branch (1879–1958)
Cather, Willa (1873–1947)
Clark, William (1770–1838)
Clyman, James (1792–1881)
Cooke, John Esten (1830–1886)

Coyner, David (*fl.* 1870s)
Glasgow, Ellen (1873–1945)
Hamner, Earl, Jr. (1923–)
Haulee, Margaret Hanley (1752–1842)
Henry, Patrick (1736–1799)
Hope, James Barron (1829–1887)
Houston, Sam (1793–1863)
Jefferson, Thomas (1743–1826)
Kinnan, Mary (1763–1848)
Lee, Henry (1756–1818)
Lee, Mary Custis (*fl.* 1850s)
Lee, Robert E. (1807–1870)
Lewis, Meriwether (1774–1809)
Lucas, Daniel Bedinger (1836–1909)
McCabe, William Gordon (1842–1920)
Madison, James (1751–1836)
Marshall, John (1755–1835)
Mason, George (1725–1792)
Munford, Robert (*fl.* 1790s)
Page, Thomas Nelson (1853–1922)
Randolph, Innes (1837–1887)
Ryan, Abram Joseph (1839–1886)
Rylant, Cynthia (1954–)
Spencer, Anne (1882–1975)
Styron, William (1925–)
Tabb, John Banister (1845–1909)
Taylor, John (1753–1824)
Terhune, Mary Virginia Hawes (1830–1922)
Thompson, John Reuben (1823–1874)
Tucker, Nathaniel Beverley (1784–1851)
Washington, Booker T. (ca. 1856–1915)
Washington, George (1732–1799)
Weems, Mason Locke (1760–1825)

Washington, D.C.
Brown, Sterling (1901–)
King, Florence (1936–)
Rawlings, Marjorie Kinnan (1896–1953)
Southworth, Emma Dorothy Eliza
    Nevitte [E. D. E. N.] (1819–1899)
Toomer, Jean (1894–1967)

West Virginia
Bryan, Daniel (*fl.* 1810s)
Cooke, Philip Pendleton (1816–1850)
Delany, Martin (1815–1882)
Hunter, Kermit (1910–)
Myers, Walter Dean (1937–)
Point, Mittie France Clark (*fl.* 1890s)
Royall, Anne Newport (1769–1854)
Wigginton, Eliot (1942–)

Outside the United States:

Benin
Vassa, Gustavus (1745–?)

Bermuda
Tucker, St. George (1752–1828)

England
Blennerhassett, Margaret Agnew (1788–?)
Catesby, Mark (1679–1749)
Hoskens, Jane Fenn (1694–?)
Kemble, Francis Anne "Fanny" (1809–1893)
Lawson, John (1674–1711)
Martineau, Harriet (1802–1876)
Parks, William (1698–1750)
Pinkney, Edward Coote (1802–1828)
Smith, Captain John (1580–1631)

France
Chateaubriand, François René, Viscomte
    de (1768–1848)
Le Petit, Father (*fl.* 1720s)
Pénicaut, Andre (*fl.* 1720s)

Germany
Lewisohn, Ludwig (1882–1955)

Greece
Hearn, Patricio Lafcadio (1850–1904)

Haiti
Audubon, John James (1780–1851)

Ireland
Adair, James (1709–1787)
McCarthy (or McCarty), Harry (?–1874)
Power, Tyrone (1797–1841)
Wilde, Richard Henry (1789–1847)

New Brunswick
Edmonds, Sarah Emma Evelyn
    (1841–1898)

Nova Scotia
Haliburton, Thomas Chandler
    (1795–1865)

Russia
Golden, Harry (1902–1981)

Scotland
Wilson, Alexander (1766–1813)

Spain
De Soto, Hernando (1496–1542)

CHRONOLOGY OF SOUTHERN LITERATURE

1612   *A Map of Virginia with a Description of the Country, the Commodities, People, Government, and Religion,* Captain John Smith

1624   *Generall Historie of Virginia, New England and the Summer Isles,* Captain John Smith

1665   *Ye Beare and Ye Cubb,* Philip Alexander Bruce

1702   *Fool's Opera,* Anthony Aston

1704   *Fleur de Lys and Calumet: Being the Pénicaut Narrative of French Adventure in Louisiana,* Andre Pénicaut

1705   *Low Character of Immigrants to Virginia,* Robert Beverley

1708   *The Sot-Weed Factor,* Ebenezer Cook

1709   *New Voyage to Carolina,* John Lawson

1711   "Self-Reliance on the Frontier," John Urmstone

1712   *The Secret Diary,* Colonel William Byrd

1722   *History and Present State of Virginia,* Robert Beverley

1728   *History of the Dividing Line,* Colonel William Byrd

1731   *The Natural History of Carolina, Florida, and the Bahama Islands,* Mark Catesby

1734   *Compleat System of Fencing,* William Parks

1736   *The Busy-Body,* Susanna Centlivre

1742   *The Compleat Housewife,* William Parks

1750   (ca.) *Flora Virginica,* John Clayton

1763   *Letters of Martha Logan to John Bartram, 1760–1763,* Martha Daniell Logan

1767   *The Disappointment, or The Force of Credulity,* Andrew Barton

1770   ca. "An Old Virginia Preacher," William Wirt

1771   *The Life and Spiritual Sufferings of That Faithful Servant of Christ, Jane Hoskens,* Jane Fenn Hoskens

1772   *Gardners Kalender,* Martha Daniell Logan

1773   *Extracts from the Virginia Charters,* George Mason

1774   *On Migration,* Mark Catesby
       A Summary View of the Rights of British America, Thomas Jefferson

1775   "Address to the Virginia Convention," Patrick Henry
       A Concise Natural History of East and West Florida, Bernard Romans

1824 *Blackbeard: A Comedy in Four Acts*, Lemuel Sawyer
      Conversations with Lafayette, George Washington Parke Custis

1825 "A Health," Edward Coote Pinkney
      Monody, on the Death of General Charles Cotesworth Pinckney, William Gilmore Simms
      Rodolph, and Other Poems, Edward Coote Pinkney
      "A Serenade," Edward Coote Pinkney
      "The Voyager's Song," Edward Coote Pinkney

1826 *The Life of General Francis Marion*, Mason Locke Weems
      Sketches of History Life and Manners in the United States, Anne Newport Royall
      Wreck of Honor: A Tragedy in Five Acts, Lemuel Sawyer

1827 *Cherokee Advocate*, Sequoyah
      Cherokee Phoenix, Sequoyah
      The Indian Prophecy, George Washington Parke Custis
      Tamerlane and Other Poems, Edgar Allan Poe

1829 *Al Aaraaf, Tamerlane, and Minor Poems*, Edgar Allan Poe
      "Israfel," Edgar Allan Poe

1830 *The Pawnee Chief*, George Washington Parke Custis
      The Railroad, George Washington Parke Custis

1831 "The City in the Sea," Edgar Allan Poe
      The Lion of the West, James Kirke Paulding
      Poems by E. A. Poe: A Second Edition, Edgar Allan Poe
      "To Helen," Edgar Allan Poe

1832 *Atalantis, a Story of the Sea*, William Gilmore Simms
      Rose Bud, Caroline Howard Gilman
      Swallow Barn, or A Sojourn in the Old Dominion, John Pendleton Kennedy
      "The Swamp Fox," William Gilmore Simms

1833 *The Book of My Lady*, William Gilmore Simms
      The Life and Adventures of Colonel David Crockett of West Tennessee, Mathew St. Clair Clarke
      Martin Faber, the Story of a Criminal, William Gilmore Simms
      "Ms. Found in a Bottle," Edgar Allan Poe
      North Point or Baltimore Defended, George Washington Parke Custis
      Sketches and Eccentricities of Col. David Crockett, Mathew St. Clair Clarke

1834 *The Eighth of January*, George Washington Parke Custis
      Georgia Scenes, Augustus Baldwin Longstreet
      Guy Rivers, William Gilmore Simms
      Narrative of the Life of David Crockett of the State of Tennessee, Thomas Chilton

1835 *Account of Colonel Crockett's Tour to the North and Down East*, Davy Crockett
      Crockett Almanack, Davy Crockett [1835–1838]
      Horse-Shoe Robinson, John Pendleton Kennedy
      Journal of an American Residence, Fanny Kemble
      The Life of Martin Van Buren, Hair-Apparent to the "Government," and the Appointed Successor of General Jackson, Davy Crockett
      The Partisan, William Gilmore Simms
      The Yemassee: A Romance of Carolina, William Gilmore Simms

1836 *Appeal to the Christian Women of the South*, Angelina Grimké
      Colonel Crockett's Exploits and Adventures in Texas, Richard Penn Smith

1836   *continued*
      George Balcombe, Nathaniel Beverley Tucker
      Pocahontas, or The Settlers of Virginia, George Washington Parke Custis
      Recollections of a Southern Matron, Caroline Howard Gilman
      The Victor's Description of the Battle of San Jacinto, Sam Houston

1837   *Letters to Catherine Beecher in Reply to an Essay on Slavery and Abolitionism
      addressed to A. A. Grimké*, Angelina Grimké
      Mellichampe, William Gilmore Simms
      Society in America, Harriet Martineau

1838   *The Birds of America*, John James Audubon
      Go Ahead Almanack, Davy Crockett
      "Let Us Go to the Woods," Caroline Howard Gilman
      Letters on the Equality of the Sexes and the Condition of Women, Sarah Grimké
      Narrative of Arthur Gordon Pym, Edgar Allan Poe
      The Poetry of Traveling in the United States, Caroline Howard Gilman
      Retrospect of Western Travel, Harriet Martineau
      Richard Hurdis: or, The Avenger of Blood, a Tale of Alabama, William Gilmore Simms
      Synopsis of the Birds of America, John James Audubon
      "William Wilson," Edgar Allan Poe

1839   *Letters of Eliza Wilkinson, during the Invasion and Possession of Charlestown, South
      Carolina, by the British in the Revolutionary War, Arranged from the Original
      Manuscripts by Caroline Gilman*, Eliza Yonge Wilkinson
      Printz Hall: A Record of New Sweden, Lemuel Sawyer

1840   *Border Beagles: A Tale of Mississippi*, William Gilmore Simms
      "The Fall of the House of Usher," Edgar Allan Poe
      Journal of a Mountain Man, James Clyman
      Love's Progress, Caroline Howard Gilman
      Tales of the Grotesque and Arabesque, Edgar Allan Poe

1841   *American Ornithological Biography*, John James Audubon and William MacGillivray
      The Kinsmen, William Gilmore Simms
      "The Murders in the Rue Morgue," Edgar Allan Poe
      *Wild Western Scenes; A Narrative of Adventures in the Western Wilderness, Forty
      Years Ago; Wherein the Conduct of Daniel Boone, the Great American Pioneer, Is
      Particularly Described*, John Beauchamp Jones

1842   *Beauchampe, or The Kentucky Tragedy, a Tale of Passion*, William Gilmore Simms
      "A Descent into the Maelstrom," Edgar Allan Poe
      Marcus Warland, Caroline Lee Whiting Hentz
      "The Masque of the Red Death," Edgar Allan Poe
      "The Mystery of Marie Rogêt," Edgar Allan Poe
      "The Pit and the Pendulum," Edgar Allan Poe

1843   "The Black Cat," Edgar Allan Poe
      "The Gold Bug," Edgar Allan Poe
      "The Tell-Tale Heart," Edgar Allan Poe

1844   *Autobiography of Lemuel Sawyer*, Lemuel Sawyer
      A Biography of John Randolph of Roanoke: With a Selection of His Speeches, Lemuel
      Sawyer
      Diegarias, Victor Séjour
      Michael Bonham, or The Fall of Bexar, William Gilmore Simms

"The Premature Burial," Edgar Allan Poe
"The Purloined Letter," Edgar Allan Poe

1845   *Helen Halsey: or, The Swamp State of Conelachita*, William Gilmore Simms
Narrative of the Life of Frederick Douglass, an American Slave, Frederick Douglass
"The Old Pioneer," Theodore O'Hara
"The Raven," Edgar Allan Poe
"The System of Dr. Tarr and Prof. Fether," Edgar Allan Poe
The Viviparous Quadrupeds of North America, John James Audubon

1846   *Areytos: or, Songs of the South*, William Gilmore Simms
Carolina Sports by Land and Water, William Elliot
"The Cask of Amontillado," Edgar Allan Poe
"A Deer Hunt," William Elliott
"The Oblong Box," Edgar Allan Poe
"The Philosophy of Composition," Edgar Allan Poe
Some Adventures of Captain Simon Suggs, Late of the Tallapoosa Volunteers,
   Johnson Jones Hooper
Writings of Hugh Swinton Legaré, Hugh Swinton Legaré

1847   "The Bivouac of the Dead, " Theodore O'Hara
"Florence Vane," Philip Pendleton Cooke
Froissart Ballads, and Other Poems, Philip Pendleton Cooke
"Histoire de la Louisiane," Charles Etienne Arthur Gayarré
The Lost Trappers, David H. Coyner
"The Mountaineer," Philip Pendleton Cooke
"My Life Is like the Summer Rose," Richard Henry Wilde
"To the Mocking Bird," Richard Henry Wilde
"Ulalume," Edgar Allan Poe

1848   *Charleston, and Her Satirists*, William Gilmore Simms
"Eureka," Edgar Allan Poe
"Haw-Blossoms," James Matthews Legaré
Orta-Undis, and Other Poems, James Matthews Legaré
"Romance of the History of Louisiana," Charles Etienne Arthur Gayarré
"To a Lily," James Matthews Legaré

1849   "Annabel Lee," Edgar Allan Poe
"The Bells," Edgar Allan Poe
"Eldorado," Edgar Allan Poe
Father Abbot, William Gilmore Simms
"For Annie," Edgar Allan Poe
Hints to the Colored People of North America, Mary Ann Shadd Cary
"My Three Years as a Shawnee Captive," Margaret Hanley Haulee
Verses of a Lifetime, Caroline Howard Gilman

1850   "I Sigh for the Land of the Cypress and Pine," Samuel Henry Dickson
Linda: or, The Young Pilot of the Belle Creole, Caroline Lee Whiting Hentz
"My Wife and Child," Henry Rootes Jackson
The Poetic Principle, Edgar Allan Poe
"Red Old Hills of Georgia," Henry Rootes Jackson
Tallulah, and Other Poems, Henry Rootes Jackson

1851   *Frederick Douglass' Paper*, Frederick Douglass
Katherine Walton: or, The Rebel's Daughter, William Gilmore Simms

1851   *continued*
       Norman Maurice, or The Man of the People, William Gilmore Simms
       The Planter's Northern Bride, Caroline Lee Whiting Hentz
       Tales of Alabama, Johnson Jones Hooper
       The Widow Rugby's Husband, a Night at the Uly Man's, and Other Tales of Alabama,
           Johnson Jones Hooper

1852   *The Anti-Slavery Harp*, William Wells Brown
       "Louisiana: Its Colonial History and Romance," Charles Etienne Arthur
           Gayarré
       "Louisiana, Its History as a French Colony," Charles Etienne Arthur Gayarré
       The Narrative of William Wells Brown; a Fugitive Slave, William Wells Brown
       *A Plea for Emigration, or Notes on Canada West, in Its Moral, Social and Political
           Aspect*, Mary Ann Shadd Cary
       The Sword and the Distaff, William Gilmore Simms
       Three Years in Europe; or, Places I Have Seen and People I Have Met, William Wells
           Brown
       "What to the Slave Is the Fourth of July?," Frederick Douglass

1853   "The Amazon and the Atlantic Slopes of South America," Matthew Fontaine
           Maury
       Clotelle: A Tale of Southern States, William Wells Brown
       The Edge of the Swamp, William Gilmore Simms
       Flush Times of Alabama and Mississippi: A Series of Sketches, Joseph Glover
           Baldwin
       The Flush Times of California, Joseph Glover Baldwin
       The Heroic Slave, Frederick Douglass
       India, Emma Dorothy Eliza Nevitte Southworth

1854   *The Americans at Home; or, Byeways, Backwoods, and Prairies*, Thomas Chandler
           Haliburton
       *The First White Man of the West, or The Life and Exploits of Col. Dan'l. Boone, the
           First Settler of Kentucky; Interspersed with Incidents in the Early Annals of the
           Country*, Timothy Flint
       The Hireling and the Slave, William John Grayson
       "History of the Spanish Domination in Louisiana," Charles Etienne Arthur
           Gayarré
       Life and Adventures of Joaquin Murieta, the Celebrated California Bandit, John
           Rollin Ridge
       Poems on Miscellaneous Subjects, Frances Ellen Watkins Harper

1855   *The Forayers*, William Gilmore Simms
       Inez: A Tale of the Alamo, Augusta Jane Evans Wilson
       My Bondage and My Freedom, Frederick Douglass
       Party Leaders, Joseph Glover Baldwin

1856   *The Banished Son and Other Stories of the Heart*, Caroline Lee Whiting Hentz
       Charlemont, William Gilmore Simms
       Eutaw, William Gilmore Simms
       "The Exalted Theme of Human Praise," Penina Moise
       Experience; or, How To Give a Northern Man a Backbone, William Wells Brown
       Hymns Written for the Use of Hebrew Congregations, Penina Moise
       "Man of the World," Penina Moise

1857   *Daniel Boone and the Hunters of Kentucky*, W. H. Bogart
       "The Daughter of Mendoza," Mirabeau Buonaparte Lamar
       "The Mocking Bird," Alexander Beaufort Meek
       Souvenirs of Travel, Celeste Le Vert
       Verse Memorials, Mirabeau Buonaparte Lamar

1858   *The Escape, or A Leap for Freedom*, William Wells Brown
       History of North Carolina, Francis Lister Hawks

1859   *Beulah*, Augusta Jane Evans Wilson
       The Cassique of Kiawah, William Gilmore Simms
       The Douglass Monthly, Frederick Douglass
       Recollections and Private Memoirs of Washington, by his Adopted Son, George
         Washington Parke Custis
       The Virginia Comedians, or Old Days in the Old Dominion, John Esten Cooke

1860   "A Plea for Union," Alexander Hamilton Stephens

1861   "The Bonny Blue Flag," Harry McCarthy
       Incidents in the Life of a Slave Girl, Written by Herself, Harriet Ann Brent Jacobs
       "My Maryland," James Ryder Randall

1862   "A Key to the Disunion Conspiracy," Nathaniel Beverley Tucker

1863   *The Black Man: His Antecedents, His Genius, and His Achievements*, William Wells
         Brown
       "Men of Color, to Arms!," Frederick Douglass
       Paddy McGann, William Gilmore Simms
       Residence on a Georgian Plantation, 1838–1839, Fanny Kemble

1864   "All Quiet along the Potomac To-Night," Thaddeus Oliver
       "The Balloon Hoax," Edgar Allan Poe
       The Creoles of Louisiana, George Washington Cable
       Declaration of the Principles of the National Emigration Convention, Martin Delany
       "Dreaming in the Trenches," William Gordon McCabe
       Ebb Tide, Joseph Glover Baldwin
       Macaria; or Altars of Sacrifice, Augusta Jane Evans Wilson
       My Cave Life in Vicksburg, with Letters of Trial and Travel, Mary Ann Loughborough
       "Somebody's Darling," Mary Ravenel de La Coste

1865   "Call to Rebellion," Henry Highland Garnet
       "Christmas Night of '62," William Gordon McCabe
       "Dixie," Albert Pike
       "The Foe at the Gates," John Dickson Bruns
       Life in Dixie during the War, Mary Ann Harris Gay
       Nurse and Spy in the Union Army, Sarah Emma Evelyn Edmonds
       "The Soldier Boy," Margaret Junkin Preston
       "Stack Arms," Joseph Blyth Allston
       "Stonewall Jackson," Henry Lynden Flash

1866   *History of Louisiana*, Charles Etienne Arthur Gayarré
       "The Jacket of Gray," Caroline Augusta Ball
       James Louis Petigru: A Biographical Sketch, William John Grayson
       The Journal of Hospital Life in the Confederate Army in Tennessee, Kate Cumming
       The Last Ninety Days of the War in North Carolina, Cornelia Phillips Spencer
       The Life of Stonewall Jackson: A Military Biography, John Esten Cooke

1866   *continued*
        Philip II of Spain, Charles Etienne Arthur Gayarré
        St. Elmo, Augusta Jane Evans Wilson
        Surry of Eagle's Nest, John Esten Cooke

1867   "The Celebrated Jumping Frog of Calaveras County," Mark Twain
        "Music in Camp," John Reuben Thompson
        The Negro in the American Rebellion: His Heroism and His Fidelity, William Wells
            Brown
        St. Twel'mo, or, The Cuneiform Cyclopedist of Chattanooga, C. H. Webb
        Sut Lovingood: Yarns Spun by a "Nat'ral Born Durn'd Fool," George Washington
            Harris
        Tiger Lilies, Sidney Lanier
        Under the Gaslight, John Augustin Daly

1868   "The Harp of Broken Strings," John Rollin Ridge
        Poems, John Rollin Ridge
        Sut Lovingood's Travels with Old Abe Linkhorn, George Washington Harris

1869   *The Cub of the Panther*, William Gilmore Simms
        Innocents Abroad, Mark Twain
        Moses: A Story of the Nile, Frances Ellen Watkins Harper

1870   *The Heir of Gaymount*, John Esten Cooke
        "How Sharp Snaffles Got His Capital and Wife," William Gilmore Simms
        An Old Fashioned Boy, Martha Farquharson Finley

1871   *Horizon*, John Augustin Daly
        A Life of Robert E. Lee, John Esten Cooke

1872   *Davy Crockett*, Frank Hitchcock Murdoch
        Roughing It, Mark Twain
        Sketches of Southern Life, Frances Ellen Watkins Harper

1873   *The Gilded Age*, Mark Twain

1874   *Our Fred: or, Seminary Life at Thurston*, Martha Farquharson Finley
        The Rising Son; or The Antecedents and Advancement of the Colored Race, William
            Wells Brown

1875   *American Ornithology; or, The Natural History of the Birds of the United States*,
            Alexander Wilson
        Cartoons, Margaret Junkin Preston
        "Corn," Sidney Lanier
        "Gone Forward," Margaret Junkin Preston
        "The Power of Prayer: or, The First Steamboat Up the Alabama," Sidney
            Lanier
        "The Symphony," Sidney Lanier

1876   *The Adventures of Tom Sawyer*, Mark Twain
        Ah Sin, the Heathen Chinee, Mark Twain and Bret Harte

1877   "Song of the Chattahoochee," Sidney Lanier

1878   *Christmas-Night in the Quarters*, Irwin Russell
        "Dancin' Party at Harrison's Cove," Mary Noailles Murfree
        "The Marshes of Glynn," Sidney Lanier
        The Mildred Books, Martha Farquharson Finley [1878–1894]
        The Romance of Rockville, Joel Chandler Harris

1879   "Jean-Ah Pouquelin," George Washington Cable
       "Lee," Dr. Francis Orrery Ticknor
       Old Creole Days, George Washington Cable
       "Virginia," Dr. Francis Orrery Ticknor
       "The Virginians of the Valley," Dr. Francis Orrery Ticknor

1880   *The Boy's King Arthur*, Sidney Lanier
       The Grandissimes, George Washington Cable
       My Southern Home; or, The South and Its People, William Wells Brown
       The Science of English Verse, Sidney Lanier
       "Sunrise," Sidney Lanier
       "Sword of Robert Lee," Abram Joseph Ryan
       Uncle Remus: His Songs and His Sayings, Joel Chandler Harris
       The White Rose of Memphis, Colonel William Clark Falkner

1881   *The Boy's Mabinogion*, Sidney Lanier
       Life and Times of Frederick Douglass, Frederick Douglass
       Madame Delphine, George Washington Cable
       The Rise and Fall of the Confederate Government, Jefferson Davis

1882   *The Boy's Percy*, Sidney Lanier
       "Compensation," John Banister Tabb
       "Kildee," John Banister Tabb
       "My Secret," John Banister Tabb
       The Prince and the Pauper, Mark Twain
       "The Snow-Bird," John Banister Tabb

1883   "The Condition of the Freedmen," Frederick Douglass
       The English Novel, Sidney Lanier
       Life on the Mississippi, Mark Twain
       Nights with Uncle Remus, Joel Chandler Harris

1884   *The Adventures of Huckleberry Finn*, Mark Twain
       Dr. Sevier, George Washington Cable
       "The 'Harnt' That Walks Chilhowee," Mary Noailles Murfree
       In the Mountains of Tennessee, Mary Noailles Murfree
       The Life and Time of Col. Daniel Boone, Hunter, Soldier, and Pioneer, Edward
           Sylvester Ellis
       Mingo and Other Sketches in Black and White, Joel Chandler Harris
       "Old Mark Langston," Richard Malcolm Johnston

1885   "The Private History of a Campaign That Failed," Mark Twain
       The Silent South, George Washington Cable

1886   *Diary from Dixie*, Mary Boykin Chesnut
       "The New South," Henry Grady

1887   *A Branch of May*, Lizette Woodworth Reese
       Free Joe and Other Georgian Sketches, Joel Chandler Harris
       In Ole Virginia, Thomas Nelson Page
       Memorials of a Southern Planter, Susan Dabney Smedes

1888   *Bonaventure*, George Washington Cable
       "Mr. Absalom Billingslea and Other Georgia Folk," Richard Malcolm Johnston
       Negro Myths from the Georgia Coast Told in the Vernacular, Charles Colcock Jones

1889   *Chita: A Memory of Last Island*, Lafcadio Hearn
       A Connecticut Yankee in King Arthur's Court, Mark Twain

1889 *continued*
      Daddy Jack the Runaway, and Other Stories Told after Dark, Joel Chandler Harris
      "If It Might Be," Kate Chopin
      Recollections of Mississippi and Mississippians, Reuben Davis
      Strange True Stories of Louisiana, George Washington Cable
      "Wiser than a God," Kate Chopin

1890 *At Fault*, Kate Chopin
      Jefferson Davis, Ex-President of the Confederate States of America; a Memoir, Varina
          Howell Davis
      The Negro Question, George Washington Cable
      "Widow Guthrie," Richard Malcolm Johnston

1891 *Jerry*, Sarah Barnwell Elliott

1892 *Iola Leroy: or, Shadows Uplifted*, Frances Ellen Watkins Harper
      The Old South, Essays Social and Political, Thomas Nelson Page
      On the Plantation, Joel Chandler Harris
      Southern Horrors: Lynch Law in All Its Phases, Ida Bell Wells-Barnett

1893 *The Reason Why the Colored American Is Not in the Columbian Exposition*, Ida Bell
          Wells-Barnett

1894 *Bayou Folk*, Kate Chopin
      "Désirée's Baby," Kate Chopin
      John Marsh, Southerner, George Washington Cable
      The Lesson of the Hour: Why Is the Negro Lynched, Frederick Douglass
      Pudd'nhead Wilson, Mark Twain
      "The Race Problem in America," Frederick Douglass
      The Sparrow's Fall and Other Poems, Frances Ellen Watkins Harper
      Tom Sawyer Abroad, Mark Twain

1895 *Atlanta Offering: Poems*, Frances Ellen Watkins Harper
      The Lee Memorial Ode, James Barron Hope
      Martyr of Alabama and Other Poems, Frances Ellen Watkins Harper
      Mr. Rabbit at Home, Joel Chandler Harris
      *A Red Record: Tabulated Statistics and Alleged Causes of Lynching in the United
          States, 1892–1893–1894*, Ida Bell Wells-Barnett
      The Story of Aaron, Joel Chandler Harris
      A Wreath of Virginia Bay Leaves, James Barron Hope

1896 "Christmas in the Confederate White House," Varina Howell Davis
      Sister Jane, Her Friends and Acquaintances, Joel Chandler Harris
      Tales of Home Folks in Peace and War, Joel Chandler Harris

1897 "Athénaïse," Kate Chopin
      The Descendant, Ellen Glasgow
      The Kentuckians, John Fox, Jr.
      A Night in Acadie, Kate Chopin

1898 *The Durket Sperret*, Sarah Barnwell Elliott
      "The Man Who Corrupted Hadleyburg," Mark Twain
      "The Miracle of Lava Cañon," O. Henry
      Music and Poetry, Sidney Lanier
      Sketches of Country Life, Francis Bartow Lloyd
      Twiddletwit: A Fairy Tale, Martha Farquharson Finley

1899 *The Awakening*, Kate Chopin
The Conjure Woman, Charles Waddell Chesnutt
"A Matter of Principle," Charles Waddell Chesnutt
Strong Hearts, George Washington Cable
"Whistling Dick's Christmas Stocking," O. Henry
The Wife of His Youth and Other Stories of the Color Line, Charles Waddell
   Chesnutt

1900 *The House behind the Cedars*, Charles Waddell Chesnutt
*The Jesuit Relations and Allied Documents: Travel and Explorations of the Jesuit
   Missionaries in New France, 1610–1791*, Father Le Petit
Mob Rule in New Orleans, Ida Bell Wells-Barnett
Negro National Anthem, James Weldon Johnson and John Rosamund Johnson
On the Wing of Occasions, Joel Chandler Harris
Poems, Frances Ellen Watkins Harper
*Thirty-One Years on the Plains and in the Mountains or, The Last Voice from the
   Plains*, Capt. William F. Drannan
The Voice of the People, Ellen Glasgow

1901 *The Cavalier*, George Washington Cable
For Charlie's Sake, and Other Ballads and Lyrics, John Williamson Palmer
"Stonewall Jackson's Way," John Williamson Palmer
Up from Slavery, Booker T. Washington

1902 *Bylow Hill*, George Washington Cable
Gabriel Tolliver, Joel Chandler Harris
Shakespeare and His Forerunners, Sidney Lanier

1903 *The Little Shepherd of Kingdom Come*, John Fox, Jr.
"A Retrieved Reformation," O. Henry
Ventures into Verse, H. L. Mencken

1904 *Deliverance*, Ellen Glasgow
The Eagle's Shadow, James Branch Cabell
"The Forgotten Man," Walter Hines Page
"The Rebuilding of Old Commonwealths," Walter Hines Page
Reminiscences of Colonial Life in Texas, Dilue Rose Harris
"The School That Built a Town," Walter Hines Page

1905 "The Gift of the Magi," O. Henry
Original Journals of the Lewis and Clark Expedition, Meriwether Lewis and
   William Clark
The Spirit of the Mountains, Emma Belle Miles
Told by Uncle Remus, Joel Chandler Harris

1906 *The Four Millions*, O. Henry

1907 *Deliverance*, James Dickey
Hearts of the West, O. Henry
*The Life and Adventures of Nat Love, Better Known in the Cattle Country as
   Deadwood Dick*, Nat Love
Uncle Remus's Magazine, Joel Chandler Harris and Julian Harris

1908 *Kincaid's Battery*, George Washington Cable
The Trail of the Lonesome Pine, John Fox, Jr.
The Wartime Journal of a Georgia Girl, Georgia Eliza Frances Andrews

1909   *Lo,* O. Henry and Franklin P. Adams
        Options, O. Henry
        "Posson Jone' and Père Raphael," George Washington Cable
        The Romance of a Plain Man, Ellen Glasgow
        "The Rose of Dixie," O. Henry

1910   *Cowboy Songs and Other Frontier Ballads,* John Lomax
        Light beyond the Darkness, Frances Ellen Watkins Harper
        "A Municipal Report," O. Henry
        "The Ransom of Red Chief," O. Henry
        Strictly Business, O. Henry
        Uncle Remus and the Little Boy, Joel Chandler Harris

1911   "The Duplicity of Hargraves," O. Henry
        The Miller of Old Church, Ellen Glasgow
        My Larger Education, Booker T. Washington

1912   *The Artist,* H. L. Mencken and George Jean Nathan
        The Autobiography of an Ex-Coloured Man, James Weldon Johnson
        O Pioneers!, Willa Cather

1913   *Collected Works,* O. Henry
        Virginia, Ellen Glasgow

1914   *Gideon's Band,* George Washington Cable
        Letters of a Woman Homesteader, Elinore Pruitt Stewart
        Smart Set: A Magazine of Cleverness, H. L. Mencken and George Jean Nathan

1915   *Letters on an Elk Hunt,* Elinore Pruitt Stewart
        Rivers to the Sea, Sara Teasdale

1916   *Book of Burlesques,* H. L. Mencken
        Life and Gabriella: The Story of a Woman's Courage, Ellen Glasgow
        The Mysterious Stranger, Mark Twain

1917   *A Book of Prefaces,* H. L. Mencken
        Songs of the Cattle Trail and Cow Camp, John Lomax

1918   *Heart of a Woman and Other Poems,* Georgia Douglas Johnson
        My Ántonia, Willa Cather
        Uncle Remus Returns, Joel Chandler Harris

1919   *The American Language,* H. L. Mencken [1919–1948]
        "The Crisis in Industry," Thomas Wolfe
        "L'Après-Midi du Faune," William Faulkner
        Poems about God, John Crowe Ransom
        Return of Buck Gavin, Thomas Wolfe

1920   "Before the Feast of Shushan," Anne Spencer
        Flame and Shadow, Sara Teasdale
        Heliogabalus, H. L. Mencken and George Jean Nathan
        "I Shall Not Care," Sara Teasdale
        The Last of the Lowries, Paul Green
        Prejudices, Second Series, H. L. Mencken
        "There Will Come Soft Rains," Sara Teasdale

1921   *Chills and Fever,* John Crowe Ransom
        "From Lang Syne Plantation," Julia Mood Peterkin

"John Redding Goes to Sea," Zora Neale Hurston
"The Merry-Go-Round," Julia Mood Peterkin

1922   "Betsy," Julia Mood Peterkin
The Book of American Negro Poetry, James Weldon Johnson
Bronze: A Book of Verse, Georgia Douglas Johnson
Carolina Chansons, Dubose Heyward
"Cat-Fish," Julia Mood Peterkin
"Cooch's Premium," Julia Mood Peterkin
Daniel Boone: Wilderness Scout, Stewart Edward White
"Ode to the Confederate Dead," Allen Tate
"The Ortymobile," Julia Mood Peterkin
"The Plat-Eye," Julia Mood Peterkin

1923   *The Shame Woman*, Lula Vollmer
Sun-Up, Lula Vollmer
"The Voodoo of Hell's Half-Acre," Richard Wright

1924   *The American Mercury*, H. L. Mencken [1924–1933]
The Autobiography of Mark Twain, Mark Twain
"Bells for John Whiteside's Daughter," John Crowe Ransom
"Drenched in Light," Zora Neale Hurston
Green Thursday, Julia Mood Peterkin
"In Aunt Mahaly's Cabin: A Folk Play for the Negro Theatre," Paul Green
The Marble Faun, William Faulkner
"Necrological," John Crowe Ransom
An Outland Piper, Donald Davidson
"Piazza Piece," John Crowe Ransom
Porgy (novel), Dubose Heyward
The Scuffletown Outlaws: A Tragedy of the Lowrie Gang, William Norment Cox
"Spectral Lovers," John Crowe Ransom

1925   *Barren Ground*, Ellen Glasgow
The Book of American Negro Spirituals, James Weldon Johnson and John
    Rosamund Johnson
Cane, Jean Toomer
The Dunce Boy, Lula Vollmer
"Heritage," Countee Cullen
Quare Medicine, Paul Green
"Spunk," Zora Neale Hurston

1926   *Angel*, Dubose Heyward
"The Artist as Southerner," Donald Davidson
Color Struck, Zora Neale Hurston
"The Eatonville Anthology," Zora Neale Hurston
First One, Zora Neale Hurston
"The Gilded Six-Bits," Zora Neale Hurston
"Last Words," H. L. Mencken
"Muttsy," Zora Neale Hurston
"Possum or Pig," Zora Neale Hurston
The Romantic Comedian, Ellen Glasgow
The Second Book of Negro Spirituals, James Weldon Johnson and John Rosamund
    Johnson

1926   *continued*
Soldier's Pay, William Faulkner
Spear, Zora Neale Hurston
"Sweat," Zora Neale Hurston
Two Gentlemen in Bonds, John Crowe Ransom

1927   *Black April*, Julia Mood Peterkin
Copper Sun, Countee Cullen
"The Creation," James Weldon Johnson
"Dead Boy," John Crowe Ransom
The Field God, Paul Green
God's Trombones: Seven Negro Sermons in Verse, James Weldon Johnson
In Abraham's Bosom, Paul Green
"Janet Waking," John Crowe Ransom
Lee in the Mountains and Other Poems, Donald Davidson
Mosquitoes, William Faulkner
Porgy (play), Dubose Heyward and Dorothy Hartzell Kuhns Heyward
"Sanctuary," Donald Davidson
The Tall Men, Donald Davidson
Trigger, Lula Vollmer

1928   *Apache Gold and Yaqui Silver*, James Frank Dobie
An Autumn Love Cycle, Georgia Douglas Johnson
Caroling Dusk, Countee Cullen
Johnny Johnson, Paul Green
Scarlet Sister Mary, Julia Mood Peterkin
Stonewall Jackson: The Good Soldier, Allen Tate
"The Vengeance of Nitrocris," Tennessee Williams

1929   "The Angel on the Porch," Thomas Wolfe
The Battle-Ground, Ellen Glasgow
Beauty Is the World, Tennessee Williams
The Black Christ, and Other Poems, Countee Cullens
The Half Pint Flask, Dubose Heyward
Jefferson Davis: His Rise and Fall, Allen Tate
John Brown's Body, Stephen Vincent Benét
Look Homeward Angel: A Story of the Buried Life, Thomas Wolfe
Mamba's Daughters, Dubose Heyward and Dorothy Hartzell Kuhns Heyward
Sartoris, William Faulkner
The Sound and the Fury, William Faulkner
They Stooped to Folly, Ellen Glasgow
A Victorian Village, Lizette Woodworth Reese

1930   *As I Lay Dying*, William Faulkner
Coronado's Children, James Frank Dobie
Flowering Judas, Katherine Anne Porter
God without Thunder, John Crowe Ransom
The Great Meadow, Elizabeth Madox Roberts
I'll Take My Stand, Fugitive Agrarian consortium
"The Jilting of Granny Weatherall," Katherine Anne Porter
Mule Bone, Zora Neale Hurston and Langston Hughes
"Old Mortality," Katherine Anne Porter

Vaquero of the Brush Country, James Frank Dobie
When a Whippoorwill, Marjorie Kinnan Rawlings

1931   *The Brass Ankle*, Dubose Heyward
"Cracker Chidlings," Marjorie Kinnan Rawlings
The House of Connelly, Paul Green
Jacob's Ladder, Marjorie Kinnan Rawlings
Penhally, Caroline Gordon
"A Rose for Emily," William Faulkner
Sanctuary, William Faulkner
"That Evening Sun," William Faulkner
These 13, William Faulkner

1932   *Bright Skin*, Julia Mood Peterkin
Ca'line, Bernice Kelly Harris
The Great Day, Zora Neale Hurston
The Laughing Pioneer, Paul Green
Light in August, William Faulkner
"Metzengerstein," Edgar Allan Poe
"A Portrait of Bascom Hawke," Thomas Wolfe
The Sheltered Life, Ellen Glasgow
Southern Road, Sterling Brown
Tobacco Road, Erskine Caldwell
Tread the Green Grass, Paul Green

1933   *A Book of Americans*, Rosemary Benét and Stephen Vincent Benét
From Sun to Sun, Zora Neale Hurston
"Gal Young 'Un," Marjorie Kinnan Rawlings
God's Little Acre, Erskine Caldwell
South Moon Under, Marjorie Kinnan Rawlings

1934   *Aleck Maury, Sportsman*, Caroline Gordon
American Ballads and Folk Songs, John Lomax and Alan Lomax
The Children's Hour, Lillian Hellman
Doctor Martino and Other Stories, William Faulkner
Jonah's Gourd Vine, Zora Neale Hurston
Man with a Bull-Tongue Plow, Jesse Stuart
The Mustang, James Frank Dobie
Permit Me Voyage, James Agee
Roll, Sweet Chariot, Paul Green
Shroud My Body Down, Paul Green
Singing Steel, Zora Neale Hurston
So Red the Rose, Stark Young

1935   "Between the World and Me," Richard Wright
Cairo! Shanghai! Bombay!, Tennessee Williams
The Enchanted Maze, Paul Green
From Death to Morning, Thomas Wolfe
Mules and Men, Zora Neale Hurston
Of Time and the River: A Legend of Man's Hunger in His Youth, Thomas Wolfe
Porgy and Bess, Dubose Heyward, George Gershwin, and Ira Gershwin
The Relation of the Alabama-Georgia Dialect to the Provincial Dialects of Great Britain, Cleanth Brooks

1935　*continued*
　　　Vein of Iron, Ellen Glasgow
　　　Wash Carver's Mouse Trap, Fred Koch, Jr.

1936　*Absalom, Absalom!*, William Faulkner
　　　"Death of a Traveling Salesman," Eudora Welty
　　　The Fugitive Kind, Tennessee Williams
　　　Gone with the Wind, Margaret Mitchell
　　　"A Mother in Manville," Marjorie Kinnan Rawlings
　　　Negro Folk Songs as Sung by Lead Belly, John Lomax
　　　Reactionary Essays on Poetry and Ideas, Allen Tate
　　　The Story of a Novel, Thomas Wolfe
　　　Who Owns America?, Fugitive Agrarian consortium

1937　*Candles to the Sun*, Tennessee Williams
　　　The Garden of Adonis, Caroline Gordon
　　　None Shall Look Back, Caroline Gordon
　　　A Southern Treasury of Art and Literature, Stark Young
　　　A Southern Treasury of Life and Literature, Cleanth Brooks
　　　Their Eyes Were Watching God, Zora Neale Hurston

1938　*The Attack on Leviathan*, Donald Davidson
　　　Beyond Dark Hills, Jesse Stuart
　　　The Fathers, Allen Tate
　　　The Hills Between, Lula Vollmer
　　　Moonshine and Honeysuckle, Lula Vollmer
　　　"An Odor of Verbena," William Faulkner
　　　Tell My Horse, Zora Neale Hurston
　　　Uncle Tom's Children: Five Long Stories, Richard Wright
　　　Understanding Poetry, Cleanth Brooks and Robert Penn Warren
　　　The Unvanquished, William Faulkner
　　　The World's Body, John Crowe Ransom
　　　The Yearling, Marjorie Kinnan Rawlings

1939　"The Field of Blue Children," Tennessee Williams
　　　The Highland Call, Paul Green
　　　The Little Foxes, Lillian Hellman
　　　Modern Poetry and the Tradition, Cleanth Brooks
　　　Moses, Man of the Mountain, Zora Neale Hurston
　　　Night Rider, Robert Penn Warren
　　　Pale Horse, Pale Rider, Katherine Anne Porter
　　　"Split Cherry Tree," Jesse Stuart
　　　Star-Spangled Virgin, Dubose Heyward
　　　Tales of the Town, O. Henry
　　　The Web and the Rock, Thomas Wolfe
　　　The Wigwam and Cabin: Life in America, William Gilmore Simms
　　　The Wild Palms, William Faulkner

1940　*Battle of Angels*, Tennessee Williams
　　　"The Birthmark," Ralph Ellison
　　　The Heart Is a Lonely Hunter, Carson McCullers
　　　"How Bigger Was Born," Richard Wright
　　　Native Son, Richard Wright
　　　"Portrait: Old South," Katherine Anne Porter

Trees of Heaven, Jesse Stuart
You Can't Go Home Again, Thomas Wolfe

1941   *A Curtain of Green and Other Stories*, Eudora Welty
Green Centuries, Caroline Gordon
The Hills Beyond, Thomas Wolfe
Let Us Now Praise Famous Men, James Agee
Longhorns, James Frank Dobie
The Mind of the South, W. J. Cash
"Mr. Toussan," Ralph Ellison
"My Side of the Matter," Truman Capote
The New Criticism, John Crowe Ransom
Our Singing Country, John Lomax
Reason in Madness, Allen Tate
Reflections in a Golden Eye, Carson McCullers
Watch on the Rhine, Lillian Hellman
"A Worn Path," Eudora Welty

1942   "The Bear," William Faulkner
Blood for a Stranger, Randall Jarrell
The Carolina Israelite, Harry Golden
Cross Creek, Marjorie Kinnan Rawlings
Cross Creek Cookery, Marjorie Kinnan Rawlings
Dust Tracks on a Road, Zora Neale Hurston
For My People, Margaret Walker
Go Down, Moses, William Faulkner
In This Our Life, Ellen Glasgow
Kentucky Is My Land, Jesse Stuart
A New Dictionary of Quotations, on Historical Principles, H. L. Mencken
"Program of the March on Washington," Philip Randolph
"Pure and Impure Poetry," Robert Penn Warren
"Recent Negro Fiction," Ralph Ellison
The Robber Bridegroom (novel), Eudora Welty
"A Tree, a Rock, a Cloud," Carson McCullers
Wave High the Banner, Dee Brown
"The Way It Is," Ralph Ellison

1943   *Brother to Dragons*, Robert Penn Warren
Guide to Life and Literature of the Southwest, James Frank Dobie
Heathen Days, 1890–1936, H. L. Mencken
The Outsider, Richard Wright
Plantation Life in the Florida Parishes of Louisiana, 1836–1846, Bennet H. Barrow
Taps for Private Tussie, Jesse Stuart
The Testament of Freedom, Thomas Jefferson
Understanding Fiction, Cleanth Brooks and Robert Penn Warren
The Wide Net, and Other Stories, Eudora Welty

1944   *Album of Destiny*, Jesse Stuart
"Flying Home," Ralph Ellison
"In a Strange Country," Ralph Ellison
"King of the Bingo Game," Ralph Ellison
The Leaning Tower and Other Stories, Katherine Anne Porter
Mongrel Mettle, Jesse Stuart

1944 *continued*
The Old Order: Stories of the South, Katherine Anne Porter
Only the Heart, Horton Foote
The Searching Wind, Lillian Hellman
"That I Had the Wings," Ralph Ellison
"The Vertical Negro Plan," Harry Golden
The Women on the Porch, Caroline Gordon

1945 *Black Boy: A Record of Childhood and Youth*, Richard Wright
"The Captive," Caroline Gordon
Dark of the Moon, Howard Dixon Richardson
The Forest of the South, Caroline Gordon
The Glass Menagerie, Tennessee Williams
Little Friend, Little Friend, Randall Jarrell
"Richard Wright's Blues," Ralph Ellison
Selected Poems, John Crowe Ransom
Understanding Drama, Cleanth Brooks and Robert Penn Warren
You Touched Me!, Tennessee Williams

1946 *All the King's Men*, Robert Penn Warren
Delta Wedding, Eudora Welty
The Fabulous Empire: Colonel Zack Miller's Story, Fred Gipson
"The Geranium," Flannery O'Connor
Local Color, Truman Capote
The Member of the Wedding, Carson McCullers

1947 *Adventures of a Ballad Hunter*, John Lomax
Another Part of the Forest, Lillian Hellman
The Common Glory, Paul Green
The Everglades: River of Grass, Marjory Stoneman Douglass
Folk Song U.S.A., John Lomax
Let Me Lie, James Branch Cabell
A Streetcar Named Desire, Tennessee Williams
The Well Wrought Urn, Cleanth Brooks

1948 *American Blues*, Tennessee Williams
Fighting Indians of the West, Dee Brown
Intruder in the Dust, William Faulkner
Life of Herod the Great, Zora Neale Hurston
Losses, Randall Jarrell
Other Voices, Other Rooms, Truman Capote
Seraph on the Suwanee, Zora Neale Hurston
Seven Tales of Uncle Remus, Joel Chandler Harris
Summer and Smoke, Tennessee Williams
The Tennessee, Donald Davidson

1949 *Hound-Dog Man*, Fred Gipson
The Limits of Poetry, Allen Tate
The Sun Comes Up, Marjorie Kinnan Rawlings
The Thread That Runs So True, Jesse Stuart

1950 *The Ben Lilly Legend*, James Frank Dobie
Children on Their Birthdays, Truman Capote
Collected Stories of William Faulkner, William Faulkner
Faith of Our Fathers, Paul Green

Hie to the Hunters, Jesse Stuart
The House of Fiction, Caroline Gordon
The Member of the Wedding (play), Carson McCullers
Requiem for a Nun, William Faulkner
The Rose Tattoo, Tennessee Williams
World Enough and Time, Robert Penn Warren

1951   *Ballad of the Sad Café*, Carson McCullers
Lie Down in Darkness, William Styron

1952   *Big Bend: A Homesteader's Story*, Fred Gipson
The Grass Harp (play), Truman Capote
Horn in the West, Kermit Hunter
Trail Driving Days, Dee Brown
Wise Blood, Flannery O'Connor

1953   *The Beatinest Boy*, Jesse Stuart
Camino Real, Tennessee Williams
"A Good Man Is Hard To Find," Flannery O'Connor
The Grass Harp (novel), Truman Capote
The Long March, William Styron
The Trip to Bountiful, Horton Foote

1954   "The Displaced Person," Flannery O'Connor
The Dollmaker, Harriette Arnow
A Fable, William Faulkner
House of Flowers, Truman Capote
The Ponder Heart, Eudora Welty
Savage Holiday, Richard Wright
A Woman Within, Ellen Glasgow

1955   *Band of Angels*, Robert Penn Warren
Big Woods, William Faulkner
Cat on a Hot Tin Roof, Tennessee Williams
"Death of the Ball Turret Gunner," Randall Jarrell
A Good Man Is Hard To Find and Other Stories, Flannery O'Connor
"Lady Bates," Randall Jarrell
Red Mule, Jesse Stuart
Selected Poems, Randall Jarrell
The Settlers West, Dee Brown
Tales of Old-Time Texas, James Frank Dobie
The Trail-Driving Rooster, Fred Gipson
Trouble in Mind, Alice Childress
Wilderness Road, Paul Green

1956   "A Christmas Memory," Truman Capote
A Death in the Family, James Agee
Hannah Fowler, Janice Holt Giles
Land beyond the River, Jesse Stuart
The Marjorie Kinnan Rawlings Reader, Marjorie Kinnan Rawlings
The Muses Are Heard, Truman Capote
Old Yeller, Fred Gipson
The Secret River, Marjorie Kinnan Rawlings
"The Turtles," Ernest J. Gaines
The Voice at the Back Door, Elizabeth Spencer

1957   *The Founders*, Paul Green
       The Hamlet, William Faulkner
       How To Read a Novel, Caroline Gordon
       Still Rebels, Still Yankees, Donald Davidson
       The Town, William Faulkner
       Yellowhorse, Dee Brown

1958   *Breakfast at Tiffany's*, Truman Capote
       The Gentle Tamers: Women of the Old Wild West, Dee Brown
       The Long Dream, Richard Wright
       The Square Root of Wonderful, Carson McCullers
       Suddenly Last Summer, Tennessee Williams

1959   *The Cave*, Robert Penn Warren
       The Mansion, William Faulkner
       Sweet Bird of Youth, Tennessee Williams

1960   *Black Like Me*, John Howard Griffin
       The Fugitive, Tennessee Williams
       "Mr. Muhammad Speaks," Alex Haley
       Period of Adjustment, Tennessee Williams
       Set This House on Fire, William Styron
       To Kill a Mockingbird, Harper Lee
       Tomorrow, Horton Foote
       The Violent Bear It Away, Flannery O'Connor
       The Woman at the Washington Zoo, Randall Jarrell

1961   *Christmas to Me*, Harper Lee
       Clock without Hands, Carson McCullers
       Night of the Iguana, Tennessee Williams
       Spencer's Mountain, Earl Hamner, Jr.

1962   *The Fetterman Massacre*, Dee Brown
       "The Heaven of Animals," James Dickey
       Hold April, Jesse Stuart
       "Just Like a Tree," Ernest J. Gaines
       A Long and Happy Life, Reynolds Price
       The Reivers, William Faulkner
       Share My World, Georgia Douglas Johnson
       To Kill a Mockingbird (screenplay), Horton Foote

1963   *Galvanized Yankees*, Dee Brown
       "I Have a Dream," Martin Luther King, Jr.
       It Is Time, Lord, Fred Chappell
       Lawd Today, Richard Wright
       "Letter from a Birmingham Jail," Martin Luther King, Jr.
       "Letters from the Earth," Mark Twain
       The Milk Train Doesn't Stop Here Anymore, Tennessee Williams
       My Brother Bill, John Faulkner
       "*Playboy* Interview: Malcolm X," Alex Haley
       Remember Me to Tom, Edwina Dakin Williams
       "Where Is the Voice Coming From?," Eudora Welty

1964   *Catherine Carmier*, Ernest J. Gaines
       Cow People, James Frank Dobie

The Keepers of the House, Shirley Ann Grau
Nigger, Dick Gregory
Shadow and Act, Ralph Ellison
Sweet as a Pickle and Clean as a Pig: Poems, Carson McCullers

1965 *Autobiography of Malcolm X*, Alex Haley
Baby, the Rain Must Fall, Horton Foote
The Ballad of the Flim-Flam Man, Guy Owen
Daughter of the Legend, Jesse Stuart
Everything That Rises Must Converge, Flannery O'Connor
In Cold Blood, Truman Capote
The Inkling, Fred Chappell

1966 *Ballad of the Free*, Margaret Walker
Beyond Defeat, Ellen Glasgow
Jubilee, Margaret Walker
Norwood, Charles Portis

1967 *Black Feeling, Black Talk*, Nikki Giovanni
Christy, Catherine Marshall
Confessions of Nat Turner, William Styron
Hurry Sundown, Horton Foote
The Man Who Cried I Am, John Williams
"May Day Sermon to the Women of Gilmer County, Georgia, by a Woman
 Preacher Leaving the Baptist Church," James Dickey
Mr. Gallion's School, Jesse Stuart
Of Love and Dust, Ernest J. Gaines
Some Part of Myself, James Frank Dobie

1968 *Bloodline*, Ernest Gaines
Coming of Age in Mississippi, Anne E. Moody
Dagon, Fred Chappell
Here's Where I Belong, Alfred Uhry
Judas, My Brother, Frank Yerby
Look Out Whitey! Black Power's Gon' Get Your Mama!, Julius Lester
Once: Poems, Alice Walker
Soul on Ice, Eldridge Cleaver
The Thanksgiving Visitor, Truman Capote
To Be a Slave, Julius Lester
"To Hell with Dying," Alice Walker
True Grit, Charles Portis
"The True Import of Present Dialogue: Black vs. Negro," Nikki Giovanni
William Styron's Nat Turner: Ten Black Writers Respond, John H. Clarke, ed.

1969 *Die Nigger Die!*, H. Rap Brown
The Foxfire Book, Eliot Wigginton
Homecoming, Sonia Sanchez
Mystery and Manners, Flannery O'Connor
An Unfinished Woman, Lillian Hellman

1970 *Black Judgement*, Nikki Giovanni
The Boo, Pat Conroy
Buckdancer's Choice, James Dickey
Bury My Heart at Wounded Knee, Dee Brown

1970   *continued*
    The Cay, Theodore Taylor
    The Homecoming, Earl Hamner, Jr.
    I Know Why the Caged Bird Sings, Maya Angelou
    The Liberty Tree, Kermit Hunter
    Losing Battles, Eudora Welty
    Old Ben, Jesse Stuart
    Prophets for a New Day, Margaret Walker
    The Third Life of Grange Copeland, Alice Walker
    To Teach, To Love, Jesse Stuart

1971   *The Autobiography of Miss Jane Pittman*, Ernest J. Gaines
    The End of the World, Walker Percy
    Enjoy, Enjoy, Harry Golden
    Gemini: An Extended Autobiographical Statement on My First Twenty-Five Years of Being a Black Poet, Nikki Giovanni
    Georgia, Georgia, Maya Angelou
    The Grass Harp (musical), Truman Capote
    "The Haunted Boy," Carson McCullers
    It's a New Day, Sonia Sanchez
    Just Give Me a Cool Drink of Water 'fore I Diiie, Maya Angelou
    Love in the Ruins: The Adventures of a Bad Catholic at a Time Near the End of the World, Walker Percy
    The Mortgaged Heart, Carson McCullers
    Re-Creation, Nikki Giovanni
    Spin a Soft Black Song, Nikki Giovanni
    "Sucker," Carson McCullers
    The World between the Eyes, Fred Chappell

1972   *How I Wrote Jubilee*, Margaret Walker
    The Optimist's Daughter, Eudora Welty
    Rambling Rose, Calder Willingham
    Small Craft Warnings, Tennessee Williams
    The Water Is Wide, Pat Conroy

1973   *Am I Blue?*, Beth Henley
    A Hero Ain't Nothin' but a Sandwich, Alice Childress
    In Love and Trouble: Stories of Black Women, Alice Walker
    "Julia," Lillian Hellman
    The Lost Colony, Paul Green
    October Journey, Margaret Walker
    Pentimento: A Book of Portraits, Lillian Hellman
    Revolutionary Petunias and Other Poems, Alice Walker
    Summer of My German Soldier, Bette Greene

1974   *A Blues Book for Blue Black Magical Women*, Sonia Sanchez
    Gather Together in My Name, Maya Angelou
    "In Search of Zora Neale Hurston," Alice Walker
    Invisible Man, Ralph Ellison
    Jericho: The South Beheld, James Dickey
    Langston Hughes, American Poet, Alice Walker
    The Memory of Old Jack, Wendell Berry
    Our Southern Landsman, Harry Golden

A Poetic Equation: Conversations between Nikki Giovanni and Margaret Walker, Margaret Walker

1975 "Charleston in the 1860s: Derived from the Diaries of Mary Boykin Chesnut," Adrienne Rich
Memoir, Tennessee Williams
Moise and the World of Reason, Tennessee Williams
Oh Pray My Wings Are Gonna Fit Me Well, Maya Angelou
The Red Devil Battery Sign, Tennessee Williams
The Robber Bridegroom (play), Alfred Uhry
Southern Ladies and Gentlemen, Florence King

1976 *The Great Santini*, Pat Conroy
Meridian, Alice Walker
No More Lies: The Myth and Reality of American History, Dick Gregory
Roll of Thunder, Hear My Cry, Mildred Taylor
Roots: The Saga of an American Family, Alex Haley
Scoundrel Time, Lillian Hellman
Singin' and Swingin' and Gettin' Merry like Christmas, Maya Angelou
WASP, Where Is Thy Sting, Florence King
"Who Then Will Speak for the Common Good?," Barbara Jordan

1977 *American Hunger*, Richard Wright
Chapeau, Alfred Uhry
Getting Out, Marsha Norman
Hear That Lonesome Whistle Blow: Railroads in the West, Dee Brown
"The Only Reason You Want To Go to Heaven," Alice Walker
A Place To Come To, Robert Penn Warren
We a BadddDDD People, Sonia Sanchez

1978 *And Still I Rise*, Maya Angelou
Cotton Candy on a Rainy Day, Nikki Giovanni
The Eye of the Story: Selected Essays and Reviews, Eudora Welty
He: An Irreverent Look at the American Male, Florence King
It's the Willingness, Marsha Norman
Little Arliss, Fred Gipson
The Roman Spring of Mrs. Stone, Tennessee Williams
Third and Oak: The Laundromat and the Pool Hall, Marsha Norman

1979 *Circus Valentine*, Marsha Norman
The Dog of the South, Charles Portis
The Habit of Being, Flannery O'Connor
I Love Myself: When I Am Laughing . . . and Then Again When I Am Looking Mean and Impressive: A Zora Neale Hurston Reader, Zora Neale Hurston
The Kingdom Within: A Spiritual Autobiography, Jesse Stuart
The Land Surveyor's Daughter, Ellen Gilchrist
Lost Sandstones and Lonely Skies, Jesse Stuart
Morgan's Daughters, Beth Henley
Roots: The Next Generation, Alex Haley
Sister, Sister, Maya Angelou
Sophie's Choice, William Styron

1980 *Barn Burning* (play), Horton Foote
The Collected Stories of Eudora Welty, Eudora Welty

1980 *continued*
The Holdup, Marsha Norman
If I Were Seventeen Again, Jesse Stuart
In Trouble at Fifteen, Marsha Norman
The Lords of Discipline, Pat Conroy
The Miss Firecracker Contest, Beth Henley
The Second Coming, Walker Percy
Swing, Alfred Uhry

1981 *Charleston*, Alexandra Ripley
Crimes of the Heart, Beth Henley
Daisy Fay and the Miracle Man, Fannie Flagg
The Heart of a Woman, Maya Angelou
In the Land of Dreamy Dreams, Ellen Gilchrist
Mary Chesnut's Civil War, Mary Boykin Chesnut
The Sanctified Church: The Folklore Writings of Zora Neale Hurston, Zora Neale
    Hurston
Something Cloudy, Something Clear, Tennessee Williams
You Can't Keep a Good Woman Down: Stories, Alice Walker

1982 *The Color Purple*, Alice Walker
Little Johnny Jones, Alfred Uhry
Miriam, Truman Capote
A Mother and Two Daughters, Gail Godwin
'night, Mother, Marsha Norman
Puella, James Dickey
Those Who Ride the Night Winds, Nikki Giovanni
Traveling On, Diane Glancy
The Wake of Jamey Foster, Beth Henley
When Sisterhood Was in Flower, Florence King

1983 *A Gathering of Old Men*, Ernest J. Gaines
Good Night Willie Lee, I'll See You in the Morning: Poems, Alice Walker
In Search of Our Mother's Gardens: Womanist Prose, Alice Walker
The Presence of Grace and Other Book Reviews, Flannery O'Connor
Tender Mercies, Horton Foote
Victory over Japan, Ellen Gilchrist

1984 *Brown Wolf Leaves the Res*, Diane Glancy
Cold Sassy Tree, Olive Ann Burns
Homegirls and Handgrenades, Sonia Sanchez
Horses Make a Landscape Look More Beautiful, Alice Walker
Oldest Living Confederate Tells All, Allan Gurganus
One Writer's Beginnings, Eudora Welty
Traveler in the Dark, Marsha Norman

1985 *America's Sweetheart*, Alfred Uhry
Confessions of a Failed Southern Lady, Florence King
The Debutante Ball, Beth Henley
I Am One of You Forever, Fred Chappell
Lonesome Dove, Larry McMurtry
*Richard Wright, Daemonic Genius: A Portrait of the Man, a Critical Look at His
    Work*, Margaret Walker
Spunk: The Selected Short Stories of Zora Neale Hurston, Zora Neale Hurston

1986   *All God's Children Need Travelin' Shoes*, Maya Angelou
         Answered Prayers: The Partial Manuscript, Truman Capote
         Driving Miss Daisy, Alfred Uhry
         Drunk with Love, Ellen Gilchrist
         Going to the Territory, Ralph Ellison
         Kate Vaiden, Reynolds Price
         The Lucky Spot, Beth Henley
         Nobody's Fool, Beth Henley
         One Age in a Dream, Diane Glancy
         The Prince of Tides, Pat Conroy
         True Stories, Beth Henley

1987   *Conversations with Flannery O'Connor*, Flannery O'Connor
         Ellen Foster, Kaye Gibbons
         Falling through Space, Ellen Gilchrist
         The Fortune Teller, Marsha Norman
         Fried Green Tomatoes at the Whistle Stop Cafe, Fannie Flagg
         New Orleans Legacy, Alexandra Ripley
         Now Sheba Sings the Song, Maya Angelou
         A Southern Family, Gail Godwin
         Steel Magnolias, Robert Harling
         Tent Meeting, Larry Larson, Levi Lee, and Rebecca Wackler
         The Thanatos Syndrome, Walker Percy
         Under a Soprano Sky, Sonia Sanchez
         Walking across Egypt, Clyde Edgerton
         The Widow Claire, Horton Foote

1988   *A Different Kind of Xmas*, Alex Haley
         Fallen Angels, Walter Dean Meyers
         Living by the Word: Selected Writings, 1973–1987, Alice Walker
         Offering, Diane Glancy
         Sacred Cows and Other Edibles, Nikki Giovanni
         Sarah and Abraham, Marsha Norman
         The Trail of Tears: The Rise and Fall of the Cherokee Nation, John Ehle

1989   *Brighten the Corner Where You Are*, Fred Chappell
         Light Can Be Both Wave and Particle, Ellen Gilchrist
         Reflections in a Jaundiced Eye, Florence King
         The Temple of My Familiar, Alice Walker
         "They Came To Stay," Maya Angelou
         This Is My Century: New and Collected Poems, Margaret Walker
         A Virtuous Woman, Kaye Gibbons

1990   *Abundance*, Beth Henley
         Clover, Dori Sanders
         Darkness Visible: A Memoir of Madness, William Styron
         Iron Woman, Diane Glancy
         Mule Bone: A Comedy of Negro Life, Zora Neale Hurston
         Signature, Beth Henley
         Warrior Marks, Alice Walker
         Why I Wrote Jubilee and Other Essays on Life and Literature, Margaret Walker

1991   *A Cure for Dreams*, Kaye Gibbons
         Finding the Green Stone, Alice Walker

1991   *continued*
     Her Blue Body Everything We Know: Earthling Poems, Alice Walker
     Lone Dog's Winter Count, Diane Glancy
     Lump It or Leave It, Florence King
     Molly Ivins Can't Say Those Things, Can She?, Molly Ivins
     Praying for Sheetrock, Melissa Fay Greene
     Scarlett, Alexandra Ripley
     The Secret Garden (play), Marsha Norman

1992   *Beth Henley: Monologues for Women,* Beth Henley
     Control Freaks, Beth Henley
     D. Boone, Marsha Norman
     Leaving Cold Sassy, Olive Ann Burns
     Missing May, Cynthia Rylant
     Possessing the Secret of Joy, Alice Walker
     With Charity for None, Florence King

1993   "The Arts and the American Dream," Barbara Jordan
     Charms for the Easy Life, Kaye Gibbons
     Having Our Say, Sarah Delany and Elizabeth Delany
     The Land Where the Blues Began, Alan Lomax
     A Lesson before Dying, Ernest J. Gaines
     "On the Pulse of the Morning," Maya Angelou
     Queen, Alex Haley
     The Streets of Laredo, Larry McMurtry
     "The Ten Commandments of Charm," Zora Neale Hurston
     "A Tidewater Morning," William Styron
     Timothy of the Cay, Theodore Taylor
     "Under the Bridge," Zora Neale Hurston
     When the Century Was Young, Dee Brown

1994   *The Delany Sisters' Book of Everyday Wisdom,* Sarah Delany and Elizabeth
      Delany
     The Good Husband, Gail Godwin
     The Importance of Pot Liquor, Jackie Torrence
     Racism 101, Nikki Giovanni

1995   *The Age of Miracles,* Ellen Gilchrist
     Beach Music, Pat Conroy
     The Florence King Reader, Florence King
     L-Play, Beth Henley
     Rhoda: A Life in Stories, Ellen Gilchrist
     The Young Man from Atlanta, Horton Foote

1996   *The Lost Laysen,* Margaret Mitchell
     The Notebook of Trigorin, Tennessee Williams
     "Rose of Lebanon," William Faulkner
     The Same River Twice, Alice Walker
     "Speech to the Democratic National Convention," Reverend Jesse Jackson

1997   *Anything We Love Can Be Saved: A Writer's Activism,* Alice Walker
     Cold Mountain, Charles Frazier
     The Death of Papa, Horton Foote
     Does Your House Have Lions?, Sonia Sanchez

Even the Stars Look Lonesome, Maya Angelou
Farewell, I'm Bound To Leave You, Fred Chappell
Flying Home and Other Stories, Ralph Ellison
The Last Night of Ballyhoo, Alfred Uhry
Where Trouble Sleeps, Clyde Edgerton

MAJOR WORKS OF SOUTHERN LITERATURE

A

Absalom, Absalom! William Faulkner, 1936

Abundance, Beth Henley, 1990

An Account of Colonel Crockett's Tour to the North and Down East, Davy Crockett, 1835

"Address to the Virginia Convention," Patrick Henry, 1775

Adventures of a Ballad Hunter, John Lomax, 1947

The Adventures of Col. Daniel Boon [sic], *Containing a Narrative of the Wars of Kentucke*, John Filson, 1784

The Adventures of Huckleberry Finn, Mark Twain, 1884

The Adventures of Tom Sawyer, Mark Twain, 1876

The Age of Miracles, Ellen Gilchrist, 1995

Ah Sin, the Heathen Chinee, Mark Twain and Bret Harte, 1876

Al Aaraaf, Tamerlane, and Minor Poems, Edgar Allan Poe, 1829

Album of Destiny, Jesse Stuart, 1944

Aleck Maury, Sportsman, Caroline Gordon, 1934

All God's Children Need Travelin' Shoes, Maya Angelou, 1986

"All Quiet along the Potomac To-Night," Thaddeus Oliver, 1864

All the King's Men, Robert Penn Warren, 1946

Am I Blue?, Beth Henley, 1973

"The Amazon and the Atlantic Slopes of South America," Matthew Fontaine Maury, 1853

American Ballads and Folk Songs, John Lomax and Alan Lomax, 1934

American Blues, Tennessee Williams, 1948

American Hunger, Richard Wright, 1977

The American Language, H. L. Mencken, 1919–1948

The American Mercury, H. L. Mencken, 1924–1933

American Ornithological Biography, John James Audubon and William MacGillivray, 1841

American Ornithology; or, The Natural History of the Birds of the United States, Alexander Wilson, 1875

Americans at Home; or, The Byeways, Backwoods, and Prairies, Thomas Chandler Haliburton, 1854

America's Sweetheart, Alfred Uhry, 1985

And Still I Rise, Maya Angelou, 1978

Angel, Dubose Heyward, 1926

"The Angel on the Porch," Thomas Wolfe, 1929

"Annabel Lee," Edgar Allan Poe, 1849
Another Part of the Forest, Lillian Hellman, 1947
Answered Prayers: The Partial Manuscript, Truman Capote, 1986
The Anti-Slavery Harp, William Wells Brown, 1852
Anything We Love Can Be Saved: A Writer's Activism, Alice Walker, 1997
Apache Gold and Yaqui Silver, James Frank Dobie, 1928
Appeal to the Christian Women of the South, Angelina Grimké, 1836
The Arator, John Taylor, 1803
Areytos: or, Songs of the South, William Gilmore Simms, 1846
The Artist, H. L. Mencken and George Jean Nathan, 1912
"The Artist as Southerner," Donald Davidson, 1926
"The Arts and the American Dream," Barbara Jordan, 1993
As I Lay Dying, William Faulkner, 1930
At Fault, Kate Chopin, 1890
Atalantis, a Story of the Sea, William Gilmore Simms, 1832
"Athénaïse," Kate Chopin, 1897
Atlanta Offering: Poems, Frances Ellen Watkins Harper, 1895
The Attack on Leviathan, Donald Davidson, 1938
The Autobiography of an Ex-Coloured Man, James Weldon Johnson, 1912
Autobiography of Lemuel Sawyer, 1844
Autobiography of Malcolm X, Alex Haley, 1965
The Autobiography of Mark Twain, Mark Twain, 1924
The Autobiography of Miss Jane Pittman, Ernest J. Gaines, 1971
An Autumn Love Cycle, Georgia Douglas Johnson, 1928
The Awakening, Kate Chopin, 1899

B

Baby, the Rain Must Fall, Horton Foote, 1965
The Ballad of the Flim-Flam Man, Guy Owen, 1965
Ballad of the Free, Margaret Walker, 1966
The Ballad of the Sad Café, Carson McCullers, 1951
"The Balloon Hoax," Edgar Allan Poe, 1846
Band of Angels, Robert Penn Warren, 1955
The Banished Son and Other Stories of the Heart, Caroline Lee Whiting Hentz, 1856
Barn Burning (play), Horton Foote, 1980
Barren Ground, Ellen Glasgow, 1925
Bastard Out of Carolina, Dorothy Allison, 1992
Battle of Angels, Tennessee Williams, 1940
Battle of Eutaw Springs and Evacuation of Charleston, William Ioor, 1807
The Battle-Ground, Ellen Glasgow, 1929
Bayou Folk, Kate Chopin, 1894
Beach Music, Pat Conroy, 1995
"The Bear," William Faulkner, 1942
The Beatinest Boy, Jesse Stuart, 1953
Beauchampe, or The Kentucky Tragedy, A Tale of Passion, William Gilmore Simms, 1842
Beauty Is the World, Tennessee Williams, 1929
"Before the Feast of Shushan," Anne Spencer, 1920
"The Bells," Edgar Allan Poe, 1849
"Bells for John Whiteside's Daughter," John Crowe Ransom, 1924
The Ben Lilly Legend, James Frank Dobie, 1950

Beth Henley: Monologues for Women, Beth Henley, 1992

"Betsy," Julia Mood Peterkin, 1922

"Between the World and Me," Richard Wright, 1935

Beulah, Augusta Jane Evans Wilson, 1859

Beyond Dark Hills, Jesse Stuart, 1938

Beyond Defeat, Ellen Glasgow, 1966

Big Bend: A Homesteader's Story, Fred Gipson, 1952

Big Woods, William Faulkner, 1955

A Biography of John Randolph of Roanoke: With a Selection of His Speeches, Lemuel Sawyer, 1844

The Birds of America, John James Audubon, 1838

"The Birthmark," Ralph Ellison, 1940

"The Bivouac of the Dead," Theodore O'Hara, 1847

Black April, Julia Mood Peterkin, 1927

Black Boy: A Record of Childhood and Youth, Richard Wright, 1945

"The Black Cat," Edgar Allan Poe, 1843

The Black Christ, and Other Poems, Countee Cullen, 1929

Black Feeling, Black Talk, Nikki Giovanni, 1967

Black Judgement, Nikki Giovanni, 1970

Black Like Me, John Howard Griffin, 1960

The Black Man: His Antecedents, His Genius, and His Achievements, William Wells Brown, 1863

Blackbeard: A Comedy in Four Acts, Lemuel Sawyer, 1824

Blood for a Stranger, Randall Jarrell, 1942

Bloodline, Ernest J. Gaines, 1968

A Blues Book for Blue Black Magical Women, Sonia Sanchez, 1974

Bonaventure, George Washington Cable, 1888

"The Bonny Blue Flag," Harry McCarthy, ca. 1861

The Boo, Pat Conroy, 1970

The Book of American Negro Poetry, James Weldon Johnson, 1922

The Book of American Negro Spirituals, James Weldon Johnson and John Rosamund Johnson, 1925

A Book of Americans, Rosemary Benét and Stephen Vincent Benét, 1933

A Book of Burlesques, H. L. Mencken, 1916

The Book of My Lady, William Gilmore Simms, 1833

A Book of Prefaces, H. L. Mencken, 1917

Border Beagles: A Tale of Mississippi, William Gilmore Simms, 1840

The Boy's King Arthur, Sidney Lanier, 1880

The Boy's Mabinogion, Sidney Lanier, 1881

The Boy's Percy, Sidney Lanier, 1882

A Branch of May, Lizette Woodworth Reese, 1887

The Brass Ankle, Dubose Heyward, 1931

Breakfast at Tiffany's, Truman Capote, 1958

Bright Skin, Julia Mood Peterkin, 1932

Brighten the Corner Where You Are, Fred Chappell, 1989

Bronze: A Book of Verse, Georgia Douglas Johnson, 1922

Brother to Dragons, Robert Penn Warren, 1953

Brown Wolf Leaves the Res, Diane Glancy, 1984

Buckdancer's Choice, James Dicky, 1970

Bury My Heart at Wounded Knee, Dee Brown, 1970

The Busy-Body, Susanna Centlivre, 1736
Bylow Hill, George Washington Cable, 1902

C

Cairo! Shanghai! Bombay!, Tennessee Williams, 1935
Ca'line, Bernice Kelly Harris, 1932
"Call to Rebellion," Henry Highland Garnet, 1865
Camino Real, Tennessee Williams, 1953
The Candidates, Robert Munford, 1798
Candles to the Sun, Tennessee Williams, 1937
Cane, Jean Toomer, 1923
"The Captive," Caroline Gordon, 1945
Carolina Chansons, Dubose Heyward, 1922
The Carolina Israelite, Harry Golden, 1941
Carolina Sports by Land and Water, William Elliot, 1846
Caroling Dusk, Countee Cullen, 1928
Cartoons, Margaret Junkin Preston, 1875
"The Cask of Amontillado," Edgar Allan Poe, 1846
The Cassique of Kiawah, William Gilmore Simms, 1859
Cat on a Hot Tin Roof, Tennessee Williams, 1955
"Cat-Fish," Julia Mood Peterkin, 1922
Catherine Carmier, Ernest J. Gaines, 1964
The Cavalier, George Washington Cable, 1901
The Cave, Robert Penn Warren, 1959
The Cay, Theodore Taylor, 1970
"The Celebrated Jumping Frog of Calaveras County," Mark Twain, 1867
Chapeau, Alfred Uhry, 1977
Charlemont, William Gilmore Simms, 1856
Charleston, and Her Satirists, William Gilmore Simms, 1848
"Charleston in the 1860s: Derived from the Diaries of Mary Boykin Chesnut,"
    Adrienne Rich, 1975
Charms for the Easy Life, Kaye Gibbons, 1993
Cherokee Advocate, Sequoyah, 1827
Cherokee Phoenix, Sequoyah, 1827
Children on Their Birthdays, Truman Capote, 1950
The Children's Hour, Lillian Hellman, 1934
Chills and Fever, John Crowe Ransom, 1921
Chita: A Memory of Last Island, Lafcadio Hearn, 1889
"Christmas in the Confederate White House," Varina Howell Davis, 1896
"A Christmas Memory," Truman Capote, 1956
Christmas-Night in the Quarters, Irwin Russell, 1878
"Christmas Night of '62," William Gordon McCabe, ca. 1865
Christmas to Me, Harper Lee, 1961
Christy, Catherine Marshall, 1967
Circus Valentine, Marsha Norman, 1979
"The City in the Sea," Edgar Allan Poe, 1831
Clock without Hands, Carson McCullers, 1961
Clotelle: A Tale of Southern States, William Wells Brown, 1853
Clover, Dori Sanders, 1990

Cold Mountain, Charles Frazier, 1997

Cold Sassy Tree, Olive Ann Burns, 1984

The Collected Stories of Eudora Welty, Eudora Welty, 1980

Collected Stories of William Faulkner, William Faulkner, 1950

Collected Works, O. Henry, 1913

A Collection of Plays and Poems, Robert Munford, 1798

A Collection of Some of the Most Interesting Narratives of Indian Warfare in the West, Containing an Account of the Adventures of Daniel Boone, One of the First Settlers of Kentucky, Samuel L. Metcalfe, 1820

Colonel Crockett's Exploits and Adventures in Texas, Richard Penn Smith, 1836

The Color Purple, Alice Walker, 1982

Color Struck, Zora Neale Hurston, 1926

Coming of Age in Mississippi, Anne E. Moody, 1968

The Common Glory, Paul Green, 1947

"Compensation," John Banister Tabb, 1882

The Compleat Housewife, William Parks, 1742

The Compleat System of Fencing, William Parks, 1734

A Concise Natural History of East and West Florida, Bernard Romans, 1775

"The Condition of the Freedmen," Frederick Douglass, 1883

Confessions of a Failed Southern Lady, Florence King, 1985

Confessions of Nat Turner, William Styron, 1967

The Conjure Woman, Charles Waddell Chesnutt, 1899

A Connecticut Yankee in King Arthur's Court, Mark Twain, 1889

Control Freaks, Beth Henley, 1992

Conversations with Flannery O'Connor, Flannery O'Connor, 1987

Conversations with Lafayette, George Washington Parke Custis, 1824

"Cooch's Premium," Julia Mood Peterkin, 1922

Copper Sun, Countee Cullen, 1927

Corn, Sidney Lanier, 1875

Coronado's Children, James Frank Dobie, 1930

Cotton Candy on a Rainy Day, Nikki Giovanni, 1978

Cow People, James Frank Dobie, 1964

Cowboy Songs and Other Frontier Ballads, John Lomax, 1910

"Cracker Chidlings," Marjorie Kinnan Rawlings, 1931

"The Creation," James Weldon Johnson, 1927

The Creoles of Louisiana, George Washington Cable, 1884

Crimes of the Heart, Beth Henley, 1981

"The Crisis in Industry," Thomas Wolfe, 1919

Crockett Almanacks, Davy Crockett, 1835–1838

Cross Creek, Marjorie Kinnan Rawlings, 1942

Cross Creek Cookery, Marjorie Kinnan Rawlings, 1942

The Cub of the Panther, William Gilmore Simms, 1869

A Cure for Dreams, Kaye Gibbons, 1991

A Curtain of Green and Other Stories, Eudora Welty, 1941

D

D. Boone, Marsha Norman, 1992

Daddy Jack the Runaway, and Other Stories Told after Dark, Joel Chandler Harris, 1889

Dagon, Fred Chappell, 1968

Daisy Fay and the Miracle Man, Fannie Flagg, 1981
"Dancin' Party at Harrison's Cove," Mary Noailles Murfree, 1878
Daniel Boone: Wilderness Scout, Stewart Edward White, 1922
Daniel Boone and the Hunters of Kentucky, W. H. Bogart, 1857
Dark of the Moon, Howard Dixon Richardson, 1945
Darkness Visible: A Memoir of Madness, William Styron, 1990
"The Daughter of Mendoza," Mirabeau Buonaparte Lamar, 1857
Daughter of the Legend, Jesse Stuart, 1965
Davy Crockett, Frank Hitchcock Murdoch, 1872
"Dead Boy," John Crowe Ransom, 1927
A Death in the Family, James Agee, 1956
"Death of a Traveling Salesman," Eudora Welty, 1936
The Death of Papa, Horton Foote, 1997
"Death of the Ball Turret Gunner," Randall Jarrell, 1955
The Debutante Ball, Beth Henley, 1985
Declaration of Causes and Necessity of Taking of Arms, Thomas Jefferson, 1775
The Declaration of Independence, Thomas Jefferson, 1776
Declaration of the Principles of the National Emigration Convention, Martin Delany, 1864
"A Deer Hunt," William Elliott, 1846
"Defence of Fort M'Henry," Francis Scott Key, 1814
The Delany Sisters' Book of Everyday Wisdom, Sarah Delany and Elizabeth Delany, 1994
Deliverance, Ellen Glasgow, 1904
Deliverance, James Dickey, 1970
Delta Wedding, Eudora Welty, 1946
The Descendant, Ellen Glasgow, 1897
"A Descent into the Maelstrom," Edgar Allan Poe, 1841
"Désirée's Baby," Kate Chopin, 1894
Diary from Dixie, Mary Boykin Chesnut, 1886
Die Nigger Die!, H. Rap Brown, 1969
Diegarias, Victor Séjour, 1844
A Different Kind of Xmas, Alex Haley, 1988
The Disappointment, or The Force of Credulity, Andrew Barton, 1767
"The Displaced Person," Flannery O'Connor, 1954
"Dissertation on Slavery: With a Proposal for the Gradual Abolition of It in the State of Virginia," St. George Tucker, 1796
"Dixie," Albert Pike, ca. 1865
Doctor Martino and Other Stories, William Faulkner, 1934
Does Your House Have Lions?, Sonia Sanchez, 1997
The Dog of the South, Charles Portis, 1979
The Dollmaker, Harriette Arnow, 1954
The Douglass Monthly, Frederick Douglass, 1859
Dr. Sevier, George Washington Cable, 1884
"Dreaming in the Trenches," William Gordon McCabe, ca. 1864
"Drenched in Light," Zora Neale Hurston, 1924
Driving Miss Daisy, Alfred Uhry, 1986
Drunk with Love, Ellen Gilchrist, 1986
The Dunce Boy, Lula Vollmer, 1925
"The Duplicity of Hargraves," O. Henry, 1911
The Durket Sperret, Sarah Barnwell Elliott, 1898
Dust Tracks on a Road, Zora Neale Hurston, 1942

E

The Eagle's Shadow, James Branch Cabell, 1904

"The Eatonville Anthology," Zora Neale Hurston, 1926

Ebb Tide, Joseph Glover Baldwin, 1864

The Edge of the Swamp, William Gilmore Simms, 1853

The Eighth of January, George Washington Parke Custis, 1834

"Eldorado," Edgar Allan Poe, 1849

Ellen Foster, Kaye Gibbons, 1987

The Enchanted Maze, Paul Green, 1935

The English Novel, Sidney Lanier, 1883

Enjoy, Enjoy, Harry Golden, 1971

The Escape, or A Leap for Freedom, William Wells Brown, 1858

"Eureka," Edgar Allan Poe, 1848

Eutaw, William Gilmore Simms, 1856

Even the Stars Look Lonsome, Maya Angelou, 1997

The Everglades: River of Grass, Marjory Stoneman Douglass, 1947

Everything That Rises Must Converge, Flannery O'Connor, 1965

"The Exalted Theme of Human Praise," Penina Moise, 1856

Experience; or, How To Give a Northern Man a Backbone, William Wells Brown, 1856

Extracts from the Virginia Charters, George Mason, 1773

The Eye of the Story: Selected Essays and Reviews, Eudora Welty, 1978

F

A Fable, William Faulkner, 1954

The Fabulous Empire: Colonel Zack Miller's Story, Fred Gipson, 1946

Faith of Our Fathers, Paul Green, 1950

"The Fall of the House of Usher," Edgar Allan Poe, 1840

Fallen Angels, Walter Dean Meyers, 1988

Falling through Space, Ellen Gilchrist, 1987

Farewell, I'm Bound To Leave You, Fred Chappell, 1997

Father Abbot, William Gilmore Simms, 1849

The Fathers, Allen Tate, 1938

Fetterman Massacre, Dee Brown, 1962

The Field God, Paul Green, 1927

"The Field of Blue Children," Tennessee Williams, 1939

Fighting Indians of the West, Dee Brown, 1948

Finding the Green Stone, Alice Walker, 1991

First One, Zora Neale Hurston, 1926

The First White Man of the West, or The Life and Exploits of Col. Dan'l. Boone, the First Settler of Kentucky; Interspersed with Incidents in the Early Annals of the Country, Timothy Flint, 1854

Flame and Shadow, Sara Teasdale, 1920

Fleur de Lys and Calumet: Being the Pénicaut Narrative of French Adventure in Louisiana, Andre Pénicaut, 1704

Flora Virginica, John Clayton, ca. 1750

The Florence King Reader, Florence King, 1995

"Florence Vane," Philip Pendleton Cooke, 1847

Flowering Judas, Katherine Anne Porter, 1930

The Flush Times of Alabama and Mississippi: A Series of Sketches, Joseph Glover Baldwin, 1853

The Flush Times of California, Joseph Glover Baldwin, 1853

"Flying Home," Ralph Ellison, 1944
Flying Home and Other Stories, Ralph Ellison, 1997
The Foe at the Gates," John Dickson Bruns, 1865
Folk Song U.S.A., John Lomax, 1947
Fool's Opera, Anthony Aston, 1702
"For Annie," Edgar Allan Poe, 1849
For Charlie's Sake, and Other Ballads and Lyrics, John Williamson Palmer, 1901
For My People, Margaret Walker, 1942
For Two Cents Plain, Harry Golden, 1959
The Forayers, William Gilmore Simms, 1855
The Forest of the South, Caroline Gordon, 1945
"The Forgotten Man," Walter Hines Page, 1904
The Fortune Teller, Marsha Norman, 1987
The Founders, Paul Green, 1957
The Four Millions, O. Henry, 1906
The Foxfire Book, Eliot Wigginton, 1969
Frederick Douglass' Paper, Frederick Douglass, 1851
Free Joe and Other Georgian Sketches, Joel Chandler Harris, 1887
Fried Green Tomatoes at the Whistle Stop Cafe, Fannie Flagg, 1987
Froissart Ballads, and Other Poems, Philip Pendleton Cooke, 1847
From Death to Morning, Thomas Wolfe, 1935
"From Lang Syne Plantation," Julia Mood Peterkin, 1921
From Sun to Sun, Zora Neale Hurston, 1933
The Fugitive, Tennessee Williams, 1960
The Fugitive Kind, Tennessee Williams, 1936

G

Gabriel Tolliver, Joel Chandler Harris, 1902
"Gal Young 'Un," Marjorie Kinnan Rawlings, 1933
Galvanized Yankees, Dee Brown, 1963
The Garden of Adonis, Caroline Gordon, 1937
The Gardners Kalender, Martha Daniell Logan, 1772
Gather Together in My Name, Maya Angelou, 1974
A Gathering of Old Men, Ernest J. Gaines, 1983
Gemini: An Extended Autobiographical Statement on My First Twenty-Five Years of Being a Black Poet, Nikki Giovanni, 1971
Generall Historie of Virginia, New England and the Summer Isles, Capt. John Smith, 1624
The Gentle Tamers: Women of the Old Wild West, Dee Brown, 1958
George Balcombe, Nathaniel Beverley Tucker, 1836
Georgia, Georgia, Maya Angelou, 1971
Georgia Scenes, Augustus Baldwin Longstreet, 1834
"The Geranium," Flannery O'Connor, 1946
Getting Out, Marsha Norman, 1977
Gideon's Band, George Washington Cable, 1914
"The Gift of the Magi," O. Henry, 1905
The Gilded Age, Mark Twain, 1873
"Gilded Six-Bits," Zora Neale Hurston, 1926
The Glass Menagerie, Tennessee Williams, 1945
Go Ahead Almanack, Davy Crockett, 1838
Go Down, Moses, William Faulkner, 1942

God without Thunder, John Crowe Ransom, 1930
God's Little Acre, Erskine Caldwell, 1933
God's Trombones: Seven Negro Sermons in Verse, James Weldon Johnson, 1927
Going to the Territory, Ralph Ellison, 1986
"The Gold Bug," Edgar Allan Poe, 1843
"Gone Forward," Margaret Junkin Preston, 1875
Gone with the Wind, Margaret Mitchell, 1936
The Good Husband, Gail Godwin, 1994
"A Good Man Is Hard To Find," Flannery O'Connor, 1953
A Good Man Is Hard To Find and Other Stories, Flannery O'Connor, 1955
Good Night Willie Lee, I'll See You in the Morning: Poems, Alice Walker, 1984
The Grandissimes, George Washington Cable, 1880
The Grass Harp (musical), Truman Capote, 1971
The Grass Harp (novel), Truman Capote, 1951
The Grass Harp (play), Truman Capote, 1952
The Great Day, Zora Neale Hurston, 1932
The Great Meadow, Elizabeth Madox Roberts, 1930
The Great Santini, Pat Conroy, 1976
Green Centuries, Caroline Gordon, 1941
Green Thursday, Julia Mood Peterkin, 1924
Guide to Life and Literature of the Southwest, James Frank Dobie, 1943
Guy Rivers, William Gilmore Simms, 1834

H
The Habit of Being, Flannery O'Connor, 1979
The Half Pint Flask, Dubose Heyward, 1929
The Hamlet, William Faulkner, 1957
Hannah Fowler, Janice Holt Giles, 1956
"The 'Harnt' That Walks Chilhowee," Mary Noailles Murfree, 1884
"The Harp of Broken Strings," John Rollin Ridge, 1868
"The Haunted Boy," Carson McCullers, 1971
Having Our Say, Sarah Delany and Elizabeth Delany, 1993
"Haw-Blossoms," James Matthews Legaré, 1848
He: An Irreverent Look at the American Male, Florence King, 1978
"A Health," Edward Coote Pinkney, 1825
Hear That Lonesome Whistle Blow: Railroads in the West, Dee Brown, 1977
The Heart Is a Lonely Hunter, Carson McCullers, 1940
The Heart of a Woman, Maya Angelou, 1981
The Heart of a Woman and Other Poems, Georgia Douglas Johnson, 1918
Hearts of the West, O. Henry, 1907
Heathen Days, 1890–1936, H. L. Mencken, 1943
"The Heaven of Animals," James Dickey, 1962
The Heir of Gaymount, John Esten Cooke, 1870
Helen Halsey: or, The Swamp State of Conelachita, William Gilmore Simms, 1845
Heliogabalus, H. L. Mencken and George Jean Nathan, 1920
Her Blue Body Everything We Know: Earthling Poems, Alice Walker, 1991
Here's Where I Belong, Alfred Uhry, 1968
"Heritage," Countee Cullen, 1925
A Hero Ain't Nothin' but a Sandwich, Alice Childress, 1973
The Heroic Slave, Frederick Douglass, 1853

Hie to the Hunters, Jesse Stuart, 1950
The Highland Call, Paul Green, 1939
The Hills Between, Lula Vollmer, 1938
The Hills Beyond, Thomas Wolfe, 1941
Hints to the Colored People of North America, Mary Ann Shadd Cary, 1849
The Hireling and the Slave, William John Grayson, 1854
"Histoire de la Louisiane," Charles Etienne Arthur Gayarré, 1847
History and Present State of Virginia, Robert Beverley, 1722
History of Louisiana, Charles Etienne Arthur Gayarré, 1866
History of North Carolina, Francis Lister Hawks, 1858
The History of the American Indian, James Adair, 1775
History of the Dividing Line, Colonel William Byrd, 1728
History of the Expedition under the Command of Captains Lewis and Clark, Meriwether
    Lewis and William Clark, 1814
History of the Revolution in South Carolina, David Ramsay, 1785
"History of the Spanish Domination in Louisiana," Charles Etienne Arthur
    Gayarré, 1854
Hold April, Jesse Stuart, 1962
The Holdup, Marsha Norman, 1980
The Homecoming, Earl Hamner, Jr., 1970
Homecoming, Sonia Sanchez, 1969
Homegirls and Handgrenades, Sonia Sanchez, 1984
Horizon, John Augustin Daly, 1871
Horn in the West, Kermit Hunter, 1952
Horse-Shoe Robinson, John Pendleton Kennedy, 1835
Horses Make a Landscape Look More Beautiful, Alice Walker, 1984
Hound-Dog Man, Fred Gipson, 1949
The House behind the Cedars, Charles Waddell Chesnutt, 1900
The House of Connelly, Paul Green, 1931
The House of Fiction, Caroline Gordon, 1950
House of Flowers, Truman Capote, 1954
"How 'Bigger' Was Born," Richard Wright, 1940
How I Wrote Jubilee, Margaret Walker, 1972
"How Sharp Snaffles Got His Capital and Wife," William Gilmore Simms, 1870
How To Read a Novel, Caroline Gordon, 1957
Hurry Sundown, Horton Foote, 1967
Hymns Written for the Use of Hebrew Congregations, Penina Moise, 1856

I

I Am One of You Forever, Fred Chappell, 1985
"I Have a Dream," Martin Luther King, Jr., 1963
I Know Why the Caged Bird Sings, Maya Angelou, 1970
*I Love Myself: When I Am Laughing . . . and Then Again When I Am Looking Mean and
    Impressive: A Zora Neale Hurston Reader*, Zora Neale Hurston, 1979
"I Shall Not Care," Sara Teasdale, 1920
"I Sigh for the Land of the Cypress and Pine," Samuel Henry Dickson, ca. 1850
If I Were Seventeen Again, Jesse Stuart, 1980
"If It Might Be," Kate Chopin, 1889
I'll Take My Stand, Fugitive Agrarian consortium, 1930
The Importance of Pot Liquor, Jackie Torrence, 1994

"In a Strange Country," Ralph Ellison, 1944

In Abraham's Bosom, Paul Green, 1927

"In Aunt Mahaly's Cabin: A Folk Play for the Negro Theatre," Paul Green, 1924

In Cold Blood, Truman Capote, 1965

In Love and Trouble: Stories of Black Women, Alice Walker, 1973

In Ole Virginia, Thomas Nelson Page, 1887

In Search of Our Mother's Gardens: Womanist Prose, Alice Walker, 1983

"In Search of Zora Neale Hurston," Alice Walker, 1974

In the Land of Dreamy Dreams, Ellen Gilchrist, 1981

In the Mountains of Tennessee, Mary Noailles Murfree, 1884

In This Our Life, Ellen Glasgow, 1942

In Trouble at Fifteen, Marsha Norman, 1980

Incidents in the Life of a Slave Girl, Written by Herself, Harriet Ann Brent Jacobs, 1861

Independence: or, Which Do You Like Best, the Peer or the Farmer, William Ioor, 1805

India, Emma Dorothy Eliza Nevitte Southworth, 1853

The Indian Prophecy, George Washington Parke Custis, 1827

Inez: A Tale of the Alamo, Augusta Jane Evans Wilson, 1855

The Inkling, Fred Chappell, 1965

Innocents Abroad, Mark Twain, 1869

An Inquiry into the Principles and Policy of the Government of the United States, John Taylor, 1814

The Interesting Narrative of the Life of Olaudah Equiano, or Gustavus Vassa, the African; by Himself, Gustavus Vassa, 1790

Intruder in the Dust, William Faulkner, 1948

Invisible Man, Ralph Ellison, 1947

Iola Leroy: or, Shadows Uplifted, Frances Ellen Watkins Harper, 1892

Iron Woman, Diane Glancy, 1990

"Israfel," Edgar Allan Poe, 1829

It Is Time, Lord, Fred Chappell, 1963

It's a New Day, Sonia Sanchez, 1971

It's the Willingness, Marsha Norman, 1978

J

"The Jacket of Gray," Caroline Augusta Ball, 1866

Jacob's Ladder, Marjorie Kinnan Rawlings, 1931

James Louis Petigru: A Biographical Sketch, William John Grayson, 1866

"Janet Waking," John Crowe Ransom, 1927

"Jean-ah Pouquelin," George Washington Cable, 1879

Jefferson Davis, Ex-President of the Confederate States of America; a Memoir, Varina Howell Davis, 1890

Jefferson Davis: His Rise and Fall, Allen Tate, 1929

Jericho: The South Beheld, James Dickey, 1974

Jerry, Sarah Barnwell Elliott, 1891

The Jesuit Relations and Allied Documents: Travel and Explorations of the Jesuit Missionaries in New France, 1610–1791, Father Le Petit, 1900

"The Jilting of Granny Weatherall," Katherine Anne Porter, 1930

John Brown's Body, Stephen Vincent Benét, 1929

John Marsh, Southerner, George Washington Cable, 1894

John Redding Goes to Sea," Zora Neale Hurston, 1921

Johnny Johnson, Paul Green, 1928

Jonah's Gourd Vine, Zora Neale Hurston, 1934
Journal of a Mountain Man, James Clyman, 1840
Journal of an American Residence, Fanny Kemble, 1835
The Journal of Hospital Life in the Confederate Army in Tennessee, Kate Cumming, 1866
Jubilee, Margaret Walker, 1966
Judas, My Brother, Frank Yerby, 1968
"Julia," Lillian Hellman, 1973
Just Give Me a Cool Drink of Water 'fore I Diiie, Maya Angelou, 1971
"Just like a Tree," Ernest J. Gaines, 1962

K

Kate Vaiden, Reynolds Price, 1986
Katherine Walton: or, The Rebel's Daughter, William Gilmore Simms, 1851
The Keepers of the House, Shirley Ann Grau, 1964
The Kentuckians, John Fox, Jr., 1897
Kentucky Is My Land, Jesse Stuart, 1952
"A Key to the Disunion Conspiracy," Nathaniel Beverley Tucker, 1862
"Kildee," John Banister Tabb, 1882
Kincaid's Battery, George Washington Cable, 1908
King of the Bingo Game," Ralph Ellison, 1944
The Kingdom Within: A Spiritual Autobiography, Jesse Stuart, 1979
The Kinsmen, William Gilmore Simms, 1841

L

"Lady Bates," Randall Jarrell, 1955
Land beyond the River, Jesse Stuart, 1956
The Land Surveyor's Daughter, Ellen Gilchrist, 1979
The Land Where the Blues Began, Alan Lomax, 1993
Langston Hughes, American Poet, Alice Walker, 1974
"L'Après-Midi du Faune," William Faulkner, 1919
The Last Night of Ballyhoo, Alfred Uhry, 1997
The Last Ninety Days of the War in North Carolina, Cornelia Phillips Spencer, 1866
The Last of the Lowries, Paul Green, 1920
Last Words, H. L. Mencken, 1926
The Laughing Pioneer, Paul Green, 1932
Lawd Today, Richard Wright, 1963
The Leaning Tower and Other Stories, Katherine Anne Porter, 1944
Leaving Cold Sassy, Olive Ann Burns, 1992
"Lee," Dr. Francis Orrery Ticknor, 1879
Lee in the Mountains, Donald Davidson, 1938
Lee in the Mountains and Other Poems, Donald Davidson, 1927
The Lee Memorial Ode, James Barron Hope, 1895
A Lesson before Dying, Ernest J. Gaines, 1993
The Lesson of the Hour: Why Is the Negro Lynched, Frederick Douglass, 1894
Let Me Lie, James Branch Cabell, 1947
"Let Us Go to the Woods," Carolina Howard Gilman, 1838
Let Us Now Praise Famous Men, James Agee, 1941
"Letter from a Birmingham Jail," Martin Luther King, Jr., 1963
"Letters from the Earth," Mark Twain, 1963
Letters of a Woman Homesteader, Elinore Pruitt Stewart, 1914

Letters of Eliza Wilkinson, during the Invasion and Possession of Charlestown, South Carolina, by the British in the Revolutionary War, Arranged from the Original Manuscripts by Caroline Gilman, Eliza Yonge Wilkinson, 1839

Letters of Martha Logan to John Bartram, 1760–1763, Martha Daniell Logan, 1763

Letters on an Elk Hunt, Elinore Pruitt Stewart, 1915

Letters on the Equality of the Sexes and the Condition of Women, Sarah Grimké, 1838

Letters to Catherine Beecher in Reply to an Essay on Slavery and Abolitionism Addressed to A. A. Grimké, Angelina Grimké, 1837

The Liberty Tree, Kermit Hunter, 1970

Lie Down in Darkness, William Styron, 1951

The Life and Adventures of Colonel David Crockett of West Tennessee, Mathew St. Clair Clarke, 1833

Life and Adventures of Joaquin Murieta, the Celebrated California Bandit, John Rollin Ridge, 1854

The Life and Adventures of Nat Love, Better Known in the Cattle Country as Deadwood Dick, Nat Love, 1907

Life and Gabriella: The Story of a Woman's Courage, Ellen Glasgow, 1916

The Life and Spiritual Sufferings of That Faithful Servant of Christ, Jane Hoskens, Jane Fenn Hoskens, 1771

The Life and Time of Col. Daniel Boone, Hunter, Soldier, and Pioneer, Edward Sylvester Ellis, 1884

Life and Times of Frederick Douglass, Frederick Douglass, 1881

Life in Dixie during the War, Mary Ann Harris Gay, ca. 1865

The Life of General Francis Marion, Mason Locke Weems, 1826

The Life of George Washington, John Marshall, 1807

Life of Herod the Great, Zora Neale Hurston, 1948

The Life of Martin Van Buren, Hair-Apparent to the "Government," and the Appointed Successor of General Jackson, Davy Crockett, 1835

A Life of Robert E. Lee, John Esten Cooke, 1871

The Life of Stonewall Jackson: A Military Biography, John Esten Cooke, 1866

The Life of Washington, with Curious Anecdotes, Equally Honourable to Himself and Exemplary to His Young Countrymen, Mason Locke Weems, 1800

Life on the Mississippi, Mark Twain, 1883

Light beyond the Darkness, Frances Ellen Watkins Harper, ca. 1910

Light Can Be Both Wave and Particle, Ellen Gilchrist, 1989

Light in August, William Faulkner, 1932

The Limits of Poetry, Allen Tate, 1949

Linda: or, The Young Pilot of the Belle Creole, Caroline Lee Whiting Hentz, 1850

The Lion of the West, James Kirke Paulding, 1831

Little Arliss, Fred Gipson, 1978

The Little Foxes, Lillian Hellman, 1939

Little Friend, Little Friend, Randall Jarrell, 1945

Little Johnny Jones, Alfred Uhry, 1982

The Little Shepherd of Kingdom Come, John Fox, Jr., 1903

Living by the Word: Selected Writings, 1973–1987, Alice Walker, 1988

Lo, O. Henry and Franklin P. Adams, 1909

Local Color, Truman Capote, 1946

Lone Dog's Winter Count, Diane Glancy, 1991

Lonesome Dove, Larry McMurtry, 1985

A Long and Happy Life, Reynolds Price, 1962

The Long Dream, Richard Wright, 1958
The Long March, William Styron, 1953
Longhorns, James Frank Dobie, 1941
Look Homeward Angel: A Story of the Buried Life, Thomas Wolfe, 1929
Look Out Whitey! Black Power's Gon' Get Your Mama!, Julius Lester, 1968
Losing Battles, Eudora Welty, 1970
Losses, Randall Jarrell, 1948
The Lost Colony, Paul Green, 1937
The Lost Laysen, Margaret Mitchell, 1996
Lost Sandstones and Lonely Skies, Jesse Stuart, 1979
The Lost Trappers, David H. Coyner, 1847
"Louisiana: Its Colonial History and Romance," Charles Etienne Arthur
    Gayarré, 1852
"Louisiana, Its History as a French Colony," Charles Etienne Arthur Gayarré, 1852
Love in the Ruins: The Adventures of a Bad Catholic at a Time Near the End of the World,
    Walker Percy, 1971
Love's Progress, Carolina Howard Gilman, 1840
Low Character of Immigrants to Virginia, Robert Beverley, 1705
L-Play, Beth Henley, 1995
The Lucky Spot, Beth Henley, 1986
Lump It or Leave It, Florence King, 1991

M

Macaria; or Altars of Sacrifice, Augusta Jane Evans Wilson, 1864
Madame Delphine, George Washington Cable, 1881
Mamba's Daughters, Dubose Heyward and Dorothy Hartzell Kuhns Heyward, 1929
"Man of the World," Penina Moise, 1856
"The Man Who Corrupted Hadleyburg," Mark Twain, 1898
The Man Who Cried I Am, John Williams, 1967
Man with a Bull-Tongue Plow, Jesse Stuart, 1934
The Mansion, William Faulkner, 1959
A Map of Virginia with a Description of the Country, the Commodities, People, Government,
    and Religion, Capt. John Smith, 1612
The Marble Faun, William Faulkner, 1924
Marcus Warland, Caroline Lee Whiting Hentz, 1852
The Marjorie Kinnan Rawlings Reader, Marjorie Kinnan Rawlings, 1956
"The Marshes of Glynn," Sidney Lanier, 1878
Martin Faber, the Story of a Criminal, William Gilmore Simms, 1833
Martyr of Alabama and Other Poems, Frances Ellen Watkins Harper, 1895
Mary Chesnut's Civil War, Mary Boykin Chesnut, 1981
"The Masque of the Red Death," Edgar Allan Poe, 1842
"A Matter of Principle," Charles Waddell Chesnutt, 1899
"May Day Sermon to the Women of Gilmer County, Georgia, by a Woman Preacher
    Leaving the Baptist Church," James Dickey, 1967
Mellichampe, William Gilmore Simms, 1837
The Member of the Wedding, Carson McCullers, 1946 (novel); 1950 (play)
Memoir, Tennessee Williams, 1975
Memoirs of the War in the Southern Department of the United States, Henry Lee, 1812
Memorials of a Southern Planter, Susan Dabney Smedes, 1887
The Memory of Old Jack, Wendell Berry, 1974

Meridian, Alice Walker, 1976

"The Merry-Go-Round," Julia Mood Peterkin, 1921

Message from the President, February 19, 1806, Meriwether Lewis and William Clark, 1806

"Metzengerstein," Edgar Allan Poe, 1832

Michael Bonham, or the Fall of Bexar, William Gilmore Simms, 1844

The Mildred Books, Martha Farquharson Finley, 1878–1894

The Milk Train Doesn't Stop Here Anymore, Tennessee Williams, 1963

The Miller of Old Church, Ellen Glasgow, 1911

The Mind of the South, W. J. Cash, 1941

Mingo and Other Sketches in Black and White, Joel Chandler Harris, 1884

"The Miracle of Lava Cañon," O. Henry, 1898

Miriam, Truman Capote, 1982

The Miss Firecracker Contest, Beth Henley, 1980

Missing May, Cynthia Rylant, 1992

Mob Rule in New Orleans, Ida Bell Wells-Barnett, 1900

"The Mocking Bird," Alexander Beaufort Meek, 1857

Modern Honor, John Blake White, 1812

Modern Poetry and the Tradition, Cleanth Brooks, 1939

Moise and the World of Reason, Tennessee Williams, 1975

Molly Ivins Can't Say Those Things, Can She?, Molly Ivins, 1991

Mongrel Mettle, Jesse Stuart, 1944

Monody, on the Death of General Charles Cotesworth Pinckney, William Gilmore Simms, 1825

Moonshine and Honeysuckle, Lula Vollmer, 1938

Morgan's Daughters, Beth Henley, 1979

The Mortgaged Heart, Carson McCullers, 1971

Moses: A Story of the Nile, Frances Ellen Watkins Harper, 1869

Moses, Man of the Mountain, Zora Neale Hurston, 1939

Mosquitoes, William Faulkner, 1927

A Mother and Two Daughters, Gail Godwin, 1982

"A Mother in Manville," Marjorie Kinnan Rawlings, 1936

The Mountain Muse: Comprising the Adventures of Daniel Boone; and the Power of Virtuous and Refined Beauty, Daniel Bryan, 1813

"The Mountaineer," Philip Pendleton Cooke, 1847

"Mr. Absalom Billingslea and Other Georgia Folk," Richard Malcolm Johnston, 1888

Mr. Gallion's School, Jesse Stuart, 1967

"Mr. Muhammad Speaks," Alex Haley, 1960

Mr. Rabbit at Home, Joel Chandler Harris, 1895

"Mr. Toussan," Ralph Ellison, 1941

"Ms. Found in a Bottle," Edgar Allan Poe, 1833

Mule Bone, Zora Neale Hurston and Langston Hughes, 1930

Mule Bone: A Comedy of Negro Life, Zora Neale Hurston, 1990

Mules and Men, Zora Neale Hurston, 1935

"A Municipal Report," O. Henry, 1910

"The Murders in the Rue Morgue," Edgar Allan Poe, 1841

The Muses Are Heard, Truman Capote, 1956

Music and Poetry, Sidney Lanier, 1898

"Music in Camp," John Reuben Thompson, 1867

The Mustang, James Frank Dobie, 1934

"Muttsy," Zora Neale Hurston, 1926

My Ántonia, Willa Cather, 1913
My Bondage and My Freedom, Frederick Douglass, 1855
My Brother Bill, John Faulkner, 1963
My Cave Life in Vicksburg, with Letters of Trial and Travel, Mary Ann Loughborough, 1864
My Larger Education, Booker T. Washington, 1911
"My Life Is like the Summer Rose," Richard Henry Wilde, 1847
"My Maryland," James Ryder Randall, 1861
"My Secret," John Banister Tabb, 1882
"My Side of the Matter," Truman Capote, 1941
My Southern Home; or, The South and Its People, William Wells Brown, 1880
"My Three Years as a Shawnee Captive," Margaret Hanley Haulee, 1849
"My Wife and Child," Henry Rootes Jackson, 1850
The Mysterious Stranger, Mark Twain, 1916
Mystery and Manners, Flannery O'Connor, 1969
"The Mystery of Marie Rogêt," Edgar Allan Poe, 1842

N
Narrative of Arthur Gordon Pym, Edgar Allan Poe, 1838
Narrative of the Life of David Crockett of the State of Tennessee, Thomas Chilton, 1834
Narrative of the Life of Frederick Douglass, an American Slave, Frederick Douglass, 1845
The Narrative of William Wells Brown; a Fugitive Slave, William Wells Brown, 1851
Native Son, Richard Wright, 1940
The Natural History of Carolina, Florida, and the Bahama Islands, Mark Catesby, 1731
"Necrological," John Crowe Ransom, 1924
Negro Folk Songs as Sung by Lead Belly, John Lomax, 1936
The Negro in the American Rebellion: His Heroism and His Fidelity, William Wells Brown, 1867
Negro Myths from the Georgia Coast Told in the Vernacular, Charles Colcock Jones, 1888
"The Negro National Anthem," James Weldon Johnson and John Rosamund Johnson, 1900
The Negro Question, George Washington Cable, 1890
The New Criticism, John Crowe Ransom, 1941
A New Dictionary of Quotations, on Historical Principles, H. L. Mencken, 1942
New Orleans Legacy, Alexandra Ripley, 1987
"The New South," Henry Grady, 1886
New Voyage to Carolina, John Lawson, 1709
Nigger, Dick Gregory, 1964
A Night in Acadie, Kate Chopin, 1897
'night, Mother, Marsha Norman, 1982
Night of the Iguana, Tennessee Williams, 1961
Night Rider, Robert Penn Warren, 1939
Nights with Uncle Remus, Joel Chandler Harris, 1883
No More Lies: The Myth and Reality of American History, Dick Gregory, 1976
Nobody's Fool, Beth Henley, 1986
None Shall Look Back, Caroline Gordon, 1937
Norman Maurice, or The Man of the People, William Gilmore Simms, 1851
North Point or Baltimore Defended, George Washington Parke Custis, 1833
Norwood, Charles Portis, 1966
The Notebook of Trigorin, Tennessee Williams, 1996
Now Sheba Sings the Song, Maya Angelou, 1987
Nurse and Spy in the Union Army, Sarah Emma Evelyn Edmonds, 1865

O

O Pioneers!, Willa Cather, 1918
"The Oblong Box," Edgar Allan Poe, 1846
October Journey, Margaret Walker, 1973
"Ode to the Confederate Dead," Allen Tate, 1922
"An Odor of Verbena," William Faulkner, 1938
Of Love and Dust, Ernest J. Gaines, 1967
Of Time and the River: A Legend of Man's Hunger in His Youth, Thomas Wolfe, 1935
Offering, Diane Glancy, 1988
Oh Pray My Wings Are Gonna Fit Me Well, Maya Angelou, 1975
Old Ben, Jesse Stuart, 1970
Old Creole Days, George Washington Cable, 1879
An Old Fashioned Boy, Martha Farquharson Finley, 1870
"Old Mark Langston," Richard Malcolm Johnston, 1884
"Old Mortality," Katherine Anne Porter, 1930
The Old Order: Stories of the South, Katherine Anne Porter, 1944
"The Old Pioneer," Theodore O'Hara, 1845
The Old South, Essays Social and Political, Thomas Nelson Page, 1892
"An Old Virginia Preacher," William Wirt, ca. 1770
Old Yeller, Fred Gipson, 1956
Oldest Living Confederate Widow Tells All, Allan Gurganus, 1984
On Migration, Mark Catesby, 1747
On the Plantation, Joel Chandler Harris, 1892
"On the Pulse of the Morning," Maya Angelou, 1993
On the Wing of Occasions, Joel Chandler Harris, 1900
Once: Poems, Alice Walker, 1968
One Age in a Dream, Diane Glancy, 1986
One Writer's Beginnings, Eudora Welty, 1984
Only in America, Harry Golden, 1958
"The Only Reason You Want To Go to Heaven," Alice Walker, 1997
Only the Heart, Horton Foote, 1944
The Optimist's Daughter, Eudora Welty, 1972
Options, O. Henry, 1909
Original Journals of the Lewis and Clark Expedition, Meriwether Lewis and William Clark, 1905
Orta-Undis, and Other Poems, James Matthews Legaré, 1848
"The Ortymobile," Julia Mood Peterkin, 1922
Other Voices, Other Rooms, Truman Capote, 1948
Our Fred: or, Seminary Life at Thurston, Martha Farquharson Finley, 1874
Our Singing Country, John Lomax, 1941
Our Southern Landsman, Harry Golden, 1974
An Outland Piper, Donald Davidson, 1924
The Outsider, Richard Wright, 1943

P

Paddy McGann, William Gilmore Simms, 1863
Pale Horse, Pale Rider, Katherine Anne Porter, 1939
The Partisan, William Gilmore Simms, 1835
Party Leaders, Joseph Glover Baldwin, 1855
The Patriots, Robert Munford, 1798

The Pawnee Chief, George Washington Parke Custis, ca. 1830
Penhally, Caroline Gordon, 1931
Pentimento: A Book of Portraits, Lillian Hellman, 1973
Period of Adjustment, Tennessee Williams, 1960
Permit Me Voyage, James Agee, 1934
Philip II of Spain, Charles Etienne Arthur Gayarré, 1866
"The Philosophy of Composition," Edgar Allan Poe, 1846
"Piazza Piece," John Crowe Ransom, 1924
"The Pit and the Pendulum," Edgar Allan Poe, 1842
A Place To Come To, Robert Penn Warren, 1977
Plantation Life in the Florida Parishes of Louisiana, 1836–1846, Bennet H. Barrow, 1943
The Planter's Northern Bride, Caroline Lee Whiting Hentz, 1851
"The Plat-Eye," Julia Mood Peterkin, 1922
Playboy Interview: Malcolm X," Alex Haley, 1963
A Plea for Emigration, or Notes on Canada West, in Its Moral, Social and Political Aspect, Mary Ann Shadd Cary, 1852
A Plea for Union," Alexander Hamilton Stephens, 1860
Pocahontas, or The Settlers of Virginia, George Washington Parke Custis, 1836
Poems, Frances Ellen Watkins Harper, 1900
Poems, John Rollin Ridge, 1868
Poems about God, John Crowe Ransom, 1919
Poems by E. A. Poe: A Second Edition, Edgar Allan Poe, 1831
Poems on Miscellaneous Subjects, Frances Ellen Watkins Harper, 1854
A Poetic Equation: Conversations between Nikki Giovanni and Margaret Walker, Margaret Walker, 1974
The Poetic Principle, Edgar Allan Poe, 1850
The Poetry of Traveling in the United States, Carolina Howard Gilman, 1838
The Ponder Heart, Eudora Welty, 1954
Porgy (novel), Dubose Heyward, 1925
Porgy (play), Dubose Heyward and Dorothy Hartzell Kuhns Heyward, 1927
Porgy and Bess (musical), Dubose Heyward, George Gershwin, and Ira Gershwin, 1935
"A Portrait of Bascom Hawke," Thomas Wolfe, 1932
"Portrait: Old South," Katherine Anne Porter, 1940
Possessing the Secret of Joy, Alice Walker, 1992
"Posson Jone' and Père Raphael," George Washington Cable, 1909
"Possum or Pig," Zora Neale Hurston, 1926
"The Power of Prayer: or, The First Steamboat Up the Alabama," Sidney Lanier, 1875
Praying for Sheetrock, Melissa Faye Greene, 1991
Prejudices, Second Series, H. L. Mencken, 1920
"The Premature Burial," Edgar Allan Poe, 1844
The Presence of Grace and Other Book Reviews, Flannery O'Connor, 1983
The Prince and the Pauper, Mark Twain, 1882
The Prince of Tides, Pat Conroy, 1986
Printz Hall: A Record of New Sweden, Lemuel Sawyer, 1839
"The Private History of a Campaign That Failed," Mark Twain, 1885
"Program of the March on Washington," Philip Randolph, 1942
Prophets for a New Day, Margaret Walker, 1970
Pudd'nhead Wilson, Mark Twain, 1894
Puella, James Dickey, 1982
"Pure and Impure Poetry," Robert Penn Warren, 1942
"The Purloined Letter," Edgar Allan Poe, 1844

Q

Quare Medicine, Paul Green, 1925
Queen, Alex Haley, 1993

R

"The Race Problem in America," Frederick Douglass, 1894
Racism 101, Nikki Giovanni, 1994
The Railroad, George Washington Parke Custis, 1830
Rambling Rose, Calder Willingham, 1972
Raney, Clyde Edgerton, 1985
"The Ransom of Red Chief," O. Henry, 1910
"The Raven," Edgar Allan Poe, 1846
Reactionary Essays on Poetry and Ideas, Allen Tate, 1936
Reason in Madness, Allen Tate, 1941
The Reason Why the Colored American Is Not in the Columbian Exposition, Ida Bell Wells-Barnett, 1893
"The Rebuilding of Old Commonwealths," Walter Hines Page, 1904
"Recent Negro Fiction," Ralph Ellison, 1941
Recollections and Private Memoirs of Washington, by his Adopted Son, George Washington Parke Custis, 1859
Recollections of a Southern Matron, Caroline Howard Gilman, 1837
Recollections of Mississippi and Mississippians, Reuben Davis, 1889
Re-Creation, Nikki Giovanni, 1971
The Red Devil Battery Sign, Tennessee Williams, 1975
Red Mule, Jesse Stuart, 1955
"Red Old Hills of Georgia," Henry Rootes Jackson, 1850
A Red Record: Tabulated Statistics and Alleged Causes of Lynching in the United States, 1892–1893–1894, Ida Bell Wells-Barnett, 1895
Reflections in a Golden Eye, Carson McCullers, 1941
Reflections in a Jaundiced Eye, Florence King, 1989
The Reivers, William Faulkner, 1962
The Relation of the Alabama-Georgia Dialect to the Provincial Dialects of Great Britain, Cleanth Brooks, 1935
Remember Me to Tom, Edwina Dakin Williams, 1963
Reminiscences of Colonial Life in Texas, Dilue Rose Harris, 1904
Requiem for a Nun, William Faulkner, 1950
Residence on a Georgian Plantation, 1838–1839, Fanny Kemble, 1863
"Resignation," St. George Tucker, ca. 1795
"A Retrieved Reformation," O. Henry, 1903
Retrospect of Western Travel, Harriet Martineau, 1838
Return of Buck Gavin, Thomas Wolfe, 1919
Revolutionary Petunias and Other Poems, Alice Walker, 1973
Rhoda: A Life in Stories, Ellen Gilchrist, 1995
Richard Hurdis: or, The Avenger of Blood, a Tale of Alabama, William Gilmore Simms, 1838
Richard Wright, Daemonic Genius: A Portrait of the Man, a Critical Look at His Work, Margaret Walker, 1985
"Richard Wright's Blues," Ralph Ellison, 1945
The Rise and Fall of the Confederate Government, Jefferson Davis, 1881
The Rising Son; or The Antecedents and Advancement of the Colored Race, William Wells Brown, 1874

Rivers to the Sea, Sara Teasdale, 1915
The Robber Bridegroom (novel), Eudora Welty, 1942
The Robber Bridegroom (play), Alfred Uhry, 1975
Rodolph, and Other Poems, Edward Coote Pinkney, 1825
Roll of Thunder, Hear My Cry, Mildred Taylor, 1976
Roll, Sweet Chariot, Paul Green, 1934
The Roman Spring of Mrs. Stone, Tennessee Williams, 1950
The Romance of a Plain Man, Ellen Glasgow, 1909
The Romance of Rockville, Joel Chandler Harris, 1878
"Romance of the History of Louisiana," Charles Etienne Arthur Gayarré, 1848
The Romantic Comedian, Ellen Glasgow, 1926
Roots: The Next Generation, Alex Haley, 1979
Roots: The Saga of an American Family, Alex Haley, 1976
Rose Bud, Carolina Howard Gilman, 1832
A Rose for Emily, William Faulkner, 1931
"The Rose of Dixie," O. Henry, 1909
"Rose of Lebanon," William Faulkner, 1931
The Rose Tattoo, Tennessee Williams, 1950
Roughing It, Mark Twain, 1872

S

Sacred Cows and Other Edibles, Nikki Giovanni, 1988
The Same River Twice, Alice Walker, 1996
The Sanctified Church: The Folklore Writings of Zora Neale Hurston, Zora Neale
    Hurston, 1981
"Sanctuary," Donald Davidson, 1927
Sanctuary, William Faulkner, 1931
Sarah and Abraham, Marsha Norman, 1988
Sartoris, William Faulkner, 1929
Savage Holiday, Richard Wright, 1954
Scarlet Sister Mary, Julia Mood Peterkin, 1928
Scarlett, Alexandra Ripley, 1934
"The School That Built a Town," Walter Hines Page, 1904
The Science of English Verse, Sidney Lanier, 1880
Scoundrel Time, Lillian Hellman, 1976
The Scuffletown Outlaws: A Tragedy of the Lowrie Gang, William Norment Cox, 1924
The Searching Wind, Lillian Hellman, 1944
The Second Book of Negro Spirituals, James Weldon Johnson and John Rosamund
    Johnson, 1926
The Second Coming, Walker Percy, 1980
The Secret Diary, Col. William Byrd, 1712
The Secret Garden (play), Marsha Norman, 1991
The Secret River, Marjorie Kinnan Rawlings, 1956
Selected Poems, John Crowe Ransom, 1945
Selected Poems, Randall Jarrell, 1955
"Self-Reliance on the Frontier," John Urmstone, 1711
Seraph on the Suwanee, Zora Neale Hurston, 1948
"A Serenade," Edward Coote Pinkney, 1825
Set This House on Fire, William Styron, 1960
The Settlers West, Dee Brown, 1955

Seven Tales of Uncle Remus, Joel Chandler Harris, 1948
Shadow and Act, Ralph Ellison, 1964
Shakespeare and His Forerunners, Sidney Lanier, 1902
The Shame Woman, Lula Vollmer, 1923
Share My World, Georgia Douglas Johnson, 1962
The Sheltered Life, Ellen Glasgow, 1932
Shroud My Body Down, Paul Green, 1934
Signature, Beth Henley, 1990
The Silent South, George Washington Cable, 1885
Singin' and Swingin' and Gettin' Merry like Christmas, Maya Angelou, 1976
Singing Steel, Zora Neale Hurston, 1934
Sister Jane, Her Friends and Acquaintances, Joel Chandler Harris, 1896
Sister, Sister, Maya Angelou, 1979
Sixes and Sevens, O. Henry, 1911
Sketches and Eccentricities of Col. David Crockett, Mathew St. Clair Clarke, 1833
Sketches of Country Life, Francis Bartow Lloyd, 1898
Sketches of History, Life and Manners in the United States, Anne Newport Royall, 1826
Sketches of Southern Life, Frances Ellen Watkins Harper, 1872
Small Craft Warnings, Tennessee Williams, 1972
Smart Set: A Magazine of Cleverness, H. L. Mencken and George Jean Nathan, 1914
"The Snow-Bird," John Banister Tabb, 1882
So Red the Rose, Stark Young, 1934
Society in America, Harriet Martineau, 1837
"The Soldier Boy," Margaret Junkin Preston, ca. 1865
Soldier's Pay, William Faulkner, 1926
Some Adventures of Captain Simon Suggs, Late of the Tallapoosa Volunteers, Johnson Jones Hooper, 1846
Some Part of Myself, James Frank Dobie, 1967
"Somebody's Darling," Mary Ravenel de La Coste, ca. 1864
Something Cloudy, Something Clear, Tennessee Williams, 1981
"Song of the Chattahoochee," Sidney Lanier, 1877
Songs of the Cattle Trail and Cow Camp, John Lomax, 1917
Sophie's Choice, William Styron, 1979
The Sot-Weed Factor, Ebenezer Cook, 1708
Soul on Ice, Eldridge Cleaver, 1968
The Sound and the Fury, William Faulkner, 1929
South Moon Under, Marjorie Kinnan Rawlings, 1933
A Southern Family, Gail Godwin, 1987
Southern Horrors: Lynch Law in All Its Phases, Ida Bell Wells-Barnett, 1892
Southern Ladies and Gentlemen, Florence King, 1975
Southern Road, Sterling Brown, 1932
Southern Treasury of Art and Literature, Stark Young, 1937
A Southern Treasury of Life and Literature, Cleanth Brooks, 1937
Souvenirs of Travel, Celeste Le Vert, 1857
The Sparrow's Fall and Other Poems, Frances Ellen Watkins Harper, 1894
Spear, Zora Neale Hurston, 1926
"Spectral Lovers," John Crowe Ransom, 1924
"Speech to the 1996 Democratic National Convention," Reverend Jesse Jackson, 1996
Spencer's Mountain, Earl Hamner, Jr., 1961
Spin a Soft Black Song, Nikki Giovanni, 1971

The Spirit of the Mountains, Emma Belle Miles, 1905
"Split Cherry Tree," Jesse Stuart, 1939
"Spunk," Zora Neale Hurston, 1925
Spunk: The Selected Short Stories of Zora Neale Hurston, Zora Neale Hurston, 1985
The Square Root of Wonderful, Carson McCullers, 1958
St. Elmo, Augusta Jane Evans Wilson, 1866
St. Twel'mo, or, The Cuneiform Cyclopedist of Chattanooga, C. H. Webb, 1867
"Stack Arms," Joseph Blyth Allston, 1865
"The Star-Spangled Banner," Francis Scott Key, 1814
Star-Spangled Virgin, Dubose Heyward, 1939
Steel Magnolias, Robert Harling, 1987
Still Rebels, Still Yankees, Donald Davidson, 1957
"Stonewall Jackson," Henry Lynden Flash, 1865
Stonewall Jackson: The Good Soldier, Allen Tate, 1928
"Stonewall Jackson's Way," John Williamson Palmer, 1901
The Story of a Novel, Thomas Wolfe, 1936
The Story of Aaron, Joel Chandler Harris, 1895
Strange True Stories of Louisiana, George Washington Cable, 1889
A Streetcar Named Desire, Tennessee Williams, 1947
The Streets of Laredo, Larry McMurtry, 1993
Strictly Business, O. Henry, 1910
Strong Hearts, George Washington Cable, 1899
"Sucker," Carson McCullers, 1971
Suddenly Last Summer, Tennessee Williams, 1958
A Summary View of the Rights of British America, Thomas Jefferson, 1774
Summer and Smoke, Tennessee Williams, 1948
Summer of My German Soldier, Bette Greene, 1973
The Sun Comes Up, Marjorie Kinnan Rawlings, 1949
Sun-Up, Lula Vollmer, 1923
"Sunrise," Sidney Lanier, 1880
Surry of Eagle's Nest, John Esten Cooke, 1866
Sut Lovingood: Yarns Spun by a "Nat'ral Born Durn'd Fool," George Washington
    Harris, 1867
Sut Lovingood's Travels with Old Abe Linkhorn, George Washington Harris, 1868
Swallow Barn, or A Sojourn in the Old Dominion, John Pendleton Kennedy, 1832
"The Swamp Fox," William Gilmore Simms, 1832
"Sweat," Zora Neale Hurston, 1926
Sweet as a Pickle and Clean as a Pig: Poems, Carson McCullers, 1964
Sweet Bird of Youth, Tennessee Williams, 1959
Swing, Alfred Uhry, 1980
The Sword and the Distaff, William Gilmore Simms, 1852
"Sword of Robert Lee," Abram Joseph Ryan, 1880
"The Symphony," Sidney Lanier, 1875
Synopsis of the Birds of America, John James Audubon, 1838
"The System of Dr. Tarr and Prof. Fether," Edgar Allan Poe, 1845

T
Tales of Alabama, Johnson Jones Hooper, 1851
Tales of Home Folks in Peace and War, Joel Chandler Harris, 1896
Tales of Old-Time Texas, James Frank Dobie, 1955

Tales of the Grotesque and Arabesque, Edgar Allan Poe, 1840

Tales of the Town, O. Henry, 1939

The Tall Men, Donald Davidson, 1927

Tallulah, and Other Poems, Henry Rootes Jackson, 1850

Tamerlane and Other Poems, Edgar Allan Poe, 1827

Taps for Private Tussie, Jesse Stuart, 1943

Tell My Horse, Zora Neale Hurston, 1938

"The Tell-Tale Heart," Edgar Allan Poe, 1843

The Temple of My Familiar, Alice Walker, 1989

"The Ten Commandments of Charm," Zora Neale Hurston, 1993

Tender Mercies, Horton Foote, 1983

The Tennessee, Donald Davidson, 1948

Tent Meeting, Larry Larson, Levi Lee, and Rebecca Wackler, 1987

The Testament of Freedom, Thomas Jefferson, 1943

The Thanatos Syndrome, Walker Percy, 1987

The Thanksgiving Visitor, Truman Capote, 1968

"That Evening Sun," William Faulkner, 1931

"That I Had the Wings," Ralph Ellison, 1944

Their Eyes Were Watching God, Zora Neale Hurston, 1937

"There Will Come Soft Rains," Sara Teasdale, 1920

These 13, William Faulkner, 1931

"They Came To Stay," Maya Angelou, 1989

They Stooped to Folly, Ellen Glasgow, 1929

Third and Oak: The Laundromat and the Pool Hall, Marsha Norman, 1978

The Third Life of Grange Copeland, Alice Walker, 1970

Thirty-One Years on the Plains and in the Mountains or, The Last Voice from the Plains,
    Captain William F. Drannan, 1900

This Is My Century: New and Collected Poems, Margaret Walker, 1989

Those Who Ride the Night Winds, Nikki Giovanni, 1982

The Thread That Runs So True, Jesse Stuart, 1949

Three Years in Europe; or, Places I Have Seen and People I Have Met, William Wells
    Brown, 1852

"A Tidewater Morning," William Styron, 1993

Tiger Lilies, Sidney Lanier, 1867

Timothy of the Cay, Theodore Taylor, 1993

"To a Lily," James Matthews Legaré, 1848

To Be a Slave, Julius Lester, 1968

"To Helen," Edgar Allan Poe, 1831

"To Hell with Dying," Alice Walker, 1968

To Kill a Mockingbird, Harper Lee, 1960

To Kill a Mockingbird (screenplay), Horton Foote, 1962

To Teach, To Love, Jesse Stuart, 1970

"To the Mocking Bird," Richard Henry Wilde, 1847

Tobacco Road, Erskine Caldwell, 1932

Told by Uncle Remus, Joel Chandler Harris, 1905

Tom Sawyer Abroad, Mark Twain, 1894

Tomorrow, Horton Foote, 1960

*A Tour through the Southern and Western Territories of the United States of North-America;
    the Spanish Dominions on the River Mississippi, and the Florida; the Countries of the
    Creek Nations; and Many Uninhabited Parts*, Viscomte de Chateaubriand, 1792

The Town, William Faulkner, 1957
Trail Driving Days, Dee Brown, 1952
The Trail-Driving Rooster, Fred Gipson, 1955
The Trail of Tears: The Rise and Fall of the Cherokee Nation, John Ehle, 1988
The Trail of the Lonesome Pine, John Fox, Jr., 1908
A Tramp Abroad, Mark Twain, 1880
Traveler in the Dark, Marsha Norman, 1984
Traveling On, Diane Glancy, 1982
Travels through North and South Carolina, Georgia, East and West Florida, William Bartram, 1792
Tread the Green Grass, Paul Green, 1932
"A Tree, a Rock, a Cloud," Carson McCullers, 1942
Trees of Heaven, Jesse Stuart, 1940
Trigger, Lula Vollmer, 1927
The Trip to Bountiful, Horton Foote, 1953
Trouble in Mind, Alice Childress, 1955
True Grit, Charles Portis, 1968
"The True Import of Present Dialogue: Black vs. Negro," Nikki Giovanni, 1968
A True Narrative of the Sufferings of Mary Kinnan, Who Was Taken Prisoner by the Shawanee Nation of Indians, Mary Kinnan, 1795
True Stories, Beth Henley, 1986
"The Turtles," Ernest J. Gaines, 1956
Twiddletwit: A Fairy Tale, Martha Farquharson Finley, 1898
Two Gentlemen in Bonds, John Crowe Ransom, 1926

U

"Ulalume," Edgar Allan Poe, 1847
Uncle Remus: His Songs and His Sayings, Joel Chandler Harris, 1880
Uncle Remus and the Little Boy, Joel Chandler Harris, 1910
Uncle Remus Returns, Joel Chandler Harris, 1918
Uncle Remus's Magazine, Joel Chandler Harris and Julian Harris, 1907
Uncle Tom's Children: Five Long Stories, Richard Wright, 1938
Under a Soprano Sky, Sonia Sanchez, 1987
"Under the Bridge," Zora Neale Hurston, 1993
Under the Gaslight, John Augustin Daly, 1867
Understanding Drama, Cleanth Brooks and Robert Penn Warren, 1945
Understanding Fiction, Cleanth Brooks and Robert Penn Warren, 1943
Understanding Poetry, Cleanth Brooks and Robert Penn Warren, 1938
An Unfinished Woman, Lillian Hellman, 1969
The Unvanquished, William Faulkner, 1938
Up from Slavery, Booker T. Washington, 1901

V

Vaquero of the Brush Country, James Frank Dobie, 1930
Vein of Iron, Ellen Glasgow, 1935
"The Vengeance of Nitrocris," Tennessee Williams, 1928
Ventures into Verse, H. L. Mencken, 1903
Verse Memorials, Mirabeau Buonaparte Lamar, 1857
Verses of a Lifetime, Carolina Howard Gilman, 1849

"The Vertical Negro Plan," Harry Golden, 1944

A Victorian Village, Lizette Woodworth Reese, 1929

The Victor's Description of the Battle of San Jacinto, Sam Houston, 1836

Victory over Japan, Ellen Gilchrist, 1983

The Violent Bear It Away, Flannery O'Connor, 1960

Virginia, Ellen Glasgow, 1913

"Virginia," Dr. Francis Orrery Ticknor, 1879

The Virginia Comedians, or Old Days in the Old Dominion, John Esten Cooke, 1859

"The Virginians of the Valley," Dr. Francis Orrery Ticknor, 1879

A Virtuous Woman, Kaye Gibbons, 1989

The Viviparous Quadrupeds of North America, John James Audubon, 1845

The Voice at the Back Door, Elizabeth Spencer, 1956

The Voice of the People, Ellen Glasgow, 1900

"The Voodoo of Hell's Half-Acre," Richard Wright, 1923

"The Voyager's Song," Edward Coote Pinkney, 1825

W

The Wake of Jamey Foster, Beth Henley, 1982

Walking across Egypt, Clyde Edgerton, 1987

Warrior Marks, Alice Walker, 1990

The Wartime Journal of a Georgia Girl, Georgia Eliza Frances Andrews, 1908

Wash Carver's Mouse Trap, Fred Koch, Jr., 1935

WASP, Where Is Thy Sting, Florence King, 1976

Watch on the Rhine, Lillian Hellman, 1941

The Water Is Wide, Pat Conroy, 1972

Wave High the Banner, Dee Brown, 1942

"The Way It Is," Ralph Ellison, 1942

We a BadddDDD People, Sonia Sanchez, 1977

The Web and the Rock, Thomas Wolfe, 1939

The Well Wrought Urn, Cleanth Brooks, 1947

When a Whippoorwill, Marjorie Kinnan Rawlings, 1930

When Sisterhood Was in Flower, Florence King, 1982

When the Century Was Young, Dee Brown, 1993

"Where Is the Voice Coming From?," Eudora Welty, 1963

Where Trouble Sleeps, Clyde Edgerton, 1997

"Whistling Dick's Christmas Stocking," O. Henry, 1899

The White Rose of Memphis, Col. William Clark Falkner, 1880

Who Owns America?, Fugitive Agrarian consortium, 1936

"Who Then Will Speak for the Common Good?," Barbara Jordan, 1976

Why I Wrote Jubilee and Other Essays on Life and Literature, Margaret Walker, 1990

The Wide Net, and Other Stories, Eudora Welty, 1943

The Widow Claire, Horton Foote, 1987

"Widow Guthrie," Richard Malcolm Johnston, 1890

Widow of the Rock and Other Poems by a Lady, Margaret Agnew Blennerhassett, 1788

The Widow Rugby's Husband, A Night at the Uly Man's, and Other Tales of Alabama, Johnson Jones Hooper, 1851

The Wife of His Youth and Other Stories of the Color Line, Charles Waddell Chesnutt, 1899

The Wigwam and Cabin: Life in America, William Gilmore Simms, 1848

The Wild Palms, William Faulkner, 1939

Wild Western Scenes; A Narrative of Adventures in the Western Wilderness, Forty Years Ago; Wherein the Conduct of Daniel Boone, the Great American Pioneer, Is Particularly Described, John Beauchamp Jones, 1841

Wilderness Road, Paul Green, 1955

William Styron's Nat Turner: Ten Black Writers Respond, 1968

"William Wilson," Edgar Allan Poe, 1838

Wise Blood, Flannery O'Connor, 1952

"Wiser than a God," Kate Chopin, 1889

With Charity for None, Florence King, 1992

The Woman at the Washington Zoo, Randall Jarrell, 1960

A Woman Within, Ellen Glasgow, 1954

The Women on the Porch, Caroline Gordon, 1944

The World between the Eyes, Fred Chappell, 1971

World Enough and Time, Robert Penn Warren, 1950

The World's Body, John Crowe Ransom, 1938

"A Worn Path," Eudora Welty, 1941

A Wreath of Virginia Bay Leaves, James Barron Hope, 1895

Wreck of Honor: A Tragedy in Five Acts, Lemuel Sawyer, 1826

Writings of Hugh Swinton Legaré, Hugh Swinton Legaré, 1846

Y

Ye Beare and Ye Cubb, Philip Alexander Bruce, 1665

The Yearling, Marjorie Kinnan Rawlings, 1938

Yellowhorse, Dee Brown, 1957

The Yemassee: A Romance of Carolina, William Gilmore Simms, 1835

You Can't Go Home Again, Thomas Wolfe, 1940

You Can't Keep a Good Woman Down: Stories, Alice Walker, 1981

You Touched Me!, Tennessee Williams, 1945

The Young Man from Atlanta, Horton Foote, 1995

MAJOR SOUTHERN AUTHORS
AND THEIR WORKS

Adair, James
The History of the American Indian, 1775

Agee, James
A Death in the Family, 1956
Let Us Now Praise Famous Men, 1941
The Morning Watch, 1951
Permit Me Voyage, 1934

Allison, Dorothy
Bastard Out of Carolina, 1992

Allston, Joseph Blyth
"Stack Arms," 1865

Andrews, Georgia Eliza Frances
The Wartime Journal of a Georgia Girl, 1908

Angelou, Maya
All God's Children Need Travelin' Shoes, 1986
And Still I Rise, 1978
Even the Stars Look Lonesome, 1997
Gather Together in My Name, 1974
Georgia, Georgia, 1971
The Heart of a Woman, 1981
I Know Why the Caged Bird Sings, 1970
Just Give Me a Cool Drink of Water 'fore I Diiie, 1971
Now Sheba Sings the Song, 1987
Oh Pray My Wings Are Gonna Fit Me Well, 1975
"On the Pulse of the Morning," 1993
Singin' and Swingin' and Gettin' Merry like Christmas, 1976
Sister, Sister, 1979
"They Came To Stay," 1989

Arnow, Harriette
The Dollmaker, 1954

Aston, Anthony
Fool's Opera, 1702

Audubon, John James
   American Ornithological Biography (coauthored by William MacGillivray), 1841
   The Birds of America, 1838
   Synopsis of the Birds of America, 1838
   The Viviparous Quadrupeds of North America, 1845

Baldwin, Joseph Glover
   Ebb Tide, 1864
   The Flush Times of Alabama and Mississippi: A Series of Sketches, 1853
   The Flush Times of California, 1853
   Party Leaders, 1855

Ball, Caroline Augusta
   "The Jacket of Gray," 1866

Barrow, Bennet H.
   Plantation Life in the Florida Parishes of Louisiana, 1836–1846, 1943

Barton, Andrew
   The Disappointment, or The Force of Credulity, 1767

Bartram, William
   Travels through North and South Carolina, Georgia, East and West Florida, 1792

Benét, Rosemary, and Stephen Vincent Benét
   A Book of Americans, 1933

Benét, Stephen Vincent
   John Brown's Body, 1929

Berry, Wendell
   The Memory of Old Jack, 1974

Beverley, Robert
   History and Present State of Virginia, 1722
   Low Character of Immigrants to Virginia, 1705

Blennerhassett, Margaret Agnew
   Widow of the Rock and Other Poems by a Lady, 1788

Bogart, W. H.
   Daniel Boone and the Hunters of Kentucky, 1857

Brooks, Cleanth
   Modern Poetry and the Tradition, 1939
   The Relation of the Alabama-Georgia Dialect to the Provincial Dialects of Great Britain, 1935
   A Southern Treasury of Life and Literature, 1937
   Understanding Drama (coauthored by Robert Penn Warren), 1945
   Understanding Fiction (coauthored by Robert Penn Warren), 1943
   Understanding Poetry (coauthored by Robert Penn Warren), 1938
   The Well Wrought Urn, 1947

Brown, Dee
   Bury My Heart at Wounded Knee, 1970
   The Fetterman Massacre, 1962
   The Fighting Indians of the West, 1948
   Galvanized Yankees, 1963
   The Gentle Tamers: Women of the Old Wild West, 1958

Hear That Lonesome Whistle Blow: Railroads in the West, 1977
The Settlers West, 1955
Trail Driving Days, 1952
Wave High the Banner, 1942
When the Century Was Young, 1993
Yellowhorse, 1957

Brown, H. Rap
Die Nigger Die!, 1969

Brown, Sterling
Southern Road, 1932

Brown, William Wells
The Anti-Slavery Harp, 1852
The Black Man: His Antecedents, His Genius, and His Achievements, 1863
Clotelle: A Tale of Southern States, 1853
The Escape, or A Leap for Freedom, 1858
Experience; or, How To Give a Northern Man a Backbone, 1856
My Southern Home; or, The South and Its People, 1880
The Narrative of William Wells Brown; a Fugitive Slave, 1851
The Negro in the American Rebellion: His Heroism and His Fidelity, 1867
The Rising Son; or The Antecedents and Advancement of the Colored Race, 1874
Three Years in Europe; or, Places I Have Seen and People I Have Met, 1852

Bruce, Philip Alexander
Ye Beare and Ye Cubb, 1665

Bruns, John Dickson
"The Foe at the Gates," 1865

Bryan, Daniel
The Mountain Muse: Comprising the Adventures of Daniel Boone; and the Power of Virtuous and Refined Beauty, 1813

Burns, Olive Ann
Cold Sassy Tree, 1984
Leaving Cold Sassy, 1992

Byrd, Col. William
History of the Dividing Line, 1728
The Secret Diary, 1712

Cabell, James Branch
The Eagle's Shadow, 1904
Let Me Lie, 1947

Cable, George Washington
Bonaventure, 1888
Bylow Hill, 1902
The Cavalier, 1901
The Creoles of Louisiana, 1884
Dr. Sevier, 1884
Gideon's Band, 1914
The Grandissimes, 1880
"Jean-ah Pouquelin," 1879

Cable, George Washington, *continued*
    John Marsh, Southerner, 1894
    Kincaid's Battery, 1908
    Madame Delphine, 1881
    The Negro Question, 1890
    Old Creole Days, 1879
    "Posson Jone' and Père Raphael," 1909
    The Silent South, 1885
    Strange True Stories of Louisiana, 1889
    Strong Hearts, 1899

Caldwell, Erskine
    God's Little Acre, 1933
    Tobacco Road, 1932

Capote, Truman
    Answered Prayers: The Partial Manuscript, 1986
    Breakfast at Tiffany's, 1958
    Children on Their Birthdays, 1950
    "A Christmas Memory," 1956
    The Grass Harp (musical), 1971
    The Grass Harp (novel), 1951
    The Grass Harp (play), 1952
    House of Flowers, 1954
    In Cold Blood, 1965
    Local Color, 1946
    Miriam, 1982
    The Muses Are Heard, 1956
    "My Side of the Matter," 1941
    Other Voices, Other Rooms, 1948
    The Thanksgiving Visitor, 1968

Cary, Mary Ann Shadd
    Hints to the Colored People of North America, 1849
    *A Plea for Emigration, or Notes on Canada West, in Its Moral, Social and Political
        Aspect*, 1852

Cash, W. J.
    The Mind of the South, 1941

Catesby, Mark
    The Natural History of Carolina, Florida, and the Bahama Islands, 1731
    On Migration, 1747

Cather, Willa
    My Ántonia, 1918
    O Pioneers!, 1913

Centlivre, Susanna
    The Busy-Body, 1736

Chappell, Fred
    Brighten the Corner Where You Are, 1989
    Dagon, 1968
    Farewell, I'm Bound To Leave You, 1997

I Am One of You Forever, 1985
The Inkling, 1965
It Is Time, Lord, 1963
The World between the Eyes, 1971

Chateaubriand, Viscomte de
A Tour through the Southern and Western Territories of the United States of North-America; the Spanish Dominions on the River Mississippi, and the Florida; the Countries of the Creek Nations; and Many Uninhabited Parts, 1792

Chesnut, Mary Boykin
Diary from Dixie, 1886
Mary Chesnut's Civil War, 1981

Chesnutt, Charles Waddell
The Conjure Woman, 1899
The House behind the Cedars, 1900
"A Matter of Principle," 1899
The Wife of His Youth and Other Stories of the Color Line, 1899

Childress, Alice
A Hero Ain't Nothin' but a Sandwich, 1973
Trouble in Mind, 1955

Chilton, Thomas
Narrative of the Life of David Crockett of the State of Tennessee, 1834

Chopin, Kate
At Fault, 1890
"Athénaïse," 1897
The Awakening, 1899
Bayou Folk, 1894
"Désirée's Baby," 1894
"Emancipation: A Life Fable," 1869
"If It Might Be," 1889
A Night in Acadie, 1897
"Wiser than a God," 1889

Clarke, Mathew St. Clair
The Life and Adventures of Colonel David Crockett of West Tennessee, 1833
Sketches and Eccentricities of Col. David Crockett, 1833

Clayton, John
Flora Virginica, ca. 1750

Cleaver, Eldridge
Soul on Ice, 1968

Clyman, James
Journal of a Mountain Man, 1840

Conroy, Pat
Beach Music, 1995
The Boo, 1970
The Great Santini, 1976
The Lords of Discipline, 1980
The Prince of Tides, 1986
The Water Is Wide, 1972

Cook, Ebenezer
The Sot-Weed Factor, 1708

Cooke, John Esten
The Heir of Gaymount, 1870
A Life of Robert E. Lee, 1871
The Life of Stonewall Jackson: A Military Biography, 1866
Surry of Eagle's Nest, 1866
The Virginia Comedians, or Old Days in the Old Dominion, 1859

Cooke, Philip Pendleton
"Florence Vane," 1847
Froissart Ballads, and Other Poems, 1847
"The Mountaineer," 1847

Cox, William Norment
The Scuffletown Outlaws: A Tragedy of the Lowrie Gang, 1924

Coyner, David H.
The Lost Trappers, 1847

Crockett, Davy
An Account of Colonel Crockett's Tour to the North and Down East, 1835
Crockett Almanacks, 1835–1838
Go Ahead Almanack, 1838
*The Life of Martin Van Buren, Hair-Apparent to the "Government," and the Appointed
Successor of General Jackson,* 1835

Cullen, Countee
The Black Christ, and Other Poems, 1929
Caroling Dusk, 1928
Copper Sun, 1927
"Heritage," 1925

Cumming, Kate
The Journal of Hospital Life in the Confederate Army in Tennessee, 1866

Custis, George Washington Parke
Conversations with Lafayette, 1824
The Eighth of January, 1834
The Indian Prophecy, 1827
North Point or Baltimore Defended, 1833
The Pawnee Chief, ca. 1830
Pocahontas, or The Settlers of Virginia, 1836
The Railroad, 1830
*Recollections and Private Memoirs of Washington, by his Adopted Son, George
Washington Parke Custis,* 1859

Daly, John Augustin
Horizon, 1871
Under the Gaslight, 1867

Davidson, Donald
"The Artist as Southerner," 1926
The Attack on Leviathan, 1938
Lee in the Mountains and Other Poems, 1927
An Outland Piper, 1924

"Sanctuary," 1927
Still Rebels, Still Yankees, 1957
The Tall Men, 1927
The Tennessee, 1948

Davis, Jefferson
The Rise and Fall of the Confederate Government, 1881

Davis, Reuben
Recollections of Mississippi and Mississippians, 1889

Davis, Varina Howell
"Christmas in the Confederate White House," 1896
Jefferson Davis, Ex-President of the Confederate States of America; a Memoir, 1890

de La Coste, Mary Ravenel
"Somebody's Darling," ca. 1864

Delany, Martin
Declaration of the Principles of the National Emigration Convention, 1864

Delany, Sarah, and Elizabeth Delany
The Delany Sisters' Book of Everyday Wisdom, 1994
Having Our Say, 1993

Dickey, James
Buckdancer's Choice, 1970
Deliverance, 1970
"The Heaven of Animals," 1962
Jericho: The South Beheld, 1974
"May Day Sermon to the Women of Gilmer County, Georgia, by a Woman
    Preacher Leaving the Baptist Church," 1967
Puella, 1982

Dickson, Samuel Henry
"I Sigh for the Land of the Cypress and Pine," ca. 1850

Dinsmore, Elsie
The Mildred Books, 1878–1844
An Old Fashioned Boy, 1870
Our Fred, 1847

Dobie, James Frank
Apache Gold and Yaqui Silver, 1928
The Ben Lilly Legend, 1950
Coronado's Children, 1930
Cow People, 1964
Guide to Life and Literature of the Southwest, 1943
The Longhorns, 1941
The Mustang, 1934
Some Part of Myself, 1967
Tales of Old-Time Texas, 1955
A *Vaquero of the Brush Country*, 1930

Douglass, Frederick
"The Condition of the Freedmen," 1883
The Douglass Monthly, 1859
Frederick Douglass' Paper, 1851

Douglass, Frederick, *continued*
 The Heroic Slave, 1853
 The Lesson of the Hour: Why Is the Negro Lynched, 1894
 Life and Times of Frederick Douglass, 1881
 "Men of Color, to Arms!," 1863
 My Bondage and My Freedom, 1855
 Narrative of the Life of Frederick Douglass, an American Slave, 1845
 "The Race Problem in America," 1894
 "What to the Slave Is the Fourth of July?," 1852

Douglass, Marjory Stoneman
 The Everglades: River of Grass, 1947

Drannan, Captain William F.
 Thirty-One Years on the Plains and in the Mountains or, The Last Voice from the Plains, 1900

Edgerton, Clyde
 Raney, 1985
 Walking across Egypt, 1987
 Where Trouble Sleeps, 1997

Edmonds, Sarah Emma Evelyn
 Nurse and Spy in the Union Army, 1865

Ehle, John
 The Trail of Tears: The Rise and Fall of the Cherokee Nation, 1988

Eliot, William
 Carolina Sports by Land and Water, 1846

Elliott, Sarah Barnwell
 The Durket Sperret, 1898
 Jerry, 1891

Elliott, William
 "A Deer Hunt," 1846

Ellis, Edward Sylvester
 The Life and Time of Col. Daniel Boone, Hunter, Soldier, and Pioneer, 1884

Ellison, Ralph
 "The Birthmark," 1940
 "Flying Home," 1944
 Flying Home and Other Stories, 1997
 Going to the Territory, 1986
 "In a Strange Country," 1944
 Invisible Man, 1947
 "King of the Bingo Game," 1944
 "Mr. Toussan," 1941
 "Recent Negro Fiction," 1941
 "Richard Wright's Blues," 1945
 Shadow and Act, 1964
 "That I Had the Wings," 1944
 "The Way It Is," 1942

Falkner, Colonel William Clark
 The White Rose of Memphis, 1880

Faulkner, John
  My Brother Bill, 1963

Faulkner, William
  Absalom, Absalom!, 1936
  As I Lay Dying, 1930
  "The Bear," 1942
  Big Woods, 1955
  Collected Stories of William Faulkner, 1950
  Doctor Martino and Other Stories, 1934
  A Fable, 1954
  Go Down, Moses, 1942
  The Hamlet, 1957
  Intruder in the Dust, 1948
  "L'Après-Midi du Faune," 1919
  Light in August, 1932
  The Mansion, 1959
  The Marble Faun, 1924
  Mosquitoes, 1927
  "An Odor of Verbena," 1938
  The Reivers, 1962
  Requiem for a Nun, 1950
  "A Rose for Emily," 1931
  "Rose of Lebanon," 1996
  Sanctuary, 1931
  Sartoris, 1929
  Soldier's Pay, 1926
  The Sound and the Fury, 1929
  "That Evening Sun," 1931
  These 13, 1931
  The Town, 1957
  The Unvanquished, 1938
  The Wild Palms, 1939

Filson, John
  The Adventures of Col. Daniel Boon [sic], *Containing a Narrative of the Wars of Kentucke*, 1784

Finley, Martha Farquharson
  The Mildred Books, 1878–1894
  An Old Fashioned Boy, 1870
  Our Fred: or, Seminary Life at Thurston, 1874
  Twiddletewit: A Fairy Tale, 1898

Flagg, Fannie
  Daisy Fay and the Miracle Man, 1981
  Fried Green Tomatoes at the Whistle Stop Cafe, 1987

Flash, Henry Lynden
  "Stonewall Jackson," 1865

Flint, Timothy
  The First White Man of the West, or The Life and Exploits of Col. Dan'l. Boone, the First Settler of Kentucky; Interspersed with Incidents in the Early Annals of the Country, 1854

Foote, Horton
  Baby, the Rain Must Fall, 1965
  Barn Burning (play), 1980
  The Death of Papa, 1997
  Hurry Sundown, 1967
  Only the Heart, 1944
  Tender Mercies, 1983
  To Kill a Mockingbird (screenplay), 1962
  Tomorrow, 1960
  The Trip to Bountiful, 1953
  The Widow Claire, 1987
  The Young Man from Atlanta, 1995

Fox, John, Jr.
  The Kentuckians, 1897
  The Little Shepherd of Kingdom Come, 1903
  The Trail of the Lonesome Pine, 1908

Frazier, Charles
  Cold Mountain, 1997

Fugitive Agrarian consortium
  I'll Take My Stand, 1930
  Who Owns America?, 1936

Gaines, Ernest J.
  The Autobiography of Miss Jane Pittman, 1971
  Bloodline, 1968
  Catherine Carmier, 1964
  A Gathering of Old Men, 1983
  "Just Like a Tree," 1962
  A Lesson before Dying, 1993
  Of Love and Dust, 1967
  "The Turtles," 1956

Garnet, Henry Highland
  "Call to Rebellion," 1865

Gay, Mary Ann
  Life in Dixie during the War, ca. 1865

Gayarré, Charles Etienne Arthur
  "Histoire de la Louisiane," 1847
  History of Louisiana, 1866
  "History of the Spanish Domination in Louisiana," 1854
  "Louisiana: Its Colonial History and Romance," 1852
  "Louisiana, Its History as a French Colony," 1852
  Philip II of Spain, 1866
  "Romance of the History of Louisiana," 1848

Gibbons, Kaye
  Charms for the Easy Life, 1993
  A Cure for Dreams, 1991
  Ellen Foster, 1987
  A Virtuous Woman, 1989

Gilchrist, Ellen
  The Age of Miracles, 1995

Drunk with Love, 1986
Falling through Space, 1987
In the Land of Dreamy Dreams, 1981
The Land Surveyor's Daughter, 1979
Light Can Be Both Wave and Particle, 1989
Rhoda: A Life in Stories, 1995
Victory over Japan, 1983

Giles, Janice Holt
Hannah Fowler, 1956

Gilman, Caroline Howard
"Let Us Go to the Woods," 1838
Love's Progress, 1840
The Poetry of Traveling in the United States, 1838
Recollections of a Southern Matron, 1837
Rose Bud, 1832
Verses of a Lifetime, 1849

Giovanni, Nikki
Black Feeling, Black Talk, 1967
Black Judgement, 1970
Cotton Candy on a Rainy Day, 1978
Gemini: An Extended Autobiographical Statement on My First Twenty-Five Years of Being a Black Poet, 1971
Racism 101, 1994
Re-Creation, 1971
Sacred Cows and Other Edibles, 1988
Spin a Soft Black Song, 1971
Those Who Ride the Night Winds, 1982
"The True Import of Present Dialogue: Black vs. Negro," 1968

Gipson, Fred
Big Bend: A Homesteader's Story, 1952
The Fabulous Empire: Colonel Zack Miller's Story, 1946
Hound-Dog Man, 1949
Little Arliss, 1978
Old Yeller, 1956
The Trail-Driving Rooster, 1955

Glancy, Diane
Brown Wolf Leaves the Res, 1984
Iron Woman, 1990
Lone Dog's Winter Count, 1991
Offering, 1988
One Age in a Dream, 1986
Traveling On, 1982

Glasgow, Ellen
Barren Ground, 1925
The Battle-Ground, 1929
Beyond Defeat, 1966
Deliverance, 1904
The Descendant, 1897
In This Our Life, 1942
Life and Gabriella: The Story of a Woman's Courage, 1916

Glasgow, Ellen, *continued*
 The Miller of Old Church, 1911
 The Romance of a Plain Man, 1909
 The Romantic Comedian, 1926
 The Sheltered Life, 1932
 They Stooped to Folly, 1929
 Vein of Iron, 1935
 Virginia, 1913
 The Voice of the People, 1900
 A Woman Within, 1954

Godwin, Gail
 The Good Husband, 1994
 A Mother and Two Daughters, 1982
 A Southern Family, 1987

Golden, Harry
 The Carolina Israelite, 1941
 Enjoy, Enjoy, 1971
 For Two Cents Plain, 1959
 Only in America, 1958
 Our Southern Landsman, 1974
 "The Vertical Negro Plan," 1944

Gordon, Caroline
 Aleck Maury, Sportsman, 1934
 "The Captive," 1945
 The Forest of the South, 1945
 The Garden of Adonis, 1937
 Green Centuries, 1941
 The House of Fiction, 1950
 How To Read a Novel, 1957
 None Shall Look Back, 1937
 Penhally, 1931
 The Women on the Porch, 1944

Grady, Henry
 "The New South," 1886

Grau, Shirley Ann
 The Keepers of the House, 1964

Grayson, William John
 The Hireling and the Slave, 1854
 James Louis Petigru: A Biographical Sketch, 1866

Green, Paul
 The Common Glory, 1947
 The Enchanted Maze, 1935
 Faith of Our Fathers, 1950
 The Field God, 1927
 The Founders, 1957
 The Highland Call, 1939
 The House of Connelly, 1931
 In Abraham's Bosom, 1927

"In Aunt Mahaly's Cabin—A Folk Play for the Negro Theatre," 1924
Johnny Johnson (coauthored by Kurt Weill), 1928
The Last of the Lowries, 1920
The Laughing Pioneer, 1932
The Lost Colony, 1937
Quare Medicine, 1925
Roll, Sweet Chariot, 1934
Shroud My Body Down, 1934
Tread the Green Grass, 1932
Wilderness Road, 1955

Greene, Bette
Summer of My German Soldier, 1973

Greene, Melissa Fay
Praying for Sheetrock, 1991

Gregory, Dick
Nigger, 1964
No More Lies: The Myth and Reality of American History, 1976

Griffin, John Howard
Black Like Me, 1960

Grimké, Angelina
Appeal to the Christian Women of the South, 1836
Letters to Catherine Beecher in Reply to an Essay on Slavery and Abolitionism Addressed to A. A. Grimké, 1837

Grimké, Sarah
Letters on the Equality of the Sexes and the Condition of Women, 1838

Gurganus, Allan
Oldest Living Confederate Widow Tells All, 1984

Haley, Alex
The Autobiography of Malcolm X, 1965
A Different Kind of Xmas, 1988
"Mr. Muhammad Speaks," 1960
"*Playboy* Interview: Malcolm X," 1963
Queen, 1993
Roots: The Next Generation, 1979
Roots: The Saga of an American Family, 1976

Haliburton, Thomas
The Americans at Home; or, Byeways, Backwoods, and Prairies, 1854

Hamner, Earl, Jr.
The Homecoming, 1970
Spencer's Mountain, 1961

Harling, Robert
Steel Magnolias, 1987

Harper, Frances Ellen Watkins
Atlanta Offering: Poems, 1895
Iola Leroy: or, Shadows Uplifted, 1892
Light beyond the Darkness, ca. 1910
Martyr of Alabama and Other Poems, 1895

Harper, Frances Ellen Watkins, *continued*
    Moses: A Story of the Nile, 1869
    Poems, 1900
    Poems on Miscellaneous Subjects, 1854
    Sketches of Southern Life, 1872
    The Sparrow's Fall and Other Poems, 1894

Harris, Bernice Kelly
    Ca'line, 1932

Harris, Dilue Rose
    Reminiscences of Colonial Life in Texas, 1904

Harris, George Washington
    Sut Lovingood: Yarns Spun by a "Nat'ral Born Durn'd Fool," 1867
    Sut Lovingood's Travels with Old Abe Linkhorn, 1868

Harris, Joel Chandler
    Daddy Jack the Runaway, and Other Stories Told after Dark, 1889
    Free Joe and Other Georgian Sketches, 1887
    Gabriel Tolliver, 1902
    Mingo and Other Sketches in Black and White, 1884
    Mr. Rabbit at Home, 1895
    Nights with Uncle Remus, 1883
    On the Plantation, 1892
    On the Wing of Occasions, 1900
    The Romance of Rockville, 1878
    Seven Tales of Uncle Remus, 1948
    Sister Jane, Her Friends and Acquaintances, 1896
    The Story of Aaron, 1895
    Tales of Home Folks in Peace and War, 1896
    Told by Uncle Remus, 1905
    Uncle Remus: His Songs and His Sayings, 1880
    Uncle Remus and the Little Boy, 1910
    Uncle Remus Returns, 1918
    Uncle Remus's Magazine (coauthored by Julian Harris), 1907

Haulee, Margaret Hanley
    "My Three Years as a Shawnee Captive," 1849

Hawks, Francis Lister
    History of North Carolina, 1858

Hearn, Lafcadio
    Chita: A Memory of Last Island, 1889

Hellman, Lillian
    Another Part of the Forest, 1947
    The Children's Hour, 1934
    "Julia," 1973
    The Little Foxes, 1939
    Pentimento: A Book of Portraits, 1973
    Scoundrel Time, 1976
    The Searching Wind, 1944
    An Unfinished Woman, 1969
    Watch on the Rhine, 1941

Henley, Beth
Abundance, 1990
Am I Blue?, 1973
Beth Henley: Monologues for Women, 1992
Control Freaks, 1992
Crimes of the Heart, 1981
The Debutante Ball, 1985
L-Play, 1995
The Lucky Spot, 1986
The Miss Firecracker Contest, 1980
Morgan's Daughters, 1979
Nobody's Fool, 1986
Signature, 1990
True Stories, 1986
The Wake of Jamey Foster, 1982

Henry, O.
Collected Works, 1913
"The Duplicity of Hargraves," 1911
The Four Millions, 1906
"The Gift of the Magi," 1905
Hearts of the West, 1907
Lo (coauthored by Franklin P. Adams), 1909
"The Miracle of Lava Cañon," 1898
"A Municipal Report," 1910
Options, 1909
"The Ransom of Red Chief," 1910
"A Retrieved Reformation," 1903
"The Rose of Dixie," 1909
Sixes and Sevens, 1911
Strictly Business, 1910
Tales of the Town, 1939
"Whistling Dick's Christmas Stocking," 1899

Henry, Patrick
Address to the Virginia Convention, 1775

Hentz, Caroline Lee Whiting
The Banished Son and Other Stories of the Heart, 1856
Linda: or, The Young Pilot of the Belle Creole, 1850
Marcus Warland, 1852
The Planter's Northern Bride, 1851

Heyward, Dubose
Angel, 1926
The Brass Ankle, 1931
Carolina Chansons, 1922
The Half Pint Flask, 1929
Mamba's Daughters (coauthored by Dorothy Hartzell Kuhns Heyward), 1929
Porgy (novel), 1925
Porgy (play) (coauthored by Dorothy Hartzell Kuhns Heyward), 1927
Porgy and Bess (coauthored by George Gershwin and Ira Gershwin), 1935
Star-Spangled Virgin, 1939

Hooper, Johnson Jones
Some Adventures of Captain Simon Suggs, Late of the Tallapoosa Volunteers, 1846
Tales of Alabama, 1851
The Widow Rugby's Husband, A Night at the Uly Man's, and Other Tales of Alabama, 1851

Hope, James Barron
The Lee Memorial Ode, 1895
A Wreath of Virginia Bay Leaves, 1895

Hoskens, Jane Fenn
The Life and Spiritual Sufferings of That Faithful Servant of Christ, Jane Hoskens, 1771

Houston, Sam
The Victor's Description of the Battle of San Jacinto, 1836

Hunter, Kermit
Horn in the West, 1952
The Liberty Tree, 1970

Hurston, Zora Neale
Color Struck, 1926
"Drenched in Light," 1924
Dust Tracks on a Road, 1942
"The Eatonville Anthology," 1926
First One, 1926
From Sun to Sun, 1933
"The Gilded Six-Bits," 1926
The Great Day, 1932
I Love Myself: When I Am Laughing . . . and Then Again When I Am Looking Mean and Impressive: A Zora Neale Hurston Reader, 1979
"John Redding Goes to Sea," 1921
Jonah's Gourd Vine, 1934
Life of Herod the Great, 1948
Moses, Man of the Mountain, 1939
Mule Bone (coauthored by Langston Hughes), 1930
Mule Bone: A Comedy of Negro Life, 1990
Mules and Men, 1935
"Muttsy," 1926
"Possum or Pig," 1926
The Sanctified Church: The Folklore Writings of Zora Neale Hurston, 1981
Seraph on the Suwanee, 1948
Singing Steel, 1934
Spear, 1926
"Spear," 1993
"Spunk," 1925
Spunk: The Selected Short Stories of Zora Neale Hurston, 1985
"Sweat," 1926
Tell My Horse, 1938
"The Ten Commandments of Charm," 1993
Their Eyes Were Watching God, 1937
"Under the Bridge," 1993

Ioor, William
Battle of Eutaw Springs and Evacuation of Charleston, 1807
Independence: or, Which Do You Like Best, the Peer or the Farmer, 1805

Ivins, Molly
  Molly Ivins Can't Say Those Things, Can She?, 1991

Jackson, Henry Rootes
  "My Wife and Child," 1850
  "Red Old Hills of Georgia," 1850
  Tallulah, and Other Poems, 1850

Jackson, Reverend Jesse
  "Speech to the 1996 Democratic National Convention," 1996

Jacobs, Harriet Ann Brent
  Incidents in the Life of a Slave Girl, Written by Herself, 1861

Jarrell, Randall
  Blood for a Stranger, 1942
  "Death of the Ball Turret Gunner," 1955
  "Lady Bates," 1955
  Little Friend, Little Friend, 1945
  Losses, 1948
  Selected Poems, 1955
  The Woman at the Washington Zoo, 1960

Jefferson, Thomas
  Declaration of Causes and Necessity of Taking of Arms, 1775
  The Declaration of Independence, 1776
  A Summary View of the Rights of British America, 1774
  The Testament of Freedom, 1943

Johnson, Georgia Douglas
  An Autumn Love Cycle, 1928
  Bronze: A Book of Verse, 1922
  The Heart of a Woman and Other Poems, 1918
  Share My World, 1962

Johnson, James Weldon
  The Autobiography of an Ex-Coloured Man, 1912
  The Book of American Negro Poetry, 1922
  The Book of American Negro Spirituals (coauthored by John Rosamund
      Johnson), 1925
  "The Creation," 1927
  God's Trombones: Seven Negro Sermons in Verse, 1927
  "The Negro National Anthem" (coauthored by John Rosamund Johnson), 1900
  The Second Book of Negro Spirituals (coauthored by John Rosamund
      Johnson), 1926

Johnston, Richard Malcolm
  "Mr. Absalom Billingslea and Other Georgia Folk," 1888
  "Old Mark Langston," 1884
  "Widow Guthrie," 1890

Jones, Charles Colcock
  Negro Myths from the Georgia Coast Told in the Vernacular, 1888

Jones, John Beauchamp
  *Wild Western Scenes; A Narrative of Adventures in the Western Wilderness, Forty Years
      Ago; Wherein the Conduct of Daniel Boone, the Great American Pioneer, Is
      Particularly Described*, 1841

Jordan, Barbara
"The Arts and the American Dream," 1993
"Who Then Will Speak for the Common Good?," 1996

Kemble, Fanny
Journal of an American Residence, 1835
Residence on a Georgia Plantation, 1838–1839, 1863

Kennedy, John Pendleton
Horse-Shoe Robinson, 1835
Swallow Barn, or A Sojourn in the Old Dominion, 1832

Key, Francis Scott
"Defence of Fort M'Henry," 1814
"The Star-Spangled Banner," 1814

King, Florence
Confessions of a Failed Southern Lady, 1985
The Florence King Reader, 1995
He: An Irreverent Look at the American Male, 1978
Lump It or Leave It, 1991
Reflections in a Jaundiced Eye, 1989
Southern Ladies and Gentlemen, 1975
WASP, Where Is Thy Sting, 1976
When Sisterhood Was in Flower, 1982
With Charity for None, 1992

King, Martin Luther, Jr.
"I Have a Dream," 1963
"Letter from a Birmingham Jail," 1963

Kinnan, Mary
A True Narrative of the Sufferings of Mary Kinnan, Who Was Taken Prisoner by the Shawanee Nation of Indians, 1795

Koch, Fred, Jr.
Wash Carver's Mouse Trap, 1935

Lamar, Mirabeau Buonaparte
"The Daughter of Mendoza," 1857
Verse Memorials, 1857

Lanier, Sidney
The Boy's King Arthur, 1880
The Boy's Mabinogion, 1881
The Boy's Percy, 1882
"Corn," 1875
The English Novel, 1883
"The Marshes of Glynn," 1878
Music and Poetry, 1898
"The Power of Prayer: or, The First Steamboat Up the Alabama," 1875
The Science of English Verse, 1880
Shakespeare and His Forerunners, 1902
"Song of the Chattahoochee," 1877
"Sunrise," 1880
"The Symphony," 1875
Tiger Lilies, 1867

Larson, Larry
Tent Meeting (coauthored by Levi Lee and Rebecca Wackler), 1987

Lawson, John
New Voyage to Carolina, 1709

Le Petit, Father
The Jesuit Relations and Allied Documents: Travel and Explorations of the Jesuit Missionaries in New France, 1610–1791, 1900

Le Vert, Celeste
Souvenirs of Travel, 1857

Lee, Harper
Christmas to Me, 1961
To Kill a Mockingbird, 1960

Lee, Henry
Memoirs of the War in the Southern Department of the United States, 1812

Legaré, Hugh Swinton
Writings of Hugh Swinton Legaré, 1846

Legaré, James Matthews
"Haw-Blossoms," 1848
Orta-Undis, and Other Poems, 1848
"To a Lily," 1848

Lester, Julius
Look Out Whitey! Black Power's Gon' Get Your Mama!, 1968
To Be a Slave, 1968

Lewis, Meriwether, and William Clark
History of the Expedition under the Command of Captains Lewis and Clark, 1814
Message from the President, February 19, 1806, 1806
Original Journals of the Lewis and Clark Expedition, 1905

Lloyd, Francis Bartow
Sketches of Country Life, 1898

Logan, Martha Daniell
The Gardners Kalender, 1772
Letters of Martha Logan to John Bartram, 1760–1763, 1763

Lomax, Alan
American Ballads and Folk Songs (coauthored by John Lomax), 1934
The Land Where the Blues Began, 1993

Lomax, John
Adventures of a Ballad Hunter, 1947
American Ballads and Folk Songs (coauthored by Alan Lomax), 1934
Cowboy Songs and Other Frontier Ballads, 1910
Folk Song U.S.A., 1947
Negro Folk Songs as Sung by Lead Belly, 1936
Our Singing Country, 1941
Songs of the Cattle Trail and Cow Camp, 1917

Longstreet, Augustus Baldwin
Georgia Scenes, 1834

Loughborough, Mary Ann
My Cave Life in Vicksburg, with Letters of Trial and Travel, 1864

Love, Nat
The Life and Adventures of Nat Love, Better Known in the Cattle Country as Deadwood Dick, 1907

McCabe, William Gordon
"Christmas Night of '62," ca. 1865
"Dreaming in the Trenches," ca. 1864

McCarthy, Harry
"The Bonny Blue Flag," ca. 1861

McCullers, Carson
The Ballad of the Sad Café, 1951
Clock without Hands, 1961
"The Haunted Boy," 1971
The Heart Is a Lonely Hunter, 1940
The Member of the Wedding (novel), 1946
The Member of the Wedding (play), 1950
The Mortgaged Heart, 1971
Reflections in a Golden Eye, 1941
The Square Root of Wonderful, 1958
"Sucker," 1971
Sweet as a Pickle and Clean as a Pig: Poems, 1964
"A Tree, a Rock, a Cloud," 1942

McMurtry, Larry
Lonesome Dove, 1985
The Streets of Laredo, 1993

Marshall, Catherine
Christy, 1967

Marshall, John
The Life of George Washington, 1807

Martineau, Harriet
Retrospect of Western Travel, 1838
Society in America, 1837

Mason, George
Extracts from the Virginia Charters, 1773

Maury, Matthew Fontaine
"The Amazon and the Atlantic Slopes of South America," 1853

Meek, Alexander Beaufort
"The Mocking Bird," 1857

Mencken, H. L.
The American Language, 1919–1948
The American Mercury, 1924–1933
The Artist (coauthored by George Jean Nathan), 1912
A Book of Burlesques, 1916
A Book of Prefaces, 1917
Heathen Days, 1890–1936, 1943
Heliogabalus (coauthored by George Jean Nathan), 1920
Last Words, 1926
A New Dictionary of Quotations, on Historical Principles, 1942

Prejudices, Second Series, 1920
Smart Set: A Magazine of Cleverness (coauthored by George Jean Nathan), 1914
Ventures into Verse, 1903

Metcalfe, Samuel L.
A Collection of Some of the Most Interesting Narratives of Indian Warfare in the West, Containing an Account of the Adventures of Daniel Boone, One of the First Settlers of Kentucky, 1820

Miles, Emma Belle
The Spirit of the Mountains, 1905

Mitchell, Margaret
Gone with the Wind, 1936
The Lost Laysen, 1996

Moise, Penina
"The Exalted Theme of Human Praise," 1856
Hymns Written for the Use of Hebrew Congregations, 1856
"Man of the World," 1856

Moody, Anne E.
Coming of Age in Mississippi, 1968

Munford, Robert
The Candidates, 1798
A Collection of Plays and Poems, 1798
The Patriots, 1798

Murdoch, Frank Hitchcock
Davy Crockett, 1872

Murfree, Mary Noailles
"The Dancin' Party at Harrison's Cove," 1878
"The 'Harnt' That Walks Chilhowee," 1884
In the Mountains of Tennessee, 1884

Myers, Walter Dean
Fallen Angels, 1988

Norman, Marsha
Circus Valentine, 1979
D. Boone, 1992
The Fortune Teller, 1987
Getting Out, 1977
The Holdup, 1980
In Trouble at Fifteen, 1980
It's the Willingness, 1978
'night, Mother, 1982
Sarah and Abraham, 1988
The Secret Garden, 1991
Third and Oak: The Laundromat and the Pool Hall, 1978
Traveler in the Dark, 1984

O'Connor, Flannery
Conversations with Flannery O'Connor, 1987
"The Displaced Person," 1954
Everything That Rises Must Converge, 1965

O'Connor, Flannery, *continued*
  "The Geranium," 1946
  "A Good Man Is Hard To Find," 1953
  A Good Man Is Hard To Find and Other Stories, 1955
  The Habit of Being, 1979
  Mystery and Manners, 1969
  The Presence of Grace and Other Book Reviews, 1983
  The Violent Bear It Away, 1960
  Wise Blood, 1952

O'Hara, Theodore
  "The Bivouac of the Dead," 1847
  "The Old Pioneer," 1845

Oliver, Thaddeus
  "All Quiet along the Potomac To-Night," 1864

Owen, Guy
  The Ballad of the Flim-Flam Man, 1965

Page, Thomas Nelson
  In Ole Virginia, 1887
  The Old South, Essays Social and Political, 1892

Page, Walter Hines
  "The Forgotten Man," 1904
  "The School That Built a Town," 1904
  "The Rebuilding of Old Commonwealths," 1904

Palmer, John Williamson
  For Charlie's Sake, and Other Ballads and Lyrics, 1901
  "Stonewall Jackson's Way," 1901

Parks, William
  The Compleat Housewife, 1742
  The Compleat System of Fencing, 1734

Paulding, James Kirke
  The Lion of the West, 1831

Pénicaut, Andre
  *Fleur de Lys and Calumet: Being the Pénicaut Narrative of French Adventure in
      Louisiana*, 1704

Percy, Walker
  *Love in the Ruins: The Adventures of a Bad Catholic at a Time Near the End of the
      World*, 1971
  The Second Coming, 1980
  The Thanatos Syndrome, 1987

Peterkin, Julia Mood
  "Betsy," 1922
  Black April, 1927
  Bright Skin, 1932
  "Cat-Fish," 1922
  "Cooch's Premium," 1922
  "From Lang Syne Plantation," 1921
  Green Thursday, 1924
  "The Merry-Go-Round," 1921

Porter, Katherine Anne, *continued*
 The Leaning Tower and Other Stories, 1944
 "Old Mortality," 1930
 The Old Order: Stories of the South, 1944
 Pale Horse, Pale Rider, 1939
 "Portrait: Old South," 1940

Porter, William Sydney. *See* Henry, O.

Portis, Charles
 The Dog of the South, 1979
 Norwood, 1966
 True Grit, 1968

Preston, Margaret Junkin
 Cartoons, 1875
 "Gone Forward," 1875
 "The Soldier Boy," ca. 1865

Price, Reynolds
 Kate Vaiden, 1986
 A Long and Happy Life, 1962

Ramsay, David
 History of the Revolution in South Carolina, 1785

Randall, James Ryder
 "My Maryland," 1861

Randolph, Philip
 "Program of the March on Washington," 1942

Ransom, John Crowe
 "Bells for John Whiteside's Daughter," 1924
 Chills and Fever, 1921
 "Dead Boy," 1927
 God without Thunder, 1930
 "Janet Waking," 1927
 "Necrological," 1924
 The New Criticism, 1941
 "Piazza Piece," 1924
 Poems about God, 1919
 Selected Poems, 1945
 "Spectral Lovers," 1924
 Two Gentlemen in Bonds, 1926
 The World's Body, 1938

Rawlings, Marjorie Kinnan
 "Cracker Chidlings," 1931
 Cross Creek, 1942
 Cross Creek Cookery, 1942
 "Gal Young 'Un," 1933
 Jacob's Ladder, 1931
 The Marjorie Kinnan Rawlings Reader, 1956
 "A Mother in Manville," 1936
 The Secret River, 1956
 South Moon Under, 1933

The Sun Comes Up, 1949
When a Whippoorwill, 1930
The Yearling, 1938

Reese, Lizette Woodworth
A Branch of May, 1887
A Victorian Village, 1929

Rich, Adrienne
"Charleston in the 1860s: Derived from the Diaries of Mary Boykin Chesnut," ca. 1975

Richardson, Howard Dixon
Dark of the Moon, 1945

Ridge, John Rollin
"The Harp of Broken Strings," 1868
Life and Adventures of Joaquin Murieta, the Celebrated California Bandit, 1854
Poems, 1868

Ripley, Alexandra
Charleston, 1981
New Orleans Legacy, 1987
Scarlett, 1991

Roberts, Elizabeth Madox
The Great Meadow, 1930

Romans, Bernard
A Concise Natural History of East and West Florida, 1775

Royall, Anne Newport
Sketches of History, Life and Manners in the United States, 1826

Russell, Irwin
Christmas-Night in the Quarters, 1878

Ryan, Abram Joseph
"The Sword of Robert Lee," 1880

Rylant, Cynthia
Missing May, 1992

Sanchez, Sonia
A Blues Book for Blue Black Magical Women, 1974
Does Your House Have Lions?, 1997
Homecoming, 1969
Homegirls and Handgrenades, 1984
It's a New Day, 1971
Under a Soprano Sky, 1987
We a BadddDDD People, 1977

Sanders, Dori
Clover, 1990

Sawyer, Lemuel
Autobiography of Lemuel Sawyer, 1844
A Biography of John Randolph of Roanoke: With a Selection of His Speeches, 1844
Blackbeard: A Comedy in Four Acts, 1824
Printz Hall: A Record of New Sweden, 1839
Wreck of Honor: A Tragedy in Five Acts, 1826

Séjour, Victor
  Diegarias, 1844

Sequoyah
  Cherokee Advocate (Elias Boudinot, editor), 1927
  Cherokee Phoenix (Elias Boudinot, editor), 1927

Simms, William Gilmore
  Areytos: or, Songs of the South, 1846
  Atalantis, a Story of the Sea, 1832
  Beauchampe, or The Kentucky Tragedy, a Tale of Passion, 1842
  The Book of My Lady, 1833
  Border Beagles: A Tale of Mississippi, 1840
  The Cassique of Kiawah, 1859
  Charlemont, 1856
  Charleston, and Her Satirists, 1848
  The Cub of the Panther, 1869
  The Edge of the Swamp, 1853
  Eutaw, 1856
  Father Abbot, 1849
  The Forayers, 1855
  Guy Rivers, 1834
  Helen Halsey: or, The Swamp State of Conelachita, 1845
  "How Sharp Snaffles Got His Capital and Wife," 1870
  Katherine Walton: or, The Rebel's Daughter, 1851
  The Kinsmen, 1841
  Martin Faber, the Story of a Criminal, 1833
  Mellichampe, 1837
  Michael Bonham, or The Fall of Bexar, 1844
  Monody, on the Death of General Charles Cotesworth Pinckney, 1825
  Norman Maurice, or The Man of the People, 1851
  Paddy McGann, 1863
  The Partisan, 1835
  Richard Hurdis: or, The Avenger of Blood, a Tale of Alabama, 1838
  "The Swamp Fox," 1832
  The Sword and the Distaff, 1852
  The Wigwam and Cabin: Life in America, 1848
  The Yemassee: A Romance of Carolina, 1835

Smedes, Susan Dabney
  Memorials of a Southern Planter, 1887

Smith, Captain John
  Generall Historie of Virginia, New England and the Summer Isles, 1624
  A Map of Virginia with a Description of the Country, the Commodities, People, Government, and Religion, 1612

Smith, Richard Penn
  Colonel Crockett's Exploits and Adventures in Texas, 1836

Southworth, Emma Dorothy Eliza Nevitte
  India, 1853

Spencer, Anne
  "Before the Feast of Shushan," 1920

Spencer, Cornelia Phillips
The Last Ninety Days of the War in North Carolina, 1866

Spencer, Elizabeth
The Voice at the Back Door, 1956

Stephens, Alexander Hamilton
"A Plea for Union," 1860

Stewart, Elinore Pruitt
Letters of a Woman Homesteader, 1914
Letters on an Elk Hunt, 1915

Stuart, Jesse
Album of Destiny, 1944
The Beatinest Boy, 1953
Beyond Dark Hills, 1938
Daughter of the Legend, 1965
Hie to the Hunters, 1950
Hold April, 1962
If I Were Seventeen Again, 1980
Kentucky Is My Land, 1952
The Kingdom Within: A Spiritual Autobiography, 1979
Land beyond the River, 1956
Lost Sandstones and Lonely Skies, 1979
Man with a Bull-Tongue Plow, 1934
Mongrel Mettle, 1944
Mr. Gallion's School, 1967
Old Ben, 1970
Red Mule, 1955
"Split Cherry Tree," 1939
Taps for Private Tussie, 1943
The Thread That Runs So True, 1949
To Teach, To Love, 1970
Trees of Heaven, 1940

Styron, William
The Confessions of Nat Turner, 1967
Darkness Visible: A Memoir of Madness, 1990
Lie Down in Darkness, 1951
The Long March, 1953
Set This House on Fire, 1960
Sophie's Choice, 1979
"A Tidewater Morning," 1993

Tabb, John Banister
"Compensation," 1882
"Kildee," 1882
"My Secret," 1882
"The Snow-Bird," 1882

Tate, Allen
The Fathers, 1938
Jefferson Davis: His Rise and Fall, 1929
The Limits of Poetry, 1949

The Mysterious Stranger, 1916
The Prince and the Pauper, 1882
"The Private History of a Campaign That Failed," 1885
Pudd'nhead Wilson, 1894
Roughing It, 1872
Tom Sawyer Abroad, 1894
A Tramp Abroad, 1880

Uhry, Alfred
America's Sweetheart, 1985
Chapeau, 1977
Driving Miss Daisy, 1986
Here's Where I Belong, 1968
The Last Night of Ballyhoo, 1997
Little Johnny Jones, 1982
The Robber Bridegroom (play), 1975
Swing, 1980

Urmstone, John
"Self-Reliance on the Frontier," 1711

Vassa, Gustavus
The Interesting Narrative of the Life of Olaudah Equiano, or Gustavus Vassa, the African; by Himself, 1790

Vollmer, Lula
The Dunce Boy, 1925
The Hills Between, 1938
Moonshine and Honeysuckle, 1938
The Shame Woman, 1923
Sun-Up, 1923
Trigger, 1927

Walker, Alice
Anything We Love Can Be Saved: A Writer's Activism, 1997
The Color Purple, 1982
Finding the Green Stone, 1991
Good Night Willie Lee, I'll See You in the Morning: Poems, 1984
Her Blue Body Everything We Know: Earthling Poems, 1991
Horses Make a Landscape Look More Beautiful, 1984
In Love and Trouble: Stories of Black Women, 1973
In Search of Our Mother's Gardens: Womanist Prose, 1983
"In Search of Zora Neale Hurston," 1974
Langston Hughes, American Poet, 1974
Living by the Word: Selected Writings, 1973–1987, 1988
Meridian, 1976
Once: Poems, 1968
"The Only Reason You Want To Go to Heaven," 1997
Possessing the Secret of Joy, 1992
Revolutionary Petunias and Other Poems, 1973
The Same River Twice, 1996
The Temple of My Familiar, 1989
The Third Life of Grange Copeland, 1970
"To Hell with Dying," 1968

Walker, Alice, *continued*
 Warrior Marks, 1990
 You Can't Keep a Good Woman Down: Stories, 1981

Walker, Margaret
 Ballad of the Free, 1966
 For My People, 1942
 How I Wrote Jubilee, 1972
 Jubilee, 1966
 October Journey, 1973
 Prophets for a New Day, 1970
 Richard Wright, Daemonic Genius: A Portrait of the Man, a Critical Look at His Work, 1985
 This Is My Century: New and Collected Poems, 1989
 Why I Wrote Jubilee and Other Essays on Life and Literature, 1990

Warren, Robert Penn
 All the King's Men, 1946
 Band of Angels, 1955
 Brother to Dragons, 1953
 The Cave, 1959
 Night Rider, 1939
 A Place To Come To, 1977
 "Pure and Impure Poetry," 1942
 Understanding Drama (coauthored by Cleanth Brooks), 1945
 Understanding Fiction (coauthored by Cleanth Brooks), 1943
 Understanding Poetry (coauthored by Cleanth Brooks), 1938
 World Enough and Time, 1950

Washington, Booker T.
 My Larger Education, 1911
 Up from Slavery, 1901

Webb, C. H.
 St. Twel'mo, or, The Cuneiform Cyclopedist of Chattanooga, 1867

Weems, Mason Locke
 The Life of General Francis Marion, 1826
 The Life of Washington, with Curious Anecdotes, Equally Honourable to Himself and Exemplary to His Young Countrymen, 1800

Wells-Barnett, Ida Bell
 Mob Rule in New Orleans, 1900
 The Reason Why the Colored American Is Not in the Columbian Exposition, 1893
 A Red Record: Tabulated Statistics and Alleged Causes of Lynching in the United States, 1892–1893–1894, 1895
 Southern Horrors: Lynch Law in All Its Phases, 1892

Welty, Eudora
 The Collected Stories of Eudora Welty, 1980
 A Curtain of Green and Other Stories, 1941
 "Death of a Traveling Salesman," 1936
 Delta Wedding, 1946
 The Eye of the Story: Selected Essays and Reviews, 1978
 Losing Battles, 1970

One Writer's Beginnings, 1984
The Optimist's Daughter, 1972
The Ponder Heart, 1954
The Robber Bridegroom (novel), 1942
"Where Is the Voice Coming From?," 1963
The Wide Net, and Other Stories, 1943

White, John Blake
Modern Honor, 1812

White, Stewart Edward
Daniel Boone: Wilderness Scout, 1922

Wigginton, Eliot
The Foxfire Book, 1969

Wilde, Richard Henry
"My Life Is like the Summer Rose," 1847
"To the Mocking Bird," 1847

Wilkinson, Eliza Yonge
Letters of Eliza Wilkinson, during the Invasion and Possession of Charlestown, South Carolina, by the British in the Revolutionary War, Arranged from the Original Manuscripts by Caroline Gilman, 1839

Williams, Edwina Dakin
Remember Me to Tom, 1963

Williams, John
The Man Who Cried I Am, 1967

Williams, Tennessee
American Blues, 1948
Battle of Angels, 1940
Beauty Is the World, 1929
Cairo! Shanghai! Bombay!, 1935
Camino Real, 1953
Candles to the Sun, 1937
Cat on a Hot Tin Roof, 1955
"The Field of Blue Children," 1939
The Fugitive, 1960
The Fugitive Kind, 1936
The Glass Menagerie, 1945
Memoir, 1975
The Milk Train Doesn't Stop Here Anymore, 1963
Moise and the World of Reason, 1975
Night of the Iguana, 1961
The Notebook of Trigorin, 1996
Period of Adjustment, 1960
The Red Devil Battery Sign, 1975
The Roman Spring of Mrs. Stone, 1950
The Rose Tattoo, 1950
Small Craft Warnings, 1972
Something Cloudy, Something Clear, 1981
A Streetcar Named Desire, 1947
Suddenly Last Summer, 1958

Williams, Tennessee, *continued*
    Summer and Smoke, 1948
    Sweet Bird of Youth, 1959
    "The Vengeance of Nitrocris," 1928
    "A Worn Path," 1941
    You Touched Me!, 1945

Willingham, Calder
    Rambling Rose, 1972

Wilson, Alexander
    American Ornithology; or, The Natural History of the Birds of the United States, 1875

Wilson, Augusta Jane Evans
    Beulah, 1859
    Inez: A Tale of the Alamo, 1855
    Macaria; or Altars of Sacrifice, 1864
    St. Elmo, 1866

Wirt, William
    "An Old Virginia Preacher," ca. 1770

Wolfe, Thomas
    "The Angel on the Porch," 1929
    "The Crisis in Industry," 1919
    From Death to Morning, 1935
    The Hills Beyond, 1941
    Look Homeward Angel: A Story of the Buried Life, 1929
    Of Time and the River: A Legend of Man's Hunger in His Youth, 1935
    "A Portrait of Bascom Hawke," 1932
    The Return of Buck Gavin, 1919
    The Story of a Novel, 1936
    The Web and the Rock, 1939
    You Can't Go Home Again, 1940

Wright, Richard
    American Hunger, 1977
    "Between the World and Me," 1935
    Black Boy: A Record of Childhood and Youth, 1945
    "How 'Bigger' Was Born," 1940
    Lawd Today, 1963
    The Long Dream, 1958
    Native Son, 1940
    The Outsider, 1943
    Savage Holiday, 1954
    Uncle Tom's Children: Five Long Stories, 1938
    "The Voodoo of Hell's Half-Acre," 1923

Yerby, Frank
    Judas, My Brother, 1968

Young, Stark
    So Red the Rose, 1934
    Southern Treasury of Art and Literature, 1937

CHRONOLOGY OF FILMS OF MAJOR WORKS OF SOUTHERN LITERATURE

1916   *Pudd'nhead Wilson*

1931   *Huckleberry Finn*

1935   *So Red the Rose*

1938   *The Adventures of Tom Sawyer*

1939   *Gone with the Wind*
         Huckleberry Finn

1941   *The Little Foxes*

1943   *Cabin in the Cotton*
         Watch on the Rhine

1946   *The Searching Wind*
         Song of the South
         The Yearling

1948   *Another Part of the Forest*

1949   *All the King's Men*
         Intruder in the Dust
         The Sun Comes Up

1950   *The Glass Menagerie*
         Native Son

1951   *A Streetcar Named Desire*

1952   *The Member of the Wedding*

1954   *The Wanton Countess*

1955   *Rose Tattoo*

1956   *Baby Doll*

1957   *Band of Angels*
         Orpheus Descending

1958   *Cat on a Hot Tin Roof*
         The Long Hot Summer

1959   *Porgy and Bess*
         The Sound and the Fury
         Suddenly Last Summer

1960   *All the Way Home*
         Huckleberry Finn
         Sanctuary
         The Sound and the Fury
         Tomorrow

1961   *Breakfast at Tiffany's*
         The Children's Hour
         The Pit and the Pendulum
         The Roman Spring of Mrs. Stone
         Summer and Smoke

1962   *Sweet Bird of Youth*
         To Kill a Mockingbird

1963   *Old Yeller*
         The Sky Is Gray
         Spencer's Mountain

1964   *The Masque of the Red Death*
         Night of the Iguana

1965   *Baby, the Rain Must Fall*

1966   *A Christmas Memory*
         This Property Is Condemned

1967   *Hurry Sundown*
         In Cold Blood
         Reflections in a Golden Eye

1968   *Boom*
         The Heart Is a Lonely Hunter
         The Thanksgiving Visitor

1969   *Last of the Mobile Hotshots*
         The Reivers
         True Grit

1973   *Tom Sawyer*

1974   *The Autobiography of Miss Jane Pittman*

1974 *continued*
Conrack
Huckleberry Finn

1977 *A Hero Ain't Nothin' but a Sandwich*
Julia

1978 *Summer of My German Soldier*
Tiger Tail

1979 *Gal Young 'Un*
The Great Santini
I Know Why the Caged Bird Sings

1980 *Barn Burning*
The Lords of Discipline

1981 *The Prince of Tides*

1982 *The End of August*
Sophie's Choice

1983 *Pudd'nhead Wilson*

1985 *The Color Purple*
The Trip to Bountiful

1986 *Crimes of the Heart*
Native Son
'night, Mother

1987 *A Gathering of Old Men*
The Glass Menagerie

1989 *Driving Miss Daisy*
Miss Firecracker
Steel Magnolias

1990 *The Ballad of the Sad Café*
Cold Sassy Tree

1991 *Fried Green Tomatoes at the Whistle*
Stop Cafe
Rambling Rose

1993 *The Adventures of Huckleberry Finn*

1994 *A Worn Path*

1997 *Bastard Out of Carolina*
The Grass Harp

PRIMARY SOURCES
Books

Agee, James. *A Death in the Family*. New York: Bantam, 1969.

———. *Let Us Now Praise Famous Men*. New York: Ballantine, 1960.

———. *The Morning Watch*. New York: Ballantine, 1966.

Allison, Dorothy. *Bastard Out of Carolina*. New York: Dutton, 1992.

Angelou, Maya. *All God's Children Need Travelin' Shoes*. Boston: G. K. Hall, 1986.

———. *Gather Together in My Name*. New York: Random House, 1974.

———. *I Know Why the Caged Bird Sings*. New York: Bantam, 1970.

———. *Now Sheba Sings the Song*. New York: Dial Books, 1987.

———. *On the Pulse of the Morning*. New York: Random House, 1993.

———. *Poems*. New York: Bantam Books, 1993.

Arnow, Harriette. *The Dollmaker*. New York: Avon Books, 1972.

Audubon, John James. *Audubon's America*. Boston: Houghton Mifflin, 1940.

Audubon, John Woodhouse. *Audubon's Western Journal 1849–1850*. Tucson: University of Arizona, 1984.

Baldwin, Joseph Glover. *The Flush Times of California*. Athens: University of Georgia, 1966.

Benét, Rosemary, and Stephen Vincent Benét. *A Book of Americans*. New York: Farrar & Rinehart, 1933.

Benét, John. *John Brown's Body*. Cutchogue, N.Y.: Buccaneer Books, 1982.

Berry, Wendell. *The Memory of Old Jack*. New York: Harcourt Brace Jovanovich, 1974.

Bledsoe, Jerry. *Bitter Blood*. New York: Onyx Books, 1988.

Bontemps, Arna, ed. *Great Slave Narratives*. Boston: Beacon Press, 1969.

Brooks, Cleanth, and Robert Penn Warren. *Understanding Poetry*. New York: Holt, Rinehart & Winston, 1976.

Brown, Dee. *Bury My Heart at Wounded Knee*. New York: Henry Holt, 1970.

———. *The Fetterman Massacre*. Lincoln: University of Nebraska Press, 1962.

———. *The Gentle Tamers: Women of the Old Wild West*. Lincoln: University of Nebraska, 1958.

———. *Hear That Lonesome Whistle Blow: Railroads in the West*. New York: Touchstone, 1977.

———. *Wave High the Banner*. Philadelphia: Macrae-Smith, 1945.

———. *When the Century Was Young*. Little Rock, Ark.: August House, 1993.

Burns, Olive Ann. *Cold Sassy Tree*. New York: Dell, 1984.

———. *Leaving Cold Sassy*. New York: Ticknor & Fields, 1992.

Cable, George Washington. *The Grandissimes*. New York: Sagamore Press, 1957.

———. *The Negro Question*. New York: Charles Scribner's Sons, 1898.

———. *Old Creole Days*. New York: Charles Scribner's Sons, 1890.

———. *The Silent South*. Montclair, N.J.: Patterson Smith, 1969.

Caldwell, Erskine. *God's Little Acre*. New York: Signet Books, 1933.

———. *Tobacco Road*. New York: Signet, 1940.

Capote, Truman. *A Capote Reader*. New York: Random House, 1987.

———. *In Cold Blood: A True Account of a Multiple Murder and Its Consequences*. New York: New American Library, 1965.

———. *Local Color*. New York: Random House, 1946.

Carmony, Neil B., ed. *Afield with J. Frank Dobie: Tales of Critters, Campfires, and the Hunting Trail*. Silver City, N.Mex.: High-Lonesome Books, 1992.

Cash, Wilbur J. *The Mind of the South*. New York: Alfred A. Knopf, 1941.

Cather, Willa. *My Ántonia*. Boston: Houghton Mifflin, 1977.

———. *O Pioneers!* In *American Pioneer Writers*. New York: Gallery, 1991.

Chappell, Fred. *I Am One of You Forever*. Baton Rouge: Louisiana State University Press, 1985.

Chesnut, Mary. *Mary Chesnut's Civil War*. New Haven, Conn.: Yale University Press, 1981.

———. *The Private Mary Chesnut: The Unpublished Civil War Diaries*. New York: Oxford University Press, 1984.

Childress, Alice. *A Hero Ain't Nothin' but a Sandwich*. New York: Avon Books, 1973.

Chopin, Kate. *The Awakening and Selected Stories*. New York: Penguin, 1983.

Clark, Barrett, gen. ed. *America's Lost Plays*. Bloomington: Indiana University, 1963.

Clyman, James. *Journal of a Mountain Man*. Missoula, Mont.: Mountain Press, 1984.

Conroy, Pat. *Beach Music*. Garden City, N.Y.: Doubleday, 1995.

———. *The Great Santini*. New York: Bantam, 1987.

————. *The Lords of Discipline*. Boston: Houghton Mifflin, 1980.

————, intro. *Military Brats: Legacies of Childhood inside the Fortress*, by Mary Edwards Wertsch. Bayside, N.Y.: Altheia Productions, 1991.

————. *The Prince of Tides*. Boston: Houghton Mifflin, 1986.

————. *The Water Is Wide*. New York: Bantam, 1987.

Coyner, David H. *The Lost Trappers*. Norman: University of Oklahoma, 1995.

Crockett, David. *A Narrative of the Life of David Crockett*. Cincinnati: U. P. James, 1834.

————. *The Tall Tales of Davy Crockett*. Knoxville: University of Tennessee, 1987.

Custis, George Washington Parke. *Pocahontas, or The Settlers of Virginia* in *Representative American Plays*. New York: D. Appleton-Century, 1938.

————. *Recollections and Private Memoirs of Washington*. Washington, D.C.: William H. Moore, 1859.

Delany, Sarah L., and A. Elizabeth Delany. *The Delany Sisters' Book of Everyday Wisdom*. New York: Dell, 1994.

————. *Having Our Say: The Delany Sisters' First 100 Years*. New York: Dell, 1993.

Dickey, James. *Buckdancer's Choice*. Middletown, Conn.: Wesleyan University Press, 1965.

————. *Deliverance*. New York: Dell, 1970.

————. *Self-Interviews*. Garden City, N.Y.: Doubleday, 1970.

Dobie, Frank. *Apache Gold & Yaqui Silver*. Austin: University of Texas Press, 1990.

————. *The Ben Lilly Legend*. Austin: University of Texas Press, 1978.

————. *The Mustangs*. Boston: Little, Brown, 1952.

Douglass, Frederick. *Autobiographies*. New York: Library of America, 1994.

————. *Narrative of the Life of Frederick Douglass, an American Slave*. New York: New American Library, 1968.

Douglass, Marjory Stoneman. *The Everglades: River of Grass*. New York: Rinehart, 1947.

Drannan, William F. *Thirty-One Years on the Plains and in the Mountains*. Chicago: Rhodes & McClure, 1900.

Edgerton, Clyde. *Raney*. New York: Ballantine, 1985.

————. *Walking across Egypt*. Chapel Hill, N.C.: Algonquin Books of Chapel Hill, 1987.

Ehle, John. *Trail of Tears: The Rise and Fall of the Cherokee Nation*. New York: Anchor, 1988.

Ellison, Ralph. *Invisible Man*. New York: Vintage, 1952.

Evans, Augusta Jane. *St. Elmo*. Tuscaloosa: University of Alabama Press, 1992.

Faulkner, William. *Absalom, Absalom!* New York: Vintage, 1990.

————. *As I Lay Dying*. New York: Vintage, 1964.

———. *Collected Stories*. New York: Vintage, 1977.

———. *Country Lawyer*. Jackson: University Press of Mississippi, 1987.

———. *Go Down, Moses*. New York: Random House, 1991.

———. *Intruder in the Dust*. New York: Random House, 1972.

———. *Light in August*. New York: Vintage, 1985.

———. *The Mansion*. New York: Random House, 1959.

———. *The Portable Faulkner*. New York: Penguin, 1967.

———. *Sartoris*. New York: New American Library, 1964.

———. *The Sound and the Fury*. New York: Vintage, 1984.

———. *The Town*. New York: Random House, 1957.

Flagg, Fannie. *Daisy Fay and the Miracle Man*. New York: Warner Books, 1981.

———. *Fried Green Tomatoes at the Whistle Stop Cafe*. New York: McGraw-Hill, 1987.

Foote, Horton. *The Widow Claire*. In *Best American Plays, Ninth Series, 1983–1992*. New York: Crown, 1993.

Frazier, Charles. *Cold Mountain*. New York: Atlantic Monthly Press, 1997.

Gaines, Ernest J. *The Autobiography of Miss Jane Pittman*. New York: Bantam, 1971.

———. *Bloodline*. New York: Dial Press, 1968.

———. *A Gathering of Old Men*. New York: Vintage, 1983.

———. *A Lesson before Dying*. New York: Alfred A. Knopf, 1993.

Gassner, John, ed. *Best Plays of the American Theatre*. New York: Crown, 1967.

Gibbons, Kaye. *Ellen Foster*. New York: Vintage, 1990.

Gilchrist, Ellen. *The Age of Miracles*. Boston: Little, Brown, 1995.

———. *Drunk with Love*. Boston: Little, Brown, 1986.

———. *Falling through Space*. Boston: Little, Brown, 1987.

———. *I Cannot Get You Close Enough*. Boston: Little, Brown, 1990.

———. *In the Land of Dreamy Dreams*. Fayetteville: University of Arkansas Press, 1981.

———. *Rhoda: A Life in Stories*. Boston: Little, Brown, 1995.

———. *Victory over Japan*. Boston: Little, Brown, 1983.

Giles, Janice Holt. *Hannah Fowler*. Boston: Houghton Mifflin, 1956.

Gilman, Caroline. *The Poetry of Traveling in the United States*. New York: S. Colman, 1838.

Giovanni, Nikki. *Cotton Candy on a Rainy Day*. New York: William Morrow, 1978.

———. *Racism 101*. New York: William Morrow, 1994.

Gipson, Fred. *Old Yeller*. New York: Harper & Row, 1956.

Glasgow, Ellen. *The Battle-Ground*. Garden City, N.Y.: Dougleday, Doran, 1929.

———. *The Collected Stories of Ellen Glasgow*. Baton Rouge: Louisiana Press, 1963.

———. *They Stooped to Folly: A Comedy of Morals*. New York: Literary Guild, 1939.

———. *The Woman Within*. New York: Hill & Wang, 1954.

Godwin, Gail. *A Southern Family*. New York: Avon Books, 1987.

Golden, Harry. *Enjoy, Enjoy!* New York: Permabooks, 1961.

———. *For Two Cents Plain*. New York: World Publishing, 1959.

———. *Only in America*. New York: World Publishing, 1958.

———. *Our Southern Landsman*. New York: G. P. Putnam's Sons, 1974.

Grau, Shirley Ann. *The Keepers of the House*. Greenwich, Conn.: Fawcett Crest, 1964.

Green, Paul. *In Abraham's Bosom*. In *The Literature of the South*. Chicago: Scott, Foresman, 1952.

———. *The Lost Colony: A Symphonic Drama in Two Acts*. Chapel Hill: University of North Carolina, 1937.

———. *Quare Medicine*. In *North Carolina Drama*. Richmond, Va.: Garret & Massie, 1956.

Greene, Bette. *Summer of My German Soldier.* New York: Bantam, 1973.

Greene, Melissa Fay. *Praying for Sheetrock*. Reading, Mass.: Addison-Wesley, 1991.

Griffin, John Howard. *Black Like Me*. New York: New American Library, 1976.

Gurganus, Allan. *Oldest Living Confederate Widow Tells All*. New York: Alfred A. Knopf, 1989.

———. *White People*. New York: Alfred A. Knopf, 1991.

Haley, Alex. *The Autobiography of Malcolm X*. New York: Ballantine, 1964.

———. *A Different Kind of Christmas*. New York: Doubleday, 1988.

———. *Queen: The Story of an American Family*. New York: William Morrow, 1993.

———. *Roots: The Saga of an American Family*. Garden City, N.Y.: Doubleday, 1976.

Hamner, Earl, Jr. *The Homecoming*. New York: Random House, 1970.

———. *Spencer's Mountain*. Cutchogue, N.Y.: Buccaneer Books, 1961.

Harling, Robert. *Steel Magnolias*. New York: Dramatists Play Service, 1988.

Harris, Joel Chandler. *Uncle Remus, His Songs and His Sayings.* New York: Penguin, 1982.

Hellman, Lillian. *The Collected Plays of Lillian Hellman*. Boston: Little, Brown, 1971.

———. *Pentimento*. Boston: Little, Brown and Co., 1973.

————. *Scoundrel Time*. New York: Bantam, 1976.

————. *An Unfinished Woman*. Boston: Little, Brown, 1969.

Henley, Beth. *Beth Henley: Four Plays*. Portsmouth, N.H.: Heinemann, 1992.

————. *Crimes of the Heart*. New York: Penguin, 1981.

————. *Monologues for Women*. Toluca Lake, Calif.: Dramaline Publications, 1992.

Henry, O. *The Complete Works of O. Henry*. Garden City, N.Y.: Doubleday, 1953.

————. *Heart of the West*. Pleasantville, N.Y.: Reader's Digest, 1993.

————. *O. Henry: Selected Stories*. New York: Book-of-the-Month Club, 1994.

Heyward, Dubose. *Porgy*. New York: George H. Doran, 1929.

Hurston, Zora Neale. *The Complete Stories*. New York: HarperCollins, 1995.

————. *Dust Tracks on a Road*. New York: HarperPerennial, 1991.

————. *Mule Bone: A Comedy of Negro Life*. New York: HarperPerennial, 1991.

————. *Their Eyes Were Watching God*. New York: Harper & Row, 1990.

Ivins, Molly. *Molly Ivins Can't Say Those Things, Can She?* New York: Random House, 1991.

Jacobs, Harriet. *Incidents in the Life of a Slave Girl*. New York: Oxford University Press, 1988.

Jarrell, Randall. *The Complete Poems*. New York: Farrar, Straus & Giroux, 1969.

King, Florence. *The Florence King Reader*. New York: St. Martin's, 1995.

————. *Lump It or Leave It*. New York: St. Martin's, 1990.

————. *Reflections in a Jaundiced Eye*. New York: St. Martin's, 1989.

————. *Southern Ladies and Gentlemen*. New York: St. Martin's, 1993.

Larson, Larry, Levi Lee, and Rebecca Wackler. *Tent Meeting*. New York: Dramatists Play Service, 1987.

Lee, Harper. *To Kill a Mockingbird*. New York: Warner Books, 1960.

Lester, Julius. *To Be a Slave*. New York: Scholastic, 1968.

Lewis, Meriwether, and William Clark. *The Journals of Lewis and Clark*. Cambridge, Mass.: Riverside, 1953.

————. *Lewis and Clark Journals*. New York: Atherton, 1922.

Lomax, Alan. *The Land Where the Blues Began*. New York: Pantheon, 1993.

Lomax, John. *Adventures of a Ballad Hunter*. New York: Macmillan, 1947.

Lomax, John, and Alan Lomax. *American Ballads and Folk Songs*. New York: Macmillan, 1934.

Love, Nat. *The Life and Adventures of Nat Love*. Baltimore, Md.: Black Classic Press, 1988.

McCullers, Carson. *The Ballad of the Sad Café and Other Stories*. New York: Bantam, 1951.

————. *The Heart Is a Lonely Hunter*. New York: Bantam, 1967.

————. *The Member of the Wedding* (novel). New York: Bantam, 1973.

————. *The Member of the Wedding* (play). In *Famous American Plays of the 1940s*. New York: Dell, 1960.

————. *Reflections in a Golden Eye*. Boston: Riverside Press, 1941.

McMurtry, Larry. *Lonesome Dove*. New York: Pocket Books, 1985.

Marshall, Catherine. *Christy*. New York: Avon Books, 1967.

Mencken, H. L. *The Impossible H. L. Mencken*. New York: Anchor Books, 1991.

————. *The Vintage Mencken*. New York: Vintage, 1983.

Mitchell, Margaret. *Gone with the Wind*. New York: Warner, 1964.

Moody, Anne. *Coming of Age in Mississippi*. New York: Dell, 1968.

Myers, Walter Dean. *Fallen Angels*. New York: Scholastic, 1988.

Norman, Marsha. *'night Mother*. New York: Hill & Wang, 1983.

O'Connor, Flannery. *The Habit of Being*. New York: Farrar, Straus & Giroux, 1979.

————. *Mystery and Manners*. New York: Farrar, Straus & Giroux, 1969.

————. *Three by Flannery O'Connor*. New York: Signet, 1983.

Owen, Guy. *The Ballad of the Flim-Flam Man*. New York: Pocket Books, 1967.

Peterkin, Julia. *Bright Skin*. Dunwoody, Ga.: Bobbs-Merrill, 1973.

————. *Scarlet Sister Mary*. New York: Grosset & Dunlap, 1928.

Poe, Edgar Allan. *Selected Stories and Poems*. New York: Airmont, 1962.

Porter, Katherine Anne. *The Collected Stories of Katherine Anne Porter*. New York: Harcourt, Brace & World, 1965.

Portis, Charles. *True Grit*. New York: New American Library, 1968.

Price, Reynolds. *Kate Vaiden*. New York: Ballantine, 1986.

————. *A Long and Happy Life*. New York: Avon Books, 1961.

Rawlings, Marjorie Kinnan. *Cross Creek*. New York: Charles Scribner's Sons, 1942.

————. *Jacob's Ladder*. Coral Gables, Fla.: University of Miami Press, 1950.

————. *The Sojourner*. New York: Charles Scribner's Sons, 1953.

————. *South Moon Under*. New York: Charles Scribner's Sons, 1933.

————. *When the Whippoorwill*. New York: Charles Scribner's Sons, 1940.

————. *The Yearling*. New York: Charles Scribner's Sons, 1970.

Ripley, Alexandra. *Scarlett*. New York: Warner Books, 1991.

Roberts, Elizabeth Madox. *Black Is My Truelove's Hair*. New York: Viking Press, 1938.

————. *The Great Meadow*. Nashville, Tenn.: J. S. Sanders, 1930.

Ruark, Robert. *The Old Man and the Boy*. New York: Crest Books, 1957.

Rylant, Cynthia. *Missing May*. New York: Orchard Books, 1992.

———. *Waiting to Waltz . . . a Childhood*. New York: Bradbury, 1984.

Sanchez, Sonia. *Does Your House Have Lions?* Boston: Beacon Press, 1997.

———. *Under a Soprano Sky*. Trenton, N.J.: Africa World Press, 1993.

Sanders, Dori. *Clover*. New York: Fawcett Columbine, 1990.

Simms, William Gilmore. *The Yemassee: A Romance of Carolina*. New Haven, Conn.: College & University Press, 1964.

Smith, John. *Captain John Smith's America: Selections from His Writings*. New York: Harper & Row, 1967.

Spencer, Elizabeth. *The Voice at the Back Door*. New York: Signet Books, 1956.

Stewart, Elinore Pruitt. *Letters of a Woman Homesteader*. Boston: Houghton Mifflin, 1988.

———. *Letters on an Elk Hunt*. Boston: Houghton Mifflin, 1979.

Stuart, Jesse. *The Best-Loved Short Stories of Jesse Stuart*. New York: McGraw-Hill, 1982.

———. *Daughter of the Legend*. New York: McGraw-Hill, 1965.

———. *Hie to the Hunters*. New York: McGraw-Hill, 1950.

———. *My Land Has a Voice*. New York: McGraw-Hill, 1966.

———. *The Thread That Runs So True*. New York: Charles Scribner's Sons, 1949.

Styron, William. *The Confessions of Nat Turner*. New York: Random House, 1967.

———. *Darkness Visible: A Memoir of Madness*. New York: Vintage, 1990.

———. *Lie Down in Darkness*. Indianapolis: Bobbs-Merrill, 1951.

———. *Set This House on Fire*. New York: Random House, 1960.

———. *Sophie's Choice*. New York: Random House, 1979.

———. *A Tidewater Morning: Three Tales from Youth*. New York: Random House, 1993.

Taylor, Mildred. *Roll of Thunder, Hear My Cry*. New York: Dial Books, 1984.

Taylor, Peter. *In the Miro District and Other Stories*. New York: Alfred A. Knopf, 1977.

Taylor, Theodore. *The Cay*. New York: Avon Books, 1970.

———. *Timothy of the Cay*. New York: Avon Books, 1993.

Torrence, Jackie. *The Importance of Pot Liquor*. Little Rock, Ark.: August House, 1994.

Twain, Mark. *The Adventures of Huckleberry Finn*. New York: Airmont, 1962.

———. *The Adventures of Huckleberry Finn*. New York: Random House, 1996.

———. *The Adventures of Tom Sawyer*. New York: Airmont, 1962.

———. *The Autobiography of Mark Twain*. New York: HarperPerennial, 1959.

———. *The Gilded Age*. Garden City, N.Y.: Nelson Doubleday, n.d.

———. *Letters from the Earth*. New York: Harper & Row, 1962.

———. *Life on the Mississippi*. New York: Oxford University Press, 1990.

———. *A Pen Warmed Up in Hell: Mark Twain in Protest*. San Bernardino, Calif.: Borgo Press, 1991.

———. *Pudd'nhead Wilson*. New York: New American Library, 1964.

———. *A Tramp Abroad*. New York: Harper & Brothers, 1906.

Twain, Mark, and Bret Harte. *California Sketches*. New York: Dover, 1991.

Uhry, Alfred. *Driving Miss Daisy*. New York: Theatre Communications Group, 1988.

Vollmer, Lula. *Sun-Up*. In *Representative American Plays from 1767 to the Present Day*. New York: D. Appleton-Century, 1938.

Walker, Alice. *The Color Purple*. New York: Pocket Books, 1982.

Walker, Margaret. *Jubilee*. New York: Bantam, 1966.

Warren, Robert Penn. *All the King's Men*. San Diego, Calif.: Harcourt Brace Jovanovich, 1974.

Welty, Eudora. *The Collected Stories of Eudora Welty*. New York: Harcourt Brace Jovanovich, 1980.

———. *Losing Battles*. New York: Random House, 1970.

———. *One Writer's Beginnings*. Boston: G. K. Hall, 1984.

———. *The Optimist's Daughter*. New York: Random House, 1972.

———. *The Robber Bridegroom*. Garden City, N.Y.: Doubleday, Doran, 1942.

Wigginton, Eliot, ed. *The Foxfire Book*. Garden City, N.Y.: Anchor Books, 1970.

Williams, Tennessee. *Androgyne, Mon Amour*. New York: New Directions, 1977.

———. *The Glass Menagerie*. New York: New Directions, 1949.

———. *Memoirs*. New York: Doubleday, 1975.

———. *A Streetcar Named Desire*. New York: New American Library, 1947.

———. *Summer and Smoke*. In *Best American Plays*. New York: Crown, 1952.

Willingham, Calder. *Rambling Rose*. New York: Delacorte, 1972.

Wolfe, Thomas. *The Complete Short Stories of Thomas Wolfe*. New York: Charles Scribner's Sons, 1987.

———. *Look Homeward, Angel*. New York: Modern Library, 1957.

———. *Of Time and the River*. New York: Grosset & Dunlap, 1935.

Wright, Richard. *American Hunger*. New York: Harper & Row, 1977.

———. *Black Boy*. New York: HarperPerennial, 1966.

———. *Native Son and How "Bigger" Was Born*. New York: HarperPerennial, 1991.

PRIMARY SOURCES

Articles and Short Works

Angelou, Maya. "They Came To Stay," *National Geographic*, August 1989, 208.

———. "Why I Moved Back to the South," *Ebony*, February 1982, 130-134.

Byrd, William. "The History of the Dividing Line," in *Southern Writers: Selections in Prose and Verse*. New York: Macmillan, 1905.

———. "The Secret Diary," in *The Literature of the South*. Chicago: Scott, Foresman, 1952.

Capote, Truman. "A Christmas Memory," in *Focus on Literature: America*. Boston: Houghton Mifflin, 1978.

Delany, Sarah L, and A. Elizabeth Delaney. "200 Years of Wisdom from the Delany Sisters," *Family Circle*, 1 February 1995, 40-43.

Douglass, Frederick. "The North Star," in *The Negro Almanac*. Detroit: Gale Research, 1989.

———. "Prejudice against Color," in *The Faber Book of America*. Boston: Faber & Faber, 1992.

———. "Speech to the American Anti-Slavery Society," in *The American Reader*. New York: HarperCollins, 1990.

———. "What to the Slaves Is the Fourth of July?," in *The American Reader*. New York: HarperCollins, 1990.

Faulkner, William. "The Bear," in *The United States in Literature*. Glenview, Ill.: Scott, Foresman, 1985.

———. "Rose of Lebanon," in *New Stories from the South*. Chapel Hill, N.C.: Algonquin Books, 1996.

———. "A Word to Young Writers," in *Faulkner: Selected Writings*. New York: Holt, Rinehart & Winston, 1969.

Gaines, Ernest J. "Miss Jane and I," *Callaloo*, May 1978, 23–38.

Gordon, Caroline. "The Captive," in *The Literature of the South*. Chicago: Scott, Foresman, 1952.

Harris, Joel Chandler. Uncle Remus stories in *The Literature of the South*. Chicago: Scott, Foresman, 1952.

Henry, O. "A Municipal Report," in *The Literature of the South*. Chicago: Scott, Foresman, 1952.

Henry, Patrick. "Speech to the Virginia Convention, March 1775," in *Southern Writers: Selections in Prose and Verse*. New York: Macmillan, 1905.

Houtchens, C. J. "The Word According to Maya Angelou," *USA Weekend*, 8–10 October 1993, 4–7.

Hunter, Kermit. "Out of History . . . A Lesson," *Unto These Hills* program, 1967, 24–27.

Hurston, Zora Neale. *Dust Tracks on the Road*. In *American Literature: The Makers and the Making*. New York: St. Martin's, 1973.

———. "How It Feels To Be Colored Me," in *The Norton Anthology of Literature by Women*. New York: W. W. Norton, 1985.

———. "Sweat," in *The Norton Anthology of Literature by Women*. New York: W. W. Norton, 1985.

Ivins, Molly. "Commentary: Behold the Powell Bubble," *Lincoln (Nebraska) Star*, 27 September 1995.

Jefferson, Thomas. "The Declaration of Independence," in *The Literature of the South*. Chicago: Scott, Foresman, 1952.

———. "The Testament of Freedom" (oratorio), Randall Thompson, composer. Boston: E. C. Schirmer Music, 1944.

Jordan, Barbara. "The Arts and the American Dream," in *Representative American Speeches, 1992–1993*. Bronx, N.Y.: H. W. Wilson, 1993, 111–117.

Key, Francis Scott. "The Star-Spangled Banner," in *Southern Writers: Selections in Prose and Verse*. New York: Macmillan, 1905.

Lomax, John. "Starving to Death on a Government Claim," in *Accent: U.S.A.* Chicago: Scott, Foresman, 1965.

McCullers, Carson. "Sucker," in *The Short Story and You*. Lincolnwood, Ill.: National Textbook Company, 1986.

"Mike Fink and Davy Crockett," in *Annals of America: 1840*. Chicago: Encyclopedia Britannica, 1968, 574–575.

Peterkin, Julia. "A Proudful Fellow," in *Contemporary Southern Prose*. Boston: D. C. Heath, 1940.

Porter, Katherine Anne. "The Jilting of Granny Weatherall," in *The United States in Literature*. Glenview, Ill.: Scott, Foresman, 1985.

Stuart, Jesse. "Hair," in *Contemporary Southern Prose*. Boston: D. C. Heath, 1940.

———. "What America Means to Me," *Reader's Digest*, August 1982, 33–36.

Twain, Mark. "The Jumping Frog," Wakefield, R.I.: Moyer Bell, 1985.

Walker, Alice. "Listen to Your 'Inner Twin,'" *USA Weekend*, 19–21 January 1996, 15.

———. "The Only Reason You Want To Go to Heaven," *On the Issues*, Spring 1997, 16–23, 54–55.

Warren, Robert Penn. "Sila," *Atlantic*, March 1980, 70–71.

Wilkinson, Eliza. "Letters," in *Southern Writers: Selections in Prose and Verse*. New York: Macmillan, 1905.

Audiovisuals

Benton, Robert. *Places in the Heart*. Video. Farmington Hills, Mich.: Fox Video, 1985.

Capote, Truman. *The Grass Harp*. Video. New York: New Line Home Video, 1997.

Flagg, Fannie. *Fried Green Tomatoes at the Whistle Stop Cafe*. Universal City, Calif.: Universal, 1991.

Gaines, Ernest J. *The Autobiography of Miss Jane Pittman*. New York: Broadway Video Enterprises, 1993.

Haley, Alex, "Alex Haley Tells the Story of His Search for Roots." Disc recording. Deerfield, Ill.: Warner Brothers Records, 1 December 1977.

Harling, Robert. *Steel Magnolias*. Video. New York: Columbia/Tri-Star, 1989.

Henley, Beth. *Crimes of the Heart*. Video. Irving, Calif.: Lorimar, 1986.

McCullers, Carson. *The Heart Is a Lonely Hunter*. Video. New York: Warner, 1968.

O'Connor, Flannery. *Wise Blood*. Video. Artificial Eye, 1979.

Twain, Mark. "The Celebrated Jumping Frog of Calaveras County." Audiocassette and guide. Prince Frederick, Md.: Recorded Books, 1995.

Uhry, Alfred. *Driving Miss Daisy*. Video. New York: Warner/Zanuck, 1989.

Warren, Robert Penn. *Band of Angels*. Colorized video. Burbank, Calif.: Warner Home Video, 1993.

Willingham, Calder. *Rambling Rose*. Video. New York: Carolco, 1991.

Internet

Audubon, John James. *Birds of America*. http://quality.cqs.ch/~rrb/Audubon.html, 1995.

Crockett, Davy. "Colonel Davy Crockett Delivering His Celebrated Speech to Congress on the State of Finances, State Officers, and State Affairs in General." www.midget/towson.edu/%7Eduncan/crockett.htm, 30 July 1996.

Davis, Jefferson. "Inaugural Address and Farewell Address." http://funnelweb.utcc.utk.edu/~hoemann/jdinaug.html, 25 March 1997.

Davis, Varina. "Christmas in the Confederate White House," *New York World*, 13 December 1896. http://www.access.digex.net/~bdboyle/confed.xmas, 24 March 1996.

de Tocqueville, Alexis. *Democracy in America*. http://darwin.clas. virginia./edu~tsawyer/DETOC.home.html, 8 October 1996.

Hellman, Lillian. *The Children's Hour*. http://www.public.iastate.edu/~spires/child.htm, 4 May 1997.

Jackson, Jesse. "After the Million Man March." http://apme.com/jackson.htm, 16 January 1996.

———. "Speech to the 1996 Democratic National Convention." http://www.inmotion-magazine.com/jjdn.html, 5 September 1996.

Jordan, Barbara. "Democratic Convention Keynote Address." http://www.elf.net/bjordan/keynote.html, 19 January 1996.

Mencken, H. L. "Hills of Zion." http://physserv/physics.wisc.edu/~shalizi/mencken/html, 16 March 1996.

———. "Last Words." http://www.bigeye.com/mencken.html, 23 November 1996.

Simms, William Gilmore. "Katherine Walton: or, The Rebel's Daughter," *Godey's Lady's Book*, November 1850. http://www.history.rochester.edu/godeys/12-50/kw.htm, 21 November 1995.

Stuart, Jesse. "The Split Cherry Tree." http://applecity.com/Kids/stories/cherry.html, 3 March 1997.

Twain, Mark. "The Noble Red Man." www.amren.com/indian.htm, 7 June 1996.

"William Faulkner." http://cortex.uchc.edu/~dcarroll/cpbk/mtghs/faulkner.html, 14 February 1997.

"William Faulkner on the Web." http://www.mcsr.olemiss.edu/~egjb/faulkner/faulkner.html, 14 February 1997.

BIBLIOGRAPHY

Adams, Agatha Boyd. *Paul Green of Chapel Hill*. Chapel Hill: University of North Carolina Library Press, 1951.

Adamson, Lynda G. *Recreating the Past: A Guide to American and World Historical Fiction for Children and Adults*. Westport, Conn.: Greenwood Press, 1994.

Afro-American Writers after 1955: Dramatists and Prose Writers. Detroit: Gale Research, 1985.

Ambrose, Stephen E. *Undaunted Courage: Meriwether Lewis, Thomas Jefferson, and the Opening of the American West*. New York: Simon & Schuster, 1996.

Anderson, Madelyn K. *Edgar Allan Poe: A Mystery*. New York: Franklin Watts, 1993.

Anderson, Michael, et al. *Crowell's Handbook of Contemporary Drama*. New York: Thomas Y. Crowell, 1971.

Arner, Robert D. *The Lost Colony in Literature*. Raleigh, N.C.: Department of Cultural Resources, 1985.

Asante, Molefi K., and Mark T. Mattson. *Historical and Cultural Atlas of African Americans*. New York: Macmillan, 1992.

Auchincloss, Louis. *Pioneers and Caretakers: A Study of Nine American Women Novelists*. Minneapolis: University of Minnesota Press, 1965.

Babb, Valerie-Melissa. *Ernest Gaines*. New York: Twayne Publishers, 1991.

Bain, Robert, et al., eds. *Southern Writers: A Biographical Dictionary*. Baton Rouge: Louisiana State University Press, 1979.

Baker, Houston A., Jr., ed. *Twentieth Century Interpretations of Native Son*. Englewood Cliffs, N.J.: Prentice-Hall, 1972.

Baldanza, Frank. *Mark Twain: An Introduction and Interpretation*. New York: Barnes & Noble, 1961.

Barger, James. *William Faulkner: Modern American Novelist and Nobel Prize Winner*. Charlotteville, N.Y.: SamHar Press, 1989.

Barksdale, Richard, and Keneth Kinnamon. *Black Writers of America*. New York: Macmillan, 1972.

Barth, J. Robert, ed. *Religious Perspectives in Faulkner's Fiction: Yoknapatawpha and Beyond*. Notre Dame, Ind.: University of Notre Dame Press, 1989.

Bartlett, John. *Familiar Quotations*. Boston: Little, Brown, 1992.

Beatty, Richmond Croom, et al., eds. *The Literature of the South*. Chicago: Scott, Foresman, 1952.

Benét, Rosemary, and Stephen Vincent Benét. *A Book of Americans*. New York: Farrar & Rinehart, 1933.

Benton, William, publ. *Annals of America*. Chicago: Encyclopedia Britannica, 1968.

Bernard, André. *Now All We Need Is a Title: Famous Book Titles and How They Got That Way*. New York: W. W. Norton, 1955.

Bigelow, Gordon E. *Frontier Eden: The Literary Career of Marjorie Kinnan Rawlings*. Gainesville: University of Florida Press, 1966.

Blain, Virginia, Isobel Grundy, and Patricia Clements. *The Feminist Companion to Literature in English*. New Haven, Conn.: Yale University, 1990.

Blair, Everetta Love. *Jesse Stuart: His Life and Works*. Columbia: University of South Carolina Press, 1967.

Blair, Walter. *Tall Tale America*. New York: Coward-McCann, 1944.

Blankenship, Russell. *American Literature as an Expression of the National Mind*. New York: Henry Holt, 1931.

Bloom, Harold, intro. *Edgar Allan Poe*. New York: Chelsea House, 1985.

———. *James Dickey*. New York: Chelsea House, 1987.

———. *Kate Chopin*. New York: Chelsea House, 1987.

———. *Mark Twain*. New York: Chelsea House, 1986.

———. *Richard Wright*. New York: Chelsea House, 1987.

———. *Richard Wright's Native Son*. New York: Chelsea House, 1988.

———. *William Faulkner*. New York: Chelsea House, 1986.

———. *Zora Neale Hurston*. New York: Chelsea House, 1986.

———. *Zora Neale Hurston's "Their Eyes Were Watching God."* New York: Chelsea House, 1987.

Bloom, Lynn Z. "Maya Angelou." In *Dictionary of Literary Biography*. Vol. 38. Detroit: Gale Research, 1985.

Blotner, Joseph. *Faulkner: A Biography*. New York: Random House, 1978.

———. *Robert Penn Warren: A Biography*. New York: Random House, 1997.

Blum, Daniel. *A Pictorial History of the American Theatre, 1900–1951*. New York: Greenberg, 1951.

Boas, Franz, preface. *Mules and Men*. Bloomington: Indiana University Press, 1978.

Bogle, Donald. *Blacks in American Films and Television*. New York: Garland, 1988.

Bonner, Thomas. *The Life and Adventures of Beckwourth*. Lincoln: University of Nebraska Press, 1972.

Bonner, Thomas, Jr. *The Kate Chopin Companion*. Westport, Conn.: Greenwood Press, 1988.

Bontemps, Arna, ed. *American Negro Poetry*. New York: Hill & Wang, 1974.

Books for Children: 1960–1965. Chicago: American Library Association, 1966.

Boorstin, Daniel J. *The Americans: The Colonial Experience*. New York: Vintage, 1965.

———. *The Americans: The Democratic Experience*. New York: Vintage, 1974.

———. *The Americans: The National Experience*. New York: Vintage, 1958.

———. *The Creators: A History of Heroes of the Imagination*. New York: Vintage, 1992.

Boren, Lynda S., and Sara D. Davis, eds. *Kate Chopin Reconsidered: Beyond the Bayou*. Baton Rouge: Louisiana State University Press, 1992.

Botkin, B. A., ed. *A Treasury of American Folklore*. New York: Crown, 1944.

Bowler, Ellen, et al. *The American Experience*. Upper Saddle River, N.J.: Prentice-Hall, 1996.

Bradbury, John. *Renaissance in the South*. Chapel Hill: University of North Carolina Press, 1963.

Bradbury, Malcolm, gen. ed. *The Atlas of Literature*. London: De Agostini Editions, 1996.

Breitman, George. *The Last Year of Malcolm X*. Pittsburgh, Pa: Merit, 1967.

———. *Malcolm X: The Man and His Ideas*. Pittsburgh, Pa.: Merit, 1965.

Brockett, Oscar G. *History of the Theatre*. Boston: Allyn & Bacon, 1968.

Brooks, Cleanth, R. W. B. Lewis, and Robert Penn Warren, eds. *American Literature: The Makers and the Making*. New York: St. Martin's, 1973.

Brown, Carolyn S. *The Tall Tale in American Folklore and Literature*. Knoxville: University of Tennessee Press, 1987.

Brown, Dee. *Wave High the Banner*. Philadelphia: Macrae-Smith, 1945.

Bruck, Peter, ed. *The Black American Short Story in the Twentieth Century: A Collection of Critical Essays*. Amsterdam: B. R. Gruner, 1977.

Brunvand, Jan Harold, ed. *American Folklore: An Encyclopedia*. New York: Garland, 1996.

Buck, Claire, ed. *The Bloomsbury Guide to Women's Literature*. New York: Prentice-Hall, 1992.

Budd, Louis J. *Critical Essays on Mark Twain*. Boston: G. K. Hall, 1983.

Budd, Louis J., and Edwin H. Cady, eds. *On Poe*. Durham, N.C.: Duke University Press, 1993.

Burdick, Jacques. *Theater*. New York: Newsweek Books, 1974.

Burns, Landon C. *Pat Conroy: A Critical Companion*. Westport, Conn.: Greenwood Press, 1996.

Butler, Robert. *Native Son: The Emergence of a New Black Hero*. Boston: Twayne Publishers, 1991.

Cady, Edwin H., ed. *Literature of the Early Republic*. San Francisco: Rinehart Press, 1967.

Calhoun, Richard J., and Robert W. Hill. *James Dickey*. Boston: Twayne Publishers, 1983.

Carr, Virginia Spencer. *The Lonely Hunter: A Biography of Carson McCullers*. Garden City, N.Y.: Doubleday, 1975.

Carson, Clayborne. *Malcolm X: The FBI File*. New York: Carroll & Graf, 1991.

Chapman, Abraham, ed. *Black Voices*. New York: New American Library, 1968.

Chapman, Mary Lewis, ed. *Literary Landmarks: A Guide to Homes and Memorials of American Writers*. Williamsburg, Va.: Literary Sketches Magazine, 1974.

Christ, Carol P. *Diving Deep and Surfacing: Women Writers on Spiritual Quest*. Boston: Beacon Press, 1980.

Clark, Emily. *Innocence Abroad*. New York: Alfred A. Knopf, 1931.

Clarke, Graham, ed. *Edgar Allan Poe: Critical Assessments*. New York: Routledge, 1991.

Clarke, John Henrik, ed. *William Styron's Nat Turner: Ten Black Writers Respond*. Boston: Beacon Press, 1968.

Clinton, Catherine, ed. *Half Sisters of History: Southern Women and the American Past*. Durham, N.C.: Duke University Press, 1994.

Coad, Oral Sumner, and Edwin Mims, Jr. *The American Stage*. New Haven, Conn.: Yale University, 1929.

Colbert, David. *Eyewitness to America*. New York: Pantheon, 1997.

Cook, Richard M. *Carson McCullers*. New York: Frederick Ungar, 1975.

Cowie, Alexander. *The Rise of the American Novel*. New York: American Book, 1951.

Crystal, David. *The Cambridge Encyclopedia of Language*. New York: Cambridge University Press, 1987.

———. *The Cambridge Encyclopedia of the English Language*. New York: Cambridge University Press, 1995.

Culley, Margo, ed. *A Day at a Time: The Diary Literature of American Women from 1764 to the Present*. New York: Feminist Press, 1985.

Cunliffe, Marcus. *American Literature since 1900*. London: Sphere Books, 1987.

Current Biography. New York: H. W. Wilson, 1961.

Davidson, Cathy N., and Linda Wagner-Martin. *The Oxford Companion to Women's Writing*. New York: Oxford University Press, 1995.

Davis, Richard Beale, et al. *Southern Writing: 1585–1920*. New York: Odyssey Press, 1970.

Davis, Sara de Saussure, and Philip F. Beidler, eds. *The Mythologizing of Mark Twain*. Tuscaloosa: University of Alabama, 1984.

De Montreville, Doris, and Elizabeth D. Crawford, eds. *Fourth Book of Junior Authors and Illustrators*. New York: H. W. Wilson, 1978.

Derr, Mark. *The Frontiersman: The Real Life and the Many Legends of Davy Crockett*. New York: William Morrow, 1993.

Deur, Lynne. *Indian Chiefs*. Minneapolis: Lerner, 1972.

Dictionary of Literary Biography. Vols. 2, 33, 35. Detroit: Gale Research, 1978, 1984, 1985.

Dictionary of Literary Biography Yearbook: 1986. Detroit: Gale Research, 1987.

Dockstader, Frederick J. *Great North American Indians*. New York: Van Nostrand Reinhold, 1977.

Dodds, Barbara. *Negro Literature for High School Students*. Champaign, Ill.: National Council of Teachers of English, 1968.

Dorman, James. *Theater in the Ante Bellum South*. Chapel Hill: University of North Carolina Press, 1967.

Dorson, Richard M. *American Folklore*. Chicago: University of Chicago Press, 1959.

Drabble, Margaret, ed. *The Oxford Companion to English Literature*. New York: Oxford University Press, 1985.

Ehle, John. *Trail of Tears: The Rise and Fall of the Cherokee Nation*. New York: Anchor Books, 1988.

Ehrlich, Eugene, and Gorton Carruth. *The Oxford Illustrated Literary Guide to the United States*. New York: Oxford University Press, 1982.

Eliade, Mircea, ed. *The Encyclopedia of Religion*. New York: Macmillan, 1987.

Elliott, Jeffrey M., ed. *Conversations with Maya Angelou*. Greenwood: University Press of Mississippi, 1989.

Ellis, Joseph J. *American Sphinx: The Character of Thomas Jefferson*. New York: Alfred A. Knopf, 1997.

Emerson, Everett. *American Literature, 1764–1789: The Revolutionary Years*. Madison: University of Wisconsin Press, 1977.

———. *The Authentic Mark Twain: A Literary Biography of Samuel L. Clemens*. Philadelphia: University of Pennsylvania Press, 1985.

Estell, Kenneth, ed. *The African-American Almanac*. Detroit: Gale Research, 1993.

Evans, Chad. *Frontier Theatre*. Victoria, B.C.: Sono Nis Press, 1983.

Evans, Elizabeth. *Anne Tyler*. New York: Twayne Publishers, 1993.

Fabre, Michel. *Richard Wright: Books and Writers*. Jackson: University Press of Mississippi, 1990.

Faust, Langdon Lynne. *American Women Writers*. New York: Ungar, 1988.

Fetterley, Judith. *American Women Regionalists*. New York: W. W. Norton, 1992.

Foerstel, Herbert N. *Banned in the U.S.A.: A Reference Guide to Book Censhorship in Schools and Public Libraries*. Westport, Conn.: Greenwood Press, 1994.

Foreman, Grant. *Sequoyah*. Norman: University of Oklahoma Press, 1938.

Forkner, Ben. *Southern Reader*. Atlanta: Peachtree Publications, 1986.

Fowler, Virginia C. *Conversations with Nikki Giovanni*. Jackson: University Press of Mississippi, 1992.

————. *Nikki Giovanni*. New York: Twayne Publishers, 1992.

Fraistat, Rose. *Caroline Gordan as Novelist and Woman of Letters*. Baton Rouge: Louisiana State University Press, 1984.

Fuller, Muriel, ed. *More Junior Authors*. New York: H. W. Wilson, 1961.

Fulton, Maurice Garland, ed. *Southern Life in Southern Literature*. New York: Ginn & Company, 1917.

Gallay, Alan, ed. *Voices of the Old South: Eyewitness Accounts, 1528–1861*. Athens: University of Georgia Press, 1994.

Gamse, Albert, arr. *World's Favorite Folk Songs*. New York: Ashley Publications, 1961.

Gassner, John, and Edward Quinn, eds. *The Reader's Encyclopedia of World Drama*. New York: Thomas Y. Crowell, 1969.

Gaudet, Marcia, and Carl Wooten. *Porch Talk with Ernest Gaines: Conversations on the Writer's Craft*. Lafayette: Louisiana State University, 1990.

Gayle, Addison, Jr. *Richard Wright: Ordeal of a Native Son*. Garden City, N.Y.: Anchor Press, 1980.

————. *The Way of the New World: The Black Novel in America*. New York: Doubleday, 1975.

Georgiou, Constantine. *Children and Their Literature*. New York: Prentice-Hall, 1969.

Gilbert, Sandra M., and Susan Gubar, eds. *The Norton Anthology of Literature by Women*. New York: W. W. Norton, 1985.

Gillespie, John, and Diana Lembo. *Junior Plots: A Book Talk Manual for Teachers and Librarians*. New York: R. R. Bowker, 1967.

Goring, Rosemary, ed. *Larousse Dictionary of Writers*. New York: Larousse Kingfisher Chambers, 1994.

Graff, Henry F., ed. *The Presidents: A Reference History*. New York: Charles Scribner's Sons, 1996.

Gremstead, David. *Melodrama Unveiled: American Theater and Culture 1800–1850*. Berkeley: University of California Press, 1968.

Grenander, M. E. *Ambrose Bierce*. New York: Twayne Publishers, 1971.

Grigson, Geoffrey, ed. *The Concise Encyclopedia of Modern World Literature*. New York: Hawthorn Books, 1963.

Griswold, Jerry. *The Classic American Children's Story: Novels of the Golden Age*. New York: Penguin, 1992.

Gross, Theodore L. *The Heroic Ideal in American Literature*. New York: Free Press, 1971.

————. *Literature of American Jews*. New York: Free Press, 1973.

Guilds, John Caldwell, ed. *Nineteenth-Century Southern Fiction*. Columbus, Ohio: Charles E. Merrill, 1970.

Hall, Donald, and D. L. Emblen. *A Writer's Reader*. Boston: Little, Brown, 1985.

Hallowell, John. *Between Fact and Fiction: New Journalism and the Nonfiction Novel*. Chapel Hill: University of North Carolina Press, 1977.

Hanes, Colonel. *Bill Pickett*. Norman: University of Oklahoma Press, 1989.

Harlow, Alvin F. *Joel Chandler Harris (Uncle Remus): Plantation Storyteller*. New York: Julian Messner, 1941.

Harris, Leon A. *The Fine Art of Political Wit*. New York: E. P. Dutton, 1964.

Hart, James D. *The Oxford Companion to American Literature*. New York: Oxford University Press, 1983.

Hartnoll, Phyllis, ed. *The Oxford Companion to the Theater*. New York: Oxford University Press, 1983.

Haskins, Jim. *The Harlem Renaissance*. Brookfield, Conn.: Millbrook Press, 1996.

Hazard, Lucy Lockwood. *The Frontier in American Literature*. New York: Thomas Y. Crowell, 1927.

Hemenway, Robert. *Zora Neale Hurston: A Literary Biography*. Champaign: University of Illinois Press, 1977.

Hendrick, George. *Katherine Anne Porter*. New York: Twayne Publishers, 1965.

Herron, Ima Honaker. *The Small Town in American Literature*. Durham, N.C.: Duke University Press, 1939.

Herzberg, Max J. *The Reader's Encyclopedia of American Literature*. New York: Thomas Y. Crowell, 1962.

Hewitt, Barnard. *Theatre U.S.A.: 1665–1957*. New York: McGraw-Hill, 1959.

Hibbard, Addison, ed. *Stories of the South, Old and New*. Chapel Hill: University of North Carolina Press, 1931.

Hicks, Jack. *In the Singer's Temple: Prose Fictions of Barthelme, Gaines, Brautigan, Piercy, Kesey, and Kosinski*. Chapel Hill: University of North Carolina Press, 1981.

Higgs, Robert J., and Ambrose N. Manning, eds. *Voices from the Hills: Selected Readings of Southern Appalachia*. New York: Frederick Ungar, 1975.

Hill, Herbert, ed. *Anger and Beyond*. New York: Harper & Row, 1966.

Hill, Jane. *Gail Godwin*. New York: Twayne Publishers, 1992.

Hine, Darlene Clark, et al., eds. *Black Women in America: An Historical Encyclopedia*. Bloomington: Indiana University Press, 1993.

Hitchcock, H. Wiley, and Stanley Sadie, eds. *The New Grove Dictionary of American Music*. New York: Macmillan, 1980.

Hoffman, A. J. *Twain's Heroes, Twain's Worlds*. Philadelphia: University of Pennsylvania Press, 1988.

Hoffman, Miriam, and Eva Samuels. *Authors and Illustrators of Children's Books*. New York: R. R. Bowker, 1972.

Hogg, Peter. *Slavery: The Afro-American Experience*. London: British Library, 1979.

Holloway, Karla F. *The Character of the Word*. Westport, Conn.: Greenwood Press, 1987.

Hornsby, Alton. *African American Chronology*. Detroit: Gale Research, 1994.

Hornstein, Lillian Herlands, ed. *The Reader's Companion to World Literature*. New York: New American Library, 1973.

Howard, Lillie P. *Zora Neale Hurston*. Boston: Twayne Publishers, 1980.

Howe, Irving. *William Faulkner: A Critical Study*. New York: Vintage, 1952.

Hoyle, Bernadette. *Tar Heel Writers I Know*. Winston-Salem, N.C.: John F. Blair, 1956.

Hoyt, Harlowe R. *Town Hall Tonight: Intimate Memories of the Grassroots Days of the American Theatre*. Englewood Cliffs, N.J.: Prentice-Hall, 1955.

Hudson, Arthur Palmer. *Humor of the Old Deep South*. New York: Macmillan, 1936.

Hudson, Theodore R. *A History of Southern Literature*. Lafayette: Louisiana State University Press, 1985.

Hughes, Glenn. *A History of American Theatre 1700–1750*. New York: Samuel French, 1951.

————. *The Story of the Theatre*. New York: Samuel French, 1938.

Hughes, Langston, and Milton Meltzer. *A Pictorial History of the Negro in America*. New York: Crown, 1968.

Humphries, Jefferson, ed. *Conversations with Reynolds*. Jackson: University Press of Mississippi, 1991.

Inge, Tonette Bond, ed. *Southern Women Writers: The New Generation*. Tuscaloosa: University of Alabama, 1990.

Jackson, George Pullen. *White Spirituals in the Southern Uplands: The Story of the Fasola Folk, Their Songs, Singings, and "Buckwheat Notes."* Chapel Hill: University of North Carolina Press, 1933.

Johnson, Allen, and Dumas Malone, eds. *Dictionary of American Biography*. New York: Charles Scribner's Sons, 1930.

Jones, Ann Goodwyn. *Tomorrow Is Another Day: The Woman Writer in the South, 1859–1936*. Baton Rouge: Louisiana State University Press, 1981.

Jones, James Earl, and Penelope Niven. *James Earl Jones: Voices and Silences*. New York: Touchstone, 1993.

Jones, John. *Mississippi Writers Talking I*. Jackson: University of Mississippi Press, 1982.

————. *Mississippi Writers Talking II*. Jackson: University of Mississippi Press, 1983.

Kaplan, Justin, gen. ed. *Mister Clemens and Mark Twain: A Biography*. New York: Simon & Schuster, 1966.

Karanikas, Alexander. *Tillers of a Myth*. Madison: University of Wisconsin Press, 1966.

Katz, Ephraim. *The Film Encyclopedia*. New York: Perigee Books, 1982.

Kerber, Linda K. *Women of the Republic: Intellect and Ideology*. New York: W. W. Norton, 1986.

Kesterson, David B., ed. *Critics on Mark Twain*. Baltimore, Md.: University of Maryland Press, 1979.

Ketchin, Susan. *The Christ-Haunted Landscape: Faith and Doubt in Southern Fiction*. Jackson: University Press of Mississippi, 1994.

King, Richard H. *A Southern Renaissance: The Cultural Awakening of the American South, 1930–1955*. Oxford: Oxford University Press, 1980.

Kingston, Carolyn T. *The Tragic Mode in Children's Literature*. New York: Columbia University Teachers College Press, 1974.

Kirkpatrick, D. L., ed. *Twentieth-Century Children's Writers*. New York: St. Martin's, 1983.

Klein, Leonard S., ed. *Encyclopedia of World Literature in the Twentieth Century*. New York: Frederick Ungar, 1981.

Koch, Frederick H. *Carolina Folk-Plays*. New York: Henry Holt, 1922.

Koloski, Bernard, ed. *Approaches to Teaching Chopin's the Awakening*. New York: Modern Language Association, 1988.

Krutch, Joseph W. *Edgar Allan Poe: A Study in Genius*. Irvine, Calif.: Reprint Service, 1992.

Kunitz, Stanley J. *Twentieth Century Authors*. New York: H. W. Wilson, 1942.

Kunitz, Stanley J., and Howard Haycraft. *American Authors: 1600–1900*. New York: H. W. Wilson, 1938.

Lamar, Howard R., ed. *The Reader's Encyclopedia of the American West*. New York: Harper & Row, 1977.

Laskin, David. *A Common Life: Four Generations of American Literary Friendship and Influence*. New York: Simon & Schuster, 1994.

Lavender, David. *The Way to the Western Sea*. New York: Harper & Row, 1988.

Lederer, Katherine. *Lillian Hellman*. Boston: Twayne Publishers, 1979.

Leeming, David Adams. *The World of Myth*. New York: Oxford University Press, 1990.

Lefler, Hugh T., and William S. Powell. *Colonial North Carolina: A History*. New York: Charles Scribner's Sons, 1973.

Leisy, Ernest E. *The American Historical Novel*. Norman: University of Oklahoma Press, 1950.

Levine, Miriam. *A Guide to Writers' Homes in New England*. Cambridge, Mass.: Apple-Wood Books, 1984.

Levine, Robert. *Conspiracy and Romance: Studies in Brockden Brown, Cooper, Hawthorne, and Melville*. London: Cambridge University Press, 1989.

Lewis, David Levering. *When Harlem Was in Vogue*. New York: Alfred A. Knopf, 1981.

Lewis, Kate Porter. *Alabama Folk Plays*. Chapel Hill: University of North Carolina Press, 1943.

Loban, Walter, et al. *Adventures in Appreciation*. New York: Harcourt, Brace & World, 1958.

Lockerbie, D. Bruce, gen. ed. *Faulkner: Selected Writings*. New York: Holt, Rinehart & Winston, 1969.

———. *Poe*. New York: Holt, Rinehart & Winston, 1969.

Low, W. Augustus, and Virgil A. Clift, eds. *Encyclopedia of Black America*. New York: Da Capo, 1981.

Lowe, James. *The Creative Process of James Agee*. Baton Rouge: Louisiana State University Press, 1994.

Lyons, Mary E. *Sorrow's Kitchen: The Life and Folklore of Zora Neale Hurston*. New York: Macmillan, 1990.

Lyttle, Richard B. *Mark Twain: The Man and His Adventures*. New York: Atheneum, 1994.

McArthur, Tom, ed. *The Oxford Companion to the English Language*. New York: Oxford University Press, 1992.

McHenry, Robert. *Liberty's Women*. Springfield, Mass.: G. & C. Merriam, 1980.

McPherson, Dolly. *Order Out of Chaos: The Autobiographical Works of Maya Angelou*. New York: Peter Lang, 1990.

McVoy, Lizzie Carter, ed. *Louisiana in the Short Story*. Baton Rouge: Louisiana State University, 1940.

Maggio, Rosalie, comp. *The Beacon Book of Quotations by Women*. Boston: Beacon Press, 1992.

————. *The New Beacon Book of Quotations by Women*. Boston: Beacon Press, 1996.

Magill, Frank N., ed. *Cyclopedia of World Authors*. New York: Harper & Brothers, 1958.

Magnusson, Magnus, gen. ed. *Cambridge Biographical Dictionary*. New York: Cambridge University Press, 1990.

Malin, Irving, ed. *Truman Capote's* In Cold Blood: *A Critical Handbook*. Belmont, Calif.: Wadsworth Publishing, 1968.

Malone, Dumas, ed. *Dictionary of American Biography*. New York: Charles Scribner's Sons, 1933.

Manning, Carol. *With Ears Opening like Morning Glories*. Westport, Conn.: Greenwood Press, 1985.

Marquardt, Dorothy A., and Martha E. Ward. *Authors of Books for Young People*. New York: Scarecrow, 1979.

Marshall, Sara. *The South*. New York: Charles Scribner's Sons, 1979.

Martin, Mick, and Marsha Porter. *Video Movie Guide 1995*. New York: Ballantine, 1995.

Martin, Wendy, ed. *New Essays on* The Awakening. New York: Cambridge University Press, 1988.

Meigs, Cornelia, ed. *A Critical History of Children's Literature*. New York: Macmillan, 1969.

Meyers, Jeffrey. *Edgar Allan Poe: Life and Legacy*. New York: Macmillan, 1992.

Miller, James, et al. *The United States in Literature*. Glenview, Ill.: Scott, Foresman, 1987.

Miller, Jordan Y. *Twentieth Century Interpretations of* A Streetcar Named Desire. New York: Prentice-Hall, 1971.

Minter, David. *William Faulkner: His Life and Work*. Baltimore, Md.: Johns Hopkins, 1982.

Moates, Marianne M. *A Bridge of Childhood: Truman Capote's Southern Years*. New York: Henry Holt, 1989.

Monaco, James, ed. *The Encyclopedia of Film*. New York: Perigee, 1991.

Moody, Richard. *Dramas from the American Theatre*. Cleveland: World Publishing, 1966.

Morris, Roy, Jr. *Ambrose Bierce: Alone in Bad Company*. New York: Crown, 1995.

Morrison, Samuel E. *The European Discovery of America: Southern Voyages*. New York: Oxford University Press, 1974.

Mullane, Deirdre. *Crossing the Danger Water: Three Hundred Years of African-American Writing*. New York: Anchor Books, 1993.

Nance, William L. *The Worlds of Truman Capote*. New York: Stein & Day, 1970.

Nathiri, N. Y., ed. *Zora! A Woman and Her Community*. Crystal River, Fla.: Sentinel, 1991.

The National Cyclopedia of American Biography. Ann Arbor, Mich.: University Microfilms, 1967.

Nevins, Allan. *The Emergence of Modern America*. Chicago: Quadrangle, 1955.

Nicoll, Allardyce. *The Development of the Theatre*. New York: Harcourt, Brace, 1937.

O'Brien, John, ed. *An Interview with Black Writers*. New York: Liveright, 1973.

O'Connor, Richard. *Bret Harte: A Biography*. Boston: Little, Brown, 1966.

O'Connor, William V. *William Faulkner*. Ann Arbor, Mich.: Books Demand UMI, 1989.

Papke, Mary E. *Verging on the Abyss: The Social Fiction of Kate Chopin and Edith Wharton*. Westport, Conn.: Greenwood Press, 1990.

Parker, R. B., ed. *The Glass Menagerie: A Collection of Critical Essays*. New York: Prentice-Hall, 1983.

Parks, Edd Winfield. *Southern Poets*. New York: Phaeton Press, 1970.

Parsons, Thornton H. *John Crowe Ransom*. New York: Twayne Publishers, 1969.

Patterson, Lotsee, and Mary Ellen Snodgrass. *Indian Terms*. Englewood, Colo.: Libraries Unlimited, 1994.

Payne, Ladell. *Black Novelists and the Southern Literary Tradition*. Athens: University of Georgia Press, 1981.

Pederson, Jay. *African American Almanac*. Detroit: Gale Research, 1994.

Perkins, David, ed. *Books of Passage*. Asheboro, N.C.: Down Home Press, 1997.

Perkins, George, et al., eds. *Benét's Reader's Encyclopedia of American Literature*. New York: HarperCollins, 1991.

Petry, Alice Hall. *A Genius in His Way: The Art of Cable's Old Creole Days*. Cranbury, N.J.: Associated University Presses, 1988.

Ploski, Harry A., and James Williams, eds. *The Negro Almanac*. Detroit: Gale Research, 1989.

Poe, Clarence, and Charles Aycock Poe. *Poe-Pourri: A North Cavalcade*. Dallas: Taylor Publishing, 1987.

Popkin, Michael, ed. *Modern Black Writers*. New York: Frederick Ungar, 1978.

Porter, A. P. *Jump at de Sun: The Story of Zora Neale Hurston*. Minneapolis: Carolrhoda, 1992.

Porter, Dorothy. *Early Negro Writing: 1760–1837*. Baltimore, Md.: Black Classic Press, 1995.

Powell, Brenda. *African American Biography*. Detroit: Gale Research, 1994.

Powell, Dannye Romine. *Parting the Curtains: Interviews with Southern Writers*. Winston-Salem, N.C.: John F. Blair, 1994.

Prideaux, Tom. *World Theatre in Pictures*. New York: Greenberg, 1953.

Pritchard, William H. *Randall Jarrell: A Literary Life*. New York: Farrar, Straus & Giroux, 1990.

Pyron, Darden Asbury. *Southern Daughter: The Life of Margaret*. New York: Oxford University Press, 1991.

Quarles, Benjamin. *Frederick Douglass*. Englewood Cliffs, N.J.: Prentice-Hall, 1968.

Quinn, Arthur Hobson. *American Fiction: An Historical and Critical Survey*. New York: D. Appleton-Century, 1936.

———. *Representative American Plays from 1767 to the Present Day*. New York: D. Appleton-Century, 1938.

Rampersad, Arnold. *The Life of Langston Hughes*. New York: Oxford University Press, 1986.

Rankin, Hugh F. *The Theater in Colonial America*. Chapel Hill: University of North Carolina Press, 1965.

Rasmussen, R. Kent. *Mark Twain A to Z: The Essential Reference to His Life and Writings*. New York: Facts on File, 1995.

Ravitch, Diane, ed. *The American Reader: Words That Moved a Nation*. New York: HarperCollins, 1990.

Rawson, Hugh, and Margaret Miner, comps. *The New International Dictionary of Quotations*. New York: Mentor, 1986.

Redding, J. Saunders. *On Being Negro in America*. Indianapolis, Ind.: Bobbs-Merrill, 1951.

Reilly, John M., ed. *Twentieth-Century Interpretations of* The Invisible Man. New York: Prentice-Hall, 1970.

Ricks, Christopher, and William L. Vance. *The Faber Book of America*. London: Faber & Faber, 1992.

Ridge, Martin. *Atlas of American Frontiers*. Chicago: Rand McNally, 1993.

Roberts, Vera Mowry. *On Stage: A History of Theatre*. New York: Harper & Row, 1962.

Roginski, Jim. *Behind the Covers: Interviews with Authors and Illustrators of Books for Children and Young Adults*. Englewood, Colo.: Libraries Unlimited, 1985.

Rohill, Frank. *The World of Melodrama*. University Park: Pennsylvania State University Press, 1967.

Rollyson, Carl. *Lillian Hellman: Her Legend and Her Legacy*. New York: St. Martin's, 1988.

Rose, Cynthia. *Native North American Almanac*. Detroit: Gale Research, 1994.

Rouse, Blair. *Ellen Glasgow*. New Haven, Conn.: College and University Press, 1962.

Ruas, Charles. *Conversations with American Writers*. New York: Alfred A. Knopf, 1985.

Rubin, Louis D., Jr. *Gallery of Southerners*. Baton Rouge: Louisiana State University Press, 1982.

———. *George W. Cable: The Life and Times of a Southern Heretic*. New York: Pegasus, 1969.

Rubin, Louis D., Jr., and Robert D. Jacobs. *South: Modern Southern Literature in Its Cultural Setting*. New York: Dolphin Books, 1961.

Rubin, Louis D., Jr., et al. *The History of Southern Literature*. Baton Rouge: Louisiana State University Press, 1985.

Ruland, Richard, and Malcolm Bradbury. *From Puritanism to Postmodernism: A History of American Literature*. New York: Penguin, 1991.

Russell, Sharman Apt. *Frederick Douglass*. New York: Chelsea House, 1988.

Rutherford, Mildred Lewis. *The South in History and Literature: A Hand-Book of Southern Authors*. Atlanta, Ga.: Franklin-Turner, 1907.

Sackett, Susan. *The* Hollywood Reporter *Book of Box Office Hits*. New York: Billboard Books, 1996.

Salzman, Jack, et al., eds. *Encyclopedia of African-American Culture and History*. New York: Simon & Schuster, 1996.

Schlesinger, Arthur Meier. *The Rise of the City*. New York: Macmillan, 1971.

Schor, Edith. *Visible Ellison*. Westport, Conn.: Greenwood Press, 1993.

Shalit, Gene, ed. *Laughing Matters: A Celebration of American Humor*. Garden City, N.Y.: Doubleday, 1987.

Shapiro, Miles. *Maya Angelou*. New York: Chelsea House, 1993.

Sheffey, Ruthe T., ed. *Zora Neale Hurston Forum*. Milwaukee, Wis.: Morgan, 1992.

Sherr, Lynn, and Jurate Kazickas. *Susan B. Anthony Slept Here: A Guide to American Women's Landmarks*. New York: Random House, 1994.

Shrader, Dorothy. *Steamboat Legacy*. Hermann, Mo.: Wein Press, 1993.

Shuker, Nancy. *Maya Angelou*. Englewood Cliffs, N.J.: Silver-Burdett, 1990.

Silverman, Kenneth. *Edgar A. Poe: Mournful and Never-Ending Remembrance*. New York: HarperCollins, 1991.

Simonini, R. C., Jr., ed. *Southern Writers: Appraisals in Our Time*. Charlottesville: University Press of Virginia, 1961.

Skaggs, Peggy. *Kate Chopin*. New York: Macmillan, 1985.

Slater, Eileen. *Literature and the Language Arts*. St. Paul, Minn.: EMC/Paradigm Publishing, 1996.

Smith, C. Alphonso. *Southern Literary Studies: A Collection of Literary, Biographical, and Other Sketches*. Port Washington, N.Y.: Kennikat Press, 1967.

Smith, Jessie Carney, ed. *Notable Black American Women*. Detroit: Gale Research, 1992.

Snead, James. *Figures of Division: William Faulkner's Major Novels*. New York: Routledge Chapman and Hall, 1986.

Snodgrass, Mary Ellen. *Celebrating Women's History*. Detroit: Gale Research, 1996.

———. *Characters from Young Adult Literature*. Englewood, Colo.: Libraries Unlimited, 1991.

———. *Crossing Barriers: People Who Overcame*. Englewood, Colo.: Libraries Unlimited, 1993.

———. *The Encyclopedia of Satire*. Santa Barbara, Calif.: ABC-CLIO, 1996.

———. *Encyclopedia of Utopian Literature*. Santa Barbara, Calif.: ABC-CLIO, 1995.

———. *Late Achievers: Famous People Who Succeeded Late in Life*. Englewood, Colo.: Libraries Unlimited, 1992.

———. *Literary Maps from Young Adult Literature*. Englewood, Colo.: Libraries Unlimited, 1995.

———. *Wise Words: A Guide to Language Arts through Aphorism*. Birmingham, Ala.: GCT, 1990.

Snyder, Gerald S. *In the Footsteps of Lewis and Clark*. Washington, D.C.: National Geographic Society, 1970.

Something about the Author. Vols. 2, 11, 65. Detroit: Gale Research, 1972, 1977, 1991.

Spearman, Walter. *North Carolina Writers*. Chapel Hill: University of North Carolina Library Press, 1953.

Spiller, Robert E., and Harold Blodgett, eds. *The Roots of National Culture*. New York: Macmillan, 1939.

Spoto, Donald. *The Kindness of Strangers: The Life of Tennessee Williams*. New York: Little, Brown, 1985.

Stein, Rita. *A Literary Tour Guide to the United States: South and Southwest*. New York: William Morrow, 1979.

Stephens, Robert O. *The Family Saga in the South: Generations and Destinies*. Baton Rouge: Louisiana State University Press, 1995.

Stewart, John L. *The Burden of Time: The Fugitives and Agrarians*. Princeton, N.J.: Princeton University Press, 1965.

———. *John Crowe Ransom*. Minneapolis: University of Minnesota Press, 1962.

Stewart, Paul W., and Wallace Y. Ponce. *Black Cowboys*. Broomfield, Colo.: Phillips Publishing, 1986.

Stick, David. *Roanoke Island: The Beginnings of English America*. Chapel Hill: University of North Carolina Press, 1983.

Straub, Deborah Gillan, ed. *Voices of Multicultural America: Notable Speeches Delivered by African, Asian, Hispanic, and Native Americans, 1790–1995*. Detroit: Gale Research, 1996.

Stuckey, W. J. *The Pulitzer Prize Novels: A Critical Backwood Look*. Norman: University of Oklahoma Press, 1966.

Sullivan, Jack. *Horror and the Supernatural*. New York: Viking Penguin, 1986.

Sullivan, Walter. *The War the Women Lived: Female Voices from the Confederate South*. Nashville, Tenn.: J. S. Sanders, 1995.

Sundquist, Eric J. *Faulkner: The House Divided*. Baltimore, Md.: Johns Hopkins University Press, 1985.

Thomas, Henry, and Dana Lee Thomas. *Living Biographies of Famous Novelists*. Garden City, N.Y.: Blue Ribbon Books, 1943.

Thorp, Willard. *A Southern Reader*. New York: Alfred A. Knopf, 1955.

Tischler, Nancy M. *Tennessee Williams*. Austin, Tex.: Steck-Vaughn, 1969.

Toth, Emily. *Kate Chopin: A Life of the Author of* The Awakening. New York: Morrow, 1993.

Townsend, John Rowe. *A Sense of Story: Essays on Contemporary Writing for Children*. New York: Lippincott, 1971.

———. *Written for Children: An Outline of English Language Children's Literature*. New York: Lippincott, 1965.

Traveller Bird. *Tell Them They Lie*. Los Angeles: Westernlore, 1971.

Trent, W. P., ed. *Southern Writers: Selections in Prose and Verse*. New York: Macmillan, 1905.

Trent, William Peterfield, et al., eds. *The Cambridge History of American Literature*. New York: Macmillan, 1946.

Trotman, James C. *Richard Wright: Myths and Realities*. New York: Garland, 1989.

Turnbull, Andrew. *Thomas Wolfe*. New York: Charles Scribner's Sons, 1968.

Twentieth-Century Children's Writers. New York: St. Martin's, 1983.

Urdang, Lawrence, ed. *Timetables of American History*. New York: Simon & Schuster, 1981.

Van Doren, Mark, ed. *An Anthology of World Poetry*. New York: Harcourt, Brace, 1936.

Video Hound's Golden Movie Retriever. Detroit: Visible Ink, 1994.

Wadlington, Warwick. *Reading Faulknerian Tragedy*. Ithaca, N.Y.: Cornell University Press, 1987.

Wagenknecht, Edward. *Cavalcade of the American Novel*. New York: Holt, Rinehart & Winston, 1952.

———. *Henry Wadsworth Longfellow: His Poetry and Prose*. New York: Continuum, 1986.

Waldman, Carl. *Who Was Who in Native American History*. New York: Facts on File, 1990.

Walker, Alice, ed. I Love Myself When I Am Laughing: *A Zora Neale Hurston Reader*. New York: Feminist Press, 1979.

———. *In Search of Our Mothers' Gardens*. New York: Feminist Press, 1983.

Walker, John, ed. *Halliwell's Film Guide*. New York: HarperPerennial, 1996.

Walker, Margaret. *Richard Wright: Daemonic Genius*. New York: Warner, 1988.

Wall, Cheryl A. *Women of the Harlem Renaissance*. Bloomington: Indiana University Press, 1995.

Walser, Richard, ed. *North Carolina Drama*. Richmond, Va.: Garrett & Massie, 1956.

Wann, Louis, ed. *The Rise of Realism*. New York: Macmillan, 1933.

Ward, Martha E., and Dorothy A. Marquardt. *Authors of Books for Young People*. Metuchen, N.J.: Scarecrow, 1979.

Warfel, Harry. *American Novelists of Today*. New York: American Book, 1951.

Warren, Robert Penn. *Who Speaks for the Negro?* New York: Random House, 1965.

Washington, Mary Helen. *Invented Lives: Narratives of Black Women, 1860–1960*. New York: Anchor Books, 1987.

Watts, Jerry G. *Heroism and the Black Intellectual: Ralph Ellison, Politics and the Dilemmas of Afro-American Intellectual Life*. Chapel Hill: University of North Carolina, 1994.

Weales, Gerald. *Tennessee Williams*. Minneapolis: University of Minnesota Press, 1965.

Weatherford, Doris. *American Women's History*. New York: Prentice-Hall, 1994.

Webb, Constance. *Richard Wright: A Biography*. New York: G. P. Putnam's Sons, 1968.

Welland, Dennis. *The Life and Times of Mark Twain*. New York: Crescent Books, 1991.

Wester, Olga. *Literary and Library Prizes*. New York: R. R. Bowker, 1970.

Westling, Louise. *Sacred Groves and Ravaged Gardens: The Fiction of Eudora Welty, Carson McCullers and Flannery O'Connor*. Athens: University of Georgia Press, 1985.

Wexler, Alan. *Atlas of Westward Expansion*. New York: Facts on File, 1995.

Whitt, Jan. *Allegory and the Modern Southern Novel*. Macon, Ga.: Mercer University Press, 1994.

Wiggins, Robert A. *Ambrose Bierce*. Minneapolis: University of Minnesota Press, 1964.

Wilkins, Thurman. *Cherokee Tragedy: The Story of the Ridge Family and of the Decimation of a People*. New York: Macmillan, 1970.

Williams, John A. *The Most Native of Sons: A Biography of Richard Wright*. Garden City, N.Y.: Doubleday, 1970.

Wilson, Charles Reagan, and William Ferris, eds. *Encyclopedia of Southern Culture*. Chapel Hill: University of North Carolina Press, 1989.

Wintle, Justin, and Emma Fisher. *The Pied Pipers: Interviews with the Influential Creators of Children's Literature*. London: Paddington Press, 1974.

Witalec, Janet. *Native North American Literature*. Detroit: Gale Research, 1994.

Witcover, Paul. *Zora Neale Hurston*. New York: Chelsea House, 1991.

Yates, Janelle. *Zora Neale Hurston: A Storyteller's Life*. Staten Island, N.Y.: Ward Hill, 1991.

Audiovisual Sources

Burns, Ken. "Thomas Jefferson." Documentary. PBS-TV, 7 March 1997.

Contemporary Authors. CD-ROM. Detroit: Gale Research, 1994.

DISCovering Authors. CD-ROM. Detroit: Gale Research, 1993.

Foote, Horton. "Old Man." Teleplay. *Hallmark Hall of Fame*, CBS-TV, 9 February 1997.

"Frederick Douglass." Documentary. *Biography*, Arts and Entertainment, PBS-TV, 5 February 1997.

"Richard Wright—Black Boy." Video. Mississippi Educational TV/BBC, 1994.

"William Faulkner: A Life on Paper." Documentary. Mississippi Educational TV/ PBS-TV, 17 December 1979.

"Zora Is My Name!" Video. *American Playhouse*, PBS-TV, 14 February 1990.

Articles and Monographs

Adams, Phoebe-Lou. "Brief Reviews—Having Our Say," *Atlantic*, October 1993, 131.

"Alex Haley's Epic Drama 'Queen' Stars Halle Berry," *Jet*, 15 February 1993, 34–39.

Angelou, Maya, and Carol E. Neubauer. "Interview," *Massachusetts Review*, Summer 1987, 286–292.

Astor, Brooke. "The Delany Sisters' Book of Everyday Wisdom," *New York Times Book Review*, 11 December 1994, sec. 7, p. 22.

Auchincloss, Louis. "The Jefferson Enigma," *Newsweek*, 24 February 1997, 61.

———. "A Morality Play That Retains Its Punch," *New York Times*, 23 March 1997, 6H, 13H.

Auchmutey, Jim. "Statue Stumps Faulkner Town," *Atlanta Journal-Constitution*, 9 March 1997, M1, M3.

Bailey, Paul. "Black Ordeal," *Observer*, 1 April 1984.

Baker, Jean-Claude. "Mastering the Art of Living," *New York Times Book Review*, 5 December 1993, sec. 7, p. 5.

Banerjee, Sujata. "The Many Lives of Maya Angelou," *Baltimore Evening Sun*, 14 December 1990.

Banks, Dick. "'Liberty Tree' Could Revise History Books," *Charlotte Observer*, 12 July 1970, n.p.

Becker, Laurence A. "'The Jilting of Granny Weatherall': The Discovery of Pattern," *English Journal*, December 1966, 1164–1169.

"Before Jamestown and Plymouth Rock," in *The Lost Colony 1990 Souvenir Program.* Roanoke Island, N.C.: Roanoke Island Historical Association, 1990.

Bell-Russel, Danna C. "Audio Review—*The Delany Sisters' Book of Everyday Wisdom*," *Library Journal*, 15 April 1995, 136.

Benson, Sheila. "Horton Foote," *Modern Maturity*, November–December 1996, 52–57.

Blythe, LeGette. "Tom Wolfe's Papa: He Had Compassion, Loved Family, Fun and the Children," *Charlotte Observer*, 25 October 1964, 1B, 12B.

Boger, Mary. "Negro Author's Whisper Has Risen to a Roar," *Charlotte Observer*, 31 March 1968, 9G.

———. "O. Henry: Sad but Charming," *Charlotte Observer*, 19 July 1970, n.p.

Bontemps, Arna. "From Eatonville, Florida, to Harlem," *New York Herald Tribune*, 22 November 1942.

Bordsen, John. "Lost Horizons," *Charlotte Observer*, 13 April 1997, 1G, 8G, 10G.

Bottoms, David. "Remembering James Dickey," *Atlanta Journal-Constitution*, 26 January 1997, B1.

Boyle, Thomas E. "Frederick Jackson Turner and Thomas Wolfe: The Frontier as History and as Literature," *Western American Literature*, Winter 1970, 276.

Brock, Brenda. "Biography—Having Our Say," *Library Journal*, 15 September 1993, 83.

Brooks, Charlotte Kendrick. "Teacher's Guide to *The Color Purple*." New York: Washington Square Press, 1985.

Brown, Tony. "Horton Foote Doesn't Give a Hoot about Fame—Just Writing Plays," *Charlotte Observer*, 9 February 1997, 1F–4F.

———. "'Papa': A Family Draws Us into Their Lazy, Downward Spiral," *Charlotte Observer*, 11 February 1997, 1E–2E.

Bryant, Jerry H. "Ernest J. Gaines: Change, Growth, and History," *Southern Review*, 1974, 863.

———. "From Death to Life: The Fiction of Ernest J. Gaines," *Iowa Review*, Winter 1972, 106–120.

Buchanan, Sally A. "Favorite Reads: Nonfiction—Having Our Say," *Wilson Library Bulletin*, December 1994, 28.

Burns, Ken. "What Thomas Jefferson Means Today," *USA Weekend*, 14–16 February 1997, 4–6.

"Celebrated Writer Comes Home," *Jackson Mississippi Clarion-Ledger*, 25 October 1985, n.p.

Collum, Danny Duncan. "Nature and Grace: Flannery O'Connor and the Healing of Southern Culture," *Sojourner's*, December 1994/January 1995, n.p.

"The Confessions of Nat Turner" *Time*, 13 October 1967.

Corliss, Richard. "Invincible Man," *Time*, 25 April 1994, 90.

Correll, John T. "'Horn in West' Debut Finds Many Hickoryites Taking Part in Historic Pageant," *Hickory (N.C.) Daily Record*, 4 July 1961.

Crenson, Matt. "Doctor Theorizes Rabies, Not Liquor, Killed Author Poe," *USA Today*, 12 September 1996, 8A.

"The Curse and the Hope," *Time*, 17 July 1964, 44–48.

Cwiklik, Robert, and T. Lewis. "Sequoyah and the Cherokee Alphabet," *School Library Journal*, April 1990, 128–129.

Daniels, Lee A. "A Critical Tradition," *Emerge*, July/August 1994, 51–53.

Desruisseaux, Paul. "Ernest Gaines: A Conversation," *New York Times Book Review*, 11 June 1978, 45.

Doar, Harriet. "Editor of the Golden Words," *Charlotte Observer*, 25 May 1969, 6G.

———. "Katherine Anne Porter: 85, but No Old Lady," *Charlotte Observer*, 8 June 1975, 4B.

Dolmetsch, Carl R. "The Baltimore Sage in a Silly Century," *Saturday Review*, 13 September 1969, 27–28.

Donahue, Deirdre. "Health, Happiness the 'Delany' Way," *USA Today*, 8 December 1994, D6.

Donaldson, Scott. "Revisiting His Tidewater Childhood Haunts," *USA Today*, 9 November 1993, 5D.

Dummett, Clifton O. "Book Reviews—Having Our Say," *Journal of the American Dental Association*, December 1993, 27–28.

Farley, Christopher John, "Flying Lesson," *Time*, 13 January 1997, 76.

"Faulkner's Legacy: Honor, Pity, Pride," *Life*, 20 July 1962, 4.

"First Novel: Mocking Bird Call," *Newsweek*, 9 January 1961, 83.

Fleming, Anne Taylor. "The Private World of Truman Capote," *Charlotte Observer*, 1 October 1978, 1F–4F.

Foster, Lee. "Sequoyah: The Cherokee Genius," *American West*, November–December 1981, 24–25.

Franklin, Nancy. "Partners in Time—Having Our Say," *New Yorker*, 25 April 1995, 118–119.

Gabbert, Leslie S. "'Cold Sassy Tree': A New Solution to an Ancient Problem," *ALAN Review*, Fall 1992, 18–19.

Gage, Carolyn. "Tara and Other Lies," *On the Issues*, Spring 1997, 34–36.

Gaines, Ernest J. "Miss Jane and I," *Callaloo*, vol. 1, 1978, 23.

Gaines, Kevin. "Living History Bears Witness," *New York Times*, 2 April 1995, sec. 2, p. 5.

Gary, Kay. "Golden Sheds Gentile Cliches," *Charlotte Observer*, 10 December 1972, 5F.

Gerber, Philip L. "Review of *The Autobiography of Miss Jane Pittman*," *Saturday Review*, 1 May 1971, 40.

Giles, Jeff. "The Delany Sisters Tell All," *Newsweek*, 1 November 1993, 54.

Gillett, Rupert. "'Horn in the West,' Youngest N.C. Historical Drama, Opens," *Charlotte Observer*, 29 June 1952, 6D.

Girson, Rochelle. "Sidelights on Invisibility," *Saturday Review*, 14 March 1953, 49.

"Gold Mountain," *Newsweek*, 28 July 1997, 64–65.

Goldsmith, Sarah Sue. "Learning To Love Gilchrist's Anna," *Baton Rouge (LA) Morning Advocate*, 18 December 1988, n.p.

Gossett, Polly Paddock. "After 7 Years, Instant Success," *Charlotte Observer*, July 23, 1994, 1A, 11A.

Greene, A. C. "Female with a Head on Her," Austin (Tex.) *American-Statesman*, 8 July 1968.

Groer, Annie. "King Accuses Colleague of Plagiarism," *Charlotte Observer*, 20 August 1995, 6C.

Hamilton, Charles V. "'Nat Turner' Reconsidered: The Fiction and the Reality," *Saturday Review*, 22 June 1968, 22–23.

Hamilton, Edith. "Faulkner: Sorcerer or Slave?" *Saturday Review*, 12 July 1952, 8–9, 39–41.

Hammons, Lyle. "Writer's Style, Comments Jolt Students at Governor's School," *Little Rock (AK) Gazette*, 23 July 1984, n.p.

Hargrove, Nancy D. "The Tragicomic Vision of Beth Henley's Drama," *Southern Quarterly*, Summer 1984, 54–70.

Harper, Michael S. and John Wright, eds. "A Ralph Ellison Festival," *Carleton Miscellany*, Winter 1980.

"Heart of the West" (publicity flier), *Reader's Digest*, 1993.

Hearth, Amy Hill. "Bessie and Sadie: The Delany Sisters Relive a Century," *Smithsonian*, October 1993, 144–164.

Hendrix, Vernon. "World-Famous Authors Were Childhood Pals," *Advertiser Journal*, 11 October 1964.

Hicks, Granville. "The Critic behind the Ruffian," *Saturday Review*, 7 September 1968, 31–32.

———. "Facets of Faulkner," *Saturday Review*, 13 July 1968, 23–24.

———. "Literary Horizons: Flannery O'Connor," *Saturday Review*, 10 May 1969, 30.

———. "The Volcanic Mr. Wolfe," *Saturday Review*, 3 February 1968, 23–24, 66.

Hill, Pati. "Truman Capote Interview," in *Writers at Work*. New York: Viking, 1958.

Hoffman, Preston. "Book Sounds," *Wilson Library Bulletin*, February 1995, 85–86.

"Home-Grown Giant," *Time*, 10 February 1968.

"'Horn in the West' To Hold Catawba County Night," *Newton (N.C.) Observer-News-Enterprise*, 27 July 1990, 9.

Hutchinson, Stuart, ed. "Mark Twain: Critical Assessments." Brochure. East Sussex, England: Helm Information, n.d.

Johnson, Claudia Durst, et al. *"To Kill a Mockingbird:* Then and Now," *English Journal*, April 1997, 1–16.

Johnson, Greg. "Workmanlike Look at Warren," *Atlanta Journal-Constitution*, 9 March 1997, L8.

Jones, Dr. H. G. "Now Tom Wolfe Can Go Home," *Hickory Daily Record*, 20 March 1974, 6B.

Kakutani, Michiko. "Time and Emotions Shape Welty's Southern Landscape," *Charlotte Observer*, 27 July 1980, 4F.

"Keeping Posted: Edgar Allan Poe," *Saturday Evening Post*, January/February 1976, 89.

Kelly, Patricia P. "Recommended: Carson McCullers," *English Journal*, October 1982, 67–68.

Kennedy, Joanne. "For Those Who Are Loyalists of Ellen Gilchrist," *Norfolk Virginian-Pilot*, 4 December 1988, n.p.

Kleinberg, Eliot. "Claimants Grasp at 'Yearling' Author's Manuscripts," *Charlotte Observer*, 23 September 1990, 19A.

Koenig, Rhoda. "Review—Having Our Say," *New York Magazine*, 20 September 1993, 66–67.

Kohler, Dayton. "Carson McCullers: Variations on a Theme," *English Journal*, October 1951, 415–422.

Laney, Ruth. "Southern Sage Savors His Rise to Success," *Emerge*, May 1994, 66–67.

Lask, Thomas. "Giant in the Land," *New York Times*, 13 February 1968.

Laughlin, Karen L. "Criminality, Desire, and Community; A Feminist Approach to Beth Henley's *Crimes of the Heart*," *Women and Performance*, 1986, 35–51.

Lee, Harper. "Christmas to Me," *McCall's*, December 1961, 63.

———. "Love—In Other Words," *Vogue*, 15 April 1961, 64.

———. "When Children Discover America," *McCall's*, August 1964.

"The Legend and Facts of Daniel Boone," *Horn in the West Souvenir Program*, 1972, 8–9.

Lewis, David Levering. "Maya Angelou: From Harlem to the Heart of Africa," *Washington Post*, 4 October 1981.

"Literary Laurels for a Novice," *Life*, 26 May 1961, 78A–78B.

"The Lost Colony." Playbill. Roanoke, Va.: Roanoke Island Historical Association, 1990.

Lyons, Gene. "First Person Singular," *Newsweek*, 18 February 1985, 81–83.

Lyons, Richard D. "'Invisible Man' Author Ralph Ellison Dies at 80," *Charlotte Observer*, April 17, 1994, 2C.

McKnight, C. A., and Dannye Romine. "The Mind of a Southerner: The Man and the Book," *Charlotte Observer*, 10 July 1977, 1C–4C.

Maddocks, Melvin. "Root and Branch," *Time*, 10 May 1971, 12, 18.

Magnier, Bernard. "Ernest J. Gaines," *UNESCO Courier*, April 1995, 5–7.

Martin, Amis. "MacPosh," *New Statesman*, 2 September 1973, 205–206.

Maschal, Richard. "The Carolinas Roots of Ralph Ellison," *Charlotte Observer*, 4C.

Meckler, Laura. "Zora Neale Hurston's Unknown Work Found," *Charlotte Observer*, 17 December 1996, 6A.

Moore, Lenard D. "Just Another City," *Small Press Review*, November 1987, 13–14.

Moore, Trudy S. "Two Black Sisters," *Jet*, 18 October 1993, 34–37.

Morris, Willie. "Faulkner's Mississippi," *National Geographic*, March 1989, 312–339.

Morrow, Lance. "A Prophetic Delver: James Dickey," *Time*, 3 February 1997, 75.

Mulligan, Hugh A. "Reporter Recalls Dramatist," *Hickory (N.C.) Daily Record*, 24 September 1990, 7D.

Myers, Leslie R. "Celebrated Writer Comes Home," *Jackson (Miss.) Clarion-Ledger*, 25 October 1985, n.p.

Nemy, Enid. "Broadway: 'The Miss Firecracker Contest,'" *New York Times*, 27 July 1984, C2.

North Carolina Authors: A Selective Handbook, University of North Carolina Library Extension Publication, October 1952.

Nudd, Timothy. "The Actors Say," *Village Voice*, 18 April 1995, 86.

Oliver, Stephanie. "Maya Angelou: The Heart of the Woman," *Essence*, May 1983, 112–115.

"Pardon Asked for O. Henry in Theft," *Charlotte Observer*, 3 December 1958, n.p.

Paterson, Judith. "Interview: Maya Angelou—A Passionate Writer Living Fiercely with Brains, Guts, and Joy," *Vogue*, September 1982, 416–417, 420, 422.

Pearson, Richard. "Jesse Stuart Dies: Author of 'Taps for Pvt. Tussie,'" *Washington Post*, 19 February 1984, B14.

Peterson, V. R. "An Interview with Ernest Gaines," *Essence*, August 1993.

Pierpont, Claudie Roth. "A Society of One: Zora Neale Hurston, American Contrarian," *New Yorker*, 17 February 1997, 80–91.

Polter, Julie. "Obliged To See God," *Sojourner's*, December 1994/January 1995.

Price, Reynolds. "James Dickey, Size XL," *New York Times Book Review*, 23 March 1997, 31.

Quarles, Benjamin. "Frederick Douglass: Challenge and Response," in *Encyclopedia of Black America*. New York: Da Capo, 1981.

"Ralph Ellison Profile," *New Yorker*, 22 November 1976.

Rhodes, Richard. "Mattie Ross's True Account," *New York Times Book Review*, 7 July 1968.

Rich, Frank. "Theater: 'Firecracker,' a Beth Henley Comedy," *New York Times*, 28 May 1984, A11.

Richardson, H. Edward. "Jesse Stuart Remembered," *Arizona Quarterly*, Summer 1984, 101–121.

Roberston, Nan. "Georgia Dynamo in 'Firecracker,'" *New York Times*, 12 November 1984, C2.

Rogers, V. Collum. "Beth Henley: Signature of a Non-Stop Playwright," *Back Stage*, 24 March 1995, 23.

Romine, Dannye. "The Golden Touch," *Charlotte Observer*, 1 October 1978, 1B, 12B.

Rubin, Louis, Jr. "Faulkner: Masterful Work about the Master," *Charlotte Observer*, 24 March 1974, 4B.

Schickel, Richard. "Jagged Flashes of Inspiration: 'The Miss Firecracker Contest,' by Beth Henley," *Time*, 11 June 1984, 80.

Schroeder, Patricia R. "Locked behind the Proscenium: Feminist Strategies in *Getting Out* and *My Sister in This House*," *Modern Drama*, March 1989, 104–114.

Shaffner, Claire. "For Those Who Like Downright Good Story-Telling," *Charlotte Observer*, 12 April 1970, 5F.

"Shangri-La South," *Time*, 4 May 1970, 100.

Sheldon, W. Lynn, Jr. "The Days of Edgar Allan Poe," *Historic Traveler*, October/November 1995, 34–41, 72.

Sheppard, R. Z. "An A-Plus in Humanity," *Time*, 20 March 1993.

Simon, John. "Theater: Having Our Say," *New York Magazine*, 1 May 1995, 67.

Smith, Sidonie Ann. "The Song of a Caged Bird: Maya Angelou's Quest after Self-Acceptance," *Southern Humanities Review*, Fall 1973.

Snow, Richard F. "A Century as Sisters—Having Our Say," *American Heritage*, December 1993, 97.

"Southern Cross," *Times Literary Supplement*, 16 March 1973, 303.

"Southerner Ellen Gilchrist Is the Book World's Belle," *People*, 11 February 1985, 74, 77.

Spencer, Jenny S. "Norman's *'night Mother:* Psychodrama of Female Identity," *Modern Drama*, September 1987, 364–375.

Stearns, David Patrick. "Recently Revealed Works Headed to Stage, Print," *USA Today*, 4 September 1996, 1–2D.

Steinberg, Sybil. "Review of *Cold Sassy Tree*," *Publishers Weekly*, 9 November 1984.

Stepto, R. B. "The Phenomenal Woman and the Severed Daughter," *Parnassus: Poetry in Review*, Fall–Winter 1979.

Sterling, Dorothy. "The Soul of Learning," *English Journal*, February 1968, 166–180.

Stithem, Marsha A. "Olive Ann Burns and 'Cold Sassy Tree' in the High School Classroom," *English Journal*, December 1994, 81–84.

Stoelting, Winifred L. "Human Dignity and Pride in the Novels of Ernest Gaines," *CLA Journal*, December 1971, 348–358.

Stone, Emily Whitehurst. "The Ties That Bind: Three Women Writers in Conflict in the South," *Charlotte Observer*, 29 September 1985, n.p.

Stuttaford, Genevieve. "Nonfiction—Having Our Say," *Publishers Weekly*, 5 July 1993, 54.

Styron, William. "As He Lay Dead, a Bitter Grief," *Life*, 20 July 1962, 39–42.

Summer, Bob. "Interview with Ernest Gaines," *Publishers Weekly*, 24 May 1993, 62–63.

————. "PW Interviews: Olive Ann Burns," *Publishers Weekly*, 9 November 1984, 66–67.

————. "Review of 'Leaving Cold Sassy,'" *Publishers Weekly*, 16 November 1992.

Swift, James V. "Steamboating: Transshipment on the Missouri River," in *Gone West*. St. Louis, Mo.: Jefferson National Expansion Memorial, n.d., 10–13.

Walker, Alice. "In Search of Zora Neale Hurston," *Ms.*, March 1975.

————. "A South without Myths," *Sojourner's*, December 1994/January 1995, n.p.

Walser, Richard. "Bernice Kelly Harris, Storyteller of Eastern Carolina" (pamphlet). Chapel Hill: University of North Carolina Press, 1955.

Warren, Tim. "A More Visible Ellison," *Atlanta Journal-Constitution*, 9 February 1997, E1.

Watson, Bruce. "If His Life Were a Short Story, Who'd Ever Believe It?" *Smithsonian*, January 1997, 92–102.

Wells, Dean Faulkner. "A Christmas Remembered," *Parade*, 21 December 1980, 4–5.

"Where an Alphabet Was Born: The Sequoyah Birthplace Museum, Vonore, Tennessee," *Southern Living*, April 1988, 33.

White, Robert A. "Pat Conroy's 'Gutter Language': Prince of Tides in a Lowcountry High School," *English Journal*, April 1992, 19–22.

Williams, Joan. "Twenty Will Not Come Again," *Atlantic*, May 1980, 58–65.

Wolff, Geoffrey. "Daddy's Little Avenger," *Washington Post*, 6 July 1968.

————. "Talking to Trees," *Newsweek*, 16 June 1969; 3 May 1971.

Wynn, Rhoda. "Paul Green: Deep Roots of Artistic Expression from a Native Son," in *The Lost Colony 1990 Souvenir Program*. Roanoke Island, N.C.: Roanoke Island Historical Association, 1990.

Young, Tracy. "Off the Cuff: Ellen Gilchrist," *Vogue*, September 1986, 415–418.

Zorotovich, Prudy. "Recommended: Eudora Welty," *English Journal*, January 1983, 67–68.

Internet

"Alice Walker Web Page," http://www.utexas.edu/~mmaynard/Walker/walker.htm, 3 May 1996.

Armstrong, M. J. "John James Audubon," http://rmc-www.library.cornell.edu/HFJ/Aud.Folio.html, 22 August 1996.

"Augusta Evans Wilson," http://www.asc.edu/archives/famous/awilson.html, 28 March 1996.

"The Ballad of Davy Crockett," www.cs.monash.edu.au/~tbp/disney/lyrics/tv/davy, 30 July 1996.

"Bierce Papers," http://sunsite.berkeley.edu:8008/findaids/Berkeley/bierce/1.toc, 24 June 1996.

"Black and White Perspectives on the American South," http://www. gactr.uga.edu/GCQ/gcqwin95/blackwhite.html, 5 February 1997.

Briggs, Cassandra. "Louisiana Literature," http://www.lacollege.edu/classes/en446/prefiled/gaines/forms.html, 5 February 1997.

"Daniel Boone," www.berksweb.com/boonetext.html, 27 September 1996.

"Daniel Boone: American Pioneer and Trailblazer," www.lucidcafe.com/lucidcafe.library/95nov/boone.html, 27 September 1996.

"David 'Davy' Crockett," www.numedia.tddc.net/sa/alamo/crockett.html, 30 July 1996.

Dobie, J. Frank. *Guide to Life and Literature of the Southwest*. Dallas: SMU Press, 1952. www.islandmm.com/llsw/llswp.htm, 16 August 1996.

"Driving Miss Daisy—Background," http://www.nchcpl.lib.in.us/ICT/DAISY/Background.html, 3 December 1996.

Dunlap, Steve. "Freedom Page: Banned Books and Other Media," http://www.bluehighways.com/freedom/banned books.html, 1 December 1996.

"Edenton History FAQs," http://www.edenton.com/history/miscfact.htm, October 1995.

"Edgar Allan Poe," http://iptweb.com/www/lib/authors/poe.html, 19 February 1997.

"Edgar Allan Poe," http://www.parec.com/edganapk.htm, 19 February 1997.

"Edgar Allan Poe National Historic Site," http://www.nps.gov/edal/humble 2.htm, 19 February 1997.

Erb, Jane. "Porgy and Bess," http://www.classicalnet/~music/comp.1st/works/gershwin/porgy&bess.html, 17 June 1996.

"Eudora Welty," http://www.cssc.olemiss.edu/welty/homepage.html, 27 April 1996.

"Eudora Welty," http://www.intercall.net/~anthony/welty.htm, 7 May 1996.

Faragher, John Mack. "Chronology," from *Daniel Boone: The Life and Legend of an American Pioneer*, http://xroads.virginia.edu/~hyper/CONTEXTS/Boone/chronolo.html, 10 November 1995.

Fichtner, Margaria. "Read It Like a Native: 100 Books about Florida," *Miami Herald*, http://wc3.webcrawler.com/select/newsrc.57.html, 29 July 1996.

"Flannery O'Connor," http://www.gac.peachnet.edu/library/~sc/focfaq.html, 26 February 1997.

"Frederick Douglass," http://www.webcom.com/~bright/source/fdougla.html, 4 March 1997.

"Frederick Douglass and John Brown," http://jefferson.village.virginia.ed/jbrown/douglass.html, 4 March 1997.

Gener, Randy. "Randy Reports," *New York Theatre Wire*, http://www.nytheatre-wire.com/genruhry.htm, 3 February 1997.

"George W. Cable," http://www.sehs.lane.edu/sehs/infos/menwomen/Cable.html, 7 November 1994.

Gislason, Eric J. *Virgin Land: The American West as Symbol and Myth*, http://xroads.virginia.edu/~HYPER/HNS/synoptic.html, 27 September 1996.

"Goat Cart Sam, aka Porgy," http:darwin.clas.virginia.edu/~kh4d/porgy.html, 5 December 1996.

Gullette, Alan. "Ambrose Bierce, Master of the Macabre." www.creative.net/~alang/lit/horror/bierce.sht, 24 June 1996.

Hecimovich, Greg A. "Notes on Literature, Miscegenation, and the Body Politic in the Jim Crow South," http://www.vanderbilt.edu/AnS/english/English104W-15.html, 20 February 1997.

Hines, Cragg. "Barbara Jordan Lived as Pioneer and Prophet," *Houston Chronicle*, http://www.chron.com/content/chronicle/page1/96/01/18/jordannu/html, 1996.

"The Historian's Gallery: Margaret Mitchell and 'Gone with the Wind' Memorabilia," http://www.nr-net.com/history/hggwtw.htm, 1 January 1997.

Hooks, Rita. "Conjured into Being: Zora Neale Hurston's *Their Eyes Were Watching God*," http://splavc.spjc.cc.fl.us/hooks/zoraint.html, 12 February 1997.

"Inspirational Short Stories To Warm Your Heart," http://applecity.com/Kids/stories/index.html, 11 September 1996.

"James Branch Cabell Biography," http:exlibris.ubs.vcu.edu/jbc/speccoll/mss/jbc/jbc.html, 17 January 1996.

"The Jesse Stuart Foundation," http://www.mis.net/jsf, 7 March 1997.

"The Jesse Stuart State National Preserve," http://www.state.ky.us/agencies/nrepc/ksnpc/jessup.htm, 7 March 1997.

"Joel Chandler Harris," http://xroads.virginia.edu/~UG97/remus/jch.html, 6 September 1996.

Johns, Vicki Slagle. "Written with a Flourish," http://loki.ur.ulk.edu/alumnus/winter96/local.html, 31 March 1996.

Jokinen, Anniina. "Anniina's Alice Walker Page," http://www.netreach/net/~alchemy/alicew, 15 October 1996.

"Kate Chopin: *The Awakening*," http://mchip00.med.nyu.edu/lit-med/html, 8 October 1996.

"The Kate Chopin Project," www.lacollege.edu, 31 March 1996.

"Kate Chopin's *The Awakening*," http://wrt.syr.edu/html, 16 May 1995.

"The Katherine Anne Porter Room," http://www.itd.umd.edu/UMS/UMCP/ARCV/kapbib.html, 23 August 1995.

Koppelman, Robert S. "Robert Penn Warren's Modernist Spirituality," http://www.system.missouri.edu/upress/spring1995/koppelma.htm, 27 April 1997.

Lieb, Patricia. "Rawlings House Is a Visit to a Past Era," www.writeonmag.com/rawlings.html, 6 December 1996.

"Looking Homeward: A Thomas Wolfe Photo Album," http://www.system.missouri.edu/upress/otherbooks/teicher.htm, 29 November 1995.

"The Lost Colony," www.204.107.79.7/lost.html, 18 May 1996.

"The Lost Colony: America's Beginning," www.outerbanks-nc.com/lostcolony/, 18 May 1996.

McGloughlin, Bill. "Flannery O'Connor," http://www.ils.unc.edu/flannery.html, 31 January 1997.

"The Margaret Mitchell House," http://www.gwtw.org, 3 July 1996.

"Marjorie Kinnan Rawlings," http://karamelik.eastlib.ufl.edu/html, 9 September 1996.

"Marjorie Kinnan Rawlings Society," www.clas.ufl.edu/english/Rawlings.Society/rawlings.html, 24 December 1996.

"Mary Boykin Chesnut," http.//www.historic.com/schs/chsdiar.2.html, 15 June 1996.

Massey, Jane Le Marquand. "Kate Chopin as Feminist: Subverting the French Androcentric Influence," http://elwing/otago.ac.nz:888/html, 19 November 1996.

Miguel, Maribeth. "Captivity Theme: A Thing of the Past," www.en.utexas.edu/~maria/cooper/captivit.htm, 14 August 1996.

Mitchell, Jason P. "Tin Jesus; The Intellectual in Selected Short Fiction of Flannery O'Connor," http://sunset.backbone.olemiss.edu/~jmitchell/flannery.html, 5 December 1995.

Mitgang, Herbert. "Lillian Hellman's FBI File," http://dept.lenglish.upen.edu/~afilreis/50s/hellman-per-fbi.html, 19 August 1996.

"Mockingbird Website and Home Page," http://pwnetwork.pwcs.edu, 15 April 1997.

"Molly Ivins on American Politics," http://www.rivertext.com/caferead.molly.html, 23 October 1996.

"Molly Ivins's Biography," http://www.arlington.net/system/static.content/bios/ivins.htm, 4 December 1996.

Musick, John R. "Pocahontas: A Story of Virginia, 1890," www.darwin.clas.virginia.edu/~jab3w/pocanew5.html, 18 May 1996.

Neuendorf, David W. "Davy Crockett on Social Spending," www.seidata.com/~neusys/colm0009.html, 1995.

Nickerson, Megan. "Romanticism in *The Awakening*," http:www.assumption.edu/html, 28 July 1996.

Noble, Mike. "A Biography of Alexis de Tocqueville," http:oasis.bellevue.k12.wa.us/sammamish/sstudies.dir/hist_docs.dir.html, 1995.

O'Shea, Brian. *Joel Chandler Harris Home Page*, http://www.ajc.com/staff/oshea/preswalk.html, 8 December 1996.

"Our Culture—Famous People: Southern Louisiana," http://hob.com/louisiana/culturefamousesla.html, 5 February 1997.

"Outdoor Drama," www.unc.edu/depts/outdoor/index.html, 19 May 1996.

"Pat Conroy Biography," http://www.bdd.com/athwk/bddathwk.cgi/107-18-95/profile, 4 December 1996.

Perkins, Donald. "Barbara Jordan," http://www.rice.edu/armadillo/Texas/jordan.html, 22 January 1996.

Price, Christopher S. "Scouting Out Racism," http://www.vanderbilt.edu/AnS/english/English104W-15/chrisp-rewrite-tokill.htm, 31 January 1996.

Rice, Alan. "Portrait of Frederick Douglass," http://www.keele.ac.uk/depts/as/Portraits/rice.douglass.html, 4 March 1997.

"Richard Wright—Black Boy," http://www.itvs.org/programs/RW/more_info.html.

"Richard Wright—Black Boy," http://www.pbs.org/rwbb/teachgd.html.

"Richard Wright: 1908–1970," http://educeth.ethz.ch/english/ReadingList/EducETH-Wright.Richard.html.

Robinson, Forrest G. "An 'Unconscious and Profitable Cerebration': Mark Twain and Literary Intentionality," http//sunsite.berkeley.edu:8080/scan/ncl-e/503/articles/robinson.art503.htm, 7 June 1996.

Rose, Julie K. "Daniel Boone: Myth and Reality in American Consciousness," http://xroads.virginia.edu/~HYPER/HNS/Boone/Smithhome.html, 10 November 1995.

"Rowan Oak," http://www.ci.oxford.ms.us/group4/rowanOak/faulkner.html, 14 February 1997.

"Scarlett Lives On!" http://www.student.mckenna.edu/student/ns/tpham/gwtw.html, 22 November 1996.

Singleton, Carole W. "The Metaphysical Dilemma of 'Bein' Alive, Bein' a Woman and Bein' Colored,'" http://www.bobsest,com/wcaat/metaphy.html, 20 May 1996.

Skube, Michael. "Searching for Scout," http://www.yall.con/thearts/quill/harper.htm, 20 February 1997.

Smykowski, Adam. "Symbolism in Harper Lee's 'To Kill a Mockingbird,'" http://www.vanderbilt.edu/AnS/english/English104W-15/tokillamockingbird/index.htm, 20 February 1997.

Stilton, Robert. "Pocahontas: The Evolution of an American Narrative," www.cup.cam.ac.uk/titles/c/0521469597.html, 18 May 1996.

Thomas, Sandra. "Frederick Douglass: Abolitionist/Editor," http://www. history.rochester.edu/class/DOUGLASS.html, 4 March 1997.

"Thomas Wolfe Homepage," http://www.mainsrv.main.nc.us/buncombe/wolfe.html, 15 December 1996.

"Thomas Wolfe Memorial," http://www.unca.edu/asheville/wolfe.html, 28 February 1997.

"Thomas Wolfe Web Site," http://cms.uncwil.edu/~connelly,wolfe.html, 24 January 1997, 27 April 1997.

"Voices from the Maps: Zora Neale Hurston," http://english.cla.umn.edu/lkd/vfg/Authors/ZorahNealeHurston, 12 February 1997.

Webb, John. "H. L. Mencken," http://w3.one.net/~muir/hlm0.html, 25 August 1995.

Zeno, Sara. "James Agee," http://www.sgi.net/marbles/zeno.agee.html, 1995.

BIBLIOGRAPHY

"Zora Neale Hurston," http://www.ceth.rutgers.edu/projects/hercproj/hurston/front.htm, 12 February 1997.

"Zora Neale Hurston," http://www.detroit.freenet.org/gdfn/sigs/l-corner-world/hurston/html, 12 February 1997.

ILLUSTRATION CREDITS

138   Photofest

143   AP/Wide World Photos

146   Vandamm Studio. Photofest

159   Kevin Geil. AP/Wide World Photos

182   Diana Ossana. AP/Wide World Photos

185   UPI/Corbis-Bettmann

188   Corbis-Bettmann

201   AP/Wide World Photos

206   Columbia Pictures, 1952. Photofest

209   UPI/Corbis-Bettmann

221   AP/Wide World Photos

228   Talbot. Photofest

237   AP/Wide World Photos

242   From a portrait by Cummings, 1893. Corbis-Bettmann

251   AP/Wide World Photos

254   Vandamm Studio. Photofest

259   Corbis-Bettmann

265   AP/Wide World Photos

271   AP/Wide World Photos

276   Erik S. Lesser. AP/Wide World Photos

282   Aimee Du Pont. Corbis-Bettmann

307   Eileen Darby. Photofest

315   Don Heiny. AP/Wide World Photos

328   AP/Wide World Photos

337   Marty Reichenthal. AP/Wide World Photos

ILLUSTRATION CREDITS

INDEX

[Note: Page numbers in **boldface** denote major entry headings. Numbers in brackets indicate illustrations.]